EAGLE ENTANGLED

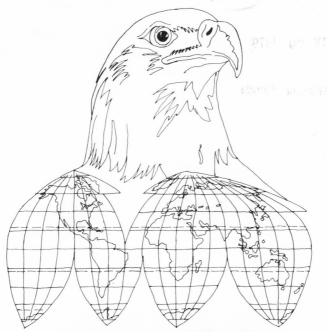

EAGLE ENTANGLED
U.S. Foreign Policy in a Complex World

Edited by
Kenneth A. Oye Donald Rothchild Robert J. Lieber
University of California, Davis

Written under the auspices of the Institute of
International Studies, University of California, Berkeley.

Longman
New York and London

EAGLE ENTANGLED
U.S. Foreign Policy in a Complex World

Longman Inc., New York
Associated companies, branches, and representatives throughout the world.

Copyright © 1979 by Longman Inc.

Developmental Editor: Nicole Benevento
Interior and Cover Design: Tim McKeen
Manufacturing and Production Supervision: Louis Gaber
Composition: Book Composition Services
Printing and Binding: Maple Press

Library of Congress Cataloging in Publication Data

Main entry under title:

Eagle entangled.

    1.   United States—Foreign relations—1977-
—Addresses, essays, lectures. 2. Carter, Jimmy,
1924-   —Addresses, essays, lectures.
I. Oye, Kenneth A., 1949-   II. Rothchild,
Donald S. III. Lieber, Robert J., 1941-
E872.E2   327.73   79-10319
ISBN 0-582-29003-1
ISBN 0-582-29002-3 pbk.
Manufactured in the United States of America

CONTRIBUTORS

LAWRENCE T. CALDWELL is associate professor of political science at Occidental College. He has been a research associate at the IISS in London and a visiting professor and director of European study at the National War College. He published *Soviet-American Relations: One-Half Decade of Detente* in 1975 and plans to publish a volume for the Council on Foreign Relations on Soviet-American Relations in the 1980s.

ALEXANDER DALLIN is professor of history and political science at Stanford University. He was director of the Russian Institute at Columbia University from 1962 to 1967 and Adlai E. Stevenson Professor of International Relations there from 1966 to 1971. He has written and edited many books, the most recent being *Political Terror in Communist Systems* (with George W. Breslauer).

BANNING GARRETT is a co-founder of *Internews* and contributes reports on military and strategic affairs. He has written on China policy and strategic matters for *Le Monde Diplomatique, Inquiry,* and other publications. He is a participant in several policy colloquia at the University of California's Institute for International Studies.

ERNST B. HAAS is Robson Research Professor of Government at the University of California, Berkeley. He is principal investigator of Studies on International Scientific and Technological Regimes, Institute of International Studies. His most recent book is *Scientists and World Order* (with M. P. Williams and D. Babai).

ROBERT O. KEOHANE is professor of political science at Stanford University. He wrote the chapter that appears in this book when he was a fellow of the Center for Advanced Study in the Behavioral Sciences, Stanford, California. He is co-author with Joseph S. Nye of *Power and Interdependence: World Politics in Transition* and editor of the quarterly journal *International Organization.*

STEPHEN D. KRASNER is an associate professor in the Department of Political Science at the University of California, Los Angeles. He is the author of *Defending the National Interest: Raw Materials Investments and American Foreign Policy,* as well as numerous articles in scholarly journals.

NANCY I. LIEBER is a lecturer at the University of California, Davis. Her publications include "Politics of the French Left: A Review Essay," *American Political Science Review;* "Ideology and Tactics of the French Socialist Party," in *Government and Opposition;* and *Contemporary Politics: Europe.* At present she is working on a study of Eurosocialism.

ROBERT J. LIEBER is professor and chair of the Department of Political Science at the University of California, Davis. He has been a research associate at the Harvard Center for International Affairs, visiting fellow at St. Antony's College, Oxford, and at the University of Essex, and associate of both the Atlantic Institute and the Centre d'Etudes et de Recherches Internationales (Paris). He is the author of *British Politics and European Unity, Theory and World Politics, Oil and the Middle East War: Europe in the Energy Crisis,* and co-author of *Contemporary Politics: Europe.* His latest research concerns international energy problems and advanced industrial societies: determinants of openness or closure in international political economy.

ABRAHAM F. LOWENTHAL, former director of studies at the Council on Foreign Relations, now heads the Latin American program at the Woodrow Wilson International Scholars in Washington. Dr. Lowenthal has also worked at Harvard, Brookings, Princeton, and the Ford Foundation. His publications include *The Dominica Intervention, The Peruvian Experiment,* and numerous articles.

MICHAEL MANDELBAUM is assistant professor of government and research associate of the Center for Science and International Affairs at Harvard University. In 1976–77 he was a Rockefeller Foundation fellow in the humanities and research associate of the Research Institute on International Change at Columbia University. He is the author of *The Nuclear Question: The United States and Nuclear Weapons* and co-author of *Nuclear Weapons and World Politics.*

MICHAEL NACHT is assistant director of the Center for Science and International Affairs and lecturer in public policy at the John F. Kennedy School of Government, Harvard University. He is also co-editor of the quarterly journal *International Security.*

KENNETH A. OYE is lecturer in political science at the University of California, Davis, and co-chair of the International Political Economy Colloquium at the Institute of International Studies, University of California, Berkeley. He has taught as a lecturer in public administration at the John F. Kennedy School of Government, Harvard University. His dissertation work at Harvard is on the politics of the interwar monetary system.

DONALD ROTHCHILD is professor of political science at the University of California, Davis. He has lectured at universities in Uganda, Kenya, Zambia, and Ghana. His most recent books are *Racial Bargaining in Independent Kenya* and (with Robert L. Curry, Jr.) *Scarcity, Choice and Public Policy in Middle Africa.*

WILLIAM SCHNEIDER is associate professor of government at Harvard University and research fellow at the Harvard Center for International Affairs. He has published a number of articles on public opinion and voting behavior and recently co-authored a history of American racial attitudes, *From Discrimination to Affirmative Action* (with S. M. Lipset). Professor Schneider is currently engaged in a study of voting behavior in the U.S. and Western Europe and plans to work with the Chicago Council on Foreign Relations in connection with its 1979 survey of U.S. public opinion and foreign policy.

STEVEN L. SPIEGEL is associate professor of political science at the University of California, Los Angeles. He is author of *Dominance and Diversity: The International Hierarchy* and co-author of *The International Politics of Regions: A Comparative Approach.* He was a member of the Brookings Institution Middle East Study Group in 1975 and 1976 and is currently writing *The War for Washington: The Other Arab-Israeli Conflict.*

CONTENTS

PREFACE

Analysts of contemporary American foreign policy frequently exaggerate the range of choice open to a President or an administration. While joining others in drawing attention to the tactical, strategic, and stylistic deficiencies of the Carter administration's foreign policy, we seek to distinguish between transitory and enduring problems. To this end we have interpreted the flappings of the eagle in the context of the thicket of constraints and contradictions in which it is enmeshed.

Part 1 contains analyses of the attributes of the thicket. The introductory chapter examines the interlocking phenomena of the erosion of U.S. dominance of economic and security affairs, the proliferation of international issues affecting the interests of the United States, and the emergence of serious tradeoffs across issues. The Carter administration's approach to foreign policy is then described and critiqued as an adaptation to the international environmental characteristics. The problem of developing a foreign policy suited to an increasingly complex international environment is compounded by characteristics of the domestic setting of foreign policy. Chapter 2 describes the distinctly nonconsensual state of contemporary public opinion on matters of foreign policy, analyzes the significance of this lack of consensus as a constraint on foreign policy, and assesses the feasibility of generating broad-based support for *any* American foreign policy.

The major themes established in part 1 are reflected in chapters on ten important regional and functional problems. The range of subjects treated reflects the broadening of American foreign policy interests to include new functional areas such as nuclear proliferation, human rights, and international economic relations. Chapters on functional and regional problems relate American interests, capabilities, and policies in one specific area to contradictory and correlative interests in other areas, the general contraction of American power, and extant domestic interests. If a hologram of an object is shattered, each fragment contains a complete image of the object from the fragment's original perspective. Each of the ten fragments of foreign policy examined in depth in this volume embody the constraints and contradictions of the whole.

To ensure that each regional and functional specialist proceeded with sensitivity to the broader context of foreign policy, this has been a collaborative effort from the beginning. Manuscripts were circulated in formative stages. Preliminary drafts of chapters were presented and discussed at the Conference on Contemporary Issues in American Foreign Policy, held at the Institute of International Studies of the University of California at Berkeley in June 1978. Chapters were revised to incorporate themes that evolved from our discussions.

We acknowledge with gratitude the contribution of the Institute of International Studies to this undertaking. Without the administrative and financial support of the institute, the implications of serious tradeoffs across issue areas could not have been assessed through intensive intellectual contact across contributors. We thank Director Carl Rosberg, Associate Director Robert Price, and Assistant Director Harry Kreisler for their support. Cleo Stoker, Karin Beros, and Bodine Webster of the Institute's administrative staff deserve credit for their efficient and friendly handling of arrangements for the Conference. Finally, Valoyce Gage of the Department of Political Science staff at the University of California at Davis merits high praise for her unstinting assistance in preparing and circulating manuscripts.

Davis, California   *Kenneth A. Oye*
February 1979   *Donald Rothchild*
                                                              Robert J. Lieber

EAGLE ENTANGLED

Part I
OVERVIEW

1

THE DOMAIN
OF CHOICE

International Constraints and Carter Administration Foreign Policy

Kenneth A. Oye

Change the context and you change the problem.
                                                    Jean Monnet

The Carter administration has been vexed and perplexed by two interlocking changes in international relations. The continuing *diffusion of power* in the international system has created a frustrating gap between the means and ends of American foreign policy. The United States was a hegemonic power in the years between the end of the Second World War and the height of the Indochina conflict. America's extraordinary military, economic, and political dominance has ended, and this basic change has necessitated adjustments in American policy. As the limits of power have become evident, the domain of choice has narrowed. American foreign policy must be increasingly sensitive to distinctions between vital and peripheral interests and what can be influenced and what must be accepted.

The task of developing a foreign policy keyed to these distinctions has been made

The author acknowledges with gratitude the advice and support of Donald Rothchild, Robert Keohane, Ernst Haas, Steve Krasner, Robert Lieber, and George Downs. The approach taken in this essay was strongly influenced by the theories developed by Robert Keohane and Joseph Nye in Power and Interdependence (*Boston: Little, Brown, 1977*).

3

more difficult by the *greater complexity* of foreign affairs. International issues affecting American interests have multiplied, and connections across issues have proliferated and oscillated. The complexity of contemporary international relations has increased the uncertainty of the basic estimates of means, ends, and tradeoffs that are the building blocks of policy. Maneuvering within a shrinking domain of choice has been complicated by this widening zone of uncertainty.

The foreign policy of the Carter administration can be evaluated as a necessarily imperfect solution to this dual problem. Numerous critics of the administration frequently characterize its foreign policy as unfocused, inconsistent, unstable, and ineffective. This chapter argues that the essence of the problem is structural. The lack of focus of American policy is largely a consequence of the multiplication of issues affecting national interests. The inconsistency of policy reflects the proliferation of connections between issues that have created tradeoffs across those interests. The fluctuations of policy are largely products of the instability of these tradeoffs. The ineffectiveness of policy follows from the confluence of contracting power, expanding interests, and increasing complexity. This does not imply that Carter administration foreign policy is beyond criticism, but rather that a simple change in tactics, or in Presidents, cannot alleviate frustration that is rooted in the setting of American foreign policy.

INTERNATIONAL CONTEXT: POWER DIFFUSION, ISSUE PROLIFERATION, AND ISSUE INTERDEPENDENCE

References to the limits of American power and the increasing complexity of international relations have been standard features of major official statements on foreign policy since 1970 and may well be shopworn features of the 1984 State of the Nation Address. Richard Nixon and Henry Kissinger presided over the "end of the postwar world" and began to adjust policy to "an increasingly complex and heterogeneous world." [1] Jimmy Carter and Zbigniew Brzezinski speak of a "new world" where "we can no longer expect that the other 150 nations will follow the dictates of the powerful," a world in which "we can no longer separate the traditional issues of war and peace from the new global questions of justice, equality, and human rights." [2] These bipartisan truisms possess more than a modicum of truth, but they fail to emphasize the connection between eroding American hegemony and the increasing complexity of contemporary international relations. The evident proliferation of international issues affecting American interests and the bewildering and unstable set of connections across foreign policy concerns are partially epiphenomenal, manifestations of underlying changes in the distribution of power.

Power Diffusion

The trappings of American power (e.g., warheads, tanks, missile submarines, and gross national product) have not diminished. Rather, the end of American hegemony reflects the dispersion of power as other nations' capabilities have increased relative to those of the United States. This diffusion of power was inevitable. Nevertheless, American excesses and successes in foreign policy during the period of U.S. hegemony accelerated changes in the basic distribution of world power on military, economic, and ideological planes. The exercise of power by administrations attempting to satisfy the often inconsistent requirements of U.S. security interests, economic interests, and national character frequently dissipated that power. This analysis emphasizes the significance of American policy relative to autonomous change, by stressing the effects of prior policy on the domain of choice open to later decision makers.

Military

The postwar objectives of American national security policy were defined, minimally, as containment of the Soviet Union and its clients and, maximally, as suppression of any revolutionary change that might threaten American economic interests or increase Soviet influence. The successful use of nuclear brinksmanship at the conclusion of the Korean war, during the Cuban missile crisis, and in the 1973 Yom Kippur war provided the Soviet Union with a rationale for accelerating development of at least an assured second-strike capacity. Soviet attainment of nuclear parity reduced or eliminated American ability to engage in nuclear brinksmanship to influence actual or potential conventional military confrontations. As a consequence, faith in the credibility of American nuclear deterrence in areas of Soviet conventional superiority is now somewhat less than total.

When potential antagonists each possess an assured second-strike capability, most military theorists argue that conventional-force balances become critical. Although frequently exaggerated, Soviet conventional forces have increased significantly in quality over the past five years as Soviet military expenditures have matched and exceeded those of the United States. At present, the United States appears to retain a qualitative technological advantage and the Soviets a quantitative advantage. What can no longer be assumed is U.S. conventional military superiority outside the immediate vicinity of Warsaw Pact nations.

American military intervention in Indochina both exemplified the limits of American power and contributed to the erosion of that power. Three administrations defined the conflict in Indochina as a test of the credibility of American security guarantees throughout the world. When American intervention failed to destroy revolutionary nationalism in Indochina, that credibility was reduced. This was true not so much because of the failure of the intervention per se; the *costs* of intervening, in human life and money, were as important as the outcome of the intervention. Public disillusionment with costly military intervention persists. While it does, the War Powers Act of 1973 effectively precludes prolonged military intervention by presidential fiat.

American covert intervention in the internal politics of other nations—facilitating coups in South Vietnam and Chile, funding right-wing political activities in Italy, seeking to assassinate leaders in the Congo and Cuba—had a mixed record of successes and failures. However, the disclosure of these actions produced a public

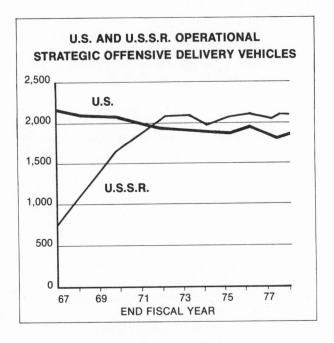

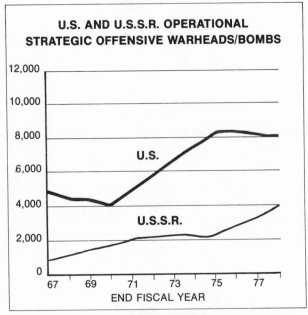

FIGURE 1.1. Soviet-American Strategic Balance

SOURCE: U.S. Department of State Bulletin, April 1978.

and legislative reaction in America that may preclude their use in the immediate future. Moreover, publicity about these activities has generally struck a deep nationalistic chord in target nations; reaction to such covert actions has frequently increased the resistance of these states to American influence.

The sharp increase in military expenditures by developing nations portends a continuing dispersal of military power. Arms purchases by OPEC nations have received the most publicity, but the importation of arms by the non-OPEC Third World has doubled (in constant prices) between 1960 and 1975. Though no Third World nation is likely to become a new superpower, and local rivalries often explain sharp increases in military imports, these weapons would materially increase the costs of any American intervention. For example, several oil producers could bloody, if not defeat, the "quick intervention and occupation forces" advocated by some academics and hinted at by Henry Kissinger in a 1975 interview. The acquisition of nuclear weapons and delivery systems for tactical use would make intervention even more costly.

In the aggregate, these changes in the distribution of military capabilities are significant. For the first time since the end of the Second World War, the United States is *not* free.

Economic

The erosion of U.S. dominance of the international economic system is largely a result of a successful American foreign economic policy and a costly American security policy. The United States attained its two principal postwar economic foreign policy objectives: (1) the reconstruction and development of Western Europe and Japan and (2) the creation and maintenance of an open international economic order. Attaining the first objective created economic partners who have become rivals as well. Reaching the second objective led to a more complete integration of the United States into the world economy. The resulting interdependence continues to confer economic benefits on the United States in terms of static and perhaps dynamic efficiency, but it imposes constraints on American economic and security policy. American decision makers from Truman through Ford regarded an activist, globalist foreign policy as a precondition for the creation and maintenance of an open international economic order. The expenditures that are concomitants of an activist security policy have had costs in terms of other interests, however: economic productivity, growth, and technological change. Deficit financing of massive military expenditures has contributed to domestic inflation and international monetary instability.

For twenty-five years after World War II, U.S. foreign economic policy accorded well with American security goals and American values, as well as with American economic interests. The recovery and growth of Western Europe and Japan were seen as reducing the probability of Soviet subversion; providing markets for American goods, services, and capital; and reflecting the generosity of the American people. Creation of an open international economic order was seen as forestalling warfare over markets and raw materials between competing trading blocs, conferring significant economic benefits on the United States as the most advanced and prosperous economy, and reflecting American commitment to the principles of the free market.

Euro-Japanese recovery was facilitated by large infusions of economic assistance, trade preferences, and formation of the Common Market (EEC). American security policy may have had the unintended side effect of retarding U.S. economic development relative to that of the EEC and Japan. In the period between 1960 and 1975, the United States spent over $1 trillion on defense. Under a reasonably credible American nuclear umbrella, members of the EEC spent $390 billion and the Japanese $27 billion over that same period. Other factors partially account for disparities in investment, productivity growth, and output growth, but the strength of the association between military expenditures and the economic indicators in table 1.1 is provocative.[3]

TABLE 1.1

MILITARY EXPENDITURES, PRODUCTIVITY AND GROWTH, 1960–73

| | Ratio to Real Output | | Produc-tivity Growth Rate [b] (%) | Output Growth Rate (%) |
	Military Expend-itures (%)	Invest-ment [a] (%)		
United States	8.1	13.6	3.3	4.1
United Kingdom	5.6	15.2	4.0	2.9
France	4.8	18.2	6.0	5.9
West Germany	3.9	20.0	5.8	5.5
Italy	3.1	14.4	6.4	5.2
Canada	2.8	17.4	4.3	5.4
Japan	0.9	29.0	10.5	10.8

SOURCE: Ruth Leger Sivard, ed., *World Military and Social Expenditures 1977* (Leesburg, VA: WMSE Publications, 1977).
[a] Nonresidential fixed investment.
[b] Manufacturing output per manhour.

Public research and development expenditures are equally revealing. In 1975 aerospace and defense research and development expenditures by the EEC totaled $3.6 billion, while the United States spent $11.7 billion. Other research and development expenditures totaled $10.3 billion by the EEC and $6.8 billion by the United States.[4] That the technological lead of the United States over other advanced industrial societies seems to be shrinking should come as no surprise. The guns-butter tradeoff is real.

Most decision makers favor sidestepping tradeoffs, when possible, and American Presidents are not exceptions. Attempting to fudge the guns-butter tradeoff through deficit financing, irrespective of levels of aggregate demand, has become a hallowed tradition that has contributed to the diffusion of American power by tightening the financial constraint and increasing the intensity of contradictions across objectives of

American policy. The most important example is President Johnson's handling of the taxes–Great Society–Vietnam war tradeoff by deliberately underestimating the costs of the war. This triggered a significant rise in the rate of inflation and contributed to an increase in inflationary expectations that continues to exacerbate the classic inflation-unemployment tradeoff.

The international monetary effects were equally significant. For twenty-five years, the United States retained the option of running balance-of-payments deficits, secure in the knowledge that dollars leaving the United States would be held by foreign governments as reserve assets or used as international currency in commercial transactions and that the value of the dollar would be reasonably constant. Under this dollar exchange standard, the seigniorage accrued to the sovereign, and the sovereign's domestic economic policy was unconstrained by international economic considerations. President Johnson's method of financing the Indochina war increased the inflation rate and triggered an outflow of dollars in excess of the international demand for liquidity. As a consequence, national and transnational actors became less willing to hold dollars. Although the United States was able to check the ensuing currency crisis by persuading foreign governments to stop converting dollars into gold in 1968, the dollar exchange standard collapsed in 1971. The abuse of the privilege of printing internationally acceptable money changed the nature of the sovereign's prerogative. Under the current international monetary system, the United States continues to run large balance-of-payments deficits, but the value of the dollar in terms of other currencies is anything but constant, and domestic antiinflationary planning is complicated by fluctuations in the value of the dollar. Although the privilege of seigniorage continues, the autonomy of U.S. domestic economic planning has been substantially reduced.

The United States attained the second fundamental objective of postwar foreign economic policy by fashioning and maintaining an open international economic order where goods and capital could flow relatively freely. The extent of U.S. integration in the open world economy it created is crudely reflected in the following figures: Total U.S. trade increased from $35 billion in 1960 to $270 billion in 1977 (from $50.9 billion to $191 billion in constant 1972 dollars).[5] Over the same period, exports as a proportion of GNP increased from 4 to 6.2 percent, and imports as a proportion of GNP climbed from 3 to 7.8 percent [6] (and to approximately 10 percent in 1978). At the present time, one of every eight manufacturing jobs in the United States and one of every three acres of American farmland depend on exports. Two-thirds of American imports are raw materials or goods that the United States cannot readily produce.[7] The increase in American dependence on imported petroleum, from 19 percent of consumption in 1960 to 47 percent in 1977, is the foremost example. While the significance of trade increased, the distribution of trade by partner changed. From 1971 to 1976, the proportion of U.S. imports from OPEC states increased from 5 to 22 percent, while imports from developed states dropped from over 73 to 54 percent. OPEC's share of American exports increased from 5 to 10 percent, while the share of developed states dropped from 70 to 63 percent.[8] Rapid growth in Europe and Japan, the oil price increase, and industrialization of the upper tier of non-oil-producing Third World nations caused a *decline* in U.S. trade as a proportion of world trade; American exports as a proportion of world exports dropped from 18.2 to 12.1 percent.[9] In short, the relative importance of the United States in world trade has declined.

Under the open international economic order, direct foreign investment also increased, though less dramatically. Between 1960 and 1976, American direct foreign investment (net capital outflows) increased from $1674 million to $4596 million (in constant 1972 dollars, from $2436 million to $3259 million). The stock of U.S. direct foreign investment in 1976 amounted to $137 billion. Foreign direct investment in the United States increased much more rapidly, from $141 million to $2176 million (in constant 1972 dollars, from $205 million to $1543 million). In 1976, the stock of direct foreign investment in the United States amounted to over $30 billion.[10]

As the U.S. stake in the world economy expanded, the economic policy choices of other nations increasingly affected the interests of the United States. American dependence on imported petroleum is an obvious example. The value of the dollar is partially determined by how Saudi Arabia denominates petroleum prices and where Saudi Arabia places its currency reserves. American growth and inflation rates are affected by OPEC's oil-pricing policies *and* by the macroeconomic decisions of the EEC nations and Japan. Other nations' policies on direct foreign investment and trade affect the worth of $137 billion of American capital.

American ability to affect other nations' calculations of their national economic interests, although still significant, has declined. What was formerly a unique American asset in international economic negotiations—access to high technology, a massive market, and immense amounts of capital—can now be provided by the EEC and Japan. Moreover, the fact that U.S. interests are affected by the actions of others to an unprecedented extent provides other nations with potential levers to move the United States. The conjunction of the expansion of American international economic interests and the contraction of American ability to protect those interests has increased American vulnerability.

Although the difference between the near-unipolarity of the post–World War II order and the fragmentation of power in the contemporary international system is significant, the power of other nations is limited in range and depth. The Soviet Union is a military superpower, but its influence in international economic affairs is minimal. The Common Market nations and Japan have become economic superpowers, but their influence in international security is not great. OPEC nations may control petroleum and petrodollars, but their military influence is at most regional (Iran, Nigeria) and, more generally, limited to raising the costs of invasion. Non-oil-producing Third World nations exercise, at most, some control over access to their markets, their commodities, and their manufactured goods, as well as some local military influence. In all these cases, power is limited to one issue area or one locality.

Moreover, the logic of interdependence in security and economic spheres cuts both ways. Although differences in the internal form of government make the symmetry imperfect, the Soviet Union and the United States share a mutual interest in avoiding direct confrontation. Nuclear and conventional parity is not the equivalent of superiority, and the Soviet Union is not a global military hegemon. The guns-butter tradeoff is not an artifact of economic system, as evidenced by grumbling over the quality and quantity of Soviet consumer goods. Finally, perhaps because of the costs of protracted military intervention in the Third World, the Soviets have not used their troops as invasion forces outside the Warsaw Pact nations.

While the United States may be vulnerable to other nations' economic policy choices, the exploitation of that vulnerability would entail significant costs. Increasing economic interdependence has intensified the European, Japanese, OPEC, and non-oil-producing Third World stake in American economic actions. The economies of these other states, as well as the U.S. economy, have evolved under conditions of interdependence, and the disruption of international economic relations would entail significant self-inflicted economic costs. By virtue of economic size and diversity, the United States is *less* dependent on international trade than are other advanced industrial and most developing nations. Finally, while the United States cannot dictate the structure of the world economy, American action is a necessary, though not sufficient, precondition for the perpetuation, renovation, or revolution of the existing international economic order.

The United States remains the only nation that can claim to be both an economic and military superpower. Nevertheless, the United States is no longer the only economic *or* military superpower. The erosion of American dominance over all aspects of international relations does not portend the end of American influence. The role of the United States in international relations has simply become that of a more normal state, with interests to be protected with limited means.

Issue Proliferation

American foreign policy concerns have mushroomed in the past ten years. International issues and associated crises and conflicts seem to be increasing in numbers, if not always in significance, at an astounding rate. What are the driving forces behind the broadening agenda of U.S. international interests?

As indicated in the preceding section, international economic interdependence has increased the costs and benefits that are external to the interests of any one nation's economic policies. Increasing governmental sensitivity to the effects and side effects of other nations' economic policies has led to attempts to ensure that such externalities are internalized. For example, macroeconomic stabilization and growth, once a domestic economic issue, now lies at the center of advanced industrial nations' economic summitry. Price levels of domestic American petroleum and natural gas concern Western Europe and Japan because of their direct and indirect effects on the stability of the dollar, the value of currency reserves, the price of petroleum internationally, the levels of inflation and unemployment in those countries, and the accessibility of markets for their exports. Economic interdependence has created these new issues and has added to the significance of traditional international economic issues such as money, trade, and investment.

The advanced industrial nations' struggle over the management of interdependence has been a short-term, nonviolent dispute over degrees of prosperity. Attention to problems such as nuclear proliferation and the global Malthusian dilemma has been triggered by fear of potentially violent long-term struggle over matters of life and death. Inchoate concern has been crystallized by contemporary events. The Indian detonation of a "peaceful nuclear explosive" in 1974, the exponential growth of the nuclear power industry, and the potential use of by-products of nuclear energy in the production of weapons have increased the immediacy of the problem of nuclear proliferation. For some, the existence of malnutrition has been dramatized by crises (e.g., famines in Bangladesh and the Sahel). For others, the limits to growth imposed by finite resources, as analyzed by the Club of Rome, were foreshadowed by the atmosphere of quiet desperation that prevailed at the time of the Arab oil embargo, and by the three years of economic stagnation that followed the OPEC price increase. Precise calculation of national advantage associated with long-term "world order" issues is impossible. Such calculations are likely to be rendered invalid by changes in technology, changes in the distribution of power, and the intrinsic unpredictability of acts of desperation. Nevertheless, the global interest in avoiding possible nuclear struggle over finite resources is clear.

Concern over economic interdependence and the long-term global dilemma accounts for but a small proportion of the issues crowding the agenda of American foreign policy. The diffusion of power is the driving force behind many new issues. As American dominance has declined, latent conflicts have become manifest, and manifest conflicts have become manifestly more significant. Dissatisfaction per se does not create an international issue. But the expression of dissatisfaction by actors who can affect important interests of other states can create an international issue. Black African dissatisfaction with racism in the white minority regimes of southern Africa is not a recent development. The likelihood of Soviet activity in southern Africa and U.S. reliance on black African petroleum and minerals have increased over the past five years, however, as has American official attention to southern Africa. As American dominance over Latin America has eroded, American attention to some Latin American problems has increased. Latin American nations have long viewed the Panama Canal Zone as a vestige of imperialism. The priority attached to renegotiating treaties with Panama and the decline of American dominance are tightly associated. American attention to the Middle East in the 1970s has increased in proportion to the apparent power of the oil-producing Arab states. Third World dissatisfaction over the existing international distribution of wealth is long-standing. The North-South dialogue over commodity stabilization, trade preferences, debt rescheduling, technology transfer, and aid did not receive much official attention until American economic interests were affected by dependence on a more powerful Third World. In the security sphere, increases in Soviet power account for the centrality of arms control to the past three administrations and the more recent resurgence of interest in conventional military issues. The intensification of official interest in NATO parallels Soviet attainment of nuclear parity and augmentation of Warsaw Pact forces. Most Americans thought Diego Garcia was a cigar until control of the Indian Ocean was elevated to the status of an "official concern" after the Soviet Navy developed into more than a coastal defense force. The regional conflict between Somalia and Ethiopia over the Ogaden is ancient, and secessionist movements in Eritria and Shaba have been attempting to break away from Ethiopia and Zaire for over a decade. In part, these disputes have been elevated to prominent places on the agenda of American policy because some antagonists have turned to a more active and distinctly more powerful Soviet Union. The diffusion of power and the proliferation of issues intertwine.

Issue Interdependence

Power contraction and interest expansion have strained the edifice of American foreign policy. But not all parts of the building are subject to equal stress. As inhabitants, we have an obvious interest in assessing how weakness in one area can affect the integrity of the whole, and how bricks and beams can be moved from areas of strength to shore up areas of weakness. These concerns are addressed in the section on structural connections across issues. That neighbors should be concerned about common supporting walls is understandable. That we and they should seek to influence each other's plans for construction and renovation is eminently predictable. Cross-issue linkage strategy is often the instrument of diplomacy chosen to project influence.

Issue interdependence bears directly on what has become the major theme of academic writing on the Carter administration's foreign policy. Articles by Stanley Hoffmann and Thomas Hughes in *Foreign Policy* [11] correctly assert that the management of contradictions is a central task of foreign policy. American support for Israel and American interest in Arab petroleum, petrodollar reserves, and trade are often held to be inconsistent. The reduction of world consumption of petroleum may increase the rapidity of nuclear proliferation. Accommodation to Third World demands for a more equitable international economic order may exacerbate existing problems in the northern economic system. The list may be readily extended. The current administration is impaled on the horns of many contradictions, and their management is perhaps the most painful task of American foreign policy. This discussion of issue interdependence assumes that the effective management of contradictions must be based on an analysis of the causes of contradictions. Sections on tactical and structural issue interdependence offer a partial explanation of why contradictions have emerged. The analysis of causes then provides a basis for the management of contradictions.

Tactical Issue Linkage

The tactic of cross-issue linkage, of joining otherwise unrelated issues for bargaining purposes, occupies a central position in contemporary diplomacy. The irregularity of the diffusion of power has left many nations with power concentrated on one issue and interests spread across many issues. This distribution of power and interest provides a strong impetus to the use of cross-issue linkage, as nations strive to transmit power from an area of strength to secure objectives in areas of weakness.

For instance, Saudi Arabia has tacitly linked maintenance of petroleum production at levels "in excess of financial needs" to the American sale of high-performance fighter aircraft. The Organization of Arab Petroleum Exporting Countries (OAPEC) embargo of 1973–74 linked supply of petroleum to Western policies on the Arab-Israeli conflict. A coalition of Third World states linked support for creation of the Special Drawing Right * to increases in the flow of developmental assistance.

The United States has also used issue linkage to impose tradeoffs on others. Kissingerian détente was premised on the linkage of American food, trade, and credits to Soviet "restraint" in its international activities. Senator Henry Jackson and Representative Charles Vanik linked East-West trade issues to Soviet relaxation of restrictions on emigration. President Eisenhower used linkage against the British in 1956, by making American support for a floundering pound contingent on British withdrawal from the Suez invasion. More recently, nations that are not of great economic or military significance to the United States and violate human rights have been confronted by the Carter administration's linkage of security assistance and human rights.

The United States is both "linker" and "linkee." How should America approach tradeoffs created by other nations? How should the U.S. use linkage diplomacy to project power from areas of strength into areas of weakness? To structure inquiry into the uses and abuses of linkage tactics, it is useful to distinguish between two classes of linkage strategy:

> Backscratching: *promises to refrain from doing something one believes to be in one's interest, if compensated; and threats to do something one believes to be in one's interest, unless compensated.*

> Blackmailing: *threats to do something one does not believe to be in one's interest, unless compensated; and promises to refrain from doing something one does not believe to be in one's own interest, if compensated.*[12]

In both categories, the linker threatens to inflict a cost or promises to refrain from inflicting a cost on the linkee. The distinction hinges on the interest of the linker in the threatened or promised action. In backscratching, the linker is requesting compensation for refraining from actions that are in his best interest. In blackmailing, the linker is requesting compensation for refraining from actions that are *not* in his best interest. The tacit Saudi Arabian linkage between maintenance of petroleum production at levels "in excess of financial needs" and American arms sales is an example of backscratching. The OAPEC embargo, an action that was not in and of itself in the interest of the OAPEC states, is an example of blackmailing.

When confronted by a tactical linkage, what considerations should affect decisions on the management of the tradeoff? Some offers may be intrinsically unacceptable. Though the calculation and comparison of interests can be difficult in practice, the compensation requested may simply outweigh whatever is offered in return. It is also evident that in negotiations, actors will strive to minimize their concessions and maximize their gains. Even these bland generalizations take on life, and devilish complexity, in the detailed analyses in later chapters in this volume. The distinction between backscratching and blackmailing produces less obvious generalizations on linkage diplomacy. When the interest in whatever is offered outweighs the compen-

---

* An artificial reserve asset, issued by the International Monetary Fund.

sation requested, the distinction should affect decisions on the management of the tradeoff. Let us consider the differences in a simplified two-actor world (i.e., ignoring the effects of linkage on third parties).

Does the creation of the linkage increase or decrease the level of satisfaction the linkee can attain? Under backscratching, the linkee at worst will be as well off as he would have been without the offer, and can be better off than if the offer had not been made. Were it not for the linkage, the other actor would simply go ahead with the action threatened. By joining issues, the linker offers the linkee the option of weighing interests in each issue and compensating the linker for foregoing an action the linker would otherwise undertake. If the linkage is not accepted, both parties are as well off as they would have been without the linkage. If the linkage is accepted, both parties are better off then they would have been had the linkage not been offered. In backscratching, linkage increases the level of satisfaction both the linker and linkee can attain. Under blackmailing, the linkee is better off *without* the offered linkage. Were it not for the linkage, the other actor would not even consider going ahead with the action threatened; the definition of blackmailing is requesting compensation for refraining from doing something one would *not* otherwise do. Although the essence of backscratching lies in the mutuality of benefits, blackmailing is distinctly asymmetrical. Blackmailing generally lowers the level of satisfaction the linkee can attain. Whereas the linkee may reject specific backscratching offers and accept specific blackmailing offers, *linkees should be predisposed toward encouraging backscratching and discouraging blackmailing.*

How does the linker's credibility affect the linkee's decision to accept or reject the tradeoff? Under backscratching, the linkee can be certain that if the offer is rejected, the linker will make good on the threat by proceeding to do what would be in his best interests to do. If the offer is accepted, however, the linkee must be concerned about the credibility of the linker's promise to refrain from acting in his own best interests. The credibility issue centers on the linkee's fear of the linker's reneging once the offer is accepted.

Under blackmailing, the linkee can be certain that if the offer is accepted, the linker will refrain from doing something he would otherwise not do, undoubtedly with some sense of relief. If the offer is rejected, however, the linkee must be concerned about the credibility of the linker's threat to act in a fashion not in the linker's own interests. The credibility issue centers on the hope that the blackmailer will not make good the threat to engage in mutually disadvantageous activity.

Although reneging or backing down has advantages in any single encounter, the trader values his reputation for honesty and the blackmailer values his reputation for apparently irrational ruthlessness because each expects to be involved in future encounters. The potential victim of blackmailing also has a reputation to protect. Given the proliferation of international issues and interests, the number of potential actions with the characteristics of imposing costs on the linkee and not necessarily being in the interest of the linker is large. As argued, the linkee has a strong interest in discouraging blackmailing, because that form of linkage lowers the level of satisfaction the linkee can attain. By increasing the probability of future blackmail, accession to extortion has very high long-term costs to the linkee.

From a welfare perspective, undisguised blackmail is likely to produce the worst of all worlds. The victim has an interest in reducing his vulnerability to future threats, and is likely to reject the offer. The blackmailer has an interest in bolstering his credibility, and is likely to execute the threat. By its nature, blackmail tends to become an ultimate test of credibility, with corrosive effects on the atmosphere of international relations and the interests of both blackmailer and victim.

For better or for worse, world politics revolves around power rather than global welfare. The two forms of linkage have different long-term effects on the linker's leverage over the linkee. What linkee reactions are likely to be triggered by blackmailing? Were it not for the linkage, the blackmailer would not consider undertaking the threatened action, and there would be little incentive for the linkee to adopt defensive measures. Blackmailing creates an incentive for the linkee to minimize his sensitivity to the actions of the linker, and thereby reduces the blackmailer's leverage in future encounters. The OAPEC embargo triggered modest defensive actions by the advanced industrial states; even a threat of embargo would have induced the West to undertake steps to reduce its dependence on Arab oil. Backscratching provides the linkee with an opportunity to compensate the linker for refraining from an action that would otherwise occur; were it not for the linkage, the linkee would seek to reduce his sensitivity. Where the linkee's cost of compensation is less than the cost imposed by the threatened action, backscratching reduces the preexisting incentive of the linkee to adopt defensive measures. Saudi Arabian production in excess of national needs lessened the urgency of conservation efforts; in the absence of linkage, the cutback in production and resulting increase in oil prices would have triggered more intensive conservation efforts and thereby reduced·Western dependency on Saudi Arabian oil. Blackmailing tends to dissipate leverage, while backscratching perpetuates dependency. All other things being equal, blackmailing is a power expenditure, whereas backscratching is a power investment.

The domestic characteristics of the United States and the objective requirements of linkage diplomacy are not complementary. Backscratching involves sacrificing interests in one area to secure benefits in another. In the United States, the interest traded off is likely to be well organized and well equipped with congressional and bureaucratic allies. The very act of trading off issues is likely to entail significant domestic political costs, as the Carter administration has discovered. Under backscratching, linker and linkee frequently attempt to exaggerate the magnitude of their concessions to secure an edge in negotiations. This will always increase fear of reneging. Use of this negotiating tactic by the United States would also strengthen the hand of domestic groups whose interests lie in the issue to be sacrificed.

If their credibility is to be maintained over future encounters, successful backscratchers should not renege and unsuccessful blackmailers should not back down. The fragmentation of power within the United States has paradoxical effects on the nation's credibility. On the one hand, presidential ability to make good on promises or threats may be undermined. For example, the much-delayed energy program was promised to the other advanced industrial societies in exchange for greater stimulation of their economies. Both sides failed to make good on their promises. Kissinger's linkage between trade and Soviet foreign policy presumably included an implicit promise that trade would not be reused as a lever on other issues. The Jackson-Vanik amendment would have violated such a promise. On the other hand, the linkage between economic cooperation with the Soviet Union and cessation of Soviet activity in Africa, made by President Carter in his Wake Forest speech, may have been made *more credible* by the President's inability to control a Congress predisposed toward making the linkage.

The possibility of blackmailing the Soviets by making SALT II contingent on a more restrained Soviet foreign policy is also affected by congressional strength. An undisguised linkage would not be credible given the strong American, as well as Soviet, interest in SALT II relative to African issues. Nevertheless, significant uncertainty over senatorial ratification of the proposed SALT II treaty increases the credibility of the threat. At the same time, making the threat would have the effect of reducing the probability of ratification by increasing senatorial doubts about the merits of the treaty, *and* would make the treaty a hostage of insurgent movements the Soviets may not control. The doubts would be magnified if the President sought to bolster the credibility of a blackmailing strategy by disguising it as backscratching, that is, by attempting to convince the Soviets that treaty ratification would not be in the American interest. The administration would probably not convince the Soviets; however, more than one-third of the Senate would probably believe that SALT II was not in the American interest, and ratification of the treaty *irrespective* of Soviet activity would become problematical.

These real and hypothetical examples underscore one simple point: whereas the international diffusion of power has increased the incidence and significance of linkage tactics, the domestic fragmentation of power has greatly complicated American management of linkage.

Structural Connections

Not all tradeoffs are deliberately created in the course of bargaining. Structural connections between issues can also create tensions across objectives. The economists' Phillips curve describes a tradeoff between inflation and unemployment, created by the relationship of each to a number of factors including aggregate demand. Conventional arms sales inherently increase the level of violence of regional warfare. Such arms sales also spread the fixed costs of research and development and tooling up over a longer production run, and thereby lower the unit cost of weapons to the American military, improve the American balance of trade, and under some circumstances reduce the probability of regional warfare. Satisfaction of Third World demands for free access to the markets of advanced industrial societies by expansion of the Generalized System of Preferences (GSP) would produce the complementary benefit of reducing the prices of some goods. The expansion of trade preferences would also impose an adjustment burden on labor in affected industries, with potentially high domestic political costs. The development of nuclear energy may be a precondition for reduction of world consumption of oil. The by-products of nuclear fuel reprocessing can be diverted to the production of nuclear weapons, however, and thus increase the probability of nuclear proliferation.

The management of structural tradeoffs across issues requires more than the simple assignment of priorities to issues. Decision making on tradeoffs created by tactical linkage should be informed by sensitivity to the class of linkage strategy producing the tradeoff; successful management of structurally produced tradeoffs depends on careful analysis of the underlying cause of the apparent contradiction.

For example, the apparent tradeoff between nuclear proliferation and petroleum consumption may be moderated by policies that weaken the structural connection between the issues. By developing alternative energy sources, controlling access to the nuclear fuel cycle, or developing reprocessing technology that does not produce near-weapons-grade by-products, the tension between the two objectives may be reduced, though probably not eliminated.

When policies to mitigate structural tradeoffs are inconceivable or ineffective, the relative interest in incompatible objectives must be assessed and a choice made. The choice is contingent on the context. In his discussion of U.S. African policy, Donald Rothchild argues that mutually reinforcing idealist and economic goals should be given primacy over traditional security objectives; he also observes that this hierarchy of interests should not guide American policy on the Middle East. One cannot answer the question "Which is more important, inflation or unemployment?" without information on the inflation rate, the unemployment rate, and other economic and political variables. When goals conflict, the determination of priorities depends on the marginal satisfaction of each objective and the connections between each objective and other goals. Even when structural connections across issues are known to create tradeoffs, it may be inappropriate to resolve the tradeoffs on an a priori basis.

Uncertainty

The rational management of tradeoffs created by tactical and structural connections between issues is complicated by the instability of the connections. Tactical linkages between issues are exceedingly difficult to predict. The OAPEC embargo, the Third World link between Special Drawing Rights and development assistance, the Eisenhower administration linkage between monetary policy and Suez, and the Carter administration link between security-supporting assistance and human rights were not anticipated by the linkees. Tactical linkage is intrinsically difficult to predict, and tadeoffs created by tactical linkage are inherently unstable. The presence or absence of a tactical linkage rests on the inclinations and shrewdness of the linker and the linkee. Although one can identify opportunities for issue linkage by examining the distribution of interests and capabilities, the number of potential backscratchings is enormous and the number of potential blackmailings even larger. Only a fraction of the opportunities are likely to be acted on, and aside from observing what linkages have been constructed in the past, no clear criteria have emerged for predicting patterns of issue linkage.

Of the structural connections discussed above, only the Phillips curve has been estimated with any precision. The relationship between inflation and unemployment has varied over time, as higher inflation rates have come to be associated with any specific unemployment rate. Economists differ in their analyses of the causes of the tradeoffs and the effects of policies on tradeoff characteristics, and even argue over the existence of the tradeoff over the long run. The other structural connections discussed above appear to be even more unstable. The connection between a pair of objectives may be contingent on a third or fourth variable; these interaction effects can produce changes in the intensity and even the direction of a tradeoff. For example, the direction of the connection between regional stability and arms transfers may be affected by a host of considerations including patterns of regional alliances, specific characteristics of leaders and governments, conflicts of interest within the region, and extraregional power distribution. The effect of GSP on labor in affected domestic industries is also unstable; the strength of the association is likely to be affected by general levels of domestic economic activity, skills of workers, mobility of capital and labor in the affected industry, and quantity and quality of adjustment assistance.

The unpredictability of tactical linkage and the instability of structural linkage are parts of a larger problem. The current quality and ultimate imperfectability of social science research impose limits on our ability to define and estimate tradeoffs, interests, and power. But while the scholar is restricted to observation, the practitioner may engage in prudent experimentation. Foreign policy initiatives may be designed to acquire information and reduce uncertainty. The scholar may sit back and wrestle with theoretical and methodological issues, but the practitioner must formulate policy. If uncertainty cannot be reduced significantly, policy should be made less sensitive to misinformation or limited information. The Carter administration has grappled with an insufficiency of power and knowledge, and its policy choices must be understood in terms of both problems.

CARTER ADMINISTRATION FOREIGN POLICY

There is no Carter Doctrine or Vance Doctrine or Brown Doctrine because of a belief that the environment we are looking at is far too complex to be reduced to a doctrine in the tradition of post–World War II American foreign policy. Indeed, the Carter approach to foreign policy rests on a belief that not only is the world far too complex to be reduced to a doctrine, but that there is something inherently wrong with having a doctrine at all.[13]

—Leslie Gelb, *Assistant Secretary of State*

The problem does not lie so much in defining these goals as in managing complexity when they may come into conflict–striking a balance among competing objectives. . . . Our approach is to make constant, pragmatic, case by case decisions, seeking the most constructive balance among our interests and adjusting our tactics as circumstances change.[14]

—Anthony Lake, *Director of the Policy Planning Staff, Department of State*

Conventional wisdom notes that the Carter administration is blessed with many foreign policies but has no foreign policy. The administration's initial approach to international relations assumed that the difficult problem of developing a coherent and realistic set of policies for an exceedingly complex world could be avoided by dividing the problem into more tractable components. As a corollary, early administration tactics aimed at preserving or increasing the separateness of issues. The administration established no hierarchy of objectives, used the tactic of cross-issue linkages sparingly, and developed distinct policies for each issue.

This disaggregative approach to foreign policy also had a strong domestic political rationale. The administration needed the support of a Democratic Congress on its foreign and domestic policy, but congressional opinion on foreign policy is fragmented. Setting priorities and using linkage entail significant domestic political costs. Some factional interest must be sacrificed. By separating the strands of foreign policy, the administration sought to avoid shattering the Democratic congressional coalition it depended on for support.*

If the issues had been independent or mutually supporting, the consequences of disaggregation might not have been serious. In the light of tactical and structural tradeoffs, the incoherence of American foreign policy produced instability in the specific components of foreign policy and, perhaps most seriously, fostered equivocation on the fundamental question of adaptation to the reality of declining power and expanding interests.

There is no overarching framework which might provide larger meaning to the components of the Carter administration's foreign policy. To *understand* contemporary foreign policy, it is useful to view the components as specific responses to specific problems. To *critique* administration foreign policy, it is necessary to look at the relationship of the parts to the whole.

Components of Policy

The Carter administration's response to the diffusion of military power—the equivalence of Soviet-American nuclear and conventional forces and the limitations on American ability to intervene in the Third World—has many faces. The administration sought to stabilize and formalize "mutual assured destruction" by developing weapons systems that are relatively invulnerable to attack, such as the cruise missile, Trident, and MX, and by continuing the SALT II negotiations. Carter has attempted to lessen the effects of nuclear parity on other areas of foreign policy by continuing the Mutual Balanced Force Reduction talks, strengthening NATO conventional forces, and programming a 3 percent real increase in defense spending over the next four years.[15]

The administration's response to limitations on U.S. capacity for prolonged intervention in the Third World has been to rely on a three-tiered strategy. Third World security policy has been reordered by (1) an increase in American toleration of revolutionary nationalism in "nonvital areas" and an attendant decrease in the use of overt and covert intervention for counterrevolutionary purposes; (2) a modest increase in the resources devoted to strengthening regional power centers, such as Nigeria, Iran, Saudi Arabia, Indonesia, India, Venezuela, and Brazil, which may be in a position to serve as possible partners of the United States; and (3) a purported increase in the mobility of American conventional strike forces, to permit "light-

---

* For further discussion of "valence" issues and American foreign policy, see chapter 2.

ning" preemptive intervention in threatened "vital areas," such as the Middle East.

The administration's response to the dual problem of increasing international economic interdependence and diffusing economic power has been consistent in its commitment to the principles of economic liberalism. For example, the administration has sought to trade off lower American tariffs on manufactured goods for lessened EEC and Japanese restrictions on agricultural commodities. On the tightly interconnected North-North economic issues of trade, money, employment, inflation, growth, and energy, the administration has, as Robert Keohane argues later in this volume, "struggled to make others adjust." But the pursuit of national advantage has been tempered by the professed American core interest in maintaining the open economic system it fashioned after the Second World War. Initially, the administration encouraged the devaluation of the dollar to increase the competitiveness of American exports and reduce the balance of payments deficit without resorting to domestic austerity measures. In the fall of 1978, the accelerating decline in the value of the dollar intensified domestic inflation and threatened the stability of the international economic order. The administration intervened to check the slide of the dollar and raised the discount rate. A vigorous domestic neomercantile reaction to increasing foreign economic competition would also pose a threat to openness; exceptions to the international economic liberalism of the administration, such as the negotiation of "orderly marketing agreements" to soften the effects of foreign competition and the creation of "trigger prices" that would activate restrictions on underpriced foreign steel imports, were motivated by fear of more protectionist measures Congress might pass.

The administration has responded to Third World dissatisfaction with the existing distribution of benefits in the international economic system by making limited concessions. For example, the United States accepted self-financing commodity stabilization agreements that cannot be readily transformed into cartels and acquiesced slightly to demands for redistribution of power in international rule-making organizations. The concessions have been relatively inexpensive, in terms of American economic interests, and may have been viewed by the administration as the minimal price the United States must pay to ensure continued integration of the South in the world economy. The long-stalled energy program was intended as a direct response to the most painful North-South problem—dependency on imported petroleum.

The administration recognized that it lacked a domestic consensus on foreign policy. It confronted this problem by replacing anticommunism with idealism as a basis for sanctifying American foreign policy. This was expressed most clearly in President Carter's address at the University of Notre Dame. Anticommunism was explicitly set aside as the central theme of foreign policy: "we are now free of that inordinate fear of communism which led us to embrace any dictator who joined us in that fear." Essentially idealistic policies were announced on many issues. A commitment to human rights, a reduction of conventional arms sales, and a reorientation of foreign aid toward the satisfaction of basic human needs may be rationalized in terms of long-term economic and security interests. But the administration's initial position on each of these issues is better understood as an expression of both the values of the President and his administration's perceptions of American values. By way of contrast, the limited American concessions on the North-South economic dialogue and the commitment to checking nuclear proliferation are best viewed as pragmatic actions with strong idealistic overtones.

These changes in American foreign policy objectives were paralleled by changes in the style of American foreign policy. The idealism of the Carter administration was to be that of a morality of means as well as ends. Kissinger's penchant for secrecy and deception was to be ended. In Carter's words, "Our policy must be open and candid." The amoral Kissingerian diplomacy was to be replaced by "a policy based on constant decency in its values." The esoteric Kissingerian diplomacy was to be supplanted by a more democratic foreign policy "that the American people both support and understand." The excesses of past policy on Indochina and Allende's Chile were denounced: "We fought fire with fire, never thinking that fire is better fought with water." Initial administration policy was marked by a strong aversion to the use of a frequently employed instrument of Kissingerian foreign policy: clandestine intervention in the affairs of other nations. Kissinger's favorite tactic—cross-issue linkage—can also be incompatible with a morality of means. To enhance future credibility, successful backscratching and unsuccessful blackmailing involve doing what is *not right* on one issue to secure an advantage on another issue. The Carter administration made little use of linkage tactics in its first year for this reason, as well as to maintain the separateness of issues. Through its positions on some issues and its general foreign policy style, the Carter administration distanced itself from the *Realpolitik* of the previous administrations.

Contradictions and Change

Initially, the Carter administration's approach to international relations was agnostic in the sense that the administration was noncommittal and undogmatic on the characteristics of connections across the strands of its foreign policy. Orthodox beliefs on tradeoffs across issues were set aside. The administration sought to develop policies that were reasonable responses to particular problems and resolve contradictions between policies as they emerged. The pages that follow center on emerging tensions between the components of the administration's foreign policy and on the changing approach of the administration to foreign affairs.

Connections Between Policies

The clearest contradictions in the current administration's foreign policy are products of structural and tactical issue interdependence. Arguments about the proper course of foreign policy are often debates over the sign and intensity of connections between objectives of foreign policy. First, few objectives are of consummatory interest. The importance of most foreign policy goals is instrumental and must be based on the assessment of connections to other objectives. Second, attaining one goal may compromise another. The side effects of a successful policy on one issue can undermine or negate progress on another issue. Each chapter in this volume seeks to define American interests and critique American policy with sensitivity to these connections.

Chapters on Soviet-American relations and on human rights focus on the connection between the protection of human rights in the Soviet Union—a core component of the idealistic thrust of Carter foreign policy—and SALT II negotiations and the overall structure of détente. The idealistic objective of promoting a more just international economic order may conflict with domestic economic objectives and may exacerbate trade tensions between advanced industrial societies. Analysis of American policy toward China discusses the triangle of Soviet-American-Chinese relations that creates complementary and contradictory connections between American policies toward both communist powers.

At this point, let us examine some possible contradictions that are relevant to several later chapters. The administration's emphasis on partnership with such "newly influential" nations as Saudi Arabia, Venezuela, Nigeria, Iran, Indonesia, Brazil, and India is understandable given the diffusion of military and economic power. Nevertheless, many leaders of these potential regional power centers may be unable to retain control of their states, much less their regions. At present, only Brazil and India possess both the internal stability and military strength to function as poles of stability in their regions. Nigeria and Indonesia are beset by sectionalism. The Shah of Iran was opposed by an eclectic set of groups ranging from ultrafundamentalist Muslims through liberal-constitutionalists to Marxists. Others are militarily weak. Saudi Arabia is vulnerable to neighboring Iran and perhaps even Iraq, and may be threatened by subversion from radical Shiite, Baathist, and leftist neighbors and its large Yemeni and Palestinian labor force. Venezuela is reasonably stable and prosperous but has neither the military nor the economic strength to be considered a regional power.

Actions that might be undertaken to strengthen these potential regional power centers can negate other objectives of the administration. The transfer of large quantities of high-quality conventional weapons conflicts with the objective of controlling conventional arms sales. The infusion of economic assistance conflicts with the administration's commitment to reorienting foreign aid toward basic human needs. Direct foreclosure of political threats to the stability of the regimes conflicts with the administration's repudiation of clandestine intervention. Toleration of repressive actions by these regimes conflicts with the administration's human rights objectives. Secondary actions that follow from the regional hegemones policy are antithetical to idealistic objectives of the administration.

One important debate bridges the chapters on Third World regions and Europe. Substantial criticism has been directed at the administration's initial noninterventionist stance on revolutionary nationalism. This debate has centered on the connection between the internal ideological and economic evolution of other nations and the political, economic, and military interests of the United States. Both conservative internationalists and neo-Marxists hold the nature of the connection to be clear. The anticommunist cites the connection as a rationale for intervention; the neo-Marxist cites the connection as an explanation of American foreign policy. With the notable exception of "human rights," early Carter administration foreign policy was based on the assumption that the internal evolution of other nations can be disassociated from the vital interests of the United States. As befits an administration that may be characterized as "nondoctrinal," the pragmatic nationalism of other states was seen as transcending matters of ideology. In economic terms, the administration's belief in the mutuality of benefits from economic interchange permitted the deduction that *pragmatic* states will continue to be participants in an international economic order irrespective of ideology, simply because it is in their interest to do so. The revolutionary Neto government of Angola has stationed a relatively large proportion of the Cuban troops to protect Gulf Oil operations in Cabinda, which provide nearly all of Angola's foreign exchange. The radical Touré government of Guinea and the Fria mining company, a multinational corporation, agreed that Guinea would own 49 percent of the shares and receive 65 percent of the profits of Fria's Guinean subsidiary.[16] Vietnam has turned to European national oil companies for the development of offshore petroleum, and those companies in turn rely heavily on American technology and equipment. The People's Republic of China is negotiating with American oil companies about development of its offshore reserves, with Japanese banks and trading companies for foreign credits, with several multinational corporations in the matter of a free trade zone in China, and with a Pan American subsidiary for construction, financing, and operation of a luxury hotel chain. The West remains the principal source of technology and capital and the principal market for goods produced. The administration's view of Third World regimes as having a stake in reaching mutually beneficial arrangements with the West, irrespective of ideology, has some empirical support.

Nationalism was held to reduce the consequences of most internal developments on American national security. If states are interested in preserving national autonomy and avoiding control by the United States and the Soviet Union, their form of government may be immaterial to the balance of Soviet-American military power. Eurocommunists are likely to be more fearful of Soviet hegemony and the Brezhnev doctrine than of American military power. Third World states or insurgent groups may, for a variety of reasons, turn to the Soviet Union for military assistance or to proxies of the Soviet Union for troops. But the repudiation of the Soviet Union by Ghana, the Sudan, Egypt, and Somalia indicate that "client" states' East-West orientation can change rapidly. The increase in autonomy that makes the internal evolution of other states less susceptible to American control may lessen the consequences of this loss of control.

This is not to argue that the administration prefers leftist nationalism to its alternatives; rather, the Carter administration differs from its predecessors in believing that the economic and military consequences of leftist nationalism do not outweigh the costs of intervention. Even if this belief is correct, contradictions between the Administration's policy of toleration and other objectives may be created by congressional dissatisfaction over a "do nothing" policy. For example, Senator S. I. Hayakawa sought to blackmail the administration by linking his vote on ratification of the Panama treaties to the adoption of a more interventionist American policy in Africa. Ratification of the SALT II treaty may be endangered if conservative internationalists in the Senate link that issue to a more explicitly interventionist American foreign policy or a less interventionist Soviet foreign policy.

Many additional instances of possible tensions between components of administration foreign policy are examined in later chapters of this book. The American interest in each international issue is real. American international interests have proliferated, and the officially sanctioned agenda of American foreign policy has been expanded to encompass many of these new interests. Unfortunately, the tensions across the strands of American foreign policy are also real. The situation necessitates choices between unpleasant alternatives. The key issue centers on the administration's handling of contradictions across its foreign policies.

Evolution of Strategy

The administration initially sought to postpone consideration of contradictions across its foreign policies. When an inconsistency in objectives became manifest or when hard decisions on the allocation of foreign policy resources could not be postponed, contradictions were resolved on a piecemeal basis. As a consequence, policies on specific regional and functional issues seemed to change in response to the "pragmatic ordering of priorities" of the week. Variations in policy attributable to changing circumstances, acquisition of information on the characteristics of specific issues, and changing tradeoffs across objectives were magnified by the ad hoc adjustment of priorities. Observers have pointed to flipflops on human rights, conventional arms sales, Eurocommunism, southern Africa, the Horn of Africa, diplomatic recognition of Cuba and Vietnam, the neutron bomb, normalization of relations with the People's Republic of China, nuclear proliferation, strategic arms limitations, and the Middle East. Policy instability on a range of issues undermined American credibility, confused attentive elites in and out of the administration, and befuddled both adversaries and allies.

The Carter administration confronts a hidden tradeoff, for the instability of policy cannot be reduced without costs. The administration's strategy of not addressing tradeoffs until they emerge—not setting rigid priorities—has some merit. First, one cannot predict on a priori grounds patterns of tactical issue linkage, and structural connections between issues are often contingent on third factors. Although pundits have argued that each of the contradictions discussed above should have been anticipated, the intensity of specific contradictions could not have been known in advance. By waiting for contradictions to emerge, the Carter administration did not *unnecessarily* sacrifice interests to attain other interests. Second, by not making its ordering of preferences clear at the outset, the administration may have slightly enhanced its ability to conduct effective linkage diplomacy. Potential blackmailers cannot calibrate their threats accurately when they have only a rough idea of what relative value their victim is likely to place on the issues to be joined. Backscratching partners will have difficulty calculating what exchange will be minimally acceptable to the Carter administration. The current administration's resolution of this tradeoff between costs and benefits of its style of decision making has been of dubious quality. Nevertheless, much of the current criticism of oscillations in Carter administration foreign policy should be tempered by the recognition of this tradeoff between flexibility and stability.

As the costs of instability became clear, the administration dampened its foreign policy oscillations. A trend may be emerging. What was most distinctive about the foreign policy of the Carter administration—idealist objectives, tolerance of leftist revolutionary nationalism, and relatively open decision making—eroded as conflicts with traditional security and economic concerns emerged and as the domestic political salience of those traditional concerns became manifest. The initial enthusiasm for protecting human rights in all nations became far more selective. Progress on idealistic North-South issues entailing significant economic costs—granting free access to northern markets by dramatic expansion of the GSP, increasing aid to one percent of GNP, and reorienting aid toward basic human needs—was minimal. While some arms sales were cancelled, the objective of reducing transfers of conventional arms was scaled down dramatically as the economic, political, and military benefits of sales became apparent. The administration's tolerant attitude toward revolutionary nationalism in Africa triggered a sharp reaction among conservative internationalists in Congress, and the administration tempered its toleration, though it has not returned to the explicitly counterrevolutionary policy of past administrations. The promised "open and candid" foreign policy had the effect of revealing inevitable disputes within the administration. This contributed to the image of blundering and ineptness and to some of the errors in policy implementation that bedeviled the administration. All speeches must now be cleared by the White House. The Carter administration sought to stabilize its foreign policy by emphasizing traditional realist objectives and approaches, where realism and idealism failed to coincide.

But realism is not an unambiguous guide for policy, and Carter policy has continued to fluctuate. In 1978 two unpopular authoritarian regimes of the right faced mass insurrections. The administration's changing policies on Iran and Nicaragua were torn by the tradeoff between supporting an existing regime satisfying some American interests and cultivating possible successors. When rioting and strikes first crippled Iran's petroleum-based economy, the administration expressed confidence in the shah's ability to ride out the crisis and shipped teargas, fuel, and messages of support to the shah. As popular discontent over the distribution of economic benefits and the shah's autocratic style of rule fused with Islamic fundamentalism, the shah's ability to retain power—with or without American support—appeared increasingly problematical. However, the attenuation of American support was likely to undermine the credibility of American commitments to the governments of other "new influentials," without excising memories of twenty-five years of intimate American relations with the shah from the minds of the opposition. When the fall of the shah appeared imminent, the administration shifted its policy. In January of 1979, President Carter encouraged the shah to take a "vacation" abroad, issued stern warnings against foreign involvement in Iran's internal crisis, and equivocated in supporting the shah's hand-picked successor, Prime Minister Shahpour Bakhtiar. After several weeks of minimal American comment on the Iranian situation, a shaky coalition between Bakhtiar and the military emerged and the administration threw official support to the new prime minister. A week later, the Bakhtiar government fell; the Ayatollah Khomeini's shadow prime minister, Mehdi Bazargan, assumed office. On the following day, President Carter announced that the United States would "honor the will of the Iranian people" and seek friendly relations with the new regime.

In the summer of 1978, a Carter administration letter commending the Somoza government for progress in the field of human rights was followed by rioting in Nicaragua. The riots, strikes, and armed rebellion spread rapidly, and the Somoza regime made extensive use of torture, aerial bombardment of urban areas, and summary execution as it sought to repress the broadly based insurrection. As Somoza appeared ready to fall, the administration shifted its policy. By autumn, the

United States had confronted Somoza with an embargo on arms, a reduction in economic aid, and restrictions on international credits, as well as a diplomatic campaign to force Somoza to resign and call free elections.[17] When Somoza's regime survived and refused to call elections, the administration intensified its campaign by further reducing economic aid and by withdrawing Peace Corps volunteers and diplomatic staff. Nevertheless, the shift in American policy—from lukewarm support to opposition—was based, in part, on administration perceptions of the long-term viability of the regime and the prospects for increasing the strength of the more moderate elements of the opposition.

The meandering course of American policy on Iran and Nicaragua exemplifies the difficulties inherent in the transition from a hegemonic international position. No policy chart of massive intervention by American or proxy troops seemed likely to guarantee the status quo, and the costs of intervention appeared to outweigh the uncertain benefits of temporarily forestalling change. The need to choose among support, equivocation, and opposition was created by American inability to determine outcomes consistent with American interests. The fluctuations in Carter policy followed from the need to adjust to events that were not susceptible to American control.

The administration's initial disinclination to link issues gave way as the limits of American power became evident. It is difficult to maintain the separateness of issues in the face of gaps between interests and influence on many important specific issues. For example, the administration resorted to linkage in the Egyptian–Saudi Arabian–Israeli fighter aircraft package in order to secure continuing Egyptian moderation, penalize Israeli intransigence, and reward Saudi Arabian economic policies that coincided with American economic interests. When American inability to control Soviet activity in Africa became apparent, the political salience of the conservative internationalist reaction within Congress increased. The administration then linked East-West trade and technology transfer to Soviet African policy. American inability to control Soviet treatment of dissidents was demonstrated by the Shcharansky and Ginsberg trials, and both public and Congress expressed outrage. The administration then canceled a computer sale and temporarily held up sale of technology necessary for completion of an oil-drilling-bit manufacturing plant in the USSR. The administration expressed an initial interest in moving toward normal diplomatic relations with Cuba. As American inability to control Cuban activity in Africa became apparent, the United States linked movement toward diplomatic recognition to Cuban restraint in Africa. In each instance, linkage tactics were used when the limits on American influence in key areas of foreign policy became clear.*

Substantial disagreement exists within the administration over the American interest in each of these actions. The administration's initial reluctance to use linkage was partially motivated by a desire to avoid domestic political repercussions that might result from sacrificing interests in one area to pursue another foreign policy objective. The most publicly visible domestic political costs were produced by the Middle East fighter aircraft package. That deal engendered mistrust of the administration among American Jews and led to the resignation of the administration's liaison to the Jewish community. The manipulation of trade and technology transfers

---

* For the reactions of linkees to these actions, see chapters 7 and 12.

to pressure the Soviet Union on human rights and African issues revealed a fundamental disagreement between the National Security Council and the Departments of Commerce and State. Zbigniew Brzezinski and Samuel Huntington of the National Security Council see the world largely in terms of competition between the Soviet Union and the United States. To these men, the U.S. interest in selling oil-drilling equipment and computers is negative; these products are seen as increasing Soviet strength relative to that of the United States. In comparison with Brzezinski and Huntington, officials in the Departments of Commerce and State are more sensitive to other foreign policy concerns. In their view, oil-drilling technology would increase Soviet oil-producing capacity and thereby ease the world petroleum crunch that may develop in the middle to late 1980s. These officials also argue that linkage would harm U.S. commercial interests without denying anything to the Soviets, for other advanced industrial societies could also transfer relevant technology. The internal dispute spilled over into Congress when Huntington of the National Security Council asked Senator Daniel Moynihan to pressure the administration to manipulate technology transfer.

Secondary policies to support linkage can create contradictions across ends. A policy that emphasizes trade concessions, credits, and technology transfers as leverage to secure concessions from the Soviet Union, without consideration of the interests and capabilities of possible alternate suppliers, is on the face of it simplistic and ill considered. Yet American ability to control alternative sources of goods, credits, and technology in Western Europe and Japan is severely limited. If Soviet concessions are not forthcoming, the ultimate effectiveness of linkage will depend on U.S. ability to secure the acquiescence of other advanced industrial states to a return to the days of the long blacklist of restrictions on East-West trade. U.S. pressure to that end could endanger North-North negotiations on energy, macroeconomic coordination, trade, and investment, and thereby trigger further domestic disputes over policy.

The administration's decisions to link (or not link) on particular issues are only the proximate cause of internal disputes. The existence of an *option to link* inevitably produces wrangling over whether that option should be exercised in specific cases. The administration's initial disavowal of linkage was intended to deny the existence of the option and thereby circumvent attendant internal conflict.

Which uses of linkage are blackmailing and which are backscratching? The distinction rests on the linker's perception of interest in the promised or threatened action, and as argued, substantial disagreement exists within the administration over the American interest in each action. Advocates of linkage in the Soviet and Cuban cases—Brzezinski and Huntington—argue against both technology transfers to the Soviet Union and the diplomatic recognition of Cuba, irrespective of the possible use of these issues as leverage. Hence, to these advocates of linkage, the act of linking would be backscratching—demanding compensation for something they would not otherwise have the United States do. The opponents of linkage in the Soviet cases—officials at Commerce and State—see an American interest in selling technology and would therefore see the linkage as blackmailing.

In the Soviet case, the opponents of linkage see linkage as conflict exacerbating. This conclusion follows logically from their view of the American interest in the actions to be manipulated; blackmailing *is* conflict exacerbating. That the proponents of linkage do not see it as conflict exacerbating follows from their view of the costs to the United States of the action to be manipulated; backscratching will not necessarily intensify conflict.

Calculations of linkage credibility under the Carter administration are indirectly affected by the category of linkage. We must focus first on the Byzantine problem of assessing whether supporters or opponents of linkage are ascendant when execution of a threat or delivery on a promise is called for. If Brzezinski and Huntington control the administration's foreign policy, a threat to terminate technology transfer unless compensated is credible. Indeed, some argue that linkage in this case is a pretext for terminating technology transfer and that the advocates of "linkage" hope that it will not be successful so that the threat can be executed. The issue of credibility would center on the possibility of reneging if the desired compensation from the Soviets was forthcoming. If opponents of linkage control foreign policy, a threat to terminate technology transfer unless compensated may not be credible, but there would be little question as to the credibility of the corresponding promise to proceed with technology transfer if Soviet concessions were forthcoming.

The Carter administration's use of linkage has been essentially reactive, not part of a comprehensive strategy. As a consequence, one asset—East-West trade and technology transfer—has been linked to Soviet policy on such disparate matters as human rights and Africa, and may well be linked to SALT before the end of the administration. Like the former Director of the Office of Management and Budget, the administration as a whole has seemed to believe that more than one deal can be secured with the same collateral. This technique can produce obvious benefits—until the bank is audited or a deal goes sour.

This same general approach to stretching limited resources has been paralleled in other areas of administration foreign policy. The tension between often contradictory ends and limited means spawned many of the problems that bedeviled early Carter foreign policy. The administration has reordered its shopping list of ends as contradictions and constraints have emerged, but its approach to reordering priorities has been piecemeal and reactive. Only after reaching the checkout counter has the shopper looked at the prices and trimmed the list. Nevertheless, the administration may claim that not all prices were posted and that some prices were changed, as it scrambles to return some goods to the shelf.

CONCLUSIONS

The foreign policy of the Carter administration has been shaped by emerging constraints and contradictions that are largely environmental in origin. The significance of these factors has been revealed by the painful twists and turns of a foreign policy best interpreted as a series of responses to a sequence of dilemmas. In every instance, the situation has necessitated choice between unattractive alternatives. The dilemmas are of more enduring interest than the specific policy choices of the administration, for in the absence of significant structural changes, the basic attributes of the situation will persist and confound future administrations.

In what ways is the situation susceptible to change? With few exceptions, the Carter administration has reacted to its environment without seeking to alter it. The exceptions are illustrative of the possibilities and limitations of a foreign policy directed at expanding the domain of choice and reducing complexity. The Carter administration sought to reduce U.S. sensitivity to future OAPEC blackmailing by raising domestic energy prices, providing incentives for conservation, encouraging development of alternative energy supplies, and stockpiling petroleum against the possibility of embargo. An effective comprehensive energy program would have yielded the collateral benefit of reducing oil imports and improving the American balance of trade, thereby easing monetary and trade conflict among the advanced industrial states. Not all side effects of the program are as benign. Higher energy costs would exacerbate inflation; the development of nuclear alternatives to oil could conflict with the administration's antiproliferation program; and the development of alternative energy sources, encouragement of conservation, and acquisition and maintenance of a strategic petroleum reserve would require significant federal expenditures. Public and congressional opinion on the costs and benefits of the program was deeply divided. The administration sought to forge a domestic consensus in support of the energy package by releasing CIA forecasts of widespread oil shortages in the 1980s and by identifying the program as "the moral equivalent of war." To secure congressional support, the President reinforced rhetoric with old-fashioned logrolling; in one ironic case, he traded off the location of a breeder reactor for a senator's vote on the energy bill.* The energy program passed without the critical crude oil equalization tax—the provision that would have raised domestic energy prices to international levels and thereby encouraged conservation and the development of alternative energy sources. Other costly provisions of the program, including the strategic petroleum reserve, are under review as the administration strives to reduce the federal budget deficit under its antiinflation program. Environmentalists have continued to oppose the development of nuclear power, and there is increasing evidence of an ominous structural connection between coal-based electricity production and long-term climatic change.[18] At the end of 1978, oil industry officials were projecting a steady rise in American oil imports, despite the somewhat less-than-comprehensive energy program.[19] The fate of the energy program reveals the limits of choice; this policy, designed to ease contradictions, became ensnared in contradictions.

In the second half of 1978, accelerating devaluation threatened to end the dollar's role as the principal international reserve asset and medium of exchange, while increasing Soviet military spending further undermined American military power. The administration adopted policies to enhance American economic and military power simultaneously. International economic advisers developed a three-pronged program to reverse the fall of the dollar, while security advisers planned a significant increase in defense spending.

The administration's international monetary initiatives included the following measures.

---

* Restricting development of the breeder reactor was one component of early administration nuclear proliferation policy.

1. The administration sought to reduce the balance-of-trade deficit by expanding American exports. Carter's advisers hoped that greater domestic productivity and the recent sharp fall in the value of the dollar would increase the competitiveness of American goods. In August the Commerce Department began an export promotion campaign to capitalize on the attractiveness of American exports priced in devalued dollars.

2. In November the administration sought to control speculation against the dollar, which had contributed to further erosion of the dollar. Through gold sales and international borrowing, American monetary authorities assembled a $30 billion pool to support the dollar on international currency markets. In addition, the Treasury Department planned to issue bonds denominated in foreign currencies in order to provide an incentive for speculators to place assets in the United States.

3. More fundamentally, the administration sought to reduce inflation and restrict growth of the U.S. money supply, at the risk of triggering a recession. In the absence of fiscal and monetary restraint, Phase II wage-price guidelines seemed to be incapable of controlling inflation or checking the slide of the dollar. In November the Federal Reserve tightened monetary policy and the President announced that he would reduce the federal budgetary deficit from an estimated $64 billion in fiscal year 1979 to $30 billion in fiscal 1980.

The monetary and fiscal restraint at the core of this program is likely to produce a recession. Recession tends to increase unemployment and attendant domestic social expenditures while reducing revenues as taxable national income falls. If previous postwar recessions serve as a reliable guide, administration policies will produce a $100 billion budgetary deficit, should a recession be engendered.[20] In the face of declining revenues and increasing domestic social spending, the administration would find it difficult to reduce budgetary deficits, yet international monetary policy would be seriously compromised by such deficits. Thus the administration's commitment to checking the decline of the dollar may prove hard to honor, even before considering the effects of increased military spending.[21]

In November of 1978 the administration also moved to increase American military power. All members of NATO had promised to increase defense spending by 3 percent. After some equivocation—the administration considered limiting the American increase to 3 percent of NATO-related defense spending—the President announced a new $1 billion per year civil defense program and a $12.5 billion supplement to the defense budget. If the administration chooses to procure weapons developed under the supplement, far heavier outlays for new weapons systems will swell the defense budget in future years.

How do the administration's plans for increasing military and economic power mesh? First, if the export campaign is to succeed without further devaluation of the dollar, American domestic productivity must increase. Yet, as argued earlier, military spending seems to have significant costs in terms of civilian productivity. Second, if the administration is to increase defense spending while reducing budgetary deficits, it must program offsetting cuts in domestic spending or increase taxes. The administration cut $15 billion out of the "normal growth" of domestic social programs and postponed plans for overhauling the federal welfare system and initiating a national health insurance program.[22] If monetary and fiscal restraint produces a recession, however, further reductions in domestic spending may be impolitic, if not impossible. Tax increases may run afoul of the domestic political constraint exemplified by Proposition 13 and reflected in federal tax reduction legislation passed in 1978. The only international monetary measure not directly compromised by increased military spending is the antispeculation program. Nevertheless, gold reserves are finite, international borrowing cannot continue indefinitely, and Treasury notes denominated in foreign currencies entail an obligation to repay in foreign currencies. The antispeculation program is, at best, a supplement to the other components of administration international monetary policy, and those other measures are weakened by increased defense spending. Although it is possible to bolster American military or economic power, it may be difficult to enhance both simultaneously.

The ideal of a general strategy keyed to the acquisition of power and the mitigation of contradictions is alluring. But such a strategy would be difficult to conceptualize and even more difficult to execute. Individual policies that might accord with such a general strategy become entangled in the same thicket of constraints and contradictions from which the Carter administration has been unable to escape. The very attributes of the situation that make such a strategy attractive may make that strategy impracticable. To return to the statement by Jean Monnet, quoted at the outset of this chapter, changing the context would change the problem. From the perspective of American decision makers, inability to change the context *is* the problem.

NOTES

1. Richard M. Nixon, "United States Foreign Policy for the 1970s," *Department of State Bulletin,* 13 March 1972.
2. Commencement address delivered by President Carter at the University of Notre Dame, 22 May 1977, as quoted in the *New York Times,* 23 May 1977.
3. This tradeoff between investment and military expenditures is not rigid. Given differences in national preferences for consumption, it is not surprising that the proportion of real output devoted to the sum of military expenditures and investment varies. However, the sums (U.S. 21.7%, UK 20.8%, France 23.0%, West Germany 23.9%, Italy 17.5%, Canada 20.8%, and Japan 29.9%) are markedly less diverse than are the statistics in table 1.1. Differences in business cycle phases may account for some disparities in productivity and output growth rates, but these effects should be partially washed out over the thirteen years of the observed period. Some reduction in variance may be attributed to statistical artifact.
4. Ruth Leger Sivard, *World Military and Social Expenditures 1977* (Leesburg, Va.: WMSE Publications, 1977), p. 11.
5. U.S. Department of State, *The Trade Debate* (Washington D.C.: Government Printing Office, 1978), p. 3.
6. U.S. Department of Commerce, *International Economic Indicators,* March 1978, p. 60.
7. Anthony Lake, "Managing Complexity in U.S. Foreign Policy," speech to the San Francisco World Affairs Council, 14 March 1978, as distributed under U.S. Department of State, Bureau of Public Affairs, Speech Series.
8. *Economic Report of the President, January 1978* (Washington D.C.: Government Printing Office, 1978).

9. Commerce, *International Economic Indicators,* March 1978, p. 58.
10. Ibid., pp. 76–77.
11. *Foreign Policy,* no. 29 (Winter 1978) and no. 31 (Summer 1978).
12. Kenneth A. Oye, "On Backscratching and Blackmailing: Cross-Issue Linkage Strategies and International Political Economy" (paper presented at the International Studies Association West Convention, 1977).
13. Leslie Gelb, in a speech at the Twenty-third Annual National Security Seminar at the U.S. Army War College, 8 June 1977, as quoted in *Parameters* 7, no. 3 (July 1977).
14. Lake, "Managing Complexity."
15. Bernard Weinraub, "White House Plans Rise to $124 Billion in Military Budget: Move Buoys Pentagon Aides," *New York Times,* 16 November 1978.
16. Donald Rothchild and Robert Curry, *Scarcity, Choice and Public Policy in Middle Africa* (Berkeley: University of California Press, 1978). "Radical" African nations with close ties to the Soviet Union have frequently been more accommodating to international investors than have their "moderate" counterparts. For a discussion of the economic policies of leftist Benin, Congo/Brazzaville, Guinea, Angola, and Mozambique, and of moderate Nigeria, Zaire, Zambia, Ghana, and Sierra Leone, see Robert M. Price, *U.S. Foreign Policy in Sub-Saharan Africa: National Interests and Global Strategy,* Policy Papers in International Affairs, No. 8 (Berkeley: Institute of International Studies, 1978).
17. The arms embargo may also serve as a demonstration of the limits of American power; Israel shipped arms to Somoza over the expressed objections of the administration.
18. While particulates produced by coal burning may be reduced by existing pollution control devices, the reduction of sulfates is more difficult and the substantial reduction of carbon dioxide is impossible. For a given amount of heat, coal produces about 24% more carbon dioxide than oil and 76% more than natural gas. Increases in atmospheric carbon dioxide may produce a "greenhouse effect"—the elevation of mean global temperature and the alteration of weather patterns. See Tom Alexander, "New Fears Surround the Shift to Coal," *Fortune,* 20 November 1978.
19. James Tanner, "U.S. Oil Imports Appear to Be Climbing; Industry Aides Expect Rise to Continue," *Wall Street Journal,* 15 November 1978.
20. For further discussion of the effects of recession on the federal budgetary deficit, see Citibank, "Congress Puts a Leash on the Deficit," *Monthly Economic Letter,* November 1978. The federal deficit may be widened further if the antiinflationary policy succeeds. Inflation moves taxpayers into higher tax brackets. This automatic source of additional revenues depends on continuing inflation.
21. Recession would also reduce demand for imports, and produce a short-term improvement in the balance of trade.
22. "Carter Will Delay Major Spending Plans Due to Fight Against Inflation, Aides Say," *Wall Street Journal,* 15 November 1978.

2

THE NEW INTERNATIONALISMS

Public Opinion and American Foreign Policy

Michael Mandelbaum and William Schneider

Before he went to Washington to serve as Jimmy Carter's assistant for national security, Zbigniew Brzezinski was working on a book to be called *America in a New World*. Indeed, the problems and challenges faced by the current administration seem different from the ones that dominated international politics for three decades after the end of World War II. In wrestling with these problems and attempting to meet these challenges, however, the Carter administration has lacked a resource held by its predecessors in conducting the nation's affairs, namely, a domestic consensus for foreign policy. For almost a quarter of a century Americans were united in support of resistance to the spread of communism, by war if necessary, under the leadership of Presidents with considerable leeway to conduct the nation's business abroad.

The cold-war consensus is gone. What has taken its place? How do Americans see international politics? How do they define the requirements for the nation's security? What constraint does public opinion place upon foreign policy? What do Americans consider their nation's proper role in this new world? Is there any consensus on anything in our foreign policy?

We can go a good way toward answering these questions by examining the 1976 presidential campaign. Public opinion tends to crystallize in a national election because the campaign takes on the structure of a debate. Also, political leaders assess public opinion better during election campaigns than they do from polls.

An earlier version of this chapter appeared in International Security, *Winter 1978. The authors are indebted to The Lehrman Institute of New York City and its director, Nicholas X. Rizopoulos, for assistance in revising it.*

Campaigners shape their policies with an eye on past elections because they expect to run again in the future.

In what sense can campaigns be characterized as debates? The two major-party candidates in a presidential campaign usually avoid taking controversial stands. They concentrate on "valence" issues, those where everyone is on the same side; they extol peace, abhor corruption, and commit themselves to a policy of controlling inflation while reducing unemployment. Candidates address these issues because voters care about them, but also because they will automatically lose votes by taking sides on divisive issues. Valence issues dominate only the second part of a presidential contest—the general election—when the candidate's task is to knit together a broad coalition of voters and when he is at pains to avoid giving people a reason to vote against him.

In the first stage of the contest, the nominating process, which includes the primaries, the task is different. Several aspirants share a general outlook. The successful candidate must find a way to stand out in the crowd. He must identify and mobilize his own constituency. Candidates often do this by forthrightly addressing "position" issues, those questions that have alternative sides, such as busing, Vietnam policy, or defense spending.

The year 1976 was a watershed year for foreign policy opinion trends. It brought to the fore two issues over which there is fundamental disagreement—détente and antimilitarism. Both issues involve basic conflicts of principle. *Détente* involves America's stance vis-à-vis international communism. Should the United States attempt to resolve differences with communist countries through negotiation, a policy that assumes an attitude of international "toleration," or should it base its foreign policy on the notion of implacable opposition and unresolvable differences between two world views? *Antimilitarism* relates more to tactical issues: military priorities in America's domestic and foreign policy. Antimilitarists oppose large-scale defense spending, military aid, military intervention, and CIA subterfuge; their opponents endorse military priorities in the name of national security.

These two issues arose from the country's principal foreign policy experiences during the Nixon and Ford administrations—the improvement of relations with the Soviet Union and China, and the sustained American role in the Vietnam war. There is an ideological link between détente and antimilitarism: the political left tends to be both antimilitary and pro-détente, whereas the right is anti-détente and promilitary. What has kept the two issues distinct is the inconsistent ideological thrust of the previous Republican administration's foreign policy. The Nixon-Ford-Kissinger foreign policy gave rise to an antimilitary protest from the left and an antidétente protest from the right. Both controversies played an important role in the 1976 presidential primaries, each in a different party.

The election campaign brought into focus a diffuse, nonideological foreign policy issue: the role of morality in America's relations with other countries. Candidate Jimmy Carter pledged a stronger moral commitment in foreign policy and thereby voiced a widespread popular unease over the Republicans' *Realpolitik*. But the antimilitary and antidétente protest movements were, like most protest movements, profoundly moralistic. Their abiding strength presents the Carter administration, and any administration in the foreseeable future, with the difficult task of finding a new consensual basis for foreign policy while avoiding divisive ideological conflict.

DÉTENTE AND THE REPUBLICANS

Détente was a central issue in Ronald Reagan's nearly successful challenge to the incumbent President of his own party. Reagan used opposition to détente to roll up victories in primaries and conventions in the South and West—the same states that had spearheaded Barry Goldwater's drive to the Republican nomination twelve years earlier. Foreign policy dissent was important in 1964 just as it was in 1976. Indeed, it has played a central role in the internal struggles of the Republican party for over twenty years.

The split between the Taft and Eisenhower wings of the party in 1952 reflected a basic division over isolationism. Senator Taft represented the historically isolationist midwestern wing of the party. General Eisenhower represented the eastern internationalist wing, in a direct line of descent from Thomas A. Dewey and Wendell Willkie. After the climactic confrontation at the 1952 convention, the midwestern wing of the party continued its steady conversion to an internationalist outlook. Conservative isolationism largely disappeared in the Eisenhower years because, with the onset of the cold war, America's role in world affairs changed. Internationalism no longer implied alliance with the "left" (Britain and Russia against Germany), rather, it was interpreted to mean leadership of the Free World in a global battle against communism.

The Reagan forces believed that the Ford administration was not fighting that battle vigorously enough. President Ford responded to Reagan's attack on détente, the centerpiece of the foreign policy he had inherited from Richard Nixon, by retreating from it. From his defeat in North Carolina to his narrow victory at the Kansas City convention, Ford abandoned the policy by bits and pieces, like a captain throwing his ship's cargo overboard in order to keep from sinking. He dropped "détente" from his political vocabulary and substituted "peace through strength." He kept Secretary of State Kissinger, who was prominently identified as the architect of détente, out of sight as much as possible. Ford allowed the Strategic Arms Limitation Talks (SALT II), the most pressing piece of business outstanding between the United States and the Soviet Union, to remain stalled. Finally, he accepted an amendment to the party platform that all but repudiated the relationship with the Soviets he and his predecessor had worked so hard to fashion. The amendment was entitled "Morality in Foreign Policy," as if to signify that that element had been ignored in the original Ford-Kissinger platform. Ford conceded the battle over détente in order to win the war over the nomination.

Reagan's views on the Soviet Union came closer to the main currents of Republican opinion than did Secretary Kissinger's policies. Polls show that opposition to détente is concentrated among conservatives, and conservatives have become the controlling influence in the Republican party. Among Republican voters in ten contested primaries polled by NBC News (seven of them won by Ford), more agreed than disagreed with the statement "While Gerald Ford has been President, the United States has fallen behind Russia in military strength" (37 percent agreed and 34 percent disagreed, on the average). This was scarcely a vote of confidence by Republicans in their own party's foreign policy. In fact, in 1976 feelings about Kissinger more than any other issue divided Republicans into Ford and Reagan supporters. In primary after primary, a steady majority of those who disapproved of

Kissinger's performance as secretary of state voted for Reagan, whereas those who approved of Kissinger voted consistently for Ford.

What is interesting about the fate of détente among Republicans is not that they rejected it in the spring and summer of 1976 but that the party was induced to support it for the five preceding years. In part this is explained by party loyalty. Nixon and Ford did what leaders of the British Conservative party often managed in the past—they kept their constituents united in support of liberal initiatives primarily because, for the rank and file, party loyalty overrode ideological convictions. Harold Macmillan, for example, put his party on record in favor of decolonization despite the enthusiasm, or at least nostalgia, for the empire felt by most Tories. But decolonization was a self-liquidating policy. Once begun, it was difficult to reverse. Republican support for détente was less enduring. With the party no longer in control of the White House, many congressional and rank-and-file Republicans turned against their own policy of détente, just as the Democrats turned against the Vietnam war when it was no longer being managed by a Democratic administration.

President Carter did not find it easy to rally Republican support for improving relations with the Soviet Union—through another SALT accord, for instance—or with the People's Republic of China, by breaking formal ties with Taiwan in order to establish them with Peking. As was the case with the Panama Canal treaties, few Republicans were moved by the fact that the initiative and continuing support for these measures came from Republican administrations. When the Democrats are in office, they become Democratic policies. And Republicans who are conservative, as most are, do not favor them.

Conservatives, as noted, are both anti-détente and promilitary. Conservative Republicans found little to complain about in the military policy of their party's administration. Nixon and Ford almost literally bought off conservative opposition with higher levels of military spending than liberals wanted and forceful policies in Vietnam and Cambodia. Thus the Reaganites used opposition to détente as a protest issue. Their promilitarism, while equally strong, simply lacked this edge of protest. Reagan did make an effort to stimulate promilitary protest over the Panama Canal, but Ford and Kissinger showed no inclination to confront Reagan over that issue.

Ratification of two treaties giving control of the canal to Panama was made more difficult because a Democratic President signed them. Despite the endorsement of Ford and Kissinger, a majority of Republicans voted against the treaties. A Republican President could have expected the support of Democrats, most of whom favored the treaties on principle, and Republicans, who did not favor them but would have been reluctant to defy (and embarrass) a chief executive of their own party.

Anti-détente and promilitary sentiment are also found among Democratic conservatives. In 1976, the principal Democratic spokesman for conservatism in foreign policy was Senator Henry Jackson of Washington. Jackson entered the 1976 Democratic primaries as a harsh critic of the Republican administration's policies toward the Soviet Union, as well as a man sympathetic to high levels of military spending. But Jackson's foreign policy views had a limited appeal in the Democratic party. Détente was not unpopular with Democrats, however much they disapproved of the ways the Republicans carried it out. Ironically, the 1976 Democratic platform was far less critical of the Ford administration's relations with the Soviet Union than was the Republican document.

The votes Senator Jackson won probably had more to do with his positions on other issues. Trade unionists and party regulars saw Jackson as a strong supporter of full-employment policies, including high defense spending; older Jewish voters sympathized more with Jackson's commitment to Israel than with the foreign policy orientation behind it.

The Jackson candidacy did not survive the spring primaries, and no other Democrat emerged to pick up the anti-détente standard. Though the conservative viewpoint on détente had some intellectual influence in the Democratic party, there were few protest votes to be mined among the party's rank and file by appealing to cold-war hostility. The Democrats had experienced their own foreign policy protest movement some years earlier, however, and the impact of those dramatic events could still be felt in 1976.

ANTIMILITARISM AND THE DEMOCRATS

"Antimilitarism" covers a wide variety of specific opinions: low esteem for the armed forces; opposition to military intervention in the affairs of other nations; distrust of military alliances, military aid, and troop commitments abroad; and support for arms control and disarmament. The antimilitary reaction arose from the American war in Indochina. It is a direct extension of the old antiwar movement. With the war over, the antimilitary attitude remains, in opposition to military spending and a desire to cut the defense budget, in hostility to the CIA and all its works, and in rejection of U.S. support for right-wing dictatorial regimes. To liberals, antimilitarism represents the lesson of the Vietnam war.

In 1976 one of the most striking features of the long string of Democratic primaries from New Hampshire to California was the *minimal* role played by antimilitarism. A principal reason has already been noted: there was no war to be against. Antimilitarism remained a kind of litmus test for left-wing Democrats, but there was no broader protest energy behind the issue, and therefore few votes.

This does not suffice to explain why the Democrats were largely silent on the subject of antimilitarism. For even if antimilitary sentiment is important only to the party's left wing, several candidates were competing with Morris Udall for primacy on the left. It is difficult to resist the conclusion that the omission of this issue was deliberate.

Whether or not this was so, the Democrats had good reason to avoid antimilitarism: *it was not a dead issue but a potentially explosive and polarizing one.* Feelings about Vietnam still ran deep in 1976 and might have split the party once again. The memory of George McGovern's experience was fresh, and painful. McGovern lost because he campaigned on an issue that split the party wide open. No one wanted to resurrect the bitterness and cynicism of the 1972 campaign. Antimilitarism, in short, was associated with divisiveness, and that charge, after the experiences of 1968 and 1972 when the Democrats virtually handed the election over to Richard Nixon, would have been enough to discredit any Democratic candidate in 1976. Also, liberals were no doubt sensitive to the fact, documented by many polls, that the national strength of antimilitarism was receding.[1]

The overriding issue in the second half of the primary campaign was Jimmy Carter himself. Surprisingly, even his liberal opponents—Udall, Jerry Brown, and Frank Church—did not try to rally opposition to Carter on the grounds that he was sympathetic to military causes. Carter was certainly more conservative on military questions than his liberal opponents, if only because he avoided taking outright antimilitary positions, but he had taken care not to identify himself so emphatically with promilitary causes as to make himself unacceptable to the party's left wing. Had Henry Jackson emerged from the early primaries as the frontrunner, liberals in the party would have been considerably more zealous in their efforts to stop him— perhaps going so far as to split the party. But the anti-Carter movement, such as it was, did not stress the antimilitary theme.

At the 1976 national convention, the Democrats made a valiant collective effort to erase the painful memory of Vietnam; it was an unmentionable subject, as Richard Nixon and Watergate had been for the Republicans. When the Vietnam issue forced itself on the floor, as in the appeal for amnesty for draft evaders, the old bitterness and division showed signs of surfacing. But Carter, moving to conciliate antimilitary sentiment on the left, agreed to support a general pardon for draft evaders and accepted a platform plank calling for a $5 billion to $7 billion cut in the defense budget.

THE GENERAL ELECTION AND "KISSINGERISM"

Although the Republican and Democratic party platforms differed sharply over foreign policy, the two men who were nominated were "moderates." Each placed himself as close as possible to the middle of the road on foreign policy and resisted all pressures to move to one side or the other.

Jimmy Carter and Gerald Ford avoided the divisive implications of détente and antimilitarism. They debated foreign policy in "valence" terms. They disagreed about performance—Ford's past performance, Carter's likely future performance— rather than about goals. Carter criticized the Ford record of negotiations with the Soviet Union on the grounds that the United States had been "out-traded." In the idiom of mass marketing, the challenger was offering the same product but at a better price. Ford, in turn, tried to use the mild antimilitary positions Carter had taken to tar him with the charge of "weakness." Carter moved resolutely to the high middle ground on the question of defense spending. Pressed to say whether guns or butter would receive first claim on the public treasury in a Carter administration, the candidate responded that the two needs "must go hand in hand, but the security of this nation has got to come first."

Some of the most extensively discussed foreign policy questions were important because of their salience to specific domestic constituencies. Both candidates courted the Jewish vote with ostentatious proclamations of friendship and support for Israel. Carter took issue with the Ford record on Cyprus, with an eye to the ballots of Greek-Americans. Each promised, for the benefit of the nation's farmers, that there would be no more embargoes on the sale of grain abroad.

In fact, Ford and Carter were probably closer to each other on foreign policy than on other issues. Ford could hardly have been expected to support the anti-détente, anti-Kissinger bias of his party's platform, and Carter was clearly uneasy with the antimilitary impulse strongly felt in some sections of the Democratic party.

An interesting feature of the 1976 presidential election, and perhaps the most important harbinger of future public attitudes toward foreign policy, was Henry Kissinger's role. Policies he had become closely associated with were at the center of the debate about foreign affairs, and his personal fate mirrors the role that foreign policy played during the long months of the 1976 campaign and is likely to play in the future.

The right on the American political spectrum is, as noted, anti-détente and pro-military; the left is just the reverse. Kissinger confused matters: he was widely and correctly perceived as being promilitary and pro-détente. This inconsistency helps explain Kissinger's initial popularity and his subsequent role, especially in 1976, as an object of controversy. Though always uneasy about détente, the Republican right was willing to accept Kissinger and even applaud him because of his "toughness" in Vietnam. If his attitude toward communists was exceptionable, his advocacy of military power was beyond reproach. The Democratic left distrusted him for the same reason—his unreconstructed militarism and his casuistry in the Vietnam negotiations. Yet opposition from the left remained subdued during most of Kissinger's tenure in office, as if liberals were temporarily struck dumb by his feat of singlehandedly ending the cold war. The Vietnam cease-fire in 1973 and Kissinger's 1974–75 shuttle diplomacy in the Middle East boosted his popularity to record levels for a public figure.

In the last two years of his term Kissinger suffered criticism from both sides. He himself did not change; but both the left and the right shifted their attention to the issues on which each opposed him. The right was no longer willing to accept détente for the sake of a few memories of bombing raids and Cambodian incursions. For liberals, who never gave Kissinger more than grudging respect, the virtues of détente ceased to outweigh his "militarist" policies in Chile, South Korea, and elsewhere. And they remembered Vietnam.

President Ford kept Kissinger virtually hidden during the primaries. During the general election campaign, Kissinger became noticeably more visible because his popularity in the electorate as a whole had remained high. Most voters agreed with him on détente and on military policy, and his feats of negotiation made him a powerful symbol of one of Mr. Ford's principal campaign themes in the fall—peace. Kissinger was, in sum, a liability for the Ford administration during the primaries, the "position issue" stage of the campaign, and an asset during the general election, when "valence issues" took over.

TWO VERSIONS OF INTERNATIONALISM

Opposition to Kissinger has an importance that goes beyond the outcome of the 1976 presidential election. In the criticism of him that came from the right and the left it is possible to discern two nascent world views that have begun to grow into full-blown alternatives both to the *Realpolitik* of the Kissinger years and to each other. These world views, liberal internationalism and conservative internationalism, stem from a fundamental division within the international-minded American public over the proper goals and methods of U.S. foreign policy.

The principal historical shift in American foreign policy took place immediately after World War II when the country committed itself to an active role in international affairs as the leader of the Western democracies against the forces of totalitarianism. This policy was supported by a broad consensus within the political elite and among the internationalist public. Since World War II, no important political figure has advocated the kind of isolationism that characterized American foreign policy for most of this country's history. Internationalist opinion has grown steadily since 1940, although a residue of isolationism remains in the mass public, mostly among the poor and the poorly educated (who in fact pay little attention to foreign affairs).[2]

A split is now emerging within the internationalist public between liberal and conservative versions of internationalism. Most Americans continue to agree that the United States should take an active role in world affairs, but there is no longer agreement on what role it should be. The experiences of Vietnam and détente have created ideological divergence over both the goals and the methods of American foreign policy. It is appropriate to think of foreign policy attitudes as arrayed along two dimensions, an internationalist-isolationist dimension (*whether* the United States should play an active role in world affairs) and a cross-cutting liberal-conservative dimension (*what kind* of role it should play). Data from a survey of U.S. public opinion and foreign policy carried out in December 1974 and January 1975 by Louis Harris on behalf of the Chicago Council on Foreign Relations help to define these world views more precisely.[3]

In the survey, respondents were shown a card listing eighteen "possible foreign policy goals that the United States might have." Respondents were asked, "For each one, would you please say whether you think that *should* be a very important foreign policy goal, a somewhat important goal, or not an important goal at all?" A principal components factor analysis of the responses (using oblique rotation) revealed that the goals tended to cluster into two groups. The first group included the following goals:

"keeping peace in the world" (87 percent of the sample labeled this a "very important" foreign policy goal)

"securing adequate supplies of energy" (79 percent)

"fostering international cooperation to solve common problems, such as food, inflation, and energy" (70 percent)

"worldwide arms control" (69 percent)

"helping solve world inflation" (67 percent)

"combating world hunger" (62 percent)"

"maintaining a balance of power among nations" (54 percent)

"strengthening the United Nations" (50 percent)

"helping to improve the standard of living in less developed countries" (41 percent)

These goals contrast with those listed below, which tended to form a separate cluster:

"containing Communism" (considered a "very important" goal of U.S. foreign policy by 58 percent of the sample)

"protecting the interests of American business abroad" (42 percent)

"strengthening countries who are friendly toward us" (40 percent)

"defending our allies' security" (36 percent)

"protecting weaker nations against foreign aggression" (31 percent)

"helping to bring a democratic form of government to other nations" (30 percent)

"promoting the development of capitalism abroad" (19 percent)

Both sets of goals are clearly international-minded, but those on the first list are consistently nonaggressive. They tend to be economic in character (food, inflation, energy), humanitarian (combating hunger, aiding less developed countries), and oriented toward peace (arms control, balance of power, the United Nations). Each commits the United States to a world role of *cooperative* internationalism, which is one facet of post-World War II internationalism. The other facet comprises the more aggressive cold-war goals on the second list: America as the leader of the Free World alliance against communism. These goals are certainly internationalist, but they represent a *competitive* version of internationalism. For instance, the economic goals on the second list—"promoting . . . capitalism" and "protecting the interests of American business abroad"—are defensive of free enterprise against antagonistic systems and values. The same sense of competition and antagonism characterizes the political goals, which include "containing Communism" and promoting democracy in other countries. These goals also emphasize a military commitment to other nations: to "strengthen," "defend," and "protect" our allies against aggression. The second list expresses the *interventionist* thrust of American foreign policy since World War II; it calls not merely for cooperation with other countries to serve mutual needs but also for the promotion of democracy and free enterprise and the protection of these values against communism.

Since both sets of goals describe the post-1945 internationalist consensus, it is not surprising to find that the two factors were positively correlated ($r = .29$). Those more supportive of cooperative internationalism also tended to be more favorable toward interventionism.[4]

Every respondent was given two factor scores, one on cooperative internationalism and one on interventionism. Factor scores are standardized, with the sample mean set at zero. Anyone with a positive factor score on internationalism was *relatively* favorable toward that value, whereas those with negative factor scores were *relatively* unfavorable. The first group was defined as the internationalist public (i.e., those who were more favorable toward internationalism than the average American). Fifty-seven percent of the 1975 sample were internationalist by this definition. Internationalists were then divided into two groups, distinguished by their views on interventionism. *Conservative internationalists* had positive scores on internationalism and interventionism; they represent the strongest supporters of the cold-war internationalist consensus. *Liberal internationalists* had positive scores on internationalism but *not* on interventionism; they represent the new variety of internationalism that has emerged in the post-Vietnam era, one that rejects militaristic and interventionist values but continues to favor an active U.S. role in the world. The residual category, those with negative scores on the internationalism factor, were labeled simply *noninternationalists*. Because internationalism and interventionism were positively correlated, it is not surprising to find that the conservative internationalist category was larger than the liberal internationalist category, 33 as compared with 24 percent. That left 43 percent of the sample in the residual category of noninternationalists.

The category of noninternationalists is admittedly heterogeneous. One could divide noninternationalists into conservatives and liberals, but there seems to be little point in doing so because the whole category is relatively uninterested in foreign affairs. Still, the terms "conservative isolationism" and "liberal isolationism" would not be unfamiliar to those who follow foreign policy debates. The problem is that these categories do not characterize major segments of public opinion. Ideological isolationism is relatively rare today, although indifference to foreign affairs is not. Conservative isolationists, once a major force in American politics, were largely converted to internationalism by the cold war. Nor is there much evidence today of the progressive isolationist tradition that once included such influential liberals as Hiram Johnson and Robert LaFollette.

"Neo-isolationism" on the left has been the subject of some discussion in recent years. This view, identified with certain radicals, holds that since the United States is always on the side of reaction and repression, it would be better if this country stayed out of world affairs entirely. Conservatives sometimes use "neo-isolationist" as a pejorative, to attack liberal internationalist positions. Thus, Ronald Reagan tried to characterize supporters of the Panama Canal treaties as neo-isolationists who wanted the United States to give up its world responsibilities. In fact, the neo-isolationist charge is usually a misreading of liberal internationalism, which argues that the United States should play a different kind of world role from the conservative internationalism of the cold war. The world role envisioned by liberal internationalists is discussed in the pages that follow.

The demographic and political characteristics of the three opinion groups are shown in table 2.1. Liberal internationalists were relatively young and well educated; over half the respondents in the liberal internationalist category had gone to college, compared with 30 percent of the other two groups. Noninternationalists were the oldest and least well educated group. The division between liberal and conservative internationalists has little to do with race; blacks are less internationalist generally, probably because they have had less opportunity for education than whites. The division between liberal and conservative internationalists does have something to do with region: southerners were underrepresented among liberal internationalists and overrepresented among conservative internationalists. Cold-war values clearly receive stronger support in the South, despite the fact that southern respondents tend to be lower in socioeconomic status and therefore, one would expect, less international-minded.

The absence of any differences in partisanship is striking. The chi-square test reveals no significant difference in partisanship between liberal internationalists, conservative internationalists, and noninternationalists $(p > .50)$. The impressive

TABLE 2.1

DEMOGRAPHIC AND POLITICAL CHARACTERISTICS
OF FOREIGN POLICY OPINION GROUPS

	Liberal Internationalists $N = 366$ (%)	Conservative Internationalists $N = 502$ (%)	Noninternationalists $N = 655$ (%)	Total Sample ($N = 1523$) (%)
Education				
Less than twelve years	20	31	37	31
High school graduate	27	39	33	33
College	53	30	30	36
	100	100	100	100
Age				
Under 30	36	28	26	29
31 through 64	51	58	56	56
65 and older	13	14	18	15
	100	100	100	100
Race				
Nonwhite	8	13	17	13
Region				
South	18	31	29	27
Party Identification				
Democrat	46	46	45	45
Independent	36	32	36	35
Republican	18	22	19	20
	100	100	100	100
Ideology				
Liberal	37	13	22	23
Moderate	42	52	48	48
Conservative	21	35	30	29
	100	100	100	100
Interest in Foreign Affairs (Index)				
Low	29	36	51	40
High	43	44	31	40

difference, as one might expect, is in terms of *ideology*. Liberal internationalists showed a disproportionate tendency to identify themselves as liberals, whereas conservatives were appropriately overrepresented in the conservative internationalist category ($p < .0001$). Still, in all three groups, as in the sample as a whole, a plurality of respondents identified themselves as moderates.

Each respondent was also asked how much attention he paid to eleven events related to foreign policy, including problems in the Middle East, the World Food Conference, the war in Cyprus, the British elections, "what's happening in Vietnam these days," and "congressional debates on foreign defense spending." The responses were used to create an index of interest in foreign affairs. Liberal internationalists and conservative internationalists showed relatively high interest in foreign affairs; noninternationalists were distinctively low in interest. There was no evidence that interest produced greater liberalism or greater conservatism on balance—only greater internationalism. The fifth of the sample highest in interest tended to be not only the most internationalist but also the most *divided* in its ideological views, 40 percent conservative internationalists and 30 percent liberal internationalists, both categories significantly larger than in the sample as a whole.

Tables A.1 through A.10 in the Appendix (pp. 71–86) show the responses of conservative internationalists, liberal internationalists, and noninternationalists to many other questions asked in the 1974–75 survey. By examining the patterns of responses to these questions, one can identify issues that divide the opinion groups and create different coalitions among them. Thus, the emphasis in the analysis that follows is on the *differences among the three groups*. In many cases, the most interesting differences are across questions rather than across groups (i.e., in the "marginals," or the responses of the total sample to each question). As any experienced survey researcher knows, however, marginals are extremely sensitive to the way in which the question is worded and in which answers are categorized, and to the particular time when the survey was taken. Concentrating on the differences among the groups calls attention to those "signals" that evoke a consistently positive or negative response from each group; such reactions are likely to persist across different surveys and different questions.[5]

The data in tables A.1 to A.10 reveal several response patterns, which may be illustrated by examining five questions on the subject of human rights. The five questions are shown in table 2.2. The first four questions in the table are excerpted from table A.4. Respondents were asked to "agree strongly, agree somewhat, disagree somewhat, or disagree strongly" with a series of "statements people have made about international affairs today." All four statements deal with the topic of U.S. pressure on behalf of human rights in other countries. What is useful about these statements for illustrative purposes is that each elicited a different response pattern from the three opinion groups defined above. Table 2.2 shows the percentage of each group who agreed strongly with each statement.

The first statement in table 2.2 was the most general: "The U.S. should put pressure on countries which systematically violate basic human rights." The statement gave no further specification of what countries, what kinds of violations, or what kinds of pressure. Just over one third (35 percent) of the sample agreed strongly with this statement, and an additional third (32 percent) agreed somewhat. Only 21.5 percent disagreed. (The remainder, on this as on all other questions, said "don't know" or "not sure.") Despite the general popularity of this position, table 2.2 reveals that it was more popular among the two internationalist groups than among noninternationalists. That the statement avoids any controversial "signals" is evidenced by the absence of any significant difference between liberal and conservative internationalists; both were strongly in favor of U.S. pressure against countries that violate human rights—without further specification. Noninternationalists were more dubious about such a commitment. The notion of the United States "putting pressure" on other countries, for whatever reason, represents an active internationalist policy. Noninternationalists are simply reluctant to get involved in other countries' affairs. Thus, this first statement evoked a division along internationalist

TABLE 2.2

RESPONSE PATTERNS TO
FIVE HUMAN RIGHTS QUESTIONS

	Liberal Interna- tional- ists	Conserv- ative Interna- tional- ists	Non- interna- tional- ists
1. *Q.7d(4): Internationalist* "The U.S. should put pressure on countries which systematically violate basic human rights."			
Percent agree strongly	40%	42%	27%
2. *Q.7d(2): Conservative coalition* "It's morally wrong for the United States to support a military dictatorship that strips its people of their basic rights, even if that dictatorship will allow us to set up military bases in that country."			
Percent agree strongly	61	47	45
3. *Q.7a(h): Liberal coalition* "How the Soviet Union handles the treatment of the Jews or other minority groups is a matter of internal Soviet politics, and none of our business."			
Percent agree strongly	17	11	18
4. *Q.7a(e): Mixed* "We should take a more active role in opposing the policy of apartheid—that is, racial separation—in South Africa."			
Percent agree strongly	24	16	11
5. *Q.7c(6): Ideological* "Here's a list of international events that the United States has been involved in in recent history. For each, please tell me whether you think it was a proud moment in American history, a dark moment, or neither a proud moment nor a dark moment. . . ." "CIA involvement in Chile"			
Percent "dark moment"	60	31	37

lines but not along ideological lines. The general theme of human rights is clearly popular among internationalists of all persuasions, especially because liberals and conservatives can read into such a question their own lists of "countries which systematically violate basic human rights." These responses provide a clue as to why the human rights issue was so popular during Jimmy Carter's presidential campaign, for it was an issue that allowed the candidate to maintain his preferred posture of ideological ambiguity.

Inevitably, campaign rhetoric must give way to policy. When the human rights issue is further specified, as in the other questions in table 2.2, ideological differences appear. For instance, the second statement holds that the United States should not support "a military dictatorship" that violates the human rights of its citizens even if that dictatorship allows us to set up military bases on its territory. Three quarters of the sample agreed, half of them strongly. It seems that this policy is even more popular than the first one. It is also more controversial. Table 2.2 shows a division between liberal and conservative internationalists: 61 percent of liberal internationalists agreed strongly that "it is morally wrong" for the United States to support such military dictatorships; the figure for conservative internationalists, 47 percent agreeing strongly, was not much higher than for the first statement. Military dictatorships that allow the United States to set up military bases are invariably right-wing and therefore strongly opposed by liberal internationalists. Conservative internationalists do not support such regimes, but their agreement with this statement (71 to 21 percent) was less intense than that of liberals (82 to 14 percent). Conservative enthusiasm for human rights in this case was probably also affected by the explicit consideration that the United States may have a military interest in maintaining good relations with these countries.

Thus, a tentative conclusion would be that liberals and conservatives differ over the nature of the regimes that are the most serious violators of human rights and the degree to which U.S. human rights policy should be modified by considerations of military interest. The first statement in table 2.2, which raised neither of these considerations, stimulated a coalition of internationalists against noninternationalists. The second statement brought together a "conservative coalition" in which conservative internationalists and noninternationalists showed relatively less enthusiasm for a human rights policy than did liberal internationalists. In other words, liberal internationalists expressed a deviating opinion. That statement 2 was broadly popular, given the wording of the question and the timing of the survey, is less significant than the fact that it raised issues that divided liberal and conservative internationalists and brought conservative and noninternationalist opinion together.

The third statement created just the opposite coalition—conservative internationalists were the deviating group. This statement makes reference to the repression of Jews and other minority groups by the Soviet Union. It takes the position that Soviet treatment of minority groups is a matter of "international Soviet politics" and "none of our business." Here, the pro-human rights position was to disagree. The sample was closely divided in this case, 47 percent disagreeing and 41 percent agreeing.[6] On this issue, liberals were less inclined to take the pro-human rights position than conservatives were. The percentage difference is small, but it reverses the pattern shown in statement 2, namely, greater liberal enthusiasm for human rights. Liberals were probably fearful that U.S. interference with Soviet treatment of minorities would endanger détente, a cherished liberal commitment, just as conservatives were reluctant to endorse a human rights policy that might conflict with U.S. military interests. To be sure, liberal internationalists were no more favorable to Soviet repression than conservatives were in the case of military dictatorships. What these results show is that the relative enthusiasm of liberals and conservatives for a human rights policy depends on what countries are involved and what other U.S. interests are at stake.

The first three questions in table 2.2 produced coalitions of two opinion groups against the third. The first question allied all internationalists behind a *general* human rights position, with noninternationalists less supportive. The second question joined conservatives and noninternationalists, who showed less support for a human rights policy than did liberals. The third question joined liberals and noninternationalists, with conservatives the most supportive of human rights. Noninternationalists were relatively unenthusiastic about any human rights policy. Thus, when either liberals or conservatives oppose a human rights policy for ideological reasons, they can usually find allies from among the 43 percent of the public who are noninternationalists and do not want to interfere in other countries' affairs.

Questions 4 and 5 in table 2.2 produced disagreement among all three opinion groups. This can occur, for example, when noninternationalists are at one extreme but there is also a significant difference between liberals and conservatives, as in the fourth question. Question 4 proposes that the United States take a more active role in opposing apartheid in South Africa. Noninternationalists were the least likely to agree strongly. What differentiates question 4 from question 1 is that question 4 also shows a significant difference of opinion between liberal and conservative internationalists. Liberals were more likely than conservatives to favor opposition to apartheid. It is not surprising to find an ideological difference over apartheid in South Africa, but it is notable that conservative internationalists were more favorable toward this statement than noninternationalists. The reason is that statement 4 has internationalist as well as ideological content. The statement not only calls for an opinion on apartheid but also raises the question of whether the United States should be more active in its opposition to the South African policy of racial separation. Such an activist policy is more distasteful to noninternationalists than to conservative internationalists. In such a "mixed" pattern, alternative coalitions are possible. If the issue were posed in more ideological terms, conservatives would probably ally with noninternationalists. If the issue were more internationalist (and ideologically neutral) in content, then the two internationalist groups might move closer together. An example of the latter policy might be U.S. mediation between the opposing sides, as in Rhodesia, to help bring about a mutually acceptable settlement.

The fifth question in table 2.2 drives conservative and liberal internationalists to opposing extremes, with noninternationalists in the middle. This occurs when an issue is overwhelmingly ideological. In such cases, the difference between liberal and conservative internationalists is greater than the difference between either group and noninternationalists. Question 5, which is excerpted from table A.10, asks whether "CIA involvement in Chile" was a proud moment or a dark moment in American history. Sixty percent of liberal internationalists labeled this event a dark moment, whereas only half as many conservative internationalists felt the same way.

The pattern is similar to that shown in statement 2, except that in statement 5, conservative internationalists were farther from liberal internationalist opinion than noninternationalists were. There is little internationalist content to this question. The assessment of CIA involvement in Chile, which liberals consider a major instance of U.S. violation of human rights, destroys any basis of agreement between liberal and conservative internationalists. Agreement was strongest in the case of statement 1, a vague, generalized commitment to human rights, ideal as a campaign statement but devoid of specific policy content. Liberal-conservative differences intensified as human rights policies became more specific and, inevitably, more controversial. Ideological differences were greatest in the one question that asked respondents to evaluate, not a hypothetical policy, but an actual event.

SOURCES OF CONFLICT
IN FOREIGN POLICY

The Chicago Council survey was administered a year before the Carter campaign or the human rights issue became the focus of national attention. Nevertheless, the data accurately predict both the breadth of appeal the human rights issue was eventually to have and the limits of its appeal when defined in terms of specific policies. The following discussion attempts to identify other issues and themes from the survey that are likely to provoke ideological contention. Throughout, the purpose is to distinguish *internationalist* themes, which tend to unite those attentive to, and traditionally supportive of, foreign policy, from *ideological* themes, which divide liberal and conservative internationalists. These themes are grouped into three general categories: the U.S. role in the world, U.S. relations with allies, and U.S. relations with communist countries.

U.S. Role in the World

Activism

Whether the United States should play an active role in world affairs is a defining element of internationalism. A clear-cut internationalist response can be observed in table A.1, question 4f: "Do you think it will be best for the future of the country if we take an active part in world affairs, or if we stay out of world affairs. Indeed, this bedrock isolationist attitude was expressed by only one third of noninternationalists. Is there, in fact, overwhelming support for internationalism?

Question 7a(b) in table A.4 reveals the limits of internationalism. When offered the statement, "America's real concerns should be at home, not abroad," a majority of internationalists and two thirds of noninternationalists agreed *strongly*. The sample as a whole agreed overwhelmingly with this statement, 87 to 11 percent. Thus, there seems to be support for active U.S. participation in the world, but an equally clear sense of priorities: our "real concerns" should be domestic, not international. Americans support an active international role as long as it is consistent with domestic priorities.

Both questions produced agreement among internationalists, with little difference between liberals and conservatives. It would seem that "activism," in and of itself, is not ideologically controversial. Nevertheless, a third formulation of the "activist" position revealed an ideological difference. Question 7*a*, statement *a*, in table A.4, defined activism in stronger terms than the two questions cited above: "The United States has a real responsibility to take a very active role in the world." This statement divided internationalists and noninternationalists more deeply than did the previous two, but it also divided conservative and liberal internationalists. Two thirds of conservative internationalists agreed strongly with this position, compared with about half of liberal internationalists. While moderate activism is not controversial, "strong" activism is. The notion that America has a "real responsibility" to take a "very active" role in the world seems to cause some liberal internationalists—and most noninternationalists—to hesitate, as if these terms connote an excessive degree of commitment. Conservative internationalists seem to support a stronger degree of commitment than do liberals.

Evaluation of U.S. Policy

Table A.1 includes a particularly interesting question: whether the United States "has generally been a force for good or a force for evil in its foreign policies since World War II" (Q.4*g*). An impressive two thirds of the sample said that this country has generally been a force for good. Conservative internationalists were notably more likely than either of the other groups to feel this way. What is surprising is how few in this survey—8 percent—were willing to say that U.S. foreign policy since World War II has, on the whole, been a force for "evil." Ten percent of noninternationalists and only 9 percent of liberal internationalists expressed this view. Liberal internationalists tended to volunteer the response that American foreign policy has been a force for *both* good and evil since World War II. Thus, no evidence here indicates that any group takes a deeply negative view of U.S. foreign policy, but liberals and noninternationalists do not share the unbridled enthusiasm of conservatives.

The Foreign Policy Process

Table A.2 includes several questions concerning the institutions and processes of U.S. foreign policy. For instance, question 2*e* asked respondents whether Congress was playing too strong or too weak a role, as compared with the President, in determining foreign policy. Liberal internationalists definitely favored a stronger foreign policy role for Congress. Half of them felt that Congress was playing too weak a role, compared with about one third of conservatives and noninternationalists who felt this way. In part, this pattern is explained by memories of the Vietnam war, which was carried on by the executive branch over many congressional objections. Also, in 1975, the time of the survey, the White House was in the hands of the Republicans, a party much less congenial to liberal foreign policy views than the Democrats, who controlled Congress.

If the President (or the Presidency) was mistrusted by liberals, what about Secretary of State Kissinger? Question 14*a* asked respondents to rate Kissinger's performance in office. The ideological ambiguity of Kissinger's foreign policy has already been discussed. It is difficult to hypothesize whether he should have been given a higher job rating by conservatives or by liberals. The undeniable fact is that Kissinger was a committed internationalist—and this is precisely what shows up in the data. Secretary Kissinger was rated higher by internationalists than by noninternationalists, but there was no significant difference between the ratings given him by conservative and liberal internationalists. Both had reasons for admiring and for distrusting him, and in the end they seem to have balanced out: Kissinger's performance was ideologically ambiguous, and so was the public's response. Only noninternationalists found little to admire in Kissinger's performance.

The one institution of U.S. foreign policy about which there was no ambiguity was the CIA. Every question that mentioned the CIA produced an ideologically polarized response. The assessment of CIA involvement in Chile has been noted. The same pattern occurred when respondents were asked to rate the job of the CIA "as the chief intelligence agency of the U.S. government" (Q.13*b*, table A.2). The sample was closely divided, with 31 percent giving the CIA a positive rating (excellent or pretty good) and slightly more, 39 percent, giving the CIA a negative rating (only fair or poor). But the net rating given by conservative internationalists was positive (11 percent more positive than negative), whereas the net rating given by liberal internationalists was negative (24 percent more negative than positive). The rating given by noninternationalists (14 percent net negative) fell in between. The same thing happened when respondents were asked whether "the CIA should or should not work inside other countries to try to strengthen those elements that serve the interests of the U.S. and to weaken those forces that work against the interests of the U.S." (Q.13*c*, table A.2). Forty percent of liberal internationalists said that the CIA should *not* do this, compared with 17 percent of conservative internationalists. Noninternationalists, 24 percent of whom said that the CIA should not carry on such activities, were again in between. Thus, while there was some ideological disagreement over the balance of power between the President and Congress, conservative and liberal internationalists were much more deeply polarized over the role of the CIA, an issue that has profoundly disrupted the internationalist consensus.

Power in International Relations

Table A.4 includes a number of statements concerning the role of power in international relations. Support for a "powerful" United States would seem to be a component of internationalism, but the evidence reveals much more complexity in public thinking. For instance, *non*internationalists hold a strongly power-oriented view of international relations and are consistently favorable toward the notion of the United States as a predominant world power. Conservative internationalists also tend to favor American power, but for different reasons.

Is power politics outmoded? Noninternationalists were the least likely to think so in the Chicago Council survey. In statement 7*d*(1), noninternationalists were the most likely to agree strongly that "having the power to get what you want is what really counts today" and the least likely to agree strongly that ". . . the old ideas of power politics and power alliances between countries have grown out-of-date"

(Q.7*d*[8]). In both cases, liberal internationalists showed the greatest inclination to reject power politics (i.e., to disagree with the first statement and agree with the second). Thus, power politics is a "mixed" signal. It is more widely accepted by noninternationalists than by internationalists, and by conservatives than by liberals.

But there is a difference between the conservative and the noninternationalist view of power. The noninternationalist view is captured by question 7*a*(*d*): "We should build up our own defenses and let the rest of the world take care of itself." This statement produced a reverse internationalist response; both categories of internationalists rejected it in about equal proportions. But a third of noninternationalists agreed strongly with this classic isolationist view. According to this position, American power should be used to keep us from having to get involved with the rest of the world; a strong and powerful United States would not have to bother with other countries, and they would not dare bother us.

Another expression of this "Fortress America" attitude is question 7*d*(3): "The U.S. is rich and powerful enough to go it alone, without getting involved in the problems of the rest of the world." Here again, noninternationalists were the most likely to agree strongly. In this case, conservative internationalists were more favorable than were liberal internationalists. Conservatives probably responded positively to the signal that the United States is "rich and powerful" and *need not* get involved with other countries (i.e., we *could* do so if we wanted, and not, as in the earlier statement, we *should* do so).

Conservatives tend to favor the active use of American power as a world leader rather than an isolated fortress. Consider for example, the ambiguous statement of question 7*d*(5):

> *The only way peace can exist in this world is when a country like the United States who wants peace is strong enough to back up warnings to possible aggressor nations that they can't get away with aggression.*

This statement produced a conservative coalition; a majority of conservative internationalists and noninternationalists agreed strongly with it, compared with only 35 percent of liberal internationalists. To noninternationalists, the statement probably meant that, if we are strong, other nations will not commit aggression *against us.* Conservative internationalists, however, might have read this statement as a U.S. commitment to act as "policeman to the world," to use American power to protect *others* from aggression.

This interpretation is supported by responses to other statements that explicitly defined the United States as having the world policeman role. Consider, for instance, question 7*d*(12):

> *The United Nations is good in theory, but the real way to keep peace in the world is to have the super powers such as the United States and the Soviet Union agree that they will not allow other countries to wage war.*

This statement prescribes an activist use of American power, an issue on which conservatives and noninternationalists part company. Only 27 percent of noninternationalists were in strong agreement in this case, compared with 43 percent of conservative internationalists.

Moreover, only 29 percent of liberal internationalists agreed strongly with this view. For one thing, the statement is critical of the United Nations because it implies that UN sanctions are good "in theory" but ineffective in practice. The statement is also "military" in tone ("the super powers . . . will not allow other countries to wage war") and hegemonic in implication (the United States and the Soviet Union must agree to police the world). By contrast, liberal internationalists were the most likely to agree with the following statement, one with much the same meaning:

> *With our improving relations with the Soviet Union, we should work more closely with the Russians to keep smaller countries from going to war. (Q.7a[i])*

This last statement makes reference to détente and has the tone of international cooperation rather than force. Both categories of internationalists tended to favor this view. Noninternationalists, distrustful of an active U.S. role in policing the world, were still distinctly unfavorable.

Thus, in sum, conservative internationalists and noninternationalists agree in their support for U.S. power but disagree over the uses to which that power should be put.

Hegemony

Noninternationalists believe that American power should isolate this country from the rest of the world. Conservative internationalists believe that American power should make this country a world leader. Throughout the Chicago Council survey, conservative internationalists were strongly responsive to the idea of U.S. world leadership. This is shown most clearly in question 4*b*, where respondents were asked whether they felt the United States *ought* "to play a more important and powerful role as a world leader" ten years from now. Conservative internationalists favored a more important role for the United States over a less important role by 43 to 14 percent (table A.1). By contrast, among liberal internationalists and noninternationalists, roughly equal percentages felt that the United States should play a more and a less important role as a world leader.

Conservative internationalists also gave the United Staters a higher rating as a current world leader. The sample was asked whether the United States plays "a more important and powerful role as a world leader today" as compared with ten years earlier (Q.4*a*, table A.1), and whether the U.S. is respected more or less today. In both cases, the sample as a whole gave a negative view. Thirty-nine percent felt that the U.S. role as a world leader had become less important, compared with 28 percent who thought that it had become more important; and by a margin of 64 to 12 percent, respondents felt that the United States today was respected less rather than more. In each case, conservative internationalists were the most positive group. They were the most likely to feel that the United States is respected and is a world leader today and that it ought to be a more powerful world leader in the future.

Table A.3 conveys this same message indirectly but convincingly. Respondents were asked "how important . . . you feel it is for the United States to be a world leader" in each of ten separate areas ranging from military strength and moral values to scientific progress and support for international organizations. What is striking about the responses is that conservative internationalists were the most likely to say that it is "very important" for the United States to be a world leader in *every one* of the ten areas. This included five "controversial" areas, in which liberals were much less likely than conservatives to say that the United States should be a world leader: military strength, moral values, standard of living, "ability to give political leadership to other like-minded countries," and "willingness to make military commitments to other countries and to keep them." The pattern also held up in areas where liberal opinion was much more favorable: economic strength, scientific and technical progress, "skill in negotiating settlements that avoid war," foreign economic aid, and support for international organizations like the UN. In each of these areas, too, conservatives were the most favorable to the idea of U.S. world leadership. Clearly, what conservative internationalists favored was *U.S. world leadership itself,* no matter what the area of endeavor. Liberals were much more selective in their responses and tended to favor world leadership in some areas (avoiding war, achieving scientific progress) but not in others (moral values, military strength). Noninternationalists tended to support U.S. world leadership in areas of "strength" (economic strength, military strength, standard of living) and in the avoidance of war but not in areas of cooperation, aid, and alliance with other countries.

U.S. Relations with Allies

International Cooperation

Noninternationalists want the United States to be strong and independent—not interdependent. For instance, slightly over half the sample agreed strongly with the idea, axiomatic to internationalists, that "international cooperation is the only way we can make progress" in solving problems like food, energy, and inflation which are "so big that no country can solve them alone" (Q.7*d*[15], table A.4). Noninternationalists tended to agree with this "fact," but without much enthusiasm. Only 39 percent of noninternationalists expressed strong agreement, compared with over 60 percent of liberal and conservative internationalists.

This same pattern showed up in questions on international organization. That internationalists were more favorable to international organization than noninternationalists is certainly not surprising, but the weakness of ideological differences on this subject is. When asked whether the "U.S. role in the founding of the United Nations" was a proud moment or a dark moment in American history (Q.7*c*[1], table A.10), both liberal and conservative internationalists called it a proud moment by overwhelming margins—89 to 2 percent among liberal internationalists, 88 to 3 percent among conservative internationalists. Noninternationalists were less enthusiastic, but a substantial majority (73 to 6 percent) still called the founding of the UN a proud moment. The absence of any ideological difference over the UN is remarkable, given the fact that the UN has often been the focus of attacks by conservative pressure groups. The domination of the UN by Third World countries that are often hostile to the United States would seem to give conservatives increased cause for resentment, but little resentment shows up among conservative *internationalists* in this survey.

While the UN is manifestly a source of pride to most Americans, there is less support for giving up power to "international organizations." Only 27 percent of the sample agreed strongly that "we should conduct more and more of our foreign affairs through genuinely international organizations" (Q.7a[f], table A.4) and only 21 percent agreed strongly that the only way to keep peace in the world is for the United States and other countries "to give up their own power to a truly international organization that will have the military power to enforce peace" (Q.7d[14], table A.4). In both cases internationalists were somewhat more favorable than noninternationalists, and liberal internationalists were more favorable than conservative internationalists—but only by a few points. The theme of international organization, even when it comes close to the idea of world government, does not seem to be an important issue of contention between liberal and conservative internationalists.

Alliances

International organization implies a cooperative effort among many nations to solve common problems, including the problem of peace. Free World, communist, and Third World nations are all members of the UN. An international organization with "the military power to enforce peace" would necessarily include both Free World and communist countries. Alliances, on the other hand, are coalitions of certain countries in opposition to others. Is the principle of alliance more controversial than that of international organization?

Several questions about alliances were included in table A.5. Question 9a asked whether the United States should make more of its major foreign policy decisions "on its own" or "mainly consult with . . . major allies before making major foreign policy decisions." The sample endorsed consultation with major allies over making decisions on our own by 51 to 39 percent. Predictably, noninternationalists were more favorable to making decisions on our own, which they favored over consultation by a small margin. Both groups of internationalists favored consultation with allies, but conservatives were somewhat more favorable. Thirty-six percent of liberal internationalists and 33 percent of conservative internationalists thought that we should make major foreign policy decisions on our own. This difference is small, but it contrasts with the fact that liberals were more likely than conservatives to feel that "we should conduct more and more of our foreign affairs through genuinely international organizations" (Q.7a[f], table A.4). The idea of consulting with *allies* introduces a new aspect to international cooperation.

Other questions in table A.5 elaborate different forms of alliance relationships. Question 14b asked whether the United States, Canada, Western Europe, and Japan should "get together to develop strategies which would make us less dependent on the decisions of the foreign oil-producing countries." This idea was overwhelmingly popular (79 percent of the sample favored it) and nonideological. It was supported by 85 percent of both liberal and conservative internationalists. A similar internationalist pattern occurred in the case of question 16, which asked which of three policies the United States should follow if America, Western Europe, and Japan were faced with another oil embargo by the Arab states. This question produced a close division between two answers: (1) sharing our oil with Europe and Japan, "even if it means less oil for Americans," an option favored by 40 percent of the sample; and (2) going it alone and leaving Europe and Japan to "fend for themselves," an option favored by 38 percent. Internationalists favored sharing oil with our allies, whereas noninternationalists felt that we should look out for ourselves. Again, there was no significant difference between liberal and conservative internationalists. Only 6 percent of the sample chose the third option, "Invade the oil-producing countries"; indeed, this policy was chosen by a mere 7 percent of conservative internationalists.

Both questions involved *economic* cooperation among allies. When the focus shifts to *political and military* cooperation, ideological differences become more pronounced. NATO is the principal political and military alliance of the United States. Question 11a asked whether the U.S. commitment to NATO should be increased, decreased, kept "as it is now," or whether the United States should withdraw from NATO entirely. Only 4 percent of the sample wanted to increase our commitment to NATO and only 7 percent thought we should withdraw. Exactly half the sample felt that we should maintain our commitment as it is now, while 13 percent favored a decrease in that commitment. Conservative internationalists were notably more enthusiastic about NATO than were liberal internationalists or noninternationalists. Conservative internationalists favored keeping or increasing our commitment over decreasing it by a margin of 53 percent. This margin was 28 percent among liberal internationalists and 24 percent among noninternationalists. Thus, on the NATO issue, a liberal coalition materializes. NATO is a costly international commitment and therefore less popular among noninternationalists. It is also an anticommunist political and military commitment and therefore less popular among liberal internationalists.

The notion that the political and military aspect of alliances divides liberals and conservatives helps explain certain findings that would otherwise be puzzling. Consider statements 7d(9) and 7d(10) in table A.4. The first says that ". . . we should try to maintain close ties and friendly relations with the countries from which our people's ancestors came"; the second proposes, more specifically, that the United States keep a close relationship with "those countries that have similar traditions and appreciation of freedom, such as England and France." Internationalists supported these views more than noninternationalists did, but in each case conservative internationalists were notably more favorable than were liberals. On the face of it, these statements seem to be high-minded and nonideological. Yet both imply a political alliance among Western democracies, countries from which most Americans' ancestors came that have "similar traditions and appreciation of freedom." These statements have an anticommunist, anti-Third World bias that limits their support among liberal internationalists. They offend the notion of pluralism, which is a central element in the liberal internationalist world view.

Foreign Aid

Almost no Americans oppose humanitarian aid to other nations. The sample was virtually unanimous in supporting "our giving emergency food and medical supplies to other nations in cases of natural disasters." Fully 90 percent of noninternationalists supported such aid, which implies no political commitment or involvement.

Support for foreign economic aid was not so widespread. A bare majority of the sample, 53 percent, said that the United States should give economic aid to other nations "for purposes of economic development and technical assistance." Foreign economic aid is clearly an internationalist issue. Such aid was supported by over 60 percent of liberal and conservative internationalists with no significant difference between them, but by only 40 percent of noninternationalists.

The same pattern shows up in question 7c (table A.10), which listed several instances of U.S. foreign aid programs and asked respondents whether each was a proud moment or a dark moment in American history: "U.S. sending emergency food to Bangladesh," "the founding of the Peace Corps," "the Marshall Plan of aid to Europe," and "the Berlin airlift." A majority called each of these a proud moment in American history, a sentiment that in each case was substantially higher among internationalists than among noninternationalists. Interestingly, there were no significant differences between the reactions of liberal and conservative internationalists to these events, even the Berlin airlift and the Marshall Plan, which were highly political in nature. It is likely that, especially with the passage of time, these policies are seen as more nearly humanitarian ("relief") than political.

Despite the widespread sense of pride in these instances of American generosity, foreign aid is not popular with the American public. In this survey as in many others, foreign aid was named as a federal program that should be "cut back first" in comparison with other forms of spending. In the Chicago Council survey, respondents felt that foreign economic aid should be cut back rather than expanded by a margin of 56 to 10 percent. One reason for this unpopularity can be seen in table A.6. Question 3g asked once again whether respondents favored foreign economic aid, but this time the stipulation was added, "if you could be sure that the economic aid we sent to countries abroad ended up helping people of those countries." In this case, support for foreign economic aid rose to almost 90 percent of liberal and conservative internationalists and to two thirds of noninternationalists. Internationalists were still relatively more favorable, but support had risen in all three groups by about 25 percent. Apparently one reason why foreign economic aid is so unpopular is that Americans do not believe it accomplishes its objective, namely, to improve the lives of people in other countries.

A program that is even more unpopular than foreign economic aid is foreign military aid. The survey respondents chose "military aid to other nations" as the federal spending program they wanted to "cut back first" over twelve other programs; and an enormous majority, 70 to 3 percent, favored cutting back rather than expanding such aid. Only 22 percent said they favored "giving military aid to other nations," and only 35 percent favored "*selling* military equipment to other nations" (Q.3i and 3k, table A.6; emphasis in original).

Not only does support decline in the case of military aid but the pattern of support also changes. The reaction to military aid is much more ideological than the reaction to economic aid. As noted, liberal and conservative internationalists tended to support foreign economic aid at about the same rate. But conservatives were twice as favorable as liberals to giving military aid to other nations (33 as compared with 16 percent). Conservatives were also more favorable to selling military equipment to other nations (40 as compared with 34 percent). An internationalist coalition supports foreign economic aid, but that coalition splits on the issue of military aid. In the latter case, liberal internationalists and noninternationalists join in opposition. As with alliance relations, the internationalist consensus breaks down when political and military considerations are introduced. That is true even when economic aid is made subject to political criteria. For example, statement 7a(c) in table A.4 proposed that "we should give foreign aid only to our friends, and not to countries who criticize the United States." Conservatives and noninternationalists were most likely to support this political definition of foreign aid, whereas liberal internationalists were significantly less favorable.

U.S. Relations with Communists

Military Policy

Any reference to the military produces immediate ideological division. One of the most common indicators of antimilitary sentiment is the question of defense spending. Question 10d (table A.1) in the Chicago Council survey asked respondents whether they thought defense spending should be expanded, cut back, or kept about the same. There was not much sentiment for expanding the defense budget, even among conservative internationalists, a majority of whom felt that defense spending should be kept about the same. Thirty-three percent of conservative internationalists favored cutting back defense spending. This percentage was twice as high among liberal internationalists, with noninternationalists falling in between. Attitudes toward defense spending followed an ideological pattern, not an internationalist pattern. Defense spending and the CIA were the two issues that divided liberal and conservative internationalists most deeply.

The question of military intervention was posed in general terms in question 6a, where respondents were asked what the United States should do "if friendly countries are attacked." Four alternatives were proposed, in descending order of "toughness" and degree of American commitment: (1) we should send military aid, economic aid, and, if necessary, American troops and manpower; (2) we should send military aid and economic aid but no American troops or manpower; (3) we should send economic aid but no military aid and no American troops or manpower; or (4) we should not send any aid—military, economic, or American troops. The most popular response was the second—military and economic aid but no American troops or manpower—chosen by 37 percent of the sample. About equal numbers of respondents, 22 and 23 percent, favored choices 1 and 3; only 9 percent felt that no form of aid should be sent.

The ideological alignment on this question was also clear. The "toughest" response—send all three forms of aid, including U.S. troops—produced a liberal coalition against it; conservative internationalists tended to favor this option, but it met with little approval from either liberal internationalists or noninternationalists. The liberal coalition showed a preference for option 3; liberal internationalists and noninternationalists were more likely to want to send only economic aid, whereas conservatives tended to reject this option in favor of the stronger ones. The intermediate choice—military and economic aid but no troops—drew support from both liberal and conservative internationalists. Indeed, liberals were actually a bit more favorable to option 2, which included military aid, than were conservatives, because it was presented as an *alternative* to sending troops. One might say that conservatives favored option 2 *or more*; liberals favored option 2 *or less*. Both rejected option 4, which was to send no aid at all. Indeed, only one in eight noninternationalists said that the United States should do nothing "if friendly countries are attacked."

The deep ideological division over the issue of military intervention is confirmed repeatedly in question 8 (table A.7). Respondents were asked "what circumstances might justify U.S. military involvement, including the use of U.S. troops." A list of twelve different circumstances was presented, ranging from "if Canada were invaded," which 77 percent of the sample felt would justify U.S. military involvement, to "if the Soviet Union attacked Yugoslavia," which only 11 percent felt would justify U.S. military involvement. In every single case on the list, conservative internationalists were significantly more favorable to military involvement than were either of the other two groups.

In only one circumstance did a majority of the sample feel U.S. military involvement would be justified: "if Canada were invaded." Support for military intervention dropped sharply, to 32–39 percent, in the following cases: "if Western Europe were invaded," "if the Russians took over West Berlin," and "if Cuba invaded the Dominican Republic." "If Israel were being defeated by the Arabs," 27 percent of the sample favored U.S. military intervention, whereas 21 percent favored such involvement "if the Arabs cut off the oil supply to Western Europe." In all other circumstances—six out of the list of twelve—less than 20 percent of the sample favored U.S. military involvement. Support for military involvement thus tends to be greater in areas geographically close to the United States (Canada, Latin America) and in Western Europe, where the United States has a military alliance and has already intervened militarily in two world wars.

Ideological division over military issues was also revealed in question 7c (table A.10), which asked respondents to evaluate several past military interventions as either "proud moments" or "dark moments" in American history. Conservative internationalists expressed the most pride in each intervention. The strongest polarization occurred in response to the most recent interventions—Korea, Vietnam, and the Dominican Republic. The powerful impact of Vietnam can be seen in the responses to that issue. No one felt positive about the Vietnam experience. Conservative internationalists called it a dark moment rather than a proud moment by a margin of 66 to 12 percent. Noninternationalists felt substantially the same way—67 to 7 percent. The feelings expressed by liberal internationalists were the most profoundly negative; 86 percent called Vietnam a dark moment and only 3 percent a proud moment. In the case of the Korean war, polarization was less extreme. Liberal internationalists called Korea a dark rather than a proud moment by 45 to 16 percent and conservative internationalists did so by 37 to 28 percent. Even in the two least controversial involvements—"Kennedy's handling of the Cuban missile crisis" and "the U.S. role in World War II"—conservative internationalists expressed the greatest pride. In these cases, the noninternationalists, not the liberals, expressed the least pride.

These findings help explain the response to another case tested in question 7c, "American support of Israel during the October 1973 war." Conservative internationalists were the most likely to call this a proud rather than a dark moment in

American history, by a 45-point margin. The margin among liberal internationalists was somewhat lower, 32 points; noninternationalists who called this a proud moment outnumbered those who called it a dark moment by 20 percentage points. This is a mixed pattern, in which internationalists were more favorable than noninternationalists and conservative internationalists were more favorable than liberals. Thus the Israel issue evokes a somewhat weaker ideological response than Korea, Vietnam, or the Dominican Republic. This corresponds to the fact that U.S. military involvement was "weaker" in the Middle East war. The United States gave Israel military aid but did not send any troops. Generally, when respondents are asked about "military aid to Israel" or "military intervention in the Dominican Republic," there is a predictable ideological response to the word "military," just as there is a predictable noninternationalist response to the suggestion of foreign entanglement. Such questions involve a complex mix of signals and should not be read as simply showing feelings toward "Israel" or "the Dominican Republic."

Pluralism

Pluralism, along with antimilitarism, is a core element of the liberal internationalist world view. The basic assumption of pluralism in the international system, as in the domestic system, is that different ideologies should coexist in an atmosphere of mutual toleration. It should not be the U.S. purpose to destroy or even deny the legitimacy of opposing ideologies. One of the best indicators of this pluralistic outlook is question 7d, statement 7: "We should have the same kind of dedication to the spread of political freedom and private enterprise of business in the world as the Russians and Chinese have for the spread of communism in the world." A majority of conservative internationalists agreed strongly. But only 38 percent of liberal internationalists felt the same way. Noninternationalists also showed limited enthusiasm for this view; only 34 percent agreed strongly with it. This statement articulates a belief central to cold-war internationalism, that the United States should match the communists in ideological zeal. That liberal internationalists show little more support for this position than do noninternationalists reveals how sharply that consensus has been broken.

A more general pluralistic outlook can be discerned in the responses to question 7b in table A.8. Here, respondents were asked whether, "if there is some advantage to the United States in it," we should recognize, "back," or trade with countries of a different ideological persuasion. In three of the cases specified in the question, the different ideological persuasion was identifiably left-wing: whether it is justified for the U.S. "to establish trade relations with communist countries," "to recognize democratic left-wing governments when they come to power," and "to back socialist governments that respect the basic political rights of their people." A fourth case had conservative connotations: "to back governments which believe in our free enterprise system but not in democracy." In every case, liberal internationalists were the most likely to feel that such policies were justified. Conservative internationalists were consistently less favorable than liberals, even in the case of backing "governments which believe in our free enterprise system but not in democracy." But conservative internationalists were always more favorable than noninternationalists, presumably because of the specification that "there is some advantage to the United States" in each policy.

The consistency of these responses indicates that every question tapped the same underlying attitude: a willingness to tolerate ideological diversity in the world. Interestingly, the fifth case listed in question 7b produced no difference of opinion among the three groups. Very few respondents felt that it was justified for the United States "to back authoritarian governments that have overthrown democratic governments," even if it were in our interest to do so. What differentiates this case from the others is the connotation of illegitimacy (i.e., an authoritarian government that has come to power illegally, by "overthrowing" a democratic government). Even conservative internationalists, who do not insist that a government be democratic in order for the United States to support it, are predisposed against regimes that come to power through violence.

Détente

Détente is closely related to pluralism. Basically, détente means a relaxation of tensions between the United States and the communist world. Exactly what this policy implies is a matter of some disagreement. Does it mean that we no longer regard communism as a threat? that we are willing to deal with communist countries on the same basis as we deal with other countries? that the United States will tolerate communism as a legitimate political ideology suitable for other nations?

All internationalists tend to support détente to a certain extent, but when the pluralist implications of détente are spelled out in detail, significant disagreement emerges between liberal and conservative internationalists. The key event in détente, President Nixon's trip to Communist China, was praised by both liberal and conservative internationalists as a proud moment in American history—62 to 6 percent among liberals and 66 to 8 percent among conservatives (Q.7c[3], table A.10). Noninternationalists were somewhat less enthusiastic but still positive, 53 to 12 percent. The principal conviction that leads internationalists to support détente is expressed in the following statement:

> The big breakthroughs in peacemaking in the future will come less from agreements with traditional allies and more from agreements in learning to live together with traditional enemies. (Q.7d[13], table A.4)

Just over half of conservative and liberal internationalists agreed strongly with this statement, while only 33 percent of noninternationalists did so. Internationalists also tended to agree with a similar statement in this series:

> In a nuclear age, when the whole world can be blown up, we have to overcome old animosities and ideological differences and learn to live with countries such as the Soviet Union and China. (Q.7d[11], table A.4)

The second statement introduces ideological considerations and, unlike the first, makes specific reference to the two leading communist powers. Thus, a more ideological response is evinced—66 percent of liberal internationalists and 55 percent of conservative internationalists agreed strongly with the second position. Noninternationalists were still far behind (36 percent in strong agreement).

What is interesting, however, is that conservative internationalists showed such strong support for both these positions, just as they expressed remarkable pride in Nixon's trip to China. As noted, it is undoubtedly important that détente was initiated by a Republican administration under a President with impeccable anticommunist credentials. It is also likely that some degree of "conversion" occurred among conservative internationalists, certainly not to a pluralist position, but to an acceptance of communism as a fact not likely to be reversed by American foreign policy. The key phrase in both statements above was that the United States should "learn to live with" Russia and China. The major impact of détente may be to have converted conservative internationalists from crusading anticommunism to an acceptance of the necessity of peaceful coexistence. The Vietnam experience certainly must have convinced many cold warriors that resistance to communism in all parts of the world is a costly and difficult policy.

Learning to live with communism is not the same as trusting the communists. Liberal internationalists are still more willing than conservatives to believe that long-term agreements with the communists will work. About two thirds of liberal internationalists felt it was possible for the United States to reach "long-term agreements to keep peace" with Russia and China (Q.11b and 11d, table A.9) and the same proportion favored "the U.S. establishing full diplomatic relations with Cuba" (Q.13a, table A.9). In each case, about half of conservative internationalists and noninternationalists felt the same way. The ideological difference notwithstanding, it is striking that as many as half of conservative internationalists and noninternationalists were willing to endorse these positions.

The strongest ideological polarization occurred in question 12b (table A.9), when respondents were asked whether it would be a threat to the United States if each in a series of six countries or areas were to go communist. The countries fell into two groups. At least two thirds of the sample felt it would be a threat to the United States if "Western European countries," "Latin American countries," or Japan were to go communist. Only about half the sample felt it would be a threat if "African countries," Italy, or Portugal were to go communist. (One must assume that Italy and Portugal are not the countries most people have in mind when they think of "Western European countries.") In each case, there was a wide gap between conservative and liberal perceptions of communism as a threat. Over 80 percent of conservative internationalists saw a threat to the United States if Western Europe, Latin America, or Japan were to go communist; the figure among liberal internationalists was 58–59 percent. Over 60 percent of conservative internationalists thought it would be a threat to the United States if Africa, Italy, or Portugal were to go communist; that view was shared by only 32–38 percent of liberal internationalists. The responses of noninternationalists were always in between, thereby creating a clear pattern of ideological polarization.

There is thus a deep cleavage between liberal and conservative internationalists over the threat posed by communism. For conservatives, what appears to have changed is not conservative attitudes toward communism, but conservative attitudes toward U.S. foreign policy. Conservatives still see world politics as a fundamental conflict of values between East and West, but they no longer feel that the United States can lead a crusade against communism by force of arms. The conservative view of détente is that we must learn to live with the communists, trusting them only as far as is necessary for the sake of peace, playing one communist power off against the others, dealing with them to our mutual advantage, but never losing sight of the essentially competitive nature of our relationship and never conceding the legitimacy of their values or intentions. The internationalist consensus in support of détente really goes no farther than this.

AN INTERPRETATION

From these survey findings and the foreign policy debate in the 1976 presidential election, it is possible to assemble a picture of the two internationalist world views.

Conservative internationalism pictures the world primarily in East-West terms: democracy versus tyranny, capitalism versus communism, freedom versus repression. Conservatives are suspicious of détente and the abandonment of the cold war as fundamentally immoral, and they seek an American foreign policy committed once again to the containment, if not the rollback, of world communism.

For conservative internationalists, the nation's security lies in aggressive American leadership of the Free World military alliance. It is an interventionist foreign policy that reads the Vietnam experience as "a failure of nerve." The conservative world view holds that the East-West confrontation should remain the moral focus of American foreign policy. Conservatives attack détente as a kind of "cartel" agreement whereby the two superpowers agree to limit competition in order to stabilize the market and protect their interests (the cartel's charter is the Helsinki Treaty). They do not believe that the Free World should be happy with what it has, or that the Soviets can be trusted to restrain themselves. The burgeoning of authoritarianism in the Third World is seen as evidence that détente can harm the cause of freedom, and there is great alarm, expressed most forcefully by Daniel Patrick Moynihan, over the way smaller, less democratic countries have begun to try to "push around" the United States at the United Nations and elsewhere. Conservative internationalists include Republicans who expressed their opposition to détente by voting for Ronald Reagan but for whom the Ford foreign policy was sufficiently promilitary, and Democrats whose suspicions of détente make them a minority within their party and whose promilitary views, while more widely shared, were muted in 1976 for the sake of party unity.

If conservative internationalists took Kissinger to task for not having been sufficiently attentive to the East-West confrontation, liberal internationalists attacked him as having been too preoccupied with such issues. Liberal internationalists, who are largely Democrats but include the dwindling band of liberal Republicans, define America's national security differently from the conservatives: they argue for internationalism as a necessity, they emphasize economic and humanitarian issues, and they reject a hegemonic role for the United States.

Much of liberal internationalism is directed against the drift of the left in the United States toward a kind of neo-isolationism. Liberal internationalists reject such a view as irresponsible and selfish. They note that the United States already has so many dealings with other countries, and that the line between domestic and foreign policy has become sufficiently blurred, that there is no practical possibility of retreating from the rest of the world.

Liberal internationalists think of international problems more in economic terms than has been customary in the past. They reject what they regard as Secretary Kissinger's excessive concern with military and strategic problems. The old "balance of power" politics, they believe, is not only irrelevant to the world's economic situation, but actually dangerous. (Kissinger was, of course, widely recognized as inexpert on international economic problems and therefore not interested in them.) Liberal internationalists want American leaders to think in global terms. For them the pressing issues are global in scope: the scarcity of natural resources, environmental and oceanic pollution, and international economic inequality. They tend to regard the common problems facing all of humanity as considerably more urgent than the ideological differences between countries. They claim it is irresponsible to fight among ourselves when "spaceship earth" is running out of fuel.

Liberal internationalists want the United States to take an active part in international affairs, but they reject a hegemonic role. The Vietnam experience and the energy crisis are seen as evidence that hegemony is no longer feasible. A new world order must come into being based on "global interdependence" of some kind. The idea of interdependence incorporates the antimilitary bias of the left because military power, the source of hegemonic influence, is no longer a critical resource. Liberal internationalists do not disapprove of détente. They want, rather, to extend it. Ideological and political differences among countries need to be tolerated, they assert, in order to address common global problems. They do not approve of communism or other forms of authoritarianism. Yet they believe that the United States must learn to live with them for the sake of larger world interests. They are, in the parlance of domestic politics, true pluralists.[7]

Although these two world views were not really "debated" in 1976, both have begun to attract attention and interest. Versions of each view have been put forward by articulate and influential people, although not in pure form. A conspicuous forum for liberal internationalism has been the quarterly journal *Foreign Policy,* and several members of its editorial board have joined the Carter administration. Although conservative internationalism is often associated with the Reagan wing of the Republican party, some of the most important essays advancing that point of view have been published in *Commentary* magazine, by writers not usually considered conservative in areas other than foreign policy. Moreover, both points of view found their way into the 1976 party platforms. The "Morality in Foreign Policy" amendment to the Republican platform was a statement of conservative internationalism. The Democratic platform accused the Republican administration of "a balance-of-power diplomacy suited better to the last century than to this one":

> *Instead of efforts to foster freedom and justice in the world, the Republican Administration has built a sorry record of disregard for human rights, manipulative interference in the internal affairs of other nations, and, frequently, a greater concern for our relations with totalitarian adversaries than with our democratic allies.*

The document includes a section on "The Challenge of Interdependence," and Jimmy Carter himself proclaimed in the third television debate with Gerald Ford that the United States should move from a foreign policy based on "balance of power" to one based on "global cooperation."

After the election, both conservative internationalists and liberal internationalists formed official lobbying groups to promote their points of view. The liberals organized New Directions as an international counterpart to Common Cause. Its founders included Robert S. McNamara, Margaret Mead, and Norman Cousins. According to its executive director, Russell W. Paterson, "You can't separate our problems into 'domestic' and 'foreign' anymore. That's the message we want to get across—and do something about quickly." The conservatives founded the Committee on the Present Danger, which warns against the threat the Soviet Union continues to pose and advocates higher levels of American defense spending. Its initial co-chairmen were David Packard, an industrialist who was deputy secretary of defense in the Nixon administration and is a prominent Republican, and Lane Kirkland, secretary-treasurer of the AFL-CIO, who supported Carter.

Liberal and conservative internationalists see the world differently. But they come together on one critical point: *each demands that American foreign policy have a moral basis, something that both regard as conspicuously missing from Henry Kissinger's diplomacy.* Both sides want to make America's role in the world a cause again—either warm-blooded or warm-hearted—rather than the cold, bloodless calculation of competing interests, a policy whose chief practitioner and principal symbol has been Henry Kissinger.

Here they may find some sympathy in mass opinion. Although Kissinger was always respected and admired for his formidable diplomatic achievements, many Americans came to feel that the nation was drifting away from its principles abroad as well as at home. There was always a cynical element in Kissinger's "shuttle diplomacy" as he rushed back and forth between Russia and China, Saigon and Paris, Israel and Egypt, South Africa and Rhodesia. As Nathan Glazer put it:

> *The United States is probably the only major country in the world in which it is taken quite as a matter of course that people will talk seriously about the relation of the nation's values to its foreign policy. We in this country seem to believe, first, that there is something distinctive about our values . . . and, second, that these values do, or should, affect our foreign policy.*[8]

LIBERALS, CONSERVATIVES, AND THE CARTER FOREIGN POLICY

The division in public opinion about foreign policy made itself felt from the earliest days of the Carter administration. Both liberals and conservatives are represented in Democratic ranks, and so the division took the form of civil strife within the Democratic party. Even before Carter took office, the party's antimilitary left was angry at the appointment to major foreign policy positions in the Cabinet and on the White House staff of "establishment" figures tainted by association with the

Vietnam war. Promilitary conservatives were dismayed by the appointment of Ambassador Andrew Young and several "unreliable" younger people to second-rank foreign policy positions.

After the inauguration the Congress became the principal arena in which the ongoing contest between liberal and conservative internationalists was played. They clashed early in the life of the administration, over the nomination of Paul Warnke to be head of the Arms Control and Disarmament Agency and chief American delegate to the Strategic Arms Limitation Talks (SALT).

Warnke was prominently identified as a liberal internationalist. Conservatives doubted that he would negotiate firmly enough with the Russians to protect American interests. They were also alarmed by the liberal tilt to the Carter foreign policy appointments. After a vigorous lobbying campaign on both sides, forty senators voted against giving Warnke the SALT post. They included both conservative Republicans (e.g., Jesse Helms of North Carolina and Robert Dole, the 1976 vice-presidential nominee) and Democrats of strong liberal bent on domestic matters but whose attitudes on international issues are conservative (e.g., Henry Jackson and Daniel Patrick Moynihan). Although the fifty-eight favorable votes were enough to pass the nomination, they fell short of the two-thirds majority that would be required to ratify a second SALT agreement, and served notice that conservative opinion will have to be taken into account in such negotiations.

The Carter administration's first approach to the Soviets on strategic armaments recouped some of the political ground that had been lost in the fight over the Warnke appointment. The proposal to make substantial cuts in both Soviet and American arsenals that Secretary of State Cyrus Vance took to Moscow in March 1977 pleased both wings of foreign policy opinion. Liberals were delighted at the prospect of real reductions in armaments rather than the high ceilings permitting existing weapons to remain, and planned new ones to be built, that previous rounds of SALT have produced. Conservatives were happy because the Carter plan called for limits on Soviet weapons they find particularly threatening, and because the new President vowed to "hang tough" behind his proposals.

But the initial Carter SALT proposal failed, and its failure demonstrated the difficulty of bridging the gap between liberal and conservative internationalists. The Russians did not like the March proposal. They rejected it brusquely and sent Secretary Vance and his party home in a way that emphasized their displeasure. The search for an agreement along the lines of the "deep cuts" proposal was abandoned. Failure to reach any SALT agreement would have disturbed liberal internationalists. An agreement along different lines, which was acceptable to the Soviets, seemed unacceptable to conservatives. The Carter administration found itself having to offend one side or the other. This was not true of SALT alone. The split between liberals and conservatives is broad. It covers a wide range of questions: how to deal with the beleaguered white regimes in southern Africa; whether and how far to press Israel to relinquish territory captured in 1967; what economic concessions, if any, to make to the less developed countries; and what to do about the growing strength of communist parties in Western Europe.*

---

* Not coincidentally, these issues are at the center of subsequent chapters in this volume. See chapters 4, 9, 11, and 12.

This split between liberal and conservative internationalism is not only broad but also deep, because both liberals and conservatives make moral claims for their points of view. People feel strongly about moral issues and therefore they are notoriously difficult to compromise. In addition, there is no consensus on what is moral. Both sides of the foreign policy debate want the United States to promote human rights abroad; however, conservatives see communist governments as the worst offenders against human rights, whereas liberals see right-wing dictatorships allied with the United States as the proper targets of human rights campaigns.

Deeply divided public opinion on foreign policy complicates the conduct of the nation's affairs abroad for three related reasons. First, the methods whereby previous Presidents have either papered over comparable divisions or brought harmony out of contentiousness are not likely to work for Carter. This is so especially because, second, he is not practicing an ideologically consistent foreign policy. On some issues he gives a liberal lead; on others he acts in conservative fashion. (A comparison between the Carter policy on SALT and on the sale of nonnuclear weapons abroad illustrates this necessary inconsistency.) Third, public opinion in general plays a larger role in the formation and management of foreign policy than has hitherto been the case.

Jimmy Carter is not the first American President who has had to direct the nation's foreign policy at a time when public opinion is unfocused. The split between liberal and conservative internationalism is far from the deepest division in American history, nor is it the first that lends itself neither to compromise nor evasion. It is singular, however, in that the methods for coping with domestic division that succeeded in the past are not likely to be available in the future.

Paying lip service to a controversial goal is one way to placate enthusiasts without giving offense to opponents. George Washington made good use of this technique. In his day, the American republic was a revolutionary state, as devoted to spreading the principles of liberalism throughout the world as the Soviet Union would be to the international triumph of communism 150 years later. Yet, when it came to acting on these principles, Washington balked. He declined to side with revolutionary France against Britain on the grounds that neutrality better served the interest of American security.

This decision did not sit well with ideologically fervent Americans. They disputed Washington's right to proclaim neutrality without congressional approval, and the controversy gave rise to the debate at the end of the *Federalist Papers* between "Helvidius" and "Pacificus" that has come down to us as one of the earliest significant discussions of presidential power over foreign policy.

The nation's first President steered a middle course between the claims of principle and the demands of security by proclaiming that the survival and prosperity of the republic would serve as a beacon to others. America's mission was to exist as an example that others could follow. The United States did its duty to its ideals by practicing liberalism in one country.

A similar approach may well permit Carter to discharge the obligation he has assumed to support the protection of human rights throughout the world. A few speeches on the subject, an occasional meeting with a Soviet dissident, and public statements on behalf of selected political prisoners may suffice to redeem his pledge to carry out an active human rights policy in the eyes of those to whom he made it.

After all, the Carter administration cannot force the Czech government to allow the performance of works by playwrights deemed subversive. Nor can it compel the Soviet Union to grant cultural autonomy to non-Russian nations under its control. It probably cannot even coax or coerce the Chilean generals to hold elections that are genuinely free, any more than eighteenth-century Americans could convert Europe to liberal practices. Nor can it even afford seriously to try. By his symbolic support of human rights, however, President Carter can get credit, as did George Washington, for being faithful to American ideals. On other issues symbolic gestures will not suffice.

A second solution to the problem posed by a divided public opinion on foreign policy is to forge a national consensus around one of the two (or more) conflicting points of view. Franklin D. Roosevelt before World War II, and Harry Truman afterward, presided over a nation split between the proponents of an active American role in Europe and the champions of abstention from European affairs. Both Presidents managed to override strong isolationist impulses.

They did so by riding the tide of events. In 1941 the Japanese attacked Pearl Harbor, and the case for isolation collapsed. Between 1945 and 1950, the Soviet Union's conspicuous and brutal conscription of Eastern Europe into the Soviet sphere of influence reinforced Harry Truman's efforts to keep the United States engaged in European affairs. It is difficult to imagine a series of events that would emphatically validate or discredit either liberal or conservative internationalism in the foreseeable future. Conservatives will continue to believe that the cold war still rages; liberals will hold that its importance, when compared with other issues, has faded.

In the absence of events that would galvanize public opinion in one way or the other, Carter and his successors might, in theory, align themselves with one of the two sides of the foreign policy debate and lead it into political combat, hoping to prevail over the other, not with the assistance of dramatic events, but by the force of argument. They might, that is, endeavor to form a consensus through the exercise of presidential leadership.

But this path, too, seems closed. Judging from its first two years in office, the Carter administration is unlikely to allow either the press of events or the logic of policy, or even the momentum of its own beliefs and commitments, to propel it in one consistent direction. Nor is any man who remains close enough to the center of the spectrum of American public opinion to be elected President likely to chart a consistent course. There will be different approaches to different issues. The United States will not conduct an ideologically consistent foreign policy. Sometimes it will please liberals and outrage conservatives; sometimes the distribution of satisfaction and dismay will be reversed. This oscillation will further complicate the task of securing domestic support for foreign policy.

Two issues with which the Carter administration has wrestled illustrate the impossibility of gliding over contentious questions and offering consistent leadership to the American people. They are the Strategic Arms Limitation Talks (SALT) and the sale of nonnuclear armaments to foreign countries.

After the Soviet rebuff of the initial proposals, the administration took a liberal direction. Conservatives became upset. Two ways of placating them were possible.

One was to wring concessions from Moscow that would satisfy the conservatives' standards for SALT. This did not happen.

A second was by unilateral increases in the American strategic forces. While this would have pleased conservatives, it would have been costly, it would have jeopardized prospects for further agreement with the Soviet Union, and it would have been unwelcome to liberals.

In the case of SALT, the administration found itself caught between the strongly held and sharply conflicting attitudes about nuclear weapons and about the Soviet Union held by liberal and conservative internationalists. When it came to the sale of nonnuclear armaments all over the world, the administration was trapped not so much between these two constituencies as between the liberal convictions of candidate Carter and the illiberal imperatives of the world in which President Carter must conduct American foreign policy.

Liberals regard armaments as comparable to narcotics: dangerous, expensive, and addictive commodities whose trade ought to be tightly controlled, if not completely stifled. Mr. Carter seemed to agree with this assessment. Soon after taking office he announced the goal of reducing American arms sales to other countries and set forth some guidelines for achieving it, such as progressively decreasing annual dollar values of arms exports. His administration then scrambled to evade those guidelines, for the guidelines conflicted with other goals of American foreign policy.

The recipients fell into three categories. For each category, U.S. armaments turned out to serve one or more purposes that the Carter administration was loathe to subvert. The first category of recipients includes the European members of NATO, Japan, and perhaps Israel. After thirty years these nations qualify as "traditional" allies of the United States. Neither wing of foreign policy public opinion begrudges the armaments that these nations obtain.

Into the second category fall states whose requests for armaments are not entirely popular. But the fulfillment of these requests is a lesser evil for the United States than the consequences of refusing them. For example, American military assistance to South Korea and Taiwan serves as a cover for the dilution of an American defense commitment. It is like a divorce settlement for a union—the defense commitment—consummated in the flush of anticommunist fervor in the 1950s, a union that has gone sour, along with the policy of resisting communism in Asia that produced it. For South Korea and Taiwan—and perhaps for Israel and Brazil as well—a regular supply of nonnuclear armaments may also serve to check an appetite for nuclear weapons.

The third category of recipients includes two countries whose purchases account for much of the dramatic increase in American arms sales in the late 1970s: Iran and Saudi Arabia. Neither has been a particular favorite of liberal or conservative internationalists; liberals disapproved of both governments because of their autocratic character; it remains to be seen whether the new "Islamic republic" of Iran will be significantly less repressive than the previous regime. Conservatives have resented the role of Iran and Saudi Arabia in increasing the price of oil.

But the Nixon and Ford administrations struck a bargain with these countries that the Carter administration so far has not been willing to break. In return for assured supplies of oil and friendly political ties in a crucial—because oil-soaked—part of the world, the United States has given Iran and Saudi Arabia the freedom to browse at will in American military storehouses. The relationship between the United States and the Islamic republic in Iran has not been defined at this writing, but given the anti-Americanism manifested by Khomeini's revolutionary movement, it is unlikely that the browsing privileges will continue for Iran. It is now even more unlikely that the United States will cut off these browsing privileges for Saudi Arabia.

The Carter administration cannot please all of the people all of the time. Few governments can. But the administration cannot consistently please, or displease, the same people.

The cleavage in public opinion will hobble the conduct of foreign policy not only because it is deeper and less readily mended than the divisions of the past but also because the way foreign policy is made and carried out has changed in the last decade, so as to give greater significance to these divisions than ever before.

American foreign policy has become more democratic in the sense that international issues now directly engage the interests and emotions of large numbers of people. (Economic issues are the foremost example.*) Ethnic and national loyalties are now marshaled for international as well as national and local purposes. In this sense, the distinction between domestic and international issues is crumbling.

The "democratization" of foreign policy encompasses another, related change. Even when foreign policy is not closely related to local issues—and the concerns of liberal and conservative internationalists do not involve the projection of local interests into the international sphere—the demand to have a say in it has become more insistent and widespread. The general salience of public opinion, as well as its particular content in 1979, complicates the task of guiding America's relations with other countries.

Political scientists have made this general point about domestic politics. They have noted a tradeoff between the level of participation and the stability of political systems (and in some cases have earned a reputation for conservatism by clearly preferring stability). According to this line of argument, the greater the number of people at the helm, the more difficult it is to steer the ship.

When foreign policy was the preserve of the few, it was relatively easy to conduct (although not necessarily to conduct well). Now that it is everybody's business, conducting it may prove impossible. The result of democratization may be "friction," "overheating," and "breakdown." Jimmy Carter, the engineer, is fond of applying some of these terms to problems in political life. For these problems there may be no straightforward, efficient solution, of the kind that an engineer might prefer. President Carter wants a foreign policy as good as the American people. But when the American people disagree about what is good, the result may be no foreign policy at all.

---

* See chapter 3.

APPENDIX

TABLE A.1

U.S. ROLE IN WORLD AFFAIRS [a]

	Liberal Interna- tional- ists (24%)	Conserv- ative Interna- tional- ists (33%)	Non- interna- tional- ists (43%)	Total Sample (N = 1523)
Question 4f Do you think it will be best for the future of the country if we take an active part in world affairs, or if we stay out of world affairs?				
Active part	74%	76%	54%	66%
Question 4g Taking into account the well-being of people throughout the world, do you feel that the United States has generally been a force for good or a force for evil in its foreign policies since World War II?				
Good	60	82	57	66
Evil	9	3	10	8
Neither	7	3	9	6
Both	17	7	11	11
Question 4a Do you think the United States plays a more important and powerful role as a world leader today compared to ten years ago, a less important role, or about as important a role as a world leader as it did ten years ago?				
More important	21	39	24	28
Less important	49	34	36	39

[a] Figures in tables A.1 through A.10 show the percent of each foreign policy opinion group giving that response. Thus, 74 percent of liberal internationalists said it would be "best for the future of the country if we took an *active part* in world affairs."

TABLE A.1 (continued)

U.S. ROLE IN WORLD AFFAIRS [a]

	Liberal Interna- tional- ists (24%)	Conserv- ative Interna- tional- ists (33%)	Non- interna- tional- ists (43%)	Total Sample (N = 1523)
Question 4b				
Do you feel that the United States ought to play a more im- portant and powerful role as a world leader ten years from now than it does today, a less impor- tant role, or about as important a role as a world leader as it does today?				
More important	29	43	28	33
Less important	27	14	23	21
Question 4d				
Do you think that the United States is respected more in the world today than it was ten years ago, is respected less, or is respected about as much now as it was ten years ago?				
Respected more	9	17	10	12
Respected less	72	55	66	64
Question 10d				
Do you think that we should ex- pand our spending on national defense, keep it about the same as it is now, or cut back our de- fense spending?				
Expand	7	19	12	13
Cut back	46	23	32	32

TABLE A.2

INSTITUTIONS OF U.S. FOREIGN POLICY

	Liberal Interna-tional-ists (24%)	Conserv-ative Interna-tional-ists (33%)	Non-interna-tional-ists (43%)	Total Sample (*N* = 1523)
Question 2e In general, compared to the role of the President, do you feel that Congress is playing too strong a role in determining foreign policy, too weak a role, or about the right role it should play?				
Too weak a role	50%	35%	34%	38%
Question 14a How would you rate the job Henry Kissinger is doing as Secretary of State—excellent, pretty good, only fair, or poor?				
Excellent	39	39	27	34
Pretty good	41	43	40	41
Only fair or poor	18	14	25	20
Question 13b How would you rate the job the CIA is doing as the chief intelligence agency of the U.S. government—excellent, pretty good, only fair, or poor?				
Excellent/Pretty good	23	43	26	31
Only fair/Poor	47	32	40	39
Question 13c In general, do you feel that the CIA should or should not work inside other countries to try to strengthen those elements that serve the interests of the U.S. and to weaken those forces that work against the interests of the U.S.?				
Should not	40	17	24	26

TABLE A.3

U.S. LEADERSHIP ROLE

	Liberal Interna- tional- ists (24%)	Conserv- ative Interna- tional- ists (33%)	Non- interna- tional- ists (43%)	Total Sample (*N* = 1523)
Question 5a				
People have different ideas about the role of the United States in the world. How important do you feel it is for the United States to be a world leader in . . . —very important, somewhat important, or hardly important at all?				
Percent "very important"				
1. Economic strength	78%	87%	70%	78%
2. Military strength	57	84	63	68
3. Scientific and technologi- cal progress	82	86	67	77
4. Moral values	57	75	53	62
5. Standard of living	56	79	57	64
6. Ability to give political lead- ership to other like-minded countries	47	70	41	52
7. Skill in negotiating settle- ments that avoid war	88	94	70	82
8. Willingness to make military commitments to other countries and to keep them	25	55	27	36
9. Willingness to give economic aid to other countries	41	51	21	36
10. Support of international or- ganizations, such as the U.N.	60	70	37	54

TABLE A.4

GENERAL VIEWS ON INTERNATIONAL AFFAIRS

	Liberal Interna- tional- ists (24%)	Conserv- ative Interna- tional- ists (33%)	Non- interna- tional- ists (43%)	Total Sample (*N* = 1523)
Question 7d I'd like to read you some statements people have made about international affairs today. For each, tell me whether you tend to agree strongly, agree somewhat, disagree somewhat, or disagree strongly.				
Percent "agree strongly"				
1. While every country feels that what it believes is right, when you boil it down in world affairs, having the power to get what you want is what really counts today	29%	32%	36%	33%
2. It's morally wrong for the United States to support a military dictatorship that strips its people of their basic rights, even if that dictatorship will allow us to set up military bases in that country	61	47	45	50
3. The U.S. is rich and powerful enough to go it alone, without getting involved in the problems of the rest of the world	11	19	27	21
4. The U.S. should put pressure on countries which systematically violate basic human rights	40	42	27	35
5. The only way peace can exist in this world is when a country like the United States who wants peace is strong enough to back up warnings to possible aggressor nations that they can't get away with aggression	35	56	58	43

TABLE A.4 (continued)

GENERAL VIEWS ON INTERNATIONAL AFFAIRS

	Liberal Interna- tional- ists (24%)	Conserv- ative Interna- tional- ists (33%)	Non- interna- tional- ists (43%)	Total Sample (N = 1523)
6. Countries gain power when they have something that other countries need from them, such as the way the Arabs have gained power through oil	65	65	50	58
7. We should have the same kind of dedication to the spread of political freedom and private enterprise of business in the world as the Russians and Chinese have for the spread of com- munism in the world	38	58	34	43
8. In an age of nuclear war- fare, the old ideas of power politics and power alliances between countries have grown out-of-date	28	25	22	25
9. America is a melting pot of people from different coun- tries and, wherever possi- ble, we should try to main- tain close ties and friendly relations with the countries from which our people's ancestors came	36	44	21	32
10. It is important in foreign af- fairs for us to keep a close relationship with those countries that have similar traditions and appreciation of freedom, such as En- gland and France	46	61	34	46
11. In a nuclear age, when the whole world can be blown up, we have to overcome old animosities and ideological differences and learn to live with countries such as the Soviet Union and China	66	55	36	50

TABLE A.4 (continued)
GENERAL VIEWS ON INTERNATIONAL AFFAIRS

	Liberal Interna- tional- ists (24%)	Conserv- ative Interna- tional- ists (33%)	Non- interna- tional- ists (43%)	Total Sample (*N* = 1523)
12. The United Nations is good in theory, but the real way to keep peace in the world is to have the super powers such as the United States and the Soviet Union agree that they will not allow other countries to wage war	29	43	27	33
13. The big breakthroughs in peacemaking in the future will come less from agreements with traditional allies and more from agreements in learning to live together with tradi- tional enemies	55	51	33	44
14. In the long run, the only way to keep peace in the world is when nations, including the United States, are will- ing to give up their own power to a truly interna- tional organization that will have the military power to enforce peace	28	23	15	21
15. Problems like food, energy and inflation are so big that no country can solve them alone, and international cooperation is the only way we can make progress in solving these problems	64	60	39	52
Question 7a (same as Q. 7*d* above)				
Percent "agree strongly"				
a. The United States has a real responsibility to take a very active role in the world	52	66	37	50
b. America's real concerns should be at home, not abroad	52	53	67	58

TABLE A.4 (continued)

GENERAL VIEWS ON INTERNATIONAL AFFAIRS

	Liberal Interna- tional- ists (24%)	Conserv- ative Interna- tional- ists (33%)	Non- interna- tional- ists (43%)	Total Sample (N = 1523)
c. We should give foreign aid only to our friends, and not to countries who criticize the United States	24	39	35	34
d. We should build up our own defenses and let the rest of the world take care of itself	18	18	34	25
e. We should take a more active role in opposing the policy of apartheid—that is, racial separation—in South Africa	24	16	11	16
f. We should conduct more and more of our foreign affairs through genuinely international organizations	34	30	21	27
g. With our improving relations with the Soviet Union and China, there is little chance for world war anymore	6	8	6	7
h. How the Soviet Union handles the treatment of the Jews or other minority groups is a matter of internal Soviet politics, and none of our business	17	11	18	15
i. With our improving relations with the Soviet Union, we should work more closely with the Russians to keep smaller countries from going to war	46	40	25	35

TABLE A.5

RELATIONSHIPS WITH ALLIES

	Liberal Internationalists (24%)	Conservative Internationalists (33%)	Noninternationalists (43%)	Total Sample (*N* = 1523)
Question 9a Do you feel that the United States should mainly make its major foreign policy decisions on its own, or do you feel it should mainly consult with its major allies before making major foreign policy decisions?				
On its own	36%	33%	46%	39%
Consult allies	55	59	42	51
Question 11a Some people feel that NATO has outlived its usefulness, and that the United States should withdraw militarily from NATO, the military organization of Western Europe and the U.S. Others say that NATO has discouraged the Russians from trying a military takeover in Western Europe. Do you feel we should increase our commitment to NATO, keep our commitment what it is now, decrease our commitment but still remain in NATO, or withdraw from NATO entirely?				
Increase/Keep as now	56	66	45	55
Decrease/Withdraw	28	13	21	20

TABLE A.5 (continued)

RELATIONSHIPS WITH ALLIES

	Liberal Interna- tional- ists (24%)	Conserv- ative Interna- tional- ists (33%)	Non- interna- tional- ists (43%)	Total Sample (N = 1523)
Question 14b It has recently been suggested that the oil-consuming nations such as the United States, Canada, Western Europe, and Japan, get together to develop strategies which would make us less dependent on the deci- sions of the foreign oil- producing countries. Do you favor or oppose such coopera- tive efforts on the part of oil- consuming nations?				
Favor	85	85	71	79
Question 16 If the United States, Western Europe, and Japan were faced with another oil embargo by the Arab states, which of these policies do you think we should adopt?				
1. Share our oil with Europe and Japan, even if it means less oil for Americans	48	45	30	40
2. Go it alone, and let Europe and Japan fend for them- selves	34	34	45	38
3. Invade the oil-producing countries	5	7	6	6

TABLE A.6

FOREIGN AID

	Liberal Interna- tional- ists (24%)	Conserv- ative Interna- tional- ists (33%)	Non- interna- tional- ists (43%)	Total Sample (*N* = 1523)
Question 3d On the whole, do you favor or oppose our giving *economic* aid to other nations, for purposes of economic development and technical assistance?				
Favor	65%	62%	40%	53%
Question 3g If you could be sure that the economic aid we send to coun- tries abroad ended up helping people of those countries, would you then favor or oppose our giving such economic aid?				
Favor	89	87	67	78
Question 3h On the whole, do you favor or oppose our giving emergency food and medical supplies to other nations in cases of natural disasters, such as floods or earthquakes?				
Favor	95	95	90	93
Question 3i On the whole, do you favor or oppose our giving *military* aid to other nations?				
Favor	16	33	17	22
Question 3k On the whole, do you favor or oppose our government *selling* military equipment to other na- tions?				
Favor	34	40	31	35

TABLE A.7
U.S. MILITARY INTERVENTION

	Liberal Internationalists (24%)	Conservative Internationalists (33%)	Noninternationalists (43%)	Total Sample (*N* = 1523)

Question 8
There has been a lot of discussion about what circumstances might justify U.S. military involvement, including the use of U.S. troops. Do you feel if . . . , you would favor or oppose U.S. military involvement?

Percent *in favor of* U.S. military involvement

	Liberal	Conservative	Non	Total
1. Canada were invaded	77%	87%	70%	77%
2. Western Europe were invaded	35	53	31	39
3. North Vietnam launched a major attack against Saigon	5	19	8	11
4. Israel were being defeated by the Arabs	23	38	22	27
5. The Soviet Union attacked Yugoslavia after Tito's death	8	16	8	11
6. The Russians took over West Berlin	32	45	25	33
7. Communist China invaded Formosa (Taiwan)	11	27	14	17
8. North Korea attacked South Korea	9	24	10	14
9. Communist China attacked India	14	24	12	16
10. The Arabs cut off the oil supply to Western Europe	15	28	19	21
11. Castro's Cuba invaded the Dominican Republic in the Caribbean	29	42	27	32
12. The Arabs cut off the oil supply to Japan	10	18	13	14

TABLE A.7 (continued)
U.S. MILITARY INTERVENTION

	Liberal Interna- tional- ists (24%)	Conserv- ative Interna- tional- ists (33%)	Non- interna- tional- ists (43%)	Total Sample (*N* = 1523)
Question 6a Now let me hand you this card with four statements on it. Please read these four state- ments and tell me which *one* comes closest to describing your own view of what the United States should do *if friendly countries are* attacked.				
1. The United States should send *military aid, economic aid,* and, if necessary, send *American troops and man- power.*	16	38	16	23
2. We might send some *military aid* as well as *economic aid,* but we should not involve any American troops or manpower.	43	40	31	37
3. We might send some *economic aid,* but we should not send military aid and should not involve any American troops or man- power.	28	12	27	22
4. The United States should *not* send any military aid or economic aid, and should *not* send any American troops or manpower.	7	5	13	9

TABLE A.8

TOLERANCE OF INTERNATIONAL DIFFERENCES

	Liberal Interna- tional- ists (24%)	Conserv- ative Interna- tional- ists (33%)	Non- interna- tional- ists (43%)	Total Sample (N = 1523)
Question 7b If there is some advantage to the United States in it, do you feel it is justified or not for us:				
Percent "justified"				
1. To establish trade relations with communist countries	74%	61%	50%	60%
2. To recognize democratic left-wing governments when they come to power	56	41	34	42
3. To back governments which believe in our free enterprise system but not in democracy	52	45	39	45
4. To back socialistic govern- ments that respect the basic political rights of their people	73	62	46	58
5. To back authoritarian gov- ernments that have over- thrown democratic govern- ments	12	12	11	12

TABLE A.9

ATTITUDES TOWARD COMMUNISM

	Liberal Interna- tional- ists (24%)	Conserv- ative Interna- tional- ists (33%)	Non- interna- tional- ists (43%)	Total Sample (N = 1523)
Question 12b If . . . were to become com- munist, do you think this would be a threat to the United States or not?				
Percent "threat"				
1. Western European countries	59%	84%	68%	71%
2. Japan	58	80	63	67
3. African countries	38	65	48	51
4. Latin American countries	58	80	66	69
5. Italy	35	63	48	50
6. Portugal	32	60	46	47
Question 11d Do you think it is possible for the United States and Com- munist China to reach long- term agreements to keep peace, or do you think that this is not possible?				
Possible	65	56	50	56
Question 11b Do you think it is possible for the United States and Russia to reach long-term agreements to keep peace, or do you think that this is not possible?				
Possible	70	58	53	59
Question 13a All in all, do you favor or oppose the U.S. establishing full dip- lomatic relations with Cuba?				
Favor	69	50	45	53

TABLE A.10

RECENT FOREIGN POLICY EXPERIENCES

	Liberal Interna- tional- ists (24%)	Conserv- ative Interna- tional- ists (33%)	Non- interna- tional- ists (43%)	Total Sample (N = 1523)

Question 7c

Here's a list of international events that the United States has been involved in in recent history. For each, please tell me whether you think it was a proud moment in American history, a dark moment, or neither a proud moment nor a dark moment.

Percent "proud"/"dark"

```
% proud
       % dark
```

	Liberal Internationalists (24%)	Conservative Internationalists (33%)	Non-internationalists (43%)	Total Sample (N = 1523)
1. U.S. role in the founding of the United Nations	89 2	88 3	73 6	82 4
2. U.S. role in the Korean war	16 45	28 37	20 42	22 41
3. Nixon's trip to Communist China	62 6	66 8	53 12	59 9
4. U.S. role in the Vietnam war	3 86	12 66	7 67	8 72
5. The Berlin airlift	57 5	57 6	44 9	52 7
6. CIA involvement in Chile	3 60	8 31	7 37	7 41
7. Kennedy's handling of the Cuban missile crisis	52 19	56 16	49 19	52 18
8. U.S. involvement in the Dominican Republic	5 29	14 15	8 20	10 20
9. U.S. role in World War II	69 13	73 10	64 15	68 13
10. The founding of the Peace Corps	87 1	87 1	72 3	80 2
11. The Marshall Plan of aid to Europe	62 4	65 3	44 8	55 6
12. U.S. sending emergency food to Bangladesh	85 0	83 2	66 5	76 3
13. American support of Israel during the October 1973 war	39 7	54 9	35 15	42 11

NOTES

1. According to Gallup polls reported by Potomac Associates, support for defense spending increased significantly from 1972 to 1976. In 1972, 42 percent of Americans felt that defense spending should be reduced or "ended altogether"; only 9 percent favored an increased defense budget (37 percent felt that defense spending should be kept at the same level). In 1974, sentiment for a reduced defense budget had fallen to 37 percent, with 17 percent favoring an increase in defense spending. In 1976, support for a larger defense budget (28 percent) was stronger than support for a reduction (24 percent). The Potomac Associates analysts reported that self-designated liberals in 1976 were one of three population groups (along with blacks and young people) that favored a significantly lower level of defense spending, whereas conservatives registered the highest level of support for defense spending of any group surveyed. See Walter Slocombe, Lloyd A. Free, Donald R. Lesh, and William Watts, *The Pursuit of National Security: Defense and the Military Balance* (Washington, D.C.: Potomac Associates, 1976), pp. 38–39.
2. See William Schneider, "Public Opinion and Foreign Policy: The Beginning of Ideology?" *Foreign Policy*, no. 17 (Winter 1974–75): 88–120. On recent trends in foreign policy attitudes, see Robert W. Tucker, William Watts, and Lloyd A. Free, *The United States in the World: New Directions for the Post-Vietnam Era?*" (Washington, D.C.: Potomac Associates, 1976), pp. 19–40; and Daniel Yankelovich, "Cautious Internationalism: A Changing Mood Toward U.S. Foreign Policy," *Public Opinion* 1 (March/April 1978): 12–16.
3. Just over 1500 respondents were interviewed in a nationwide sampling of voting-age adults. The questionnaire covered a wide variety of foreign policy attitudes and issues, with most interviews lasting between one and two hours. Interviewing took place while President Ford was in office and Henry Kissinger was secretary of state. The major events of 1974 included the oil crisis and gasoline shortages at the beginning of the year, President Nixon's resignation in August, the November congressional elections that resulted in large-scale Democratic gains, and the most severe year-long economic recession since the 1930s. American military involvement in Vietnam had ended by late 1974, although the fall of Saigon and the final communist takeover did not occur until a few months after the survey, in the spring of 1975.

    We wish to thank the Chicago Council on Foreign Relations for permission to use the data from this survey. Neither the Council nor anyone associated with it bears any responsibility for the analysis and interpretations presented here.
4. For example, consider those goals that correlated significantly with *both* factors. The factor loadings for these four goals were as follows:

	Cooperative Internationalism	Interventionism
"Defending our allies' security"	.43	.57
"Protecting weaker nations against foreign aggression"	.48	.55
"Strengthening countries who are friendly toward us"	.51	.55
"Maintaining a balance of power among nations"	.53	.40

    All four goals relate to military security and hostility toward enemy powers. They are alliance goals, and the idea of alliance includes both antagonism toward a common enemy and cooperation and mutuality of interest among allies. Note that the "aggressive" component declines and the "mutuality" component rises as one goes down the list.
5. Defense spending is a good example. In the 1974–75 Chicago Council survey, two questions about defense spending were asked. On the first question, asked early in the survey, respondents were given a printed card that listed thirteen different government programs.

The interviewer said, "Here is a list of present federal government programs. For each, I'd like you to tell me whether you feel it should be expanded, cut back, or kept about the same." "Defense spending" was second on the list, after "aid to education." Forty-one percent of the sample said that defense spending should be cut back. Later in the interview, respondents were asked, "Do you think that we should expand our spending on national defense, keep it about the same as it is now, or cut back our defense spending?" Only 32 percent of *the same respondents* thought that defense spending should be cut back. Apparently sentiment for cutting back defense spending rose when the question was asked in the context of competing federal programs, rather than as an isolated issue. Moreover, the second question was asked after respondents had been forced to think about foreign policy issues for a considerable period of time.

Attitudes toward defense spending have also shown a tendency to shift markedly over time. See, for instance, Bruce M. Russett, "The Revolt of the Masses: Public Opinion on Military Expenditures," in *New Civil-Military Relations,* ed. John P. Lovell and Philip S. Kronenberg (New Brunswick, N.J.: Trans-action, 1974), pp. 57–88. The Gallup poll uses the following question to measure public sentiment toward defense spending: "There is much discussion as to the amount of money the government in Washington should spend for national defense and military purposes. How do you feel about this: Do you think we are spending too little, too much, or about the right amount?" In late January 1976, 36 percent of a nationwide sample said that the government was spending too much for defense. In July 1977, the percentage saying "too much" had fallen to 23 percent. The percentage saying "too much" fell among white respondents from 36 in 1976 to 22 in 1977, while the percentage of black respondents saying "too much" fell from 44 to 33. That almost half the blacks interviewed (44 percent) thought that the government was spending too much on national defense was true only at the time of the 1976 poll. That black respondents were more likely than white respondents to favor cutting back defense spending was true in both polls.

For a comprehensive report of the findings of the Chicago Council survey, see John A. Rielly, ed., *American Public Opinion and Foreign Policy 1975* (Chicago: Chicago Council on Foreign Relations, 1975).

6. This close division seems to have persisted. A Gallup poll of 515 Americans was taken on 12–13 July 1978, just as the verdict in the Ginzberg case was being announced. Respondents were asked, "Do you think the President and other U.S. leaders should criticize the Soviet Union for violating the human rights of its citizens, or do you feel that it is none of our business to criticize the Soviets for their treatment of Soviet citizens?" The sample was about evenly divided, 49 percent saying that it is "none of our business" and 43 percent saying that U.S. leaders should criticize Soviet violations of human rights. When asked, "Would you favor or oppose U.S. efforts to influence the Soviet Union's policy regarding the human rights of Soviet citizens by bringing that policy into negotiations on other issues between the two countries?" the division was again close, 44 percent favoring such pressure and 41 percent opposing it. (Results reported in *Newsweek,* 24 July 1978, p. 23.)

7. Partisanship, in the parlance of domestic politics, is the opposite of pluralism. Partisanship means polarization and "taking sides," whereas pluralism involves tolerance and accommodation. Partisans seek to defeat the other side; pluralists try to find a way of getting along together. For an insightful essay by a conservative internationalist that applies the *partisan* analogy to international politics, see Daniel Patrick Moynihan, "Party and International Politics," *Commentary,* February 1977, pp. 56–59.

8. "American Values and Foreign Policy," *Commentary,* July 1976, p. 32.

Part II
FUNCTIONAL PROBLEMS

3

U.S. FOREIGN ECONOMIC POLICY TOWARD OTHER ADVANCED CAPITALIST STATES:

The Struggle to Make Others Adjust

Robert O. Keohane

To people with a romantic turn of mind, economic policy is surely the dismal side of foreign affairs. Economic issues are sometimes dubbed "low politics," in contrast to the "high politics" of military and security policy. The phrase suggests, if not the burlesque of "low comedy," at least a dull grubbiness characteristic only of the narrowly self-seeking or the pedantically unimaginative. Yet dismal or not, American foreign economic policy may determine the course of national and world prosperity. Moreover, there are strong links between "low politics" and "high politics," as illustrated by the impact of the world depression of the 1930s on the political conflicts of that period. Foreign economic policy is not "mere economics." Since

I am grateful to Shannon Salmon for research assistance; to numerous colleagues for comments on an earlier draft; and particularly to Robert J. Art, Ernst B. Haas, Stephen Krasner, Abraham Lowenthal, and Kenneth Oye for their criticisms and advice. Research support for this paper was provided by the German Marshall Fund of the United States, by Stanford University, and, through the Center for Advanced Study in the Behavioral Sciences, by National Science Foundation grant BNS-76-22943.

disputes between governments over economic issues are dealt with politically—through bargaining and the exercise of power—as well as through economic policy, the analysis of foreign economic policy cannot safely be left to economists.

The advanced capitalist countries have not been very successful in managing the world economy during the 1970s. Continued failure would adversely affect numerous American objectives—political as well as economic—during the 1980s. Thus the Carter administration has faced, and will continue to face, uncomfortable foreign economic policy choices with potentially serious and far-reaching consequences. This chapter examines some of the dilemmas confronting the Carter administration, and assesses its responses to them during its first twenty-one months in office. It focuses entirely on relations among the advanced capitalist states; Stephen Krasner discusses relations between these states and poorer countries in chapter 4.

The importance of foreign economic policy makes it a subject of controversy and an area of crucial policy choice. By the same token, however, the real interests and motivations of participants are likely to be obscured by rhetorical argumentation and tactical maneuvering. Assertions by spokesmen for governments and interest groups about the reasons for their own policies may be misleading, and their characterizations of the effects of current policies, and alternatives to it, are often even less reliable guides to the true situation. It is therefore necessary, before assessing the Carter administration's policies in financial, trade, and energy policy, to develop an analytical scheme that will help us to interpret the chaotic flow of events. We need to seek what has been called, in another context, a "thick description" of the situation: an understanding that encompasses the meaning of actions as well as their surface manifestations.[1]

The first half of this chapter provides the basis for a description in the rest of the chapter of the Carter administration's performance during its first twenty-one months in office. My analytical scheme is organized around three fundamental problems that would be faced by any U.S. government in the field of foreign economic policy: (1) specifying basic objectives; (2) resolving various conflicts among its policies; and (3) creating a balance between the resources at its disposal, on the one hand, and the constraints imposed by the external environment, politics in the United States, and limitations of knowledge, on the other. I assume that the United States is, and will remain for the foreseeable future, a nonrevolutionary power with a capitalist economic system. My purpose is to analyze both what any U.S. government will seek to accomplish in these circumstances and the dilemmas that will confront it when choices are possible. I make no policy recommendations. Nor am I arguing on behalf of the goals I ascribe to policy makers, or in favor of the capitalist economic system they attempt to maintain. My purpose is analytical and interpretive rather than prescriptive or didactic.

MAJOR OBJECTIVES OF U.S. FOREIGN ECONOMIC POLICY

By major objectives I mean those foreign economic policy objectives that any nonrevolutionary U.S. government, responding to the interests of individuals and groups within the United States, would find it desirable to pursue. These major objectives are rooted in long-term political and economic interests. Even though the government will find it desirable to pursue such objectives, it may not always be able to do so; other goals may conflict with these objectives, or the requisite resources and skills to accomplish them may not be available. Yet a failure to achieve major foreign economic policy objectives will entail costs for the United States: national economic targets may not be attained, and other objectives may be adversely affected as well. If the domestic economy suffers, so will the party in power.[2]

The fundamental objective of U.S. economic policy is to assure national prosperity, defined in terms of economic growth, full employment, and a reasonably stable price level. American foreign policy as a whole seeks to maintain an international environment in which U.S. interests (as defined by the government) are protected at relatively low cost. Foreign economic policy deals with the intersection of these concerns; its basic goal is to assure the international conditions conducive to national prosperity. For this to be accomplished, two subobjectives must be met: the major economic and political partners of the United States must be prosperous, and the United States must successfully maintain its influence over international economic outcomes.

Prosperity Abroad

With the announcement of the European Recovery Program (Marshall Plan) in 1947, the United States explicitly came to regard the prosperity of its major allies as a policy objective. From the beginning, this goal had a political-military as well as an economic basis; without prosperity in Europe and Japan, the ability of the United States to maintain close ties with stable governments in those areas—and therefore to contain Soviet expansion—would be jeopardized. Since 1947, American foreign economic policies have always taken the international economy into account, although substantial policy changes have taken place. Since 1960, the external sector has loomed increasingly large for the U.S. economy. Foreign dollar holdings have increased immensely, and foreign trade as a proportion of gross national product has more than doubled.[3] Thus the economic rationale for attempting to foster prosperity in other market economies has been strengthened even as political and economic difficulties have become more severe.

Between 1947 and 1958, the United States attempted to aid reconstruction, first in Europe, then in Japan, by providing aid to those areas and purchasing goods from them. Under the Truman administration, the Marshall Plan stimulated European recovery and alleviated the dollar shortage. What the Marshall Plan failed to accomplish was achieved by the boom that accompanied the Korean war. In the mid-1950s, the United States opened its doors to Japanese products and urged its European allies (with only partial success) to do likewise. By 1958, European currencies were convertible once again, the dollar shortage had ended, and Japan was beginning her spectacular economic growth.

The period between 1959 and 1964 is now regarded as a "golden age" of symmetrical prosperity. Economic growth took place in Europe, Japan, and the United States, while inflation hovered around 2 percent annually.[4] The Kennedy administration propounded the "dumbbell theory" of U.S.–European cooperation, which stressed the symmetry of situation and responsibilities between the United States and the European Community. (The metaphor was meant to conjure up weightlifting, not cynical thoughts about the intelligence of policy makers!) During this period, the United States adopted more liberal foreign trade legislation, and the Kennedy Round of tariff talks (which was to end successfully in 1967) was begun. Although academic economists warned about potential instabilities in the international financial system, policy makers believed that these could be controlled effectively. Between 1959 and 1964, American policy no longer attempted, virtually singlehandedly, to lead the world toward prosperity; this was now to be accomplished by moving arm in arm with Europe (with Japan, still a junior partner, tagging along behind).

This benign period came to an end with the expansion of the Vietnam war in 1965. At this point disruption came from the United States, when the Johnson administration's reluctance to increase taxes to pay for its war in Southeast Asia led to excess demand and inflation. As a result, the U.S. balance of payments deteriorated sharply, calling into question the nation's ability to maintain the value of the dollar and eventually leading to its devaluation in 1971. Although the Nixon administration gradually reduced the American war effort, it deliberately stimulated the economy in preparation for the 1972 elections, contributing to the excessive boom of 1972–73 and to huge U.S. external deficits. Between 1970 and 1973, the U.S. external deficit accounted for $54 billion of new international liquidity. Between 1965 and 1973, the United States was a major disruptive force in the world economy, as a result of its war- and election-induced fiscal and monetary policies.[5]

In the next period, between late 1973 and 1976, the major shock to the world economy came not from the United States but from the oil-exporting countries. Large increases in oil prices accentuated disarray in financial markets and contributed to the sharpness of the recession, which Western governments had engineered in order to reduce high rates of inflation. American efforts to maintain world prosperity during this period focused on reducing inflation at home while promoting the "recycling" of oil revenues abroad to avert a financial crash and severe world depression. Private financial markets provided most of the loanable funds, but the International Monetary Fund (IMF) was also used to assist weak economies that had suffered from the sudden oil-price rise.

The accession to power of the Carter administration led to policy shifts. The new administration focused its attention initially on accelerating the rate of growth of the advanced industrial countries, in particular of the strong economies of Germany and Japan. The defensive, "disaster-limiting" strategy of the Ford administration was replaced by a more expansionary approach, attempting to put the world economy, as well as the United States, on a renewed path to growth.

U.S. Influence

From the American perspective, maintaining world prosperity is not sufficient. It is also necessary to ensure that particular American interests are safeguarded. World prosperity would not be satisfactory to the U.S. government if it were financed by real losses of American income and assets.

Very small countries can protect their interests only through changes in their own internal economic policies: as they cannot influence the policies of others significantly, they must adjust to change themselves. Powerful states, on the other hand, often have alternatives: they can use their power to force others to bear some of the costs of adjustment to change. The effects of adverse changes in the world economy on one's own citizens can sometimes be cushioned by inducing others to shoulder some of the burdens. Thus the protection of American interests may depend, in international negotiations, not only on the invisible hand of economic competition, or even on the velvet glove of gentle persuasion, but on the sinewy hand (if not necessarily the iron fist) of national power. Implicit and explicit political bargains lie behind patterns of international economic transactions; the United States, like other important actors, finds it useful to maintain influence over international economic events.

Immediately after World War II, the United States was an economic and political Gulliver among the Lilliputians of Europe and Japan. It accounted for 40 percent of world gross national product in 1950 and was the only potential source of large-scale aid to countries devastated by the war. Between 1950 and 1975, as its share of world GNP fell to 25 percent, the United States became less able, *by itself,* to determine the course of events.[6] Consultation and agreement became increasingly necessary; and challenges from other advanced capitalist states, on particular issues, increasingly likely.

Yet what is most striking is the continued leadership role of the United States. Only France has explicitly challenged American dominance; and France has been too weak, and its policies too closely tied to distinctively French interests, to play this role effectively. Thus, in the international monetary area, after five years of turmoil and bargaining, the arrangements made at Rambouillet in November 1975 and in Kingston in January 1976 satisfied essential American demands at the expense of those who favored pegged exchange rates or at least more systematic constraints on the United States as the key-currency country.[7] U.S. ties with Saudi Arabia and Iran, its political-military influence in the Middle East, and its *relatively* less dependent position in petroleum make the United States the most important actor in the energy area and accentuate European and Japanese dependence on American policy. The International Energy Agency (IEA) is a result of American initiative, and the United States remains the moving force behind the organization. The United States is also at the center of financial networks that have "recycled" OPEC's investments to states with current account deficits.[8]

The United States remains the leader because its allies depend on it. None of them has the strength, energy, or self-confidence to replace it, nor do they (with the sporadic exception of France) seem to have the desire to do so. The United States provides a structure of world order, however unsteady, on which they depend. Franz Schurmann has perceptively pointed out that "there are so many unexpected sources of support for the American Empire. . . . In 1973 a whole array of nations, once intent on restraining America's violent adventurism, came to fear what could happen if the world order, for which America was the core, collapsed."[9] Or, in colloquial American language, "you can't beat something with nothing."

Yet leadership, or dominance, also has costs. Dominant powers have to defend not only their own dominant positions but also the system, or international regimes, they have helped construct. When the dominant power cannot rely on coercion, secondary powers will be tempted to "cheat" on the system, acting as "free riders" who benefit from the overall order but avoid paying for its construction or maintenance. As the adherence of these states to the system becomes more important (e.g., as they become more important economically), the leader may need to provide them with larger and larger concessions. Yet granting these concessions may undermine the uniquely dominant position of the leader. Thus a difficult, potentially contradictory cycle is set in motion: concessions to keep the regime functioning may undermine the power of the leading power, which is itself the strongest supporter of the existing regime.[10]

In the systemic role of the hegemonic power, we thus see contradictory forces. Leaders must pay the price of leadership by providing more than their share of collective goods; this is a potential source of weakness. But the fear of an empire's collapse, or a set of international regimes premised on the dominance of one country, works powerfully in the hegemonic power's favor. Relations between the hegemon and its partners can become a multifaceted bargaining game in which, at the level of resources, weakness leads to further weakness (as resources are dissipated to support the regime), but at the psychological level, weakness leads to strength (as erosion of the regime increases fears among dependent secondary states about the collapse of the system). This bargaining game is complicated by a peculiar "politics of partnership" in which the great power and secondary states find themselves at odds on the content, although not the form, of cooperation. The leading state seeks to persuade the increasingly important secondary states to "share the burdens of leadership" by supporting the system, *without* attempting to redesign or reorient the system to their advantage. For their part, the secondary states either persist in defining themselves as "small powers" long after that is appropriate (as Japan has) or demand a greater role in making decisions for a system they are asked to support (as in the case of Germany under Chancellor Schmidt).

To maintain its influence, the United States needs to follow a three-sided strategy. Like all great powers, it must attempt to maintain or increase its tangible power resources; it must develop power resources through internal effort and limit its dependence on others. The United States must therefore be wary of increasing imports of petroleum, particularly from the Middle East, which could undermine U.S. influence. Second, any American administration must cultivate belief in its indispensability—by taking initiatives, making concessions on particular issues for the sake of building international regimes, and ensuring that Washington remains at the hub of the multiple networks that link OECD (Organization for Economic Cooperation and Development) countries with one another. Secretary of State Kissinger's proposals for an International Energy Agency during 1974 helped assure that the United States would continue to play a central role in energy politics and would not be pushed to one side by a Euro-Arab dialogue.[11] Finally, it is important that governments allied with or dependent on the United States not take American strength and leadership for granted, for if they do, they will be unwilling to contribute fully to the costs of the American-centered regime. Thus it is in America's interest to be slightly unpredictable, particularly if Congress can be blamed. Up to a point, an American administration's bargaining position is strengthened if it can demand concessions on the grounds that if they are not forthcoming, Congress may take precipitous adverse action that might undermine American leadership and turn the United States toward isolationism or protectionism. The unpredictability of Congress (especially to foreigners) makes it a power asset for the United States; American administrations can employ "threats that leave something to chance," with Congress providing the necessary random element for this technique to work. U.S. pressure on Japan over trade issues during the last months of 1977 illustrated this technique in action.[12]

Thus the United States can be expected to act to maintain its influence, as well as to search for prosperity. Policy makers talk about assuring prosperity and order more than they reveal their attempts to maintain or increase their political influence. To analyze questions of influence, the observer has to rely more on analysis of what policy makers do, and less on what they say, than in the other areas. In undertaking this sort of analysis, attention must be paid to intangible as well as tangible sources of influence.

CONFLICTS AND TRADEOFFS AMONG POLICIES

We are used to thinking about policy in dichotomous, mutually exclusive terms. "Foreign policy" and "domestic policy" are discussed separately, or "economic motivations" are contrasted with their "political" counterparts. In discussions of "foreign" economic policy, these dichotomies serve us badly.

In the 1970s it has become conventional wisdom that foreign and domestic policy are closely intertwined. Certainly this requires little demonstration in the economic realm. International monetary policies affect the domestic money supply and inflation in numerous countries; the reverse is also the case. The key to an effective international role for the United States in energy is its "domestic" energy policy. An effective domestic energy policy would also improve the macroeconomic impact of the United States on the world economy. Effective action on energy is a precondition for substantially reducing the current account imbalances created by huge American oil imports and might allow the United States to redirect some of its financial stimulus to the exports of countries that need it more. Without such a policy, the cleverest policy at the international level will be only of marginal value. In the trade field, domestic pressures—in steel, textiles, shoes, and electronics—have led to the formulation of new international policies, which will affect both the domestic economy and America's international relations.

Thus *foreign* economic policy by itself cannot deal effectively with the problems faced by the United States in the world economy. Domestic measures must be taken as well, with costly adjustments imposed on some sectors of the population at home. An effective foreign economic policy depends on an effective overall economic policy.

Even people who accept close linkages between domestic and foreign policies frequently draw a sharp contrast between "economics" and "politics." Thunderous mock battles take place between analysts who believe that political motivations are primary and those who contend that the "real objectives" of policy makers are economic.[13] Yet, for contemporary statesmen, as for the mercantilists of the seventeenth and eighteenth centuries, power is a necessary condition for plenty.[14] This was true in the immediate postwar period, and it is true now. In the late 1940s, the exercise of American power was required to build international economic arrangements consistent with the structure of American capitalism; conversely, U.S. military strength depended *in the long run* on close economic as well as political ties between the United States on the one hand and Western Europe and Japan on the other. In the same manner, in the 1970s it is futile to ask, for instance, whether the United States proposed the International Energy Agency for the sake of coping with energy problems or because it wished to reinforce its political influence. Effective international action on energy questions was impossible without U.S. leadership; conversely, American influence and prestige would be increased by leading a successful energy effort. Insofar as power is a necessary means for the attainment of actors' objectives in world politics, it attains, as Arnold Wolfers taught us, a status similar to that of an end in itself.[15] Power and wealth are in the long run complementary goals.

U.S. policy makers are therefore not required to make choices between power and wealth over the long term. Their challenge is different: to devise strategies in which economic gains reinforce political influence, and vice versa. In the short run, this may mean bolstering one's power at the expense of particular economic objectives, or the reverse. But over the long run, wealth (at least in the form of a productive, thriving economy) is a source of power; and power, in a world without guarantees of order and justice, may be necessary to keep one's wealth secure.

The key tradeoff for the United States in the late 1970s and early 1980s, as for mercantilist statesmen in the eighteenth century and American leaders in the late 1940s, is not between power and wealth but between the *long-term* power-wealth interests of the state, and *short-term* interests, whether of the society as a whole or of individual merchants, workers, or manufacturers. The United States is not the only country that has been unable to formulate long-term goals without making concessions to shot-term economic interests. Jacob Viner observes that in Holland during the seventeenth and eighteenth centuries, "where the merchants to a large extent shared directly in government, major political considerations, including the very safety of the country or its success in wars in which it was actually participating, had repeatedly to give way to the cupidity of the merchants and their reluctance to contribute adequately to military finance." [16] In Britain also, "the autonomy of business connections and traditions," according to Viner, cut across long-term state interests. During the Marshall Plan years, American administrators had to deal with the "special demands of the American business and agricultural community that expected direct and early profit from the program—and who were well-represented in Congress . . . . The general goals of multilateral trade were certainly in the interests of all these constituencies; yet they, unlike the State Department, were willing to undermine the achievement of the general aim for even the smallest immediate gain." [17] Throughout the 1950s, '60s, and '70s, U.S. administrations have found it difficult to implement their designs for international economic regimes under American leadership in the face of opposition from affected sections of the public with strong representation in Congress.

In economic development, the conflict between short-run and long-run objectives arises in choices between consumption on the one hand and savings or investment on the other. When the economy underinvests, it is favoring the present over the future. One can use similar concepts in discussing power. A state invests in power resources when it binds allies to itself or creates international regimes in which it plays a central role. During the 1930s, Germany followed a "power approach" to trade questions, changing the structure of foreign trade so that its partners would be vulnerable to its own actions.[18] After World War II, American policy had a broader geographical focus and was less coercive, but it also involved power investment. The United States absorbed short-run economic costs, such as those imposed by discrimination in the early 1950s against American goods in Europe, for the sake of long-term political and economic gains. The United States established international governing arrangements (or "regimes") that revolved around Washington, and on which its allies in Europe and Japan were highly dependent.

Power disinvestment may also take place; power can be consumed and not replaced. Governments faced with changes in the world economy may use their power to shift the costs of adjustment to change to the inhabitants of weaker states, for example, by imposing tariffs or quotas on imports. In the short run, this may benefit certain groups at home (although others will suffer indirectly). In the long run, however, such actions are likely to weaken the economic base of the protectionist countries by creating inefficient, high-cost industries. In such an event, power disinvestment has taken place.

The use of power by leading states to protect the immediate interests of some of their citizens may also reduce the incentives for weaker states to remain dependent on their powerful partners, as the following example illustrates. U.S. governments throughout most of the postwar period have sought to ensure that Japan remained a regular and major importer of American agricultural products. Not only was this beneficial for American farmers and for the U.S. economy; the benefits that Japan derived from these arrangements, and its dependence on American food, served as potential sources of U.S. influence over Japanese policy. Yet in 1973 the United States temporarily restricted exports of soybeans to Japan, in an attempt to restrain inflation at home. This attempt to export inflation led the Japanese to begin to diversify their sources of supply by encouraging soybean production in Brazil; the result is likely to be some reduction in American economic power over Japan.

The question whether to invest in additional power resources, or to consume some of those that one has accumulated, is a perennial issue of foreign policy, cutting across issue areas. U.S. influence in the international monetary system will depend to a great extent on maintenance of rough equilibrium on current account; even for the reserve-currency country, it is difficult to maintain one's power if one runs large and persistent current account deficits. Reducing the current account deficit to a manageable size implies some sacrifice of current consumption; maintaining a huge deficit requires a less obvious, but equally important, consumption of American power resources. In the energy area, the United States could continue to let its imports of petroleum grow rapidly, drawing on its international credit standing to finance them and on its influence over major OPEC countries to assure that the oil kept flowing. By this means, it could maintain current consumption patterns, at least for some time; but its power position vis-à-vis other major industrialized countries, as well as toward OPEC, would gradually erode. Power disinvestment would be taking place. In the trade field, the United States has traditionally invested in an open international trading regime by foregoing the temporary advantages (at least to one sector of the economy or another) to be gained by protectionist measures. Increasingly, however, the AFL-CIO and affected industries such as steel and textiles (where some protectionist measures were taken even in the 1960s) have demanded curbs on imports. Merely threatening such curbs might increase American influence abroad. Systematic implementation of them on a large scale, however, would be likely to reduce American influence over the world trade regime. In this respect, at least, such measures would also represent power disinvestment.

I conclude that every U.S. government will have to fashion an economic policy that is simultaneously a "domestic" and a "foreign" policy and that each government will have to seek both power and plenty. The most important set of *choices* any government will face, across a range of policy areas, has to do with the relative weighting of the short-run versus the long-run, of consumption (of wealth or power) versus investment. Any analysis of foreign economic policy must assess the extent to which investments, in power as well as in production, are being made or dissipated.

RESOURCES AND CONSTRAINTS AFFECTING POLICY

The United States is the most important state in the OECD on virtually every issue that arises. This is in part a result of its material resources. Although the disparities have been declining over the last quarter century, the United States still has by far the largest and the most technologically advanced economy in the Western world. It is relatively more self-sufficient in energy than any of its partners in the International Energy Agency, except for Britain, Canada, and Norway. (Nevertheless, its imports of oil are much greater in absolute amount than those of any other country.) The diversity and size of the American economy probably ensures that the United States would be damaged less by a disruption of world trading relationships than would any of its partners.

Other factors buttress American preeminence. As argued above, Japan and the major European countries still look to the United States for leadership and support, although Germany, in particular, shows more independence than it did before the 1970s. Moreover, American political-military power represents a power resource for the United States in dealing with its allies. If "actual strangulation" of the industrialized countries (to use Henry Kissinger's expression) were to be attempted by Middle Eastern oil producers, only the United States could effectively retaliate with force. The high costs to great powers of using force in the contemporary world would make this policy a reluctant last resort, but the fact remains that of the advanced capitalist states, only the United States would have the option.[19]

The United States does face serious constraints on its ability to pursue a successful foreign economic policy. To some extent these reflect the growing independence of its allies as well as the increasing assertiveness of others, such as the oil exporting countries. Yet some significant constraints on U.S. policy stem not from policies of other states but from other causes.

One set of constraints on U.S. policy is the result of domestic pluralism. Interest groups clash with one another as well as with the President. Domestic oil companies and consumers in the northeastern United States both claim to want an "effective energy policy," but the former demand market-set prices and the latter insist on paying less than an unregulated market would require. Each side may prefer *no* energy policy to victory by its opponents. The result may be a stalemate or an ineffective compromise. Domestic interest groups constrain American policy in the trade field, as well as in energy. Indirectly, by demanding growth with only moderate inflation, domestic pressures have set the parameters for international monetary and growth policy. The structure of the U.S. government, with a powerful Congress representing particular regional and sectoral interests, reinforces the impact of well-organized, even if relatively small, domestic interests on U.S. foreign economic policy.[20]

Also of great importance are constraints imposed by the proliferation of issues, and the multiple linkages among them. Chapter 1 emphasized this point; it is only necessary to reinforce it with some examples here. Within the realm of foreign economic policy, policies adopted to attain one set of objectives, such as energy self-sufficiency, may adversely affect other goals, such as noninflationary economic growth. To complicate matters, noneconomic issues may have major effects on the success of foreign economic policy. U.S. policy toward Israel is clearly linked to energy policy by major oil producers, in particular Saudi Arabia. Even the Panama Canal treaty has affected foreign economic policy, by so preoccupying the U.S. Senate and requiring so much attention from the President during the first four months of 1978 that even less progress was made on the energy bill than one might have expected. The issues of growth policy, trade policy, and energy policy are never actually faced by policy makers in the relatively clear and simple form in which they are posed later in this chapter.[21]

The last set of constraints is the least discussed, although nonetheless of considerable significance. U.S. policy makers face problems of insufficient knowledge in shaping foreign economic policy. No one sufficiently understands the complexities of international political economy to be able to predict accurately the effects of a given change of economic policy by the OECD countries as a whole, much less the effects of change in U.S. policy alone. To what extent will increases in domestic money supplies, or international liquidity, affect inflation rates in the industrialized countries? Can stimulative policies be devised that will promote investment and growth without markedly increasing the rate of inflation—or is no such option available? Are "structural policies," to reshape or reorganize certain industries through government action, necessary for the advanced industrial countries to resume their pattern of prosperity? How would democratic publics react to tightly disciplined governmental policies that reduced the rate of growth of government budgets and government services and that favored profits and investments over wage increases in allocating shares of the national product?[22] Neither economists nor political scientists have adequately addressed these issues, and policy makers find themselves without informed guidance when they have to make decisions. This is particularly true of macroeconomic policies for noninflationary growth, but to some extent it applies to energy (where forecasts of energy supply and demand in the future vary considerably) and trade (where estimates of the viability of certain established industries, such as steel in the United States, also differ).

These constraints do not make the United States a "helpless giant" in foreign economic policy. They do limit the ability of any administration to achieve its purposes, and a politically prudent administration will to some extent tailor its publicly announced objectives to these limitations on its power.

At the risk of some oversimplification, the major foreign economic policy issues facing the United States can be placed within three categories: (1) growth policy, (2) trade policy, and (3) energy policy. *Growth policy* (or macroeconomic policy) seeks to promote real economic growth, at relatively full employment and with relatively low rates of inflation; the primary instruments to achieve these results are monetary and fiscal policy. *Trade policy* focuses on particular industrial or agricultural sectors that seem to be threatened either by imports or by barriers against American exports abroad. It has a more specific focus than growth policy. *Energy policy* must deal not only with the financial problems raised by high levels of oil imports (imports of petroleum cost the United States about $45 billion in 1977) but also with the political vulnerabilities that dependence on imports may produce.

To some extent the distinction among growth, trade, and energy policies is artificial. Japan could stimulate additional production abroad not only by lowering trade barriers but also by increasing its growth rate (thus increasing imports). A given level of economic growth in the United States would have different implications for exchange rates if the U.S. level of energy imports were closer to $25 billion than to $45 billion. Competitive advantages in particular industries, such as steel, are affected by relative energy prices in major industrial countries and by relative exchange rates, as well as by trade barriers per se. For purposes of clarity in exposition and organization it is useful to analyze the three areas separately, but the connections among them should not be forgotten.

Growth policy, trade policy, and energy policy are discussed in successive sections of this chapter, but each section has a similar analytical structure. I first consider the *initial objectives* of the Carter administration in the issue area. Then I examine the *constraints on policy implementation*—what made it difficult to attain the initial objectives—along with the resources available to mold events. Finally, I examine the *dilemmas* facing the United States in each area, in relation to American objectives of simultaneously maintaining prosperity in the United States and abroad, and American influence over events.

THE CARTER ADMINISTRATION GROWTH STRATEGY

Throughout its tenure, the administration of President Gerald Ford fought inflation as "public enemy number one." During 1976, this emphasis was consistent with conventional wisdom among the advanced industrial states; in July of that year, the

OECD Economic Outlook warned that in the recovery then taking place, "the balance of the risks may well be on the side of a stronger expansion than forecast," with inflationary consequences.[23] By the beginning of 1977, however, economic observers were becoming more concerned about sluggishness than about excessive expansion. The December issue of the *Outlook* asked the strong countries of the OECD (particularly Germany, Japan, and the United States) to "bear in mind the fact that world demand movements are on the low side." [24]

The Carter administration was responsive to this advice both at home and in its foreign economic policy. Within its first two weeks in office, the administration proposed an economic stimulus program, whose key element was a $50 tax rebate to virtually every American. Treasury Secretary Blumenthal, presenting this program before a House committee, emphasized the "international economic context in which this program should be viewed." After reviewing the unemployment and growth problems of industrial countries, Secretary Blumenthal explicitly coupled domestic U.S. economic policy with its foreign economic policy:

> *In solving these problems, all countries must work together. The Carter Administration believes strongly in such collaboration and will strive to foster it. Today, for example, it is important that those stronger countries, like the United States, Germany, and Japan, work together to expand as rapidly as is consistent with sustained growth and the control of inflation.*
>
> *By adopting this stimulus program, the United States will be asserting leadership and providing a better international economic climate. We will then ask the stronger countries abroad to follow suit. This program itself implicitly calls on them to undertake stimulus efforts of proportionately similar amounts to ours.[25]*

The Carter administration's economic stimulus package was in domestic political trouble from the start, opposed by the chairman of the Board of Governors of the Federal Reserve System, Arthur F. Burns, by much of U.S. business, and by a large number of congressmen. During the winter and early spring, economic indicators in the United States turned upward and economic growth seemed to be resuming, furnishing further arguments for opponents of the plan. It was withdrawn by the Carter administration before the end of April.[26]

Despite the collapse of the American stimulus program, the United States continued its efforts to persuade Germany and Japan to increase their rates of economic growth. At the London Economic Summit Conference in May, Germany and Japan nominally agreed to take measures to expand their economies along with the United States, but it soon became evident that these targets would not be met. Germany promised to attain 5 percent economic growth during 1977, and Japan 6.7 percent. In the end, the German growth rate was only about 2.5 percent and the Japanese rate about 5 percent. In contrast, the United States approximately met its 5.8 percent target. The ineffectiveness of U.S. pressure was also suggested by the trends of growth rates during the year. German and Japanese growth fell sharply as 1977 wore on. Moreover, Germany continued to run a small current account surplus of about $2 billion, while the Japanese were amassing a huge surplus of over $10 billion. Meanwhile, the United States had a $20 billion deficit.[27] By the end of the year, it was clear that the "locomotive" strategy of the Carter administration—by which the strong economies would pull the world out of recession—had failed. In

February, the OECD Economic Policy Committee agreed on a "convoy" approach, according to which "convalescent" economies, such as those of Britain, France, and Italy, were to expand their economies faster, along with the United States, Germany, and Japan. Yet in view of the reluctance of the German and Japanese governments to take strong expansionary measures, the new program—formally labeled the Coordination Reflation Action Program—could cynically be regarded as no better than its acronym.[28]

The crucial constraints on American policy in this affair were found in the resistance of the German and Japanese governments to American interference in what they regarded as their domestic economic affairs. This resistance was apparent early, although it was expressed differently by the two governments, reflecting Germany's less vulnerable political-economic position and its more forthright national style.

The Germans expressed their resistance and resentment consistently. Chancellor Helmut Schmidt declared in January 1977 that Germany could not do any more to expand and that all countries should be asked to expand cautiously together, rather than following the OECD's and Carter administration's "locomotive" strategy, by which the stronger countries would pull the rest along. Chancellor Schmidt argued that since German economic performance—on both unemployment and inflation—was better than that of the United States, Germany required no lectures on economic policy from the American government.[29] Germany rejected American pleas at a March meeting of the OECD's Economic Policy Committee, and later that month a U.S. Senate staff report advised that "to the extent that U.S. economic strategy is premised upon a coordinated economic expansion of the strong economies of the United States, West Germany and Japan as a means of pulling up the weaker European economies, it is probably mistaken." [30] According to the report, high German officials saw the problems of weaker OECD economies, such as Britain, France, and Italy, as being caused primarily by domestic conditions that other countries could not correct. The German government did adopt some mild stimulative policies during the year, but they were minor and did not prevent the growth rate from continuing to decline. By late 1977, German spokesmen had become more biting in their characterizations of the Carter administration's strategy: Germany's chief delegate to an OECD meeting in November characterized the locomotive theory as "naive," and Chancellor Schmidt warned his Common Market colleagues that prosperity could not be restored by printing money but required thrift and hard work.[31] If anything, pressures from the United States seem to have hardened the German stand.

The Japanese followed similar policies, but without the didactic rhetoric favored by Chancellor Schmidt and members of his government. The Japanese government committed itself to aim for a 6.7 percent growth rate in 1977 and took some relatively minor and ineffective steps to stimulate its domestic economy and reduce its balance-of-trade surplus. As late as the annual meeting of the IMF on September 26–30, the Japanese minister of finance said that the 6.7 percent growth target was appropriate for 1977, although it was clear that this would not be attained. Japan sought to appear cooperative, while following a more conservative path than the United States or the OECD would have liked.[32]

By the end of 1977, the failure of the Carter administration's "locomotive" strategy had exposed a difficult dilemma for American foreign economic policy. In the absence of effective coordination among the advanced industrialized countries, expansionary economic policies in the United States would contribute to extremely large American current account deficits without necessarily assuring prosperity abroad. Even if the United States could finance its deficits indefinitely without creating grave monetary instability, it would be acquiring external liabilities—thus engaging in power disinvestment—without achieving its objective of world prosperity or acquiring countervailing external assets. It would not even necessarily secure political "goodwill" for its economic sacrifices, and it would be in a weak position to cope with future adversity. No prudent American government could complacently accept such a prospect.

Since financing a huge deficit indefinitely would be politically unwise, it was necessary either for the United States to adjust to world economic conditions or for other states to adjust to the United States. This is essentially what the "locomotive" debate was about: the United States wanted Germany and Japan to make the most painful adjustments, while the governments of those countries sought to impose the costs of adjustment on the United States. In international economic relations, power often manifests itself as the ability to force others to bear costs of adjustment to change.[33]

When it became clear in the fall of 1977 that Germany and Japan could not be persuaded to follow expansionary policies, the United States took actions, or failed to take actions, that had the effect of forcing some costs onto its partners: it began a well-publicized campaign to reduce the Japanese current account surplus, and it allowed the dollar to depreciate on world financial markets.

In November, an American mission to Tokyo reportedly demanded that Japan within three weeks publicly announce commitments to reduce its current account surplus; about three weeks later, Japan sent a delegation to Washington with a package of concessions drawn up by a cabinet reshuffled in the wake of the American ultimatum.[34] U.S. officials claimed that this move reflected American concern for the health of the international economic system, which was jeopardized by Japan's huge surplus, as well as domestic pressures within the United States. They also asserted that the negotiations were amicable.

Japanese officials and observers, however, expressed surprised concern that the huge United States should put so much pressure on Japan, which considers itself to be a relatively small, vulnerable country struggling to maintain its economy in adverse circumstances. They emphasized the failure of American exporters to concentrate seriously on the Japanese market, and the structural difficulties (such as those in agriculture) that make it impossible for Japan to liberalize its policies as rapidly as the United States desires. The Carter administration policy may have been handled in a more conciliatory way than the "Nixon shocks" of 1970–71, but like the controversies over textiles and exchange rates in those years, the United States was exercising its superior power over the highly vulnerable Japanese.[35] In both cases, it appeared to United States officials that the power investments it had made for years—supporting Japan politically, militarily, and economically while making it asymmetrically dependent on the United States—should pay dividends in this time of economic need. Thus, when economic losses to the United States (or certain sectors of the U.S. population) became significant political issues domestically, and when Japanese policies seemed to destabilize the international economy, the American administration was willing to draw on its power resources.

American actions carried certain long-term political risks. If Japan should attempt to change the structure of its production and foreign trade, and its political ties, to become less dependent on the United States in the long run—and if it could successfully do so—the U.S. influence over Japanese policy would decline. Thus it was important from the U.S. perspective not to make the threat too harsh. On the other hand, effective persuasion could have political as well as economic rewards, domestically and in Europe. From a political perspective, American actions could be seen as an attempt to use some "excess power" vis-à-vis Japan both to serve short-term domestic objectives and to strengthen the international economic system, thereby reinforcing the positio of relatively conservative regimes, with which the U.S. had strong ties, in economically weak countries such as France, Italy, Portugal, and Spain.

The second major way by which costs could be forced on to others would be to let the dollar depreciate by following a policy of "benign neglect" of the dollar in world financial markets. By making exports cheaper in foreign currency, and imports into the United States more expensive in dollar terms, such a depreciation would tend, over time, to reduce the U.S. deficit while reducing export surpluses of strong currency countries. Of course, it would also have the negative consequences of increasing the U.S. inflation rate and worsening the terms of trade. During the summer and fall of 1977, it appeared that the Carter administration was following this course; Secretary Blumenthal was even accused of "talking the dollar down." Responding to fierce criticisms during the winter from European governments and Japan, U.S. officials professed greater concern about the dollar's decline, and in early January the Treasury and the Federal Reserve Board announced that they would intervene from time to time on foreign exchange markets in support of the dollar.[36] It quickly became evident, however, that the United States was not prepared to support the dollar at any given level, only, as the Council of Economic Advisers put it, "to act forcefully when market conditions become disorderly." An agreement between the United States and Germany in March—announced after a long build-up—had a similarly limited purpose. The administration did "not believe it is appropriate to maintain any particular value for the dollar." [37]

It is not surprising that the markets were reported to be asking, "Does the United States really mean to support the dollar, or is it just going through the motions?" [38] A good case could be made that the policy of the Carter administration was really one of "disguised benign neglect." The administration believed that supporting the dollar at present levels would be extremely costly and would probably fail; but it was no longer politic to view the dollar's decline with equanimity or to express disdain for European and Japanese fears that they would be hurt by exchange rate changes. Thus the United States continued to require Europe and Japan (and OPEC, since OPEC assets were largely in dollars and the price of oil was dollar-denominated) to bear the burden of adjustment—while the rhetoric changed. Sugar coating was put on the pill.[39]

A policy of continued economic expansion at home, plus "benign neglect" on the foreign exchange markets, could only have been sustained if American leaders were willing to accept both higher inflation rates domestically (as a result of expansionary policies coupled with the falling exchange rate) and conflict with U.S. allies. The latter may have been acceptable; the former became unacceptable as inflation rates in the spring of 1978 rose above double-digit annual levels. Domestic fiscal and monetary policy turned toward greater restraint: the proposed tax cut was reduced in size, and interest rates rose. Correspondingly, the United States now abandoned its high-growth alliance with the OECD secretariat: In late May the United States opposed a secretariat plan for coordinated stimulation of world economic growth, with the chairman of the Council of Economic Advisers arguing that rising inflation and the huge American trade deficit made it impossible for the United States to expand its rate of growth further.[40] Not only was the locomotive policy now dead—the leading locomotive had applied its brakes.

During the summer and fall of 1978 it became evident that the brakes had not been applied hard enough to satisfy the foreign exchange markets. The dollar fell sharply across all other major currencies, culminating in sharp declines at the end of October. Finally, on November 1, 1978, the Carter administration reacted by announcing a sudden policy shift: domestic interest rates were sharply increased and the United States adopted new policies that represented "a commitment to massive intervention, if necessary," in the foreign exchange markets. One high-level Treasury official commented that "the time comes when you can't let Adam Smith completely alone."[41] The American government was willing to risk a serious recession in 1979 for the sake of reducing the rate of inflation and stabilizing the dollar on international markets. The reversal of policy from that of February 1977 was now virtually complete. The struggle by the United States to force costs of adjustment on to others had been unsuccessful, since the effects of the dollar's precipitous decline had been more severe than the administration could tolerate. As Arthur Okun commented after the November 1 measures were announced, "The gnomes of Zurich got their way."[42]

The international aspects of this story can be analyzed with the help of a rudimentary game theoretical presentation. The struggle between the United States, Germany, and Japan can be represented as a simple two-actor bargaining game, as indicated in figure 3.1. Each actor—the United States on one hand, Germany and Japan on the other—can select a strategy of expansion or one of restraint. Each combination of strategies has implications for current account deficits or surpluses, inflation, and unemployment. In the chart, "best results" are indicated by double plus signs, "worst results" by double negative signs, and neutral effects by zeros. The payoffs to the United States are indicated, in each box, by the notations to the upper left of the diagonal line; the payoffs to Germany and Japan by the notations to the lower right.

Allocation of current account deficits and surpluses approximates a zero-sum situation, insofar as each country prefers to run surpluses (as has been the almost universal tendency of governments, despite the advice of most economists). If both actors expand, the effects are neutral; but actors exercising restraint while their partners expand can expect to show current account improvement, and vice versa. Performance on the unemployment dimension is not zero-sum. Both sides will do

FIGURE 3.1

AN INTERNATIONAL, MACROECONOMIC
POLICY COORDINATION GAME

GERMANY AND JAPAN

	Policy:	Expansion	Restraint
	Expansion	I	II

	Outcome Dimensions:	U.S. / G. & J.	U.S. / G. & J.
	Current account	0 / 0	− − / + +
UNITED	Inflation	− / −	− / +
STATES	Unemployment	+ + / + +	+ / −

	Restraint	IV	III

	Outcome Dimensions:	U.S. / G. & J.	U.S. / G. & J.
	Current account	+ + / − −	0 / 0
	Inflation	+ / −	+ / +
	Unemployment	− / +	− − / − −

NOTE: For the United States, situation I dominates situation II and situation IV dominates situation III. For Germany and Japan, situation I dominates situation IV
and situation II dominates situation III. Other choices depend on the governments' weightings of various objectives.

best when they are both following expansionary policies, and worst when they are
both exercising restraint. In the diagram, I assume that unemployment is influenced
more by national or regional policy than by the other party's policies; for instance,
the United States performs better on the unemployment dimension when it is
expanding and its partners exercising restraint (as in 1977) than vice versa. Finally,
with respect to inflation, I assume that inflation will be higher with expansionary
than with contractionary policies worldwide; but inflation will also be severe, under
floating exchange rates, for countries following expansionary policies when their
partners are exercising restraint (since their exchange rates will tend to depreciate
and thereby increase the cost, in local currency, of imported goods).

From the diagram it can be seen that for the United States, situation I dominates
situation II, and situation IV dominates situation III. That is, a movement from II to
I or III to IV would improve U.S. performance on some dimensions without hurting
it on any others. Thus German and Japanese expansion is good for the United
States. For Germany and Japan, situation I dominates situation IV and situation II
dominates situation III: American expansion is good for them.

Now we are in a position graphically to reinterpret the macroeconomic disputes
of 1977 and 1978. In 1977 the world economy was in situation II, with the United
States expanding rapidly while Germany and Japan grew slowly. The United States
sought, through pressure on those countries, to move to situation I. Germany and
Japan resisted, largely out of fear of inflation, although expansion would have helped

their employment situations. So the world stayed in situation II. As the United States moved toward restraint, the world moved toward situation III in the diagram, and closer to a new world recession.

The irony of this result is that situation III is the only one that is clearly inferior to at least one other solution *for both sides*. For the United States, III is dominated by IV; for Germany and Japan, III is dominated by II. Moreover, judging from its strenuous attempts to get Germany and Japan to act as locomotives in 1977, the United States (at least the Carter administration, if not Wall Street) prefers I to III as well. So do the weaker European countries, who are neither part of the figure 3.1 game nor particularly influential in actual policy discussions. But the United States, faced with an unacceptable situation II, could only move *unilaterally* to III. In the absence of effective policy coordination, the United States, Germany, and Japan all achieve suboptimal results; and the weak, poorly represented countries (several European countries plus the less developed countries) face what is for them a potentially difficult international economic situation.[43]

The international debates and negotiations over macroeconomic policy during 1977–78 illustrate the potential for conflict hidden in Secretary Blumenthal's call for international economic collaboration (see page 103). Because the perceived interests of the major countries diverged, no conflict-free solution was possible. The problem was not simply one of "educating" the Germans and Japanese to their "true interests" as defined by liberal, neo-Keynesian economists of the OECD and the United States. On the contrary, for there to be agreement, power would have to be successfully exercised.

Yet it was difficult for the United States to exert its power successfully. Applying pressure threatened to intensify international economic conflict and strain relations with close allies. The ultimate weapon of pressure—depreciation of the dollar—exacerbated conflict, increased risks of protectionist actions abroad, and threatened to accelerate American inflation. By November 1978, it seemed that the United States was no longer trying to force adjustments on to others, but that it was emphasizing the fight against inflation at home. Yet, essentially uncoordinated policies of restraint by all three major powers would, if earlier forecasts by American officials proved correct, lead to a recession that could have been avoided by coordinated action. The exercise of power may have been costly and dangerous; the failure effectively to exercise power would have serious consequences as well.

The United States could conceivably attempt to solve its macroeconomic problems by adopting protectionist trade measures. These would have to be accompanied by an effective energy policy (because a protectionist United States in all likelihood would not be allowed by other countries to run surpluses on trade in manufactured goods and capital account to finance $45 billion worth of oil imports). Few economists or high officials in the Carter administration regarded protectionism as an effective response to macroeconomic difficulties. Yet ongoing changes in the structure of foreign trade were causing dislocations, with serious domestic political consequences. The pressure to "do something" was strong. It is to the area of trade that we now turn.

THE CARTER ADMINISTRATION AND THE POLITICS OF TRADE

When Jimmy Carter came into office in January 1977, foreign trade was already the focus of some of the hardest-fought battles in Washington. Since 1934, American Presidents had consistently promoted lower tariffs and freer trade. Protectionist sentiment was persistent, particularly in Congress; yet forces favoring freer trade continued to gain support between 1934 and the early 1960s. These political changes, aided by American economic successes in the first two postwar decades, culminated in the passage of the Trade Expansion Act of 1962 and the successful conclusion of the Kennedy Round of multilateral trade negotiations in 1967. Even at the time when the liberal traders were successful, important U.S. industries such as iron and steel, textiles, and footwear were coming under pressure from imports, and protectionist sentiment began to increase. Indeed, textiles had already been exempted from the liberal provisions of the 1962 Trade Act. The AFL-CIO changed from an antiprotectionist to a protectionist stance during the late 1960s. In 1971, in conjunction with his international monetary measures, President Nixon imposed a temporary 10 percent surcharge on American imports. Although the Congress in 1974 passed a trade act authorizing the President to make large reductions in tariffs, this legislation contained a number of relatively restrictive provisions that had been absent from the 1962 act. Legislators were clearly laboring under intensive cross-pressures on trade issues.[44] The direct effects of particular trade measures were highly visible and specific, and could be readily perceived by industrialists, union officials, and members of the general public. Unlike international monetary politics, trade was not perceived as an esoteric issue area that had to be interpreted by squabbling bands of arcane economists. Whether for these or other reasons, trade attracted more domestic controversy than issues of exchange rates and the international monetary system even though the latter may have been more important for the economy as a whole.[45]

The initial policy pronouncements and actions of the Carter administration in the trade field were consistent with the liberalism of previous Presidents. Under Carter, the United States continued to press for further reductions in trade barriers at the Multilateral Trade Negotiations in Geneva. In March Undersecretary of State-Designate Richard N. Cooper cautioned Congress against taking a protectionist path:

> *Imports are a natural scapegoat for what is basically deficient total demand. Import restrictions, however, will never work collectively—unemployment will only be exported. Thus far Governments have generally followed prudent trade policies, but the possibility of protectionism is real. Trade restrictions would spread in the current environment, and it could easily take another decade to get back to where we are today.*[46]

In April Carter rejected recommendations by the international Tariff Commission to impose restrictions on imports of color television sets and shoes, incurring the wrath of George Meany, president of the AFL-CIO.[47]

The need to make concessions to protectionist forces was evident from the reactions to these early Carter decisions. Over the next few months, his special trade representative, Robert Strauss (former chairman of the Democratic National Committee), developed a policy of "free but fair trade," in which Orderly Marketing Agreements (quotas disguised as "voluntary" agreements) would be used to help politically influential industries hardest hit by imports. Under an OMA, the United States arranges with its major suppliers for them to limit their exports, and the agreement is then filed under the provisions of the General Agreement on Tariffs and Trade (GATT). For instance, since most recent growth in shoe imports has come from Taiwan and South Korea, the United States decided to negotiate an OMA with these nations instead of ordering general import restrictions. A similar agreement was made with Japan covering color television sets.[48]

During the past decade, less developed countries such as South Korea, Taiwan, and Brazil have been increasingly successful exporters to the United States and other industrialized countries. This pattern is no longer confined to items of peripheral importance but extends to basic industrial products, such as steel. Structural changes in world trade and production patterns account for many of the disruptions felt in industrialized countries, and the effects of these changes on particular industries are exacerbated by the low level of aggregate demand in the advanced industrial states.[49] Pressures for increasing protectionism are by no means likely to be temporary. As long as manufacturing industries continue to develop in the Third World, these pressures are apt to continue, if not increase.

The difficulties confronting proponents of a liberal trade policy were illustrated graphically by events in the steel industry during the summer and fall of 1977. Bethlehem Steel announced a quarterly loss of $477 million in August; in September, steel firms announced layoffs of thousands of workers, including 5000 workers at one plant near Youngstown, Ohio.[50] Officials of the steel industry, union leaders, and congressmen from affected areas immediately called for restrictions on imports and other protection for the industry. U.S. Steel filed an "anti-dumping complaint" against virtually the entire Japanese steel industry, charging that it sold steel below cost in the United States.

Critics of the industry argued that many of its troubles were its own fault and that the timing of the layoffs reflected industry efforts to reduce long-term costs, as well as problems of weak demand and import competition. They could also point out that imports of steel were not growing dramatically; during the first eight months of 1977, imports accounted for under 16 percent of the U.S. market, less than their percentage in 1968. In 1968, however, the U.S. economy was still benefiting from the long boom of the 1960s; and heavy industry received an additional boost from the Vietnam war. By 1977, on the contrary, unemployment and unused capacity were much higher. The costs of imports to workers and industrialists were correspondingly more severe. Regardless of the merits of various arguments, the key political fact was that industry and union leaders, many congressmen, and much of the public identified imports as the key problem.[51]

Under strong pressure, the Carter administration hastily developed a plan to protect the industry—defending the plan, not on the grounds that it was good in itself, but that it was less harmful than the feasible alternatives—in particular, import quotas. The key point in the plan was to establish a "reference price" for steel based on the cost of production in Japan, the most efficient foreign producer. An accelerated antidumping investigation will be initiated immediately if imported steel is sold in the United States below the reference price. Reference prices were set at about 5.7 percent below the average price of comparable American steel products in the eastern United States. By April 1978, actual prices for steel in the United States had risen about 15 percent, and talks were under way among the United States, the European Community, and Japan to produce a "world steel agreement." Steelmakers from lese developed countries were excluded from these negotiations.[52]

Under intense pressure, the Carter administration had retreated from its liberal stand of the winter and spring to a "defense of liberalism through moderate protectionism." It was attempting, in its dealings with the European and Japanese steel industries and governments, as well as in the Orderly Marketing Agreements, to do what Undersecretary Cooper said in March 1977 was not possible: to make import restrictions "work collectively."

We saw that in the area of macroeconomic, or growth, policy, the Carter administration was caught between its desire for sustained and relatively rapid economic growth and the resistance of foreign governments to its plans for attaining that objective consistent with international financial equilibrium. A similar dilemma loomed on the trade side, although in this case the affected industries, both in the United States and abroad, were more directly involved. Domestic pressure for protection was vociferous; advocates of erecting barriers to imports specifically criticized foreign governments and industries. Thus in December, AFL-CIO President George Meany argued:

> *Foreign trade is the guerrilla warfare of economics—and right now the United States economy is being ambushed. Free trade is a joke and a myth. And a Government trade policy predicated on old ideas of free trade is worse than a joke–it is a prescription for disaster. The answer is fair trade, do unto others as they do unto us—barrier for barrier—closed door for closed door.*

Meany also implied that the costs of allowing free trade in steel would not be limited to wealth but would extend to power as well. Like the mercantilists of the seventeenth and eighteenth centuries, he perceived that being materially dependent on a potential adversary would weaken one's autonomy and power. He argued that imported steel is cheaper

> *because foreign countries subsidize their steel industries so they can undercut United States companies. Of course, when the United States steel industry is destroyed, the United States would become dependent on foreign sources, and without a steel industry of our own, the foreign countries could charge whatever they want.*[53]

On the monetary-macroeconomic-growth side, the principal focus of debate was domestic, with international problems seen as indirect though powerful constraints on domestic policy in the long run. On the trade side, by contrast, foreign economic policy questions were at the forefront of attention. Moreover, the growth policy debate was dominated by economists; all were in favor, in principle, of an open world economy. Arguments over trade policy, by contrast, were conducted primarily by industry and union officials and congressmen, not by economists. These people were much less reticent than economists about expressing clearly protectionist sentiments.

In part, the arguments about trade policy had to do with whether protectionism would serve the goal of national prosperity. The AFL-CIO and industries such as steel said it would; neo-classical economists and administration spokesmen such as Richard Cooper and Robert Strauss argued that protectionism would damage prosperity by leading to retaliation against American exports and inefficiency at home. The policy debate also rested to some extent on the *relative priority* that should be given to competing foreign policy objectives—in particular, to national prosperity in the short run versus world order, with its implications for long-run prosperity. One could believe that protectionism would bring economic gains, at least in the short run, without favoring such a course of action—if one thought that such a step would undermine the American-centered structure of world order and eventually, therefore, bring economic as well as political trouble to the United States. According to this argument, protectionist policies would decisively damage U.S. relations with developing countries and jeopardize U.S. ties with its allies in the OECD. The long-run political and economic arguments could be used to counter the protectionists' short-run emphasis on jobs.

Yet the implications of a long-run argument were not that simple. A sophisticated neo-mercantilist version of the protectionist argument could be constructed. According to this view, imports of steel would eventually weaken the American steel industry to a point at which the industrial base of the United States would be undermined and its power in the world eroded. A United States that had become merely an affluent service economy, an economy of hamburger chains and investment banks, would indeed be a "pitiful, helpless giant" in a competitive and conflict-ridden world political economy. Although advocates of protectionism generally stressed the short term, focusing on jobs and profits, they could also make a long-term political argument for their position.

Thus the economic controversies over the effects of liberal trade in a world of highly organized, government-supported industry were not the only issues behind the dilemmas of American policy. There were also two different, although implicit, answers to the question, What is a secure base of political influence in contemporary world politics? Administration spokesmen and their allies outside government argued that U.S. autonomy and influence could be secured only within a structure of world order, and that particular sacrifices should be made to assure that such a structure were developed. "World order politics" should be the guiding motif of American policy.[54] To the neo-mercantilists, however, international politics remains a realm of self-help politics, and *national* power in a traditional, material sense is a sine qua non for security and influence.

The interesting thing about this debate is that both sides may be right, under different conditions. World order has the quality of a self-reinforcing equilibrium, or self-fulfilling prophecy. As long as governments and other significant actors believe that order will be maintained—and in particular that the major power or powers upholding it are willing to make the necessary sacrifices to maintain it—strong measures to discipline violators will be unnecessary. "Investments in world order"—providing orderly regimes for interaction, and incentives for participation by major governments—will be more productive than investments in national material bases of power. It will make more sense to buy South Korean steel and Saudi Arabian oil than to protect one's own steel industry or develop expensive sources of domestic petroleum. Since liberal economists *assume* that a structure of world order exists, they naturally favor this open course of action; as long as that assumption is sensible, or sufficiently self-reinforcing, they are wise to do so.

Yet, when the fabric of world order becomes frayed, it can unravel quickly. At this point, national material sources of power become more important, as they did during the 1930s, and confidence placed in international regimes seems increasingly empty. Governments that "insured themselves" against this eventuality by reducing their dependence on others are then in a better position than those who did not. The irony is that by protecting themselves against the consequences of a world collapse (e.g., by protectionist measures), they may have helped to bring on the demise of the benign international regime. Even they may therefore be in worse positions than if they had supported the system.[55]

The dilemmas posed by these potential dynamics are most difficult for great powers, for they have both the most choice and the greatest effects on the system. If the United States decided that the structures of world order created after World War II were collapsing and acted accordingly, those structures would assuredly break down. Whether the analysis had been correct or not, it would have been (if accompanied by action) self-fulfilling. From a long-term political standpoint, therefore, a turn toward full-fledged protectionism (as opposed to concessions to protectionist sentiment here and there within the context of a liberal world economy) could well be a decisive and irrevocable step with broad implications for the political and security issues discussed elsewhere in this book, as well as for international economic relations.

ENERGY POLICY IN THE CARTER ADMINISTRATION

In April 1977 President Carter submitted an extensive energy program to the Congress. This measure was considered by the administration to be its most important piece of legislation; and to a considerable extent, it was justified on grounds of foreign policy. To a significant degree, the weaknesses in the U.S. international political-economic position could have been rectified by more effective energy policies. In 1978 Americans were still paying prices well below world levels for energy; gasoline for automobiles, for instance, was less than half as expensive to American consumers than to their counterparts in Europe and Japan. U.S. oil imports increased 20 percent in 1976 and 18 percent in 1977, so that by 1977 they amounted to almost 48 percent of U.S. consumption and cost a total of $45 billion, compared with $8.5 billion in 1973. American levels of oil consumption, relative to gross domestic product, were high by OECD standards.[56] American balance-of-payments problems could not be solved without effective measures to control the growth of oil imports, if not to reduce them in absolute terms. Moreover, as the United States became increasingly dependent on Middle Eastern petroleum supplies, the American ability to influence events in the Middle East and resist pressure from oil-producing Arab states would be likely to decline. President Carter thus worried not only about the dollar but also about "the serious security implications of becoming increasingly dependent upon foreign oil supplies which may for some reason be interrupted." [57]

America's allies strongly supported the administration's plans. Members of the International Energy Agency (which include all major advanced capitalist countries except France) had been urging the United States to take strong energy measures before the Carter plan was announced, and continued to express their concern about American action. As a Canadian minister put it, "It will be very difficult for other countries to adopt stringent energy policies if someone could say, 'If the U.S. won't do it, why should we?' I think there would be the gravest of consequences if the Carter administration isn't successful in getting substantially what it proposed." [58] The large and growing energy consumption of the United States was particularly worrisome in view of forecasts that at present rates of growth in oil consumption, serious shortages would appear in the 1980s, accompanied, it was feared, by sharp increases in price.[59] U.S. energy conservation performance, which was poor between 1973 and 1976, was seen to require improvement through legislation.

As in trade, the major constraint on administration policy was posed by domestic politics. In energy, however, the President had to take new initiatives, whereas in trade, protectionist critics of the administration demanded the changes. Energy legislation had to be proposed, on which billions of dollars of costs (to consumers) and profits (to producers) would depend. The Carter energy package sought to reduce the energy growth rate through conservation measures, such as an increase in the gasoline tax, a tax on automobiles not meeting federal mileage standards, incentives to homeowners to insulate their houses, and taxes on industrial use of oil and natural gas. The Ford administration had put less stress on conservation measures. In a reversal of preelection promises, Carter asked that federal price controls on natural gas, as well as oil, be retained and extended to intrastate gas, although prices of natural gas would be allowed to rise somewhat. Ford had favored an end to federal regulation of oil and gas prices.[60]

Although most provisions of the Carter plan passed the House of Representatives, it ran into difficulty in the Senate. The plan's retention of price controls on natural gas and oil, and its tax provisions, were opposed by a large part of the domestic oil industry. Moreover, it was seen by senators from the South and West as unduly favorable to the Northeast, which is more heavily represented in the House than in the Senate, and which benefited further in the House from the power of the Speaker, who came from Massachusetts. If the plan had been adopted, present wide disparities between the cost of energy in the Southwest and the Northeast would have been narrowed greatly—to the disadvantage of southwestern industry. Carter's tax proposals would have relatively benefited consumers in the Northeast, who use less energy per capita than residents of other sections of the country.[61]

Carter's energy plan therefore came to be seen in sectoral and sectional terms. It

TABLE 3.1

KEY PROVISIONS OF THE CARTER ENERGY PROGRAM AND THEIR FATE IN CONGRESS

Proposal (April 1977)	Result (October 1978)
Increase in gasoline tax	No such provision adopted (defeated in both House and Senate)
Tax on "gas-guzzling" cars	Approved, beginning with 1980 models; not applicable to trucks or vans
Extension of natural gas price controls, with higher price ceiling	Compromise approved providing for price controls on intrastate gas, but for all price controls to be removed by 1985
Tax on crude oil	No such provision adopted (defeated in Senate finance committee)
Tax credits for home insulation	Approved

SOURCE: *The Economist* (London), 21 October 1978, p. 36.

NOTE: Indication that the Carter administration proposal was "approved" does not imply that all provisions of the final legislation were identical with the proposal of the administration; but rather that the essential provisions of the administration's proposal were retained.

was not debated merely on a technical level—what policies would be most effective in stimulating conservation and production of energy? It became linked to fundamental issues of income distribution and interpersonal equity, as well as to environmental concerns. From a single-issue point of view, some energy programs seemed to be clearly in the "public interest," particularly on foreign policy grounds. Whether Carter's plan was optimal could be contested, but if the goal was reduced energy dependence, this program was better than no measure at all. Members of the public, and their representatives in Congress, did not see the issue from this perspective. To oil company executives in Houston or senators from Louisiana, corporation profits, and prospects for reelection, were at stake; to consumers in Massachusetts, natural gas prices were more salient than abstractions about energy dependence; and to many environmentalists, the first priority was to halt the further development of nuclear power. Whatever its economic merits or faults, the administration package did not command an effective coalition; too many contradictory concerns impinged on the energy bill. Despite the strong foreign policy rationale for the program (on grounds of long-run power as well as short-run and long-run prosperity), and the international support it had gathered, it was the victim of domestic politics.

In October 1978, after seemingly interminable negotiations in the U.S. Senate, Congress passed energy legislation, which President Carter signed. Table 3.1 indicates what happened to the major provisions of the legislation the President had described, eighteen months earlier, as "the moral equivalent of war." The humorous columnist Art Buchwald summarized the results by imagining an interview with the general in charge of the war against wasting fuel. Surveying the ruins, the general regretfully declares: "We had to destroy the energy bill to save it." [62]

The fate of the energy program reminds us that foreign economic policy issues are inherently linked to other domestic issues that seem more important to influential groups and industries in the United States. When these domestic issues are salient to large numbers of people, foreign policy concerns are likely to carry little weight with the U.S. Congress, even when they are highly relevant to decisions. An American in the IEA secretariat recalls that when he asked Senator Henry Jackson whether the IEA's views had any influence in Congress, he "got a big horselaugh." [63] During the 1980s the United States will confront many foreign economic policy issues in which domestic and foreign policy considerations are intertwined. Examination of policy making in the late 1970s suggests that, at least where Congress is involved, foreign policy interests will get short shrift.

CONCLUSION

The problems of the Carter administration during its first two years illustrate what happens when intentions, however good, meet reality in foreign economic policy. To some extent the Carter administration created problems for itself by proclaiming expansionary macroeconomic policies that it could not implement either domestically or internationally, and by failing to devise politically acceptable energy legislation and lobby effectively for it during 1977. Yet the major difficulties faced by the Carter administration were not entirely the results of its own blunders but were inherent in the nature of American political institutions and the position of the United States in the world. They are likely to persist in the future.

It will continue to be hard for the United States to maintain prosperity at home and abroad. In part this reflects difficulties of coordinating policies among advanced industrial states, which have been discussed in this chapter. Other forces are also at work. The advanced industrial countries are now being required to pay more attention to events outside their own sphere, and in some ways to adjust to these changes rather than always being able to impose the costs of adjustment on others. The oil-price rises of 1973–74 and the impact of the Organization of Petroleum Exporting Countries (OPEC) on world politics provide the most obvious examples. Of comparable importance, but less noticed, is the shift in comparative advantage in certain major industrial sectors—textiles, steel, and some areas of electronics—toward the more advanced Third World countries. This phenomenon is discussed more fully in the next chapter, and it will increasingly affect not only "North-South relations" but also the industrial structure of the North. The reaction of the industrialized countries may well be defensive, protectionist, and discriminatory against poorer countries that have successfully followed the advice of Harvard- or Chicago-trained economists.

Internal tensions within capitalist countries are also important. Contemporary capitalism coexists uneasily with democratic institutions; it is difficult to make capitalism run smoothly and still achieve the levels of social welfare and equity of income distribution that democratic publics expect. Tensions and contradictions abound and will continue to manifest themselves in "political" as well as "economic" ways. Thus important constraints will be imposed by domestic politics, as well as by conflicting state policies, the existence of multiple, competing issues, and knowledge limitations of decision makers.

Conflicts will continue to exist among objectives. As the economists are fond of saying, there is no "free lunch," although politicians are adept at creating illusions that such a feast can be provided (with payment at least deferred until after the next election). Even when we adopt a national, or "public interest" point of view, conflicts arise among objectives. Even if we agree that in the long run it does not make sense to choose between power and wealth, we may disagree on how much preference to give to the immediate over the distant future; in economists' terms, personal and national "discount rates" may differ. Keynes's reminder, "in the long run we are all dead," reminds us that there should probably be *some* discount rate, but it hardly tells us what it should be. Even if we should agree on this, different policy prescriptions would follow from different estimates of the long-run costs of various policies. For instance, would aggressive U.S. pressure on Japan to reduce its trade surplus undermine world order, U.S. influence, and prosperity in the long run? Would protectionism help or hinder attempts to maintain national prosperity? Would such protectionism increase U.S. influence in the future by protecting the American industrial base, or would it reduce U.S. influence by undermining the structure of world order that America now dominates?

These problems are simple in comparison with the issues that arise when we no longer assume that all political actors analyze foreign policy issues in terms of a known "national interest." People look at foreign economic policy issues, as they do other issues, in terms of their own interests, and often interpret "the national interest" in these terms. Thus it is not surprising that members of the foreign policy elite usually care more about long-term foreign policy questions, and less about jobs in Ohio, than steelworkers in Youngstown. Nor is it difficult to understand why positions taken on President Carter's energy policy so often follow the lines of class, industrial, and regional interest.

This brings us to a restatement of the key theme of this essay: the politics of foreign economic policy (both domestic and international) involves contention over who will bear the costs of adjusting to change. We can only attain our "thick description" of events by looking beyond the pious statements and universalistic rhetoric to the interests served by policy. We have seen that policy disputes between advanced capitalist countries on monetary and trade issues reflect struggles by governments to force the costs of adjustment on to others. In domestic political controversies, such as those on trade and energy matters, tangible interests are also at stake—in these cases, of competing groups rather than governments. In both situations we will only be misled if we believe that the arguments are essentially disputes over doctrine, principle, or ideology, or that the central problem is how to interpret world interests. On the contrary, conflicts of interests, as perceived by the participants, are at the heart of the political struggle. These interests combine aspirations to power and wealth. They are in some areas, and at some times, complementary. Thus coalitions are formed and agreements are made. But the interests of autonomous actors never completely coincide; hence, there is always some political contention, even in harmonious relationships.

In the 1980s, the United States will continue to be subject to adverse foreign economic pressures. These pressures—whether the result of slow growth abroad, export campaigns aimed at the American market, or high energy prices—will have political repercussions at home. Domestic groups will demand that other governments adjust their policies to American needs. Although the United States is powerful, it is not all-powerful, and forcing such adjustments on to others will be difficult. Whether successful or not, it will lead to tough negotiations, verbal recriminations, and a certain amount of international bad feeling. Thus attempts at policy coordination will lead to conflict. American foreign economic policy under President Carter and his successors will be judged according to its success in keeping international conflict manageable while retaining domestic political support and maintaining U.S. influence as well as fostering prosperity at home and abroad. The foreign economic policy kitchen will be hot; success will come to those who can turn out the goodies without setting off an explosion.

NOTES

1. Clifford Geertz, *The Interpretation of Cultures* (New York: Basic Books, 1973).
2. There is well-documented evidence for the United States, at least, that electorates punish political parties, and political leaders, for failing to increase real per capita income. See Edward R. Tufte, *Political Control of the Economy* (Princeton, N.J.: Princeton University Press, 1978).
3. In 1960 imports plus exports amounted to under 7 percent of gross national product; in 1977 they amounted to over 14 percent. See *Economic Report of the President* (Washington, D.C.: Government Printing Office, January 1978); calculated from tables B-1, B-97, and B-99, pp. 257, 368, and 371.
4. *Towards Full Employment and Price Stability,* a report to the Organization for Economic Development and Cooperation (OECD) by a group of independent experts, chaired by Paul McCracken (Paris: OECD, 1977), p. 42. Henceforth cited as McCracken Report.
5. Ibid., pp. 44–65. For a discussion of President Nixon's attempts to assure his reelection by sharply increasing personal income before the 1972 election, see Tufte, *Political Control of the Economy.*
6. Marina v. n. Whitman, "Sustaining the International Economic System: Issues for U.S. Policy," *Princeton Essays in International Finance,* no. 121 (June 1977): 8.
7. Benjamin J. Cohen, *Organizing the World's Money: The Political Economy of International Monetary Relations* (New York: Basic Books, 1977).
8. For a brief discussion of the reconstruction of the international monetary system between 1973 and 1976, see Robert O. Keohane and Joseph S. Nye, *Power and Interdependence: World Politics in Transition* (Boston: Little, Brown, 1977), pp. 82–86. For more extensive analysis, see Cohen, *Organizing the World's Money.* The statement about American dominance in the International Energy Agency is documented in Robert O. Keohane, "The International Energy Agency: State Influence and Transgovernmental Politics," *International Organization,* Autumn 1978.
9. Franz Schurmann, *The Logic of World Power* (New York: Pantheon, 1974), p. xxiii.
10. This cycle is clearer in the sphere of international monetary politics than in trade or energy. Both Britain and the United States faced problems such as these as reserve currency countries. See Fred Hirsch and Michael Doyle, "Politicization in the World Economy and Necessary Conditions for an International Economic Order," in *Alternatives to Monetary Disorder,* ed. Hirsch et al. (New York: McGraw-Hill for the Council on Foreign Relations, 1977).

11. Henry R. Nau, "U.S. Foreign Policy in the Energy Crisis," *Atlantic Community Quarterly* 12 (Winter 1974–75): 426–39; and Pierre Hassner, "Europe and the Contradictions in American Policy," in *America as an Ordinary Country*, ed. Richard Rosecrance (Ithaca: Cornell University Press, 1976), pp. 60–86.

12. Nevertheless, a strong argument could be made now that the unpredictability of American policy has been carried well beyond the point at which it confers advantages on the United States. As Stephen Krasner has pointed out to me, if Congress ultimately blocks the President's policy, the result can be "like throwing the steering wheel out the window in a game of chicken." For a brilliant discussion of the "threat that leaves something to chance," see Thomas C. Schelling, *The Strategy of Conflict* (New York: Oxford University Press, 1960).

13. Consider, for instance, the arguments between "orthodox" historians and "revisionists" about the origins of the cold war. Orthodox historians often ignored underlying economic objectives, but the revisionists have often committed a similar monistic error (with a different factor considered crucial) by searching for "real" economic motivations behind every policy. For an example of the latter in an otherwise impressive work, see Joyce Kolko and Gabriel Kolko, *The Limits of Power: The World and United States Foreign Policy, 1945–1954* (New York: Harper & Row, 1972).

14. For a classic statement of this argument, with reference to the seventeenth and eighteenth centuries, see Jacob Viner, "Power versus Plenty as Objectives of Foreign Policy in the Seventeenth and Eighteenth Centuries," *World Politics* 1, no. 1 (October 1948).

15. Arnold Wolfers, "Power and Influence: The Means of Foreign Policy," and "The Pole of Power and the Pole of Indifference," in *Discord and Collaboration: Essays on International Politics* (Baltimore: Johns Hopkins University Press, 1962).

16. Viner, "Power versus Plenty," p. 20.

17. Kolko and Kolko, *The Limits of Power*, pp. 444–45.

18. See Albert O. Hirschman, *National Power and the Structure of Foreign Trade* (Berkeley, Calif.: University of California Press, 1945; reissued, 1969), p. 47.

19. For a fuller discussion of the complexities of using force in the contemporary world, see Keohane and Nye, *Power and Interdependence*, pp. 11–19.

20. Stephen D. Krasner, "United States Foreign Economic Policy: Unravelling the Paradox of External Strength and Internal Weakness," in *Between Power and Plenty: Foreign Economic Policies of Advanced Industrial States*, ed. Peter J. Katzenstein (Madison: University of Wisconsin Press, 1978). This book was first published as Vol. 31, no. 4, of *International Organization* (Fall 1977).

21. I am indebted to Abraham Lowenthal for observing that an earlier draft of this chapter did not make this point clearly.

22. For discussions of some of these issues, see the McCracken Report, and the critique in Robert O. Keohane, "Economics, Inflation, and the Role of the State: Political Implications of the McCracken Report," *World Politics* 31, no. 1 (October 1978).

23. *OECD Economic Outlook*, no. 19 (July 1976): 9. For a statement of the Ford Administration view, see Secretary of State Kissinger's speech to the OECD, 21 June 1976.

24. *OECD Economic Outlook*, no. 20 (December 1976): 12.

25. U.S. Congress, House, *Conduct of Monetary Policy: Hearings before the Committee on Banking, Finance and Urban Affairs*, 95th Cong., 1st sess., 2 February 1977, p. 9.

26. Burns' views appear in ibid., p. 93. Discussions of reasons for the demise of Carter's economic stimulus package can be found in the *New York Times*, 1 May 1977, sect. 3, p. 1, and sect. 4, p. 2.

27. In 1977, OPEC states had a collective current account surplus of about $35 billion, which was projected to decline to $20–25 billion in 1978. The counterpart to this OPEC surplus was a large deficit on current account for OECD countries as well as non-oil countries. See Morgan Guaranty Trust Co., *World Financial Markets*, February 1978; and *Annual Report of the Council of Economic Advisors* (published with the *Economic Report of the President*) (Washington, D.C.: Government Printing Office, January 1978), tables 15, 16, and 18. For final figures on the U.S. current account deficit, see the *Wall Street Journal*, 23 March 1978.

28. A discussion of this Economic Policy Committee meeting appears in the *New York Times,* 28 February 1978.

29. *New York Times,* 20 and 24 January 1977. The U.S.–German difference on questions of inflation was by no means new. West German Minister of Economics Ludwig Erhard told President Eisenhower in 1958, "Whereas the Germans, because of their history, always worried about inflation, the Americans, because of their history, always worried about depression. The resulting danger was that America would overrespond to threats of recession and cause serious inflation in the long run." Herbert Stein, *The Fiscal Revolution in America* (Chicago: University of Chicago Press, 1969), p. 340.

30. *U.S. Foreign Economic Policy Issues: The United Kingdom, France, and West Germany, A Staff Report Prepared for the Use of the Subcommittee on Foreign Economic Policy of the Committee on Foreign Relations, U.S. Senate* (Washington, D.C.: Government Printing Office, 1977). The quoted passage appears on p. 31. For an account of the Economic Policy Committee meeting, see *New York Times,* 3 March 1977.

31. *New York Times,* 22 November and 7 December 1977. Reports of German economic stimulus packages appeared in the *New York Times,* 23 March and 15 September 1977.

32. For reports of the Japanese position, see, for instance, *New York Times,* 21 January and 5 August 1977; *IMF Survey,* 10 October 1977; *Economist,* 1 October 1977.

33. These costs of adjustment are not purely objective; they depend on policy-makers' values and interests as well as on economic facts. Within a country, certain groups may benefit by changes viewed by others, or by governmental leaders, as costs; Japanese consumers, for instance, would benefit as consumers from reductions of import barriers on cheap agricultural products from the United States. For the purposes of this analysis, however, policy-makers' utility functions are taken as the standards by which costs are assessed. If a government resists a policy change, imposition of it is regarded as a cost to that government even though some of its citizens might benefit thereby.

34. *New York Times,* 22 November and 7 December 1977.

35. My sources for these statements are interviews and conversations in Washington and Tokyo during March 1978. For a discussion of the 1969–71 period, see I. M. Destler, Priscilla Clapp, Hideo Sato and Haruhiro Fukui, *Managing an Alliance: The Politics of U.S.–Japanese Relations* (Washington, D.C.: Brookings, 1976).

36. *New York Times,* 5 January 1978, p. 1.

37. *Report of the Council of Economic Advisers* (Washington D.C.: Government Printing Office, 1978), p. 124.

38. See Leonard Silk, "The U.S.–German Action: Markets Are Unconvinced," *New York Times,* 14 March 1978, pp. 47, 59.

39. It is impossible to confirm whether these were the "real motivations" of policy makers, so the argument for this point of view remains speculative. It should also be noted that policy-makers' views sometimes change; reports in the spring of 1978 suggest that Secretary Blumenthal, in particular, became more worried about the effects of the dollar's decline in the late winter of that year. Some of these reports ascribed this heightened concern to moves by central banks to sell dollars in large quantities, and to complaints from Saudi Arabia. See *Economist,* 1 April 1978.

40. *New York Times,* 1 June 1978, p. 47.

41. The first quotation is from the Undersecretary of the Treasury for Monetary Affairs, Anthony Solomon, and appears in the *Wall Street Journal,* 2 November 1978. The second quotation is from an anonymous Treasury Department official; see the *San Francisco Chronicle,* 2 November 1978.

42. *San Francisco Chronicle,* 2 November 1978.

43. Thus, although there are some differences in the structure of the game, the outcome of this international economic policy game is like that of the classic "Prisoners' Dilemma" game often used in discussions of bargaining: in the absence of effective coordination, results are suboptimal for both players. An extra twist in this game is that those actors affected by the game, but not participating in it, do especially badly.

44. For a lucid recent account, see Krasner, "U.S. Commercial and Monetary Policy." For a

classic analysis of the politics of foreign trade in the 1950s, see Raymond A. Bauer, Ithiel de Sola Pool, and Lewis Anthony Dexter, *American Business and Public Policy: The Politics of Foreign Trade* (Chicago: Aldine-Atherton, 1963).

45. See Keohane and Nye, *Power and Interdependence,* pp. 121, 253 *n.*

46. U.S. Congress, Senate, *Statement of Undersecretary for Economic Affairs-Designate Richard N. Cooper, before the Subcommittee on Foreign Economic Policy of the Senate Foreign Relations Committee,* 18 March 1977 (Department of State Press Release), p. 3.

47. *New York Times,* 7 April, 1977.

48. *New York Times,* 13 June 1977.

49. See Morgan Guaranty Trust Co., *World Financial Markets,* September 1977 and January 1978; *New York Times,* 24 September 1977.

50. *New York Times,* 21 September 1977; *Wall Street Journal,* 27 October 1977.

51. For figures on imports as a percentage of consumption, see *New York Times,* 17 October 1977. For a discussion of factors other than imports that influenced the timing of layoffs, see the 1978 *Report of the Council of Economic Advisers,* p. 136. Reports on contentions of "dumping" can be found in the *New York Times,* 14 October 1977, and the *Wall Street Journal,* 25 November 1977.

52. For the reference pricing system, see the 1978 *Report of the Council of Economic Advisers,* p. 137; and *New York Times,* 4 January 1978, p. A1. For a discussion of the trilateral discussions on a steel agreement, see "Towards a World Steel Cartel," *Economist* (London), 29 April 1978, p. 95.

53. Both quotations are from the *New York Times,* 9 December 1977.

54. See Stanley Hoffmann, "The Uses of American Power," *Foreign Affairs,* October 1977, pp. 28–48. For a critique of the Carter administration's first year, see Hoffmann, "The Hell of Good Intentions," *Foreign Policy,* no. 29 (Winter 1977–78): 3–26.

55. Like the macroeconomic game described in the previous section, this recalls the famous "prisoners' dilemma" situation in game theory.

56. For the 1973 and 1977 import figures, see the 1978 *Economic Report of the President,* p. 7; for percentage import growth, see the *New York Times,* 14 March 1978, p. 1. In 1975, U.S. total energy requirements per unit of gross domestic product were larger than those of all but five IEA countries. See *OECD Observer,* no. 83 (September/October 1976): 5. Furthermore, average daily oil consumption between 1973 and the first half of 1977 rose 7.5 percent in the United States, but fell in other major OECD countries. See *Wall Street Journal,* 31 October 1977. Oil imports in the first quarter of 1978, however, fell 14 percent from the first quarter of 1977, largely due to the flow of Alaskan oil in the latter year. See *Wall Street Journal,* 20 April 1978.

57. *New York Times,* 14 October 1977.

58. *Wall Street Journal,* 7 October 1977.

59. One such forecast is found in *The Energy Outlook to 1985* (Paris: OECD, 1977). The U.S. Central Intelligence Agency made a similar projection. It should be noted that many economists disagree. See, for instance, Robert S. Pindyck, "OPEC's Threat to the West," *Foreign Policy,* no. 30 (Spring 1978).

60. For a comparison of the Carter and Ford Energy plans, see *Congressional Quarterly Weekly Review,* 23 April 1977.

61. *New York Times,* 20 October 1977.

62. *The Economist* (London), 21 October 1978, p. 36.

63. Interview, IEA Secretariat, Paris, November 1977.

4

NORTH-SOUTH ECONOMIC RELATIONS

The Quests for Economic Well-Being and Political Autonomy

Stephen D. Krasner

A striking aspect of the current international system is the involvement of states whose power capabilities are very unequal. Since the evolution of the modern state system in the sixteenth and seventeenth centuries, there have always been large and small states defined in terms of geographic area or population. But never, before 1945, have very large disparities in the level of economic development been a central characteristic of the system. Most lesser developed areas were colonized, formally or informally, during the nineteenth century by the more developed and powerful countries of North America and Europe. Today, virtually all areas of the Third World (of Asia, Africa, and Latin America) have gained at least formal inde-

I would like to thank the members of the Colloquium on National Control of International Movements of the Institute for International Studies in Berkeley, as well as the other contributors to this volume, especially Robert Keohane and Abraham Lowenthal, for their comments. An earlier version of this chapter was written for a series of meetings organized at the Woodrow Wilson Latin American Center by Abraham Lowenthal. My debt to the work of Robert W. Tucker, partcularly his The Inequality of Nations *(New York: Basic Books, 1977), is not adequately reflected in the footnotes. The completion of this chapter was facilitated by a grant from the Rockefeller Foundation.*

pendence. In many international organizations all states exercise the same formal power; Benin, the United States, Afghanistan, and the Soviet Union each cast one vote. A central problem of the countries of the southern hemisphere, the Third World, has been to find some way of coping with their international weakness: how to gain some control over aspects of the international system, particularly the international economic regime, that vitally affect their political stability and economic well-being. Another and more obvious problem has been how to enhance the economic well-being of their inhabitants, many of whom live below subsistence levels.

The alleviation of external vulnerability and the enhancement of economic well-being are not necessarily correlated, particularly in the Third World. Many of these countries are so weak that even rapid levels of growth will not lessen their vulnerability to political, economic, or military disturbances from the international environment. Rapid economic growth may even make these countries more vulnerable to foreign influence by disrupting traditional political and social patterns and further enmeshing them in the world economy. Growth may mean more trade with the rest of the world and greater levels of capital and technology transfer, developments that could make less developed countries (LDCs) more susceptible to external perturbations or pressures.[1]

This chapter argues that the countries of the Third World have adopted a two-track strategy. On track A they have pursued goals related to economic well-being. Although not oblivious to questions of autonomy while pursuing this track, they have been willing to trade autonomy for greater economic transfers from the North to the South. Examples include the creation of international commodity agreements, the renegotiation of foreign debt, and the treatment accorded multinational corporations. On track B, the LDCs have tried to deal directly with their vulnerability in the international system. Here their fundamental objective has been to enhance their influence in international organizations that can alter the rules and norms governing the international economic regime. Here economic transfers have been unacceptable unless they were accompanied by fundamental changes in institutional arrangements.

The two tracks are distinguished not only by their objectives but also by the arenas and actors involved. Track A has been pursued in nonuniversal international forums in which the actors are individual states, multinational corporations, and international organizations, particularly international financial agencies. Examples include the negotiation of standby agreements between the International Monetary Fund and particular states, the renegotiation of concession agreements of foreign corporations, the imposition through national legislation of restrictions on the activities of foreign businesses, debates among primary-product exporting countries about market shares in international cartels and commodity agreements, the negotiation of credit terms between multinational banks and Third World countries, and the conclusion of bilateral or multilateral trading agreements between more and less developed states. Track B has been pursued in universal international forums in which the actors are groups of states, particularly in the South. Various aspects of the New International Economic Order have been presented in a wide range of forums including the UN Conference on Trade and Development, the UN General

Assembly, the UN Industrial Development Organization, and the Law of the Seas (LOS) Conference. Here the LDCs have presented a unified position through the Group of 77, an organization formed at the 1964 meeting of the UN Conference on Trade and Development (UNCTAD), which now includes more than a hundred members. The primary manifestation of efforts by poorer countries to enhance their international autonomy has been a set of proposals labeled the New International Economic Order (NIEO).

In interpreting demands that have been made by the South, most analysts and policy makers in the North have committed one fundamental error: they have assumed that track A with its pragmatic economic orientation encompasses all the demands of the Third World. They have ignored the more radical implications of track B. Thus, they have interpreted the NIEO as a reformist program designed to increase the transfer of economic resources within existing institutional structures rather than an effort to revise these structures. For instance, a story by a leading economic correspondent of the *New York Times* described the Paris Conference on International Economic Cooperation (a set of meetings held in 1976 and 1977 among developing countries, members of the Organization of Oil Exporting States [OPEC], and advanced market economy countries) as a forum for discussing "a more equitable sharing of the world's wealth." [2] Robert McNamara, president of the World Bank, has argued that "it is relatively unimportant whether the assistance (to less developed countries) is to take the form of commodity agreements, debt relief, trade concessions, bilateral or multilateral financing—or any particular combinations of these—provided the overall total is adequate." [3] Observers in industrial countries make frequent analogies to domestic economic movements, such as the development of labor unions and efforts to increase welfare payments, that have taken place in the wealthier countries. John Sewell of the Overseas Development Council (a private Washington-based organization devoted to improving relations with the Third World) has stated that the demands of the LDCs bear "some similarity to the emergence of organized labor in this country in the late 1920s and 1930s." [4] One author has maintained that in the area of technology the LDCs are engaging in "consumerism." [5] Another has stated that UNCTAD should be viewed as a "trade union movement." [6] The NIEO is seen as a response to an economic crisis, a failure of the existing system to operate fairly and effectively in the Third World. A UN official has written that "acute poverty, chronic unemployment and endemic undernourishment continued in most (developing countries), or even worsened, and their economic dependence on the metropolitan countries was perpetuated and even extended into new areas." When these facts were recognized in the 1960s, the Third World "could not but conclude that a new economic order was necessary, an order that would explicitly recognize the needs and conditions of the developing countries." [7]

This chapter demonstrates that the prevailing wisdom is incorrect because it underestimates the importance of political goals to less developed countries. The Third World is not interested only in improving its material well-being; it is also interested in enhancing its autonomy. That objective is as important as economic goals. The countries of the South cannot be bought off simply by higher levels of resource transfers because such transfers, at any level that is politically feasible, would not do much to reduce the international weakness and vulnerability of most Third World states; even with much higher levels of growth, most states of the South would still be unable to insulate themselves from capricious changes in the international economic system.

THIRD WORLD AUTONOMY AND THE NEW INTERNATIONAL ECONOMIC ORDER

Proposals for the NIEO, the premier manifestation of track B, emerged during the 1970s from a series of meetings attended by Third World states. The NIEO involved the grafting of two historical roots. The first was the nonaligned movement; the initial meeting of nonaligned countries was held in Bandung in 1955 to carve out an independent political position for Third World countries, one that would allow them to avoid falling under the sway of either the communist or the Western bloc. The second root was the Group of 77, formed at the first UNCTAD meeting in 1964. Its purposes were economic, for once the independent political stance that was the touchstone of the nonaligned group took up economic concerns, it was a short step to rejecting an economic regime that reflected the goals and values of the advanced market economy countries, particularly the United States. The notion of collective and individual economic self-reliance for the Third World, of a break with the extant world economy, was first voiced at a meeting of nonaligned countries at Lusaka in 1970.[8]

At Algiers in 1973 a de facto merger took place between the nonaligned countries and the Group of 77. This conference adopted an Economic Declaration and an Action Program for Economic Cooperation that provided the basis for the Declaration on the Establishment of a New International Economic Order and the Program of Action on the Establishment of a New International Economic Order, which were adopted at the Sixth Special Session of the UN General Assembly in May 1974. This was the first special session to deal with economic issues. The Charter of Economic Rights and Duties of States was adopted in December 1974 at the twenty-ninth regular General Assembly session. The Seventh Special Session held in 1975 adopted a resolution on Development and International Economic Cooperation. Additional statements on North-South relations were approved at UNCTAD meetings in Santiago in 1972 and Nairobi in 1976, at a conference on raw materials in Dakar in February 1975, and at a UN Industrial Development Organization session in Lima in March 1975.[9] These resolutions elaborated the goals that have become associated with the NIEO and have set the agenda for track B discussions between the North and the South since the early 1970s.

The NIEO envisons basic changes across a wide variety of issue areas:

Trade. The Group of 77 wants preferential and nonreciprocal treatment, such as the removal of tariff and nontariff barriers that impede their exports to more industrial states even though these barriers remain in place for exports from more advanced countries. LDCs also want the right to regulate their own imports to facilitate an autochthonous process of industrial development.

Raw materials. The Group of 77 calls for changes that would basically alter the way in which raw materials move across international boundaries. LDCs have asserted the right to exercise sovereignty over raw materials production within their borders by nationalizing foreign corporations and establishing, without external interference, appropriate levels of compensation. The Charter on Economic Rights and Duties of States (passed by the UN General Assembly over objections from some industrialized states) provides that states have the right to form international commodity cartels that are not subject to retaliation from consuming countries. More recently, attention has been focused on an integrated commodity program prepared by the UNCTAD secretariat. A key element in that program would be the creation of a common fund for stabilizing and raising commodity prices. The Group of 77 wants this fund to support not only buffer stocks for commodities when consumers and producers had already reached agreement (e.g., the International Tin Agreement and the International Cocoa Agreement) but also to make loans to support commodities not covered by specific agreements, as well as to provide funds for diversification, productivity improvement, market promotion, and the enhancement of the role of LDCs in marketing and distribution. The Group of 77 has stated that it wants decisive control over any fund established. In a related area, the mining of minerals from the deep seabed, the Group of 77 has made proposals that would give its members effective control over any international seabed authority created to regulate such activities.

Capital flows. In the area of foreign aid, the Third World emphasizes higher and less restricted capital flows from the North to the South. The Second UN Development Decade (adumbrated in a 1970 UN General Assembly resolution) set a target for capital transfers equal to 1 percent of the gross national product (GNP) of the industrialized countries, with 70 percent of this figure granted on concessional terms. LDCs have called for the rescheduling or cancellation of some debt obligations. They have asked for a link between the creation of any new international liquidity by the International Monetary Fund and aid for poorer areas. Mahbub ul Haq, an official of the World Bank who has recently emerged as a prominent critic of the current international economic system, has proposed creating a World Development Authority with the power to collect taxes at the global level and distribute receipts to less affluent areas. At the UN Disarmament Conference held in 1978 the Group of 77 proposed a tax on the industrialized nations (INs), to be used for aid, based on arms expenditures.[10]

Technology transfers. The Third World seeks a new code regulating the transfer of technology, most of which is now controlled by multinational corporations, made binding on private firms as well as governments. The proposed code would eliminate restrictions on the use of technology now imposed by multinational corporations (MNCs), such as prohibitions on the export of products produced with a particular technology because such exports might compete with the firm's sales in other countries. It would give less developed states preferential access to technology, as well as the right to discriminate against foreign corporations. The basic principle underlying the Third World position is that technology is part of the common heritage of mankind and not a proprietary right of the organization that develops it.

Decision making. The South also explicitly demands "the right to participate fully and effectively in the international decision-making process in the solution of world economic, financial and monetary problems." [11] In effect, this would mean moving away from arrangements based on weighted voting determined by economic size and toward arrangements based on one-nation-one-vote dictated by the principle of the sovereign equality of all states. Haq states that "the long-term solution is to change the institutional system in such a way as to improve the access of the poor to economic opportunities." He goes on to argue that "the Third World has to make it quite clear in its future negotiations that what is at stake is not a few marginal adjustments in the international system; it is its complete overhaul." [12]

The set of changes proposed by the Third World are not marginal reforms. They would not merely enhance the flow of resources to the South. They would fundamentally alter institutional arrangements, both formal and informal, governing the international movement of goods and services. If the NIEO were accepted, the countries of the North would have less control. MNCs would have less discretion over resources they formally owned. More decisions would be made by international organizations in which the South enjoys an effective majority. The South justifies its demands by the contention that the extant system is illegitimate because it is unfair and exploitative: unfair because the weakness of poorer countries has made it impossible for them to defend their interests adequately; and exploitative because richer countries have appropriated the wealth of poorer ones.

It should not be surprising that the countries of the South are concerned about mitigating their vulnerability or that they have made institutional changes a fundamental part of their NIEO program. The South's concern with vulnerability and weakness reflects the enormous disparities in power resources that typify the present international system. Never before have countries with such dramatic differences in power enjoyed even formal equality as sovereign states.

Measuring relative power resources is a perennial problem for students of international relations. There is no simple summary statistic that adequately covers all aspects of the problem. Resources, and conversely vulnerabilities, vary from one issue area to another.[13] The best single indicator of national power resources, because it summarizes data on levels of economic development and population size and is readily available, is a measure of aggregate economic activity, such as a country's GNP. Table 4.1 shows GNP levels for almost all the world's countries.

Differences between countries of the North and countries of the South are staggering. China, with the largest GNP of any Third World country, is the only Third World country that could lay claim to great power status; yet the GNP of the United States is 5.64 times larger. Countries thought of as regional hegemones do not have impressive GNPs compared with most industrialized countries. The GNPs of India and Brazil (the two largest after China) are about the same as those of Spain and Poland; Iran's rivals Belgium's; Saudi Arabia and Nigeria have GNPs similar to those of Denmark and Finland. Few countries of the Third World can play a major role in the international system; almost all are subject to military, economic, and political pressures that can threaten their economic and political well-being.

In attempting to cope with their weakness and vulnerability, the less developed countries have made international organizations the centerpiece of their strategy. In

TABLE 4.1

DISTRIBUTION OF GROSS NATIONAL PRODUCT
(number of countries)

Level of GNP 1975 (billions of dollars)	INs	LDCs	Total
Above 1000	1	0	1
500–1000	1	0	1
250–500	2	1	3
125–250	5	0	5
65–125	4	2	6
30–65	9	4	13
15–30	6	6	12
7–15	3	17	20
3–7	0	15	15
1–3	3	28	31
Below 1	0	41	41
Total	34	114	148

SOURCE: Derived from figures in World Bank *Atlas*, 1977.

established organizations such as the World Bank and the IMF they have tried to alter voting rules to enhance their influence. In organizations established during the 1970s, such as the International Fund for Agricultural Development (IFAD), or in the proposed integrated fund for commodities and the international seabed authority, the Group of 77 has sought effective control.

International organizations have assumed such a prominent role for the less developed countries because even high-levels of resource transfers will do no more than marginally change the power position of most Third World countries. The gap between the North and the South is too large; few LDCs can bridge it by simply increasing their own national resource capabilities. Control over international organizations is, for the Group of 77, a potential substitute for national weakness. By enhancing their influence in these organizations, LDCs may be able to alleviate the uncertainty and vulnerability that threatens their political and economic stability. Moreover, international organizations are one decision-making arena where LDCs already have considerable leverage and access. Here, power in the form of votes is frequently allocated equally among all states: one nation, one vote. In sum, the states of the Third World have acted in much the same way as states have always acted: they have tried to enhance their power in the international system.

If this interpretation is correct, then the North-South confrontation is likely to be more persistent and acerbic than is generally realized. Those who see the South motivated only by economic considerations believe that more economic generosity from the North will ultimately lead to a stable and mutually acceptable situation. Scholars and policy makers who hold this position have not underestimated the difficulty of increasing transfers, for there is considerable resistance in the United States to more foreign aid, greater liberalization of technology transfers, and increased trade concessions. Nevertheless, they have argued that by educating the public to the benefits for the United States of a more equitable and stable international economic order, American policy might be more forthcoming. If, however, the NIEO focuses on political vulnerability, not material well-being, even a more liberal American attitude on economic matters will not reduce tensions. The Third World's demand for political concessions, associated with voting power in international organizations, will be even more difficult to secure from the advanced countries than will an increase in the transfer of wealth.

ECONOMIC WELL-BEING AND PRAGMATIC THIRD WORLD BEHAVIOR

This discussion of the NIEO is not meant to imply that the program encompasses all relations between the rich and the poor. On the contrary, discussions of NIEO proposals in universal international forums often have little relationship to most issues raised by ongoing North-South economic transactions. Political vulnerability is a central concern to less developed states, but it is not their only concern. Improving economic well-being is also a basic objective, one that LDCs have pursued regardless of the impact on basic institutional structures.

In this quest many LDCs have been remarkably successful; track A has not been a failure. The economic performance of the Third World has been far better than is generally realized; indeed, in many ways it is remarkable and unprecedented. At the least, the impact of the postwar international economic regime on less developed areas must be regarded as complicated and differentiated, not simply as a drag on the progress of poorer countries or an engine of exploitation.

Many nonindustrialized countries have enjoyed substantial rates of growth, the most obvious nations being the oil exporters. Here an alteration in bargaining power between host-country governments and multinational corporations, coupled with a shift in market conditions that favored producers over consumers, made it possible for a number of Third World states to quadruple the price of oil in the winter of 1973–74. The consequences for the rest of the world, as well as for the OPEC states (some accumulated large amounts of foreign exchange reserves and pushed their per capita incomes to levels substantially above those in even the richest industrialized nations), are very much with us. In 1975, GNP per capita in North America was $7100. Table 4.2 shows the per capita incomes for states that are members of OPEC, as well as their real per capita growth rate. A few very rich oil-exporting countries are not, of course, typical of the Third World. Nevertheless, the OPEC experience indicates that the liberal international economic regime, which persisted with little challenge into the early 1970s, did not always benefit richer countries and damage poorer ones.

Some non-oil LDCs have experienced rapid economic growth; others have stagnated. Tables 4.3 and 4.4 show the distribution of per capita growth rates for less developed and industrialized market economy countries.

Most LDCs have enjoyed respectable rates of per capita economic growth, with 57 percent recording rates of 2 percent or above for the 1960–75 period and 52 percent for the 1970–75 period. Industrialized nations have done better, and none has experienced a negative growth rate, whereas 13 percent of LDCs had negative

TABLE 4.2

OPEC INCOME AND GROWTH

	1975 GNP per capita (U.S. dollars)	Real GNP Growth Rates	
		1960–75	1970–75
Algeria	840	1.8	4.3
Ecuador	550	3.4	6.1
Gabon	2,250	5.0	7.8
Indonesia	200	2.4	3.5
Iran	1,550	8.1	13.3
Iraq	1,100	3.3	6.7
Kuwait	14,710	−2.9	−3.3
Libya	5,510	10.5	3.9
Nigeria	320	3.4	5.3
Qatar	8,570	4.1	−0.4
Saudi Arabia	3,060	6.6	4.1
United Arab Emirates	13,500	13.7	1.6
Venezuela	2,140	2.2	1.5

SOURCE: Figures from World Bank *Atlas*, 1977.

TABLE 4.3

REAL AVERAGE ANNUAL PER CAPITA GNP GROWTH RATES FOR NON-OIL LDCs [a]
(number of countries in each category; percentage of total in parentheses)

	Less than 0	0–1.9	2–3.9	4–5.9	6+
1960–75	10 (13%)	22 (29%)	30 (40%)	9 (12%)	4 (5%)
1970–75	18 (22%)	22 (31%)	22 (31%)	7 (10%)	8 (11%)

SOURCE: Derived from figures in World Bank *Atlas*, 1977.
[a] Includes only those countries whose population exceeds one million.

TABLE 4.4

REAL AVERAGE ANNUAL PER CAPITA GNP GROWTH RATES FOR INDUSTRIALIZED MARKET ECONOMY COUNTRIES [a]
(number of countries in each category; percentage of total in parentheses)

	Less than 0	0–1.9	2–3.9	4–5.9	6+
1960–75	0	0	13 (65%)	5 (25%)	2 (10%)
1970–75	0	7 (35%)	8 (40%)	5 (25%)	0

SOURCE: Derived from figures in World Bank *Atlas*, 1977.
[a] Includes only those countries whose population exceeds one million.

TABLE 4.5

GDP GROWTH RATES

Time Period	1950–60	1960–65	1965–70	1965–73
Real average annual rate of growth for GDP of industrialized countries	4.1	5.2	4.7	4.6
Number of LDCs with higher rates of growth	42	42	51	53
Number of LDCs with lower rates of growth	40	45	37	36

SOURCE: Derived from figures in World Bank *World Tables,* 1976, pp. 392–97.

average annual per capita growth rates for the 1960–75 period, and 22 percent had negative rates for the 1970–75 period. In aggregate terms the per capita growth experience of the Third World since 1950 has been about the same as that of the North, with both areas growing at a little over 3 percent.[14]

In comparison with the wealthier countries, LDC performance looks much more impressive if absolute rather than per capita figures are compared. In aggregate terms the real rates of growth for the Third World have been higher for total output, agricultural output, and manufacturing output than the rates for the industrialized world.[15] Table 4.5 compares the aggregate growth rate of industrialized countries with that of individual LDCs. This table indicates that, since 1965, most countries of the South have grown faster than those of the North. This is not to deny that overpopulation is a severe problem; indeed, a comparison of table 4.5 with tables 4.3 and 4.4 highlights how severe a constraint it is. Population growth is inherently a domestic rather than an international problem, however. Altering the international economic regime will not directly affect the rate of reproduction.[16]

National income accounts are not the only measure of well-being, and in many ways are misleading because they do not include nonmarket transfers, thus giving a downward bias to figures for less developed states. An alternative way to assess well-being is to investigate physical and social indicators such as life expectancy, infant mortality, and education. In these terms the countries of the Third World have done well, even reducing the absolute gap with the North. A comparison between Latin America and the United States based on several indicators of health, education, and communication found that the gap decreased 18 percent between 1940 and 1950, 21 percent between 1950 and 1960, and 25 percent between 1960 and 1970.[17]

The preceding discussion does not claim that this is the best of all possible worlds for the countries of the South. The basic point is that existing institutional arrangements have not been manifestly detrimental for a substantial number of LDCs; economic growth has not been incompatible with the postwar international regime. Thus, it is not surprising that LDCs have pursued pragmatic policies primarily designed to improve their economic performance in some arenas, while in others they have pushed the NIEO, with its emphasis on radically altering institutional structures. Track A has been followed in many issue areas, among them the effort to regulate the activities of multinational corporations. Here, LDCs have been willing to weigh autonomy and vulnerability against greater economic benefits; they have focused on intertemporal changes in their own economic well-being rather than on cross-national comparisons with wealthier and more powerful areas.

Perhaps no issue has confronted the less developed countries with such cross-cutting pressures as that of regulating multinational corporations (MNCs). Multinationals offer poorer areas many attractions: they provide otherwise unavailable technology; they enjoy access to markets of wealthier areas; and when they first enter a region, they usually commit their own capital. For an LDC the entrance of multinational corporations often seems a great bonanza; it brings resources from outside the country that would not otherwise be available and mobilizes resources (primarily labor) from within the country that would otherwise remain dormant.

Yet this is far from the whole story, particularly after a foreign firm is established and local actors become more familiar with its operations. MNCs are an alien presence associated with the imperial past because of their ties with former colonial countries. Reliance on private capitalism conflicts with socialist ideologies that help to legitimate many regimes in Third World countries. MNCs may engage in unfair transfer pricing, in which they charge their own affiliates prices for imports and exports different from those charged on the world market. They may bring inappropriate technology into less developed countries because they transfer what is available in their home countries rather than adjust to local conditions; the most frequently voiced complaint is that the technology used by MNCs is too capital intensive and thus fails to utilize domestic labor fully. MNCs also may distort local tastes through their control of advertising, pushing products that are inappropriate for the host areas. An egregious example of this was Nestlé's marketing of baby formula in Africa. Given the poor sanitary conditions in the area, bottled formula was far more dangerous to babies than breast milk. Finally, foreign firms may undermine local businesses and weaken the development of indigenous entrepreneurial skills because local firms cannot compete with the multinationals. Although the importance of each of these considerations varies across countries and industries, all are of great concern to political leaders in less developed countries.[18]

How can LDCs respond to the multinationals? The most extreme response, one that assures national autonomy but sacrifices economic benefits, would be to exclude them altogether. China and Burma have in the past moved far in this direction, but it is not the typical pattern. Almost all Third World countries continue to allow MNCs to operate within their borders, and at the same time try to regulate their activities. Tables 4.6 and 4.7 show pattern of MNC investment in the Third World.

There has hardly been a break in relations between MNCs and the Third World. These aggregate figures do, however, mask a change in the kind of investment that is taking place: investment in extractive industries has declined sharply in the 1970s (primarily because of nationalizations) whereas that in manufacturing and banking has risen. For instance, in 1973 U.S. direct investment in extractive industries was 36 percent of all LDC investment, but by 1976 it had dropped to 18 percent; during the same period manufacturing investment had risen from 34 percent to 39 percent, and services (banking and insurance) had risen from 30 percent to 43 percent.[19]

The response of the South to MNCs has varied greatly depending on the

TABLE 4.6

DIRECT INVESTMENT STOCK IN
DEVELOPING COUNTRIES
(billions of U.S. dollars)

	1967	1971	1975
OPEC countries	9.1	11.6	15.6
Tax havens [a]	2.3	3.9	8.9
Other LDCs	21.4	27.8	43.7
Total	32.8	43.3	68.2

SOURCE: United Nations, *Transnational Corpo-rations in World Development, A Re-examination* (New York, 1978), p. 254.

[a] Bahamas, Barbadoes, Bermuda, Cayman Islands, Netherlands Antilles, and Panama.

TABLE 4.7

AVERAGE ANNUAL DIRECT INVESTMENT FLOWS FROM
INDUSTRIALIZED COUNTRIES TO LDCs
(millions of U.S. dollars)

1965–67	1970–72	1973	1974	1975	1976
2245	3883	6711	7084	10494	7593

SOURCE: United Nations, *Transnational Corporations in World Development, A Re-examination* (New York, 1978), p. 249.

economic interests and ideological proclivities of different countries. At the present time states such as Chile, Argentina, Egypt, and Tunisia place virtually no restrictions on the activities of MNCs. Others apply strict regulations. India, for example, imposes a ceiling of 40 percent for the equity participation of foreign corporations in Indian firms; this measure recently led Coca Cola and IBM to leave the country rather than conform with Indian law. Iran and Malaysia limit foreign equity participation to 49 percent. The Andean Common Market, which encompasses a number of Latin American countries, has probably passed the most extensive regulations to control multinationals; these include limits on profit remittances and the transfer of majority ownership to local nationals after fifteen or twenty years. In general, LDCs have tried to gain greater control over capital flows from multinationals, have encouraged the purchase of local products rather than imports, have required some degree of local processing, have regulated the employment of foreign nationals, and have attempted to get foreign enterprises to unbundle their technology.[20]

In sum, in attempting to deal with multinational corporations the less developed countries have adopted complicated and variegated strategies that involve tradeoffs between benefits offered by foreign enterprises and economic and political costs that accompany such investment. This kind of behavior, which it typical of track A, contrasts with the fundamental emphasis on reducing vulnerability and enhancing autonomy manifest in the NIEO. Actors and goals differ in these two forms of LDC strategy. Whereas the regulation of multinational enterprises primarily takes place through national legislation, the effort to implement the NIEO is made at universal international forums. Track A is typified by a multiplicity of public and private actors; track B by a unified southern bloc.

THE RESPONSE OF THE NORTH

The General Pattern

The wealthier industrialized countries have confronted two kinds of demands from the Third World, one oriented toward coping with the international vulnerability and the other with improving economic performance. The first set of demands involves cross-national comparisons, the second intertemporal ones.

The wealthier countries have responded to pressure from the South by trying to cope with track A demands while ignoring track B ones. They have made compromises on a number of specific issues but have not accepted basic alterations in the rules and norms governing the international economic regime proposed by the Third World. They have generally rejected redistribution of voting power in international organizations that would give the South effective control.

In the area of LDC treatment of multinational corporations, the industrialized states have been compelled to accept higher levels of host-country controls. This has been the result, not of a change in sentiment, but of a recognition that there is little that developed countries can do to protect foreign investors. Over time, real power resources have shifted from the multinationals to host-country governments, particularly in raw materials exploitation. When corporations first enter an underdeveloped country, their capital, knowledge of the market, and technical expertise give them a strong bargaining advantage. Host-country nationals eventually develop technical and marketing sophistication of their own, and capital can be internally generated. Moreover, the political resentment felt against large foreign investors makes them tempting targets for political elites seeking to enhance their domestic political support. Since the mid-1960s, the result of these trends has been an epidemic of nationalizations of raw materials industries in developing countries. In oil, copper, bauxite, and other commodities, the government of the home country, not the multinational, now makes the basic economic decisions.[21]

During the 1960s, the United States was resistant to greater assertion of control by host countries. The Hickenlooper Amendment, enacted in 1962, called for the mandatory cutoff of foreign aid to any country that did not provide prompt and adequate compensation to nationalized American investors. The United States tried to use economic pressure to force Peru to reach a satisfactory agreement with a subsidiary of Exxon. By the early 1970s, American policy makers realized they had little leverage. Economic pressure tended to undermine multinational American corporations because it led to nationalist reactions. The United States adopted a more conciliatory attitude toward foreign control or takeover of American investors.[22]

In the area of trade, the industrialized countries have accepted the principle that the LDCs should have preferential treatment. This has been reflected in the establishment of a Generalized System of Preferences (GSP) by the EEC, the United

States, Japan, and other wealthy countries. The GSP eliminates or reduces tariffs on certain manufactured products exported from LDCs while it holds to the full rate on goods from other industrialized nations. Virtually all GSP programs enacted by wealthier countries are hemmed in with restrictions, such as prior quantitative limitations on the value of a product covered and the exclusion of products that might harm domestic producers. Nevertheless, these programs offer substantial advantages to LDC exporters on a wide range of goods. In 1977 the United States granted preferences on goods valued at about $4 billion.[23]

The United States also has moved closer to the position advocated by the Third World in international commodity agreements. During most of the postwar period, the United States opposed such arrangements, claiming they distorted international markets.[24] The only agreement endorsed by the United States for a product exported primarily by LDCs was the International Coffee Agreement, first concluded in 1962. Under pressure from the Third World, however, American policy makers adjusted their position on this issue. In early 1976 the United States signed a new version of the Coffee Agreement and joined the International Tin Agreement. Some progress has been made toward the conclusion of agreements for rubber and tea. Aside from these raw materials, American leaders have also suggested that bauxite and iron ore might be suitable for international control. After holding that commodities should be considered on a case-by-case basis, the United States agreed in June 1977, at the conclusion of the Conference on International Economic Cooperation, that a common fund for commodities should be a "key instrument in attaining the agreed objectives of the (UNCTAD) Integrated Programme for Commodities." [25]

The industrial nations have also made some concessions to the Third World on capital flows. In 1977 and 1978 Canada, Germany, Great Britain, Japan, Sweden, the Netherlands, and the United States agreed to cancel some LDC debts.[26] Moreover, during the mid-1970s the impact of higher oil prices on developing countries was mitigated by an increase in capital flows from the North. Most of these additional credits were from commercial rather than public sources, however, and they carried substantial interest rates. The pattern of capital flows to the LDCs is shown in table 4.8. Although the increase in funds has come primarily from private institutions, there has been some state involvement; the U.S. government has officially guaranteed a substantial proportion of funds lent to LDCs by private banks.[27]

When it comes to sharing decision-making power in international institutions, the United States and other wealthy countries have shown some flexibility. They have been willing to accept some mutual veto systems that give both the North and the South the power to block decisions. For example, in international commodity councils such as the International Coffee Council, a measure cannot be approved unless it has the support of both producing and consuming countries, voting separately. In international financial institutions such as the World Bank, the International Monetary Fund, the Inter-American Development Bank, and the Asian Development Bank, the division of voting power strictly according to financial contribution has eroded over time. Contributions to highly concessionary facilities such as the International Development Agency (IDA) of the World Bank, the Asian Development Fund of the Asian Development Bank, and the Fund for Special Operations of the

TABLE 4.8

NET DISBURSEMENTS FROM INDUSTRIALIZED COUNTRIES
TO LDCs AND MULTILATERAL INSTITUTIONS

	1970	1971	1972	1973	1974	1975	1976	1977
Total flows as a percent of GNP	.73	.76	.73	.75	.78	1.02	.98	.93
Official development assistance as a percent of GNP	.34	.35	.33	.30	.33	.35	.33	.31
Private and other official flows as a percent of GNP	.40	.42	.40	.44	.45	.65	.65	.62

SOURCE: World Bank *Annual Report,* 1976, p. 100; Federal Reserve Bank of Chicago, *International Letter* 19 November 1976; IMF *Survey,* 3 July 1978.

Inter-American Development Bank (which account for about 25 percent of lending from these institutions) are usually not counted in the allocation of voting power. Thus, the United States does not get any additional voting power as a result of its contributions to concessionary facilities; only the IDA has a separate voting arrangement, and even here LDCs have more power than in the World Bank itself. The proportion of votes needed to approve many decisions in the Board of Governors of the IMF has been raised to 85 percent, giving LDCs an effective veto. In 1972 the central forum for the discussion of reform of the international monetary system, the Committee of 10, was expanded to the Committee of 20 to accommodate nine developing countries. The most recently created financial agency, the billion-dollar International Fund for Agricultural Development (IFAD), gives equal voting power to industrialized countries, OPEC members, and the Third World.

These examples of more forthcoming policies do not imply that the United States has accepted all the demands of the Third World. This is hardly the case. The actual level of concessionary, as opposed to commercial, capital transfers is only about half the .7 percent of industrial nation GNP agreed to at the beginning of the Second UN Development Decade in 1970. The United States is in arrears in its contributions to a number of international financial institutions, particularly the International Development Agency, a major source of funds for the poorest countries. The United States has not joined the International Cocoa Agreement, claiming that the organization's mechanism for controlling the market is too cumbersome, and has refused to make voluntary contributions to the international tin buffer stock. It has rejected the Group of 77's plan for an ambitious common fund for commodities, which could initiate its own action rather than simply respond to requests from independent commodity councils. Although LDCs have been given more power in existing financial institutions, they rarely have the voting power to pass their own programs; all they can do is block proposals from the wealthier nations. Power on the Board of Governors of the World Bank is still distributed differently than power in the UN General Assembly.

The Carter Administration

There has been considerable policy continuity within the United States on North-South issues. The Carter administration has elaborated, but not extended in any fundamental way, the initiatives taken during the Ford-Kissinger period. Although the United States accepted a number of Third World demands during the late 1960s and early 1970s (e.g., the allocation of SDRs to LDCs and the generalized system of preferences for exports from developing areas), the tone of American policy was antagonistic until a speech by Henry Kissinger in April 1975. In this address Kissinger indicated greater American sympathy for the plight of the Third World and specifically endorsed a more conciliatory attitude toward international commodity agreements, a position that led to considerable antagonism with William Simon's Treasury Department.

The Carter administration has made no basic shifts. The attitude toward commodity agreements has been more consistently favorable since the rift was healed between State and Treasury. At the CIEC in June 1977 the United States endorsed a common fund for commodities; under Kissinger, the United States indicated it would only discuss such questions on a case-by-case basis. There has been no breakthrough on individual commodity agreements, however, and the North and the South are still far apart on the nature of a common fund. The Carter administration has made a new departure in expressing a willingness to cancel some debts of the poorest LDCs and has indicated it would like to augment its support for international financial institutions, but it is far from certain that the latter initiative will secure congressional approval.

The continuity in American policy under Carter was somewhat surprising; before they entered government, many officials in the new administration had endorsed a forthcoming attitude toward the Third World. Assistant Secretary of the Treasury for International Affairs C. Fred Bergsten had argued that cooperation with the Third World was essential because of the threat of commodity cartels and the need for LDC cooperation in international organizations. One of the shibboleths of the new administration has been the concept of world order, which implies that the Third World (as well as the first and second) must reach some modus vivendi if a stable international regime is to be established.[28] Kissinger had been criticized by policy makers in the Carter administration for excessively concentrating on great power relations. Yet the change in personnel brought about by the 1976 election has not led to any decisive change in policy.

The failure of the United States to arrive at a satisfactory settlement with the South, or even to chart a course that might plausibly lead to such an outcome, is a function of the fundamental differences that divide the rich and the poor. LDC policies designed to enhance economic performance over time can result in many areas of agreement, but this is not true for an NIEO oriented toward mitigating the vulnerability of the South in the international system. The South's desire to enhance its well-being is a nonzero-sum situation in which actors from rich and poor countries can both gain, but the effort to increase autonomy is a zero-sum situation: greater power for the South means less power for the North. The North may compromise on questions of economic well-being, but it will not compromise on those related to autonomy. Track A rolls through a large area of common ground; track B leads to a head-on collision.

THE LAW OF THE SEAS DEBATE

An issue that highlights the clash between North and South inherent in the NIEO program is the Law of the Seas (LOS). Since the early 1970s, the LOS Conference has been trying to conclude an agreement that would establish new international rules for oceans. These talks have covered an extremely complex set of issues including coastal economic zones, passage through straits, scientific exploration, and deep seabed mining. Agreement has been reached on all but the last two points; seabed mining is the most contentious. The conference has deadlocked on the issue of control of mineral nodules containing commercial quantities of nickel, copper, manganese, and cobalt. These potato-sized rocks are found in many places on the ocean floor, but the most promising deposits are in the Pacific Ocean.

The United States and other industrialized countries have made a number of concessions related to seabed mining. They have accepted the principle that the seabed is the common heritage of mankind (previous international practice held that resources not owned by anyone could be claimed by anyone capable of developing them). They have acceded to a mutual veto system in any international seabed authority created. They have accepted twenty-year production limitations on copper and nickel to protect the markets of land-based LDC producers. They have endorsed an arrangement that would share exploitation of the nodules between an international enterprise acting directly for the international community and private multinational corporations. They have expressed willingness to allocate a proportion of the profits from seabed mining to international development needs. These concessions have not moved the Group of 77 to endorse a new treaty for the oceans. The Third World has insisted on effective control over any seabed authority created and a major role for the enterprise in the exploitation of manganese nodules.[29]

The LOS negotiations are an example of a tradeoff between marginal economic transfers on the one hand and more effective control on the other. An effective majority in the international authority would, at least formally, give the Third World a good deal of control over various practices and principles related to the resources of the sea. Failure to reach agreement will leave the Third World countries with nothing. If the conference fails, the industrialized nations will probably go ahead, either on the basis of national legislation or limited international agreements, to create their own regime for the sea.

This LOS impasse is not the only example of Third World willingness to forgo an increase in seabed resources for more effective political control. The seabed regime that would have benefited the Third World most was one that restricted economic zones to a narrow coastal bank, leaving a large proportion of the ocean's fish, oil, and hard mineral wealth under international control. Had the economic zone been limited to twelve miles instead of two hundred, one economist has estimated that the oceans could have generated $4.5 billion in revenues a year for development needs.[30] This is not a trivial sum. Yet the possibility of a narrow coastal economic zone was never seriously entertained by the Group of 77 largely because a number of Latin American states were at the forefront of efforts to extend national control over the oceans.

Another example of the Third World's desire for effective control, rather than simply economic transfers, was the rejection of a 1970 American proposal to create an international trusteeship zone between the 200-meter isobath and the end of the continental margin. This zone would have remained under the sovereignty of the coastal state. Some proportion of the revenue generated in the trusteeship zone would, however, have been given over to international development purposes. As virtually all of the oceans' most valuable resource, petroleum, is within a coastal zone extending 200 miles or to the edge of the continental shelf (the provision of the current draft text), but only 55 to 70 percent is within the 200-meter isobath, acceptance of the American proposal could have meant a significantly larger share of resource transfers to the Third World than will be the case if the present draft treaty is accepted.[31] The American proposal would not have meant any increase in political control for the Third World, however.

The LOS conference offers a clear example of the importance that the Third World attaches to enhancing autonomy. Contrary to most issues associated with the NIEO, the LOS negotiations have offered a clear tradeoff between greater transfers of resources within the present regime and a new regime that would give the states of the Third World effective control as well as more income. The countries of the South have opted for the second path even though it may leave them with no resources from the deep seabed. The LOS negotiations are an instance of track B strategy that virtually precludes compromise between the North and the South.

POWER CAPABILITIES AND THE INTER-NATIONAL ECONOMIC REGIME

The Distribution of Power

Confronted with a large bloc of poor countries interested in changing the exercise of power, not merely in improving their economic well-being, what should the response of the United States be? Should the North try to accommodate track B as well as track A? The answer depends on the answer to an antecedent question: has there been a fundamental shift in the underlying distribution of power in the world system?

A few words of clarification are necessary on the distinction between the actual exercise of power and underlying power capabilities. The underlying power of a state is a reflection of its economic endowments and productive capacity (GNP is one summary indicator) and the relationship between its endowments and those of other countries. These relationships establish the relative opportunity cost of changing an established pattern of behavior. If country A can change its commercial policies toward country B at small cost, but country B would suffer a sharp loss in income, then country A has the underlying capabilities to exercise power over country B. The leaders of country A can demand or suggest that country B change its behavior in a certain way, lest B suffer economic damage because A changes trading relationships.[32]

Aside from power relationships resulting from dyadic ties, underlying capabilities also determine the ability of a state, or group of states, to establish and maintain a given international economic system or regime. Economic transactions will not take place simply because there are economic gains to be had—or at least they will not take place at high levels. To develop the kinds of complicated exchanges that take place in a modern market economy, national or international, some political entity must be capable of establishing and maintaining rules and norms. Some state must be capable of providing a medium of exchange that can offer the liquidity and confidence necessary to sustain a high level of exchange.[33] Once these arrangements are actually established, the political power behind them may become masked; indeed, as habits and institutions develop, the direct exercise of political power becomes less necessary. Nevertheless, underlying power capabilities are critical for the establishment of a new system, and they determine whether that system can be maintained if it comes under attack.

The underlying distribution of power capabilities among states is changing all the time, albeit usually slowly. Some countries enjoy faster rates of growth than others. Technological innovations are made that benefit industries in specific geographic areas. New sources of raw materials are discovered.

The actual pattern of behavior in the world economic system, the rules and norms governing the movement of goods, services, labor, technology, and capital, does not change in such a continuous fashion. Practices tend to be established at particular historical junctures. In the past, these junctures usually have been marked by wars that destroyed existing systems. Most of the rules and norms for the present international economic system were initiated in the period immediately after the Second World War when the United States enjoyed an unprecedented level of underlying power capability. The economies of Europe and Japan were destroyed; much of the Third World was not yet independent.

An international economic regime is likely to be stable when there is congruence between underlying power capabilities and actual practices: when the system operates in a way that benefits those states that have the most power, it is not likely to change. A system is likely to be unstable when there is a lack of congruence between underlying power capabilities and actual practices: when the operations of the system fail to benefit those that have the power to change it.[34]

When there is a growing incongruence between underlying capabilities and existing practice, statesmanship demands that an effort be made to bring them back into some kind of alignment. The true skill of the statesman lies in discerning the underlying distribution of power capabilities and trying to establish a regime congruent with them. The statesman does this through diplomacy. The soldier does it through war. It has generally been the soldier that has brought about adjustment in the system.

With respect to the Third World's demand for a New International Economic Order, a program I have tried to show is an effort to alleviate weakness and vulnerability and not merely a set of reformist measures to increase the transfer of wealth, the question is: has there been a fundamental shift in the underlying power capabilities of the South? If such a shift has not taken place, then acceptance of the Third World's track B demands will create an inherently unstable system. If the Third World does not have the underlying power capabilities to sustain their vision of a new regime, such a regime is bound to come under persistent attack.

Clearly, in one issue area an underlying shift in power capabilities has taken place and there has been a dramatic change in norms and practices: petroleum. Over time, the bargaining position of the host-country governments increased relative to that of the multinational oil companies. The host countries increased their technical skill, knowledge of the market, and capital.

This process occurred in other raw materials industries (the result was a change in the pattern of ownership and control), but in petroleum something else happened. The underlying power capabilities of the host countries changed not only with respect to multinational corporations but also with respect to consumers. OPEC controlled a large proportion of world oil exports, demand for petroleum proved to be inelastic, and at least some of the larger producers (notably Saudi Arabia, Kuwait, Abu Dhabi and Libya) had enough foreign exchange reserves to allow them to take the risk of withholding oil from the market. OPEC has become an effective cartel. The underlying change in power capabilities has been reflected in a change in who determines the price and level of production of oil and the institutions (state-owned corporations versus multinationals) that have formal ownership of petroleum reserves.

If similar changes in underlying power capabilities have taken place in other issue areas, then the United States and the industrial countries should accept the New International Economic Order presented by the Third World. Resistance can lead only to instability and persistent confrontation. But there is no compelling evidence that such a shift in underlying capabilities has taken place. Some observers have argued that OPEC is only the beginning; cartels will be established in a number of other raw materials.[35] But exporters have had only limited success. The bauxite-exporting countries have substantially increased their taxes on multinational corporations. Nevertheless, this seems to be more an example of price gouging than of true cartel behavior: Jamaica and other producing countries have been able to take advantage of monopoly profits not exploited by multinational corporations. In the face of the global recession in the mid-1970s the bauxite-exporting states backed away from some of their demands, such as payment guarantees regardless of production. Furthermore, the International Bauxite Association (IBA) has failed to agree on general production controls, the mark of a true cartel.[36] Phosphorous producers (Morocco accounts for 70 percent of world export) were able to raise prices in the 1970s. And producer organizations have been formed for a wide number of commodities, most recently natural rubber.

Nevertheless, major efforts to control the market by actually limiting production and export have failed. The most important of these failures is CIPEC, the International Council of Copper Exporting Countries. In June 1976, after several years of trying to maintain copper prices in the face of a weak market, Chile, one of CIPEC's major members, opposed continuation of a 15 percent production cutback.[37] In general, commodity price movements have been closely associated with global economic conditions. Using 1970 as an index equal to 100, the prices of nineteen internationally traded industrial materials rose to a peak of about 240 in mid-1974, fell to a trough of about 140 at the end of 1975, and rose to nearly 200 in the spring of 1977.[38] When sharp individual price increases have occurred, as in the case of coffee or cobalt, they have been more the result of external events (a frost in Brazil, civil war in Zaire) than of conscious market manipulation.

I do not mean to argue that the erosion of underlying American power capabilities has not been accompanied by some increase in the ability of the Third World to influence the world economic system. The industrial states, including the United States, do not exercise the same power they had in the recent past. But the power of the Third World is primarily negative; it is the ability to deny, to foul up the existing machinery, rather than to create a stable new order. For example, the large amount of debt being accumulated by a few nonoil industrial nations could lead to a serious banking crisis if defaults become widespread. The failure to generate funds for investment in new sources of raw materials could lead to future shortages. The failure to cultivate export crops, such as cocoa, could lead to declining yields and higher world prices. The inability to secure Third World acceptance at international forums where the one-nation-one-vote principle prevails, such as the LOS conference, could prevent the conclusion of new arrangements for the world system.

The emphasis LDCs have placed on control over international organizations itself reflects the absence of any fundamental alteration in underlying power capabilities. Voting power in such organizations could offer some leverage, some ability to enhance autonomy. If the LDCs possessed resources they could unilaterally manipulate, they would almost certainly have acted on their own, just as the oil-exporting states have done. Absent such resources, they have had to turn to the best option available to them—control over international organizations—even if it is not a very good one. By this option they may raise and stabilize commodity prices, change the rules governing technology transfer, and make capital flows larger and more automatic. Control of international organizations is a substitute, albeit a far from perfect one, for the kind of leverage that usually comes from domestic resources, from a nation's size and productive assets.

This substitute is available in the first place, not because of the policies of LDCs, but because of the power and style of the United States. By and large the current set of international organizations reflects American efforts to create a stable international order after the Second World War. International organization and international law suited the bureaucratic legalistic proclivities of American policy makers.[39] They also helped to veil the raw power resources that were the actual foundation of the regime and thereby contributed to legitimating it. Even though American power has declined, America's style and the organizations it created have persisted. For instance, rather than try to reach agreement with like-minded states on ocean issues, American policy makers accepted a negotiating format that linked complex and logically unrelated problems (e.g., innocent passage through straits and deep seabed mining) and that included all states, not just littoral ones. American leaders have persisted in looking to universal forums to construct new rules and norms for the international system; because they have taken such processes seriously, less developed countries have had the opportunity to use these same settings to enhance their autonomy.

Thus, there has been no fundamental shift in underlying power capabilities. To ameliorate their international vulnerability, weaker states have adopted a strategy that focuses on control over international organizations. Through such control they hope to alter rules and norms governing the international economic regime. The clearest manifestation of this policy is the NIEO. Acceptance by the wealthier states of Third World demands would be a mistake because practices and underlying capabilities would be incongruent. Control over international organizations offers the South as a whole its best chance for enhancing autonomy, but law and organization are weak foundations on which to build a stable international regime.

CONCLUSIONS

Although areas of possible compromise between the United States and particular less developed countries exist, this does not imply that if new policies are successfully implemented (e.g., commodity agreements for copper or iron ore), large numbers of Third World states will accept the existing economic order or challenges similar to those embodied in proposals for a NIEO will cease. Progress on track A does not mean that the Third World will abandon track B. The current international system poses unique problems. Never before have states at such radically different levels of development been so intimately involved with one another. At the beginning of the nineteenth century, differences in per capita income between poor and rich countries were on the ratio of about 1:2; they are now about 1:30. Even with rapid rates of economic growth in the Third World between now and the year 2000, the gap between rich and poor will diminish in relative terms but still grow absolutely.[40]

This differential poses problems for the regimes of the Third World. Growth may enhance material well-being, but political leaders will still find themselves in a vulnerable position, in part because of external developments. Sharp changes in commodity prices, or conditions imposed by foreign creditors, can exacerbate the political instability endemic in virtually all Third World countries. Since most policy makers cannot enhance their autonomy by equalizing underlying power capabilities because the gap with the rich is already too great, they are likely to continue to press for direct changes in power within international organizations. Such changes might help compensate for their inherent weakness. This effort, which is reflected in the NIEO, will continue to generate basically unresolvable conflict between the North and the South. Relations will improve during some periods and deteriorate during others (often as a function of whether universal international meetings in any given period are relevant to NIEO issues), but the international weakness and vulnerability that afflicts almost all LDCs, and their efforts to compensate for this condition, will continue to be a central characteristic of the international system.

NOTES

1. For a discussion of the destabilizing effects of growth, see Samuel P. Huntington, *Political Order in Changing Societies* (New Haven: Yale University Press, 1968), pp. 47–53; and Mancur Olson, Jr., "Rapid Growth as a Destabilizing Force," *Journal of Economic History* 23 (December 1963).
2. *New York Times*, 11 February 1977, p. D1.
3. Ibid., 15 January 1977, p. 33.
4. John W. Sewell, "The United States and World Development, 1977," in *The United States and World Development, Agenda 1977* (Washington, D.C.: Overseas Development Council, 1977), p. 8.
5. G. K. Helleiner, "International Technology Issues: Southern Needs and Northern Responses," in *The New International Economic Order: The North-South Debate*, ed. Jagdish N. Bhagwati (Cambridge, Mass.: MIT Press, 1977), p. 298.
6. Robert L. Rothstein, *The Weak in the World of the Strong: Developing Countries in the International System* (New York: Columbia University Press, 1977), p. 145.
7. Karl P. Sauvant, "Introduction," in *The New International Economic Order: Confrontation or Cooperation between North and South?* ed. Karl P. Sauvant and Hajo Hasenpflug (Boulder, Colo.: Westview Press, 1977), p. 3.
8. Ibid., p. 5; and Roger D. Hansen, "Major U.S. Options on North-South Economic Relations: A Letter to President Carter," in Sewell, *The United States and World Development*, p. 28.
9. Sauvant, "Introduction," p. 6; Catherine B. Gwin, "The Seventh Special Session: Toward a New Phase of Relations Between the Developed and Developing States?" in Sauvant and Hasenpflug, *The New International Economic Order*, pp. 102–3; U.S. Senate, Committee on Finance, *United States International Trade Policy and the Trade Act of 1974*, Committee Print, 94th Cong., 2d sess. (Washington, D.C.: Government Printing Office, 1976), pp. 5–6.
10. Mahbub Ul Haq, *The Poverty Curtain: Choices for the Third World* (New York: Columbia University Press, 1976), pp. 187–97.
11. United Nations General Assembly Res. 3281 (XXIX), art. 10.
12. Haq, *The Poverty Curtain*, pp. 165, 168.
13. For a discussion of issue structuralism, see Robert O. Keohane and Joseph S. Nye, *Power and Interdependence: World Politics in Transition* (Boston: Little, Brown, 1977), pp. 49–54.
14. United Nations, *Transnational Corporations in World Development: A Re-examination*, E/C.10/38 (20 March 1978), p. 205.
15. World Bank *Annual Report*, 1976, pp. 96–97.
16. Robert Paarlberg, "Domesticating Global Management," *Foreign Affairs* 54 (April 1976).
17. James Wilkie, "The Narrowing Social Gap: Latin America and the United States, 1940–1970," *Statistical Abstract of Latin America*, Supplement no. 8 (Los Angeles: UCLA Latin American Center, forthcoming).
18. For a discussion that is generally sympathetic to the multinationals, see Raymond Vernon, *Storm over the Multinationals* (Cambridge, Mass.: Harvard University Press, 1977), chap. 7; for one that is unsympathetic, see Richard J. Barnet and Ronald E. Müller, *Global Reach: The Power of the Multinational Corporations* (New York: Simon and Schuster, 1974), pt. 2.
19. United Nations, *Transnational Corporations*, p. 242.
20. Vernon, *Storm over the Multinationals*, chap. 7; and United Nations, *Transnational Corporations*, pp. 182–87.
21. Raymond Vernon, *Sovereignty at Bay* (New York: Basic Books, 1971), chap. 2.
22. For a discussion, see Stephen D. Krasner, *Defending the National Interest: Raw Materials Investments and American Foreign Policy* (Princeton: Princeton University Press, 1978), chap. 7.

23. IMF, *Survey*. 23 June 1975, pp. 186–89; Office of the Special Trade Representative, press release #263, 1 March 1978.
24. The United States has supported international agreements for grain, a commodity it exports.
25. State Department, news release, April 1976, testimony of Assistant Secretary Jules Katz; IMF, *Survey*. 17 May 1976 and 23 January 1978; *Wall Street Journal*. 14 December 1977, p. 30; UNCTAD, TD/IPC/CF/CONF/L.5.
26. *New York Times*. 13 October 1977, p. 3; 6 March 1978, p. D1.
27. Ibid., 15 November 1976, p. 47.
28. C. Fred Bergsten, "The Threat from the Third World," *Foreign Policy* 11 (Summer 1973). For a less forthcoming view by another administration official, see Richard N. Cooper, "A New International Economic Order for Mutual Gain," *Foreign Policy* 26 (Spring 1977).
29. For a discussion of the Law of the Seas negotiations, see Edward Miles, ed., *Restructuring Ocean Regimes: Implications of the Third United Nations Conference on the Law of the Sea*. which appeared as a special issue of *International Organization* 31 (Spring 1977), esp. the article by Robert L. Friedheim and William J. Durch, "The International Seabed Resources Agency Negotiations and the New International Economic Order."
30. Richard N. Cooper, "The Oceans as a Source of Revenue," in Bhagwati, *The New International Economic Order*.
31. International Economic Studies Institute, *Raw Materials and Foreign Policy* (Washington, D.C.: The Institute, 1976), p. 233.
32. The classic discussion is Albert Hirschman, *National Power and the Structure of Foreign Trade* (Berkeley: University of California Press, 1946). See also Kenneth N. Waltz, "The Myth of Interdependence," in *The International Corporation*. ed. Charles P. Kindleberger (Cambridge, Mass.: MIT Press, 1970); and Klaus Knorr, *The Power of Nations* (New York: Basic Books, 1975).
33. Charles P. Kindleberger, *The Great Depression* (Berkeley: University of California Press, 1973); Fred Hirsch, "Is There a New International Economic Order?" *International Organization* 30 (Summer 1976).
34. For a discussion of congruence, see Robert O. Keohane and Joseph S. Nye, "World Politics and the International Economic System," in *The Future of the International Economic Order: An Agenda for Research*. ed. C. Fred Bergsten (Lexington: Heath, 1973), pp. 133–40.
35. "The Threat from the Third World." For counterarguments, see Stephen Krasner, "Oil Is the Exception," *Foreign Policy* 14 (Spring 1974); Bension Varon and Kenji Takeuchi, "Developing Countries and Non-Fuel Minerals," *Foreign Affairs* 52 (April 1974); and Tony Smith, "Changing Configurations of Power in North-South Relations since 1945," *International Organization* 31 (Winter 1977).
36. *Wall Street Journal*. 14 June 1976, p. 14.
37. Ibid.
38. Federal Reserve Bank of Chicago, *International Letter*. no. 335 (15 July 1977).
39. Stanley Hoffman, *Gulliver's Troubles or the Setting of American Foreign Policy* (New York: McGraw-Hill, 1968), pt. 2; and Henry A. Kissinger, *American Foreign Policy: Three Essays* (New York: Norton, 1969), pp. 29–34.
40. P. N. Rosenstein-Rodan, "The Have's and Have Not's Around the Year 2000," in *Economics and World Order: From the 1970s to the 1990s*. ed. Jagdish N. Bhagwati (New York: Macmillan, 1972). Rosenstein-Rodan estimates that in the year 2000, with rapid growth, the total GNP of Asia, Africa, and Latin America (in 1965 U.S. dollars) will be $2116 billion. The estimate for the GNP of the United States in the year 2000 (in 1965 U.S. dollars) is $2880 billion. The corresponding per capita figures are $427 for the less developed world and $9650 for the United States.

5
CONTROLLING NUCLEAR PROLIFERATION

Michael Nacht

OUTLINING THE PROBLEM

Concern over the spread of nuclear weapons has persisted among governments, international organizations, and individual scholars and strategists since the detonation of the two atomic bombs on Japan in August 1945. For the most part, national governments have maintained a narrow focus. They have concentrated on the feasibility and desirability of acquiring an independent nuclear weapons capability and have considered the probable effect of this acquisition on neighboring states, particularly those nations judged to be potential adversaries. International organizations, seeing the problem in a broader context, have attempted, with limited success, to devise legal and political barriers that would reduce the likelihood of nuclear proliferation. Independent analysts, the least constrained, have sought to explore the fundamental characteristics of the nuclear proliferation process and to speculate about its impact on world order.

These considerable efforts notwithstanding, a global consensus has never developed on either the definition of the term "nuclear proliferation" or the nature and desirability of its consequences. What does it mean to say that a particular nation is a "nuclear weapon state"? That it has stockpiled sufficient amounts of weapons-grade material so that in a short period of time it could assemble one or several nuclear weapons? That it has in its possession an inventory of nuclear weapons? That it has detonated a nuclear weapon? That it has married a stockpile of nuclear weapons to a fleet of delivery vehicles, producing a formidable nuclear force in military terms?

Each definition has its supporters. For many years the internationally accepted norm was that only states that had detonated a nuclear device—the United States, the Soviet Union, Great Britain, France, the People's Republic of China and, most recently, India—were classified as nuclear weapons states. Now it is common to find Israel, which has never exploded a nuclear weapon, cited as a member of the "nuclear club" because of the widespread belief that it has obtained sufficient amounts of weapons-grade material from the operation of its Dimona reactor (and other sources) to have assembled tens and perhaps hundreds of nuclear bombs.

This definitional ambiguity explains in part why great controversy surrounds the appropriate measures to be adopted to curb the spread of nuclear weapons: without an accepted definition of the disease, there can be no widespread support for the cure. The problem is even conceptually messier than definitional ambiguity would suggest, however, for many governments, particularly in the developing world, deny that there is a disease to be cured. A frequent observation within less developed countries is that the stabilizing condition of mutual deterrence is a dominant feature of the Soviet-American relationship because of the enormous nuclear arsenals possessed by both powers. Smaller countries argue that this condition need not be unique to the superpowers and that the spread of nuclear weapons to many other nations will enhance regional stability as mutual deterrence relationships develop between regional rivals. The view that nuclear proliferation would be a source of stability in international politics has been supported by Pierre Gallois, the noted French strategist, and Morton Kaplan, the prominent American political scientist, among others. Arguments to the contrary, emphasizing the highly unstable character of many political systems and the lack of effective instruments of command and control necessary to safeguard nuclear weapons are often dismissed as self-serving attempts to perpetuate a condition of "nuclear haves" and "nuclear have-nots."

The distinction between "horizontal" and "vertical" proliferation is an added complication. The nuclear weapon states, especially the United States and the Soviet Union, have maintained a commitment to modernize their nuclear forces qualitatively and quantitatively—"vertical proliferation"—while attempting to curb the acquisition of nuclear weapons by nonnuclear states—"horizontal proliferation." Indeed, all nuclear weapon states have acted to prevent further proliferation once they themselves had the bomb. Nonnuclear nations have considered this behavior by the nuclear weapon states as highly discriminatory. Some governments of nonnuclear states have argued that until vertical proliferation is halted and reversed, the demands of the nuclear states to curb horizontal proliferation are inherently illegitimate.

The nuclear proliferation problem is compounded by the fact that various motivating forces operate among the nuclear threshold countries, and so it is futile to search for a panacea. In the contemporary period three forces seem to dominate: security, power, and prestige. Some states see their sovereignty threatened and consider nuclear weapons to be the ultimate safeguard of their security. Israel, South Africa, South Korea, Pakistan, and Taiwan fit best in this category. According to the logic attributed to the governments of these states, they each would, in extremis, threaten to use nuclear weapons against their enemies, and by so doing, would deter attacks that would otherwise destroy them. Other states—Brazil and Iran * are prime examples—seem to seek regional hegemony or perhaps even superpower status and consider the possession of nuclear weapons as part of the political-military arsenal needed to achieve their goal. A third class of states—Libya and Uganda are often cited—ostensibly wish to acquire nuclear weapons primarily for the prestige thought to accrue to leaders of nuclear nations and the consequent enhanced role this would permit them to play in international affairs. In addition, powerful domestic forces could act on some governments in the direction of nuclear weapons acquisition, such as the "technological imperative" of demonstrating an ability to enter the nuclear age, the desire of a powerful military establishment to flex its muscles, or the perceived electoral benefits to a leader in domestic difficulty.

It is extremely demanding for the United States, or any nation, to fashion a coherent and effective nuclear nonproliferation policy, not only for the reasons cited here, but also because of the tradeoffs inherent with other policies. An aggressive nuclear nonproliferation policy runs the risk of exacerbating relations with allies who see nuclear energy-related aspects of the policy as a threat to the well-being of their domestic nuclear industries. Conventional arms transfers are often sought by nuclear threshold nations as the "price" of remaining nonnuclear. How high a price in conventional arms should be paid to support the nonproliferation policy? What of the domestic repercussions of promoting a policy perceived as threatening to the U.S. nuclear industry at precisely the same time as the nation is attempting to find alternatives to OPEC (Organization of Petroleum Exporting Countries) oil supplies? What of the risks run in alienating developing nations who also seek to become independent of OPEC but find themselves confronted by a U.S. nonproliferation policy that would severely curtail the growth of their indigenous nuclear industries?

President Carter has chosen to confront these issues directly. Consistent with his background as engineer and businessman, Carter as President has emphasized a willingness to grapple with technological issues and has demonstrated a tendency to impose management structures on complex problems. To distance his administration's foreign policy from those of its immediate predecessors—a familiar course of action in American presidential politics—he has permitted balance-of-power diplomacy to give way to global architecture, at the same time eschewing amoral pragmatism in favor of high moral principles.

Nowhere has this emphasis on technology, management, globalism, and morality converged more dramatically than in his administration's efforts to prevent the spread of nuclear weapons to nonnuclear states. Starting with the 1976 presidential campaign and continuing through his first term, Carter has made a point of placing nuclear proliferation near the top of his foreign policy concerns. In the process he has developed a policy that is deep in technical detail; some would say so deep that it has lost sight of the fundamentally political nature of the nuclear proliferation problem. Carter's policy is geared to institution building and the establishment of an

---

* The domestic instability that arose in Iran in the latter months of 1978 strongly suggests, however, that the country's foreign policy goals and economic development plans will be severely curtailed in the years ahead.

international consensus so that the spread of nuclear weapons can be managed even if it cannot be stopped. In promoting this approach the President and members of his administration have stressed repeatedly that the policy deserves support precisely because it addresses a global problem, one that poses a fundamental challenge to the existing international order, a challenge governments have a moral responsibility to meet head-on. To understand how and why the Carter policy took the shape it did requires an appreciation of the historical development of the issue, as well as a rudimentary understanding of pertinent technological considerations.

THE HISTORICAL CONTEXT

In June 1946, less than a year after the United States dropped two atomic bombs on Japan, Bernard Baruch went before the United Nations and offered a choice "between the quick and the dead." Baruch was the U.S. representative to the UN Atomic Energy Commission, a body established to ensure that atomic energy was used only for peaceful purposes. The Baruch Plan called for the creation of an international organization to control all nuclear-related activities: ownership of nuclear materials, management of nuclear fuel cycle operations, inspection of nuclear facilities, and determination of violations and sanctions against violators. The Soviet Union unfortunately construed the plan as a means by which the United States could retain its nuclear weapons monopoly. Because this ran counter to the established Soviet aim of acquiring its own nuclear arsenal, the plan was rejected.

Over the next several years the United States worked vigorously to develop its nuclear stockpile, including thermonuclear weapons, while protecting the "secret" of the bomb. In 1953, however, with the Soviet Union and Great Britain now also nuclear weapon states, President Eisenhower launched the "Atoms for Peace" program, which was designed to enlist American cooperation in the promotion of civilian nuclear power programs abroad. With American nuclear technology developing rapidly, this initiative also had enormous economic implications for the fledgling American nuclear energy industry. This was an important international development not only because it stimulated interest in, and acquisition of, nuclear energy facilities by many nations but also because it held the promise of moving states into the "nuclear age." At the time this was viewed with virtual universality as a highly prestigious status, in domestic and international terms, and a most coveted objective. Indeed, it is important to emphasize that in the mid- to late 1950s several European nations, particularly the Federal Republic of Germany, enthusiastically embraced civilian nuclear power for its own benefits and also as compensation for its unilateral decision to forgo the acquisition of nuclear weapons.

The spread of nuclear weapons was not halted, however. France, for a variety of political, cultural, and security reasons, became the fourth member of the nuclear club in 1958, and the People's Republic of China was widely rumored to be about to follow suit. Substantial alarm arose that the world was on the verge of rapid nuclear weapons proliferation. Among the most noted cries of alarm came from C. P. Snow in 1960:

We know with the certainty of statistical truth that if enough of these weapons are made—by enough different states—some of them are going to blow up. Through accident, madness, or folly—but the motives do not matter. What does matter is the nature of the statistical fact. . . . [This] is not a risk but a certainty. . . . The arms race between the US and the USSR not only continues but accelerates. Other countries join in. Within at the most six years China and several other states will have a stock of nuclear bombs. Within at most ten years some of these bombs are going off.[1]

Snow was correct about China, which detonated its first nuclear device in 1964; otherwise, he was in error. Over the next ten years no other nation detonated a nuclear device and not a single weapon was used in anger.

In retrospect several reasons may explain the pessimism of the 1960s.[2] Alliance structures provided sufficiently credible security guarantees to dissuade some states from acquiring nuclear weapons while constraining the behavior of others who retained an interest in developing a nuclear option. Economic, technological, and manpower deficiencies were more formidable for some nuclear threshold states to overcome than was generally appreciated by those who were sounding the proliferation alarm. A few states that neither suffered from these deficiencies nor were constrained by alliance relationships could not identify a security need the acquisition of nuclear weapons would meet. Finally, and of singular importance, the amount of weapons-grade material available for the fabrication of nuclear weapons by nonnuclear states was not large.

Nonetheless, in response to the building concern over the problem, the United States took the lead in establishing further international barriers to the spread of nuclear weapons. Working in concert with the Soviet Union, the United States formulated the Nuclear Nonproliferation Treaty (NPT), which was signed by several nations in 1968 and entered into force in 1970. The NPT prohibited nuclear weapon states party to the treaty from assisting any nonnuclear state in acquiring nuclear weapons; it also prohibited nonnuclear states who were treaty members from taking any actions, alone or with others, to acquire such devices. In return, nonnuclear states who joined the treaty were promised full cooperation and assistance from the nuclear weapon states in developing their capabilities to utilize nuclear energy for peaceful purposes. Great Britain joined the United States and the Soviet Union in ratifying the treaty; France and the People's Republic of China, the other two nuclear powers, failed to participate. During the next few years membership in the NPT climbed rapidly to almost one hundred states, but there were several key omissions: Israel, Egypt, India, Pakistan, Argentina, Brazil, and South Africa, to name a few. The treaty remained controversial. Many developing nations criticized it as inherently discriminatory, perpetuating a "have" and "have not" relationship between the few nuclear weapon states and the rest of the world. Moreover, many Third World nations charged that the United States and the Soviet Union violated the treaty because they continued to add to their stockpile of nuclear weapons and delivery vehicles despite their obligations under the treaty to proceed immediately toward the goal of nuclear disarmament.

TECHNOLOGICAL CONSIDERATIONS

It has long been recognized that nations have, at least in theory, several options when considering how to obtain sufficient amounts of material to fabricate nuclear weapons. Most often, they construct facilities designed specifically to produce this material. A second option would be to obtain the material from facilities used for nuclear research. A third option is to acquire the material as a by-product of a nuclear power program. A fourth option is to obtain the material directly from other sources—through purchase, theft, or as a gift. Much of the nuclear proliferation problem centers on the composition of this material and how to close off avenues to its availability.

A nuclear weapon requires material in which nuclear fission can be induced by low-energy neutrons—so-called fissile material. The reader is probably familiar with the notion that of the substances found in nature, uranium is such a material. In fact, it is the isotope uranium-235 that has this property; and natural uranium is composed of only .7 percent U-235, the balance being U-238 and a small amount of U-234, both of which are nonfissile isotopes. To be useful in weapons the composition of the natural uranium must be changed to include a far larger percentage of U-235, normally in excess of 90 percent, although some weapons have been detonated with only about 20 percent U-235. This change in composition is termed uranium "enrichment." Because enrichment involves the physical separation of isotopes that differ in mass by tiny amounts, the process is technologically demanding and exceedingly costly.[3]

Nuclear power reactors, particularly the light water reactor developed in the United States that is likely to remain the dominant reactor design for the next twenty years, require uranium enriched to 3 percent U-235, so-called low-enriched uranium, in contrast to the "highly" enriched uranium required for nuclear weapons. Uranium enrichment technology is therefore crucial to both nuclear energy and nuclear weapons programs. From an energy perspective the enrichment task is characterized as the "front end" of the nuclear fuel cycle because it is a requirement for feeding the nuclear reactor with appropriate fuel.

Besides the process of uranium enrichment, fissile material can be produced by converting nonfissile isotopes to fissile isotopes through exposure to neutrons in the nuclear reactors themselves. As it happens, light water reactors using low-enriched uranium produce weapons-grade material as a matter of course by converting the nonfissile isotope U-238 to the fissile isotope plutonium-239, a substance not found in nature and produced only in this fashion. Similar results occur for reactors of somewhat different designs. (Reactors operating on the so-called thorium cycle use abundant quantities of thorium-232, which in turn is converted into the fissile isotope U-233.)

The plutonium produced in light water reactors is combined with other elements in the reactor's spent fuel rods and must be separated from these elements to be useful. This separation process is termed "reprocessing," a chemical technique that is technologically straightforward and economically much less demanding than enrichment. Because the separated plutonium is fissile material, it can be "recycled" into the front end of the fuel cycle as reactor fuel in lieu of low-enriched uranium.

But the separated plutonium can also be used to produce weapons directly. Hence reprocessing, the so-called "back end" of the fuel cycle, is vital both to nuclear energy and to nuclear weapons programs.

Partly as a result of technological innovation and partly stemming from the desire to become independent of uncertain uranium supplies for reactor fuel, the nuclear industry has taken major strides to develop nuclear power plants based on different reactor designs than the light water reactor—so-called breeder reactors. Although breeders are still in advanced engineering development and have yet to be proved technologically or economically feasible, their significant characteristic is that they produce more plutonium than they consume. Nuclear industry officials and energy planners see a world of breeder reactors as a world of nuclear energy self-sufficiency in which nations would be free of concern about the predictability of their uranium fuel supplies.[1] Because plutonium is an especially toxic and difficult-to-handle substance, nuclear industry personnel are particularly anxious to become involved in reprocessing as a way of familiarizing themselves with the handling of plutonium so as to be better prepared for the breeder reactor and the so-called plutonium economy expected to materialize by the 1990s. Nevertheless, a typical 1000-megawatt nuclear power plant at present produces approximately 250 kilograms of plutonium, and a nuclear weapon requires no more than 5 to 10 kilograms to be effective. Thus the notion of large numbers of reprocessing plants producing enormous quantities of plutonium that are then stored at, or transported from, reactor sites is a frightening prospect for those concerned about nuclear weapons proliferation.

CATALYTIC EVENTS AND THE FORD POLICY

Although specialists often felt that nuclear energy programs and nuclear non-proliferation were on a collision course, the broader consensus held that the NPT was sufficiently effective to contain the problem. Indeed, the International Atomic Energy Agency (IAEA) in Vienna, which was originally established in the 1950s as a result of the Atoms for Peace program, was the UN agency specifically charged with the dual responsibilities of seeing that the use of nuclear energy for peaceful purposes was facilitated, particularly to the developing countries, and at the same time that nuclear safeguards programs were implemented to ensure that nonnuclear states were in compliance with the treaty. This consensus was severely shaken by three events that took place between 1973 and 1975. The 1973 oil embargo by the Organization of Petroleum Exporting Countries underscored the vulnerability of nations dependent on external sources for energy supplies and stimulated a vigorous quest for energy independence by states the world over. Because of the widely held view that nuclear energy was the only technologically feasible alternative to fossil fuels for the balance of the century, the demand for nationally owned facilities capable of using nuclear energy for electric-power generation increased markedly. (The nature of the demand for nuclear power reactors, as of mid-1978, is summarized in table 5.1. Note the enormity of the U.S. nuclear energy program in comparison to all other states.) This demand was not limited to the reactors but included enrichment and reprocessing facilities as well, the so-called sensitive technologies of greatest concern to individuals focusing on the weapons proliferation problem.

In May 1974 the Indian government announced the explosion of a nuclear device termed a "peaceful nuclear explosion," or PNE. India, which is not a party to the

TABLE 5.1
SURVEY OF NUCLEAR POWER REACTORS

Country	Operating	Under Construction	Ordered	Total
Argentina	1	1	0	2
Austria	0	1	0	1
Belgium	3	4	0	7
Brazil	0	3	0	3
Bulgaria	2	2	0	4
Canada	9	11	4	24
Czechoslovakia	1	4	0	5
Egypt	0	0	1	1
Finland	1	3	0	4
France	14	22	12	48
German Democratic Republic	3	4	0	7
German Federal Republic	12	8	8	28
Hungary	0	4	0	4
India	3	5	0	8
Iran *	0	2	0	2
Italy	4	1	4	9
Japan	16	10	1	27
South Korea	0	3	2	5
Luxembourg	0	0	1	1
Mexico	0	2	0	2
Netherlands	2	0	0	2
Pakistan	1	0	0	1
Philippines	0	1	1	2
Poland	0	0	1	1
Rumania	0	0	1	1
South Africa	0	0	2	2
Spain	4	7	5	16
Sweden	8	2	2	12
Switzerland	3	2	1	6
Taiwan	1	5	0	6
USSR	23	12	0	35
United Kingdom	33	6	0	39
United States	68	86	47	201
Yugoslavia	0	1	0	1
34 countries	212	212	93	519

SOURCE: *Nuclear News,* August 1978, pp. 67–85.
* Note that since the publication of this issue of *Nuclear News* the domestic turmoil in Iran has resulted in the cancellation of two reactors on order, leaving only two that are under construction.

NPT, had obtained sufficient amounts of weapons-grade material to fabricate a nuclear weapon from a research reactor purchased from Canada in violation of the terms of the sale, thus demonstrating the feasibility of this path to nuclear weapons acquisition. The use of the term PNE, moreover, suggested that nations had found a different rationale for legitimizing the development of devices that are in fact indistinguishable in their effects from nuclear weapons.[5]

Then, in June 1975, after several months of detailed negotiations, the Federal Republic of Germany announced an agreement with Brazil to supply by the early 1990s a complete nuclear fuel cycle including six to eight reactors, a reprocessing plant, and an enrichment facility, in return for Brazilian payment of $8 billion. The precedential nature of this transaction, the fact that few high-level U.S. officials had been informed prior to the agreement of its magnitude and significance, and the concern that Brazil in particular was "buying in" to a nuclear weapons option led to considerable rethinking in Washington about the effectiveness of U.S. nuclear non-proliferation policy.[6]

Indeed, some months before the announcement of the German-Brazilian deal, the Ford administration had moved to convene a meeting of the major nuclear supplier nations to determine whether they could reach common agreement on export policies so that the spread of sensitive nuclear technologies, particularly to the developing nations, could be severely curtailed.[7] This group, which began meeting secretly in London in the fall of 1974 and came to be known as the London Suppliers' Club, was unable to affect the outcome of the German decision to export sensitive technologies to Brazil.

The Ford administration was reluctant to pressure one of America's closest allies to roll back a deal that was of great economic significance to the German nuclear industry; high-level officials in Washington also did not want to strain the political relationship between the two nations over an issue not directly related to NATO security concerns. Nonetheless, considerable criticism among nongovernment groups in the United States forced the Ford administration to review the deal with high-level German officials. In the 1976 presidential campaign Jimmy Carter made this a public issue and called on all nations to adopt a voluntary moratorium on the national sale or purchase of sensitive nuclear technologies. Carter also argued the need to delay commercial reprocessing in the United States until the demand, economics, and safety of the technology had been clearly demonstrated. President Ford, in response to the Carter initiatives and as a result of increased pressure from Congress, ordered a major review of the problem within the U.S. government. Just one week before the presidential election, Mr. Ford announced his decision to suspend transfers of reprocessing and enrichment technologies for an initial period of three years, as well as to defer commercial reprocessing in the United States until its implications were more fully understood.

THE CARTER INITIATIVES

Because of Carter's keen personal interest in the subject, and as a consequence of his determination to follow through on his campaign promises, immediate attention was focused on the nuclear proliferation issue by members of the new Carter administration, and attempts were made to fashion a comprehensive approach to the problem as quickly as possible. As a result, in April 1977 President Carter announced a seven-point program as the foundation of his administration's policy on nuclear power and the relationship of nuclear energy technology to the proliferation of nuclear weapons. The main points of the program were these:

An indefinite deferral of the commercial reprocessing and recycling of the plutonium produced in U.S. nuclear programs, and the decision not to use federal funds or federal government influence to complete the plant at Barnwell, South Carolina, as a reprocessing facility.

A restructuring of the U.S. breeder reactor program to give greater priority to alternative breeder designs, and deferral of the date when breeder reactors will be put into commercial use.

A redirection of funding of U.S. nuclear research and development programs to accelerate research into alternative nuclear fuel cycles that do not involve direct access to materials usable in nuclear weapons.

An increase in U.S. production capacity for enriched uranium to provide adequate and timely supply of nuclear fuels for domestic and foreign needs.

A decision to propose the necessary legislative steps to permit the United States to offer nuclear fuel supply contracts and guarantee the delivery of nuclear fuel to other countries.

Continuation of the decision to embargo the export of equipment or technology that would permit uranium enrichment and chemical reprocessing.

Endorsement of continuing discussions with supplying and recipient countries on a variety of international approaches and frameworks that would permit nations to achieve their energy objectives while reducing the spread of nuclear explosive capability. These would include exploring the establishment of an international fuel cycle evaluation (INFCE) program aimed at developing alternative nuclear fuel cycles as well as a variety of international and U.S. measures to assure access to nuclear fuel supplies and spent fuel storage for nations sharing common nonproliferation objectives.

The Carter policy as initially put forth was similar to the efforts proposed by President Ford just before the 1976 presidential election. The Carter policy reaffirmed the importance of light water reactors as the bedrock of nuclear power programs for at least the next ten years; it reaffirmed the significance of the IAEA as the organization responsible both for providing technical assistance to nonnuclear weapon states that are party to the NPT and for implementing a system of safeguards to verify that the parties to the treaty are in compliance with it; and it reaffirmed a moratorium on reprocessing in the United States.

There were a number of significant differences between the Carter and Ford proposals, however. The Carter policy provided for an indefinite deferral on reprocessing in the United States rather than a three-year deferral. Moreover, regarding breeder reactors, there was a noticeable decline in enthusiasm from Ford to Carter. While the Carter policy did not call for the cessation of research on breeders (indeed, the administration has requested and maintained a breeder research and development effort in excess of $400 million, which exceeds that of any other nation) or for other nations to forsake their breeder programs, it clearly places development of breeder reactors within the context of minimizing the spread of nuclear weapons rather than letting their designs be governed strictly by energy and economic considerations.

The INFCE, a new initiative by President Carter, was designed to provide information to prospective recipients of nuclear energy facilities on alternative fuel cycles, fuel availability, improved methods for the operation of light water reactors, and other data that would be useful in the recipient's decision-making processes. It was intended to build on the work of the London Suppliers' Club with the advantage that it would be established in such a manner as to avoid being seen as a "rich man's club," the principal deficiency of the Suppliers' Club.

The Carter administration also moved to restructure American nuclear export policy. Carter wanted nuclear export agreements to be carried out through negotiations that emphasize several criteria: a comprehensive safeguards program for all nuclear facilities (termed "full scope" safeguards), the penalty of an automatic cutoff in fuel supply and in technical assistance by the United States should the nonnuclear state detonate a peaceful nuclear explosion, the right of the United States to rule on the permissibility of the transfer of nuclear technologies from the recipient state to third parties, and the right of the United States to rule on the permissibility of the recipient state acquiring or developing an indigenous reprocessing capability. The new policy also instituted a procedural change whereby the President could override an export decision made by the Nuclear Regulatory Commission (NRC), justified on the basis of whether the NRC's decision was consistent with U.S. nonproliferation policy. This change altered the somewhat ad hoc nature that had previously characterized U.S. nuclear export decision making. And by emphasizing international fuel assurances and considering as an interim solution the establishment of an international spent-fuel depository, the Carter administration sought to increase the sensitivity of American policy to the concerns of the recipient nations.

There seemed to be, in addition, a considerable change in emphasis from Ford to Carter in how the United States would deal with its allies on nuclear matters. Despite the adoption of a visible stance in opposition to nuclear proliferation by Ford, during his administration the United States, to paraphrase one high-level official, would not sacrifice alliance relationships on the altar of nuclear nonproliferation. The Ford administration felt particularly concerned about applying too much pressure on France, the Federal Republic of Germany, and Japan with respect to their domestic nuclear energy programs and export policies, for fear of creating considerable and unnecessary tension in America's relations with these states. The Carter administration has been willing to incur such risks. As President Carter stated in an address on foreign policy at the University of Notre Dame in May 1977, "we are attempting, even at the risk of some friction with our friends, to reduce the danger of nuclear proliferation." Although initial negativism toward Carter, particularly by the West Germans, was temporarily overcome at a London summit meeting in May 1977, it is apparent from the general trends during the first few years of the Carter administration that strains in alliance relationships are likely to be a significant and perhaps even crippling by-product of American initiatives to stem the spread of nuclear weapons.[8]

INITIAL REACTIONS

Initial reactions to the Carter policy were less than enthusiastic both at home and abroad.[9] In the United States, the Carter administration found it extraordinarily difficult to gain widespread congressional support for this program. Although some of this difficulty is attributable to the general cyclical nature of executive-legislative relations, in which Carter found himself in office at a time of congressional reassertion of its legislative authority, and some of the problems were no doubt incurred because of ineptitude on the part of administration officials in dealing with the Congress, several roadblocks were policy-specific. Key congressmen were skeptical that the United States was capable of providing sufficient incentives to dissuade nonnuclear states from seeking to acquire a full nuclear fuel cycle. There was some disquietude about the overzealous approach of the administration's export policy, the "overloading" of important bilateral relationships, and the fear of nationalist reactions that might well produce exactly the opposite effect from what was intended. There was concern that the policy was not well understood and that it had been poorly explained. And, perhaps most important, many influential members of Congress were friends of the U.S. nuclear industry and saw the Carter policy as placing crippling restrictions on America's nuclear technological development and on the ability of the industry to be competitive in sales abroad.

Initial reactions outside the United States were generally unsympathetic. Only a few days after Carter's April statement, a major conference on the transfer of nuclear technology was convened in Persepolis, sponsored by the Iranian government in cooperation with the American Nuclear Society, the European Nuclear Society, and the Japan Atomic Energy Society. Although the Carter administration downplayed the significance of the conference because of the vested interests of the sponsors, who would naturally be opposed to the Carter policy, the conference attracted nearly five hundred participants from forty-one countries and expressed concerns of many governments, particularly those of the developing nations. These concerns and criticisms can be summarized as follows:

Reprocessing of fuel and recycling of fissile isotopes are essential to the operation of any breeder reactor, and the Carter suggestions that both reprocessing and recycling are unacceptable are viewed with alarm because they strike at the heart of future nuclear power programs.

Unlike the United States, many other nations cannot afford to defer use of the breeder.

The near-monopoly of uranium enrichment services by the United States is viewed by the developing nations with alarm rather than with equanimity.

The Carter policy is considered particularly threatening because it indicates that the United States plans to interfere directly in the implementation of enrichment, reprocessing, and recycling technologies in the importing nations. The importing nations desire to determine their own courses of implementation, dependent only on the rate of growth of the energy needs of the various countries, the world supply of uranium, and the policies of the uranium exporting nations.

The Carter statement is regarded by some as an abrogation of Article IV of the

NPT, which stipulates that "parties to the Treaty in a position to do so shall cooperate . . . to the further development of the applications of nuclear energy for peaceful purposes, especially in the territories of non-nuclear weapon states party to the Treaty, with due consideration for the needs of the developing areas of the world."

Restrictions on reprocessing of spent fuel are further criticized on the grounds that they will not be an effective deterrent to nuclear weapons proliferation—the price is too high for a marginally effective safeguard—and, further, that many nations are legally committed to reprocessing as the only feasible route to the safe and ultimate disposal of radioactive wastes.

The portion of the Carter policy citing the exploration of alternative breeder designs and fuel cycles is viewed with skepticism. "There are no fuel cycles which are consistent with breeding and which provide an effective technological barrier to proliferation."

The Carter policy will strengthen the political position of antinuclear power groups in the United States and other supplier nations, thereby increasing the uncertainty that commitments made by supplier nations to recipient nations can be met.

Although some progress has been made in implementing the policy, many of the arguments raised at Persepolis have continued to plague the Carter administration. These arguments have been raised in subsequent meetings of the London Suppliers' Club; in bilateral negotiations between the United States and the Federal Republic of Germany over the future of the German-Brazilian deal and German policies concerning reprocessing and the disposal of nuclear wastes; in bilateral negotiations with Japan on the future status of the Japanese reprocessing facility at Tokai; in discussions with the British on their plans to establish a reprocessing facility at Windscale; in negotiations with the French over their export policy, the future of their breeder program, and the status of the multinational facility operated by EURATOM; and in a host of other bilateral and multilateral discussions and negotiations. In short, the Carter policy was and is judged essentially to be an ineffective attempt to provide a technical fix to a largely political problem. It has been characterized as a policy of "denial" rather than one of cooperation and has exacerbated relations with America's closest allies. It has created fears in the developing world that the United States, as a leading industrial nation with great influence on the actions taken in many other countries, will undermine the ability of nations to adopt sound alternatives for their own energy supplies. The policy is considered highly discriminatory vis-à-vis the developing world and in contravention to international agreements.

PROMISE AND PERFORMANCE

Despite these initial and persistent criticisms of the Carter administration's approach to the nuclear nonproliferation problem, major efforts have been made to implement the policy and with some tangible if limited success. Although the international environment is a dynamic one, making any summary and assessment of the Carter policy subject to rapid obsolescence, basic trends can nonetheless be identified with some confidence. The policy has evolved into one having six major components, and these provide a useful framework for analysis.

Safeguards

A major element of the Carter policy has been to require full-scope safeguards in all new nuclear export agreements. This requirement has now the force of law with the passage of the Nuclear Non-Proliferation Act of 1978 in January, which has made legally binding on the U.S. government many of the provisions outlined in Carter's statement of April 1977. The law requires:

> As a condition of continued United States export of source material, special nuclear material, production or utilization facilities, and any sensitive nuclear technology to nonnuclear-weapon states, no such export shall be made unless IAEA safeguards are maintained with respect to all peaceful nuclear activities in, under the jurisdiction of, or carried out under the control of such state at the time of the export.

The administration's position is that safeguards are not merely a technical fix to monitor nuclear materials, provide physical security, and sound the alarm if material has been diverted. Safeguards are also considered to be a deterrent to the diversion of such material; if safeguards are effective, they will provide timely warning to the international community should violations actually be committed.

Such safeguards are already accepted by more than one hundred nations party to the NPT and by three states that are party to the treaty of Tlatelolco (the Latin American Nuclear Free Zone Treaty). It seems highly unlikely, however, that this standard will be universally supported. Among the supplier states, France has continued to oppose the establishment of this requirement, although it has shown greater sensitivity to the nonproliferation problem by withdrawing its offer to sell a reprocessing plant to Pakistan. French resistance on the safeguards issue, however, has meant that the Suppliers' Club has been forced to settle for a set of guidelines, published in January 1978, that fails to endorse this provision explicitly and instead limits the requirement to transferred and by-product materials. This may not turn out to be of long-term significance if an international body following from the INFCE replaces the Suppliers' Club as the major unit formulating nuclear export policy.

In the volatile Middle East, the Egyptian position is that full-scope safeguards are acceptable as long as Israel is subjected to the same criteria. Given the high probability of the existence of an Israeli nuclear weapons program and the concomitant resistance of Israeli officials to any safeguards program applied to their Dimona reactor facility, however, the prospects for implementing this policy are bleak. In India, the administration was pleasantly surprised by Prime Minister Desai's vow not to authorize the explosion of a nuclear device during his tenure in office. Nevertheless, the Indian government remains subject to the charge by its domestic political opponents that to submit to full-scope safeguards is to become a party to the discriminatory NPT system established by the United States and the Soviet Union. India and the United States seem to be on a collision course because the United States is unwilling to provide fuel and services for India's Tarapur reactor unless these safeguards are accepted. In Latin America, despite the signature by the United States to Additional Protocol I [10] of the treaty of Tlatelolco in May 1977, the treaty is in reality not in force. Brazil, for example, refuses to be bound by the treaty until several matters are resolved; Argentina has failed to ratify the treaty; and Cuba remains outside the treaty. Given tensions in the region, it seems that several states will refuse to place themselves in a position of being legally bound to accept full-scope safeguards.*

Restraints on Sensitive Technology Transfers

The administration pushed for adoption by the Suppliers' Club of restraint in the transfer of sensitive facilities, particularly reprocessing plants, and hoped that this restraint would be applied retroactively as well. The policy was not terribly success-ful in the early stages, however. The attempt to apply restraint retroactively to the transfer of nuclear technology by the Federal Republic of Germany to Brazil clearly failed,† and it remains highly uncertain how effective it will be in influencing French export policy on possible future deals with Iran and Iraq. Indeed, both the German and French positions on future agreements are ambiguous. Although Chancellor Helmut Schmidt, in a joint press conference with French President Valéry Giscard d'Estaing in mid-June 1977, announced that West Germany would not export nu-clear reprocessing technology beyond existing contracts, he noted that this decision was valid "for the time being." Moreover, difficult negotiations between the United States and Japan over the future status of the Japanese reprocessing facility at Tokai led to an agreement that permits operation of the facility "for an initial period of two years." This period terminates in the fall of 1979, and the Japanese now feel they are committed to breeder programs for their energy future and must reprocess in order to learn how to handle plutonium fuels. The Japanese do not expect to export such facilities, but as a party to the NPT with no nuclear weapons aspirations, they believe the United States should make an exception in their case and not object to Japanese reprocessing. The same is true of the British position, which endorses the commitment both to breeders and to the establishment of a reprocessing plant at Windscale. The Japanese-American agreement, the British decision to proceed with Windscale, and a Japanese arrangement to have much of its spent fuel reprocessed at Windscale and at La Hague, France, are viewed in Washington as setbacks for the administration in its attempts to prevent the spread of operational reprocessing facilities. Moreover, the American declaratory policy of restraint seems to be hurt-ing American nuclear sales abroad because the United States is viewed increasingly as an unreliable exporter of nuclear facilities.[11]

Incentives

A third component of the Carter policy has been to help other countries with their spent-fuel storage problems if they cooperate with the administration's ap-proach to nuclear energy. A multimillion-dollar program has been approved by the

---

* See chapter 10 for additional considerations relevant to Latin American concerns.

† The German-Brazilian deal is at present in an uncertain state, however, because of questions raised by Brazilian experts about its economic feasibility and desirability.

President to help less developed countries investigate nonnuclear alternatives; the 1978 Non-Proliferation Act calls for the creation of an international nuclear fuel authority (INFA) to provide fuel services and appropriate quantities of fuel to ensure fuel supply on reasonable terms to recipient nations; and the United States, in anticipation of providing low-enriched uranium to countries that forgo the full fuel cycle, is moving ahead with a new enrichment plant at Portsmouth, Ohio. The problem with these steps is that the United States is widely viewed as an untrustworthy supplier of nuclear fuel; there is strong resistance in the United States toward providing storage for the spent fuel of other nations' nuclear programs; and many of the other incentives are linked to conditions that a variety of supplier and recipient nations simply find unacceptable.

Consensus Building

This element centers on the INFCE exercise. Consensus building is an attempt to initiate a dialogue between supplier states and recipients; it clearly reflects the view that the London Suppliers' Club is at best an interim measure that will always be vulnerable to the charge of being a secret cartel. INFCE began with an organizing conference in Washington in October 1977 attended by forty nations and representatives of the IAEA, the Commission of the European Communities, the International Energy Agency, and the Nuclear Energy Agency. From Washington's perspective, INFCE should have three main goals: to investigate technologies that are proliferation-resistant, such as reprocessing techniques that do not produce pure plutonium; to create multinational institutions that can effectively manage the spread of nuclear energy technology and materials without increasing the prospect of nuclear weapons proliferation; and to buy time to produce increased amounts of enriched uranium that would be made available to recipient nations in exchange for their forgoing the development or acquisition of reprocessing facilities. The participants at the organizing conference established eight working groups—resource availability, enrichment, assurance of supply, reprocessing, fast breeders, spent-fuel management, waste disposal, fuel cycle concepts—each to be co-chaired by two or three members of INFCE. The full results from INFCE are to be reported in early 1980, but major technical fixes to the basic problems are unlikely to emerge from the exercise. It seems doubtful, therefore, whether this approach can overcome the suspicions felt by some nations and the sense of discrimination felt by others to build the sort of consensus Washington is hoping to achieve. Indeed, a major challenge facing the administration over the next several years is to reconcile the results of INFCE with the large number of bilateral agreements the United States is currently renegotiating. These renegotiations are to bring U.S. nuclear arrangements completed under the Atoms for Peace program in line with contemporary U.S. nonproliferation policy.

Domestic Policy and Legislation

From the outset the Carter policy has been based on the assumption that the United States must set the proper example in terms of its own domestic nuclear energy program if it is to have any hope of persuading other states to follow suit. In a short period of time the administration has announced the indefinite deferral of reprocessing for recycling and the intention to broaden the U.S. breeder program to investigate more proliferation-resistant breeder fuel cycles; has seen passed by the Congress the Non-Proliferation Act of 1978, which legalizes many of the administration's policy approaches; and has initiated a major technical review designed to assist in framing future U.S. domestic nuclear developments and support American international nonproliferation policy objectives.[12]

These initiatives have been carried out amid a storm of criticism from the nuclear industry and segments of the Congress allied with the industry. There is little doubt that the administration's stance was interpreted by some as a direct threat to the profitability, indeed the viability, of the U.S. nuclear industry. Despite the passage of the Non-Proliferation Act, the intense battle on Capitol Hill over the details and direction of domestic energy legislation continues. The administration has apparently won the battle to prevent the plant at Barnwell, South Carolina, from being developed as a reprocessing facility, but the debate over the status of the Clinch River Breeder Reactor has not been resolved. General reaction outside the United States, however, seems to be that America's energy needs and resources are sui generis and that U.S. decisions on domestic reprocessing and breeders are barely, if at all, relevant to the energy needs of other nations. Thus, while the policy may have been worse off if these steps had not been taken (owing to the criticism that would have been forthcoming to the effect that the United States does not practice what it preaches), many nations do not care for what the United States is preaching, independent of what it practices.

Measures to Affect Motivations

The final element of the Carter policy involves a series of attempts to affect the principal motivations states have for acquiring nuclear weapons—security interests and matters of status and prestige. Strengthening and promoting security guarantees, increasing the membership of the NPT, and converting the treaty of Tlatelolco into an effective international legal instrument are some of the bilateral and multilateral efforts endorsed by the United States to weaken security-related incentives for acquiring nuclear weapons. Completing a comprehensive test-ban treaty and an effective SALT II treaty are desired as a means of deemphasizing the apparent usefulness of nuclear weapons as tools of foreign and military policy.

There are significant problems with many of these approaches, however. In the post-Vietnam period the United States is having sufficient difficulty retaining its existing relationships with Western Europe and Japan; the prospect for acquiring new security partners seems exceedingly remote. Existing treaty arrangements with South Korea are under pressure—because of the Carter commitment to withdraw American ground troops from the Korean peninsula within five years; the treaty with Taiwan has been terminated as a consequence of the normalization of Sino-American relations. Strains have developed with Israel over Middle East policy and with Brazil as a consequence of the American position on both the German-Brazilian deal and on human rights. Attempts by the Carter administration to endorse vociferously the movement for majority rule in southern Africa has, whatever its positive effects in Black Africa, seriously strained relations between Washington and Pretoria. Consequently, American attempts to diminish the nuclear weapons appetites of several nuclear threshold states have met considerable resistance, in part because the foreign policy of the Carter administration outside the nuclear non-proliferation area has tended to be at cross purposes with this objective.*

The NPT remains intact and may well add Indonesia, Portugal, and Sri Lanka in the near future; but there has been no movement on the part of India, Brazil, France, China, or Israel to join. While the Carter policy intends to permit the transfer of nuclear technologies for peaceful purposes, it is nonetheless accused of being in violation of Article IV of the NPT. Over time, this may have the effect of weakening rather than strengthening the international legitimacy of the treaty. As noted, the treaty of Tlatelolco continues to face formidable obstacles before entering into force, and the same is true of both a comprehensive test-ban treaty and SALT II. The comprehensive test ban suffers from Soviet insistence that France and China participate, which is virtually out of the question, as well as from a desire to keep open the option to conduct peaceful nuclear explosions. Problems of verification and stockpile reliability are also important stumbling blocks to an accord. Moreover, great uncertainty remains as to the final terms of a SALT II treaty, whether the U.S. Senate would ratify it, and whether, even if ratified, it would have any significant effect on the prospects of nuclear proliferation in third countries.

CONCLUSION

The Carter administration has taken on an enormous task in trying to construct a comprehensive approach to the nuclear nonproliferation problem. It involves an incredible web of energy- and security-related issues. And it is proceeding from several premises that are far from universally shared. The view that nuclear prolifer-ation will be a destabilizing force in world politics, widely held in the United States, is rejected by key individuals whose nations are caught in the grip of intense regional conflicts. As stated at the outset, there is no global consensus on either the threat posed by nuclear proliferation or the steps that should be taken to cope with it. In several nations—France, the Federal Republic of Germany, Great Britain, and Japan—suspicion lingers that American energy-related strategies are motivated not only by a concern over the spread of nuclear weapons but also by a desire to perpetuate American dominance of the nuclear export market. The policy cuts at the heart of numerous domestic energy programs and generated great resentment initially because of the confrontational attitude taken by American officials in trying to persuade nations to support it. Although this approach has been replaced by one that stresses cooperation rather than confrontation, the scars remain. The tech-nical character of the policy, the lack of coordination between it and other foreign

---

* The reader is referred to chapter 2 for an analysis of these policies within the framework of "liberal internationalism" and for more detailed discussions of American policy toward China, Latin America, and Africa in chapters 8, 10, and 11.

policy efforts of the administration, and the general confusion that has been the trademark of the Carter Presidency in its first term have all served to damage the effectiveness of the substantive initiatives.

It should be emphasized that the Carter administration chose to influence the policy of nations where it thought it had the greatest leverage: control over the transfer of nuclear energy technologies that could be used to serve nuclear weapons programs. While continuing to pursue political-military strategies to retard nuclear proliferation, there is little doubt that the heavy technological emphasis of the nonproliferation policy will remain, despite the inconsistencies and tradeoffs it will inevitably engender. In executing the policy four long-term problems must be confronted: the assurance of uranium supplies, international arrangements for enrichment and reprocessing, spent-fuel storage and management, and nuclear-waste disposal. The ability of the administration to control the transfer of sensitive nuclear technologies will rest heavily on its success in forging international agreements to resolve these problems.

Ultimately the success of the policy must be judged on the extent to which it retards nuclear proliferation. The Carter approach has certainly heightened concern about the problem on a global scale. If the administration can adhere to its basic strategy and not fall back in the face of a variety of political and economic pressures, there is a chance—at least some chance—that the spread of nuclear weapons can be discouraged. If, as a result, the use of a nuclear weapon in anger is forestalled, it will have all been worth it. Alternatively, if the administration ultimately reverses itself, as it has on other key issues, if it continues to practice a foreign policy dominated by irritation and retreat, the likelihood of nuclear proliferation will increase appreciably.

At the outset of the Carter administration it seemed reasonable to state that in the event of a major shock to the international system—for example, the sale of a nuclear weapon, the use of a nuclear weapon in anger, or the widespread availability of advanced technologies (e.g., laser isotope separation) permitting off-the-shelf bombs to be acquired by many states in a short period of time—the United States would move aggressively to halt further nuclear proliferation, using coercive and military measures when necessary. Sanctions against new nuclear states could be expected to dominate the American reaction.[13] These nasty alternatives still seem plausible in the event the nonproliferation policy does not succeed.

NOTES

1. Sir Charles P. Snow, "The Moral Unneutrality of Science" (address to the American Association for the Advancement of Science, New York City, 27 December 1960).
2. I have reviewed these issues previously, at somewhat greater length, in "Arms and Politics: Old Issues, New Perceptions" in *Arms Control and Technological Innovation*, ed. David Carlton and Carlo Scherf (London: Croom Helm, 1977), pp. 161–69.
3. At present the dominant means of uranium enrichment is by gaseous diffusion. Gaseous-diffusion plants require enormous amounts of electricity with capital costs presently in excess of $1 billion per plant. Other techniques include gas centrifuge, now reaching commercial feasibility, as well as aerodynamic and laser techniques, which are still under research. These techniques are described in detail in Ted Greenwood et al., *Nuclear Power and Nuclear Proliferation* (London: IISS, 1976).

4. Natural uranium is available from only a few states. A study by the Organization for Economic Cooperation and Development projects that by 1985 production of natural uranium will be distributed as follows: U.S., 46 percent; South Africa, 16 percent; Canada, 13 percent; Niger, 7 percent; Australia, 6 percent; France, 4 percent; and all others, 8 percent. See *Nuclear Power: Issues and Choices. A Report of the Nuclear Energy Policy Study Group* (Cambridge, Mass.: Ballinger, 1977). This report, known as the Ford-MITRE Study, was a key document in shaping the Carter nonproliferation policy. It had its origins in a 1975 meeting at Aspen, Colorado, in which the impact of nuclear energy programs on nuclear proliferation was addressed in detail. See Michael Nacht, *Nuclear Energy and Nuclear Weapons* (Aspen: Aspen Institute for Humanistic Studies, 1976). From this meeting emerged a commitment by the Ford Foundation to support a study of nuclear energy policy. The study's findings on nonproliferation served as the basis for the Carter approach to the problem, and several authors of the report subsequently joined the administration.

5. PNEs are ostensibly useful to redirect rivers and for certain geological activities. India and the Soviet Union have retained an interest in such applications, but the United States has determined that there are no suitable uses for PNEs in the continental United States because of technical deficiencies compared to chemical explosives, as well as high social and economic costs.

6. If seen to completion, the deal would provide Brazil in fifteen years with an autonomous nuclear industry including reprocessing plants and an enrichment facility utilizing the Becker nozzle aerodynamic process developed in West Germany and ostensibly tested in South Africa. Although the West German government insisted that severe safeguards would be attached to the operation of these facilities, there was great concern in Washington that the deal would not only promote Brazilian economic development through the establishment of a sophisticated and far-reaching nuclear energy program but also that (1) it would accelerate greatly Brazil's ability to become a nuclear weapons state; (2) this development would stimulate Argentina, which has a long-established nuclear energy research community, to face the choice of being subject to possible intimidation by its rival or acquiring nuclear weapons of its own; and (3) it might possibly provide the Federal Republic of Germany with an ability to obtain nuclear weapons not produced on its own territory.

7. Originally the Club was composed of seven nations: Canada, West Germany, France, Japan, the Soviet Union, Great Britain, and the United States. It was expanded to fifteen in 1976 with the addition of Belgium, Czechoslovakia, East Germany, Italy, the Netherlands, Poland, Sweden, and Switzerland.

8. Some observers have long felt that as a consequence of these strains the Soviet Union would be the principal beneficiary of an aggressive American nuclear nonproliferation policy.

9. I have reviewed these initial reactions previously in "Global Trends in Nuclear Proliferation," in *Insecurity!: The Spread of Weapons in the Indian and Pacific Oceans,* ed. Robert O'Neill (Canberra, Australia: Australian National University Press, 1978), pp. 6–12.

10. This protocol in effect prohibits nuclear weapon states from retaining nuclear weapons in Latin American territories for which they are internationally responsible. It is not applicable to nuclear weapons in transit.

11. It has been reported, for example, that Spain may turn to Germany for nuclear facilities because of the uncertainty surrounding American commitments. See "U.S. Policy Delays Hurt Nuclear Sales," *Baltimore Sun,* 12 November 1977, p. 1.

12. This review has been termed the Non-Proliferation Alternative Systems Assessment Program (NASAP). For a sketch of its charter see John M. Deutch, *Statement on the Office of Energy Research FY 1979 Authorization,* Subcommittee on Fossil and Nuclear Energy Research, Development and Demonstration of the House Committee on Science and Technology, 8 February 1978, pp. 1–18.

13. See Michael Nacht, "The United States in a World of Nuclear Powers," *Annals of the American Academy of Political and Social Science,* March 1977, pp. 162–74.

6

HUMAN RIGHTS

To Act or
Not to Act?

Ernst B. Haas

*The Uganda Commission on Human Rights "will be charged with explaining
Uganda's position abroad and advising the Life President about the human rights
situation in the country."*

Radio Uganda as reported in
San Francisco Chronicle, 4 April 1978

*"I think that our concept of human rights is preserved in Poland much better than in
some other European nations with which I am familiar. There is a substantial
degree of freedom of the press . . . : a substantial degree of freedom of religion,
demonstrated by the fact that approximately 90 percent of the Polish people profess
faith in Christ; and an open relationship between Poland and our country and
Poland and Western European countries in trade, technology, cultural exchange,
tourism."*

President Carter in Warsaw, 30 December 1977

*"The cause of human rights is one that is shared by the leaders of both our coun-
tries. . . . The Shah has been so helpful to me as a new leader. There is no other
leader on earth who is as close a friend and ally. . . ."*

President Carter in Teheran, 31 December 1977

A murdering tyrant, a practitioner of Marxism-Leninism, an authoritarian monarch,
and an elected constitutional official all claim to share the faith in human rights. Is

*I acknowledge with gratitude the research assistance of Beverly Crawford and Jack Donnelly and the
supporting services of the Institute of International Studies, University of California, Berkeley. I also
appreciate deeply the help and advice received from Carl G. Rosberg, Robert O. Keohane, and Kenneth
Oye.*

the millennium truly at hand? Is a human right hidden in every aspiration and every policy?

The contemporary debate about human rights supports such an impression. It is said that human rights are more important than property rights. Without especially favorable treatment, women, nonwhites, and homosexuals are unable to enjoy their human rights. Forbidding the Eskimos to hunt whales is a violation of their human rights. The right to clean air and water is widely proclaimed. Palestinians have the right to their own homeland, as do Namibians, Puerto Ricans, and Basques. Workers have the right to organize and bargain collectively, free from intimidation and coercion. Multinational corporations have the right to mine the deep ocean, and governments have the right to forbid their doing so. The press has the right to gather all the news, and governments have the right to correct distortion and bias in reporting and publishing. Peoples and nations have the right to manage their natural resources, but humanity has the right to an adequate diet, basic health care, and decent housing. Some stockholders claim they have the right to realize a fair profit from their investment in enterprises'that produce the goods and services to which everybody has a right. The debate suggests that everything involves somebody's human right—and that, as often as not, the rights of individuals, corporations, nations, peoples, and governments defy reconciliation.

This is the setting in which the United States has declared that improvement in the enjoyment of human rights by citizens of *other countries* is a core objective of American foreign policy. In the post-Vietnam era of disillusionment with the ability of the United States to promote its way of life by force of arms and by the exercise of economic power, it is understandable that a new administration would seek a moral focus for a foreign policy that eschews the methods of its predecessor. It is understandable that it would seek to hold out to the American public and other nations an attractive symbol to legitimate foreign policy, free from the stigma of duplicity, domination, and defeat. This chapter proposes that it is impossible, unwise, and immoral to adopt a policy of seeking energetically and consistently to promote human rights abroad. Moreover, it demonstrates that the Carter administration was slow to realize during its first two years in office that the brave words of the politics of symbolism must yield to the more guarded acts of a policy of juggling a variety of national interests. Nevertheless, the chapter also shows when and where a more circumspect and modest policy of promoting certain human rights can be practiced fruitfully.

The Carter administration began its tenure with words that smacked of another crusade for democracy; it has settled down to a modulated tune in which the symbol of universal human rights is evoked more sparingly. Repression in China is never mentioned; support of Russian dissidents is sporadic; Sadat is a great and progressive statesman, as is the shah and the king of Saudi Arabia. No mention is made of tyranny in Zaire, and American influence is wielded in the Philippines and South Korea with more restraint than the words of Andrew Young might have suggested in 1977. We are moving uneasily between the symbolism of loud words and the reality of cautious deeds. The Carter administration has had to relearn the rules of international politics. What has been relearned?

The global meaning of "human rights" is murky and self-contradictory. No one can promote human rights without specifying *which* rights and *whose* rights are at stake. The great majority of governments is not interested in human rights protection. The means available to the United States for promoting human rights are not very effective. The role of a human rights policy within the overall conception of the national interest is far from clear. A consistent and energetic policy in the human rights field makes impossible the attainment of other, often more important, objectives of American policy. Once this was realized, something had to give. The human rights policy was the first victim of the realization that politics is the art of the possible, the practice of carefully considering the tradeoffs between competing but equally legitimate objectives.

THE GLOBAL CONTEXT

Which Rights Are "Human" Rights?

Rights come in various hues and stripes, but some rights are more basic than others. Some are preconditions for the later realization of more specific and substantive benefits; some, though substantive, seem essential to protect the most precious aspects of individual freedom and autonomy.

A conception of "basic" rights cannot be easily separated from the cultural and historical context in which it arose. American conceptions of basic rights, as expressed in the Bill of Rights, may or may not be universal; freedom may be conceived in different terms in other cultures. Since the promotion of human rights through foreign policy implies the persuasion (or coercion) of people not part of the American tradition to share our national vision, we must first determine to what extent the American conception of basic human rights is accepted elsewhere, if only in principle.

Demands, riots, and fasts do not constitute evidence of wide acceptance. The officially declared will of governments may. The most widely cited document expressive of a universal governmental will is the Universal Declaration of Human Rights, approved unanimously by the UN General Assembly in 1948. The legal significance of the declaration remains in doubt, but not its symbolic value.[1] The rights affirmed in the declaration are basic. They include the universal entitlement to rights "without distinctions of any kind" with respect to origin or status; the right to "life, liberty, and the security of person"; freedom from slavery and servitude, torture and degrading treatment, equality before the law, and the equal protection of the law; freedom from arbitrary arrest, detention, and exile; the right to a fair trial under the presumption of innocence; the right to travel freely, to be free from arbitrary interference with privacy, to seek and be granted asylum from persecution, to enjoy a nationality, to marry and found a family, to own property and not be arbitrarily deprived of it; the right to freedom of thought, conscience, and religion, and the expression and communication of ideas through any medium. Everyone also has a right to free assembly and association but cannot be compelled to join an association. People have the right to take part in government through freely chosen representatives and to equal access to the public service. "The will of the people shall be the basis of the authority of government," to be expressed in regular and genuine elections based on universal suffrage and the secret ballot. Everybody has the right to social security, to work, to the free choice of employment, to equal pay for equal work, and to form and join trade unions. All have the right to rest and leisure and to a standard of living "adequate for the health and well-being of himself and of his family," to education free of charge at the primary level and subject to the choice of the parents. Everyone also "has the right freely to participate in the cultural life of the community" and "to the protection of the moral and material interests resulting from any scientific, literary, or artistic production of which he is the author," in a "social and international order in which the rights and freedoms set forth in this Declaration can be fully realized."

This affirmation is expressed in much greater substantive and procedural detail in some twenty international conventions that are legally binding for those who ratify them. The UN adopted conventions defining and outlawing the crime of genocide (1948), defining certain political rights of women (1952), and eliminating all forms of racial discrimination (1965). UNESCO, in 1962, adopted a text outlawing discrimination in education. The International Labor Organization (ILO), among the almost one hundred fifty conventions it has adopted since 1919, included eight that define and protect basic rights: the right of agricultural workers to organize (1921), restrictions on the use of forced labor (1930), freedom of association and the right to organize (1948), collective bargaining (1949), abolition of forced labor (1957), elimination of discrimination in employment (1958), aims and standards of social policy (1962), and protection of workers' representatives (1971).

The rights defined in these conventions are comprehensive and sweeping, but they are designed to protect specific groups, such as women, students, workers, or racial minorities. The UN also adopted two major conventions that cover everybody: the covenants on civil and political and on economic, social, and cultural rights (1966). The civil and political rights include all those defined in the Universal Declaration, except for the right to property, on which the negotiators could not agree. In addition, the covenant also includes the rights of detained persons to be treated with humanity, prohibits propaganda for war and incitement to hatred, and creates rights for children and minorities. The economic and social covenant restates the same rights listed in the declaration, but instead of affirming the existence of the right as inhering in the individual, this text speaks of states "recognizing" and "taking steps to insure" the rights in question. Civil and political rights are declared to *exist;* economic and social rights are to be *promoted* by state action.[2]

The world thus seems to have a code that leaves out very little. If legal texts, UN declarations, and efforts by committed human rights activists define a consensus, there would seem to be little left to be done by the Carter administration. The chilling reports published annually by Amnesty International tell us there is a huge gap between affirmation and performance.[3] Hence we must determine which governments and which kinds of regimes practice what they preach. We must inquire whether the various rights, so eloquently and sweepingly declared, are mutually supportive or whether they, in fact, contradict one another. And we have to ask ourselves whether the declared international consensus is consistent with the American heritage of protecting and promoting basic rights.

Who Is to Enjoy Which Rights?

The American tradition in its Jeffersonian version affirms the rights of the *individual*. The individual human being is thought to be endowed with certain inalienable rights, which are to be enjoyed freely: neither the government nor other individuals are to be permitted to infringe on them. The American tradition seeks to protect the individual *against* his own government. The law is to be understood as *prohibiting the government* from infringing these rights. The underlying logic of this stance does not prevent the realization of positive benefits (in the form of new legal rights) for the individual; it creates the political framework for the freedom to demand new rights. Hence the American tradition has stressed freedom of assembly, association, speech, advocacy, the press, religion, research, and the right to vote in regular elections by means of the secret ballot. As a result of the exercise of these rights, clean air, maternity benefits, a minimum wage, and a decent dwelling can also become rights. But their realization is to be the consequence of the free play of unfettered social and political forces, *not* to be stipulated by constitutional definition or proclaimed to be inalienable and universal.

This conception of human rights is also contained in the international texts, along with some additional conceptions that may not fit the American tradition quite so well. The covenant on Civil and Political Rights, the convention Eliminating Racial Discrimination, and the ILO conventions on Freedom of Association, Collective Bargaining, Forced Labor, and Discrimination in Employment define basic rights protecting individuals *against* their governments. But in addition they contain obligations that compel government to act positively *for* the enjoyment of such rights. They contain provisions obligating governments to protect their citizens against infringement of rights. Often this calls for positive steps to bring these rights into existence in the first place. Under the Civil and Political Rights covenant, governments must prohibit warlike propaganda; they must also create rights for children and minorities. Under the Racial Discrimination convention they must act to prohibit speech and writing favoring doctrines of racial superiority and create machinery for the positive elimination of discrimination. These obligations imply infringements of rights enjoyed earlier by others.

Promoting the rights of individuals by way of positive government action is the hallmark of the UN covenant on Economic, Social and Cultural Rights. That text creates rights to work, fair wages, equal pay for equal work, to strike, to enjoy social security payments (including special assistance for mothers and children), to an adequate standard of living, to the highest attainable standard of physical and mental health, to education, and to participate in cultural life and enjoy the benefits of scientific progress. To say that individuals have a "right" to these things implies that specific quantitative targets be established and that government programs be launched and funded to implement them. To define and promote such rights—if undertaken seriously—means that the Scandinavian welfare state is to be the model for the world. That this is beyond the economic and administrative capacity of most states is obvious. It is less obvious that the very principle of basic human rights is redefined in this approach: instead of only equipping individuals to be free to fight for such benefits, the covenant commits governments to achieve these benefits on behalf of individuals. The rights cease being a discretionary matter; their affirmation shapes positive public policy. President Carter, in the first blush of enthusiastic espousal of the international human rights treaties, took no notice of these contradictions in legal concepts between Americans and others.

So far we have spoken only of the rights of individuals. The international texts are also concerned with the rights of *collectivities*. These, under the American tradition, may be protected as a matter of policy; but American jurisprudence has shied away from asserting them as a matter of constitutional entitlement. American law does single out for protection racial minorities, women, children, the handicapped, and workers. The benefits of the law are conferred on *individuals* who happen to be members of one of these classes of people, however, *not* on the entire class. A woman claiming to be the victim of discrimination in employment cannot file a complaint by virtue of being woman, but only by showing that she, as an individual who happens to be a woman, was denied employment *because* she is a woman. The controversy over racial quotas in the United States is made more acute by the bias against conferring rights on classes of people, as opposed to individuals.

Things are different in the international consensus implied by the UN texts. Rights *are* asserted for specific collectivities. The beneficiaries of the convention Outlawing All Forms of Racial Discrimination are racial and ethnic *groups* and institutions as well as persons belonging to such groups. The UN Commission on Human Rights applies the same principle to national liberation *movements*. Article 1 of the covenants singles out *peoples* as the collectivity to be endowed with rights:

> All peoples have the right of self-determination. By virtue of the right they freely determine their political status and freely pursue their economic, social and cultural development.
> All peoples may, for their own ends, freely dispose of their natural wealth and resources without prejudice to any obligations arising out of international economic cooperation, based upon the principle of mutual benefit, and international law. In no case may a people be deprived of its own means of subsistence.

States must refrain from interfering with the rights of such collectivities. Much more important, states are obligat d to act on behalf of their rights through positive administrative and judicial measures: integrate schools, prohibit the dissemination of ideas advocating racial inequality, support national liberation movements financially and otherwise, provide free education, and protect the family. Many of these positive duties apply not only to relations within states. In some instances foreign governments assume these obligations with respect to collectivites in other countries.

Matters get still more complex when we turn to the main collectivity, the state itself. International law, like municipal law, gives the state certain rights and duties. Whether these can be considered human rights is not clear. Insofar as the state is empowered to coerce the conduct of individuals, it seems to be the opposite of human rights; but when the collective right of society as embedded in the state has the effect of protecting some individuals against others, the rights of states may be proxies for human rights. In municipal law the contradiction between individual and collective rights is resolved by the judiciary; the line separating the two realms is fixed by the ebb and flow of judicial discretion. As there is no international equivalent for such judicial power, given the restricted jurisdiction of the International Court of Justice, no authoritative and consensual manner of balancing the rights of states against individual or group rights is available. We face a situation in which states *claim* to act in defense of human rights, and in making the claim they absorb the right by exercising it. The results may be ambiguous with respect to the actual enjoyment of rights by individuals and collectivities. Paradoxical as it may sound to vest the state with "human" rights, in practice it often looks that way. I shall illustrate the exercise of this claim by summarizing the current debate on the "right" of the state to *suppress and protect* terrorists, the press, and civil insurgents and regulate the economy.

The main UN texts guarantee the right to life and to political asylum. Airplane hijackers and other political terrorists claim these rights for themselves and deny them to others in the name of national self-determination and national liberation. The governments of Algeria, Libya, and South Yemen agree with the terrorists. Other governments do not, asserting instead the right of the state to use force—sometimes through armed intervention abroad—to protect itself against such acts, and thereby protect its individual citizens. Their views have been enshrined in three international conventions dealing with the return of hijacked aircraft, passengers, and crew; the extradition and prosecution of hijackers; and aircraft saboteurs. Yet, others continue to defend their policies or harboring terrorist groups by citing their obligation to support national liberation movements.[4]

An international agreement on the press has been delayed for years because the freedom to gather news cannot be reconciled with the right of the state to assure the "accuracy" of the news, a euphemism for the legitimacy of censorship. Efforts have been made to enlarge the scope of the humanitarian law of war by including civil wars and providing a bill of rights for noncombatants. Such a step would limit the ability to the state to use indiscriminate force in putting down rebellions. It is therefore not surprising that states with a history of such events have been cool toward this type of human right. On the other hand, the same states have fervently espoused the enlargement of the law of war to provide protection for combatants in "national liberation struggles"; obviously, there are "good" and "bad" civil wars, depending on whose ox is being gored.

Economic inequality is now a prominent theme in the discussion of human rights, and it too poses the issue of who enjoys the rights: the individual or the state. The UN Charter on the Economic Rights and Duties of States clearly opts for the state:

> *Every State has the sovereign and inalienable right to choose its economic system as well as its political, social and cultural systems in accordance with the will of its people, without outside interference, coercion or threat in any form whatsoever.* (Art. 1)

> *Every State has and shall freely exercise full permanent sovereignty, including possession, use and disposal over all its wealth, natural resources and economic activities.* (Art. 2, Par. 1)

The Charter, even though not legally binding, in fact corresponds to the actual practices and hopeful professions of a large number of countries.[5] It asserts some sweeping new rights, primarily for the benefit of the poorer countries: to regulate foreign investments, to control multinational corporations, to nationalize property, to be free from economic and trade discrimination practiced for political reasons, and to a status of full equality in international decision making. Conversely, it defines new duties imposed on the industrialized countries: to carry on their foreign economic relations so as to facilitate "equitable development"; to mobilize their resources and to cooperate internationally for the same purpose; to support "structural changes" in poor countries; to facilitate technological and scientific progress and the transfer of such knowledge to poor countries; to achieve complete disarmament; and to eliminate colonialism, racism, and apartheid. Again, the population as a whole, as institutionalized through the state, is the beneficiary.

The tension between the state as beneficiary and the individual is explicitly resolved in favor of the former in general international law. The UN and OAS charters clearly establish a right on the part of states to be free from the threat of intervention and external subversion; states have a duty not to intervene, not to attempt the overthrow of another government. And the meaning of the term "intervention" is constantly being stretched to include the use of financial and commercial pressure even if this involves the routine operations of multinational corporations. To be free from such threats implies the right to do something about them, to take repressive measures possibly violating the rights of individuals. Was Bolivia violating the human rights of some of its citizens in using torture and illegal imprisonment in fighting against subversion originating in Cuba? Or was the state simply exercising its right to protect itself against intervention? Is there a single standard applying to all states, or does a special set of rights favor only the socialist states? In any event, many international texts and a large number of national declarations made in the negotiation of these treaties make clear that the state reserves the right to defend "public order," "national security," or "the general welfare"; it reserves the right to protect the collectivity against challenge from within, which is seen as violating *national* constitutional or legal precepts.

The Lack of Global Consensus

In the welter of rights being asserted and claimed, we cannot be sure who accepts them. Nor can we be certain that verbal or even legal acceptance implies a willingness to take them seriously. Because the rights of individuals, groups, peoples, nations, and states are frequently in conflict, we have no way of being certain whether the individual really occupies center stage. In the past, the American attachment to human rights did not have to face this conundrum because of its firm espousal of *individual* human rights. The intellectual and legal history of liberalism was suspicious of group, national, or state rights. If we espouse the right of some collectivity to life, property, free speech, or education—and if the members of that collectivity disagree with one another over the enjoyment of these rights—we effectively work for rights *of* somebody *against* somebody else. Thus the logic of promoting collective rights contradicts the notion of protecting the rights of individuals. In the American tradition this difficulty was avoided by defining human rights in such terms as to perfect the ground rules of democratic competition. If everyone enjoys the rights of free speech, assembly, the secret vote, equality before the law, and a fair trial, and if no religion is established as authoritative, then individuals in exercising these rights will create political procedures under which the most popular view will win, until supplanted by another view that is equally popular.

Hence, in the traditional American view, priority should be given to the promotion of political and civil rights of individuals. The price one pays for this preference is the postponement of the enactment of the kinds of specific economic, social, and cultural rights found in the UN covenant. Those who exercise their political and civil rights may refuse, compromise, or delay the enactment of legislation protecting the right to social security, employment, decent housing, or full health. If, on the other hand, one wishes to give priority to economic and social rights that may themselves be controversial in any given country, the state must curtail the free exercise of political and civil rights. To do otherwise would leave the door open to democratically enacted legislation impairing economic and social rights. No wonder that contemporary socialist states have stressed economic and social over political and civil rights. The contradiction between the two sets of rights is not cleared up in the existing corpus of international agreements. The logic of collective rights violates the notion of individual rights, but the logic stressing individual political rights puts in jeopardy the enjoyment of some economic rights, while the commitment to certain collective economic and social rights makes impossible the full enjoyment of all individual political rights.

Moreover, the state still has the right to protect itself. This doctrine is much more strongly developed in law and in practice outside the United States, though American administrators and courts invoke it too. The states that most strongly espouse collective rights of an economic and social character also insist on the right of the state to punish individuals opposed to the prevailing emphasis. Traditional American policy cannot easily make its peace with this view, and denunciations of the Soviet Union challenge it frequently. Yet the conundrum remains: which sets of rights and beneficiaries are to be promoted? In pointing to the Bill of Rights as a model for the world, President Carter had to confront the actual heterogeneity of the world in which we live.

Our Heterogeneous World: Who Accepts Which Rights?

The administration seeks to protect and promote human rights in a world of rich and poor, socialist and capitalist, Hindu, Muslim, Christian, and atheist, pluralist and totalitarian. The drastic toning-down of the evangelical tone at first adopted by the administration probably owes a lot to the recognition that only one third of mankind lives under governments committed to the individual rights associated with democracy. Just over a quarter of mankind lives in economic systems able to provide most of the economic and social rights enshrined by the UN. We now demonstrate the political and economic diversity of the world in which a human rights policy must unfold.

We have the needed data for 140 states. We divide them into groups so as to capture two dimensions of interest: the place of civil and political rights of individuals in the national institutional order; and the commitment to policies involving the

TABLE 6.1

CLASSIFICATION OF WORLD'S POLITIES

	Industrialized Mixed Economy		Developing Mixed Economy		Industrialized Command Economy		Developing Command Economy	
	Popu-lation	Coun-tries	Popu-lation	Coun-tries	Popu-lation	Coun-tries	Popu-lation	Coun-tries
Competitive	18%	23	18%	18		0		0
Semicompetitive	1%	5	16%	26		0		0
Noncompetitive		0	12%	39		0	2%	9
Totalitarian		0		0	9%	7	25%	13

economic, social, and cultural rights applicable to groups and individuals. In the political dimension we distinguish between competitive, semicompetitive, noncompetitive, and totalitarian polities. The economic dimension breaks down into wealthy industrialized countries with mixed economic institutions, poor countries with mixed economic institutions, industrialized countries with socialist-command institutions, and poor countries with socialist institutions (see table 6.1).[7]

The global picture concerning the acceptance of international human rights enshrined in UN and regional conventions must be noted first. Europe is unique in widely accepting a regional code of rights; these rights are weighted in favor of protecting the individual *against* his own government. The OAS American convention, however, remains a dead letter even though it has been subject to hemisphere-wide negotiations since 1960, thus suggesting that the commitment to regional human rights codification is still largely rhetorical. Overarching texts of global scope—the two UN covenants—are not widely accepted yet. But global conventions designed to protect the rights of specific groups of clients (women, minorities, workers) are widely accepted in all parts of the world. So are texts that seek to safeguard large categories of people against specific acts of oppression (genocide, forced labor, denial of the right to organize). While racial discrimination is a subject of abhorrence, in terms of international law, to almost two thirds of the governments, only six of them also committed themselves to the concomitant principle of permitting their citizens to complain to the UN. Only 11 percent of the world's governments accept the obligation to subject itself to a complaint procedure. That number shrinks to 7 percent for the UN-sponsored and monitored texts, whereas the corresponding ratio for the European convention is 70 percent.

Looked at in terms of our clusters of polities, a clear picture emerges. Competitive/mixed economy/industrialized polities *and* totalitarian/command economy/industrialized countries almost universally accept the major texts establishing civil and political rights. Two thirds in each cluster accept the economic and social rights as well. But while about 40 percent of the competitive polities also subject themselves to the international complaint procedure, *none* of the totalitarian polities does so. Neither do the poor totalitarian countries; moreover, they are far from eager to ratify the substantive portions of the conventions. Only half of the less industrialized/poorer competitive polities accept the conventions; 10 percent accept the complaint procedure. The semicompetitive and noncompetitive polities, irre-

TABLE 6.2

INCIDENCE OF HUMAN RIGHTS VIOLATIONS, 1976–77

	Industrialized Mixed Economy	Developing Mixed Economy	Industrialized Command Economy	Developing Command Economy
Competitive	7 [a]	44 [b]	— [c]	—
Semicompetitive	80	88	—	—
Noncompetitive	—	77	—	100
Totalitarian	—	—	100	69 [d]

[a] The violators are Spain and Israel. Spain had not enacted its amnesty of political prisoners, and Israel was cited for detention without trial of suspected Arab terrorists.

[b] India was still under the "emergency regime." Colombia, Dominican Republic, Venezuela, Portugal, Turkey, and Sri Lanka were accused of various acts of illegal detention and denials of due process against political terrorists by Amnesty International, not by the United States.

[c] Dash equals not applicable.

[d] That number is low because the Amnesty report did not include South Yemen, Mongolia, and Guinea-Bissau. Somehow, it found no evidence that repression exists in North Korea. The State Department report did not include these countries because they do not receive U.S. security aid.

spective of economic institutions, tend to prefer economic and social rights to civil and political norms and all but ignore the right of aggrieved persons to file complaints with the UN. Any semblance of international consensus on these matters must surely be in the mind of the beholder. Practically nobody outside Western Europe is willing to submit to the complaint procedure. And the Soviet bloc matches its enthusiasm for accepting civil and political rights with its disdain for participating in the airing of complaints of violations. If this is the homage vice pays to virtue, the resulting hypocrisy is not likely to help the inmates of labor camps.

Obviously, governments are not eager to make full disclosures of their acts of repression; estimates of violations of human rights are therefore often inconsistent and incomplete. Two separate efforts were made to arrive at some quantitative findings about the extent to which international norms are implemented nationally.

The first survey singles out civil and political rights and is confined to materials relating to the 1976–77 period. It relies on the most recent annual report of Amnesty International [8] and the two reports submitted in 1977 and 1978 to Congress by the Department of State.[9] These reports use different definitions of human rights violations and do not cover the same countries. In table 6.2, countries cited in any of the reports were counted as violators. The numbers in the cells are the percentage of countries cited within the clusters described in table 6.1.

Our second test of the authority of international norms relies on the annual reports of the United Nations, the International Labor Organization, the Council of Europe, and the Organization of American States. Each organization has created a supervisory mechanism for monitoring the fidelity with which conventions concluded under its auspices are being implemented. These mechanisms include the obligation of each ratifying government to make an annual report on measures taken to implement the rights. In addition, the ILO possesses machinery to evaluate the reports to determine which legal obligations are being violated. Thus we know who is found guilty by the ILO. A similar machinery exists in the UN in the form of the Committee on Racial Discrimination. To date, however, this body has not issued lists of states violating the terms of the convention.

The fidelity with which ILO conventions were implemented between 1970 and 1976 is almost perfectly consistent with what one would expect on the basis of the governments' commitments to open political institutions. Almost no violations occur in OECD countries. Democratic countries that are not industrialized have a spotty record in implementing ILO conventions. All others have bad records.

Three additional multilateral forums exist for identifying violators of human rights. The European Commission on Human Rights receives complaints from individuals and governments alleging specific breaches of the European convention. Between 1970 and 1976 only two such complaints survived the stringent screening procedures of the Commission; they involved Austria and Belgium, both of which were found guilty of violating a provision of the treaty.[10] The Inter-American Commission, despite the fact that the American convention is not in force, continued to receive and investigate complaints during this period. It issued adverse reports against Bolivia, Cuba, El Salvador, Guatemala, Haiti, Honduras, Nicaragua, and Paraguay. It conducted a special investigation of Chile, which resulted in a scathing denunciation of the Pinochet government.[11] The final forum is the UN's Commission on Human Rights.

Only recently, in the long history of the UN Commission, did the member governments agree to issue annual lists of states guilty of a "persistent pattern of gross violations" of human rights. Since 1970, complaints from states, groups, and individuals, which previously had simply been received and filed without publicity or formal investigation, can be discussed in the Commission, investigated by an "impartial" body, and eventually result in a formal condemnation of the government in question. This procedure, it was hoped, would overcome the double standard in human rights discussions which had developed. The previous practice had boiled down to the exclusion from consideration of all complaints except those submitted against South Africa and the remaining colonial powers. In other words, situations of interest to the Asian, African, and Soviet-bloc countries were aired; those of interest to the West were suppressed.[12] The logic of the cold war and of the struggle for decolonization dominated the consideration of human rights issues.

Things have not measurably changed since the new procedures went into effect; the double standard continues to rule unscathed at the UN. Of all the possible violators of human rights which have been documented by other investigations, only four countries were denounced by the UN: Chile and South Africa on two occasions each, Portugal once, and Israel no less than six times. As far as the UN is concerned, genocide was not committed in Rwanda, Indonesia, and Nigeria; the Soviet Union is free of persistent and gross violations; India was always a model of democracy; Brazilian and Iranian police never used torture and illegal detention; Iraq always treated its ethnic minorities with consideration; and so on. The cold war may be receding and the struggle against colonialism has been won, but non-Western governments have lost none of their interest in using the UN to protect themselves and castigate others. And as they have the votes, why expect them to behave otherwise?

Conclusion

The global context facing an energetic American policy of promoting human rights is a bleak one. There is much rhetoric and little substantive agreement on what is meant by human rights. Many of the alleged rights run counter to the American political tradition. Many others are mutually contradictory. Only countries with an established democratic tradition are consistent and sincere practitioners of the international norms, though not even all of them accept the international texts. Multilateral machinery for bringing about national implementation of such rights works only in Western Europe, and intermittently in the Western Hemisphere. It does not work at all in the United Nations. Is it credible that American policy could successfully take on over a hundred reluctant dictatorial governments ruling two thirds of the world's population?

AMERICAN FOREIGN POLICY AND HUMAN RIGHTS

What Is the Carter Foreign Policy?

"This Administration has excellent objectives, corresponding to admirable intentions. But foreign policy is not a matter of objectives; it is a matter of strategy—the interconnection between an overall conception, a set of objectives, and specific policies." [13] That is the crux of the matter. The objectives include the continuation of détente with the Soviet Union, strategic arms control and nuclear nonproliferation, limiting the diffusion of conventional armaments, making progress toward a "new international economic order" favoring the developing countries by means of multilateral arrangements, eliminating white domination in Africa, making peace between Israel and the Arab states, *and promoting human rights.* The policies that constitute the means for attaining these objectives are the same as those practiced by any other administration: rewarding and offering incentives to your friends and allies, or treating them with benign neglect; persuading and threatening your enemies, or rewarding them for approved behavior. The way this is done remains constant: give or withhold foreign aid, raise or lower barriers to trade, promote or end "special relationships," establish or interrupt normal diplomatic contact, protest or praise the policies of others, either privately or in a splashy public forum.

The trouble is that the policies are only as good as the objectives they are supposed to serve, and the objectives are *not* mutually consistent unless they are ranked and ordered in terms of their importance to the United States. Ranking and ordering calls for an "overall conception," a generalized future state of affairs toward which these objectives are supposed to move the country and the world. Depending on what that conception is, détente might take priority over new economic agreements, or the new economic order might take priority over Africa and the Middle East. If human rights were to take first place, they would make the attainment of most of the other ojectives impossible. But if they do not take first place, where do they fit into the scheme of things? Since the Carter administration has no overall conception, it is impossible to tell. Quite rightly, Stanley Hoffmann entitles his analysis of this state of affairs as "the hell of good intentions."

We must distinguish between brave and sweeping words and actual deeds. It will become clear that a huge gap exists between what the administration's words suggest and what its actual policies have been. We turn to the words first.

How, then, does the administration describe its human rights policy? "The Carter Administration," says the Department of State, "has made an active concern for human rights throughout the world a central part of U.S. foreign policy. . . . A positive policy offers hope to those whose rights have been denied. It also serves the national interest by reasserting American ideals as the foundation of our foreign policy, encouraging respect among nations for the rule of law in international affairs, and rebuilding domestic consensus in support of our foreign policy." [14] Even though this statement does not make clear whether the national interest consists in creating respect for law abroad or appealing to a constituency at home, the rights of interest to the United States are those enshrined in "our historical documents" and in the major international texts reviewed above (none of which has been ratified by the United States to date). But more specifically they are

> *Freedom from arbitrary arrest and imprisonment, torture, unfair trial, cruel and unusual punishment, and invasion of privacy; Rights to food, shelter, health care and education; and Freedom of thought, speech, assembly, religion, press, movement, and participation in government.* [15]

In short, the United States claims to be committed to the promotion of the rights of the individual enshrined in the U.S. Bill of Rights and to a few selected economic and social rights. How does this policy fit into the other objectives of the administration?

> *The U.S. is seeking to integrate human rights considerations into its bilateral and multilateral relationships as a key element in decisionmaking. Other factors, including security and economic interests, continue to be important in defining our policy. We wish to develop a policy permitting a case-by-case approach to improve human rights situations in the most effective way possible. This policy, while concerned with progress on the full range of human rights, will continue to recognize differences among countries.* [16]

Are the "other factors" more or less important than human rights? Does a "case-by-case" approach suggest that human rights will be addressed *only if* more important objectives are not jeopardized by doing so? Or does it mean that only cases involving our enemies will be taken up? What is the "most effective way"? Is it quiet diplomacy, the UN complaint procedure, or the Belgrade Conference on the Helsinki Treaties? How can the "full range" of human rights be covered if, as we saw, these rights are mutually contradictory and often conflict with established American law and practice? If we "recognize differences among countries," do we put pressure only on nations who already practice democracy or on those who do not? Only the actual record of the administration in implementing these commitments can answer these questions.

Periodic comments by Secretary of State Cyrus Vance suggest that no consistent and systematic campaign is intended, much to the chagrin of some domestic champions of international human rights. On April 30, 1977, Vance said that "a sure formula for defeat of our goals would be a rigid, hubristic attempt to impose our values on others. . . . A doctrinaire plan of action would be as damaging as indifference." Early in February of 1978 Vance spoke of "tentative results" achieved by the policy in easing repression in some countries and reaffirmed that human rights, because of the Carter administration's emphasis, has become "a major theme of discussion" in international organizations. In the spring of 1978 the administration gave evidence of tiring of the campaign and wishing to downgrade it; it reported to Congress reluctantly on the extent of human rights violations among countries receiving U.S. aid. But in the summer of 1978 it stepped up the campaign by "speaking out" loudly during the trials of Soviet dissidents, a policy opposed by Andrew Young, who seemed more concerned about "political prisoners" in the United States. It is difficult to identify the players without a scorecard.

Methods of Influence and Their Effectiveness

What methods of influencing unwilling foreign governments does the United States have at its disposal? The methods include private remonstrances, public denunciations, appeals to international organizations, and coercive measures—cutting aid, restricting trade, and clandestine or overt military force. All have been used in the past, with very mixed results.

Making unpublicized protests against specific practices is the most commonly used method. It is also the method preferred by professional diplomats. Washington, if no grandiloquent statement of principled intention is first announced, has the option of when and where to protest. Because the lack of publicity means just that, we have no complete public record of such diplomatic protests. This protects the protesting officials against charges of failure and saves the target government the embarrassment of having to acknowledge American intervention and, possibly, compliance with it. It is said, for instance, that such protests brought about the emigration of 35,000 Jews from the Soviet Union, a figure that was cut sharply as soon as protests became public and were linked in the U.S. Senate with restrictions on trade with the Soviet Union. In any event, such protests have been recognized as a legitimate exercise of the law of humanitarian intervention for a long time. They have often led to the release from prison of individuals, the cessation of specific acts of persecution, and the granting of foreign asylum to political leaders opposing a given government. If the Carter administration had confined its policy to this method, there would be no occasion to offer these comments.

Protests can also be made publicly, by "speaking out," as the Carter administration is fond of doing. This can still be confined to a bilateral exchange: the offending government is made the subject of a remark in a speech or a press conference, or it is mentioned adversely in a report to Congress. Public protest, of course, can be accompanied by private remonstrances by the U.S. ambassador in the offending country. This was done during 1977 with some effect in order to stop torture and illegal detention in South Korea, the Phillippines, and Argentina, among others; it was attempted unsuccessfully in the case of the Soviet dissidents. The negative implications of this approach were clearly illustrated in Panama: opponents of the Panama Canal treaties and political exiles from Panama made an issue over the repressive nature of the Torrijos government; the Department of State then sought to soft-pedal the issue.

Going public can be done with even more splash by appealing to an international organization or other multilateral forum. One example was the discussion of human rights in the Belgrade meetings reviewing the Helsinki Agreements. Since more was at stake there than the relaxation of repression in Eastern Europe, American delegates had to decide to what extent they would harp on human rights violations. Their task was not made easier by the Soviet response, which sought to link the introduction of the human rights issue with a revival of the cold war. Since détente is a two-way street, denouncing one's partner in negotiations on other issues in a multilateral public forum enables the partner to link issues the United States would prefer to keep separate.

Appeals to international organizations are subject to all the vagaries discussed above and raise the issue of the double standard on human rights questions. The United States has thus been singularly unsuccessful in getting the United Nations to include on its agenda human rights violations considered serious in Washington. It has been equally unsuccessful in deleting from the agenda situations not considered serious by American diplomats, such as the case of Israel. But things are somewhat different in the Organization of American States. Its Inter-American Commission on Human Rights is a body made up of independent experts. The United States has been able to support the work of the Commission in investigating and airing violations, and in putting the collective pressure of publicity on the offending government. This method brought results in Chile and the Dominican Republic; it did not work when applied to Cuba and Paraguay.

Coercive measures on behalf of human rights have been used rarely in the past, though they were prominently discussed by the Carter administration. The simplest way of applying coercive pressure is to cut or eliminate foreign aid. In the case of military aid, or government-sanctioned sales of military equipment (usually provided on credit), a foreign government highly dependent on such supplies may be forced to mend its ways, at least for a while. It is difficult to find striking examples of the successful application of this kind of pressure because the United States has never followed such a line for a sufficiently long time. Moreover, if the United States stops a sale, France, Britain, or West Germany can always jump into the opening, not to mention the Soviet Union. That happened when Washington stopped military aid to Ethiopia and South Africa. Cutting economic aid is still more difficult, because it is not the offending government that is punished, but its needy population. The method worked when, in 1948, Washington cut off aid to Holland to force the Dutch government to grant Indonesia the right of national self-determination. The Carter administration has declared that it will *not* use economic aid as a means of pressure, though it has actually done so in Uganda, Ethiopia, and the Central African Empire.

Congress, in the enthusiasm of some of its members to use the foreign aid weapon as a way of promoting human rights, discovered during 1977 that there has been a steady trend away from bilateral toward multilateral grants and loans. Economic aid is being given increasingly by the World Bank, the International Monetary Fund, the UN Development Program, and such regional institutions as the Inter-American Development Bank. Can these institutions be used to coerce governments to stop violating human rights? In the past, the United States on occasion justified its opposition to extending multilateral aid to Cuba on the grounds that such aid would abet the continued violation of human rights. The House of Representatives adopted legislation in 1977 which, had it been passed by the Senate, would have linked financial contributions to the UN and World Bank to the withholding of multilateral aid to states in violation of human rights standards. The State Department opposed the legislation, and President Robert McNamara of the World Bank announced that U.S. contributions "tied" in such a fashion were unacceptable. Nevertheless, legislation was enacted directing the President to instruct U.S. delegates to these institutions to vote against aid projects earmarked for such countries. Multilateral aid, therefore, can be used as a method for promoting human rights only if a sufficient number of countries sides with the United States. Moreover, to the extent that foreign lending is handled by private banks and corporations, such assistance to economic development also escapes this form of leverage.

That leaves trade embargoes and armed force. The imposition of a trade embargo against Cuba simply drove that country more tightly into Soviet arms, without doing a thing for human rights. The reduction of sugar imports from the Dominican Republic in 1961, however, did have the desired effect of temporarily stopping political repression in that country. Unfortunately for the administration, few countries in the world are as dependent as the Dominican Republic, and therefore as amenable to this method of pressure. No country has ever used its armed forces to compel another only to respect human rights, though this objective has sometimes been included among other objectives when armed intervention was undertaken, as the United States did in 1965 in the Dominican Republic. The United States, along with all other industrialized countries, has resolutely refused to consider armed action to protect human rights in South Africa, though it observes the UN-ordered embargo on arms sales.[18] On the other hand, clandestine armed force was on occasion used for, and against, governments involved in human rights controversies. Thus, CIA involvement was widely suspected in the installation of the repressive Greek military regime in 1966. American involvement in the overthrow of the Allende government is established, though it cannot be proven that the United States planned to install the extremely repressive Pinochet government instead. In both cases, clearly, clandestine force was used so as to result in violations of human rights. However, the United States also gave clandestine support to regimes using force to protect themselves *against* the repressive designs of their domestic opponents; this occurred in Venezuela during the 1960s and in Portugal in 1975.

How effective have the methods been since the Carter administration took office? Our account is necessarily incomplete because we have no way of assessing any private protests that may have been launched, and because it is confined to events during 1977 and 1978. The Department of State says that "the Administration has undertaken diplomatic initiatives with many countries, urging improvement in human rights conditions. We seek to encourage and assist those governments that

have taken forthright steps toward improving human rights." [19] There is no indication of what these measures of positive reinforcement and reward have been. On a
bilateral basis, the State Department notes that the reduction or halting of military
aid is the main mode of action, whereas economic aid is to serve those who need it
most.

Over fifty countries were singled out for public criticism by the United States
during 1977–78. In a few cases the complaints took the form of statements by the
President or the secretary of state. With Eastern European countries, the forum for
denunciation was the Belgrade Conference. The bulk of the criticism was expressed
in two reports sent by the State Department to Congress in conformity with legislation that military aid might be denied to violators of human rights. Twelve countries
were subsequently mentioned as having improved their record by releasing some
prisoners, permitting some dissidents to emigrate, or promising to hold elections
some time in the future: Argentina, Haiti, Indonesia, Philippines, Uruguay, South
Korea, Paraguay, Yugoslavia, Brazil, Ecuador, Chile, and East Germany. In no case
was it maintained that the overall repressive character of these regimes had been
altered. Who among the violators suffered actual or threatened cuts in aid? Argentina, Ethiopia, Uruguay, Brazil, El Salvador, Guatemala, Nicaragua, Angola,
Mozambique, Vietnam, Cuba, Cambodia, Laos, Uganda, and Chile were mentioned
in various releases of the Department of State. The list is curious in many respects.
Angola, Mozambique, Vietnam, Cuba, Cambodia, Laos, and Uganda were not receiving any aid in the first place, though negotiations for making them eligible were
going forward in some instances. All the Latin American victims except Nicaragua
announced their refusal to seek or accept U.S. aid before action was taken in
Washington. Ethiopia's share of aid was eliminated for a variety of reasons having
little to do with human rights. [20]

The administration also moved on the multilateral front. U.S. delegate to the UN
Allard Lowenstein sought to include Soviet persecution of dissidents on the agenda
of the UN Commission on Human Rights and also talked about Uganda. Moreover,
he said that, for the first time in recent years, the Commission's debate was more
balanced because bloc voting was avoided. Encouraged perhaps by this evidence of
getting away from the double standard, President Carter renewed the earlier American proposal for the creation of the office of a UN High Commissioner for Human
Rights. He prominently raised the issue of human rights in the Western Hemisphere
in the meetings of the OAS and worked to increase the budget of the Inter-
American Commission on Human Rights, while stressing American support of the
Commission's investigation of repression in Chile.

What can we conclude from this record? There has been some marginal improvement in behavior on the part of a few countries. Nobody can tell how permanent
that change may be, but past experience with similar waves of relaxation in repression strongly suggests that, unless the regime changes basically, people released
from prison can always be rearrested. The skills of the torturer, though perhaps not
used for a while, are never forgotten. No fundamental change in the global human
rights picture can be discovered. Moreover, it has become very clear that neither
multilateral discussion and censure nor the manipulation of foreign aid has been an
effective means for persuading other governments. That leaves us with quiet di-

plomacy and its occasional successes in alleviating the fate of single victims of repression. Such had been the situation before President Carter took office; it will be the situation when he leaves it. The question is: why is this so?

THE LESSONS: THE NATIONAL INTEREST IS ELUSIVE

"Why Do We Always Support Dictators?"

The question of American support for dictatorial regimes is raised with monotonous regularity by human rights enthusiasts. Should we support only democratic countries? Such a policy would force us to curtail relations with over a hundred governments. Should we never ally ourselves with a repressive government? To do so assumes that the promotion of human rights takes precedence over all other objectives of foreign policy. Must we refrain from intervening with force—openly or clandestinely—on behalf of a repressive ruler? To abstain implies that a less repressive alternative to such a government is waiting in the wings. The Carter administration, despite its first pronouncements, has learned *not* to impose its human rights preferences on governments in Asia, Africa, Latin America, and Eastern Europe in a sweeping and consistent manner. It has moderated its policy as it realized that the national interest demands a more discriminating calculation of the costs and benefits involved in action and inaction.

Perhaps the most sobering insight has been the realization that intervention on behalf of *anybody* implies that somebody will enjoy rights at somebody else's expense, at least in any context that is not fully democratic. For instance, in Chile the Allende government was promoting the economic and social rights of the peasantry and the workers at the expense of the property rights of the middle classes by means permitting the threat of violence. The United States, in undoing the results of a democratic election, was also indirectly supporting the human rights of a segment of Chile's population. In Venezuela, support for the AD Government had the result of protecting the civil and political rights of the groups associated with the regime, against the civil and political rights of the left-wing terrorists who suffered torture and illegal detention (and who were trained and supported by Cuba). In Venezuela these acts resulted in the stabilization of a competitive political order; in Vietnam similarly inspired efforts did not. When should one act? If the answer is murky, the exercise of prudent self-restraint must result, by the nature of the world in which we live, in the support of dictatorships.

I now summarize why the administration's record has been so spotty and why the administration moderates its rhetoric with inaction. What was understood by previous administrations also became clear to Carter: international politics is not like the politics of the American civil rights movement. There is no collective guilty conscience about past misdeeds. The suffering of individuals and groups elsewhere does not evoke a sustained and energetic response. There is no body of core values, no underlying acceptance of a clear norm that can guide and inspire those who fight for the elimination of discrimination and torture. There is all too much awareness that local conditions and local values differ and justify modes of governance repugnant to the American tradition. There is no central legislature which can pass civil rights legislation and no central police force to protect civil rights leaders or keep integrated schools open. There is no Supreme Court to hand down a *Brown* v. *Board of Education.* There are no voters to punish those who ignore human rights or reward those who promote them. And none of the international pronouncements and legal texts so far adopted goes any way in the direction of creating such attitudes or institutions. Nor can they be expected to do so, given the realities of the world.

Slowly it was learned that there is a difference between working for the perfection of democracy and protecting a few selected human rights, though the distinction is far from easily observed in practice. It was learned that the means for promoting human rights are blunt and uncertain, and that it is not always wise to link them with the means appropriate for attaining other policy aims. And it was learned that the articulation of the national interest carries with it tradeoff problems. Solving such problems must result in the downgrading of human rights activities.

Promoting Democracy and Promoting Human Rights

A successful competitive order also protects and promotes specific human rights, though not necessarily all the aspirations proclaimed by the UN. If it is possible to create or protect democratic government abroad, human rights will benefit automatically. However, it does not follow that it is impossible to do something for certain human rights even in the absence of a competitive order. It might still be feasible to use the power of the United States to moderate the use of torture and illegal detention, to cite the most common abuses of civil rights. The difference between the two tasks is stark: one calls for working with basically sympathetic forces abroad; and the other means opposing the rulers of semicompetitive, noncompetitive and totalitarian countries *who have deliberately chosen to disregard human rights.*

Occasions for feasible intervention on behalf of democracy arise from time to time. But they do not occur often. Nor is their frequent recurrence likely during the remainder of this administration. The United States certainly "intervened" forcefully in behalf of democracy in its military occupation of Japan and Germany after 1945—and the intervention seems to have been eminently successful. Less dramatic and prolonged episodes are often forgotten. The United States supported a democratic revolution in Costa Rica between 1948 and 1950 with military and political aid thinly disguised under the collective security operations of the Organization of American States; the OAS was used once more to protect the fledgling democratic government of Venezuela from threats emanating from the right-wing Dominican Republic and Communist Cuba. Why can't we do these things more often?

Success in cementing democracy abroad depends on the severity of the task. The Kennedy administration, through the Alliance for Progress, sought to harness foreign aid policies systematically to the promotion of democratic societies in Latin America by stressing the participation and evolution of trade unions, peasant associations, and urban squatters' organizations. Such policies were successful in places that, for reasons unconnected with prior American policy, *had already* developed organizations, beliefs, and institutions favoring democratic government. In most instances these developments could take place because the standard of living and the mode of social and economic organization were at a level where the threshold of poverty, dependence on agriculture, rural isolation, and illiteracy had already been crossed. Successful democracy seems to require a minimum standard of living and a degree of social mobilization and awareness as essential preconditions.

These preconditions do not yet exist in most of the world. When they do prevail, I favor selective policies of intervention on behalf of democracy—always providing that such intervention *not* interfere with other important policy objectives. When the tradeoff between working for democracy and world peace, general prosperity or disarmament is clear and sharp, even this kind of intervention is dangerous. Under no circumstances should it be legitimated in the language of a global crusade based on the American heritage. Thus, intervention on behalf of democracy was justifiable in the cases cited, in Portugal, and—as recently as 1978—in the Dominican Republic. It is not now justified in the Philippines, South Africa, and Nicaragua.

What about the less sweeping policy of simply seeking to promote certain human rights? The distinction is sometimes made by spokesmen for the Carter administration. More and more they have admitted that, indeed, the global promotion of democracy is not feasible and should not be attempted. Nevertheless, they also claim that sharp tradeoffs between incompatible objectives can be avoided by stressing an active American policy of working for the cessation of the most blatant violations of human rights—torture and the indefinite imprisonment of the opponents of a regime. Is it possible to sustain the distinction and limit an active human rights policy to the suppression of these practices? If so, Carter's efforts to intervene in Argentina, South Korea, the Philippines, and Nicaragua could withstand the finding that the global setting facing democracy is dismal.

In much of the contemporary world the distinction does not stand up. No ruler will tolerate an organized opposition when he is reasonably certain that his opponents will use their liberty to overthrow him. No ruler will permit free and honest elections when he has reason to fear that the election will result in his ouster and the advent of his bitter enemies. Nor will he permit a free press, open debate, or freedom of association. The sharpness of social and political conflict determines the limits of toleration. Only countries in which it is understood that those who displace the rulers in an honest election will then *not* proceed to the wholesale incarceration of their opponents and the confiscation of their property can afford to live by the rules of our First Amendment.

As a matter of principle, a totalitarian or authoritarian ruler in a divided society cannot afford to be selectively repressive. He cannot eschew democracy as a matter of commitment and also avoid completely the convenience of torture and illegal detention. Such schizophrenia would force him to give up extracting information on conspiratorial cells from imprisoned students opposing his rule. It would mean risking assassination, hijackings, and kidnapping. It would risk public trials of opponents who could not be convicted with available evidence. Not to imprison such people in the first place, or not sending them into exile, would permit the exercise of freedom of association to oust the ruler.

These lessons apply completely only to the committed totalitarian polities, of which there were about twenty in 1978. They do not apply in full force to the thirty semicompetitive polities, or even to all noncompetitive ones. In these instances it *does* make sense to speak only on behalf of key human rights, not on the full range and not of democracy in general. In semicompetitive polities the rulers' sense of security is often considerable because there is no potentially powerful but repressed opposition. Hence, appeals and threats on behalf of illegally imprisoned individuals may be heeded. Sometimes such rulers have decided on their own to introduce gradual measures of political liberation; then they will often not oppose efforts to restrain the police. In noncompetitive polities, too, circumstances arise that make it wise for the rulers to cater to foreign criticism, if only for a short while. They will then stop the practice of torture and permit some of their enemies to go into exile instead of imprisoning them. The Carter administration's intervention on behalf of such individuals in Argentina, South Korea, the Philippines, Chile, and Indonesia was justifiable and did bring some results. The rulers did not change the regime; in all cases it remains repressive. But sensitivity to, or perceived dependence on, American goodwill had the result of making the lot of some people more bearable. How long this will last, granting the unchanged character of the regime, we cannot guess. On the other hand, attempts to speak out on behalf of key rights in South Africa, the Soviet Union, Cambodia, Cuba, or Uganda remain an empty rhetorical exercise.

In short, the nature of the target country matters. Selective measures on behalf of human rights can be effective whenever the rulers of such countries have decided by themselves to liberalize the regime, or when they feel they must bow to the United States because they would otherwise suffer some other deprivation they cannot afford, or both. What kind of deprivation? The choice of sanction brings us to the matter of the efficacy of means.

Means, Leverage, and Linkage

We confine the discussion now to efforts on behalf of core human rights in target countries offering some limited hope of success. By what means can we expect to reduce torture, illegal detention, and other violations of personal dignity, but not worry about censorship, rigged elections, suppression of trade unions, and social security payments, in such semicompetitive polities as Argentina and South Korea or in noncompetitive settings like Chile or Zaire?

Means for exerting pressure, as we saw, may be unilateral or multilateral, verbal or coercive. Multilateral means can be further subdivided into those used by the United Nations and pressure exerted by regional organizations. We can dispose of UN multilateral means very simply: they do not work. Since the violators of human rights enjoy a healthy majority in the UN, no UN action or meaningful condemnation stands a chance of being adopted. But regional organizations are more effective. Condemnation by the Council of Europe usually works because violations involved are neither gross nor persistent; they are not part of a systematic pattern of governance. When the violations are more systematic, as they were in Greece and Cyprus, the pressure of the Council of Europe is *not* adequate to bring about a change. In the OAS, as we saw, multilateral criticism, when it results from the impartial investigations of a body of independent experts, *can* influence the behavior of rulers who feel themselves extremely dependent on foreign support; in other situations such criticism is without effect.

How dependent must the violator be? This is the crucial question we must examine when we turn to unilateral measures. Dependence may mean a number of things. The Dominican Republic is highly dependent on the United States because it markets most of its sugar here under a preferential quota, has few other important exports, and relies on American private investors for much of its capital needs. Its army receives its training and weapons from the United States. Because of the length of time over which these ties have been established, and because of the vested interests created, a disruption of these transactions would leave the elite in the Dominican Republic with difficult choices of where to turn for quick alternatives. Hence, the threat from Washington to consider disruption is a potent sanction. On the other hand, Argentina's exports are more diversified and have no single dominant customer. While her armed forces are dependent on the United States, there is independent manufacturing capacity in Argentina, and weapons could be bought elsewhere. American leverage on Argentina is much weaker. Washington can threaten few sanctions that would seriously cripple Buenos Aires. South Korea is in an intermediate position. Relatively independent of the United States economically, she depends on American troops and heavy military aid for her security. Effective leverage on behalf of human rights can be exercised only if the dependence is extreme and if the means used to exercise leverage do not attempt to link issues that are as important to the United States as they are to the target country.

If leverage is to be more than a verbal slap on the wrist—which is as ineffective when used by a single country as it is when employed by the UN—it must be linked to some foreign policy issue other than human rights. Coercive means, by definition, imply that the target is being deprived of something it treasures: aid, trade, capital, military security, a special understanding, an alliance. Linkage, however, implies that the United States is *less* dependent on the target country than is true of the reverse relationship; if this is not the case, the United States is being deprived of a benefit by linking the issue of human rights to one or more of the others. Effective leverage presupposes low dependence on the part of the United States, and implies an American freedom to link or not to link issues freely. When this condition is not met, coercive means for protecting human rights are as ineffective as verbal ones. And when the target country chooses to link issues, contrary to American preferences, human rights fare worse still. This is what the Soviet Union did with success at the Belgrade Conference, forcing the United States to choose between détente and human rights and maneuvering the Carter administration into a final stance of soft-pedaling the rights of dissidents in Russia.

American dependence is illustrated in the cases of Greece, Turkey, South Korea, and the Philippines. All involve alliances against the Soviet Union and China. All involve the moral issue of whether it is a lesser evil to tolerate a noncommunist dictatorship or—through the threat of coercion on behalf of human rights—aid in the advent of a communist takeover.

Both Greece and Turkey have alternated between periods of repressive military rule and parliamentary democracy. In both there have been genuine possibilities that unruly and violence-prone government by political parties would result in a communist takeover. Both occupy a military position crucial to the defensive strategy of NATO. The emergence of communism would constitute a severe blow to the military security *and* the political values of Western Europe and the United States. When it is clear that the continuation of such domestic conditions is likely to trigger a communist takeover, acts of condoning repression are justified. Whether these conditions actually prevailed in sufficient severity in the Greece of 1966–74 is another matter. I am simply suggesting that such conditions occur and that the anti-human rights implications of the claim in favor of national security is not always a camouflage for an underlying sympathy for fascism. Then the linking of issues is not in the interest of the United States.

I doubt that the infrastructure for successful democracy exists in the Philippines, or in South Korea. I believe that the advent of totalitarianism in either is a greater evil than the continuation of authoritarian rule. I also believe that for military reasons it is genuinely important to the United States to keep both from falling into the Chinese or Soviet sphere. Again, therefore, a policy of intervening actively and publicly on behalf of human rights is not likely to be effective because the United States cannot and should not link the withdrawal of military or economic aid to the protection of human rights. Momentary concessions made by these governments to help aid bills through Congress should not be mistaken for lasting improvement, though the lot of the persecuted will be eased for a while. The administration would act wisely if it could persuade Seoul and Manila quietly to ease repressive policies without having to threaten acts of coercion which lack credibility.

Morality and Tradeoffs Among Objectives

Is the difficult lesson of how to estimate tradeoffs among competing but equally moral national objectives being learned? Does the administration recognize that the protection of human rights cannot be given priority without seriously sacrificing some other end? The measure of morality is not loud words and strongly held beliefs, but the principle of proportionality between ends and means, the principle of weighing competing but legitimate ends and choosing the most moral among them for priority attention, while doing the least harm to groups, nations, and individuals who may get in the way. Neither words nor deeds suggest that the lesson has sunk in.

Some of the greatest crimes against individual human rights have been committed by those who claim to incorporate the collective rights of peoples and nations and classes, by those who claim to be leading their followers to the utopia of equality and fraternity by shooting and exiling their opponents. Almost every national liberation movement which has led its supporters to political independence in the last twenty years, with the blessing of the United Nations, has become a repressive machine whose more fortunate victims seek asylum in the "capitalist-racist" West.

The Carter administration has to come to terms with this fact of life. It no longer speaks of giving priority to promoting human rights because this would call into question the success of other international priorities: détente, military disengagement from the Third World, economic betterment, improved health and housing, environmental protection, nuclear nonproliferation, or a stable peace in various parts of the world. The foreign leaders on whose cooperation these priorities depend are the violators of human rights. We cannot expect to change their ways with denunciations and the curtailment of aid and trade unless we are also willing to give up on other objectives.

Nor does it help to claim that our first priority is the creation of a better world order and that the observance of human rights is an essential part of such an order. Says Stanley Hoffmann:

> *The quest for human rights and the quest for world order are not identical. Ordinary world order issues may foster conflict, the ultimate objective is accommodation—compromise for survival and progress. The issue of human rights, however, by definition, breeds confrontation. Raising the issue touches on the very foundations of a regime, on its sources and exercise of power, on its links to its citizens or subjects. It is a dangerous issue—a difficult one to manipulate, because if the Carter Administration does mean what it says it means, many other nations may take this as an assertion of American hubris, an old fondness for telling others how to run their affairs. The subject of human rights almost inevitably increases tensions with our enemies. If it is pursued very avidly, it diminishes the chances of cooperation on a number of other world order issues.*[21]

Yet there may be situations in which these tensions and confrontations may be acceptable, where an active policy of using national power to coerce a violator of human rights is free of the problems we examined. Such situations involve several ingredients: the violations must be particularly brutal and widespread, their continuation arouses the strong opposition of most governments, collective or unilateral coercive measures are unlikely to interfere with the pursuit of other important foreign policy objectives, and the use of such measures will not create a bad precedent for the evolution of a more benign world order. The case for a strong American policy on behalf of human rights in Uganda ought to be examined in these terms.

There is no need to enumerate the crimes of Idi Amin. Yet his rule by mass murder is not universally condemned. Other African states, irrespective of the private sentiments of their leaders, have publicly defended Uganda and expressed their opposition to unilateral or collective sanctions. They are unlikely to intervene actively in Uganda. Legislation was adopted by Congress in 1978 designed to bring about the fall of the Amin regime by means of a unilateral American boycott on the purchase of Ugandan exports.[22] Quite possibly, such a step would be effective. Equally possible, it might arouse the active opposition of most African governments and also lead to greater Ugandan dependence on Soviet aid. In my judgment these would be entirely acceptable costs. An embargo on Ugandan coffee, in short, would pose no issue as far as the attainment of other American policy objectives are concerned. Why then did the Carter administration oppose the legislation and maintain that this mode of protecting human rights interferes with other objectives?

The justification for inaction in Uganda has to do with the creation of undesirable precedents for the future of the world order. The Carter administration, like its predecessors, prefers to keep "politics" and "economics" separate in international relations. It does not wish to make trade and financial relations dependent on political alignments and calculations in the hope of keeping them subject to the universalistic norms that have grown up since 1945—no matter that the United States has also been highly selective in its adherence to these norms. Moreover, the preference for keeping politics and economics separate also benefits American business. Why punish American traders and investors by means of an embargo for the sins of the governments of countries in which they are active? A trade embargo justified by the policy of promoting human rights could backfire badly, even if it works in the case in point. Suppose the Arab countries launch an oil embargo against the United States in the pursuit of their policy to safeguard the human rights of Palestinians? Or the organization of copper-producing nations boycotts sales to the West so as to promote the right to regulate commodity prices and corporate remittances? Remember, these are "human" rights under current UN practice!

We can only speculate on the likelihood of such events. But, then, who predicted the oil embargo of 1973 over a purely political issue? In any event, the precedent has already been set; the United States was the chief actor in its establishment in relations with Cuba and the Dominican Republic. The application of our criteria, then, offers no compelling reasons for not coercing Uganda through economic measures. Even the principle of doing the least harm to innocent bystanders argues in favor of enacting such measures. The criterion of proportionality forces us to ask who would suffer the most from such measures, granting that no great burden would be foisted on the United States. The coffee-growing peasantry is already deprived of most of its share of the revenue, so no additional suffering would be entailed. Moreover, the Ugandan economy is so precarious as to make the loss of the American market for its coffee an emergency that could harm the regime immediately. Because no moral or practical issue arises to militate against the use of economic sanctions, one might expect the Carter administration to welcome this opportunity to try a little harder. It exemplifies the "selective approach" with minimal costs. For once, there are no important tradeoffs to be considered.[23]

Another curious gap in the Carter human rights policy has been its neglect of the crime of genocide, a more serious violation of human rights than torture and illegal detention. The more serious episodes involving genocide took place before Carter took office. Today, only Brazil's policies toward its indigenous Indian population come to mind as a genocidal practice, though it is not difficult to imagine the resurgence of these policies in Africa and the Middle East. (One may think here of Shaba and the Kurds.) As far as is known, the Carter administration did not remonstrate with Brazil over the rights of the aboriginal population. One wonders whether it would take up the case of the Kurds in the event of need. As with Ugandan coffee, there is no reason not to be active on behalf of such ethnic groups when no other and more important foreign policy objective is involved and when the costs can be so distributed as to minimize harm to the innocent. Even military intervention can be justified when these conditions are met.

Toward a True Human Rights Policy

Many veterans and beneficiaries of the civil rights struggle applauded the emphasis on human rights and saw in it the extension of their concerns to Africa and Latin America. Others welcomed it as a way of showing America's continued opposition to communism without having to resort to armed threats. Many, while sharing some feeling of malaise about the feasibility of the policy, nevertheless supported it enthusiastically because they felt the need for an ethical reaffirmation, a restatement of core American values after the trauma of Vietnam and Watergate.

They have mostly been disappointed. These expectations ignore the issue of tradeoffs. They fail to recognize the global trend toward collective rights, the lack of consensus, the impatience with individual rights. Either the administration resolutely pursues human rights everywhere—which it cannot and will not do for the reasons we gave—or it promotes them "selectively," as it has in fact done. But even the selective policy has been inept and often without effect. How can we do better in recognizing the limits on promoting human rights *and* making a contribution to their improvement?

Our discussion leads to these conclusions:

1. Do not intervene on behalf of repressive regimes with military and counterinsurgency aid and symbolic gestures when no clear and present national security danger exists.

2. Use quiet diplomacy (including nonpublicized threats to manipulate aid, trade, and investments) to induce repressive rulers to moderate torture and illegal detention when such measures pose no issue of competing national objectives; but do not expect that such interventions will help democracy or result in the permanent disappearance of such practices.

3. Do not proclaim indiscriminate support for UN human rights conventions and discussions when the content and meaning of the multilateral machinery conflict with American traditions on human rights.

4. Be ready to intervene, with force if necessary, on behalf of democracy when and where the preconditions for successful democratic government seem to exist.

5. Use coercive measures to change the ways of repressive governments unlikely to develop into democracies when and where coercion does not interfere with more important policy objectives and when the lot of ordinary people is not made worse by such steps.

6. Actively promote global policies in the field of human rights when such rights command wide acceptance and are capable of being implemented.

Generous acts of commission are possible. The United States can underwrite and promote rights that *are* consistent with the American tradition and *are* compatible with all the major foreign policy objectives. They do not raise any of the nagging moral and practical issues. No problem of priorities arises. Moreover, these rights have already been legitimated by a number of recent international meetings.

Prominent among them is the right to adequate food and nutrition. The right is personal, capable of being defined in scientific terms, universal, and subject to efficient implementation through international programs and national contributions. A right to a minimal standard of health—as opposed to "full mental and physical health"—is equally realistic, and for the same reasons. Others may come to mind readily. They can be embraced by communists, fascists, liberals, and ordinary authoritarians. They are of equal appeal to Muslims, Hindus, Christians, and atheists. They threaten no government and do not pit legal and philosophical traditions against each other. I commend them to the Carter administration.

NOTES

1. Texts of the international declarations and conventions can be found in Louis B. Sohn and Thomas Buergenthal, eds., *Basic Documents on International Protection of Human Rights* (Indianapolis: Bobbs-Merrill, 1973). Subsequent quotations are from this volume.
2. In addition, the international protection and promotion of human rights is institutionalized in the Council of Europe and the Organization of American States. The European convention is much more modest in the scope of rights to bě protected than are the UN convenants, but also much more effective in implementing them. The American convention is more ambiguous in its phrasing of rights. Even though it is not yet in effect, effective work in implementation has been done by the Inter-American Commission on Human Rights. Discussions for the creation of regional human rights machinery have also taken place in Africa and in the Arab League.

   The ILO conventions of concern are: Right of Association and Combination of Agriculture Workers [No. 11]; Forced or Compulsory Labor [No. 29]; Freedom of Association and Protection of the Right to Organize [No. 87]; Application of the Principles of the Right to Organize and to Bargain Collectively [No. 98]; Abolition of Forced Labor [No. 105]; Discrimination in Respect of Employment and Occupation [No. 111]; Basic Aims and Standards of Social Policy [No. 117]; Protection and Facilities to be Afforded to Workers' Representatives in the Undertaking [No. 135].
3. See also the case studies on national policies with respect to human rights in Willem A. Veenhoven et al., eds., *Case Studies on Human Rights and Fundamental Freedoms: A World Survey*, 2 vols. (The Hague: Nijhoff, 1975). The effectiveness of the system is evaluated by Evan Luard, ed., *The International Protection of Human Rights* (New York: Praeger, 1967). For a study of experience with the major ILO convention (Freedom of Association), see Ernst B. Haas, *Human Rights and International Action* (Stanford: Stanford University Press, 1970).
4. For a full discussion of these issues, see Chalmers Johnson, "Terror," *Society*, November–December 1977, pp. 48–52.
5. The Charter was adopted by the UN General Assembly on 12 December 1974 (Res. 3281 XXIX) by a vote of 120 to 6 to 10. See *UN Monthly Chronicle*, January 1975, pp. 108–18. The General Assembly must conduct a review on the extent to which the Charter is implemented at every fifth session.
6. The European and American conventions on human rights are explicit on this point. Socialist countries customarily ward off allegations of violations of human rights by invoking the same principle. For a detailed treatment of the issue in the jurisprudence of the European Commission on Human Rights, see Frede Castberg, *The European Convention on Human Rights* (Leyden: Sijthoff, 1974), pp. 165–73.
7. The following countries were excluded from the survey: Papua-New Guinea, Tonga, Qatar, Bahrein, Maldives, Djibouti, Comoros, Solomon Islands, Belize, St. Tomé and Principe, Rhodesia, Cape Verde Islands, Seychelles, Angola, Samoa, Nauru. Population figures refer to 1973, the number of countries to 1977. Countries in each group are identified and the coding rules described in Ernst B. Haas, "Global Evangelism Rides Again," *Policy Papers in International Affairs* (Berkeley: Institute of International Studies, 1978), pp. 16–19, 48–49. The statistical materials from which the following conclusions are drawn are on pp. 20–28.
8. Amnesty International, *Report 1977*. Not everything in the report could be transposed into my analysis. Amnesty's conception of human rights does not correspond in all respects with the position taken in this paper. "Prisoners of conscience" are the beneficiaries of rights of concern to Amnesty, and the definition of such persons includes, among others, victims of the death penalty legally condemned, maltreatment of prisoners according to Amnesty's standard of fair treatment (there being no internationally accepted minimum standard) and the "harassment" of dissidents short of illegal detention and torture (as, for instance, acts of extradition of which Amnesty disapproves or condemnation of conscientious objectors to military service). Amnesty is not concerned whether such actions are well within the legal code of the state in question and are permissible under existing international law. In addition, Amnesty does not consider whether the

alleged acts are isolated instances of local brutality or form part of a systematic pattern. Political units other than sovereign states are included on their blacklist. In some instances, violators are cited even though the investigation has not been completed. As a general rule, I have accepted Amnesty's findings only when they concern acts of terrorism by security forces against dissidents, torture and detention without trial, and violations of due process during trial. I have excluded cases in which the allegation was confined to ill treatment of prisoners, and to acts not now in obvious violation of international law. No reliable assessment of the relative severity of the violations of human rights is possible on the basis of this information. By far the most common violations reported concern detention without trial and torture.

9. The Department of State released a list of 82 countries on March 13, 1977. Countries on this list receive security aid from the United States. Of these, 58 practice all or some of the following: repression of right of political expression, forceful violation of the person, freedom of travel, emigration, legal guarantees, detention. The rights of interest to the Department of State were those of life, liberty, security of home, person, and property (U.S., Congress, Senate Foreign Relations Committee, *Human Rights Report,* 95th Cong., 1st sess., March 1977). The 1978 report lists 105 countries, of which 50 are guilty of these practices (U.S., Congress, Joint Committee Print, *Country Reports on Human Rights Practices Report Submitted to the Committee on International Relations of the U.S. House of Representatives and Committee on Foreign Relations U.S. Senate by the Department of State,* 95th Cong., 2d sess., 3 February 1978). The report is careful to explain that many practices violating human rights are natural and understandable in terms of the degree of modernity and threats to internal security prevalent in some countries. Hence its tendency is to exonerate some countries condemned by Amnesty International. The 1978 report is considerably less eager to pass judgment on other countries than its predecessor was in 1977.

10. In addition, the Commission condemned Turkey for its behavior in Cyprus, but the Council of Europe failed to accept the condemnation. European Commission of Human Rights, *Decisions and Reports,* Nos. 1–5 (Strasbourg, 1975–76); European Commission of Human Rights, irregularly issued *Reports* on individual cases (Strasbourg, 1971–75).

11. Inter-American Commission on Human Rights, *Report(s) on the Work Accomplished During the Twenty-Eighth Session(s) (through Thirty-Third)* (Washington D.C.: General Secretariat of the Organization of American States, 1971–75); *Annual Report 1976* (containing information on 37th, 38th, and 39th sessions of the Commission), Doc. OEA/Ser. L/V/II.40, Doc. 5, Corr. 1, 7 June 1977. Also see *Third Report on the Situation of Human Rights in Chile,* IACHR, OEA/Ser. L/V/II.40, Doc. 10, 11 February 1977.

12. See J. Carey, *UN Protection of Civil and Political Rights* (Syracuse: Syracuse University Press, 1970), pp. 91–94, and chap. 12. United Nations, Commission on Human Rights, *Report(s) On the Twenty-Seventh (through Thirty-Second) Session(s),* ECOSOC *Official Records.* Supplements variously numbered, Fiftieth through Sixtieth Sessions, 1971–76 (Document Numbers E/4949, E/5113, E/5265, E/5464, E/5635, E/5768).

13. Stanley Hoffmann, "The Hell of Good Intentions," *Foreign Policy* 29 (Winter 1977–78): 3.

14. U.S. Department of State, *Gist.* January 1978. Chapter 2 in this volume suggests that the administration overestimated the commitment of American public opinion to an active human rights policy. However, it did not overestimate the desires of specific groups within American opinion (i.e., groups having special concerns for Latin America, Africa and the Soviet Union).

15. *Gist.* January 1978.

16. Ibid.

17. *New York Times.* 18 May 1977, p. 14; 10 February 1978, p. A14; *San Francisco Chronicle.* 5 February 1978, p. 16.

18. Until the advent of the Carter administration, the United States had not complied with the UN-ordered total trade embargo against Rhodesia. Neither had most other chrome-importing countries, including the Soviet Union.

19. *Gist.* January 1978. The administration sent to the Senate for ratification of the two UN covenants, the Genocide convention, and the convention of Racial Discrimination. President Carter also signed the American convention.

20. This material was collected on the basis of all events reported to the *New York Times*. On 7 March 1977, Warren M. Christopher and Patricia Derian told the Senate Foreign Aid Subcommittee that cutting aid was not the best way to deal with human rights violations. Instead, they urged that U.S. diplomatic personnel be given special training in human rights matters so as to be better able to use quiet diplomacy and friendly persuasion.
21. Hoffmann, "The Hell of Good Intentions," pp. 7–8.
22. Richard Ullman, "Human Rights and Economic Power: The United States versus Idi Amin," *Foreign Affairs* 56, no. 3 (April 1978). Ullman makes a most convincing case in favor of the moral and practical feasibility of a binding coffee embargo. My argument accepts and draws on his reasoning. I would add only that unless such an embargo is made a collaborative effort among all major coffee importers, a unilateral embargo might result merely in a shift of customers.
23. A parallel argument cannot be made, in my estimation, for an active human rights policy in South Africa and Rhodesia. What is at stake here are not the core human rights of concern to us, but the much more elusive "right" to national self-determination and the struggle over which nationalist group will seize control of the state eventually. Torture and illegal detention here *cannot* be separated from the larger issue of nourishing democracy. Intervention here implies taking sides on the question of who will eventually win and by what means—in a context *not* hospitable to future democracy. The administration seeks to link its ill-advised intervention with future Soviet power in Africa. This linkage, far from clarifying choices, obscures matters further because it may either help the oppressors or strengthen groups who have no interest in observing human rights once they come to power. Southern Africa makes the case for doing nothing about human rights.

Part III
AREAL PROBLEMS

7

U.S. POLICY TOWARD THE SOVIET UNION

Intractable Issues

Lawrence T. Caldwell
and
Alexander Dallin

American perceptions of this country's relationship with the Soviet Union have undergone considerable fluctuations in recent years. From the brink of conflict in the years of the "classical" cold war to the fumbling for coexistence in the Khrushchev era, from the Nixon-Kissinger détente of the early 1970s to the new tensions and alarms of the Carter years, the pivotal relationship between the superpowers has experienced more ups and downs than many observers had expected.

Soviet perceptions of the relationship, too, have fluctuated considerably, although Moscow has avoided the extremes of optimism and pessimism observed in American opinion. The narrower band within which Soviet attitudes seem to fluctuate is only partly a product of the discipline the Soviet leadership exercises over policy discussion in that country. Soviet analysis of the relationship has persistently stressed that cooperation, détente, peaceful coexistence—whichever formula is used—do *not* mitigate the class struggle. Therefore, Soviet perceptions of the relationship have been explicitly ambiguous; and there have, perhaps, been fewer surprises when expectations of cooperation have confronted the reality of conflict.

Still, the image persists that Soviet-American relations have proven less stable in the 1960s and 1970s than is good for the health of the international political system. Despite these fluctuations between outright hostility and grand shows of summit détente, there has been remarkable continuity in the relationship. The major alternative conceptions of Soviet motivations and intentions were articulated almost a generation ago. The issues confronting the Carter administration with respect to the Soviet Union do not differ fundamentally from those that complicated the choice of foreign policy during the Nixon, Johnson, Kennedy, or Eisenhower years. The United States has not faced fundamental choices in its relationship with the USSR since the Truman Presidency.

This is not to suggest that nothing new has occurred in the conduct or perception of either side. New events—real, anticipated, or imaginary—have provided new challenges and new perspectives: the Soviet strategic buildup of the mid-1970s, the human rights issue stressed by the Carter administration (at least during its first year in office), the surfacing of the energy problem in 1973, SALT, and the rivalries in Africa all provide examples of new events that have affected Soviet-American relations. Nevertheless, the fundamental issues remain concerning strategy and tactics in the conduct of American foreign policy toward the Soviet Union.

Ever since the Russian Revolution of 1917, Americans have worried about what the Soviet regime is up to. Often more obsessive than informed, this preoccupation with a potential adversary had its roots in widely taught and widely shared simplicities about the Bolsheviks and in the actions and pronouncements of the leaders in the Kremlin.[1]

Leaving aside relatively small segments at either extreme of the political spectrum, there have been extended periods of overwhelming consensus among "establishment" observers, policy makers, academic specialists, and the media about Soviet intentions and behavior. At other times there have been pervasive cleavages in Western opinion.

With the benefit of hindsight, it can be said that this American consensus, when it has existed, has not served policy well. It has often frustrated new initiatives, inhibited the willingness to test the waters, and probably caused the United States to miss opportunities whose exploitation would have required a deviant set of assumptions. This was probably true during the years of *rigor mortis* Stalinism; we will never know what effect a different American policy would have had on Soviet behavior in 1945 and 1946, or on Sino-Soviet relations from 1949 on; we are also unlikely to establish who was right and who was wrong in the arguments over Stalin's intentions in 1952 and over his overtures regarding Germany.

The same is true of the Khrushchev years. However erratic the behavior of the Soviet leader, the general thrust of his "westward" move—including the Sino-Soviet split, which many American analysts for too long refused to recognize as genuine, and his visits to the United States in 1959 and 1960—indicated the beginnings of a profound reorientation that the United States might have taken advantage of better and earlier than it did.[2]

On the American side, a sequence of overreactions propelled policy makers and public opinion from one extreme to the other. Thus the Russo-American "amity" of World War II ill-prepared the United States for the realities of postwar tensions, which soon produced the cold war. In turn, long years of hostility and suspicion gave way to exaggerated hopes and naive oversell of détente in the early 1970s. Those expectations set the stage for the reversal that the Carter administration executed in 1977–78.

The consensus on détente was more dubious and more fragile than the other instances, but in each case, what was assumed to be broad consensus turned out to be a disservice to the fresh and open-minded analysis of Soviet conduct and Soviet-American relations. Both the historical record and the principle of benefiting from an examination of alternative assumptions argue strongly for a multiple-advocacy approach to the study and understanding of Soviet-American relations.[3]

This chapter argues that the debate that heated up over Soviet-American relations during the Carter administration has, in fact, revolved around a series of persistent issues, many of which have not received adequate articulation and analytical discussion. We seek to frame these issues in a slightly different manner from the shape they normally assume in public debate, and to make some preliminary observations about their policy implications.

None of this analysis can be undertaken without our first observing how little informed the American public debate is by attempts to understand Soviet perspectives on the current stage of U.S. relations with the Soviet Union. The substantial controversy that characterizes this debate has been conducted at a level of generalization about the Soviet Union and the motivations of the Kremlin leadership that does a genuine disservice to long-term requirements for achieving increased understanding between the two societies. Although this chapter is not an appropriate place to undertake a systematic review of the assumptions underlying the American debate, it must begin with a minimal consideration of the Soviet perspective on the cooling of détente.

THE VIEW FROM MOSCOW

From Moscow's perspective the mood in Soviet-American relations began to deteriorate during the winter of 1975–76 when the relationship was first represented by Secretary of State Henry Kissinger and his influential deputy, Helmut Sonnenfeldt, as a means by which to manage the Soviet Union's emergence into the role of a global and imperial power. After January 1976, President Ford toughened his verbal position on the relationship with the Soviet Union under pressure from Ronald Reagan's challenge for the Republican presidential nomination; the CIA upwardly revised its estimates of Soviet defense spending spectacularly; the Congressional Research Service prepared an alarmist assessment of the "U.S.–Soviet military balance"; and Secretary of Defense Donald Rumsfeld issued his annual report in terms that, while not varying much in tone or substance from those of his predecessor, once again made Soviet military advances the foundation of his argument for U.S. defense spending.

Predictably, in Moscow, where détente had not recovered from the Trade Bill controversy of January 1975, the Soviets became apprehensive about how much of the noise from Washington was campaign rhetoric and how much represented a fundamental shift in American policy. There was genuine uncertainty in Moscow about the views of President Ford and candidate Jimmy Carter, and intense interest in how the outcome of the U.S. election might affect the Soviet-American relationship. There was also frustration with the alteration of mood in Washington, which seemed to place the basic shared interest between the superpowers—SALT II—in jeopardy for partisan considerations.

General Secretary Leonid Brezhnev gave one of the first signals of this perception in his report to the 25th Party Congress on February 24, 1976, when he suggested that détente had been complicated by "influential forces in the United States that have no interest either in improving relations with the Soviet Union or in international detente as a whole." [4] Brezhnev stressed his desire to bring SALT II to a conclusion and was reasonably open about his objectives: to obtain some restraint in the American B-1 bomber and Trident submarine programs.

Secretary Kissinger went to Moscow in January, and apparently he felt he had almost nailed down a SALT II agreement. On his way back to the United States via Brussels and Madrid, he spoke with cautious optimism and suggested that the numerical guidelines of Vladivostok might actually be reduced. Two factors intervened to dampen his optimism: (1) technical limits on the cruise missile evidently became an issue in Washington, then possibly between Washington and Moscow; and (2) although U.S.–Soviet differences might have been compromised without substantial danger to the strategic equation, Ford's difficulties in his quest for the Republican nomination reduced his willingness to compromise and to oppose the Pentagon. By mid-April, with the Texas, Indiana, Georgia, and Alabama primaries ahead of him and already beginning to run scared, he apparently decided (through a meeting of the National Security Council) to go public with the story that SALT II had reached an impasse and to put it on the shelf until after the national convention.

The director of Moscow's Institute for the USA and Canada, Georgy Arbatov, who has good connections with the Kremlin, urged against this move in *Pravda* on April 2.[5] During April and May the Soviet press began to take a tougher line on détente and on SALT II.[6] This shift in the Soviet position may have meant that Soviet policy was changing. More likely, the Soviet leadership had as its central purpose to warn the United States that two could play the "get tough" game and to prepare Soviet citizens for the possibility of no SALT II agreement in the near future and deteriorating relations between the two countries.

Thus, the deterioration of Soviet-American relations began to be acknowledged on both sides in 1976. Détente, as the relationship was labeled during its more positive months in 1972–74, was placed on the back burner. From Moscow's perspective, the American election was the cause. This interpretation could be protested on rather persuasive grounds. Reports of Soviet actions in Angola and Portugal were not likely to change anyone's mind about Soviet purposes—at least not any minds in places where they counted. The process of shifting political mood is subtle. Kissinger had repeatedly drawn attention to the ambiguous nature of Soviet ambitions and had consistently argued that the purpose of détente was to encourage the Soviets to see their interests better served by stressing cooperation with the United States than by emphasizing conflict. It was unlikely that Portugal or Angola changed his mind.

Soviet actions during 1975 forced Ford and Kissinger to call attention to Moscow's choice of policy, which stressed the conflict side of the relationship. This provided an opportunity for those less enthusiastic about détente to emphasize their case, to score points. Political forces, inside and outside government, favorable to cooperation with the Soviet Union went on the defensive. The whole tone of the election campaign changed. Political forces in Washington favorable to détente, then, faced a double handicap: Secretary Kissinger and the State Department were forced to stress the limits of détente, and those who had reservations about U.S.–Soviet cooperation moved to the offensive. Soviet actions in 1974–75 contributed to the shift in mood in Washington.

In this context the Carter administration came to power. Secretary of Defense Rumsfeld and President Ford left office issuing grave warnings about Soviet intentions.[7] Harvard Russian historian Richard Pipes led a study of Soviet intentions (known as "Team B") that formulated a very negative view of Soviet purposes.[8] The Committee on the Present Danger was created. Some of this intensive activity inevitably left an imprint on the formative stages of the Carter administration's Soviet policy and affected the atmosphere in which a bureaucratic scramble for mid-level positions took place in the new administration.

The Soviets understood the dangers of this process. They moved quickly but cautiously after the election. During a visit by President Ford's Treasury secretary, William Simon, in late November, Brezhnev acknowledged that the election had damaged Soviet-American relations and held out the prospect of greatly increased trade between the countries if the relationship could be gotten back on the détente track.[9] Arbatov, in a major *Pravda* article on December 11, hinted that the Soviets would be tough.[10] He warned that Washington would have to pay for the "dishes broken" during the campaign.

On January 18, 1977, Brezhnev made a major policy speech in Tula on Soviet-American relations.[11] He called the alarms sounded by Ford, Rumsfeld, and Team B "tiresome twaddle." More important, he interpreted U.S. defense programs such as the B-1, cruise missiles, and Trident submarines, and the American positions in SALT II and MBFR, as the results of hawkish influence in Washington. He stressed the need for détente, which he defined as a "willingness to resolve differences and disputes not by saber-rattling, but by peaceful means, at the negotiating table." "Détente," he said, "means a certain trust and ability to take one another's legitimate interests into account." On March 21, Brezhnev made another important speech to the Trade Union Congress in Moscow. He attacked the Carter administration's emphasis on "human rights" in the strongest possible terms:

> *Washington's assertions that it is entitled to teach others how to live cannot, I believe, be accepted by any sovereign state. . . . Let me repeat: we shall not tolerate interference in our internal affairs by anyone, under any pretext. The normal development of relations on such a basis is, of course, unthinkable.*[12]

He chided Washington for taking no constructive actions to overcome the "stagnation" in the relationship and argued that "important objective possibilities" existed for improving it.

The months from January 1976 to March 1977 were crucial in the formulation of Soviet attitudes toward its relationship with the United States. Secretary of State Cyrus Vance's mission to Moscow, with its "deep cuts" and one-sided proposals for SALT II, could not have been timed worse. The Brezhnev leadership had already given indications it would respond to American "cooling" tactics by "toughening" its own position. Knowing this, Secretary Vance took proposals to Moscow that would have required the Soviet Union to reduce its SLBM/ICBM forces under the proposed general ceilings of 1800 to 2000 missiles, that would have limited MIRVs to 550 ICBMs (precisely the number already deployed by the United States and a limit that maximized the U.S. technological lead in SLBM technology), and would have limited "large" missiles to 150 (only the Soviets had deployed them). The Soviet rejection was of unprecedented severity.

Some of Brezhnev's pique may have resulted from what he judged a double injury to his foreign policy. He saw people taking control of Washington's foreign policy apparatus who professed the intention of correcting Secretary of State Kissinger's "overemphasis" on East-West issues by upgrading trilateral relations with industrialized nations of Europe and Japan and North-South issues. In addition, Brezhnev had to face at least the irritant and possibly the real threat of Carter's "human rights" campaign. Both trends in U.S. policy—to reduce the rôle of Soviet-American relations and to force them into a human rights context—constituted strong motives for the Soviet leadership to pull the new administration back onto a bilateral track between the superpowers.

Much of what happened in the following months may have confirmed these judgments in the minds of the Politburo members. After relations had been mutually acknowledged by both sides to reach their lowest point in at least a decade during the early summer, the Carter administration signaled its willingness to take a more moderate stance in the President's Charleston speech on July 21, 1977.[13] In the fall, Vance and Foreign Minister Andrei Gromyko seemed to get SALT II back on track.[14] But the Carter administration continued to give signs of indecision— mixing "hard" with "accommodating" signals—and Moscow continued to behave as though it had decided on a policy that would move slowly on the SALT II issue but continue to assert its interests in Africa and refuse obdurately all efforts by the Carter administration to interfere in its domestic affairs. The arrest and trial of prominent dissidents, and the harassment of correspondents, suggested that the Brezhnev leadership had chosen to dissociate cooperative interests (SALT II) from conflictive ones (Africa and human rights).[15]

From Moscow's perspective, then, the issues affecting Soviet-American relations look different than from Washington's. First, the deterioration of the relationship has not been simply the product of Carter's new policies. On the contrary, it represents a cumulative trend stretching back at least to 1975. The Kremlin, moreover, sees that it exercised restraint and patience, at least until March 1977, whereas the United States sacrificed its long-term interests in cooperation with the Soviet Union to temporary political necessities.

More important, Soviet analysts made it clear that this movement toward cooler relations was initiated on the American side as a result of greater influence by the "hawks."[16] That meant that the Brezhnev leadership had a vested interest in not letting Washington use the deterioration of relations as a tool for obtaining agreements more to its liking in SALT II and MBFR, and also in preventing the success of a harder line that would, from Moscow's perspective, strengthen anti-Soviet forces within Washington's bureaucratic struggle.

On the second issue, human rights, the Politburo found itself in a serious dilemma. It had assumed since at least the spring of 1972 that a reduction of tensions between East and West would be paralleled by what it called increased "ideological vigilance" at home.[17] Thus, détente had been based on a reduction of ideological emphasis in U.S.-Soviet relations, but not at home and not in the competition for influence in the Third World. Regarding Soviet relationship with its dissidents and Soviet support for "revolutionary" movements in Africa, Asia, and Latin America, any de-emphasis on ideology directly threatened the basis of the Communist party's claim to legitimacy. From the Kremlin's perspective, détente was in essence an agreement to reduce the ideological dimensions of the cold war among the industrialized nations, but it never implied changes at home or in Soviet policy toward the Third World. Carter's human rights policy seemed to break these rules and threaten the basis of détente. The Soviet leadership had deep self-interests in deflating Carter's policy.

Finally, Moscow's leaders did not view their military programs as threatening. They pointed out that the SS-X programs, additions to combat aircraft and armor, and improvements in the Red Navy were all natural products of the Soviet acquisition of global superpower status. They argued that even considerable and responsible authorities in the West had concluded that the Soviet Union was achieving not military "superiority," but "parity." That, they argued, was the natural and inevitable condition of their new role as a power equal to the United States. It seemed unnatural that the United States should retain control of the seas and have both quantitative and qualitative superiority in strategic weapons. On the contrary, from the Soviet point of view, the overall shift of political forces in favor of socialism should be reflected in the military balance. Those in the West who did not accept this reality were, again from the Kremlin's perspective, the most "reactionary" and "anti-Soviet" among the political forces of their adversaries. As with human rights, therefore, the Soviet leadership had a strong vested interest in attempting to influence American and Western politics in a way that prevented these forces from dominating politics in Britain, France, Germany, the United States, and Japan.

None of these Soviet perceptions, of course, needs to be accepted by the United States. In fact, the purpose of maintaining an active policy of cooperation is to control the kinds of conflict implicit in these Soviet positions. But the Soviet perspective is more reasonable than is often credited in this country. It is not a mystery. It has its own logic.

Soviet policy certainly is not one of deception, one designed to "take in" the Americans while preparing for a final confrontation. Soviet perceptions revealed genuine uncertainties about American intentions during the mid-1970s, and the deterioration in Soviet-American relations has taken place against the backdrop of substantial tensions between Peking and Moscow. It has not gone unobserved in the Soviet Union that the most "anti-Soviet" voices in Washington have also called for the United States to "play the China card."

THE MAJOR ISSUES

The preceding interpretation of the way in which the Soviet leadership has read and dealt with the Carter administration, even if it approximates the Kremlin reality closely—and our knowledge permits no full confidence that it does—still does little to explain the political environment in which the Carter White House has operated. In fact, neither Moscow nor Washington responds primarily to the perceptions and actions of the other. The proximate pressures of their own political environments, even when these are engaged sharply by U.S.–Soviet relations, naturally constitute the principal concerns of both Carter and Brezhnev.

The political environment in Washington since 1974 has been extremely complicated with respect to the superpower relationship. In part the difficulties have reflected the unsettled state of American politics following the defeat in Vietnam and the disgrace of Watergate, and in part they have reflected the inevitable product of a new international environment only marginally affected by Vietnam or Watergate. First, the Soviet Union emerged during the 1970s as a global superpower. That is a fact, and adjustment to it would be difficult for the United States irrespective of other instabilities in domestic and international politics. Second, the OPEC embargo upgraded a number of issues in the New International Economic Order on the policy agendas of all industrialized states. Thus, just when the relative military power of the Soviet Union and United States seemed to be shifting in favor of the adversary, the definition of power in the international system seemed to reduce the influence of both superpowers in fundamental ways. The Carter administration, and any others that follow it during the next decade, are simply faced with the need to adjust American policy along both these critical axes at the same time.

Moreover, with respect to the bilateral relationship, the Carter administration has had to deal with a number of interconnected issues against the twin backgrounds of (1) an exaggerated sense, partly inherited from the Kissinger era, that all issues dividing Moscow and Washington were amenable to manageable resolution by direct negotiation; and (2) an exaggerated sense, only partly the product of Soviet behavior, that détente has been a failure as it ostensibly serves to camouflage a new Soviet offensive whose ultimate victim is a weakened United States. In large measure, tension between these two approaches has been responsible for the setting in which contending personalities and bureaucracies, a lack of clear vision at the top, and conflicting interpretations of events contributed to the turbulence in American policy toward the Soviet Union in 1977–78.

The issues are not all, or even for the most part, new. They have persisted since the late 1940s. They require careful rethinking.

The Issue of Linkage

The Carter administration has found itself ensnared in its own concept of linkage. It has attempted to link, or to deny that it is linking, SALT II to Africa, trade to the protection of human rights in the Soviet Union, and American domestic politics (particularly attitudes in the U.S. Senate) to any number of questions in Soviet-American relations.[18] The idea of linkage grows naturally out of the fact that the two superpowers share some interests and conflict over others. It is tempting to try to affect the Soviet Union's position on questions where our interests conflict by threatening to forfeit cooperation on questions where our interests seem to coincide.

Ultimately, linkage increases ideological conflict. The attempt to establish linkage between conflicting and cooperative interests implies that all issues are woven into an endless seam and that progress on one cannot be expected without progress on all. By tying cooperative interests to conflictive ones in this way, all issues are brought back finally to the ideological differences between the two political systems. In a curious way, the United States and Soviet Union have reversed roles. In the 1950s, especially on disarmament questions, the USSR called for "universal and complete disarmament." Presidents Eisenhower and Kennedy were frustrated by this "all or nothing" approach, which ran counter to the American pragmatic tendency to break conflicts into discrete issues and negotiate where differences did not seem irreconcilable. In the 1970s, the United States has often seemed to initiate this kind of all-or-nothing dialogue—demanding that the Soviets change their internal treatment of dissidents, alter their policy in the Middle East, or cease support for revolutionary movements in Africa as a price for making progress on strategic arms limitation or for increasing trade.

The internal debate over whether to establish linkages has often been oblique and confused. Secretary Kissinger succumbed to the temptation to establish linkages during his step-by-step efforts to obtain Soviet cooperation in securing a settlement in the Middle East, but made a persuasive argument to the Senate Foreign Relations Committee during the Trade Bill debate in 1974 against tying one moral value (control of arms competition and the risks of nuclear war) to another (the emigration of Jews from the USSR).[19] As Kissinger recognized in the latter context, but not in the former, linkage ultimately requires the setting of policy priorities: is the conflictive value to be obtained worth the risk of the cooperative value to which its resolution is tied?

Thus the debate, or nondebate, on linkages is precisely over priorities in American foreign policy toward the Soviet Union. The differences among the participants are not absolute. Probably all participants would agree that on *some* issues of potential conflict—say, the establishment of Soviet hegemony by military means over Germany or Israel—the sacrifice of any cooperative issue would be an appropriate means by which to secure leverage. Nonetheless, much of the discussion and conduct of American policy toward the Soviet Union has seemed to have an almost mindless disregard for the tough questions of priorities. It might further be argued that policy makers, who often naturally exaggerate the significance of immediate issues and pay less attention to the demands of those issues on which quiet progress is being made, are almost uniquely unsuited to make ad hoc judgments about the priorities on which all linkages must be based.

The Issue of Leverage

What does one do about the fact that the dominant culture of neither the Soviet Union nor the United States has much understanding of, and probably has strong prejudice against, the political and economic systems of the other? One of the darkest pages of American history was written over the fear that the Soviet Union was dedicated to promoting the overthrow of the American system by communist infiltration into every corner of our national life. Alexander Solzhenitsyn has irreversibly affected our generation by his portrayal of those dark chapters in Soviet life during which loyal citizens were herded into the *gulag* partly because their loyalty was presumed to be compromised by the most innocent contact with the outside world.

The issue of exercising leverage on the development of the internal system in the Soviet Union has been among the most divisive in the American debate over Soviet-American relations. Much of the discussion in the Soviet Union over détente in general and the Conference on Security and Cooperation in Europe in particular has centered precisely on the obverse of this leverage question—what the Soviets have referred to as "ideological subversion" by the West and "interference in Soviet internal affairs." [20] On the American side the issue is simply put: how high a priority should be placed on any effort to change the internal structure or domestic policies of the Soviet Communist regime and what are the prospects for promoting systemic change or the selection of domestic policies by American pressure?

The Carter administration has been particularly handicapped on this issue. The President's personal commitment to "human rights" has led to verbal and symbolic interventions on behalf of Soviet dissidents—Vladimir Bukovsky and Anatoly Shcharansky, to name the most prominent. We argued above that the form, if not the substance, of the Carter policy during the early months of 1977 contributed to an equally determined effort by the Brezhnev leadership to "cut" the human rights–SALT II linkage and communicate a tough refusal to permit "interference" in Soviet internal affairs. The administration has been caught in a dilemma that has implications for American policy extending beyond its tenure in office. Interventions by the President on behalf of individual dissidents or ethnic groups in the Soviet Union, no matter how worthy, do not get at the root problems of political repression. On the contrary, these actions may have the opposite effect: they may increase repression. It can be argued that the Soviet leadership has a vested interest in conveying precisely the message that American interference leads to more trials, harsher sentences, tougher police controls. Thus, the Carter administration, while bound by its general policy to confront evidence of human rights violations in the Soviet Union, has (1) not ameliorated the conditions it deplores and (2) has sacrificed some of the accomplishments of the previous administrations in improving Soviet-American relations.

The temptation of the Carter administration has been to have it both ways: to speak out on the egregious characteristics of the Soviet system while keeping cooperation on track. It has been a difficult line to walk. Almost any effort to alter the internal system or domestic policies of the partner-adversary in the superpower relationship opens a vast storehouse of ideological disagreement. One cannot go far down that path before being driven against the wall of Solzhenitsyn's logic: the fundamental incompatibility of communism and Western pluralism.[21] We've been against that wall before, and once our backs are to it there is precious little opportunity for cooperation on such issues as strategic arms limitation or the control of risks in global competition.

Of course the President is right. The Soviets have never failed to continue the ideological struggle on their side and have explicitly refused to abandon it.[22] There is logic to Carter's insistence that the United States also not abdicate its values in those cases where interests conflict and the incompatibilities of individual and collectivist rights become evident. But the habit of cooperation between the superpowers is not deeply rooted, and détente is fragile. It is difficult to know how far and when to push. It is inexcusable to ignore that dramatic interventions on behalf of individual dissidents by the White House constitute a challenge to the authority of the Kremlin leadership and will inevitably be construed as efforts to obtain leverage over the internal affairs of the Soviet Union. It may be cathartic to do so, or even be required for the demonstration of American determination and dedication to national values, but the risks are great and the outcomes dubious, possibly even counterproductive. Moscow intends to make sure that it is. Privately, authoritative Soviet officials have made clear that Brezhnev "could not afford to let Carter get away with it"—presumably, vis-à-vis his own Politburo associates as much as vis-à-vis the outside world. Thus, "American interference in Soviet internal affairs" may provide incentives for the Kremlin to tighten controls over the very people the U.S. policy is intended to help. Neither superpower can allow the other to obtain great or frequent leverage over its selection of domestic policy or over the nature of its internal regime without surrendering the ideological differences that legitimate its exercise of power.

The issue of leverage is broader than the question of Carter's human rights policy, but the latter has provided the sharpest example of the former. At the least, after the Soviet abrogation of the Trade Agreement in January 1975, and after the Brezhnev leadership's reaction to the Carter human rights campaign, it is obvious that the United States cannot often play its own diplomatic or economic cards to achieve leverage over the Soviet domestic politics; to do so is counterproductive at best and risks substantial interests at worst.

The Issue of Military Competition

Much of the uncertainty and dynamism in Soviet-American relations comes down finally to the question of military power. Regardless of one's assessment of the nature and meaning of Soviet military power, almost no observer in the United States disagrees with the observation that the military balance is qualitatively different in the mid-1970s from the 1950s and 1960s. Whether one judges the Soviets to have achieved superiority, to be attempting to achieve superiority, to have achieved or be aiming for parity, or still to have substantial military vulnerabilities, almost everyone agrees that the USSR in the 1970s is a global superpower capable of projecting significant and impressive military power far beyond its territorial approaches. The remarkable thing about the debate over Soviet power in the West is how little disagreement there is over this central fact.

The problem has been, and is, to judge what implications this noticeable improvement in the relative power position of the Soviet Union has for international affairs. In particular, given the persistence of political and economic competition between the superpowers, between East and West, what are the risks that their formidable military power might be brought to bear on the resolution of conflict and what are the risks of escalation to a major military confrontation? Africa has become a symbol of this question. Soviet actions in Africa following the Angolan intervention in 1974–75 constitute a qualitative alteration of Soviet foreign policy in two respects. First, the Soviet Union has not previously mounted anything on the scale of its "interference" in Africa outside its own borders and those of the states immediately contiguous to it. Second, the Soviet Union has participated in, and encouraged, a sophisticated and coordinated effort by the socialist bloc to affect the balance of power among political forces in southern Africa as the racist regimes of (Portuguese) Angola, Rhodesia, and South Africa have come under intensified pressure for majority rule. This demonstration of a willingness to use military power, albeit mostly by proxy, at such distances from Soviet borders has coincided with the actual achievement of global-power capabilities. Therefore, the question has been unavoidable in American politics of the relationship between Soviet military capabilities and political intentions. That question most passionately engages the division between right and left, liberals and conservatives in the West.

It is obvious, but not very helpful, to observe that capabilities do not provide a good indication of intentions. Although Soviet military programs and the exercise of newly established global reach cannot be demonstrated conclusively to constitute evidence of aggressive motivation or determination to gain superiority over the United States, those military capabilities do exist and decisions to procure them were taken. Thoughtful observers must address their meaning. Whatever one judges to be the motivation for their deployment, Soviet military forces also constitute real problems for NATO and American forces.

As discussed, the Carter administration came to power at a particularly impropitious moment for the impartial consideration of this relationship between Soviet power and Soviet intentions. The Soviet-backed faction in Angola had succeeded, Kissinger and Sonnenfeldt had felt obligated to call attention to the emergence of Soviet "imperial power," President Ford had retreated before attacks from the right in his own party and had sacrificed an early SALT II agreement to his own political needs, and political forces with the most hostile interpretation of Soviet military power were clearly on the offensive as the changeover from the Ford to the Carter administrations took place. This was the context of Carter's decisions on the B-1 bomber, the neutron warhead, the MX and cruise missiles. Altogether, Carter's record in demonstrating restraint in defense programs is probably better than the arms control liberals in his party had any right to expect, especially given the dynamics by which other international political issues—nuclear proliferation, the New International Economic Order, the trilateral idea, human rights—assumed relatively more importance than the bilateral Soviet-American relationship and its central dynamic, SALT II.

The Carter administration has had to develop its approach to the Soviet Union in the context of several military developments.

First, the Soviet Union has completed testing and has engaged in vigorous deployment of the SS-16, 17, 19 ICBMs and the SS-X-20 land-mobile MRBM.[23] Especially the coupling of the SS-X-18 and 19 to MIRV has seemed to threaten the viability of American Minuteman forces, and the SS-X-20 has brought NATO's deterrent and flexible response strategy under sharp reexamination. The issue of strategic balance is particularly difficult for the Carter administration. This feature of the arms race has been complicated by the interaction of technology and strategy. Although the United States has retained significant advantages in number of deliverable warheads (11,000 to 3800), by which the Soviet leadership has justified going forward with its own programs, the size of the Soviet SS-X-18 and 19 missiles has prompted some observers to question whether the Soviet Union might ultimately be tempted in certain crisis situations to launch a preemptive first strike.[24] Of course, from the Soviet point of view, American advances in missile accuracy have raised the same specter. It is a technological dilemma that an increased number of warheads on a single missile, especially if each one has counterforce accuracy, increases both the second- and first-strike credibility of the force. That is, a limited number of each side's missiles, each equipped with multiple reentry vehicles (MIRV), might be used to attack the other side's ICBMs in a first strike. Alternatively, even if relatively few missiles were to survive a first strike, if each has MIRV, the damage they can inflict is substantial; and they are assumed to pose a real second-strike deterrent threat. Therefore, MIRV technology works both to increase the deterrent effect of a second strike and to multiply the risks of war by increasing the feasibility of a first strike.

Second, the Soviet Union has modernized its navy, increasing its reach and vastly improving its capability to interdict NATO's sea lines of communication.[25] While the Soviet navy cannot be thought of as equal to the American navy, let alone combined NATO naval forces, it clearly can deny any nation dominance of the seas. Moreover, it has been steadily expanding its capability and mission. The Carter administration therefore has been under pressure to increase the size of the American navy's defense appropriation. The administration has resisted this pressure at some political cost.[26]

Third, the Carter administration has improved the army's participation in defense priorities. This has come largely as a result of Soviet efforts to upgrade their ground forces, especially in Europe. The size of Soviet forces located on the territory of the Warsaw Pact has not increased noticeably since 1968, but their capability has improved through a steady modernization program.[27] Especially Soviet armored and antiarmor forces have continued development in ways that seem to many observers not justifiable by any objective reading of the Warsaw Pact–NATO military disposition in Europe.

Finally, the military balance in Europe has been affected by a development many specialists find most disturbing. The Soviet air force has shifted emphasis from interceptors to ground-attack configurations.[28] The Su-17 Fitter C, the MiG-23 Flogger B, and the Su-19 Fencer all provide more offensive capability in terms of support for ground warfare. Combined with the inexorable improvement of Soviet armored capabilities (especially the T-62, T-72 tanks, and BMP mechanized infantry combat vehicles), the shift in Soviet air tactics suggests the extension of capabilities.

All these military developments can be argued to constitute evidence of expansionist political ambitions, as has been stated in American defense debates. The general pattern of Soviet military developments has undeniably been to increase Soviet options for "offensive" operations. Of course, these same developments can be argued simply to constitute sensible military precautions against improvements in American and NATO capabilities, as the Soviets have stated. But the mood in the United States is that improvements in Soviet capabilities have gone beyond, or will soon go beyond, those justified by the long-professed Soviet desire for parity. This alteration of mood was symbolized in early 1976 by the CIA's change in the way it costed Soviet defense expenditure, which resulted in consensus for the first time in estimates that Soviet defense spending exceeded that of the United States when both budgets were expressed in dollar equivalents.[29] That change was the product of a bureaucratic fight in which powerful elements in the CIA eventually capitulated to others in the Defense Department. But the ease with which even the attentive American public has adopted the habit of describing the Soviet defense effort as larger than that of the United States reflects a change of mood in Washington as a result of Soviet efforts in military power. The Carter administration has had to contend with an atmosphere in Washington quite different from that of its immediate predecessors, a fact not yet widely appreciated by the American public.

The Issue of International Communism

The issue of international communism has three dimensions: the Sino-Soviet relationship; the Soviet Union's position in Eastern Europe; and Moscow's approach to the nonruling Communist parties, especially in Western Europe. All are troublesome for the United States. The West generally was slow to credit the seriousness of the Chinese disagreement with the Russians, and the reason was at least partly ideological. Our own ideological biases have consistently made it difficult to acknowledge the diversity of Communist parties, and our rivalry with the Soviet Union has promoted the kind of zero-sum thinking by which "communist" gains have been misread as "Soviet" gains.

This Western habit of failing to differentiate among Communist parties has influenced the Carter administration but has been intertwined with the American approach to NATO. The concept of "Eurocommunism" has emerged in the middle 1970s, and every Western government has had to face the growth of leftist political forces in Italy, France, and on the Iberian Peninsula. The Carter administration has not been too heavy-handed in voicing its disapproval of the French and Italian Communist parties but still came in for rather strong criticism from other French and Italian political forces for "intervention" in the elections of 1978 (see chapter 9).[30] The fundamental difficulty lies in the fear that greater participation by the left in West European politics will decrease American and increase Soviet influence. That supposition needs to be reexamined rigorously.

It seems clear that American efforts to influence the outcome of elections or political arrangements in allied countries are counterproductive. Such interference produces a nationalist and anti-American reaction and may strengthen those forces least amenable to those who interfere. But the more profound reasons for restraint in articulating American preferences go beyond such immediate effects. The general trend leftward in European politics may suggest that those political cultures are changing profoundly (see chapter 9), and it is not in America's interest to be identified with traditional, change-resistant elements. More important, it is not clear that consensus exists in the American culture for intervention against communist participation in West European politics. To intervene may activate the kind of bitter political cleavages that surfaced in our political system during the late 1960s and early 1970s. That is not to say that the left is influential in American politics; rather, the issue may be posed differently in the future, with the United States seen as supporting traditional, elitist, possibly even antidemocratic elements in Europe. Both Italian and French politics provide some basis for confusing anticommunist and pro-NATO political forces with entrenched economic and political privileged classes. Should the issue be posed in that manner, the impact on American politics is by no means as certain as the actions of both the Kissinger and Carter years would imply.

This apparent American impulse to resist change in Western Europe is linked to the NATO problem. In many ways NATO is a necessary military alliance that has outlived its political utility. Both the growth of the European Community and persistent strain between the United States and its European partners have reduced the capacity of NATO for coordinated political action. Moreover, the perceived military necessity to counter a deteriorating military balance in Europe has strengthened the defense rationale for NATO. Thus, something of a division has developed within the United States and its European allies between those whose bureaucratic responsibilities lie in defense and those whose roles lie in the economic and political areas. The former have felt a sense of embattlement as they have confronted the realities of improved Warsaw Pact and Soviet capabilities and have naturally preferred the simpler world of clear-cut East-West rivalry that the military balance has continued to imply. These elements have reinforced the tendency to resist Eurocommunism. On the other hand, governmental and nongovernmental actors with political and economic responsibilities have tended to be more sensitive to American-European difficulties, and have not seemed eager to rush into the fight against the West European Communist parties.

The Soviets have had a parallel difficulty. Europe has long been the focus of Soviet campaigns to woo democratic governments away from American influence. In fact, for much of the postwar period Soviet policy in Europe has had two primary goals: to undercut American influence, and to constrain the reestablishment of German power. The Soviet effort to gain access to Western technology in the 1970s has altered these traditional bases of policy slightly, and Eurocommunism has presented the Kremlin with a difficult set of choices. On the one hand, many of the Brezhnev leadership's impulses clearly cut in the direction of supporting communist gains in Europe. These reinforce traditional ideological prejudices and offer some not altogether predictable opportunities for achieving the traditional goal of reducing American influence in Western Europe.[31] On the other hand, support for Eurocommunism has the potential for bringing the USSR into conflict with West European democratic and capitalist governments and reducing Soviet access to Japanese, American, and European trade.

More difficult, from the Kremlin's point of view, is the relationship of Eurocommunism to Eastern Europe. The effects of peaceful gains for the French and Italian Communist parties on reformist elements in Hungary, Poland, and even Germany and Czechoslovakia are ultimately unpredictable. In fact, the modification of political and economic forms in the Warsaw Pact and Comecon since 1969 have been motivated by the Soviet need to create a more cooperative framework in Eastern Europe as a hedge against the dual threats of Sino-Soviet difficulties and the dynamic political and economic demonstration effort of Western Europe.[32]

The fundamental question regarding American conceptions of Communist parties' roles in Western Europe and international communism generally is whether internal dynamics promoting diversity and experimentation are to be exploited for short-term gains against the Soviet Union, or whether these dynamics will be conceived to work toward the long-term interests of pluralism and democracy. The latter conception seems more sensible, provided these forces are not exploited in such a way as to reengage the kind of bipolar conflict that inevitably increases Soviet leverage over developments in the international communist movements.

The normalization of diplomatic relations with the People's Republic of China, dramatized by the visit of Vice Premier Teng Hsiao-ping to the United States in January–February 1979, brought to the fore yet another dispute within the Carter administration. Was the Chinese connection to be used to align the PRC with the West against the Soviet Union, or was the United States to commit itself to "evenhandedness" in dealing with the two communist giants?

While the implications of the "China card" were hard to miss—Brzezinski had in mid-1978 formulated the official view that a strong China was in the American national interest—there was concern by observers outside the NSC over the effect of normalization—or rather, the way it was handled and what it implied—on Soviet perceptions and behavior. The delay in the conclusion of negotiations for the new SALT treaty was widely seen as a consequence of the new Sino-American tie. Fears were voiced over the implications Moscow might draw from its new sense of encirclement by China, Japan, the United States, and NATO. Other circles in Washington were advocating a clear "tilt" in American policy in favor of the PRC.

It was apparent that the White House had failed to adopt and impose a single policy. On the one hand, siding with the State Department position (and vigorously encouraged to do so by his West European allies), the President in mid-January sought to assure the Soviet leadership that the U.S. would sell no arms to Peking (though the United States could not pretend to regulate or impede arms sales to China by its NATO allies). Some observers foresaw an early administration effort to repeal the 1974 Jackson-Vanik Amendment (denying most-favored-nation status to communist countries that do not permit free emigration) equally in regard to both the USSR and the PRC. Plans for the Brezhnev visit to Washington called for a style and level equivalent to those of the Chinese visit.

On the other hand, Carter had been led to misinterpret publicly the less than benign Soviet reaction to his normalization announcement. And he had presumably approved Brzezinski's insertion into the Sino-American communiqué of the condemnation of "hegemony"—the code word used by the Chinese for Soviet domination, whose use (Brzezinski was bound to know) could not but be perceived in Moscow as a clear provocation.

It was obvious that a fundamental difference over American foreign policy remained unresolved, and even a formal commitment to a policy of "balance" or "symmetry" was not likely to forestall serious questions regarding its meaning and implications in the months and years ahead.[33]

The Issue of Asymmetrical Societies

At its root, the rivalry between the United States and the Soviet Union is more than the sum of its parts. It is more than simply an ideological difference between communism and democracy, more than competition between great powers. The two societies are fundamentally different. The one is peasant-based; it is still rural in the last quarter of the twentieth century, although it has strong industrial bases collected in its cities; it has a long history of authoritarian rule and a complicated mixture of admiration and disdain for Western culture; and it is based on a tradition of collectivist values powerfully reinforced by its official Marxism-Leninism. The other society is urban and has moved beyond the traditional structures of industrialism; its frontier experience has left an indelible imprint of individualism; its centers of economic and political power are pluralist in ways unmatched by any other culture on earth; but it may have deep strains of intolerance that as yet have surfaced only occasionally. Both societies have strong ethnic, racial, and national minorities, although their approach to the problems of assimilation have been radically different. Such complicated asymmetries provide a rich breeding ground for misperception and require the modest restraint in policy that genuine humility dictates in the face of imperfect understanding.

Perhaps at the turn of the twenty-first century other issues will become more important. The power structures of both nations are essentially dominated by people of European descent; both are consumer-oriented; both have strong traditions of economic growth; and both will increasingly need access to resources outside their geographical boundaries. Neither is well adapted to profit from the shift of international power from the East-West axis to the North-South one (see chapter 6). Each has an ultimate interest in survival, but while each possesses the military power to ensure that the other cannot survive, neither is able to guarantee its own survival. They are mutual hostages. These commonalities might provide the basis for cooperation in the future, but the asymmetrical nature of their cultures will require long, persistent, and difficult efforts to avoid the most destructive manifestations of their conflicting interests and to build on their cooperative ones.

UNDERLYING ASSUMPTIONS

If we look at the major positions advocated in the United States on the cluster of issues discussed, we find that they can usefully be examined through the prism of three heuristic models suggested some years ago by other analysts of American policy toward the Soviet Union.[34] The labels often applied to these three approaches are *essentialist, mechanistic,* and *cybernetic.*

> *Generally, the essentialist approach [writes one political scientist] is almost entirely microanalytic in its explanatory orientation, describing Soviet foreign policy behavior as flowing logically from the nature of totalitarianism, just as its Soviet high-Stalinist counterpart explains American foreign policy as flowing logically from the nature of imperialism. In both cases it is not what the country in question does but what it is which is the source of conflict.*[35]

The essentialist school is thus highly determinist; it minimizes the possibility of change in the Soviet system and thus also dismisses the "reactive" elements in Soviet policy. It requires no day-to-day scrutiny of the Soviet horizon, since little if anything can ever change.

For example, some analysts of the essentialist persuasion have little difficulty recommending exploitation of diversity in international communism. In fact, they tend to overreact to signs of differentiation precisely because these are viewed as contrasting with the stasis of the Soviet Union and creating difficulties for the Soviet leadership. They also do not distinguish between using what leverage the West has for immediate, as opposed to long-term, policy goals, simply because the prospects of adaptation are thought to be slight except as a result of fundamental regime change (normally the disintegration of communist rule). Linkages, therefore, make eminent good sense. Because essentialists do not see the Soviet Union as a worthy partner in most endeavors, they regard as improbable that the sacrifice of cooperation elsewhere to gain leverage on an issue where interests conflict would forfeit anything of significant value. The essentialists, naturally, stress the asymmetries of the two societies and do not conceive that (1) the Soviet system will adapt to new conditions or (2) the shape of future international issues may broaden the basis of shared interests between the superpowers.

This model has undergone some transformation in recent years. What earlier could be disposed of as totalitarian, now requires further specification; hence a bifurcation, with some commentators (notably Alexander Solzhenitsyn) attributing the ugly essence of the Soviet system to communism whereas others (notably Richard Pipes) see it as quintessentially Russian—with a fair dose of predetermination, as the system cannot escape its heritage. Others, like Senators Moynihan and Jackson, now clothe ideological ideas in pragmatic language.

Curiously, neither of these essentialist approaches has been well or widely represented in the upper levels of U.S. government. In part this reflects the difficulty of making a persuasive case for it; in part the activist, manipulative, and pragmatic instincts of American policy makers imply a distaste for dogmatic constructs that preclude their effectiveness in advance.[36]

The second approach, which has been labeled mechanistic, had its most systematic and seminal exposition in George F. Kennan's famous "X" article. As later comments emphasized, Kennan saw Soviet expansionism much as a "fluid stream which moves constantly, wherever it is permitted to move. . . . But if it finds unassailable barriers in its path, it accepts these philosophically and accommodates itself to them." [37] It is in substance a traditional view that adversary power can and must be checked with equal or suqerior power. The concern here is with behavior rather than essences, and with force meeting force; the answer to Soviet ambitions is containment.

Members of this school may differ profoundly over the amount of American "force" required to contain the natural Soviet tendency for expansion. They tend not to be grouped as uniformly into the "big defense budget" camp as the essentialists. However, many of them are probably at least as congenial to policies of linkage. Since expansion is seen as the natural behavior of the Soviet Union—whether for ideological, nationalist, or great-power reasons—it is the momentum that must be kept in check and that results in a kind of "firefighting" strategy. Each new crisis assumes ever greater importance because Soviet success will reinforce the aggressive behavior. Therefore, analysts in the mechanistic school tend to favor considerable risks to communicate the message that aggressive behavior, say in Africa or the Middle East, cannot succeed. If this goal of demonstrating the futility of "expansion" requires sacrificing interests on which agreement has already been achieved, that price is reduced by the longer-term interests of conditioning Soviet behavior. Some advocates of this approach do not hesitate to recommend policies designed to obtain leverage over Soviet decision making, even on domestic policies, precisely because the conception is behavioral—to fail to take a position against the trials of Ginzberg or Shcharansky would promote further disregard of human rights. Others of this persuasion tend to place far less value on shaping the incentive structure for internal decisions; rather, they regard it as the proper role of American foreign policy only to contain undesirable actions in world affairs. These analysts differ in their expectations that the Soviet regime might mellow, with a possible trend among them in the direction of less optimism for moderation than Kennan originally expressed.

The various approaches that can be fitted within the "mechanistic" model have probably constituted the dominant school in Washington since World War II. It continues to be the most influential syndrome, although some of its working assumptions have been undergoing change and review. There are still those who would today, much as Kennan did thirty years ago (but would not today), call for a massive commitment of physical force to constrain, confront, and rebuff Soviet endeavors—all the more so if the recent buildup in Soviet strategic and conventional weapons is perceived as a license for Moscow to move with impunity until and unless it encounters a serious and credible challenge, a serious risk, or an exorbitant cost. Such an approach may or may not assume that Moscow is capable of reading correctly the signals sent from the United States, and may or may not believe in effective deterrence (e.g., by an invulnerable second-strike capability).

More novel and in a number of ways more sophisticated, within the "mechanistic" sector of the political spectrum, is the approach currently identified with U.S. National Security Adviser Zbigniew Brzezinski, himself a noted expert on Soviet and communist affairs.[38] He appears to give little weight to the ideological components of Soviet motivation. He is also unlike the "essentialists" in denying that the Soviet Union is "ten feet tall." He is emphatic in asserting that, overall, "they" are not ahead of "us." Indeed, by what can only be labeled a fortuitous coincidence, Brzezinski's old colleague and current adviser, Samuel Huntington, in the summer of 1977 (almost at the same time the Central Intelligence Agency made public its own projections) produced a study for the National Security Council known to insiders as PRM 10 forecasting serious problems for the Soviet Union from a slowdown in economic growth, a depletion of fossil fuel energy sources, demographic changes likely to produce a manpower shortage, and other woes.[39]

In brief, the Brzezinski approach disputes the dire forecasts disseminated by the Committee on the Present Danger. Nevertheless, and this is crucial to this school of thought, the policy inference to be drawn from the perception of a vulnerable Soviet Union is a mandate for a new brinkmanship. Since Moscow is not the monster the essentialists make it out to be, the United States can afford to pressure it. It can set new conditions for arms agreements; it can "play the Chinese card"; it can escalate the rhetoric, referring to the "innate racism" of the Russians (as President Carter did), speaking of Soviet "marauders" in Africa, and generally exceeding the bounds of conventional diplomatic proprieties. It sees nothing wrong with putting one's foot down—in fact, with putting it down harder than one's weight might warrant. The thrust of its approach to the Soviet Union suggests, too, that there is a commitment not to shy away from a confrontation (something which, as will be apparent, advocates of the third position would find unnecessary or counterproductive, short of a genuine crisis).

The third approach was labeled cybernetic because a key part of it was the belief that there was, or could be, significant feedback from Soviet experience abroad to the decision-makers' mind sets and assumptions—in effect, a learning process by which the outside world can have a significant impact on future Soviet foreign policy decisions. As William Zimmerman has commented:

> A cybernetic or organismic imagery of a state's foreign policy, however, not only (a) presupposes a reactive propensity on the part of those who act in the name of the state. It also presupposes that (b) external events have an impact on attitudes and produce structural adaptation, and that (c) attitudinal divergence and political conflict are persistent attributes of the political process even within rigidly hierarchical command systems. [40]

It also implies the existence of a Soviet system in which elite politics and group interests can find some expression and at least informally compete with rival policy preferences: Moscow is here seen no longer as the unitary purposive actor political science and propaganda stereotypes often made it out to be.

Interestingly, one of those whose writings over some fifteen years have identified him with this approach is Marshall Shulman, now Secretary of State Vance's senior adviser on Soviet affairs. Indeed, the Department of State may well be seen as a haven for specialists on Soviet affairs who hold some variant of "cybernetic" views. These involve a perception of the (1) differences, contradictions, perhaps fears and uncertainties, within the Soviet elite, and also between Moscow and other (ruling and nonruling) Communist parties; and much in the same vein as the mechanists' perception, (2) the weaknesses in the Soviet system.

This approach typically leads to the argument that American behavior and pronouncements unwittingly fuel the continual Soviet dialogue about U.S. intentions and capabilities.[41] It also prompts the view that Western policy must reward "good" Soviet behavior and punish the "bad"—perhaps an unwitting application of principles of child psychology and behavior modification to dealing with the rival superpower.[42] Such an approach does imply greater fine-tuning of analysis and greater flexibility of policy responses on the part of the American policy maker than do either the essentialist or mechanistic approaches.

The cybernetic approach also implies careful, day-to-day reading of Soviet pronouncements and behavior. The essentialist model absolves observers from the need to be bothered much by what the Soviets say, or even what they do in the short run, because these are regarded as tactical expressions of strategies long understood in the West. The mechanistic school tends to follow events closely but, despite emphasis on American verbal expressions, apparently tends to cynicism about the explanations given for Soviet policy by Soviet analysts and political figures. The cybernetic model requires difficult, often unrewarding, attention to verbal and other signals at many levels of Soviet society. More generally, this third approach assumes a more organic and pervasive interdependence between the two worlds than the other approaches would recognize.[43]

SOME CONCLUDING REMARKS

Different American images and perceptions of the Soviet system, Soviet policy, and Soviet purposes inform different policy preferences in the United States. A more extensive treatment might seek to show how each of the three approaches discussed above tends to focus on a different body of "evidence" drawn from the record of Soviet performance and pronouncements, with each group using proof selectively in support of its point of view. To suggest such a symmetry in the relationship between empirical data, interpretation, and inferences for each of the models is not to imply that the case for all is equally good, equally well founded, or equally well argued. A lot of facts, moreover, are inherently ambiguous and subject to conflicting interpretations.

It may seem surprising, in retrospect, that fundamental differences among key foreign policy figures in the Carter administration did not surface more rapidly than they did. How they will be resolved remains to be seen, but a few general points can be suggested.

The first concerns the considerable, disproportionate, and often decisive weight of American domestic politics. Its role is not ubiquitous and need not be controlling—as indeed the Carter administration's handling of the Panama Canal issue showed. By the same token, the Panama Canal treaties only underscored the extent to which such issues were hazardous to the executive branch, tended to require a mobilization of effort and attention that can rarely be brought about, and in effect paralyzed the legislative machinery for considerable stretches of time. Moreover, if the President cannot expect to win all such showdowns, even when his party controls both houses of Congress, he will not wish to risk his prestige on key foreign policy issues (such as SALT II) more often than is essential, especially as an election draws near.

For its part, the Soviet leadership failed to appreciate the impact of its behavior in the arms buildup, Africa, and the handling of dissent on American opinion. While Moscow perceived correctly that a Soviet or Cuban role in Angola or Ethiopia courted no risk of a military clash with the United States (or other major powers), it failed to understand adequately the receptivity—indeed, eagerness—of American media, politicians, and a sizable part of the public to new evidence of Soviet nastiness.[44]

No doubt these predispositions provided a particularly fertile soil, in 1978, for the overreaction—part genuine, part contrived—of various people alienated by the behavior of the Carter administration. This included some who opposed the Panama

Canal treaties, advocates of the B-1 bombers, those who opposed U.S. policy in southern Africa or had economic interests in Zaire and neighboring areas, some who deemed the postponement of neutron bomb production and deployment a serious error, and those worried about the image of vacillation and ineffectiveness projected abroad by the Carter regime.[45]

Moreover, White House officials concerned with domestic opinion discovered that a "tough" line served to recoup some of the President's waning prestige at home.[46] While hard evidence is lacking, it is understandably tempting to speculate that, in the words of one columnist:

> It's no coincidence that [Patrick] Caddell's need to change his luck has coincided with Brzezinski's success in selling the hard line. Suddenly, Caddell has discovered foreign policy and Brzezinski has discovered domestic politics. The two of them have come up with a new target for Carter, and a highly convenient one, in Russia.[47]

The fact that the secretary of state or the vice-president is often able to neutralize such an approach does not in itself invalidate the argument.

The administration's assumptions about public opinion create dangers that it will find itself hostage to its own rhetoric. White House positions perpetuate characteristic oversimplifications that have trapped and misled American policy makers since the Bolshevik Revolution. That the Soviets have their own version of the "two-camp" view, of the assumption "that he who is not with us is against us," does not justify the risks such rhetoric carries for sound policy.

This tendency of American Presidents to trap themselves, to surrender their tactical flexibility by giving themselves as hostages to the rhetoric by which they address public opinion, leads to a second general observation about the Carter policy. There has been a deeply engrained reluctance in the United States to acknowledge diversity among communists and their clients. Ever since the Stalin-Tito rift was depicted abroad as a clever game to deceive the West and U.S. officials refused to believe that a Sino-Soviet split could be real, such misperceptions have lingered in Washington. Most recently, this has affected the American view of Eurocommunism (discussed in chapter 9). The same instinct to opt for a view that posits excessive neatness in hierarchical dependence was apparent in Zbigniew Brzezinski's characterization of the Vietnamese-Cambodian fighting as a proxy war between Russia and China. It was also at the heart of the debated and ultimately embarrassing assertions—by the NSC, the CIA, and the White House—that the Katangan rebels' invasion of Zaire's Shaba Province was engineered by the Cubans, who in turn were tools of the USSR. Such a perspective allows no more for a rift between the Ethiopians and the Cubans or between the Iraqis and the Russians than it did, a few years earlier, for a break between the Sudan or Egypt and the Soviet Union. It scarcely requires elaboration to see that the tendency to deny diversity to *the* enemy may be psychologically functional but is apt to be politically inaccurate and grossly misleading. Just as Brzezinski some years ago analyzed the alternatives facing "The Soviet System [as] Transformation or Degeneration," and just as another senior associate of his in the NSC has eloquently denied the role of groups in Soviet elite politics—leading to the spurious assumption of "monolithism" on the "other" side [48]—so the homogenization of a complex set of ambiguous relationships into a rigid and simple chain of command tends to misplace responsibility and require the observer to miss opportunities to deal with components of a divided aggregation rather than with a single, streamlined whole.

If we consider the spectrum of alternative foreign policies toward the Soviet Union, we find that the most imaginative and "daring" departures are precisely those that are most difficult, or plainly impossible, to contemplate for reasons of domestic politics. Thus a more relaxed policy toward Eurocommunism, identifying it as a distinct embarrassment for Moscow and a possible magnet for Eastern European attitudes, at the least should deserve serious consideration, were it not for the virtual impossibility for the administration to saddle itself with charges of "softness" on communism that such a course would invite.

Similarly, a good case could be made for a sustained and systematic American effort to maximize U.S. or Western interaction with the Soviet Union, both to foster the reality and perception of interdependence, which would be educational as well as constraining for Soviet decision makers, and to promote in the next generation of Soviet leaders an internalized conviction that they have more to gain from getting along with the West than confronting it. This might logically extend from trade and technology to culture and education, as well as arms control. But if nothing else, such a policy would take time: even if it pays off in the long run, it would not be susceptible to "temperature taking" at will. In the meanwhile its sponsors would be subject to attacks and critiques as impractical, naive, or worse.[49]

That both the President's two major statements on U.S.-Soviet relations in the first half of 1978—the Wake Forest and Annapolis speeches—were reported by sources close to the administration and widely believed abroad to be for "domestic consumption" illustrates the danger. While Moscow continued its "patience" with American domestic political requirements at the diplomatic level, the atmosphere thus reinforced strengthened the hand of those elements in the Soviet leadership that favored the trials of dissidents and contributed to the mood within which the state security and legal apparatus seemed to disregard international public opinion about the conduct of the Orlov, Ginzburg, and Shcharansky trials.

A third general observation may be made regarding Soviet influence in the Third World. Precedents need not be compelling, but all previous experience suggests that Moscow has repeatedly succeeded in gaining *influence* in Third World countries— partly thanks to economic, military, and technical assistance— but not often for long periods of time and almost never in so great a measure that its influence could not be jeopardized and Soviet advisers ejected from the country (see chapters 10 and 11).[50] There are pandemic differences between nationalist and communist movements, in addition to a multitude of other sources of tensions and conflicts. Without any American help or advice, a number of Third World countries have over the years rid themselves of Soviet influence and personnel. Hence a good case could be made that, in areas of marginal security importance to the United States, the United States might do well to give Soviet or Cuban "instructors" enough rope to hang themselves. In practice such an approach would seem to require too relaxed a posture for too long a time, too vivid an image of American impotence or indifference, too compromising an illustration that the emperor had no clothes, to be *politically* feasible.

Finally, the sense of drift and contradiction within the Carter administration must be ascribed to failure to give clear and firm definitions of policy at the top. Carter is not the first President whose preelection statements sought to appeal both to those who wanted a "tougher" foreign policy and to those who sought a more comprehensive accommodation; a similar case could, for instance, be made for the Kennedy years. But the suspicion lingers that until late spring of 1978, at any rate, there was no clear awareness of the incompatibility of various presidential pronouncements on the Soviet Union.

If columnists and reporters can be believed, the drafts of the major presidential addresses dealing with the Soviet-American relationship can in each instance be identified primarily with the views of a particular adviser. Thus the authorship of the Carter address at the University of Notre Dame on May 22, 1977 has been attributed to National Security Adviser Brzezinski.[51] Responsibility for the reversal in emphases in the President's address in Charleston, South Carolina (July 1977), after the deterioration in Soviet-American relations in the first half of 1977, has been attributed to the additional influence of Marshall Shulman.[52] In turn, the far more belligerent comments in the Carter speech at Winston-Salem, North Carolina (March 1978), were reportedly drafted by Samuel Huntington; and the attempt to synthesize at Annapolis on June 7, 1978, was said to be largely the work of Carter himself.[53] If so, in each case the choice of speechwriter (or at least the major intellectual craftsman) greatly influenced the content insofar as U.S. policy toward the Soviet Union was concerned.

The discussion of "linkages" and SALT, in an earlier section of this chapter, provides another example of ambiguities making for confusion; and the reaction to the Carter-Brzezinski position on Zaire and Angola, as well as the Brzezinski "China card," included considerable skepticism in the Washington bureaucracy. If his Annapolis speech was an attempt by Jimmy Carter to put forth a definitive statement of U.S. policy,[54] he was bound to be disappointed. Ambiguity continued to prevail, as did the persistent syncopation between Vance and Brzezinski and other key administration figures. It is hard to avoid the conclusion that the President failed to understand the import and impact of the uncertainties created by sins of omission, as well as commission, by his own team.

The one element that has been neglected in this discussion is the Soviet counterpart to the American dialogue over "doing business with Moscow." Careful students of Soviet writings on the United States, for instance, have sought to show—and the evidence is convincing—that one cannot merely document differences in Soviet perceptions and attitudes, but can actually trace continuities and consistencies over some twenty-five years or more in Soviet images of the United States, and how each model in turn is congruent with a particular set of policy implications.[55] For our purposes it does not matter greatly whether Soviet views of the United States are most usefully grouped into two, three, or four clusters; what is clear is that there are at least two polar opposites, as well as some intermediate formulas. In substance the opposite poles are represented by the dogmatic and the pragmatic approaches, by the more hostile and the more benign; and the policy implications correspondingly range from isolationism to interaction, from conflict to cooperation. Moreover, other studies show that these diverse policy preferences are congruent with positions in ongoing Soviet policy debates over different, "linked" issues, such as the likelihood of superpower war, the need for technological and scientific innovation, the sufficiency of the Soviet defense posture, and priorities in resource allocation.[56]

An analysis of linkages between Soviet foreign policy and its domestic determinants strongly suggests the need for sensitivity to the Soviet home front on the part of foreign observers and policy makers. Some years ago, an American scholar suggested that distortions in Soviet-American relations have resulted from each side's failure to comprehend the complexity of the other's decision making.[57] No doubt there is danger in overstressing conflicts and cleavages in the Soviet elite, but we would consider it a lesser distortion than the conventional proclivity to "black-box" Soviet foreign policy outputs.

In this light it may be wrong to ask, as is often done, whether the United States can influence Soviet outlook and hence behavior. We would argue that, whether it wants to or not, and whether it knows it or not, the United States by what it says and what it does (and what it fails to say or do) inevitably contributes to the dialogue being carried on among members of the Soviet elite: the mutual perceptions of the United States and the Soviet Union are in large measure shaped by each other's behavior. The United States is thus an unwitting participant in internal Soviet assessments and arguments, much as Soviet behavior provides contending American schools with ammunition.

Though neither side likes to hear it said, one may well speak of tacit alliances between adversaries. Not only do the moderates on each side share an interest and cooperate to promote agreements deemed to be mutually beneficial—on academic exchanges or a comprehensive test ban—but others help each other in deed if not in intent. The military-industrial establishment on both sides cites the research and procurement of the other to justify its own demands for larger budgets and allocations. Indeed, it has been suggested that, in a number of areas, Soviet and American counterparts are in effect "functional bureaucratic allies" and "external pacers" for each other.[58]

More than that, even the "hawks" on both sides unwittingly cooperate to validate each other's expectations. Their commitment to worst-case analysis requires the assistance of the adversary to provide support for their self-fulfilling prophecies of doom and gloom.[59] Similar to the action-reaction phenomenon in the arms race, the affirmation of the "present danger" in the United States cannot but strengthen the hand and provide evidence cited by Soviet diehards who deny the possibility of meaningful and useful accords with the United States, and who see no evidence of American goodwill but firmly expect an eventual military showdown. In similar fashion, military men on both sides have striven to water down the ban on qualitative improvements in strategic weapons being negotiated by the arms control communities on both sides.

Only the future will tell what effect American politics, competing American models of Soviet behavior, and irresolution in the White House will have on the balance of Soviet arguments and alignments regarding Soviet-American relations. Their existence is not in doubt. What is in doubt is whether top American policy makers are sufficiently aware of this dimension of the relationship.

NOTES

1. See, for instance, Peter Filene, ed., *American Views of Soviet Russia, 1917–1965* (Homewood, Ill.: Dorsey Press, 1968); Thomas A. Bailey, *America Faces Russia* (Ithaca: Cornell University Press, 1950); Alexander Dallin, "Bias and Blunders in American Studies on the USSR," *Slavic Review*, September 1973; Lawrence T. Caldwell, *Soviet-American Relations: One Half Decade of Detente—Problems and Issues* (Paris: Atlantic Institute for International Affairs, 1976); Richard J. Barnet, *The Giants* (New York: Simon and Schuster, 1978).

2. See *Khrushchev Remembers*, 2 vols. (Little, Brown, 1970, 1974); Michael P. Gehlen, *The Politics of Coexistence* (Bloomington, Ind.: Indiana University Press, 1967); Erik Hoffmann and Frederic Fleron, eds., *The Conduct of Soviet Foreign Policy* (Chicago: Aldine/Atherton, 1972); Paul Marantz, "Prelude to Detente: Doctrinal Change under Khrushchev," *International Studies Quarterly*, December 1975; Walter LaFeber, *America, Russia and the Cold War, 1945–1971* (New York: Wiley, 1972); Thomas W. Wolfe, *Soviet Power and Europe, 1945–1970* (Baltimore, Johns Hopkins, 1970); Michel Tatu, *Power in the Kremlin* (New York: Viking, 1970).

3. See Alexander George, "The Case for Multiple Advocacy in Making Foreign Policy," *American Political Science Review*, September 1972.

4. *Pravda*, 25 February 1976.

5. Ibid., 2 April 1976.

6. See reports of U.S. protests to the Soviet government on harassment of U.S. diplomats, *New York Times*, 2, 6, and 17 April 1976; reports on Soviet microwave beaming, ibid., 2 May, 2 and 26 June 1976. For Soviet commentary, see *Literaturnaya gazeta*, 26 May 1976, and a report on Soviet charges of "anti-Soviet hysteria," *New York Times*, 16 April 1976.

7. See Secretary of Defense Donald Rumsfeld's *Annual Defense Department Report, FY 1978*, dated 17 January 1977, on which stories appeared in the January 19 editions, including the *Los Angeles Times*; and President Ford's interview in *New York Times*, 12 January 1977.

8. For a summary reported to capture the essence of the "Team B" approach, see Richard Pipes, "The Soviet Strategy for Nuclear Victory," *Washington Post*, 3 July 1977. See also the Drew Middleton article in *New York Times*, 25 June 1977, p. 7.

9. *Pravda*, 1 December 1976.

10. Georgy Arbatov, "Soviet-American Relations Today," ibid., 11 December 1976.

11. Ibid., 19 January 1977.

12. Ibid., 22 March 1977.

13. *New York Times*, 22 July 1977.

14. See Richard Burt's article in ibid., 11 October 1977.

15. The story of the Carter administration's relationship to Soviet dissidents is complex. Note the treatment of *Los Angeles Times* reporter Robert Toth (*New York Times*, 12 June 1977), *New York Times* reporter Craig Whitney, and Harold Piper of the *Baltimore Sun* (*New York Times*, 29 and 30 June 1978); see also reports of Carter's interview with Vladimir Bukovsky (*New York Times*, 2 March 1977) and his defense of Anatoly Shcharansky (*New York Times*, 14 June 1977). The trials of Shcharansky, Ginzburg, Whitney and Piper filled the papers in June–July 1978.

16. See, for example, Georgy Arbatov in *Pravda*, 3 August 1977; A. Chernyshov, "For the Benefit of the Soviet and American Peoples in the Interests of World Peace," *International Affairs*, no. 3 (March 1977): 37–46; editorial, ibid., no. 6 (June 1977): 3–10; V. F. Petrovsky, "On Current Foreign Policy Concepts of the USA," *S.Sh.A., Ekonomika, Politika, Ideologia*, no. 8 (August 1977): 9–10; Yu. F. Oleshchuk, "Nonconstructive Arguments Against Detente," ibid., no. 10 (October 1977): 33–44.

17. See, for example, speeches of M. A. Suslov to a Party Ideological Conference, *Pravda*, 21 June 1972; and Brezhnev in a reception for Fidel Castro, ibid., 28 June 1972.

18. See, for example, Brzezinski's "impromptu" session with reporters concerning the effect of Soviet actions in Africa on SALT II, *Los Angeles Times*, 2 March 1978; he justified his ideas of linkages by arguing that he favors a "detente that is genuinely comprehensive and truly reciprocal," *New York Times*, 21 March 1978, p. 16; these ideas are clearly reflected in Carter's speech at Wake Forest University, *New York Times*, 18 March 1978; on withholding U.S. trade, see *New York Times*, 27 June 1978.

19. In a statement to the Senate Foreign Relations Committee, 19 September 1974, as in U.S. State Department, *Special Report, no.* 6 (Washington, D.C., 1974).

20. The strongest statements came in the Brezhnev address to the 25th Party Congress, *Pravda,* 25 February 1976; his speeches at Tula, ibid., 19 January 1977, and to the Trade Union Congress, ibid., 22 March 1977. See also the analysis by Georgy Arbatov in ibid., 3 August 1977, and V. Kartashkin, "International Relations and Human Rights," *International Affairs,* no. 8 (August 1977); 29–38.

21. His two most eloquent statements are his speech to the AFL-CIO, *New York Times,* 1 July 1975, and to the Harvard University commencement, *Los Angeles Times,* 9 June 1978.

22. See especially Brezhnev's references to the class struggle at the 25th Party Congress, *Pravda,* 25 February 1976.

23. The best public sources on Soviet weapons deployment are the *Annual Reports* of American Secretaries of Defense. See, for example, Donald Rumsfeld, *Annual Defense Department Report, FY 1978* (Washington, D.C., 1977); Harold Brown, *Department of Defense Annual Report, Fiscal Year 1979* (Washington, D.C., 1978); also the annual editions of *Military Balance* published each fall by the International Institute of Strategic Studies of London.

24. See Rumsfeld, *Annual Defense Department Report, FY 1978,* pp. 121–22; Brown, *Department of Defense Annual Report, Fiscal Year 1979,* pp. 106–7; see also Donald H. Rumsfeld, *Annual Defense Department Report, FY 1977* (Washington, D.C., 27 January 1976), pp. 52–64; Paul H. Nitze, "Assuring Strategic Stability in an Era of Detente," *Foreign Affairs,* January 1976, pp. 207–32; Amos Jordan, "Soviet Strength and U.S. Purpose," *Foreign Policy,* Summer 1976, pp. 32–35; Colin S. Gray, "The Strategic Forces Triad: End of the Road," *Foreign Affairs,* July 1978, pp. 771–89; and his *The Future of Land-based Missiles,* Adelphi Paper, no. 140 (London, 1977).

25. See Michael MccGwire, ed., *Soviet Naval Developments: Context and Capability* (New York: Praeger, 1973); Michael MccGwire, et al., eds., *Soviet Naval Policy: Objectives and Constraints,* (New York: Praeger, 1975); and Michael MccGwire and John McDonnel, eds., *Soviet Naval Influence: Domestic and Foreign Dimensions* (New York: Praeger, 1977).

26. For example, the entire controversy surrounding President Carter's threat to veto the defense building appropriation in August 1978 revealed the difficulty. The threat was first made in a televised news conference on August 17 (see *New York Times,* 18 August 1978); excellent analysis can be found in Jack Nelson's article in the *Los Angeles Times,* 18 August 1978.

27. In addition to the annual *Military Balance,* published by the International Institute for Strategic Studies in London, see John M. Collins, *American and Soviet Military Trends Since the Cuban Missile Crisis* (Washington, D.C.: Center for Strategic and International Studies, Georgetown University Press, 1978), pp. 321–72.

28. See Robert P. Berman, *Soviet Air Power in Transition* (Washington, D.C.: Brookings, 1978), pp. 27–34.

29. CIA, *Estimated Soviet Defense Spending in Rubles, 1970–1975* (Washington, D.C., May 1976); CIA, *A Dollar Comparison of Soviet and U.S. Defense Activities* (Washington, D.C. February 1976).

30. See reports of Carter's meeting with French Socialist leader François Mitterrand, *New York Times,* 7 January 1978; the text of the U.S. position on the Italian political situation, ibid., 13 January 1978; and a State Department policy statement reported in ibid., 17 April 1977.

31. See Marshall D. Shulman, " 'Europe' versus 'Detente,' " *Foreign Affairs,* April 1967, pp. 389–402; Robert Legvold, "The Franco-Soviet Rapprochement After De Gaulle," *Survey,* Autumn 1974, pp. 67–93; Lawrence T. Caldwell, *Soviet-American Relations: One-Half Decade of Detente,* Atlantic Paper, May 1975 (Paris, 1975), pp. 24–25.

32. See Lawrence T. Caldwell, "The Warsaw Pact: Directions of Change," *Problems of Communism,* September–October 1975, pp. 1–19; Lawrence T. Caldwell and Steven E. Miller, "East European Integration and European Politics," *International Journal,* Spring 1977, pp. 352–85.

33. See *New York Times,* 26 January 1979; *Washington Post,* 28 January, 2 and 4 February

1979. Compare the following comments, made at the same meeting with business executives:

Cyrus Vance: "We believe that China has an important role to play in the search for global peace and stability. The same is true for the Soviet Union. Our national interests are best served when we seek to improve relations with both nations while protecting our vital strategic interests."

Zbigniew Brzezinski: "Normalization consolidates a favorable balance of power. . . . A fundamental choice the Soviet Union faces is whether to become a responsible partner in the creation of a global system of genuinely independent states or whether to exclude itself from global trends and derive its security exclusively from its military might and its domination of a few clients."

(*New York Times,* 16 January 1979.)

34. William Zimmerman, "Choices in the Postwar World," in *Caging the Bear,* ed. Charles Gati (Indianapolis: Bobbs Merrill, 1974); and Zimmerman, "Soviet Foreign Policy in the 1970s," *Survey* (London), no. 87 (Spring 1973). See also William Welch, *American Images of Soviet Foreign Policy* (New Haven: Yale University Press, 1970).

35. Gati, *Caging the Bear,* p. 91.

36. There are, it is true, members of Congress who have absorbed and repeated "essentialist" arguments. So have influential critics of U.S. foreign policy, such as Paul Nitze, the thrust of whose arguments, however, centers to a greater degree on Soviet power than on Soviet essence. Some "essentialist" views are reflected by individuals (e.g., in the American defense community) who oppose all technology transfers to the Soviet Union. Many of these observers, then, find the Soviet defense programs described above unambiguously to suggest the intention to achieve superiority.

37. "X" (George F. Kennan), "The Sources of Soviet Conduct," *Foreign Affairs,* July 1947, and variously reprinted.

38. On Brzezinski, see also Elizabeth Drew, "Brzezinski," *New Yorker,* 1 May 1978. We are leaving aside additional, idiosyncratic characteristics of his outlook and personality. One of these is the tendency to reduce foreign conduct to an abstract intellectual game, with postures essentially represented by verbal pronouncements and, it would seem, little else.

39. U.S. Congress, Joint Economic Committee, *Soviet Economic Problems and Prospects* (Washington, D.C., 8 August 1977); "View of Russia as Declining Power May Threaten Detente," *International Bulletin,* 15 August 1977; Kenneth Jowitt, *Images of Detente and the Soviet Political Order* (Berkeley, Calif.: Institute of International Studies, 1977); "Soviet Economic Problems and Prospects," CIA Research, July 1977.

40. Zimmerman, in Gati, *Caging the Bear,* pp. 96, 99.

41. See, e.g., Shulman's statement before the House Committee on International Relations, 26 October 1977; and "How Shulman Views Soviet Motives and Strategies," *New York Times,* 16 April 1978.

42. A recent example may illustrate the difference in approaches. When in the spring of 1978 the Soviet Union significantly increased the number of emigration visas issued to Jews wishing to leave the USSR, the reaction among American Jewish groups was divided. The American Jewish Congress favored considering the Soviet practice "a first signal of the kind we have been waiting for" and therefore advocated giving "an almost exact symbolic equivalent" by exempting credits to the USSR for grain purchases from the United States from the 1974 Trade Act. By contrast, the National Conference on Soviet Jewry, an umbrella organization speaking for a number of groups, came out in opposition to such a change of U.S. policy. Senator Henry Jackson also opposed such a change in policy. See *New York Times,* 11 June 1978.

43. See, e.g., Helmut Sonnenfeldt, "Implications for Soviet-American Relations," in *The XXV Congress of the CPSU,* ed. Alexander Dallin (Stanford, Calif.: Hoover Institution Press, 1977).

44. In return, it may be argued, American political figures have tended to underestimate the impact of *their* behavior on the ongoing debates in the Soviet political elite, as will be discussed below.

45. Such a tendency may well have been reinforced by the predisposition of journalism to

consider bad and dramatic news "newsworthy" whereas bland and balanced statements made out of cautious concerns about incomplete evidence inherently attract less attention or space.

46. "The entire Administration is surprised to discover that it is easier to gain a solid base of political support when the United States is at odds with the Soviet Union than when the two countries agree." Michael Ledeen, "Improvisations on a Theme by Henry Kissinger," *Harper's*, April 1978, p. 15. See also President Ford's statement that Carter must "take a harder line with the Soviets," *Washington Post*, 26 May 1978.

47. Eliot Janeway, in *San Francisco Examiner and Chronicle*, 4 June 1978.

48. William Odom, "A dissenting View of the Group Approach to Soviet Politics," *World Politics*, July 1976. See also his "The Militarization of Soviet Society," *Problems of Communism*, September–October 1976, with distinctly "essentialist" overtones. For the Brzezinski paper and a discussion of it, see Z. Brzezinski, ed., *Dilemmas of Change in Soviet Politics* (New York: Columbia University Press, 1969).

49. See Alexander Dallin, "The Fruits of Interaction," *Survey* (London), no. 100/101 (Summer–Autumn 1976); also Marshall Shulman, "Toward a Western Philosophy of Coexistence," *Foreign Affairs*, October 1973.

50. For an excellent discussion of Soviet vulnerabilities in its global competition with the United States and the implication for policy, see Robert Legvold, "The Nature of Soviet Power," *Foreign Affairs*, October 1977, pp. 49–71.

51. For the speech, see *New York Times*, 23 May 1977.

52. For the speech, see ibid., 22 July 1977.

53. For the speech, see ibid., 18 March 1978; and Terrence Smith in ibid., 21 March 1978 for Brzezinski's role.

54. See Murray Marder, "Behind the President's Speech," *Washington Post*, 11 June 1978.

55. See especially Franklyn Griffiths, "Image, Politics and Learning in Soviet Behavior Toward the United States" (Ph.D. dissertation, Columbia University, 1972); Robert W. Hansen, "Soviet Images of American Foreign Policy, 1960–1972" (Ph.D. dissertation, Princeton University, 1975); Donald Kelley, "The Soviet Debate on Convergence," *Polity* 6 (Winter 1973); Morton Schwartz, "Soviet Perceptions of the United States" (forthcoming, 1979); William Zimmerman, "Soviet Perceptions of the United States," in *Soviet Politics After Khrushchev*, ed. Alexander Dallin and Thomas Larson (Englewood Cliffs, N.J.: Prentice-Hall, 1969).

56. See Alexander Dallin, *Domestic Determinants of Soviet Foreign Policy* (New York: Columbia University, Research Institute on International Change, 1979). Some of the following paragraphs are based on this study.

57. Herbert Dinerstein, *Fifty Years of Soviet Foreign Policy* (Baltimore: Johns Hopkins, 1968), p. 7.

58. Colin Gray, "The Urge to Compete," *World Politics*, January 1974. See also Edward L. Warner, "The Bureaucratic Politics of Weapons Procurement," in *Soviet Naval Policy*, ed. Michael McGwire, et al. (New York: Praeger, 1975).

59. See also the comments of two recent émigrés from the Soviet Union, Boris Rabbot, in the *Washington Post*, 10 July 1977; and Alexander Yanov, in *Détente After Brezhnev* (Berkeley, Calif.: Institute of International Studies, 1977).

8

CHINA POLICY AND THE STRATEGIC TRIANGLE

Banning Garrett

The development of the Washington-Peking connection under the Carter administration underscores the fact that this administration, like its two Republican predecessors, links America's China policy closely to U.S. policy toward the Soviet Union.
After initially placing Sino-American relations low on his list of foreign policy
priorities, President Carter decided in the spring of 1978 to seek rapid improvement
in relations with Peking, in large part to gain leverage over the Soviet Union. His
decision followed the deterioration of U.S. relations with Moscow and a subsequent
search for ways to pressure the Soviets in response to their involvement in Africa,
difficulties in the SALT II negotiations, and domestic pressure to "get tough" with
the Russians. Some policy makers also saw a new U.S. initiative toward Peking as
necessary to prevent a deterioration of Sino-American relations, a new Chinese
isolationism, or even a Sino-Soviet *rapprochement*. Both American and Chinese lead-
·ers viewed normalization of relations between Washington and Peking on January 1,
1979 as a strategic as well as bilateral issue.

Washington has looked beyond China to the Soviet Union in its dealings with
Peking; the Soviets, too, have looked over their shoulders at the Chinese as they
have sought better relations with the United States in the 1970s. And China's
leadership, after bitter struggles, has decided to seek a strategic alliance with
Washington to counter what it perceives as a greater long-term threat from the
Soviet "polar bear."

This chapter describes some of the policy debates involving perceptions of this

*I would like to thank Jan Austin. Harry Harding. David M. Iton. and Kenneth Oye for their
insightful comments and suggestions in the preparation of this chapter.*

"triangular" relationship, with emphasis on America's China policy; it discusses the development of China policy and the interaction of the United States, China, and the Soviet Union under the Carter administration. Finally, it attempts to draw out some notions of the triangle as an analytical tool for analysis of these interactions and suggests some limits to the triangle analogy and some of the risks and limitations to manipulating this complex relationship.

CHANGING STRATEGIC POSTURES

The Carter administration inherited a *rapprochement* between the United States and the People's Republic of China engineered on the American side by Henry Kissinger and Richard Nixon and on the Chinese side by Chou En-lai and Mao Tse-tung. This "new relationship" with China, formalized in the 1972 Shanghai Communiqué, dramatically altered the Sino-American equation from one of hostility and confrontation to one of cooperation and pursuit of "parallel interests" on a global scale. For both the United States and China, strategic concerns about the Soviet Union were at the heart of the *rapprochement* and provided the context for decision making on "bilateral" issues.

Although Chinese Communist party interest in *rapprochement* with the United States can be traced back to the early 1940s, and although the split between China and the Soviet Union became public in the early 1960s, the strategic triangle did not become fully operative until the 1970s. The United States rejected Chinese feelers for improving relations in the 1940s and treated postliberation China first as a virtual extension of the Soviet Union and then as a more dangerous enemy than Moscow.

Following the open Sino-Soviet polemics of 1963, some U.S. strategists advocated making common cause with the Soviet Union to contain "Chinese aggression." Morton Halperin, for example, argued that the major threat to U.S. interests in Asia emanated from China, especially from Peking's newly demonstrated nuclear capability. Suggested Halperin: "In Asia, in fact, the United States may begin to find herself more and more often tacitly allied with the Soviet Union against Chinese aggression." He added that the United States "might well wish to explore with the Soviet Union the possibility of joint action to halt the Chinese nuclear program or to render it politically and militarily useless. . . . The most extreme form of joint Soviet-American action (or unilateral action by one or the other) would be a military move designed to destroy Chinese nuclear facilities. . . . If the Soviet Union should ever reach the point where she was prepared to make such a move, the United States should indicate that she has no objection to it and will not interfere in any way. But the United States needs also to consider the possibility of military action to destroy the Chinese nuclear power undertaken on her own initiative." [1] Ironically, a decade later American officials were referring to China as a "quasi ally" with which the United States had "parallel interests" in containing the Soviet Union in Asia and throughout the world. China's nuclear capability was viewed as a threat to the Soviet Union, not to the United States, and American strategists were arguing for U.S. assistance to China to help strengthen its deterrent to Soviet preemptive attack.

In the mid-1960s, U.S. policy makers often justified American military involvement in Vietnam as necessary to contain "Chinese expansionism." U.S. forces in Asia and the Pacific were deployed to meet this objective, and American global military posture was based on a "2½ war" strategy, that is, preparation to fight major wars simultaneously in Asia against China and in Europe against the Soviet Union—and at the same time to meet a "minor" contingency elsewhere, such as in Vietnam.

Dramatic events in the 1968–71 period—from the Soviet invasion of Czechoslovakia and declaration of the "Brezhnev Doctrine" to the Sino-Soviet border clashes and Kissinger's secret trip to Peking—radically shifted the strategic postures of the United States, China, [2] and the Soviet Union. American and Chinese strategic interests coalesced sufficiently to produce a nascent *rapprochement* between Washington and Peking. In 1969 the United States was able to drop from a 2½ war strategy to a 1½ war posture, no longer expecting to fight a war in Asia against China. The Chinese, who had been preparing for a possible two-front war against the United States in the south and east and against the Soviet Union in the north, could now focus their military planning on the Soviets. The Soviet Union, on the other hand, had to strengthen military forces on its eastern and western flanks simultaneously and face the prospect, however remote, that the United States would come to China's aid in the event of a Sino-Soviet war.

An intensifying Sino-Soviet split offered opportunities as well as dangers for the United States. The danger was that the Sino-Soviet border clashes in 1969 would erupt into a major, possibly nuclear, war between the giant communist powers. At worst, the United States could be dragged into such a war; even if that did not happen, a successful Soviet move to provoke leadership changes in Peking that led to a renewal of the Sino-Soviet alliance could shift the global balance of power against the United States. Nixon and his advisers saw in this situation an opportunity for the United States: by indicating American opposition to a Soviet attack against China—and rejecting possible Soviet overtures for joint U.S.–Soviet action against China's nuclear facilities reportedly made during 1969 and 1970 [3]—the United States could help head off a Sino-Soviet war. At the same time, Washington could gain new leverage over Moscow by capitalizing on Chinese receptivity to *rapprochement*. This strategy could maintain the Sino-Soviet rift while preventing Sino-Soviet war, and would give the United States the upper hand in the triangle as both Peking and Moscow sought to improve their relations with Washington. Nixon and Kissinger also hoped to find a route to a favorable settlement to the war in Vietnam by placing the conflict in the larger context of the strategic triangle and using Washington's newfound leverage over North Vietnam's supporters to try to force Hanoi to accept American terms for a settlement. The Vietnam part of this strategy failed, primarily because of Nixon and Kissinger's overestimation of Moscow's and Peking's leverage over Hanoi and underestimation of North Vietnam's military capabilities.[4] Finally, the Americans hoped that a U.S.–China reconciliation would gain Peking's support for stability in Asia while the United States reduced its force levels in the region in line with the Nixon Doctrine.

Nixon and Kissinger formally established détente with both Peking and Moscow during 1972, while the Vietnam war escalated. The Shanghai Communiqué with its antihegemony clause signed by President Nixon during his visit to China in February consolidated the Sino-American *rapprochement*. It also put Washington on record as opposing any effort by the Soviet Union to dominate China.[5] Three months later, Nixon went to Moscow, where he signed the first strategic arms limitation (SALT) agreement between the United States and the Soviet Union, thus laying the cornerstone for the structure of U.S.–Soviet détente.[6]

Nixon and Kissinger left unresolved two major issues that were passed on to the Ford and Carter administrations: how and when to follow through on the Shanghai Communiqué and fully normalize relations with Peking (which meant severing diplomatic and defense ties with Taiwan and withdrawing military personnel from the island), and whether or how to "play the China card" against Moscow beyond obtaining the advantages of the initial Sino-American *rapprochement*. Watergate weakened President Nixon and consumed his administration, inhibiting any possible move toward ending ties with Taiwan, whose conservative supporters in the United States were Nixon's last base of support toward the end of his Presidency. And President Ford, who presided over the fall of Saigon and the deterioration of détente, feared the impact of normalization on his prospects for nomination and election in 1976.

A QUIET DEBATE

When Carter took office in January 1977, normalization of relations was still on the agenda, a half decade after the signing of the Shanghai Communiqué. Within the new administration, however, the issue of establishing full diplomatic ties with Peking was less contentious than the debate over the role of American relations with China in U.S. strategy toward the Soviet Union. A focus of that debate was the establishment of ties with military implications between Washington and Peking.

The issue of intelligence sharing with China—which later became part of the debate over military ties—originated with Kissinger's initial secret visit to Peking in July 1971 when he apparently took satellite reconnaissance photos of Soviet military installations and forces along the Sino-Soviet border as an opening card in the ensuing triangular game.[7] Although the focus of his talks with Chinese leaders was on normalization of relations, that move demonstrated U.S. interest in China's security and the potential usefulness to China of the American connection.

A secret debate over military ties with China and their usefulness as a counter to the Soviet Union has continued within the government ever since. That debate has been shrouded in great mystery, and has involved the President, the secretaries of defense and state, the national security adviser, and the CIA director. Kissinger apparently ordered the first study of the question of military ties with China by the NSC staff in 1972–73, although no word of the contents of that look at the issue has become public. By late 1974, high-level officials in the Pentagon and the Central Intelligence Agency were also debating the proposition that closer relations with Peking, including military ties, could be a means of gaining leverage over the Soviet Union and improving the U.S. position in the global balance of power. A key document pointed to by proponents of such ties at that time was a study by RAND analyst Michael Pillsbury. The study, simply entitled "L-32" (its RAND designation number), was circulated among top officials in the Pentagon and the CIA. It detailed some probes the Chinese had made in the West for military aid and explored the possibility of U.S. military relations with China.[8]

This divisive controversy became public knowledge in the fall of 1975 when Pillsbury published a declassified version of "L-32" in *Foreign Policy* magazine, entitled "U.S.–Chinese Military Ties?" This was followed immediately by a leak to the *New York Times* of two CIA studies detailing Chinese approaches to U.S. corporations about purchase of military-related technology and exploring the impact of possible U.S. military aid to China on debates in Peking over the future of China's opening to the West and hostility toward the Soviet Union.[9] The *Times* story also noted that officials favoring the development of military ties with China pointed to the Pillsbury article as presenting the arguments being debated within the government.

According to Pillsbury and other analysts,[10] U.S. military ties with China could:

Provide leverage for controlling Soviet behavior in other areas of the world (e.g., Africa) and pressuring the Soviets in the SALT talks and other bilateral negotiations.

Help prevent a Sino-Soviet *rapprochement* by maintaining suspicion and tension between Peking and Moscow on the one hand, and by tying China's leaders to the current policy of tilting toward the United States on the other.

Indicate a direct U.S. interest in China's security, giving Moscow reason to fear American aid to China in the event of a new Sino-Soviet military conflict. Analysts noted that even public discussion of *possible* "military ties" creates uncertainty in Moscow that requires the Soviets to take that possibility into account in strategic planning and crisis decision making.

Provide a "payoff" to Chinese leaders for their opening to the United States, which had been stagnating on the diplomatic level since 1973, and thus bolster those in the Chinese leadership fighting to defend that policy.

Improve China's nuclear deterrent capability by providing military technology such as computers to control over-the-horizon radar and satellite cameras for photo reconnaissance of Soviet military installations. This would increase Peking's early-warning capacity, thus decreasing the danger to China of a Soviet surprise attack in a crisis, and the danger to the Soviets of a premature launch of Chinese missiles out of a fear of a Soviet preemptive strike.

Improve China's conventional military strength through the transfer of advanced weapons and weapons technology, thus bolstering China's deterrent to a Soviet conventional attack.

Continue to tie down forty to fifty Soviet divisions on the Chinese border and perhaps even cause the Soviets to increase the number of their troops in the Sino-Soviet border region, bringing a corresponding reduction in Soviet forces available for combat against NATO in Europe.

Allow the United States to move forward in relations with Peking while circumventing the thorny problem of Taiwan. The Chinese, it was argued, are more concerned with countering the Soviet Union than with establishing formal diplomatic relations with Washington, and would see strengthened Sino-American military ties as improving their military and strategic positions vis-à-vis Moscow.

Exactly what constitutes military ties with China has never been spelled out, and Soviet reaction to different suggested relations could vary widely. Pillsbury suggested a range of possibilities from which to "select initiatives that would encourage the development of a U.S.–Chinese military relationship," including: an "exchange of military academy delegations, defense attaches, and even defense ministers"; "U.S.–Chinese intelligence sharing about the Soviet Union through covert channels"; "limited military assistance to the Chinese" that was "carefully selected to maximize its anti-Soviet utility to China"; and encouragement of allied military sales to China by Washington.

Pillsbury predicted that the status of U.S.–Soviet relations would provide the context for future consideration of military ties with China. "If détente seems to be deteriorating, then the temptation to experiment with some of these initiatives would increase. A President more hostile to the Soviet Union and détente than Ford," Pillsbury wrote in his 1975 essay, "might be particularly attracted to the idea, risky as it is, of forging a close U.S.–Chinese bond in the Pacific, perhaps embracing Japan, as a new form of anti-Soviet containment." Pillsbury added that "less drastic alternatives are more attractive," such as modifying the "specious policy of 'evenhandedness' which now governs exports of advanced defense technology. The same restrictions should not apply to both the Soviet Union and China. China is not nearly as large a security threat to us as the Soviet Union is. To maintain a rough parity in the global triangle of power, we need a policy which explicitly recognizes that Peking has a legitimate interest in improving its deterrence against the threat of Soviet attack." Pillsbury mentioned, as an example, sale to China of advanced underwater listening equipment for oil exploration, which would also enhance Peking's antisubmarine-detection capability.

The primary objection raised both inside and outside government was that U.S. military ties with China, instead of leading the Soviet leadership to be more cautious and compliant, could have an adverse impact on U.S.–Soviet relations. Some opponents argued that such ties could provoke a hard-line reaction in the Soviet leadership and lead to tougher Soviet positions on SALT and other bilateral issues, an accelerated Soviet military buildup, and increased global projection of Soviet military power. Along with this, they said, would be a Soviet reconsideration of détente, which was entered into by Moscow in the early 1970s in large part to head off close Sino-American collaboration. Soviet leaders, opponents noted, might view U.S. military ties with China as the beginning of an anti-Soviet alliance between Peking and Washington. U.S. officials opposed to military relations with China have been especially concerned that such ties could undermine the SALT negotiations, which, they say, require a considerable degree of mutual trust.

These officials have also been concerned that military ties with China could dangerously increase Sino-Soviet tension; a few officials have even argued that the Soviets might launch a preemptive attack on China to head off a major Western effort to strengthen China's military capability. Proponents of military ties have responded that although the Soviets would be upset by such a Western effort, there is little they could do about it, and that an unprovoked Soviet military strike against China would not only offer little hope for success but also would lead to an extremely damaging international reaction.

The views of opponents and proponents of military ties with China frequently correlated with their assessments of a set of related issues. Those opposed to such a policy also argued that a Sino-Soviet *rapprochement* is not likely and that a limited détente between the Soviet Union and China, if it were to occur, would not be harmful to U.S. interests because it would reduce international tensions and lessen the chances of a dangerous Sino-Soviet war; that China wants neither arms nor an alliance from the United States; and that American arms sales to China would be counterproductive in their impact on U.S. relations with the Soviet Union. Those who favored extensive development of U.S.–China military ties also argued that a Sino-Soviet *rapprochement* is a real and dangerous possibility; that the Chinese do want an alliance, albeit informal, with the United States and the West against Moscow; that the Chinese do want Western arms and American military technology; and that selling arms to China would have a useful effect on the Soviets, pressuring them to be more forthcoming on bilateral and multilateral issues.

TWO MOVES TOWARD CHINA

In the midst of this ongoing debate, two major moves toward Western military ties with China occurred during the Ford administration. In December 1975 Britain agreed to sell China Rolls-Royce Spey jet engines, including both finished engines and a factory to begin producing them in China. The Spey engine is strictly for military aircraft and is used in the British version of the F-4 Phantom fighter bomber. The Chinese had first expressed interest in the Spey in 1972, but it was not until the fall of 1975 that the United States decided to acquiesce to the deal. Secretary Kissinger personally discussed the deal with British leaders and decided to allow the sale to go through, bypassing COCOM (the coordinating committee of NATO countries plus Japan and not including Iceland that was set up in 1950 to control the export of strategic goods to communist countries), in order to send a positive signal to the Chinese at a time of deteriorating relations with both China and the Soviet Union.[11] The Spey deal proved Chinese interest in Western arms purchases and appeared to set a precedent for the United States acquiescing to arms sales to China by its NATO allies.

Vice-Premier Teng Hsiao-ping was apparently in charge of running the Chinese government when the Spey deal was completed. Chairman Mao Tse-tung was ailing and Premier Chou En-lai was on his deathbed. Chou died the following month and, unexpectedly, Teng was soon purged for the second time. Hua Kuo-feng emerged as the acting premier to replace Chou, while the radicals began a brief reign in power, led by Mao's wife, Chiang Ching. The radicals favored a strict Maoist policy of self-reliance and thus opposed large-scale purchases of Western technology, including military equipment. No new arms deals with the West occurred following the Spey deal and Teng's purge. Six days after the arrest of the "Gang of Four" radical leaders on October 6, 1976 (less than a month after Mao died), the Ford administration made the second major Western move toward military ties with China.

On October 12, 1976, the National Security Council secretly approved the sale to

China of two advanced Control Data Cyber 172 computers with military applications. The Chinese request to buy the computers had been around for more than a year, but the administration decided to approve the sale as a gesture to China's post-Mao leadership. Kissinger, who had initially opposed the deal, viewed the decision as signaling both Moscow and Peking that the United States was concerned with China's security. This was intended to head off either Sino-Soviet *rapprochement* or Soviet military pressure on China during the post-Mao policy and power struggle. Approval of the Cyber deal was also a tangible "payoff" to those in the Chinese leadership who had supported the intitial opening to the United States.[12]

Kissinger, however, did not want to abandon the policy of "evenhandedness" that had guided previous American technology transfers to communist countries. Under that policy, the United States was not supposed to sell to one communist nation an item being denied to another. The administration had approved the sale to Moscow of a similar Cyber 73 computer two weeks earlier. The Cyber 172 sale to Peking nevertheless represented a de facto tilt toward China because it promised to greatly enhance Chinese technological capabilities, whereas the Soviets already had computer technology comparable to the Cyber computers. The agreed-upon use for the computers was for petroleum exploration.[13] Nevertheless, defense experts said the Cyber 172 could be used for nuclear weapons calculations, control of phased-array radars for early-warning systems, and processing underwater detection information. The virtually unprecedented consideration and approval of the sale by the NSC, with the direct participation of the President and the secretary of state, belies the administration's public statement at that time that it had been a routine decision.

In the critical period following Mao's death, the Ford administration also publicly indicated a strong concern for China's security. Kissinger said at a news conference on October 15 that "the territorial integrity and sovereignty of China is very important to the world equilibrium and we would consider it a grave matter if this were threatened by an outside power." Nine days later, Kissinger went even further, linking U.S. and Chinese security, adding that the United States "would take an extremely dim view of a military attack or even military pressure" on China.[14]

These moves toward Peking did not end the policy dispute, primarily because of the change of administration, but they did set precedents for President Carter.

THE NEW ADMINISTRATION DEBATES CHINA POLICY

When Jimmy Carter won the 1976 presidential election, Sino-American relations were in a holding pattern, U.S.–Soviet relations were deteriorating, and a major debate was raging within the government and the broader foreign policy community over Washington's policies toward both Moscow and Peking. Upwardly revised U.S. intelligence estimates of Soviet military spending and claims that the Soviets were seeking military superiority rather than parity had revived alarmist sentiments and heightened suspicions of Moscow's global intentions (see chapter 7).

With mounting hostility toward the Soviet Union and disillusionment with détente, the views of those who wanted to strengthen relations with China (including military ties) to pressure Moscow gained increasing support. But some officials within the new administration also hoped to reverse the downward trend in U.S.–Soviet relations and find new ground for building a more cooperative relationship with Moscow, especially on arms control. These officials tended to view U.S. relations with Peking as a bilateral matter and were wary of trying to play China against the Soviet Union. These tendencies would be reflected in the conflicting views of Secretary of State Cyrus Vance and the State Department on the one hand, and National Security Adviser Zbigniew Brzezinski and his NSC staff on the other. Visits to Peking by the two officials, in August 1977 and May 1978, would highlight these two policy currents within the administration and have sharply different impacts on U.S.–China relations and triangular politics.

In the weeks before Carter took office, his initial signals to Moscow and Peking emphasized an interest in pursuing détente while showing little interest in China. Carter personally affirmed to Soviet party leader Leonid Brezhnev that he shared the Soviet leader's desire for peace, nuclear disarmament, and reduction in conventional weapons. Carter promised to "move aggressively to get the SALT talks off dead center," and laid the blame on the United States for the impasse in the negotiations.[15] Carter also indicated that he wanted to improve trade relations with Moscow and appointed prodétente moderates to key Cabinet positions—Harold Brown as secretary of defense and Cyrus Vance as secretary of state.[16] At the same time, Secretary of State-designate Cyrus Vance indicated that improvement of relations with Peking would be a low priority for the new administration. Vance told *Newsweek* on December 13 that he planned to normalize relations with China, but slowly. "He does not believe there is any rush to establish relations with China," *Newsweek* reported, "since it is important to maintain a careful balance in U.S. relations with the Soviets."

Although Carter took office in January 1977 with U.S.–China relations far down the list of foreign policy priorities, the "China card" was soon pushed to the front of the presidential deck. As Lawrence Caldwell and Alexander Dallin point out (see chapter 7), Carter's outspoken human rights policy toward the Soviet Union, including a personal letter to Soviet dissident Andre Sakharov and a new SALT proposal calling for major reductions in weapons from the previously agreed-upon totals of the 1974 Vladivostok accord (which the Soviets were hoping to finalize quickly with the new administration), led to the bitter failure of a mission to Moscow by Secretary Vance in late March.

Carter responded to the impasse with the Soviets by flirting for the first time with the notion of improving U.S. ties with China to pressure the Soviet Union on SALT and other issues. Immediately after Vance returned empty-handed from Moscow, Carter made a series of highly public gestures toward Peking, including unexpectedly adding his son Chip to a congressional delegation leaving for China and letting it be known that he wanted to visit China and that the United States regularly informs the Chinese about developments in the SALT talks. Carter also ordered a major NSC review of America's China policy, including the issue of sales of military-related technology to Peking—a move that was quickly leaked to the press.[17]

IMPACT ON MOSCOW

While the Carter administration was making its first moves toward improving ties with China and considering more far-reaching measures to gain leverage over the Soviet Union, the Soviets were concluding that (1) there was virtually no hope for short-term improvement in their own relations with Peking, and (2) closer ties between Washington and Peking could pose a serious threat to Moscow. The Soviets had stopped all public criticism of China immediately after Mao's death in September 1976 and had sent their chief border negotiator, Deputy Foreign Minister Leonid Ilyichev, to Peking in November to resume the Sino-Soviet border talks broken off eighteen months earlier. But Ilyichev, who reportedly took no new proposals with him, returned empty-handed to Moscow at the end of February.[18]

China's post-Mao leadership had not stopped Chinese attacks on the Soviet Union and had continued to press for closer ties with the West to counter the Soviets. Chinese officials were quoted as saying that opposition to the Soviet Union is a "fundamental strategic policy rather than a temporary expedient for China," that "the Taiwan issue is a small matter compared with many common objectives the United States and China have"; and that Soviet expansion and a third world war are inevitable unless Brezhnev's regime is overthrown or Soviet power is checked by "joint pressure" applied by Western Europe, Japan, China, and the United States. Chinese officials also charged that the Soviets have not given up their "ambition of subjugating China" and called for a "race against time" to build up the Chinese economy,[19] providing a strategic rationale for an ambitious modernization drive.

Moscow broke its self-imposed silence on China on April 20 with charges in the foreign affairs weekly *New Times* that China's new leadership under Hua Kuo-feng was committed to following Mao's anti-Soviet foreign policy and had been whipping up "anti-Soviet hysteria."

The most important Soviet assessment of triangular relations in this period was contained in a May 14 *Pravda* article signed by I. Aleksandrov, a pseudonym representing the Party Central Committee. The Aleksandrov piece indicated the Soviet leadership had concluded that (1) the United States was seriously considering support for a major Western effort to supply China with modern arms and military technology; (2) such arms transfers would threaten Soviet security, at least in the long run; and (3) there was a danger China might succeed in pulling the United States toward an anti-Soviet alliance. The Aleksandrov article warned that any Western military aid to China would be used not only against the Soviet Union but eventually against the West as well, and called on the West to join the Soviet Union in containing Chinese ambitions. The *Pravda* article also implied that the Soviets would not sit idly by if the West began arming China, although it did not specify what action Moscow might take.[20]

The Aleksandrov statement was published less than a week before the convening of the first round of SALT talks between Vance and Soviet Foreign Minister André Gromyko since the disastrous March meeting in Moscow. Because of the timing of the statement, U.S. officials also took it as a warning that Western military aid to China could undermine the strategic arms negotiations. According to U.S. officials,

the Soviets had argued during previous SALT talks that Chinese nuclear forces
should be counted along with American strategic forces because the Soviet Union
has to be prepared to counter the Chinese simultaneously with the United States.
They also had suggested that Western military aid to China would bolster the
long-term Chinese nuclear threat to the Soviet Union.[21] Washington, on the other
hand, hoped that its recent flirtation with China would produce more Soviet flexibility in the upcoming talks. Little progress was made at the May 20–21 meeting in
Geneva, however, except that the atmosphere of the talks improved over the Moscow meeting and the two sides compromised to reach a framework for further
discussions.[22]

By publicly acknowledging their concern over American ties with Peking in such
an authoritative article as the Aleksandrov piece, the Soviets were showing their
sensitivity to U.S. pressure.[23] This admission fueled the arguments of those in the
administration who suggested that such a policy would in fact give the United States
leverage over the Soviets, whereas others interpreted the statement as a warning
that such a policy would have serious adverse repercussions.

By June, opponents of U.S. military ties with China had won the first round of
battle within the government; the administration backed away from playing the
"China card" against Moscow.[24] An initial draft of the NSC review ordered by
Carter in April, Presidential Review Memorandum (PRM) 24, recommended
against a tilt toward China in the transfer of military-related technology—i.e., continuation of the policy of "evenhandedness" in approving and denying requests for
purchase of strategic technology by China and the Soviet Union. (An administration
official later said that U.S. arms sales to China were not even officially considered
because such consideration was thought to be in itself too provocative toward the
Soviet Union.) The PRM draft was leaked to the *New York Times* on June 24, where
it was also reported that the opponents of military technology sales to China were
centered in the State Department at the China and Soviet desks, whereas supporters
of such sales came from the Pentagon, the CIA, and the NSC.[25]

PRM 24 concluded that "since the desire to head off Chinese-Western collaboration was a major impetus to the present [Soviet] leadership's policy of détente, there
is presumably a point at which the present Soviet leadership or its successors would
conclude that this policy is not achieving the desired objective. Despite the difficulties for other Soviet objectives, Moscow would then be compelled to make a fundamental reassessment of its policies toward the U.S." The draft study said that the
"severity of Soviet reaction" to a policy of U.S. facilitating transfers of military-
related equipment to China "would increase with the perceived threat to Soviet
interests. At some undefined point, Soviet perceptions of the threat of U.S.–
Chinese military collaboration would stiffen Soviet positions on even the major
issues of U.S.–Soviet relations such as SALT, especially if initial Soviet efforts to
reverse the trend failed. The Soviets might also increase tensions with China."

The leak of PRM 24's conclusions indicated to the Soviets that the administration
had ruled out the transfer of military-related technology to China. But it also warned
Moscow that such technology transfers had been considered at a high level of the
U.S. government and could be reconsidered at a later date if relations between the
United States and the Soviet Union deteriorated further.[26] In fact, PRM 24 and the

issue of military-related technology transfers to China would continue to be hotly debated within the government for almost another year.

Nevertheless, in the spring and summer of 1977 leading up to Secretary of State Vance's trip to Peking in August, PRM 24's initial conclusions represented U.S. policy. In a major Asia policy address on June 29,[27] Vance indicated that U.S.–China relations would be dealt with primarily in a bilateral rather than triangular context— that the United States had at least temporarily ended its flirtation with playing China against the Soviets. Vance promised that a constructive U.S. relationship with China "will threaten no one. It will serve only peace." At the same time, Vance assured the Chinese that the United States "will not enter into any agreements with others that are directed against the People's Republic of China." Vance concentrated his remarks on the problem of normalization of relations between Washington and Peking. He emphasized the administration's commitment to move toward full normalization of relations based on "the view expressed in the Shanghai Communiqué that there is but one China." Vance pointedly failed to mention the U.S.–Taiwan mutual defense treaty and referred only to a "peaceful settlement of the Taiwan question by the Chinese themselves." Vance also said, however, that progress toward normalization "may not be easy or immediately evident"; he called for "reciprocal efforts" on China's part to "normalize further our bilateral relationship." [28]

While the administration was signaling to Moscow that the United States would not play its China card at that time, it was also taking other steps to ease tensions with the Soviet Union. Carter backed off his tough SALT proposals and toned down his statements on human rights, which had rankled the Soviets. This policy trend culminated in a speech on U.S.–Soviet relations by Carter on July 21 at Charleston, South Carolina. Carter, who later characterized the speech as "a move toward better understanding," said he believed that "an atmosphere of peaceful cooperation is far more conducive to an increased respect for human rights than an atmosphere of belligerence or warlike confrontation." [29]

The trend toward cooling the rhetoric and signaling Washington's interest in improving ties with Moscow was reinforced by another NSC Presidential Review Memorandum, PRM 10, the main conclusions of which were leaked to the press during the summer. PRM 10, a major interagency review of the global balance of power and U.S. strategy, concluded that the growth in Soviet military and economic power was slowing down and that long-term trends favored the United States. PRM 10's conclusions contrasted sharply with Ford administration warnings of a continuing Soviet military buildup outstripping the United States and a Soviet reach for nuclear superiority.[30] The massive study concluded that the U.S.–Soviet military balance was roughly equal at present, but contrasted the strength and scope of the American economy and capacity for technological innovation with forecasts of impending Soviet capital and labor shortages. In addition, PRM 10 noted Moscow's problems with political succession, agricultural failures, and the continuing Sino-Soviet split as factors exacerbating Soviet long-term weakness and tilting the balance of power toward the United States.

The NSC study produced an initial sense of relief among arms controllers and prodétente experts and officials who were concerned that "alarmist" claims about Soviet intentions were damaging prospects for a new SALT agreement and the overall tenor of U.S.–Soviet relations. PRM 10 seemed to suggest that the United States could take a more relaxed view of the "Soviet threat" and proceed with SALT and other efforts to increase Soviet-American cooperation.

Nevertheless, the PRM 10 strategic assessment created immediate problems for Sino-American relations, which were apparent during and after Secretary Vance's trip to Peking in late August. Chinese leaders attached great importance to the Vance visit, which was to be their first direct contact with a Carter Cabinet-level official and was scheduled to begin just after the close of the Eleventh Party Congress.[31] However, the Chinese quickly made it clear that they were disappointed with the outcome of their talks with the secretary of state. Vice-Premier Teng Hsiao-ping charged that the United States had regressed from the Ford administration's position on normalization, setting back efforts to establish full diplomatic ties between Washington and Peking.[32]

U.S. officials worried that the failure to move forward in relations with China resulting from Vance's trip was more a function of fundamental differences in strategic views than of the highly publicized impasse over normalization. The conclusions of PRM 10 were a direct challenge to China's view of the United States as a declining superpower with the Soviet Union as the superpower on the ascendancy. The Chinese view provided the strategic and ideological rationale underlying Peking's efforts to establish an informal working alliance with the United States against the Soviet Union. To the Chinese, PRM 10 also raised questions about the usefulness of America as an ally if Washington failed to see the need to take a strong, aggressive global stand against Moscow.

Chinese fears that the Carter administration would not take a hard line against the Soviets but would seek a more cooperative relationship with Moscow seemed justified by progress in the SALT negotiations reported after Gromyko met with Vance and Carter in Washington in September. The President and secretary of state indicated that they were optimistic and that the Soviets had made concessions in the talks.[33] Carter told the United Nations on October 4 that the United States and the Soviet Union were within sight of a new SALT agreement, and on October 27 the President said that the general terms for a new SALT accord might be reached "within the next few weeks."

Carter's prediction was wrong; by the end of the year, hardliners inside and outside the government had combined to pressure the administration to take a new, tougher line in the SALT talks, which ultimately led the United States to withdraw compromise proposals made earlier, setting back the negotiations. Congressional and public reaction to deepening Soviet and Cuban involvement in Ethiopia's war with Somalia over the Ogaden further exacerbated U.S.–Soviet relations, which in early 1978 were in another downhill slide.

In the winter of 1977–78, the Chinese were also pressuring Carter to take a tougher line toward Moscow, suggesting that the administration was following the path of appeasement of the Soviet Union. Members of Congress visiting China in January were told by Vice-Premier Teng that the global military strength of the United States vis-à-vis the Soviet Union and Washington's determination to stand by its commitments to its allies were of more immediate concern to China than normalization of relations with America.[34] The Chinese told their foreign visitors they had been very disappointed with the development of Sino-American ties under Carter, and they viewed Vance as "anti-Chinese." [35]

WASHINGTON ACCUSED OF "APPEASEMENT"

The Chinese also questioned U.S. credibility and usefulness as an ally in major press articles. The reliability of the American commitment to Western Europe, and by implication to China, was challenged by *Peking Review:* "Today, Western Europe comes under the U.S. 'protective umbrella,' but if the Soviet Union plunges Western Europe into a blitzkrieg, no one can be sure what the U.S. reaction will be. . . . Shouldn't this make people think and take precautions?" [36] If it is doubtful that the United States would come to the defense of Western Europe in a crisis, the Chinese implied, Washington is even less likely to risk war with the Soviet Union by aiding China in the event of a Sino-Soviet conflict.[37] *People's Daily* went further, charging that "advocates of appeasement" in the West—apparently including at least some members of the Carter administration if not the President—"hope they can divert the Soviet Union to the East so as to free themselves from this Soviet peril at the expense of the security of other nations." [38]

In these attacks on the Carter administration's policy the Chinese accused the United States of

1. Underestimating "the scope and magnitude of Soviet expansion"—a clear reference to PRM 10's assessment of the global balance of power.[39]

2. Trying "to use disarmament as a means to check the speed of Soviet arms expansion and war preparations," although "neither the talks on the reduction of forces in Central Europe nor the SALT talks can stop the Soviet Union from building up its military strength."

3. Hoping to use "technical expertise, loans, and sales of grain" to "curb the Soviet Union," by making it dependent on the West. But "in so doing, they [the Americans] greatly speed up the process in which the Soviet Union is catching up with and surpassing the U.S. and Western Europe in arms and equipment."

People's Daily also hinted that Chinese leaders hoped American policy would change. The paper cited Mao Tse-tung during World War II as saying that the United States shifted from following a "Munich policy" in the Far East that undermined China's resistance to Japan to a policy of support for the Chinese resistance.

Chinese hopes for such a change in American policy brightened in early 1978 as U.S.–Soviet relations again deteriorated. The administration responded to pressures for retaliatory action against the Soviets for their military involvement in Ethiopia by hinting at linkage of SALT and other bilateral issues to Soviet behavior in Africa. A battle then ensued within the administration. Brzezinski made the most direct public suggestions of linkage, while Vance rejected the idea of linking SALT and Soviet involvement in Africa.

CARTER TALKS TOUGH TO MOSCOW

President Carter adopted a generally harder line toward the Soviets and leaned toward the Brzezinski position on linkage (except for SALT). A speech by Carter at Wake Forest University on March 17 indicated that the administration had adopted a policy toward Moscow based more on competition through a buildup of U.S. conventional forces and exercise of American economic and technological advantages than on cooperation through negotiations to halt modernization of weapons and reduce armaments. Carter also linked future Soviet-American scientific and economic cooperation to Soviet involvement in Africa and the growth of Soviet military power. The Soviet news agency Tass called the speech "alarming" and virtually accused Carter of abandoning détente. The essence of the speech, Tass said, "actually means a shift of emphasis in American foreign policy away from the earlier proclaimed course of insuring the national security of the U.S. through negotiations, through limiting the arms race and deepening détente, to a course of threats and a buildup of tensions."

Carter's Wake Forest address was prepared by Brzezinski and his staff. Brzezinski told the *Washington Post* three days before the address that the time had arrived for the United States to take a tougher stand toward Moscow to "prove we weren't soft." Brzezinski and the "hardliners" in the administration had gotten the upper hand in a matter of a few weeks. Carter was taking a tougher stand on SALT and other defense issues and was implying a linkage between trade and other bilateral ties and Soviet behavior in Africa. The final step in the move toward increasing pressure on Moscow was taken in May when Brzezinski went to China.[40] Carter's adoption of a more combative stance toward the Soviets had helped open doors in Peking.

Before the new American overtures to China, the Soviets apparently tried to reopen talks with Peking, possibly to pressure the United States by demonstrating they, too, had a "China option." Moscow sent a secret letter to the Chinese just before the opening of the Fifth National People's Congress at the end of February, proposing a joint statement on normalizing relations and resuming border negotiations. But according to Tass, which revealed the offer in March, the Chinese rejected it out of hand. The Chinese rejection apparently repeated earlier demands that Soviet troops—estimated at about half a million—be withdrawn from the border area prior to opening talks.[41] Vice-Premier Teng Hsiao-ping was quoted as saying on March 23 that there was "not a solution in sight" to the Sino-Soviet conflict.[42] The Chinese published an official rejection of the Soviet proposal on March 26, and two days later Brezhnev left for a tour of the Soviet Far East and Chinese border areas—a move that indicated the Soviets did not expect to improve ties with Peking. On April 5 Brezhnev watched Soviet military maneuvers outside the city of Khabarovsk, just twenty-five miles from the Chinese border and near the scene of fierce fighting during the 1969 border clashes.[43]

While Peking showed no interest whatsoever in easing tensions with the Soviet Union, it was sending warmer signals to Washington—apparently hoping to encourage the Carter administration's harder line toward Moscow. Chairman Hua said in his report to the National People's Congress on February 26 that although the United States and China had fundamental differences, "the two countries have quite a few points in common on some issues in the present international situation." By contrast, Hua made no mention of "points in common" with the United States in his report to the Party Congress on the eve of Vance's visit to Peking in August.

SETTING THE STAGE FOR BRZEZINSKI'S MISSION

The National People's Congress in February and March 1978 marked a turning point for China, ratifying China's post-Mao leadership and policies. The Congress gave the go ahead for Hua and Teng's ambitious program to realize the late Premier Chou En-lai's goal of making China a modern industrialized state by the turn of the century. The plans incorporated seeking large amounts of Western technology, including defense technology and weapons, for this massive drive to achieve the modernization of agriculture, industry, national defense, and science and technology.

The first report of a Western arms purchase by post-Mao China appeared in late April, less than two months after the National People's Congress meeting. Wu Hsiu-chuan, deputy chief of staff of the People's Liberation Army, told a visiting delegation of Japanese military experts that China had purchased from France an unspecified number of sophisticated HOT antitank missiles and related technology.[44] The Chinese statement proved premature—the deal had not been finalized—but the report correctly suggested that the Carter administration would not try to block arms sales to China by Western European countries, a position leaked to the press by high-level administration officials on the eve of Brzezinski's visit to Peking.[45]

The White House also leaked that the administration would allow sales to China of "gray area" dual-purpose technology that had potential military applications. It was reported that the administration had dropped the policy of "evenhandedness" and would sell to China equipment denied to the Soviet Union. In his search for a means to pressure the Soviet Union over Africa, SALT, dissidents, and other issues, Carter seemed willing in the spring of 1978 to take the risks that opponents of military-related technology sales to China had outlined in order to gain the benefits proponents said would accrue from such a policy.

These developments in Peking, Moscow, and Washington set the stage for Brzezinski's visit to China on May 20-23, 1978. The White House officially denied that Brzezinski's trip was intended to send any signals to Moscow, but administration officials said privately that the visit's primary purposes were to reassure the Chinese about U.S. defense policies vis-à-vis the Soviet Union, reaffirm Washington's desire to pursue parallel interests with China globally, keep the Soviet Union "off balance" by holding out the possibility of increasingly close Sino-American cooperation if U.S. relations with Moscow deteriorated further, reassure the Chinese about American concern for their security vis-à-vis the Soviets, and reaffirm U.S. interest in normalizing relations with China.[46]

Many of these issues were addressed publicly by Brzezinski during his Peking stay. In his opening toast he told his Chinese hosts: "We approach our relations with three fundamental beliefs: that friendship between the United States and the People's Republic of China is vital and beneficial to world peace; that a secure and strong China is in America's interest; that a powerful, confident and globally engaged United States is in China's interest." Brzezinski said that "the United States does not view its relationship with China as a tactical expedient," but rather as "derived from a long-term strategic view" as "reflected in the Shanghai Communiqué." He said the United States recognizes and shares "China's resolve to resist the efforts of any nation which seeks to establish global or regional hegemony." Brzezinski mentioned Africa, Europe, the Middle East, and Asia as areas where "we can enhance the cause of peace through consultations and, where appropriate, through parallel pursuit of our similar objectives." [47]

Brzezinski's visit provided the breakthrough that set the two countries on the path to normalization of relations seven months later. But the context of that rapid movement toward a final compromise on a formula for establishing full diplomatic ties was clearly the mutual U.S.–China interest in countering the Soviet Union on a global scale, the primary theme of Brzezinski's discussions with Chinese leaders. The anti-Soviet tenor of his mission was underscored by the not unintentionally overheard anti-Soviet jokes he made to his Chinese hosts as they climbed the Great Wall together, to the effect that whoever got to the top last would have to fight the Russians in Ethiopia.[48] Brzezinski also stressed that President Carter "is determined to join you in overcoming the remaining obstacles in the way to full normalization of our relations within the framework of the Shanghai Communiqué. The United States," Brzezinski added, "has made up its mind on this issue." And Brzezinski aides told the *New York Times* the two sides had agreed that normalization of relations was not only a bilateral matter but also strategically important to offset the Soviet Union.[49] Brzezinski told the *Times* that "the basic significance of the trip was to underline the long-term strategic nature of the United States relationship to China."

Brzezinski also departed significantly from Vance's formulation the previous June that the U.S. relationship with China "will threaten no one." In both his opening and departing toasts, Brzezinski said that "only those aspiring to dominate others have any reason to fear the further development of American Chinese relations." As both Brzezinski and Chinese leaders clearly believed the Soviets desire to "dominate others," the statement was an obvious warning to Moscow and suggested an anti-Soviet tilt in U.S. policy in contrast with Vance's earlier "evenhanded" approach.

Brzezinski and his NSC staff added to Soviet concern about his visit by leaking to the press that the sale to China of U.S. dual-purpose, military-related technology and Western arms had been discussed in Peking, and that Chinese leaders had been given detailed briefings on the SALT negotiations and on PRM 10. (Brzezinski's view of the policy implications of PRM 10, which contrasted sharply with Vance's, was that Soviet weaknesses and long-term U.S. advantages should be exploited to extract greater concessions from the Soviet Union and to contain its influence, even at the expense of possible deterioration in U.S.–Soviet relations—a view that was far more amenable to the Chinese and suggested greater American willingness to pursue a potentially provocative informal alliance with Peking against Moscow.) An NSC official in Brzezinski's delegation also discussed expanding technological exchanges and U.S. help in achieving China's goal of becoming a modern industrial state by the end of the century.[50] Chinese officials, who were dissatisfied with Vance's Peking visit, termed the talks with Brzezinski "beneficial," and were clearly pleased.[51]

PLAYING THE CHINA CARD

The intended message to Moscow resulting from Brzezinski's Peking consultations was clear: the United States had begun to "play the China card," and the Chinese had succeeded in drawing the U.S. closer into an informal global anti-Soviet alignment. How far the relationship would go was uncertain, however, especially considering the unpredictable internal politics of the Carter administration and the roller-coaster relationship between Washington and Moscow. But Brzezinski's trip signaled a new era in Sino-American cooperation—at a time of near-cold-war tension in U.S.–Soviet relations. While Washington and Moscow were sliding down a precarious slope toward confrontation in the spring of 1978, the pace of Sino-American collaboration was accelerating as the United States sought to help the Soviet's giant, hostile neighbor become "secure and strong."

On his return from Peking, Brzezinski continued his offensive against the Soviets. A few hours after a tense White House meeting between Carter and Gromyko, attended by Brzezinski and Vance, the President's national security adviser publicly charged the Soviets with violating "the code of détente" and called for "an international response" to Soviet and Cuban military activity in Africa. Carter had charged in his talks with Gromyko that the Soviets bore responsibility for the invasion of Zaire's Shaba Province by Katangese rebels—a charge Gromyko denied to reporters on the White House steps. Brzezinski also stressed in an interview on NBC's "Meet the Press" that the United States and China have "parallel interests" and said he was "troubled" by the buildup of conventional forces by the Soviet Union, including efforts "to strengthen the concentration of its forces on the frontiers of China." [52]

President Carter also stepped up his attacks on Moscow at a NATO summit meeting in Washington on May 30, charging that the Soviet military buildup in Eastern Europe "far exceeds their legitimate security needs" and calling for major increases in NATO defense spending. A week later, at Annapolis, the President challenged the Soviets to "choose either confrontation or cooperation," saying that "the United States is adequately prepared to meet either choice." Soviet President Brezhnev warned of a possible return to a "lukewarm war" if not a cold war, and the Soviet press labeled Brzezinski a "foe of détente," warning that his "basically aggressive 'tough line' "—which it viewed as expressed in Carter's Annapolis speech—is "not only fraught with the danger of a throwback to the Cold War," but also "harbors the dangers of a confrontation."

The Soviets explicitly attacked Carter's China policy. On June 25 Brezhnev charged that "recently attempts have been made in the U.S. at a high level, and in quite cynical form, to play the China card against the USSR"—a charge Carter denied two days later at a press conference.* Brezhnev called the policy "short-sighted and dangerous," and warned that "its authors may bitterly regret it." A week earlier *Pravda* had stated more explicitly that U.S. "alignment with China on an anti-Soviet basis would rule out the possibility of cooperation with the Soviet Union in the matter of reducing the danger of a nuclear war and, of course, of limiting armaments." Over the following weeks, *Pravda, Izvestia,* and the Defense Ministry's *Red Star* declared that American collusion with China would backfire against the United States and that Western military aid to Peking would ultimately be used against the West; that playing the China card would lead to a harsh Soviet reaction; and that U.S..–China military ties would not be a military threat to the Soviet Union, which is sufficiently strong to deal with any Western-aided increase in Chinese military capability.[53] Moscow commentaries also warned that the Chinese aim was to provoke a war between the United States and the Soviet Union.

Soviet officials told Western journalists privately that they were increasingly concerned that the Carter administration had decided to shelve détente in favor of forging closer ties with China. They said Washington—in search of a short-term strategic advantage—seemed to have abandoned pledges of increased trade and transfers of technology promised in the early 1970s by Kissinger to entice the Soviet Union into détente. Soviet experts suggested that Moscow would have to make foreign and domestic policy adjustments in response to the situation, which portended a shift in the balance of power and alignment of forces against it.[54]

The continuing deterioration in U.S. relations with the Soviet Union reached a near confrontation over Soviet dissidents in July. The trials of dissidents Anatoly Shcharansky and Alexander Ginsberg were held deliberately just as Vance and Gromyko met in Geneva for another round of SALT talks. Carter rejected pressure from some of his advisers and congressional hardliners to cancel the Vance-Gromyko meeting, but he made the first use of trade as a weapon in his dealings with Moscow. Carter canceled the sale of a $7 million Sperry Rand Univac computer system to the Soviet news agency Tass and agreed that henceforth all proposed technology transfers to the Soviet Union would come under NSC review. The institution of political controls over technology transfers to the Soviet Union, and the addition of oil technology transfers to the USSR to the list of strategic goods requiring export licenses, had been urged by administration hardliner Samuel Huntington, the coordinator for PRM 10. For months, Huntington had been advocating the use of oil technology transfers to the Soviets as an economic weapon against Moscow. He had outlined his strategy in an off-the-record briefing for a select gathering of government officials, scholars, and business leaders in mid-June, arguing that Soviet weakness in energy technology could be exploited in carrot-and-stick fashion to entice and coerce the Soviets into what he considered acceptable behavior in SALT, Africa, human rights, and other areas.[55]

---

* Carter himself denied he was playing China against the Soviet Union, but certainly that denial was part of the game, assuming Carter sought to avoid unnecessarily antagonizing the Soviets or admitting that the United States was using the Chinese.

The dissident trials and domestic pressure on Carter to react strongly pushed the President to adopt the Huntington plan. Carter also held up approval of a vital part of a $144 million sale by Dresser Industries of Dallas, Texas, of a drill bit factory to Moscow—a move advocated by Huntington in June, shortly after the deal was approved at a lower level in the government. The drill bits reportedly last five times as long as Soviet drill bits and would speed deep hole drilling in Siberia and help alleviate the Soviets' long-term oil production problems.[56]

Carter allowed the Dresser sale to go through, however, after bitter internal debates—including opposition from a special ad hoc Pentagon committee convened to consider the deal—and strong opposition from some members of Congress, including Senator Henry Jackson. The White House announced the decision not to block the sale on September 6, just as chief SALT negotiator Paul Warnke arrived in Moscow for a crucial round of arms talks. But the machinery was now in place in the White House for carefully controlling oil technology transfers to the Soviet Union, as demonstrated by coordination of the announcement of the sale with Warnke's arrival in Moscow—an apparent carrot to entice Soviet compromise in the arms negotiations.

While the President was tightening up on transfer of technology to the Soviet Union, he was encouraging sales of advanced technology to China. The administration did not try to block a Sperry Rand sale to Peking of two Univac 1100 series computers similar to those denied Moscow.[57] This apparent "tilt" toward China in technology transfers also was evident in reported direct government backing being given to four U.S. oil companies engaged in preliminary talks with Chinese leaders on establishing offshore drilling operations and selling oil technology to China.[58] Some reports suggested that U.S. investment in China's oil development program could range from $25 to $50 billion.[59]

Besides encouraging the involvement of U.S. corporations in sales of a wide range of high technology items and in possible joint ventures and production sharing deals with the Chinese, the administration began a highly publicized program of government-to-government science and technology exchanges. President Carter sent his science adviser, Frank Press, to Peking in July at the head of an unprecedented delegation of top scientific and technological government officials, including the heads of NASA, the National Science Foundation, the National Institute of Health, and the U.S. Geological Survey. On his return, Dr. Press held out the prospect of broad scientific and technical cooperation between the United States and China, which, he said, could serve as the "basis for growing commercial and industrial relations." Press's visit to Peking—and the reports that two Cabinet-level officials, Secretary of Energy James Schlesinger and Agriculture Secretary Bob Bergland, would visit China in the fall—contrasted sharply with Carter's decision to cancel all high-level government visits to the Soviet Union to show displeasure with the dissident trials, including cancellation of a visit by Dr. Press to Moscow scheduled for late July.

While the Press delegation's visit to Peking demonstrated the administration's commitment to helping China in its ambitious modernization goals, it also represented a new Chinese flexibility in dealing with the United States. Prior to 1978, the Chinese had shunned direct government-to-government exchanges prior to full normalization of relations. But in January they had sent a high-powered petroleum industry delegation to the United States in response to an invitation from Energy Secretary Schlesinger. Following Brzezinski's trip, the Chinese accelerated government-level exchanges to improve their access to U.S. technology and technological know-how. This included discussions to cooperate on bilateral matters ranging from sending thousands of Chinese students a year to the United States for scientific and technical training to launching a communications satellite for China.[60]

The Chinese also demonstrated a new sensitivity to the administration's domestic problems over severing ties with Taiwan to normalize relations with China. Chinese leaders refused to rule out the use of force to reunite Taiwan with the mainland, or to alter their basic demands that the United States sever diplomatic and defense ties and withdraw their remaining military personnel from the island. But they placed a new emphasis on seeking a peaceful solution to the Taiwan problem, including calls for direct negotiations with the Nationalist Chinese, and indicated that they foresaw reunification as a long process.[61] "Taiwan is a minor problem," Teng reportedly said to Brzezinski in May, "that will be solved by history." [62]

The process set in motion by China and the United States in May of 1978 culminated in the announcement on December 15, 1978, that the two countries would normalize diplomatic relations on January 1, 1979, and that Chinese Vice Premier Teng Hsiao-ping would visit Washington. The United States had met China's three conditions on Taiwan, while China agreed not to challenge a U.S. statement of concern that the Taiwan problem be solved peacefully by the Chinese themselves. The United States and China also agreed to disagree on indefinite continuation of U.S. arms sales to Taiwan, and China accepted the continuation of the U.S.–Taiwan mutual defense treaty for one year after normalization of relations between Peking and Washington. Finally, the joint communiqué announcing establishment of diplomatic ties included an "anti-hegemony" clause which both the Chinese and the Soviets viewed as directed at Moscow, although administration officials insisted publicly that normalization of relations was not aimed at the Soviet Union.

The announcement that China and the United States would soon normalize relations was made less than a week before Vance and Gromyko were scheduled to meet in Geneva for what was billed by the American side as the final round of SALT talks before a Carter-Brezhnev summit to be held in Washington in mid-January. Carter said just before the meeting, "I can say without any doubt that our new relationship with China will not put any additional obstacles in the way of a successful SALT agreement and also will not endanger our good relationship with the Soviet Union." Carter also claimed that he had received a note from Brezhnev that was "very positive in tone" and which acknowledged normalization of relations between the United States and China as contributing to world peace. The Soviet news agency Tass, however, shot back that although Brezhnev had told Carter normalization of relations between states is a "natural matter," the Soviet leader had objected to the wording of the communiqué—an obvious reference to the anti-hegemony clause—and that "the Soviet Union will follow most closely what the development of American-Chinese relations will be in practice and from this will draw appropriate conclusions for Soviet policy." The failure of the two sides to reach agreement at the Geneva meeting was attributed by administration officials as in large part the result of a Soviet desire to put off finalization of the accord—and a Carter-Brezhnev summit—until after Teng's visit to Washington in order to assess how the United States dealt with the Chinese leader. Carter acknowledged in mid-January that Soviet concern about Sino-American ties may have interfered with the completion of the SALT II treaty. The Soviets denied that U.S.–China ties were the cause of the delay, however, apparently because they did not want to acknowledge a linkage between SALT and China.

The Soviets received mixed signals from a summit of four Western leaders held in Guadeloupe January 5–6, three weeks before Teng's visit to Washington. President Carter, British Prime Minister Callaghan, West German Chancellor Schmidt, and French President Valery d'Estaing strongly endorsed a new SALT agreement and reassured the Soviets that U.S. normalization of relations with China had not altered the West's commitment to détente. But Callaghan also took that opportunity to announce Britain's decision to go ahead with plans to sell Harrier vertical-takeoff jet fighters to China as part of a $2 billion trade package.

Teng's dramatic visit to the United States on January 29 to February 5 also left the Soviets unsure of U.S. intentions. On the eve of Teng's visit, Carter said the United States would "be cautious in not trying to have an unbalanced relationship between China and the Soviet Union." And Vance had said two weeks earlier, "Our policy toward them will be balanced and there will be no tilts one way or the other, and this is an absolutely fundamental principle." But the administration conspicuously failed during Teng's visit to reject outright a call by him for an alliance against the Soviet Union embracing China, the United States, Japan, and Western Europe. "If we really want to be able to place curbs on the polar bear," Teng told *Time* in an interview published the day he was welcomed to the White House, "the only realistic thing for us is to unite." Teng also said at the White House that because the United States and China review their bilateral relations in a "long-term strategic perspective," the two sides "easily reached agreement on normalization." Teng tirelessly attacked the Soviet "hegemonists" during his stay in the United States, although he backed off from the actual word "alliance," which he had used in previous interviews, to describe his call for "common efforts" against the Soviet Union. A joint communiqué, issued at the end of Teng's stay in Washington, said the two sides reaffirmed that "they are opposed to efforts by any country or group of countries to establish hegemony or domination over others." But the communiqué also said the two sides had discussed areas of "differing perspectives" as well as those areas where they have "common interests and share similar points of view." Carter similarly distanced himself from Teng without specifying areas of disagreement when he said at a ceremony for the signing of scientific and cultural exchange agreements that "the security concerns of the United States do not coincide completely, of course, with those of China. Nor does China share our responsibilities,"—suggesting that SALT was an area of "differing perspectives."

The Soviets asked for a "clarification" of the administration's attitude toward the "incendiary statements by the Chinese guest at the White House." Brezhnev adviser Arbatov said in a CBS television interview during Teng's visit that the Chinese leader was attempting to "hammer into the minds of Americans an illusion that . . . an improvement of relations and a military-political alliance with China can be a sound alternative to détente, to arms control, to development of cooperation in the world. . . . This illusion, I think," Arbatov warned, "is dangerous even in the era of conventional warfare. It becomes tremendously dangerous in the era of nuclear warfare." He added, however, that he thought the United States was "rather far" from an alliance with China, and that he had hopes for the "common sense and political wisdom of Western countries and the American people."

DYNAMICS OF THE TRIANGLE

Although this listing of the perceptions and interactions of triangular politics in the first two years of the Carter administration is not exhaustive, it should provide a sense of the dynamics of the strategic U.S.–China–USSR triangle. Carter's decision to begin "playing the China card" followed the worsening of U.S.–Soviet relations and an administration search for a means of pressuring Moscow in response to Soviet involvement in Africa, difficulties in the SALT negotiations, human rights issues, and domestic pressure to take a harder line toward the Soviet Union.

Soviet policy toward the United States has been in large part a response to Sino-Soviet and Sino-American relations. A major if not primary motivation prompting Soviet leaders to seek détente with the United States in the early 1970s was to head off a Sino-American *rapprochement* that could result in closer collaboration between Peking and Washington than between Moscow and Washington.[63] In a worse case, Soviet leaders have feared an encirclement of the Soviet Union by a U.S.–Western Europe–Japan–China alliance, a nightmare that may have seemed to be turning into a reality for the Soviets in mid-1978. Moscow's aim has been to head off such collusion by demonstrating to Washington that the United States has more at stake in improved ties with the Soviet Union—such as cooperation on nuclear arms control with the only power that has the ability to destroy the United States— than it has with China.

For Chinese leaders, their policy toward the United States has been in large part a function of their Soviet policy—their assessment of the relative threats posed by the Soviet Union and the United States and the usefulness of the United States as a counter to the Soviet Union.[64] By tilting toward the United States, they sought to head off collusion between the United States and the Soviet Union. The Chinese have sought to sow suspicion and increase tensions between the United States and Soviet Union, as well as to improve Sino-American relations. Teng Hsiao-ping told *Time* just before his visit to Washington that although he did not oppose a SALT agreement between the United States and the Soviet Union, "one should not rely on such a thing. In seeking world peace and world stability, such agreements are neither as significant nor as useful as the normalization of relations between China and the U.S. and the peace and cooperation treaty signed between China and Japan."

These concerns of the leadership in the three countries set up a dynamic in which each country has tried to prevent collusion by the other two. In particular, China and the Soviet Union each have sought to have better relations than the other with the United States.

"Collusion and contention" has been the Chinese set of polar opposites used to describe the U.S.–Soviet relationship, with emphasis on one or the other in most periods since the early 1960s.[65] The Carter administration has used the formulation "cooperation and competition" to describe U.S.–Soviet relations, with one or the other code word emphasized by various policy makers at different points in the modulating relationship.

In short, the Soviets have viewed the Sino-American *rapprochement* as U.S.–China collusion against them, just as the Chinese have sought to undermine détente as potential, if not actual, U.S.–Soviet collusion against China. And American leaders have viewed potential Sino-Soviet *rapprochement,* however unlikely, as threatening to alter the current favorable global power alignment.

Michel Tatu, in a prophetic essay in 1970 predicting a Sino-American *rapprochement,* suggested "there will have to be a Washington-Peking dialogue, even at the risk of weakening the 'hot line' to Moscow and offending the Soviet Union. When this dialogue takes place the triangular set-up will have become fully operative. . . ." [66] Tatu set out the "theory of the game" in the following "principles":

1. The existence of an "adversary number one" leads to "objective. collusion" with number two.

2. Each of the three players aims to reduce collusion between the others to a minimum.

3. At the same time, it is in the interest of each to bluff or blackmail his chief adversary by threatening collusion with the other.

4. The surest way for any of the three to provoke the other two into collusion is to display undue aggressiveness.

Although Tatu's rules of the game provide useful insights into the dynamics of the triangle as it has developed, they also imply greater symmetry than has been the case. The positions of the players in the game are not interchangeable, and their ability to utilize the potential moves outlined in Tatu's rules has been asymmetrical. The United States has been in the most favorable position of the triangular players and is most able to take full advantage of the maneuverability suggested in Tatu's rules. (Tatu recognized that the "United States will probably be in the most advantageous position" of the three powers, but he did not incorporate this insight into his rules of the game.) The key to these U.S. advantages has been the relative permanency of the Sino-Soviet split. Sino-Soviet collusion against the United States has remained only a theoretical possibility; although the specter of *rapprochement* between Peking and Moscow has been raised in the West, no serious moves to heal the rift seem to have been made by either power since the triangle became operative with the Sino-American *rapprochement* of 1971–72. China and the Soviet Union have each sought closer ties with the United States—collusion with Washington—in competition with each other.

Both the Chinese and the Soviets want access to American and other Western technology and trade, just as both want to head off collusion by the United States with the other power against them. Each could jeopardize the Western connection it is seeking by a détente with the other, which could create Western fears of Sino-Soviet *rapprochement* and lead to a halt in the flow of technology to the East. For Moscow, Sino-Soviet détente also could provoke a greater Western military buildup in strategic and conventional forces, and for the Chinese it could force Washington to return to a 2½ war strategy. Consequently, although it is in the interest of Soviet and Chinese leaders to avoid a Sino-Soviet war by practicing crisis management in their border dispute, it may not be in either's interest to improve relations markedly—at least not at this time or under current conditions—because of the threat such a move would hold for what each clearly views as more important interests in its relations with the United States and the West.

Neither the Soviet Union nor China wants to risk altering the triangular configuration to its disadvantage through *rapprochement,* but each seeks to shift the current triangular power balance by drawing the United States into closer collaboration with it against the other. The Soviets presumably seek a more far-reaching détente with the United States that would not only expand trade, arms control efforts, and other bilateral relations but would also strain U.S.–China relations by increasing Chinese fears of U.S. appeasement of the Soviet Union and anti-China collusion between Washington and Moscow.

The Chinese, for their part, seek to draw the United States closer to a "united front" with the Second and Third Worlds against Moscow to contain and weaken the Soviets and exacerbate U.S.–Soviet conflict. Sino-American collusion against the Soviet Union would rule out anti-China collusion between Washington and Moscow, heighten U.S.–Soviet tensions, and possibly provoke a reduction in the transfer of U.S. technology, grain, and other commodities to the Soviets. It could also lead to a greater Western military buildup against the Soviet Union and possibly divert Soviet military pressure from the East to the West, or at least strain Soviet military capabilities.

In either case, the triangular position of the power that succeeded in isolating the other from the United States through forging closer ties of its own with Washington would be greatly improved, bringing a new triangular configuration—and possibly exacerbating conflict between the United States and the left-out power.

When the triangle became operative in the early 1970s, U.S. moves to improve relations with either China or the Soviet Union stimulated the other power to seek improved ties with Washington as well. Even during periods of strain in Sino-American or Soviet-American relations, Washington's relations with both Peking and Moscow have been better than have been China's and the Soviet Union's relations with each other. This has reflected both the favorable U.S. position in the triangle and a U.S. policy of overall evenhandedness that has meant refusing to tilt decisively toward either Moscow or Peking.

The United States is in the unique position of having both the greatest interest in preserving the current asymmetries of the triangular configuration and the strongest position from which to act to maintain its position. American interest in maintaining this equilibrium stems from the favorable nature of the United States position and the dangers for the United States that could result from a decisive shift to one side or the other.

Substantial improvement of U.S. relations with Moscow that appeared to Peking as anti-China collusion, for example, could strain Sino-American relations. Peking could retreat toward a new hostile isolation and possibly take aggressive actions against U.S. interests in Asia. China could also seek its own *rapprochement* with the

Soviets. At the least, Chinese leaders might no longer view Washington as a useful ally against the Soviet Union and thus be forced to reexamine their strategic policy.

But the Chinese would have to consider such actions in the light of their increasing dependence on Western supplies of technology and capital vital to China's modernization program. If an expanded U.S.–Soviet détente were to parallel continued improvement in Sino-American bilateral ties following normalization of relations, including further expansion of trade and technology transfers, then Chinese leaders would be forced to choose between assuming a posture of hostility toward the United States or accepting the new American posture toward Moscow as compatible with closer Washington-Peking relations. The Chinese might have continued access to technology from Western Europe and Japan even if they decided to cool relations with the United States. But defense ties by NATO and Japan with China are unlikely to survive U.S. disapproval, and the Chinese are seeking from the United States increasingly significant technology transfers, including military-related technologies, making the option of jeopardizing relations with America less and less acceptable.

A key problem for U.S. policy makers seeking to play the triangle is to assess the limits of Washington's maneuverability, although American policy almost certainly will continue to be based on uncertain and conflicting estimates of those limits. On the one hand, U.S. actions such as selling arms directly to China or seeking a military alliance with Peking could lead to a confrontation with the Soviet Union or other counterproductive Soviet reactions. On the other hand, easing restrictions on the sale to China of military-related defense technology and supporting arms sales to Peking by West European countries could pressure the Soviets into making gestures toward improving ties with the United States to head off further Sino-American cooperation and collusion.

The high costs of miscalculation in assessing how far the United States can tilt toward Peking (or Moscow) is likely to lead to caution if not conservatism on the part of an American President who seeks to preserve détente. Even a relatively small possibility of costly confrontations or other counterproductive Soviet reactions would seem to be unacceptable. But to a President prepared to abandon détente and even SALT, potential negative Soviet reactions from a policy of arming and allying with China (short of war) might seem worth the risk if the policy promised to increase the U.S. global position of power vis-à-vis the Soviet Union. In this case, the President might opt for a shift from triangular balance to a semipermanent alliance of the United States with China against the Soviet Union—a new "containment" strategy. The favorable U.S. position in the triangle, however, rests on American ability to induce China and the Soviet Union to compete against each other for improved relations with Washington. By allying with China, the United States would restrict its freedom of action and maneuverability in the triangle, reducing American leverage over both Moscow and Peking.

Even at a time of worsening U.S.–Soviet relations and a search for a means to pressure Moscow, proposals for forming a U.S.–China alliance would be viewed with caution. In many ways, the primary relationship is a bipolar one between Washington and Moscow. Only the Soviet Union and the United States can threaten each other's survival. The vast superiority of the two countries' nuclear arsenals sets them apart from China, as well as from the rest of the world. Their conventional military capabilities enable them both to project modern military power on a global scale. By contrast, China has only a modest nuclear force.[67] China has yet to deploy an ICBM that can deliver nuclear warheads to the United States,[68] and the Chinese cannot reach nuclear parity with America and the Soviet Union in the foreseeable future (although Chinese nuclear weapons have become sufficiently invulnerable to preemptive attack to provide a credible deterrent to a Soviet first strike). China has the largest army in the world, but it is armed with equipment twenty years behind U.S. and Soviet military technology and lacks the air and sea support for large-scale operations outside China's contiguous land areas. Most experts doubt that the Chinese armed forces could threaten a credible attack on heavily armed Taiwan, especially as long as massive Chinese deployments are committed to meeting a potential conflict with the Soviet Union. In addition, China is only beginning to deploy a blue-water navy to project Chinese naval power beyond China's coastline and into the Pacific.

For Washington and Moscow, then, it is primarily a bipolar world of military power. This military bipolarity, especially in nuclear arms, has created a perceived interest in Moscow and Washington for collaboration to try to impose some ground rules and restraints on competition and contention to regulate the arms race and prevent nuclear war. Even this relationship is asymmetrical, however: for the Soviets, Chinese nuclear and conventional forces are a threat requiring Soviet deployment of counter forces; whereas for the United States, Chinese military power is not currently viewed as threatening, and some officials see the Chinese as potential allied forces.

Another asymmetry: the economic power of the United States is unequaled by the Soviet Union both in the size of its economy and in its global economic importance. America's GNP is about twice that of the Soviet Union, and the U.S. economy has an even greater relative impact on the world economy. China's GNP is only about one sixth the size of America's, and China is only beginning to become a significant factor in the world economy. (China's modernization drive, however, is rapidly increasing the significance of the Chinese market for Western sales of capital equipment and technology, and China is likely to become increasingly important as an exporter of raw materials, especially oil and coal.) China's political influence, including the impact of its culture and its massive population, has far outstripped its military and economic power and has given the Chinese a global political importance surpassed only by the Soviet Union and the United States.

What these asymmetries suggest is that the United States has more to gain or lose in its relations with Moscow than in its relations with Peking. The Soviets are in a much stronger position to damage U.S. interests than are the Chinese, and cooperation with the Soviet Union could have an impact on a wider range of U.S. interests than could such cooperation with China. They also suggest that the United States should be more likely to move toward better ties with Moscow at the risk of damaging relations with Peking than toward closer U.S.–China ties, which could heighten tensions with the Soviet Union. Prior to Vance's abortive Moscow trip in March 1977, the Carter administration seemed to be seeking such cooperation with the Soviets while placing improvement of ties with China on the back burner. But as

U.S.–Soviet relations worsened in 1978, increasing collusion between Washington and Peking—if not an informal alliance against the Soviets—seemed to be the direction of U.S. policy

IT'S HOW YOU PLAY THE GAME

The preceding discussion of the dynamics of the triangle demonstrates the difficulty of even conceptualizing this set of relationships. Nevertheless, leaders of the three countries do view their positions and actions in triangular terms. They calculate costs and benefits, short-term and long-term gains, and tactical and strategic implications in their relations with the third power when they interact with, or signal, the second power.

The meanings of actions and perceptions are not necessarily shared in the other capitals, however, nor are they necessarily fully understood by the power taking the initiative. The Carter administration's moves toward China in the spring of 1978, for example, were in large part a matter of strategic signaling to the Soviet Union. The Soviets responded by accusing Carter of "playing the China card." But what does "playing the China card" actually mean? And is there just one China card, a card that once played cannot be played again? What the United States did fell short of playing the China card if that meant providing military aid to China or entering into an informal military alliance with Peking against the Soviets. On the other hand, the administration let it be known that it was heeding the advice of those within the government who had advocated playing the China card. What the administration did, in fact, was to appear to tilt toward China in a number of ways that were seen—and were intended to be seen—as provocative by the Soviet Union. The United States, while officially maintaining its policy of "evenhandedness" governing the transfer of strategic technology, approved sales to China of advanced dual-purpose technology with military applications that would be denied to the Soviets. The administration indicated it would not block the sale to China of "defensive" military hardware by Western European countries. The United States committed itself to giving China major support in its massive drive for modernization on a government-to-government level. In the spring and summer of 1978 the United States also gave tacit support to China's aggressive new diplomacy aimed at encircling the Soviet Union. Chinese leaders quickly finalized the Sino-Japanese peace treaty, signed August 12, after nearly six years of haggling over its antihegemony clause. The agreement was reached primarily because the Chinese decided to compromise on that clause and other issues, but the United States also encouraged the Japanese to go ahead with finalization of the document.[69] Administration officials publicly suggested that Japan, China, and the United States have a common interest in maintaining the existing balance of power in northeastern Asia to contain the Soviet Union.[70] The administration also quietly supported Chairman Hua's unprecedented visit to Romania, Yugoslavia, and Iran shortly after the Sino-Japanese accord was signed. The Soviets perceived in these moves U.S. encouragement of Chinese encirclement of the Soviet Union, including pursuit of a "parallel interest" shared by the United States and China in "destabilizing" Eastern Europe.[71] Finally, the United States announced the normalization of relations with Peking at a critical point in the SALT negotiations with Moscow.

From the Soviet point of view, was this playing *the* China card or *a* China card? Were the American moves toward collusion with China an immediate or long-term security threat, or simply a pressure tactic by Washington, or both? Was the policy reversible through jawboning—by threatening dire consequences for U.S.–Soviet relations, for China, and even directly for the United States and the West in their long-term dealings with an unreliable Peking? Or should the Soviet Union begin to take long-term countermeasures such as bolstering military forces on the Eastern and Western fronts to face more hostile and increasingly united enemies East and West? Should Moscow make an attempt to head off this collusion by making concessions to Washington in SALT and other matters, or would this simply be viewed as a sign that American policy was working to pressure the Soviet Union? The Soviets had to assess both the implications of U.S. actions and the intentions of U.S. policy makers, and they had to decide on a course or courses of action to respond to and influence Washington's moves toward Peking.

How, does Washington evaluate Moscow's reaction? Soviet actions following Brzezinski's trip to Peking could be interpreted differently and lead to different policy conclusions. Did the combined pressure of moves toward China and imposition of tighter controls of technology transfer to the Soviet Union produce Moscow's apparent attempt to improve relations in the late summer and fall on 1978, including compromises in the SALT talks to reach a new agreement? Or did the China moves further exacerbate already tense relations between Washington and Moscow, delay improvement in ties, and make that improvement far more tenuous because of deepened Soviet suspicions of U.S. intentions? Even if the Soviets were pressured successfully to make compromises in the short term, were the long-term prospects for easing tensions and expanding cooperation between the United States and the Soviet Union enhanced or set back? The evidence is not conclusive. Those favoring military ties with China, for example, argue that the events of 1978 proved their case, whereas those opposed counter that the Soviets would have been more moderate and forthcoming sooner in their dealings with the United States if they had not been provoked by American collusion with Peking. They also argue that U.S. gestures toward Moscow following the near confrontation over the dissident trials in July, including Carter's finally deciding to approve the sale of the Dresser drill bit factory to the Soviet Union in September, helped ease tensions. The Soviets may have assessed that their warnings against playing the China card had led to second thoughts in Washington. Soviet moderation may have been intended to encourage a United States move back toward a more evenhanded approach in its dealings with Moscow and Peking.

Another area of critical ambiguity concerns the limits on U.S. collusion with China. Did Brzezinski overplay America's hand—as many administration officials apparently felt—or could the United States go further in tilting toward Peking without provoking an unwanted response from Moscow? Uncertainty about the meaning of the actual Soviet response further complicates estimating likely Soviet response to future moves.

An analysis of the dynamics of the strategic triangle helps pose questions about the interactions of the three powers, but it does not provide a clear guide to finding the answers—for either the analyst or the policy maker. The ambiguities and complexities of the triangular relationship will continue to make most judgments tenuous at best. Nevertheless, recognizing that bilateral relations between any two of the three powers are likely to have a triangular component helps direct the analyst or policy maker toward a more complete understanding of the particular interaction under consideration. The triangle exists whether or not a given leader recognizes the triangular aspect of bilateral ties with either Moscow or Peking. This also suggests that despite protestations by U.S. officials that, for example, technology transfers to China are strictly a bilateral matter between Washington and Peking, such deals will be viewed and evaluated by both the Soviets and the Chinese in triangular terms. The United States is in the triangular game whether or not it wants to be a player. The Carter administration, of course, clearly wants to be in the game, although how the U.S. hand should be played will continue to be a subject of intense controversy within the government.

NOTES

1. Morton H. Halperin, *China and the Bomb* (New York: Praeger, 1965), pp. 124–25, 138. President Kennedy considered a military strike against China's nuclear facilities, according to several informed sources.
2. See Melvin R. Laird, Secretary of Defense, *Fiscal Year 1971 Defense Program and Budget* (Washington, D.C.: Government Printing Office, 20 February 1970), p. 53.
3. See the Internews *International Bulletin* (hereinafter referred to as *IB*) 5, no. 4 (27 February 1978). See also John Newhouse, *Cold Dawn: The Story of SALT* (New York: Holt, Rinehart and Winston, 1973), pp. 188–89; and H. R. Haldeman, *The Ends of Power* (New York: New York Times Books, 1978), pp. 89–94. Some officials thought the Soviet overtures were a bluff on the Soviets' part to pressure the Chinese.
4. See Gareth Porter, *A Peace Denied* (Bloomington: University of Indiana Press, 1975); and Banning Garrett, "A Peace Denied, A Peace Seized," *Indochina Chronicle,* December 1975.
5. See Robert G. Sutter, *China-Watch: Toward Sino-American Reconciliation* (Baltimore: Johns Hopkins University Press, 1978), pp. 3, 109–12.
6. See Newhouse, *Cold Dawn,* pp. 100, 168–69, on the China factor in détente and the SALT negotiations.
7. Confirmed to the author by a knowledgeable Pentagon source and a former member of Kissinger's NSC staff. In addition, China scholar Jerome Cohen wrote in the *Los Angeles Times,* 30 November 1975: "The United States may already be providing China with certain types of unpublicized military assistance, for example by sharing satellite intelligence data regarding the deployment of Soviet forces."
8. "L-32" was reviewed at the CIA by Roger Glenn Brown, a senior analyst in the Office of Political Research, among others at the agency and in the Defense Department. Brown and high-level officials at the Pentagon circulated "L-32" with comments by Pillsbury and raised an issue likely to become far more critical over the coming years. An informal group was set up at the Pentagon to study the implications of the RAND paper. In the fall of 1975, the CIA circulated two highly classified intelligence memoranda by Brown on Chinese politics and the Sino-Soviet-U.S. triangle and Chinese perspectives on importing Western military technology. Both studies provoked a contentious debate within the CIA, at the State and Defense departments, and at the NSC. The first versions of Brown's studies were made public at a seminar given by Brown at the RAND corporation in early

1975. See Thomas M. Gottlieb, *Chinese Foreign Policy Factionalism and the Origins of the Strategic Triangle* (Santa Monica: RAND R-1902-NA, November 1977), p. 11n. Gottlieb discusses Brown's thesis extensively. A short, unclassified version of Brown's studies appeared in *Foreign Policy,* Summer 1976, entitled "Chinese Politics and American Policy: A New Look at the Triangle."

9. *New York Times,* 4 October 1975. The *Times,* which had obtained the two CIA studies by Brown (see note 8), listed some of the low-key Chinese feelers to U.S. corporations for military-related high technology, including approaches to Itek for satellite cameras, to Lockheed for C-141 military transport planes, to Control Data for Cyber 172 computers, and to RCA Global Communications about radar and communications equipment.

10. Besides Pillsbury and Brown, see also Jerome Cohen, "A China Policy for the Next Administration," *Foreign Affairs,* October 1976; Ross Terrill, "China and the World: Self-Reliance or Interdependence," *Foreign Affairs,* January 1977; and A. Doak Barnett, "Military-Security Relations between China and the United States," *Foreign Affairs,* April 1977.

11. Several sources insist that the British were determined to go through with the deal and Kissinger basically acquiesced to their decision. Kissinger's office was apparently the source of the leak to the *New York Times,* 25 April 1976, which makes that point. See also *Forbes,* 1 June 1976; and *Business China,* 6 February 1976.

12. See columnist Victor Zorza in the *Washington Post,* 29 October 1976, on the power struggle over the Cyber computer deal. He notes that those supporting the sale used the same arguments as those used by Pillsbury in his *Foreign Policy* article a year earlier.

13. See *IB* 3, no. 21 (5 November 1976), for a discussion of the sale and the weak safeguards against its diversion to military uses. See also Banning Garrett, "L'Evolution des Rapports entre Les Etats-Unis et la Chine," *Le Monde Diplomatique,* January 1977. *The New York Times,* 4 October 1975, noted that the Cyber 172 was a "top of the line" computer, two categories above other computers on the restricted list. See the *New York Times,* 29 and 30 October 1976 and *Aviation Week,* 25 October 1976.

14. Kissinger also said at his October 15 news conference that the United States had not discussed arms sales with Chinese leaders. Former Secretary of Defense James Schlesinger, who was fired by President Ford in November 1975, said on 11 April 1976, on CBS's "Face the Nation," that U.S. officials had discussed in recent years giving military assistance to Peking but "there was never a formal addressing of the issue" while he was in government. He referred to China as a "quasi ally" and said of military aid to the Chinese, "I would not reject it out of hand," a statement he repeated after returning from a visit to China in September 1976. See *U.S. News and World Report,* 18 October 1976. Secretary of Commerce Eliot Richardson said on 27 May 1976 in Tokyo that the United States would be willing to discuss arms sales to China if Chinese leaders raised the subject. *Los Angeles Times,* 28 May 1976.

15. In a closed meeting with the Senate Foreign Relations Committee, 23 November 1976 (a transcript of which was later released), Carter said: "the SALT talks have in effect been recessed since early last spring, or late last winter, because of a disagreement between the Defense and State Departments and because of the fact that this was an election year."

16. In early 1977 Carter nominated Paul Warnke for the posts of chief arms negotiator and director of the Arms Control and Disarmament Agency—an appointment that became the focus of conservative forces in Congress upset with Carter's then apparent "soft" line on détente with the Soviet Union.

17. See *IB* 4, no. 8 (25 April 1977), for a listing and assessment of Carter's moves toward China after the Vance visit to Moscow.

18. Both Chinese and Soviet sources said that no progress was made in the talks. A Soviet source said that neither side offered anything new in the talks. Chinese Deputy Foreign Minister Wang Shu told *Newsweek,* 25 September 1978, that the talks had made no progress in their nine-year history. He also told *Newsweek* that China would allow the 1950 Sino-Soviet treaty to lapse in 1979, a point made a few weeks earlier by Chinese leaders to Japanese officials.

19. See *IB* 4, no. (10 23 May 1977); Michael Pillsbury, "Future Sino-American Security Ties: The View from Tokyo, Moscow and Peking," *International Security* 1, no. 4 (Spring 1977): 142.

20. *New York Times*, 15 May 1977; for complete text, see *Pravda*, 14 May 1977.

21. Pentagon SALT experts acknowledge that at some point in reductions of nuclear weapons, the relatively small number of deliverable Chinese nuclear weapons (140–160, according to the International Institute for Strategic Studies' *Military Balance*, 1978–79, p. 56. This includes 30–40 IRBMs, 30–40 MRBMs, and 80 medium bombers. The IISS also says the Chinese may have deployed a few ICBMs with a 3000-to-3500-mile range.) would be a factor for Soviet planners targeting their nuclear warheads, which have to cover U.S., French, British, and Chinese nuclear targets simultaneously.

22. Both sides made compromises to try to get the SALT talks back on track. Gromyko left the Geneva meeting saying there had been "some progress," but charging that the United States "has not given up its attempts to achieve unilateral advantage"—a charge repeated by Brezhnev on May 30; he added that no serious movement forward had been achieved. See *IB* 4, no. 12 (20 June 1977.)

23. See Pillsbury, "Future Sino-American Security Ties," on the apparent debate within the Soviet leadership over how seriously to take both the prospect and the potential impact of Western arms sales and other military ties to China. Also see Morris Rothenberg, *Whither China: The View from the Kremlin* (Washington, D.C.: Center for Advanced International Studies, University of Miami, 1977), pp. 265–66, including Soviet discussion of Pillsbury's 1975 *Foreign Policy* article proposing the idea of U.S. military ties with China. Rothenberg says: "Moscow has displayed deep and continuous concern about the Sino-American relationship developed since the advent of the Nixon Administration. It sees this relationship as, at a minimum, providing leverage for the indefinite future to both Peking and Washington in their separate struggles against Moscow, and, at a maximum, inventing a continuing specter of outright collusion between the two against the U.S.S.R. . . . the ultimate nightmare for Moscow is that the U.S. and China will work themselves into a full-scale military alliance against the U.S.S.R." (p. 251).

24. Carter's national security adviser, Zbigniew Brzezinski, asked in May whether the United States should consider sales of military equipment to China, told *U.S. News and World Report*, "I think that's an immediate policy question which I would not want to comment on."

25. Some of the same actors involved in the debate under Ford were listed by the *New York Times* as involved under Carter. For reports on the policy struggle within the government under Ford, see Victor Zorza, *Washington Post*, 9 October 1975, 12 and 26 March 1976, 4 June 1976, and 29 October 1976. Retired Admiral Elmo Zumwalt told the *Post* on August 23 (while Secretary Vance was in Peking) that Brzezinski had told him to tell Chinese leaders during his just completed visit to China that the *Times* leak on PRM 24 had been wrong, that arms sales to China had not been ruled out.

26. PRM 24 also addressed the issue of normalization of relations between the United States and China and concluded that the United States might have to accept Peking's three conditions—severance of defense ties with Taiwan, ending of diplomatic relations with Taipei, and withdrawal of all U.S. military personnel from the island—without any guarantee from China that it would not use force to reunite Taiwan with the mainland. In return, the study said, the best the United States could get would be Peking's acquiescence to a unilateral U.S. declaration of interest in a peaceful resolution of the controversy and to continued U.S. arms sales to Taiwan. See John Wallach's report for the Hearst News Service in the *San Francisco Examiner*, 26 June 1977.

27. Delivered to the Asia Society in New York.

28. Vance also said that U.S. relations with China are a "central part" of U.S. foreign policy and are important for "global equilibrium," a slight watering-down of Carter's statement at Notre Dame on May 22 (written by Brzezinski) that "we see the American-Chinese relationship as a central element of our global policy, and China as a key force for global peace." Carter's statement was the first time a President had termed relations with China a

cental element in U.S. global, rather than regional, policy—a statement calculated to worry the Soviets as well as to reassure the Chinese. The Soviets would also be disturbed by Carter's description of the Chinese as a "key force for global peace," since Moscow had a week earlier accused China of seeking to provoke a new world war.

29. The speech reportedly was written by Vance's top Soviet adviser, Marshall Shulman, who wrote in the January 1977 issue of *Foreign Affairs* that he thinks the United States is more likely to get what it wants from the Soviet Union through reduced tensions and increased cooperation rather than through confrontation and pressure tactics. See *IB* 4, no. 15 (15 August 1977), on the Carter speech and the modulations in U.S.–Soviet relations at that time.

30. See *IB* 4, no. 1 (14 January 1976), for the unfolding debate over the Soviet military threat that faced the new administration.

31. See *Issues and Studies* (Taipei), January 1978, pp. 109–16, for the apparently authentic text of a secret speech by Foreign Minister Huang Hua delivered a month before Vance's visit to Peking. Huang reportedly said "far from being a coincidence, the schedule of the [Vance] tour was arranged to show that we have attached special importance to the Sino-American talks, to instill into the U.S. government more confidence in Vance's mission, and to checkmate the Soviet revisionists. If you want to ask who will be the most nervous and uneasy about Vance's trip, in my view, it will be the Soviet revisionists, and Taiwan comes next" (p. 114).

32. The Chinese were prepared to assure the United States they would not use force to liberate Taiwan for ten years, according to Huang Hua, ibid., pp. 112–13. But the Vance mission nevertheless led to Chinese denunciations of reports they were willing to be flexible on the Taiwan issue. See *New York Times*, 7 September 1977, and also 29 August 1977, for Harrison Salisbury interview with Li Hsien-nien. U.S. officials said privately later that there had been no discussion of arms sales or even military ties with China during Vance's visit. This may have contributed to China's displeasure, and it contrasts sharply with the content of Brzezinski's discussions with Chinese leaders during his visit to Peking nine months later.

33. At a press conference on 29 September 1977, Carter also said that the Soviets had been "fairly flexible in their attitudes."

34. Senator Gary Hart (D-Colo.) to Reuters in Peking, 9 January 1978, for example.

35. K. S. Karol, cited in the *Christian Science Monitor*, 30 January 1978.

36. Jen Ku-ping, "The Munich Tragedy and Contemporary Appeasement," *Peking Review*, no. 50 (9 December 1977). This was apparently a reference to leaks from Washington that PRM 10 advocated NATO abandonment of one third of West German territory in the event of a Warsaw Pact attack—a report denied by the administration. See the *New York Times*, 6 January 1978, which says PRM 10 does not advocate such a policy.

37. The Carter administration had not yet publicly reaffirmed the commitment to China's security made by Kissinger in October 1976, although there is no public indication whether Kissinger's statements at that time had actually reassured the Chinese.

38. "Chairman Mao's Theory of the Differentiation of the Three Worlds is a Major Contribution to Marxism-Leninism," by the editorial department of *People's Daily*, translated in *Peking Review*, no. 45 (4 November 1977). Chairman Hua made a similar statement on the eve of Vance's visit to Peking in August. Hua said in his "Political Report to the Eleventh National Congress of the Communist Party of China, August 12, 1977": "There is a trend toward appeasement among those people in the West who cherish the illusion that peace can be maintained through compromises and concessions, and some even want to follow in Chamberlain's footsteps and try to divert the peril of the new tsars to the East in order to preserve themselves at the expense of others." The repetition of this line more than two months after Vance's visit indicates the Chinese were not reassured by the secretary of state on this question. See also the *New York Times*, 6 January 1978, on the "Military Posture and Force Structure Review" section of PRM 10, which cited the document saying that the notion of "establishing close links with China in an effort to divert Soviet military resources to Asia," had been considered and rejected as not feasible "in the near future."

39. Hua said in his "Political Report" that "the current strategic situation in their contention is that Soviet social imperialism is on the offensive and U.S. imperialism on the defensive."

40. Brzezinski's support for playing the China card against the Soviets is reported by Elizabeth Drew in a major profile of the national security adviser in the *New Yorker*, 1 May 1978. See also *New York Times*, 18 May 1978, on Brzezinski's desire to play China off against the Soviet Union.

41. An editorial in *Pravda*, 1 April 1978, accused the Chinese of trying to force a "unilateral withdrawal" of Soviet troops that would leave the disputed border open to Chinese invasion along "a front stretching for thousands of kilometers." *Pravda* said the Soviet population in the border areas "would remain on the old frontiers and Chinese would be given the opportunity to 'develop' these areas."

42. *Economist*, 8 April 1978.

43. Soviet negotiator Ilyichev was nevertheless sent to Peking to reopen the stalled border talks. He arrived in the Chinese capital on 26 April 1978—the day the White House announced that Brzezinski would visit Peking 20–23 May.

44. A report on his comments in Japan's *Mainichi Shimbun* was reprinted in the pro-Peking Hong Kong paper *Ta Kung Pao*, which is tantamount to Chinese confirmation of the story. See the *Wall Street Journal*, 2 May 1978. For reports during this period on Chinese interest in Western arms purchases, see *New York Times*, 14 April 1978; *Baltimore News American*, 12 April 1978; *Christian Science Monitor*, 3 and 4 May 1978; *Der Spiegel*, 15 May 1978; and *Far Eastern Economic Review*, 28 April 1978. French officials told Reuters on 20 October 1978 that China had placed an order for HOT and Milan antitank missiles and Crotale antiaircraft missiles worth $700 million during a visit to Peking by French Prime Minister Raymond Barre in January 1978. Reuters said that France was finalizing the deal, which they hoped to sign before the end of 1978. The Reuters report was released to Reuters on the eve of a visit to Paris by Soviet Foreign Minister Gromyko, who, according to *Der Spiegel* (30 October 1978) hoped to dissuade the French from completing the deal. The *Washington Post* reported on 27 October 1978 that the Soviet Union had warned France and several other Western European countries that selling arms to China was likely to result in "very big damage" to their bilateral relations with Moscow. See also the *New York Times*, 13 November 1978.

45. See *New York Times*, 18 May 1978; *Christian Science Monitor*, 22 May 1978; *Los Angeles Times*, 11 June 1978; *Washington Star*, 5 June 1978; and *U.S. News and World Report*, 12 June 1978. U.S. officials, interviewed in October 1978, insisted that reports in the spring of 1978 that the United States had decided to approve or even encourage arms sales to Peking by Western European countries were inaccurate, and that no decision had been made whether to oppose or approve such sales, contrary to various news reports that apparently emanated from the NSC staff. On 3 November 1978, however, Secretary of State Vance said in response to a question dealing with Soviet complaints about the pending French arms sale to China, that "insofar as other nations are concerned, this is a matter which each of them must decide for itself." Officials later described the U.S. position as one of "neutrality" on the issue of Western arms sales to Peking. See the *Los Angeles Times*, 7 November 1978; and the *New York Times*, 8 November 1978. U.S. officials also insisted in October 1978 that the United States had not dropped the policy of "evenhandedness" on transfer of U.S. military-related technology to China and the Soviet Union, although they acknowledged the ambiguity of recent decisions, including the sale of airborne geological scanning equipment to China and negotiations with the Chinese for sale and launching of a domestic communications satellite—neither of which would be sold to the Soviet Union.

46. *New York Times*, 27 April 1978; and *U.S. News and World Report*, 8 May 1978.

47. China publicly indicated support for the U.S. role in aiding the Western intervention in Zaire (see *Washington Post*, 20 May 1978), and Secretary Vance consulted with Chinese Foreign Minister Huang Hua in New York on 2 June before Huang left for Kinshasha to demonstrate Chinese support for the beleaguered Mobutu regime. Carter's tough stand on Zaire, blaming the Shaba rebel invasion on the Soviets and Cubans, was intended partly as

a show of toughness by the Carter administration to impress the Chinese on the eve of Brzezinski's visit.

48. See *Time* and *Newsweek,* 5 June 1978, for the prominence given to the jokes by Brzezinski, who some Chinese sailors dubbed the "Bear Tamer."

49. *New York Times*, 28 May 1978. Chinese officials later made the same point to Rep. Lester Wolff (D-N.Y.). He returned from leading a congressional delegation to Peking in mid-July saying that the Chinese, who told him they were willing to negotiate directly with Nationalist Chinese leaders, said that they want to move rapidly in normalization, which they see as a "key strategic and political move in the world arena, specifically against the Soviet Union."

50. *New York Times*, 28 May and 25 June 1978; and Evans and Novak, *Washington Post,* 22 June 1978; on administration decision-making on the issue. The *Times* reported on 18 May that administration officials were inclined to approve the sale of certain defensive arms to China by Western European countries. On 9 June 1978 the *Times* reported that the administration had agreed to a Chinese request to buy airborne geological survey equipment (with military uses for antisubmarine detection) that it will not sell to the Soviet Union. U.S. officials also told Reuters, 9 June 1978, that the same equipment would be denied the Soviets because of its potential military uses. But the *Los Angeles Times,* 10 June 1978, reported that the *New York Times* erred and that China and the Soviet Union remained in the same category for control of technology exports. The White House notified Congress 21 August 1978, in a report on international transfers of technology, that "The same ground rules that apply to the Soviet Union and other communist countries apply in the case of the People's Republic of China. These ground rules precluded the transfer of military technology and provide for the control of transfers of dual-use strategically important products and technical data." This statement does not rule out denying a given item to the Soviets that is approved for sale to China.

51. Reuters; 29 May 1978; *New York Times*, 24 May 1978.

52. The "Meet the Press" interview was taped on Saturday, 27 May and aired on Sunday, 28 May 1978.

53. See *Soviet World Outlook,* 15 August 1978. See also *New York Times,* 18 June 1978, for excerpts of a major *Pravda* statement on triangular relations. Soviet sources also told reporters, however, that China's hostility toward the Soviet Union was so great that Moscow could not allow emergence of a China modernized and armed by the West. *Pravda* also warned the Chinese of the consequences of a war with the Soviet Union. See *Washington Post,* 5 September 1978.

54. This concern was indicated publicly in an unprecedented Politburo statement on 26 August that cautioned the West against supplying arms to China, clearly suggesting that such a move would undermine efforts to reach a new SALT agreement and negotiate the reduction of forces in Central Europe at the Vienna talks. The statement was also a response to Chinese Communist party Chairman Hua Kuo-feng's trip to Romania, Yugoslavia, and Iran, which was then under way. The Politburo accused China of being a "serious threat" to peace, working for "an uncontrollable arms race," and "advertising their hostility toward the Soviet Union" in order "to gain access to NATO military arsenals." *Washington Post,* 27 August 1978.

55. See *Washington Post,* 26 June 1978; *New York Times,* 27 June 1978; and *IB* 5, no. 15 (31 July 1978). An edited version of Huntington's remarks was published in *Foreign Policy,* no. 32 (Fall 1978). Huntington left the NSC staff and returned to Harvard by the fall of 1978. Interestingly, Carter had told reporters on 26 June: "We have never tried to threaten the Soviet Union, we have never held out the prospect of increased or decreased trade if they did not or did do a certain thing we thought was best."

56. Huntington, ibid., said: "It has been estimated that Soviet oil production would today be 10–15 percent less than it is were it not for recent imports of certain types of Western technology" (p. 69). Huntington apparently was referring to a controversial CIA report which also estimated that the Soviet Union would face an oil production shortfall in the mid-1980s and become a net oil importer.

57. *China Business Review,* July–August 1978, p. 24. The *Review* said it expected the Univac

sale, announced by Sperry Rand on 29 June, to be approved by the administration despite Carter's decision on 18 July to block the sale of a virtually identical Univac to Tass, ostensibly on national security grounds.

58. *New York Times,* 20 July 1978. The companies, Exxon, Phillips Petroleum, Pennzoil, and Union Oil, were later joined by Mobil, according to the *Wall Street Journal,* 5 September 1978. ARCO oil, according to business sources, was also negotiating with the Chinese in the summer of 1978 for possible deals to build oil refineries and petrochemical complexes.

59. See *Far Eastern Economic Review,* 1 September 1978; *Washington Post,* 11 August 1978.

60. Reuters, 15 September 1978; *Washington Post,* 13 October 1978; *Washington Star,* 31 October 1978.

61. See *IB* 5, no. 19 (9 October 1978), for a roundup of Chinese moves on the Taiwan issue. See also *Far Eastern Economic Review,* 15 September 1978. See also Michel Oksenberg, "Sino-American Relations in a New Asian Context," in *Dragon and Eagle: United States-China Relations: Past and Future,* ed. Michel Oksenberg and Robert B. Oxnam (New York: Basic Books, 1978), for policy recommendations that closely parallel some of the Carter administration's China policy. Oksenberg joined Brzezinski's staff in early 1977 as the NSC China expert.

62. Quoted by Stanley Karnow, *Baltimore Sun,* 10 July 1978.

63. See, for example, Adam Ulam, *Foreign Policy,* Fall 1976; Boris Rabbot, *New York Times Magazine,* 6 November 1977; *New York Times,* 24 June 1977, on PRM 24.

64. See Gottlieb, *Chinese Foreign Policy Factionalism,* p. 124. In the late 1960s and early 1970s, the Chinese leadership was deeply divided on Sino-Soviet and Sino-American ties, with some leaders favoring easing tensions with Moscow, some favoring *rapprochement* with the U.S., and a third faction favoring equidistance from both the Soviet Union and the U.S.

65. See Gottlieb, *Chinese Foreign Policy Factionalism;* Sutter, *China-Watch;* and Michael Pillsbury, "SALT on the Dragon" (Santa Monica: RAND P-5457, April 1975).

66. Michel Tatu, "The Great Power Triangle: Washington-Moscow-Peking" (Paris: Atlantic Institute, 1970).

67. See *The Military Balance 1978–79* (London: International Institute for Strategic Studies, 1978) for comparative conventional and nuclear force levels of the three powers.

68. This was likely an intentional restraint on China's part to avoid raising fears in the United States of a direct Chinese nuclear threat. See, for example, *Washington Post,* 4 March 1976, where former Defense Intelligence Agency chief General Daniel Graham told reporters that China halted development of an ICBM capable of hitting the United States for foreign policy reasons following the 1972 visit of President Nixon to Peking.

69. *New York Times,* 24 May 1978.

70. See *New York Times,* 25 June 1978, on speech by Richard Holbrooke, assistant secretary of state for East Asian and Pacific affairs, delivered in Hawaii, 16 June 1978.

71. See for example *Washington Post,* 19 September 1978. See also *Soviet World Outlook,* 15 August 1978.

9

EUROCOMMUNISM, EUROSOCIALISM, AND U.S. FOREIGN POLICY

New Rosé in an Old Bottle?

Robert J. Lieber and
Nancy I. Lieber

America's European policy subsumes an enormous array of important but complex and vexing subjects. This chapter, rather than seeking to treat the myriad components of this policy instead focuses on the particular question of U.S. policy toward the West European left. What is thereby excluded in breadth may be more than regained in depth and perspective, however, for the pattern of contemporary American policies toward Eurocommunism and Eurosocialism illuminates some important aspects of the American-European relationship and the post–World War II alignment of superpower relations as they bear upon the European continent. The present approach also benefits from being able to provide a stable medium-term policy assessment that is not too vulnerable to sharp and frequently ephemeral oscillations. In this light, the period from the early 1970s to January 1977, under the aegis of Henry Kissinger, and then from the onset of the Carter administration to the completion of the French legislative elections of March 1978 and the defeat of the *Union de la Gauche,* constitutes a coherent whole in which a series of major policy initiatives, choices, and outcomes can be fruitfully analyzed in a broad context.

Kenneth Oye argued in chapter 1 of this book that three sets of Carter administration foreign policy perceptions or objectives coexist uneasily: idealism on general political affairs, realism on security affairs, and liberalism on international economic affairs. The lack of pattern or hierarchy among these objectives has produced instability and problems of choice and adaptation in specific areas. Policy toward Western Europe has been particularly susceptible to difficulties caused by a series of aims that could not be mutually reconciled or were thought to be unreconcilable. In addition to the problems of linkage among these objectives, the linkage between domestic and foreign policy has also proved to be obtrusive in affecting policy toward this region.

The analysis that follows discusses the nature of contemporary Eurocommunism and Eurosocialism and traces the background and inadequacies of American policy under the Kissinger administration. Then it deals with the three principal objectives of Carter administration policy and the domestic linkages that provided important feedback on those policies. After that, we analyze the nature of U.S. policy oscillations and reversals in dealing with the rapidly changing patterns of events on the European left and discuss the costs of that policy, as well as its overall implications.

EUROCOMMUNISM AND EUROSOCIALISM

In the past decade, significant developments have taken place within the Western European left, developments that have challenged the assumptions and foundations of the Nixon-Ford-Kissinger and now Carter administrations' policies toward our allies in Western Europe. No longer is the Western European left so clearly divided as it was in the postwar period between moderate Social Democratic parties and Stalinist Communist parties. Instead, several important Western European Communist parties have traveled considerable ground toward a moderate Eurocommunism, and within a number of Social Democratic/Labor parties, a movement to the left can be called Eurosocialism. Whether the Carter administration accepts or understands these changes is crucial in determining the validity and viability of its policy toward the Western European left.

Eurocommunism

In the past, American foreign policy makers have looked on Western European Communist parties as "fifth columnists" for the Soviets in their drive for global influence. By and large, this analysis was correct in the nearly monolithic era of communism—that is, until World War II and the early cold-war period. In 1948, however, Tito broke with the Soviet Union and ushered in a movement toward national and independent roads to socialism, a movement greatly furthered by the

Sino-Soviet split in the early 1960s. The latest challenge to Soviet supremacy, that of the Eurocommunists, dates from the Soviet invasion of Czechoslovakia in 1968.

Who and where are the Eurocommunists? Contrary to the label, there is no Eurocommunist specter haunting all of Europe. Rather, the phenomenon is found in three important Communist parties—the French, Italian, and Spanish—with parties in the other fifteen Western European nations either undecided, split, or against the Eurocommunist movement. The strength of the three important Communist parties varies markedly. The Spanish Communist party (PCE) is the farthest removed from actual governmental power, having received 9 percent of the vote in the June 1977 elections. The French Communist party (PCF) received 21 percent in the March 1978 legislative election, but after it had consciously adopted a line of policy that ruptured the *Union de la gauche* and damaged its chances for obtaining a share of governmental power because of its leaders' uneasiness at the prospect of becoming a junior partner of the Socialists. The Italian Communist party (PCI), with 34 percent of the vote in the June 1976 elections, already holds substantial de facto, though not formal, power in the Italian national government. It also controls many city and regional governments.

Eurocommunism is thus a limited geographical phenomenon; what, then, is its political essence? Basically Eurocommunism reflects the erosion of strict adherence on the part of Western European Communist parties to the Marxist-Leninist principles enunciated by Lenin in 1920. We can summarize Lenin's twenty-one conditions (necessary for qualification as a Communist party and membership in the Third International) into three principles: proletarian internationalism, or loyalty to the Soviet Union as the leader of the international communist movement; rejection of bourgeois democracy and in favor of the dictatorship of the proletariat; and the notion of working-class primacy in the revolutionary movement, with the Communist party as the vanguard of the proletariat. In all three areas, the Spanish, Italian, and French Communist parties have considerably "revised" their original Marxism-Leninism. First, they no longer feel bound to the Communist party of the Soviet Union (CPSU) as the guiding party, a role that in Stalin's day enabled Moscow to set strategy and manipulate individual national Communist parties. Instead, the Eurocommunists have openly declared their intention of pursuing "national roads to socialism," roads that potentially differ from those traditionally traveled by Marxist-Leninists, but roads dictated by differing national conditions. For the Eurocommunists, operating in the "bourgeois" democracies of Western Europe, the most appropriate road to power is the parliamentary, or constitutional, road, in possible coalition with other left parties and with middle-class, as well as working-class, support. Thus the Leninist strategy of seizure of power by a cadre party that proceeds to set up a dictatorship of the proletariat has been replaced by the Eurocommunists' avowed electoralism and commitment to democratic, majority rule with the protection of minority political rights after a left victory. As a joint communiqué released by the leaders of the French, Spanish, and Italian Communist parties in March 1977 stated, the Eurocommunists are now committed to

> the respect, guarantee and promotion of individual liberties of every kind: freedom
> of thought and of expression, of the press, of association, of meetings and demon-

strations, the right of free movement within and beyond national boundaries, trade union freedom and independence, the right to strike, the inviolability of privacy, the respect for universal suffrage and of the opportunity of the majority to change the government democratically, freedom of worship and of the expression of philosophical, cultural and artistic opinions and trends.

Yet, the erosion of Leninist principles, striking as it is, is by no means complete, nor completely credible, as far as it goes. For instance, the Eurocommunists, for all their forthright criticisms of the Soviet Union's violations of dissidents' political rights, rarely if ever disassociate themselves from Soviet foreign policy positions (other than those concerned with European affairs). Similarly, dramatic changes such as the elimination of the adherence to "Leninism" as a requirement for admission to the Italian and Spanish Communist parties and the official dropping of the term "dictatorship of the proletariat" from all three Eurocommunist parties' statements of intent are nonetheless rendered suspect by the continued practice (in varying degrees) of democratic centralism *within* the parties. That is, these parties by and large continue to prohibit internal party democracy, organized factions, competing conference motions, an open party press, insurgent candidates for party leadership positions, and so forth. Lastly, while Spanish Communists may be anxious to work with the (much larger) Spanish Socialist party (PSOE) and even willing to merge with them and overcome the schism of 1920, and Italian Communists may offer the extended hand of historic compromise to the Christian Democrats, yet the French Communist party retreated from its position of cooperation with the French Socialist party once it became obvious that such cooperation would benefit the Socialists at the Communists' expense. There are limits, the French Communist party replied to its Spanish and Italian Eurocommunist brethren (who were highly critical of the PCF's sabotage of a French left victory) to how far the vanguard role of the Communist party could be eroded.

So the Eurocommunists find themselves in limbo. They have exchanged their Marxist-Leninist internationalism for a stance of national independence. They have moderated their formerly Stalinist nature—yet, as they move slowly in the direction of democratization, they approach a phenomenon that already exists (and indeed has grown in the past decade): democratic socialist parties, or Eurosocialism.

Eurosocialism

Eurosocialism is associated with the recent tendency of some Western European democratic socialists to challenge the long-prevailing model of social democracy on the one hand, while continuing to shun all forms of Leninism on the other. Usually affiliated with the already existing mass Social Democratic parties, the Eurosocialists have either come to dominate those parties (most notably in France and Sweden) or at a minimum are active in their left-wings (Britain and Federal Republic of Germany). Unlike Eurocommunism, the scope of Eurosocialism includes not only virtually all of Western Europe, but also concerns parties that have held governmental power or are approaching that likelihood.

Several factors account for the rise of Eurosocialism within the European left, including the failure—in different respects—of both Western European social democracy and Soviet bureaucratic collectivism to deliver on socialist promises and ideals; the alternative modes of political participation raised by the student, women's, ecology, and other protest movements of the past decade; international changes such as the lessening of the cold war, polycentrism in the communist world, and a sense of "Europeanness" furthered by institutions such as the European Community and economic interdependence of the European states.

The essence of Eurosocialism is found in its intended movement "beyond social democracy"—movement in terms of ideology, strategy, and foreign policy. In terms of ideology, the Eurosocialists assert that social democratic policies have been inherently limited to managing capitalism in a more humane way. The resulting welfare state and managed economy systems have undeniably improved the lot of millions of people through a certain amount of income redistribution and social benefits, but these same social democratic arrangements have fostered the growth of governmental bureaucracies increasingly perceived as too large and centralized, too unresponsive and uncontrollable. In contrast, the Eurosocialists advocate policies designed to facilitate the redistribution and decentralization of economic power (e.g., increased social ownership that is not merely nationalization but municipal, regional and cooperative ownership; democratic planning; and democratization of the workplace). Such an economic program—espoused, for example, by the French PS—would go considerably further in eroding American-dominated multinationals' economic and political prerogatives than have the policies of the social democratic governments of postwar Europe.

In terms of strategy, the Eurosocialists look more favorably, or at least with more hope, on the changes within the Western European Communist parties. In some instances they seek to solidify those changes (rather than dismiss them as suspect) by working electorally and governmentally with the Eurocommunists. This debate over cooperation with the Eurocommunists has been a particularly divisive one inside the Socialist International, with the more moderate Social Democrats lining up with U.S. foreign policy makers in expressing displeasure vis-à-vis the Eurosocialists' toleration of Eurocommunism.

Finally, the Eurosocialists' international policies are substantially less Atlanticist than those of the prevailing postwar social democrats. Seeking a break with both economic and military dependence on the U.S., the Eurosocialists envisage, for the *very* long run, a pan-European neutrality with contagion into Eastern Europe of their democratic socialist model and ultimately an end to both superpowers' domination on the European continent.

THE POLICY BACKGROUND: KISSINGER AND THE EUROPEAN LEFT

Administration policy under Henry Kissinger reflected considerable hostility toward much of the Western European left, not merely its Eurocommunist components. Moderate governing Social Democratic parties, such as those of Britain and the Federal Republic of Germany, which broadly accepted the major elements of post-1948 domestic and foreign policy, were largely spared this animosity; elsewhere, parties that called into question any postwar given, even on a very modest basis, or that showed themselves willing to cooperate with parties that did so, found themselves the target of American enmity.

Thus, in France, where François Mitterrand rejuvenated the Socialist party (PS), broadening its base, increasing its share of the electorate from a weak 5 percent in 1969 to nearly 20 percent in 1973, and thereby establishing a powerful noncommunist alternative on the French left, the PS found itself at odds with the American government. In particular, its strategy of *Union de la gauche* and its Common Program of Government signed in 1972 with the French Communist party (PCF) and the small, moderate Left Radical party were regarded as unacceptable. Despite counterarguments that the alliance with communists would be one which socialists could dominate, and that it could provide a vehicle for economic and social reforms without drastically altering the course of France's previous Gaullist policies toward the Atlantic Alliance and the European Community (Common Market), the Kissinger policy perceived the leftist alliance as something to be ostracized, lest it jeopardize the internal stability of France and provide a source of Soviet contagion. More than two years in advance of the March 1978 legislative elections, opinion polls signaled the distinct possibility that the left might actually win a majority in the French National Assembly. The American reaction was to intensify opposition to this trend. For example, in early 1976 leading socialists were warned by American diplomats, privately and ominously, that the United States "would not tolerate" the establishment of a French government that included communist ministers. These and other interventions resulted not only in criticism from the left and from substantial sectors of the French press but also stirred rebuttals from Gaullist political leaders, who argued that the French people were fully capable of determining their political destinies without exterior involvement.

More broadly, the U.S. reaction reflected an inaccurate assessment of the French political situation. France has traditionally experienced political oscillations between governments, even regimes, of right and left; but since 1958 France has been governed under Gaullist and conservative auspices. Initially, the democratic left, whose main component was the Socialist SFIO, was weak, fragmented, and even discredited. This left the Communist party (PCF) as the main opposition force to Gaullism (a situation encouraged by de Gaulle himself). In the late 1960s and early '70s, however, its remarkable restructuring and rebuilding efforts allowed the PS to overtake the communists and become the largest political force on the left. Despite American fears, the PS alliance with the PCF did not at all imply a situation like that of Prague in 1948. Mitterrand and the socialists had used the Communists, not vice versa.

Programmatically, the PS saw itself as democratic socialist rather than social democratic. A socialist-dominated leftist government under François Mitterrand (himself a non-Marxist) would have been likely to pursue a set of moderate and occasionally radical reforms in a country whose inegalitarian distribution of wealth and income (OECD figures, 1976) is worse than that of Spain.[1] There would have been some use of tax policies to deal with the prevailing pattern of income distribution, substantial measures of nationalization, major efforts to improve welfare state benefits and minimum wages, and greater democratization and liberalization in both the political arena (e.g., enactment of habeas corpus) and economic life (efforts at *autogestion,* or workers' self-management). To be sure, elements of this program would have been unsettling to some individuals and groups inside France and in Western Europe and the United States. Subsequent socialist-communist disagreements over the extent of nationalization and increases in the minimum wage (the SMIC) also raised the issue of whether the left could successfully manage the French economy without serious internal divisions, as well as problems of high inflation, balance-of-payments difficulties, and capital flight. Nonetheless, by themselves, none of the major elements of the Common Governmental Program would necessarily have created a drastic rupture with France's existing pattern of a mixed economy within a democratic political system, particularly in view of the enormous international economic, financial, and commercial constraints and interdependencies within which France functions. Moreover, a leftist French government, dominated not by communists but by moderate democratic socialists, would in practice have remained a member of the Atlantic Alliance, the European Community, and other Western economic institutions. In this context, Kissinger's strictures were not only unnecessary and counterproductive, but they reflected an even worse sin: they were *unrealistic.* In particular, they threatened to earn the unnecessary hostility of what at the time seemed likely to become the next government of France.

In Italy, where the most powerful, albeit one of the most moderate and revisionist, of the Eurocommunist parties (PCI) pressed the decaying Christian Democrats (DC) who had ruled for three continuous decades, Kissinger's policies were particularly antagonistic. Not only did the administration seek to use its influence against the PCI in the June 1976 national election, but it intervened in a number of tangible and symbolic ways. These included the channeling of $7 million in covert payments to noncommunist political parties, a practice evidently not uncommon throughout much of the postwar period. The United States also signaled its determination to prevent communists from entering government through the PCI's desired "historic compromise" with the DC. In June 1976, at a Western economic summit meeting in Puerto Rico, President Ford obtained the informal agreement of the French, British, and West German governments, and the tacit cooperation of Canada and Japan, to refuse loans to Italy in dealing with its balance-of-payments deficits if a new Italian Cabinet were to contain communists. The reaction of even the DC to this was far from uniformly favorable; for example, the outgoing Christian Democratic prime minister, Aldo Moro (later murdered by terrorist Red Brigades in May 1978) strongly criticized the United States, West Germany, France, and the UK for acting in an "improper way." [2]

The Nixon-Ford-Kissinger policy toward Italy was not, however, merely anticommunist. It also involved dealings with the authoritarian right. Thus Giorgio Almirante, head of the neo-fascist MSI party, obtained a meeting in Washington with two staff members of the National Security Council,[3] even while the PCI's moderate foreign affairs authority, Sergio Segre, who supported a continuing presence for Italy in both the Common Market and NATO, was denied a visa to enter the United States in order to speak at a meeting of the Council on Foreign Relations in New York.[4] Subsequently, U.S. congressional investigations revealed that in 1972 the CIA had paid approximately $800,000 to the head of Italy's military intelligence organization, General Vito Miceli, and that the same man was later indicted on charges that he had been involved in an unsuccessful December 1970 plan to overthrow the democratically elected government of Italy. What characterizes both the Miceli payment and the denial of the Segre visa is that both incidents were not merely taken at the initiative of overzealous lower-echelon officials. The Segre visa was blocked by Kissinger's chief assistant for European policy, Helmut Sonnenfeldt, who refused to waive a provision of U.S. immigration law, and the payment to General Miceli was made evidently on orders of the U.S. ambassador to Italy, Graham Martin, against the objection of the local CIA station chief.[5]

As for the southern European dictatorships (Greece, Portugal, Spain), in the years before their demise, American policy manifested a preference for these regimes for fear of what might follow. In Greece, the Nixon administration went far beyond the dictates of strategic necessity in intimacy with, and support for, the regime of Papadopoulos and his successors. With the 1974 ouster of this regime, the United States incurred the wrath of Greek public opinion, enraged further by the ineptitude of American policy toward Cyprus (first the turning of a blind eye toward the coup against Archbishop Makarios by a former terrorist, Nikos Sampson, and then failure to deter a Turkish invasion [6]). As a result, the Greek government withdrew from the NATO integrated military command structure and negotiated the end of home-port basing for the U.S. Sixth Fleet, as well as the closing of a number of U.S. air and naval bases. By contrast, the Western Europeans (who, after the 1967 coup, froze the Greek association agreement with the EEC and expelled Greece from the Council of Europe) were able to bask in admiration.[7] Thus, even in the short run, American policy toward Greece was unrealistic.

The Portuguese and Spanish cases completed the Kissinger approach. In Portugal, the United States was reluctant to compromise its support of the Salazar and Caetano regimes or their African policies. When the 1974 upheaval finally occurred, the administration (particularly Secretary of State Kissinger, but not Ambassador Carlucci) pursued a hapless and vacillating policy, replete with tired and inappropriate—but revealing—references to Soares as a Kerensky and to the 1948 Czech case.[8] In the event, those Portuguese favoring a moderate and democratic course won out over both the Stalinist communism of the Portuguese Communist party (PCP) and an abortive right-wing coup attempt. They did so with important assistance from the Western European socialists (including the much vilified French and Swedes, as well as the Germans and British). Kissinger's policy seemed to be one of standing by Franco to the moment of his death. In the words of a dissident Spanish army officer:

> *There were thousands of ways Washington could have brought pressure on Franco to liberalize the government, without actually breaking with him. Washington never seemed willing to capitalize on the fact that Franco needed American aid and friendship at least as much as Washington needed those bases.*[9]

In view of these experiences, it is worth asking why the United States became committed to this kind of policy in the late 1960s and early to mid-'70s. First, these policies reflected a short-term stress on stability—at whatever cost. To a degree, this orientation followed logically from a conception of Europe that dated from the immediate post–World War II period and that had proved serviceable for a generation. Second, there were worries about defense. American policy makers believed that socialists' values would dictate lower political and budgetary priorities for defense and thus lead to a serious weakening of NATO and the Atlantic Alliance. In addition they viewed socialists as insufficiently hard-nosed in dealing with world problems. The specter was thus less that of "Finlandization" than of "Copenhagenization." What is more, Secretary Kissinger had postulated a new domino effect whereby a communist role in the Italian government could tempt other Europeans, including the French and Germans, to move in the same direction.[10] The presence of these communists would dangerously undermine American public support for the burdens of Atlantic defense because it would be difficult to explain why the United States should bear the costs of a military alliance against communism if communists were already inside it. To this group of concerns, a series of objections can be raised. To begin with, it is by no means clear that, in practice, socialist governments neglect defense. A government of the French left, for example, would have been likely to follow relatively Gaullist defense policies; indeed, PS defense pronouncements indicated a policy of maintaining the nuclear force while upgrading conventional forces.[11] In addition, Sweden under the socialists had one of the highest defense efforts in Western Europe (as a percentage of GNP) and moderate social democratic governments in Britain and the Federal Republic of Germany have by no means neglected defense. As for a "domino" effect, local political, economic, historical and even cultural factors are far more important in shaping national outcomes than is the example of another country. The inclusion of the Federal Republic of Germany, with states that might be tempted to include communists in its government, was simply inexplicable. Not only is there deep and widespread hostility based on the East German situation, but there are no communists in either house of the federal parliament. Finally, it may be practical to view the Atlantic Alliance as targeted not so much against a political force (communism) as against a military one (the Soviet Union). Indeed, at the height of the cold war, American military assistance to Yugoslavia recognized this, and in contemporary circumstances the long-term viability of the Alliance could be dependent on a military rather than political orientation.

Yet a third factor explained America's European policy under the Kissinger aegis. It was a kind of Spenglerian gloom—or perhaps personal pessimism—that the flow of history favored the USSR and that the Western democracies were at the same time becoming less resolute externally and decaying internally. The evidence for this, however, was rarely assembled. At a minimum, the future of Western society is hardly preordained, and the philosophical anguish of individual policy makers is no substitute for judgment about the ability of these societies to adapt to change, manage their economies, and maintain their equilibrium in a complex world. Indeed, it may be more plausible to argue an opposite proposition: the nature of Western societies enables them to adapt more readily to inevitable changes in their domestic and international environment. By contrast, the bureaucratic dictatorships of Eastern Europe impose a rigidity upon those societies, which hinders their adaptability and sets limits to their domestic support. When change does come, the absence of legitimate channels for it may well make it explosive. Thus we see cycles of explosion and repression in Eastern Europe. The outcome over successive generations is unknowable, but it is hardly plausible that these societies are the chosen vehicle of any putative forces of history.

Despite these considerations, Kissinger occasionally lapsed into speculation that communism was engulfing Europe and that, within a decade, all of its countries would probably be socialist or communist. At best, the United States would do well to seek direct alliances with the German Federal Republic and with Spain as bulwarks of anticommunism.[12] In addition, Kissinger's preference for a static Europe and his personal penchant for pessimism were joined to an instinctive predisposition for the right wing of the political spectrum. Interestingly enough, this was not the rigid anticommunism of John Foster Dulles, who could refuse to shake hands with Communist Chinese leaders at Geneva in 1954, or the crusading benign invincibility of Walt Rostow orchestrating the American escalation in Vietnam. Rather, it was a situational conservatism, capable of *Realpolitik* in dealings with Chinese and Soviet leaders but unrelentingly hostile to leftist experiments that might carry any risk of weakening the postwar paradigm of American alliance hegemony.

Conceptually, the Kissinger policy sought to freeze the postwar division of Europe in the pattern that had prevailed since 1948. Indeed, the "Sonnenfeldt Doctrine" hinted at extending a quid pro quo to the Russians: tacit noninterference by the United States in Eastern Europe in exchange for an understanding that the United States would continue to remain free to intervene in Western European politics according to is own dictates. Thus, in December 1975, Helmut Sonnenfeldt, then State Department counselor, briefed American diplomatic personnel in Europe. He is reported to have described the Soviets' inability to acquire loyalty in Eastern Europe as an "unfortunate" historical failure because "Europe is within their scope and area of natural interest," and outlined a policy in which the U.S. was to seek to encourage an "organic" relationship between the Soviet Union and its East European neighbors.[13]

Overall, the Nixon-Ford-Kissinger policies toward Europe were, in substantial measure, ineffective and unrealistic. Western Europe in the mid-1970s no longer resembled Europe in the mid-1950s. The United States increasingly lacked the means and legitimacy to intervene effectively in Western European politics or stop processes of change, no matter what direction these might take. A spheres-of-influence policy seemed increasingly outmoded, and in Western Europe, a philosophy that appeared to imply "better a Papadopoulos than a Mitterrand" needlessly alienated large sections of opinion among moderates and the democratic left. In southern Europe especially, emergence of moderate democratic regimes occurred despite U.S. policies rather than because of them. Yet in Eastern Europe, American policy seemed to convey endorsement of the Brezhnev Doctrine of limited sovereignty and deemphasize efforts at encouraging evolution in the domestic conditions or foreign policies of the Eastern European states.

THE CARTER POLICY

Reacting against policies that appeared rigidly resistant to change, as well as of dubious effectiveness, the administration of President Carter at first seemed predisposed to a significant redirection of European policy. Before the June 1976 Italian elections, four prominent senior Democratic foreign policy figures had dissented from Henry Kissinger's position on Italian Communism. George Ball, Paul Warnke, Cyrus Vance, and Zbigniew Brzezinski were associated with a position that did not perceive communist participation in Italian government as necessarily fatal to NATO. In their view, the Soviet Union could be seen as having reason to be more fearful of the rise of Western European Communist parties than was the United States. Thus Brzezinski attacked Kissinger's "apocalyptic" rhetoric, noting that it had the effect of enhancing the PCI in Italian eyes and preventing the United States from developing an informal dialogue with the PCI in the event the party achieved a share of governmental power.[14]

This early identification of President Carter's national security adviser and secretary of state with a more relaxed and tolerant policy toward Eurocommunism reflected a certain idealism in general political affairs. In this view, the nature of American constitutional ideals required faith in the democratic process, a stress on human rights abroad, an unwillingness to countenance intervention in the domestic internal affairs of other states, and a relaxed confidence that this orientation would not produce consequences inimical to the long-term interests of the United States. From this perspective, the moderate and reformist aspects of the PCI's policies seemed reassuring, as did the party's relative independence from Moscow, its abandonment of the Marxist-Leninist conception of dictatorship of the proletariat, its record of urban and regional government performance, and its role as a system player within the Italian political context. In addition, the likelihood of political change in Italy, and even its need, were implied in the remarks of no less a cautious European political figure than Helmut Schmidt, who had described the Italian Christian Democrats as "corrupt" and "burned out" after three decades of rule.[15] It seemed plausible that if the PCI achieved the status of coalition governing partner with the DC, this need not be done at the sacrifice of Italy's domestic political system nor with a drastic alteration in her foreign policy commitments. Indeed, there was reason to hope that the liabilities of having communist participation in a major Western European government for the first time since 1947 would be more than offset by the advantages stemming from the influence that a non-Soviet variant of European Communism might have in encouraging Eastern European countries to move farther away from the Soviet model and its foreign policy orbit.

This general political predisposition reflected a reaction against the excesses of American's postwar interventionism in Vietnam and elsewhere, and of CIA involvements. Its idealism also echoed the religious and moral imperatives Jimmy Carter's campaign speeches embodied. Not incidentally, it fit a coherent political criticism of Kissinger's foreign policy. As we shall see, however, once in office, Carter's foreign policy makers found it necessary to grapple with additional military and economic objectives which sometimes implied contradictory lines of policy.

From a security perspective, the Carter administration remained realist in its

predisposition. Thus, despite an emphasis on arms control and international understanding, it followed the basic postwar elements of inherited national security policy,
particularly the need to maintain a stable nuclear balance vis-à-vis the Soviet Union
and to deter any Soviet threat to the European balance of power. In this light, the
continued viability of NATO seemed essential. Even so, this security concern need
not have dictated complete hostility to the PCI or the French left, particularly to the
extent that the Atlantic Alliance could be treated as a military alliance against Soviet
national power rather than a political bulwark against communism.

A conception, implicit or explicit, of NATO as aimed primarily at maintaining a
military equilibrium in Europe could offer a means of adapting to political change in
Western Europe with a flexibility sufficient to preserve the essentials of military
security. By contrast, the Kissinger policy of adamant opposition to change in Italy,
France, and elsewhere may have made such change slightly less likely but at the cost
of raising the stakes so that in the event Eurocommunists did at some point achieve
even a share of political power, a crisis jeopardizing alliance cohesion and viability
was increasingly likely. Given the nature of pluralistic Western political systems, the
fact that change tends to occur almost ineluctably (even if for no other reason than a
growth in sentiment to "throw the rascals out"—as experienced even in Sweden
after four decades of Socialist rule), the growth in desire for change after two
decades of conservative government in France and three decades in Italy, and the
lack of means by which the United States could be certain of preventing such
change, the tradeoffs implied in Kissinger's policy seemed a bad bet in any but a
short-term perspective.

In France and Italy, the two most important and pressing countries, considerable
evidence existed that a policy stressing the fundamental military purpose of the
alliance could be viable. Although the Common Program of the French left called
for the dissolution of military blocs in Europe, this was in effect contingent on
relinquishment by the Russians of their hold on Eastern Europe. Given the extreme
unlikelihood of voluntary Soviet compliance, this meant the continuation of French
membership in the Atlantic Alliance.[16] In other respects, including refusal to rejoin
the NATO integrated military structure, defense policies of the French left implied
considerable continuity with the Gaullist pattern (which the United States had managed to tolerate throughout the 1960s and early '70s). Had the French left come to
power in the 1973 or 1978 legislative elections, its defense and foreign policies
would have been determined by socialist rather than communist ministers. And,
defense and foreign policy experts of the PS had made reasonably clear their interest
in the maintenance of the Atlantic Alliance as at least a military, if not always a
political, commitment. Thus, for example, as Charles Hernu, a leading socialist
defense authority explained:

> *The ideological basis of the Atlantic Alliance is not capitalism and its multina-
> tionals, but the respect and defense of freedom, of democracy, of political
> pluralism. To refuse a democratic alternation of power in France is to deny the
> pluralist spirit of the alliance.*[17]

In Italy, considerable evidence also existed that the alliance could be adapted to
encompass more diversity if political orthodoxy was not insisted on. Italian Com-

munist party leader Enrico Berlinguer had, in fact, explicitly accepted Italy's continued membership in NATO. In a widely cited June 1976 interview with the Italian
newspaper *Corriere Della Serra*, he stated:

> *"I feel that, since Italy does not belong to the Warsaw Pact . . . we can proceed on
> the Italian road to Socialism without any constraint. . . . I want Italy not to
> leave the Atlantic Pact. . . . I feel safer being on this side."* [18]

In other statements Berlinguer and PCI leaders elaborated their reasons for this
position, including the desire to preserve détente and the need for a European
military equilibrium as a requirement for this; and the concern that unilateral withdrawal from the alliance by Italy would alter the strategic equilibrium in an undesirable and potentially destabilizing manner.[19] As the PCI also rejected the Brezhnev
Doctrine, continued membership in NATO promised to lessen the likelihood any
Italian experiment involving socialism with a human face would suffer the fate of
Dubček and Czechoslovakia.

To be sure, the Italian situation and the PCI's position contained major elements
of uncertainty. Until 1972 the PCI's policy had been characterized by the slogan,
"Italy out of NATO, NATO out of Italy," and as Ciro Zoppo has noted, in the
minds of PCI leaders the United States, as the major capitalist nation, has continued
to remain the leading imperialist power.[20] Further, when pressed for more detailed
responses, PCI leaders have tended to take the view that no direct threats to Italy's
security exist, hence the problem of Italy's alliance loyalty remains essentially
hypothetical. Other PCI spokesmen, such as Lombardo Radice, have stressed that
this commitment depends on the United States respecting the "defensive" character
of NATO and that the alliance not be used as a vehicle for American manipulation
and "imperialist aggression." [21] Added to these concerns is the fact that in foreign
policy questions outside the European continent, particularly vis-à-vis the developing world and the Middle East, the PCI has normally followed a policy line much
more consistent with the preferences of the Soviet Union than those of the United
States. And yet, even allowing for the weight of these considerations, there is reason
to believe that NATO would not be threatened by the presence of communists in an
Italian government. Thus, in Zoppo's measured analysis:

> *". . . there are, on balance, no major negative effects on NATO security in sight
> for the immediate future. This judgment . . . would not be altered significantly
> if Italian Communists joined Christian Democrats in the government. In that
> case, the political impact on Italy would outweigh by far the consequences for
> NATO military operations. Precipitate and radical revisions in PCI military
> and defense policies towards NATO would not fit traditional PCI behavior and
> would severely undermine the PCI's tenure of office. Moreover, it is unlikely that
> the PCI will engage in unconstitutional behavior . . . .*
> *PCI participation in the governance of Italy would require neither that
> NATO set aside its commitment to democracy nor signify Soviet dominance of
> Italy."* [22]

The Nixon-Ford-Kissinger policy explicitly rejected any limited military conception of the Atlantic Alliance. Thus its broader political approach to NATO treated

Eurocommunism as unquestionably damaging to Western security. As Henry Kissinger referred to it, in a November 1975 conversation with François Mitterrand, the Atlantic Alliance was an "anticommunist alliance." [23] By contrast, the Carter foreign policy began with a more ambiguous orientation, suggesting for a time that a military conception might prevail. Within a year, however, it moved toward a more outspoken hostility toward the PCI and the French left on security grounds. In part this was conditioned by domestic political considerations in the United States, as well as by reaction against the continuing buildup and modernization of Soviet military forces in Eastern Europe and a resultant decreased willingness to entertain risks in the Western half of the continent. More broadly, it reflected a return to the political conception of NATO as anticommunist rather than merely anti-Russian. This in turn was linked to a series of major economic concerns implicit in the Carter administration's economic priorities and its attachment to maintenance of an open liberal international economic order within a preexisting international economic paradigm.

The Carter administration's attachment to a liberal international economic order, as well as the major role that the United States plays, by virtue of its economic size and power, within the IMF, GATT, OECD, and in gatherings of the leading industrial democracies, shapes its policies toward the Western European left and ensures that the United States inevitably will be involved in key decisions affecting the economic and political fate of European countries, whether or not the administration wishes to avoid direct intervention. The example of France provides a useful illustration.

Mitterrand and his leftist coalition partners were committed to a program of major reform and macroeconomic stimulus. Had they won the March 1978 legislative elections, they were pledged to create half a million jobs in their first year in office, increase minimum wages (the SMIC) by 38 percent, improve social services and unemployment benefits, and carry out nationalization of nine major industrial groups. Apart from nationalization, which would have increased the share of French GNP produced in the public sector from 11 percent to approximately 20 percent, the policies involved enhancement of economic growth and stimulation of aggregate demand. These strong reflationary policies would occur within the existing international economic setting, however, where exports account for about 16 percent of France's GNP and imports are equivalent to about 18 percent, and where monetary flows, investment, energy imports, balance-of-payments considerations, and the activities of multinational corporations are of great importance. Hench there would likely be external consequences that no French government by itself could control. Specifically, vigorous economic stimulus at a time of persistent Western stagflation would have been likely to create a sharp increase in France's import demand, to worsen the balance of payments, put downward pressure on the value of the French franc, touch off increased inflation, and together with other factors, stimulate capital flight and reduced investment. In the absence of international cooperation, including loans to help in financing balance-of-payments deficits, the government would have faced two broad choices: either abandon its domestic economic objectives (or resign) or adopt a series of stringent protectionist measures and controls. The second alternative would imply capital controls, price controls, export subsidies or import deposit schemes (à la Italy in 1976 or Britain in 1966), industrial subsidies, encouragement of import substitution, and so on. These measures would irk Germany (with its $2 billion trade surplus with France), the European Community, and the IMF (with its orthodox views of economic policy, austerity prescriptions, and preference for unemployment rather than inflation). They would also run counter to American preferences and priorities for a liberal international economy.

Conceivably, U.S. policy makers could have had the option of coming to terms with, or at least tolerating, the policies of macroeconomic stimulus in the Mitterrand program. This would have implied international financial cooperation, through the IMF and other bodies, in helping the French government cope with balance-of-payments problems, as well as a willingness to acquiesce in temporary or limited protectionist measures, perhaps within the framework of escape clauses allowed by GATT. More broadly, it would imply a willingness to cooperate with a Eurosocialist administration in order to widen areas of possible cooperation and understanding, strengthen Mitterrand's hand in dealing with the communists, encourage moderate change rather than radical disruption, and lessen the dangers of a crisis in France or the Western alliance. Alternatively, a pattern of hostility, as expressed in the June 1976 Puerto Rico summit discussions (of the Ford-Kissinger administration) on denying loans to Italy, and as conceivable in the January 1978 Carter administration stance toward Eurocommunism in France and Italy, would almost certainly have been a significant factor in precipitating a crisis. Faced with internal economic problems and external hostility of this sort, a Mitterrand government might have chosen to resign, or to curtail many of its programmatic aspirations (as successive moderate British Labour governments did in reaction to balance-of-payments problems in 1964, 1966, and 1974–75), but, given its ideological commitments and the nature of its domestic coalition with the communists, such a government could well have chosen to follow a course of action much more autarchic in nature and less cooperative toward its European and Western partners. This implies greater economic disruption than would otherwise have been the case, with potentially damaging consequences for a number of countries and risks of both domestic and international destabilization.

POLICY REVERSALS

Just as concerns over security and the maintenance of a liberal international economic order created a propensity for the Carter administration's otherwise tolerant political predisposition toward Eurocommunism and Eurosocialism to be overridden, so did conditions in the domestic political environment. The sometimes inchoate nature of the administration's foreign policy; domestic and congressional reactions to the Panama Canal treaties, as well as events in Angola, Ethiopia, and Rhodesia; concerns about cancellation of the B-1 bomber and the status of the neutron bomb; fears over Soviet weapons programs and the uncertain implications of SALT II negotiations; and generalized expressions of uncertainty about America's adaptation to a post-Vietnam, post-Watergate environment all had the effect of making it more difficult for the administration to defend a complex and long-term policy of flexibility toward Eurocommunism. By contrast, reversion to a more orthodox European policy seemed to offer temporary respite from criticisms of naiveté or insufficient hardheadedness toward a new variant of the old communist nemesis and yet to cost little in terms of resources or commitments.

Initially, the Carter administration seemed predisposed to follow the more flexible policy suggested by Brzezinski, Vance, and Warnke in the spring of 1976. It was not that Eurocommunists were positively welcomed, nor that their involvement in Italian, French, or Spanish politics or government was seen as without risks, but rather that none of these parties seemed in a position to dominate or control the countries involved and that their participation in government could be tolerated without a strong likelihood of excessive domestic or foreign policy dangers in those countries.

In December 1976, even before taking office, high-level foreign policy officials of the incoming Carter administration met privately in Washington with two leading French socialist figures (Michel Rocard and Jean-Pierre Cot). Given the PS's partnership with the PCF, this contact seemed to signal a readiness to establish broader and more positive contacts between American foreign policy makers and European leftist leaders than had been acceptable in previous years.

More concretely, in an April 1977 statement on Eurocommunism, its first official comment on the subject following Carter's assumption of the Presidency, the State Department seemed to underline the view that only communist domination of a Western European state, not just participation in its government, would be a serious cause of concern. In addition, a major foreign policy address by President Carter, his Notre Dame commencement speech on May 22, 1977, seemed to convey an overall foreign policy orientation in which the United States would take a more relaxed and less obsessive approach toward confrontation with communists. Carter spoke of a "quiet confidence" in our own political system and in democracy as a whole:

> *Being confident of our own future, we are now free of that inordinate fear of Communism which once led us to embrace any dictator who joined us in our fear. . . .*

Referring to the post-1945 world order, he added:

> *Our policy during this period was guided by two principles: a belief that Soviet expansion must be contained and the corresponding belief in the importance of an almost exclusive alliance among non-Communist nations on both sides of the Atlantic.*
>
> *That system could not last forever unchanged. Historical trends have weakened its foundations. . . .*[24]

Despite these pronouncements, distinct signs of reversion to more orthodox European policies were becoming evident. As early as the beginning of April, for example, Secretary of State Cyrus Vance made clear an American preference that French Communists not be accorded a role in government. A similar theme was implied a few weeks later by President Carter, in a newspaper interview with European reporters. Interestingly enough, the Vance statement earned a rebuke from

French President Giscard d'Éstaing, who stated in a televised news conference that he had told Vance he "thought it improper for the American government to pass judgment on the internal affairs of France in whatever way." Giscard added that Vance would have done better to confine himself to remarks that it was up to the French people to make their own choice of their leaders and their future, rather than having emphasized that the rise of Communist parties in France and Italy would create problems in relations between American and those European states.[25]

Despite this lack of favorable response in France, the perceptible hardening of U.S. policy seemed to meet a more sympathetic domestic echo. The *New York Times* editorialized that the United States should take legitimate steps to discourage European Communist power, and commented approvingly, ". . . American policy will clearly influence events. Not to intervene in any way is simply another form of intervention. It would signal American unconcern or indifference." [26] A hard-line policy was also counseled by Henry Kissinger, who, although no longer secretary of state, had retained considerable domestic influence as an *éminence grise.* In early June, Kissinger warned against the dangers of communist gains in Europe as a setback to European and world freedom. He urged that the U.S. government avoid giving the impression it saw communist successes as a foregone conclusion, as would be the case by ostentatious consultation or association, and added that, on "the most basic moral values of our civilization . . . we cannot be neutral." [27]

By this time, President Carter's formally expressed position was becoming more explicitly antagonistic to the Eurocommunists, although it still fell well short of the unrelenting hostility of Kissinger. As Carter expressed this in his interview with European reporters prior to the London summit meeting of May 1977, European voters were "perfectly capable" of making their own decisions, although the United States preferred that the governments involved remain democratic and that no totalitarian elements become either influential or dominant:

> *To summarize: we certainly prefer that the democratic parties prevail in the future. And we can encourage that process, not by interfering in electoral procedures within countries themselves but by making the system work ourselves.*[28]

This orientation of an expressed preference that communists not be elected to office, coupled with a commitment to nonintervention in the electoral process (which, concerning Italy, represented a break with nearly three decades of both overt and covert American practice), did have some basis of domestic support. For example, one June 1976 survey among a group of Americans characteristic of the attentive public in foreign policy questions found that by an approximately two-to-one margin they opposed American actions to exert political and economic pressures on Italy to prevent communists from being taken into a national government coalition. A year later, a comparable survey found 63 percent of those responding favored the continuation of present relations between the United States and French or Italian governments containing communists, provided these observed democratic principles. A plurality, 44 percent, however, agreed that the United States should make clear in advance that it would insist on excluding communists in these governments from any secret NATO activities.[29] Among the adult American population as a whole, public opinion remained somewhat less tolerant. In the national sample analyzed by Michael Mandlebaum and William Schneider (see chapter 2, question 7*b*) only 42 percent of respondents felt it would be justified for the United States "to recognize democratic left-wing governments when they come to power."

Still, the administration maintained its position, expressed, for example, by Secretary Vance, that the United States could not tell any country whom to elect, but that it clearly preferred democratic forces and would view communist domination of a Western European government with great concern. In Vance's terminology an implied distinction remained between communist *participation* in government (which was seen as conceivable) versus *domination* (which remained quite improbable). In addition, Vance continued to hold out the "possibility" that, by encouraging increased independence of Eastern Europe, Eurocommunists in government could create problems for the Soviet bloc that "would more than outweigh the damage that Eurocommunism could bring to the NATO structure." [30] However, European policy had become increasingly inconsistent. In June, for example, the State Department quietly informed François Mitterrand that President Carter would not meet with the French Socialist party leader on the latter's projected September trip to the United States. The decision was immediately leaked to the French press and seemed to signal a conscious U.S. policy of taking sides in the election. At the time, its wisdom was also open to serious question because Carter had met with the British opposition leader, Margaret Thatcher, on her visit to Washington, and the decision on Mitterrand seemed to convey hostility to a man that French public opinion polls indicated to be the next prime minister of France. Thus, far from following a policy that might have strengthened Mitterrand's hand in dealing with the PCF and encouraged a greater degree of cooperation and receptiveness on a whole range of political, security, and economic issues, the administration went out of its way to signal its hostility.

Despite the decision on Mitterrand, there remained persistent contrary elements of policy. Spanish Communist party leader Santiago Carillo was allowed to visit the United States in November 1977 and express widely and with great publicity views that had earned him the enmity of Moscow. This visit contrasted strikingly with the denial of a visa to Sergio Segre two years before.

The domestic feedback on Eurocommunism became increasingly unfavorable, particularly with the approach of the March 1978 French legislative elections and the Italian government crisis of late 1977 and early 1978. The nature of the political dialogue was reflected in former President Ford's characterization of Eurocommunism as "Stalinism in a mask and tyranny in disguise." [31] This level of stridency also characterized Henry Kissinger's depiction of Eurocommunism in a nationally televised program on the subject in early January 1978. Kissinger painted a picture of a swelling, essentially unreconstructed communist monolith threatening to engulf each major Western European nation; he implied analogies with the 1930s, the rise of fascism and Western appeasement. The ahistorical nature of this analysis, the failure to note that alone in Italy had communist support actually grown in the postwar period whereas in France the PCF had drawn a perennial 20–25 percent of the electorate and was now at a relatively low ebb, and the failure to distinguish between the possibility of gaining a role in government in perhaps one or two cases, as opposed to the extreme remoteness of actually obtaining control of an entire country, all marked this presentation as a strident polemic rather than a reasoned analysis of the real mix of conceivable outcomes and risks.[32]

Nonetheless, for an administration struggling to keep its balance in the midst of a bitter Senate debate over the Panama Canal treaties, seeking to fend off political attacks on its ostensible ineptitude in foreign policy and lack of resolution in dealing with Russians and Cubans, and headed by a President in whom opinion polls indicated the public had little confidence, the prospect of defending an unorthodox European policy could only be seen as an unwelcome additional burden of relatively low priority, particularly when general political objectives in foreign policy were set alongside conflicting or discordant security and economic priorities.

In dealing with France and Italy, the Carter administration moved to a more adamant posture. On January 3, 1978, during his visit to Paris, the American President met with Mitterrand. Despite contradictory reports on their meeting, one of which quoted Carter as praising the socialist leader and telling him the two men had "many things in common" (a remark that sent the French stock market down by more than 2 percent), American diplomatic officials in Paris indicated that Carter had warned Mitterrand—at least in general terms—against reestablishing the alliance with the PCF that had been broken off in September by communist intransigence. This admonition was followed ten days later by a vigorous intervention in the Italian situation, which had been in turmoil since December when the Andreotti government had collapsed and PCI leaders sought an increased role in a new government. After consultations in Washington between Carter, Vance, and the American ambassador to Italy, Richard Gardner, the State Department released the sharpest pronouncement the Carter administration had made on Eurocommunism. The statement asserted that "we have an obligation to our friends and allies to express our views clearly," then went on to warn that the PCI did not share democratic "values and interests" and that not only did the United States not favor communist participation in Western European governments but wished to see communist influence there reduced.[33] This intervention proved embarrassing to Christian Democratic politicians in Italy, who had been working closely in informal coalition with the PCI for many months. Indeed, the DC minority government could not introduce major legislation without consulting and obtaining the tacit consent of the PCI. In addition, the communists held the chairmanships of several important legislative committees. The arrangement had worked adequately, without jeopardizing external alliance commitments nor internal stability (beyond its already precarious situation), yet Christian Democratic leaders who had supported or participated in these arrangements were in effect being rebuked for a dangerous and highly undesirable activity, yet one for which there had been little or no viable alternative.

From a Western European perspective, the U.S. intervention did not seem to have been particularly effective or welcome (though one faction of the DC opposed to cooperation with the PCI was gratified). Apart from the German government and Chancellor Helmut Schmidt, other Western European governments were not gravely concerned at the possibility that the PCI might obtain Cabinet positions. Instead, there may have been greater worry at the deterioration of the Italian economy and increased political violence and instability. To the extent that participation by the PCI in government might be able to assist in the establishment of an incomes policy and a stronger degree of law and order, it provided the possibility of greater system stability and thus at least the chance that the risks of this change might be offset or outweighed by its benefits.[34] The American interventions also elicited some of the most unfavorable reaction in France since the height of Gaullism. Unsurprisingly, communist and socialist leaders condemned the U.S. position. But Robert Pontillon, the PS's national secretary in charge of international questions and a socialist politician long known for his close (even compromising) affinities for the United States, described the U.S. inference as "unacceptable." Edgar Faure, Speaker of the French National Assembly and a centrist, stated that "it does not conform with our concept of democracy." Michel Poniatowski, a major figure in Giscard's party, termed the U.S. pressure "shocking and inadmissable" and Giscard condemned the intervention by stating, "I have always made it a rule never to accept that anybody—and I mean anybody—interfere in French political life." [35]

Whatever the European reaction, the domestic American response provided the Carter administration with positive reinforcement. Characteristically, in an editorial rhetorically titled, "Is It Time for Communists?" the *New York Times* echoed the position expressed in the State Department's policy statement on Italy, challenged the Italian Communists to prove they "are now only Social Democrats in the tradition of Willy Brandt or Olof Palme," and observed that none of the communists, Euro- or otherwise, "share our *political and economic liberalism.*" [36] Even allowing for appropriate concerns about vestiges of Leninism, and skepticism about alliance commitments, the implication of such a stance was that not merely was orthodox Marxism-Leninism unacceptable—a venerable and unexceptionable caution—but that however fundamental the changes in European Communism, no alteration short of total conversion to moderate Social Democracy, indeed to the tenets of economic liberalism—would be acceptable. This position, which infers that between Stalinist Marxism-Leninism and the Social Democracy of a Schmidt or Callaghan there is nothing, is in fact parochial and inflexible. It fails to respond to the kind of democratic socialist currents prevalent in France—in short, to Eurosocialism—as well as implying hostility to any latent Eastern European aspirations toward socialism with a human face. It does, however, convey the kind of analysis prevalent among many in the American foreign policy community.[37] Whether it will prove to determine overall U.S. policy toward the European left remains to be seen; to the extent that it does, the flexibility and adaptability of U.S. policy toward Europe will be markedly constrained, and the chances for serious and probably unnecessary conflicts of interest with future left-of-center Western European regimes will be enhanced.

CONCLUSION

The Carter administration's policies toward the Western Euorpean left have not appeared to incur appreciable domestic political costs, particularly in the short run. Broader considerations of long-term American interests vis-à-vis Europe exist, however, by which these policies may not be without drawbacks or risks. The policy instruments that the United States possesses to determine European political outcomes, particularly election results, are limited. Had the French *Union de la gauche* managed to win the March 1978 legislative elections (as most opinion polls suggested would be the case), the United States would have incurred not only the predictable animosity of the PCF (in its present, incompletely de-Leninized form), but also would have earned the distrust of the senior coalition partner, the PS, upon whom the basis for continuation of a tolerable U.S.–French relationship would have depended. In addition, the United States had, in effect, set itself squarely against political and economic reform in a country that even the *Economist* (an eminently respectable and conservative journal) describes as evincing "the inequalities (in certain respects, not all) of a banana republic." [38]

Over the long term, the political, economic, and social health and stability of Western societies has been based on their ability to adapt to change and reform themselves. Policies that embody a restrictive view of the range of legitimate change risk alienating large numbers of European voters and political elites. If successful in opposing change, these policies threaten to contribute to ossification and stagnation—and hence ultimately to dangerous and explosive disruption at a later date. (Arguably, the problems of Italy after three decades of uninterrupted, inefficient, and corrupt rule by the DC could be one such manifestation of this, though the case is far from certain.) On the other hand, unsuccessful opposition to change risks creating an image of foreign policy failure at home and abroad while making future cooperation more difficult.

Nor should the arguments about Eastern Europe suggested in 1976–77 by Vance and Brzezinski be discarded out of hand, even though Carter's leading foreign policy officials seem to have backed away from them. In neither Eastern nor Western Europe is politics a fixed and static affair. If, for example, the PCI does at some point manage to gain a slice of formal national governmental authority in Italy beyond the considerable informal and regional power it already exercises, this has the potential result of reinforcing the revisionist and moderate currents in the PCI without threatening a communist takeover of state power along East European lines. In the French case, involving a more hard-line party, the dominant force would remain the socialists, whose leaders are highly unlikely to allow PCF control of key ministries such as Defense and Interior. (Indeed it was almost certainly the PCF's fear of being used and of playing second fiddle to the socialists that caused them to precipitate the damaging rupture of the *Union de la gauche* in September 1977, which was unconvincingly papered over on the eve of the March 1978 election.) A party such as the PCI already has substantial contact with East European Communist parties and governments and has seemed to operate as a pole of attraction for them. Its revisions, criticisms, and policies provide an alternative to the unreconstructed neo-Stalinism of the Soviet model yet without so readily laying the East Europeans open to Soviet charges of anticommunism and other sins. This holds out the prospect of enhanced change from within Eastern Europe which three decades of external Western pressure has been unable to engender. In short, there *is* reason to believe that the risks of Eurocommunist participation in Western Europe may well be counterbalanced by changes in Eastern Europe.

Further, the risks in Western Europe have almost certainly been overstated. The manner in which countries such as Italy and France are so deeply enmeshed in a web of interdependent economic, commercial, monetary trading, and even cultural relationships with their Western European and Atlantic partners makes the prospects of long-term disruptive change unlikely. Voluntary withdrawal from, for example, the European Community, would be exceptionally costly and disruptive, and dependence on highly developed trade and investment patterns is too great. Thus, even had a Mitterrand managed to take office in March 1978 and not faced American hostility, the cumulative effects of economic interdependence would have placed virtually insuperable constraints on the range of innovation and change available to a government of the left. Security constitutes yet another form of tenacious interdependence. Thus Mitterrand has observed:

> *Am I going to challenge a geographical and historical description? It is useless; France belongs to Western Europe by geography and by the web of history; she must remain loyal to it.*[39]

The French socialist leader has also been quite explicit in stating that a left government would remain a "loyal but not an integrated ally."[40]

Ironically, both the United States and the USSR have been antagonists of Eurocommunism and Eurosocialism. In a sense, each country has seemed to have a vested interest in portraying the range of choice as limited to a fairly narrow set of variations on either the Soviet or the American pattern. Such a predisposition is perhaps comforting to policy makers by virtue of its familiarity. It also reflects an effort to retain spheres of influence at a time when, as Pierre Hassner has noted, both détente and Eurocommunism have seemed to be destabilizing forces, threatening to erode the sharp division of Europe into two isolated societies, and "to liberate forces which everybody tries to manipulate . . . but which nobody can be sure of controlling in the long run."[41] One of the arguments of this chapter, however, is that the processes of change may well be ones to which the United States and Western Europe are better equipped to adapt than is the USSR.

Much depends on the definition of U.S. interests. It is far from a foregone conclusion that the vital interests of America dictate that the cautious economic policies of a Social Democratic chancellor, Helmut Schmidt, or a Labourite prime minister, James Callaghan, fall within the range of tolerable activity while those of a putative Democratic Socialist premier, François Mitterrand, would not. Questions involving the tradeoffs between unemployment and inflation, the extent of nationalization, the level of minimum wages, or experiments in economic planning and workplace industrial democracy imply enough variability and uncertainty in their answers and implications so that it is by no means certain that only the fiscal and monetary orthodoxy of the U.S. Federal Reserve Board or the austerity policies traditionally prescribed by the IMF stand between the viable patterns of Western mixed economies and welfare states, on the one hand, and economic chaos, Leninist political takeovers, or both, on the other. What, in short, is the essential *content* of U.S. interests? Must America be identified principally with conservative and orthodox economic policies, or is there room for adaptation and change without irremediable damage to Western economic prosperity and military security? Let us recall, for example, the heated and emotional antagonism directed by most business interests to the economic and social reforms of Franklin Roosevelt. This is not to argue that Berlinguer or Marchais or even Mitterrand is either more or less than a Roosevelt (such an analogy would be ethnocentric). There may, however, be isomorphisms. Who can be certain, after all, that substantial changes and reforms could not take place within Western societies and in their international economic relationships, which might not prove beneficial and functional rather than destabilizing or disfunctional?

Yet, the existing pattern of policy, if continued, almost guarantees eventual negative outcomes. Major changes did not come in Italy or France in the election years of 1976 and 1978. But future change can by no means be ruled out. If it does occur, what then? In France, the lessons of 1977–78 suggest that American hostility on the one hand, coupled with programmatic determination and the economic constraints of high energy import dependence on the other, might well have created strong pressures for a Mitterrand government to be pushed in the direction of protectionism and autarchy, with results potentially harmful to France and her European neighbors.[42] In Italy, the kind of hostility reflected in the mid-1976 Puerto Rico summit agreement to deny financial aid to a government with communists could conceivably have precipitated a crisis to discredit Berlinguer's moderate approach and strengthen the hand of a hard-line pro-Soviet minority within the PCI. In the hypothetical case of an Italian government in which the PCI actually constituted the dominant force, perhaps after some future elections in which the Communists emerged as the leading Italian party, a policy of bitter Western hostility would present such a government with the choices either of resigning or moving toward the Soviet orbit. In the economic sphere this would imply severe measures of protectionism and autarchy coupled with Soviet economic aid and trade agreements. And in the area of security, despite PCI declarations and intentions to the contrary, allied pressures might have the effect of forcing the communists into major shifts in military or foreign policy, particularly in the event of a foreign crisis.[43]

Policy is not made in a vacuum. Domestic pressures on American foreign policy making have grown in response to a series of developments, not only Vietnam, the imperial Presidency and Watergate, but also in reaction to a changing American role. It has been argued, for example, that a degree of hegemonic decline and the gradual shift in emphasis from security to economic issues have increased the relative weight of domestic structures on foreign economic policy.[44] Such a shift implies greater weight for a variety of domestic economic interests, including banks and multinational corporations, in influencing European policies. Yet little of this influence is likely to be favorable to policies of change and adaptation (i.e., to left-of-center governments in Europe). It also may be less feasible for foreign policy makers to adopt a policy that emphasizes a largely military approach to the Atlantic Alliance. Indeed, Stanley Hoffmann has argued that the security link is the political basis of the open international economy. Implicitly, an exclusive emphasis on security issues would thus be unlikely. In Hoffmann's words:

> *America's original interest in Western Europe's recovery has been transformed into an interest in Western Europe's prosperity and financial solvency, because of the very strength of the links of trade and financial involvement that make of the North Atlantic (if you'll pardon the expression) a coprosperity sphere. The political base of this "community" of advanced capitalism is the security link established in the late 40s.*[45]

As a result, PCI leaders, for example, tend to believe that in a showdown, as in Chile, the United States would use her influence to preserve her political-economic interests even at the cost of antidemocratic government.[46]

This chapter has suggested that a more flexible and relaxed American policy toward the European left is consistent with the general political idealism of the Carter administration and that such an approach would not necessarily be inimical to long-term U.S. interests. At the same time, such a policy could be effectively reconciled with realistic security concerns, particularly if the Atlantic Alliance were perceived principally in terms of its objective of deterrence and defense against Soviet military power rather than as a political bulwark against communism per se or as a vehicle for a particular type of social-economic orthodoxy. Yet the interpretation given to another Carter administration objective, the maintenance of a liberal international economic order, as well as the increased linkage between domestic and foreign policy, have enhanced the tendency toward a harder line in European policy.

The disparity among policy choices reflected by these often divergent objectives and linkages explains in substantial measure the inconsistencies and shifts in Carter policy. The end product of this vector sum of forces has been a policy that remains less neat and coherent than that of the Nixon-Ford-Kissinger period but less anachronistic and perhaps less prone to engender bitter anti-American reactions. Future developments in policy, both regionally and in response to developments in specific European countries, are likely to depend on which of the administration's objectives—political, military, or economic—is uppermost in the calculations of policy makers at the time, as well as the degree to which domestic political considerations are perceived as imposing excessive costs, or possible benefits, in response to alternative policy choices.

NOTES

1. Malcolm Sawyer, "Income Distribution in OECD Countries," *OECD Economic Outlook* (Paris, July 1976).
2. See, e.g., *New York Times*, 18 July 1976. The administration subsequently denied, in a letter by the National Security Council chief, General Brent Scowcroft, to the House of Representatives International Relations Committee, that a formal agreement had been reached, but did acknowledge that the general issue was "disscussed." Ibid., 5 August 1976. However the original account emanated from a background briefing to reporters by German Chancellor Helmut Schmidt to Washington reporters on 16 July, and was widely reported in the European press. Moro's criticism is quoted in ibid., 20 July 1976.
3. See Richard Holbrooke, "Washington Dateline: A Little Visa Problem," *Foreign Policy*, no. 21 (Winter 1975–76): 245.
4. "The 'Communist Question' in Italy," *Foreign Affairs* 54, no. 4 (July 1976): 691–707.
5. See, e.g., the account in the *New York Times*, 30 January 1976.
6. See Laurence Stern, "Bitter Lessons: How We Failed in Cyprus," *Foreign Policy*, no. 19 (Summer 1975): 34–78.
7. See, e.g., *Economist* (London), 14 August 1976.
8. See Tad Szulc, "Lisbon and Washington: Behind Portugal's Revolution," *Foreign Policy*, no. 21 (Winter 1975–76): 3–62.
9. Quoted in *New York Times*, 28 October 1975.
10. *New York Times*, 30 December 1975 and 14 April 1976.

11. See, e.g., Jacques Huntzinger, "Le PS et la défense," *Projet*, no. 104 (April 1976): 450–58. Also Charles Hernu, *Soldat-citoyen: essai sur la défense et la sécurité de la France* (Paris: La rose au poing-Flammarion, 1975), pp. 152–53.

12. See, e.g., accounts of the impression made on West German businessmen, *Wall Street Journal*, 27 October 1977, and remarks to a dismayed King Juan Carlos of Spain (then seeking to facilitate the democratization of his country), in an account by Tad Szulc, *New Republic*, 13 November 1976.

13. Sonnenfeldt and Kissinger subsequently denied that these remarks conveyed an acceptance of the Brezhnev Doctrine or of a Soviet sphere of influence in Eastern Europe.

For official summaries of remarks by Helmut Sonnenfeldt and Secretary Kissinger as well as Sonnenfeldt's congressional testimony, see U.S., Congress, House, *United States National Security Policy Vis-à-Vis Eastern Europe (The 'Sonnenfeldt Doctrine')*, *Hearings before the Subcommittee on International Security and Scientific Affairs of the Committee on International Relations*, 95th Cong., 2d sess., 12 April 1976. Also, *New York Times*, 6 April 1976. For a criticism and alternative conception, see Robert J. Lieber, "The Pendulum Swings to Europe," *Foreign Policy*, no. 26 (Spring 1977).

14. *New York Times*, 14 April 1976.

15. Ibid., 16 April 1976.

16. See Nancy I. Lieber, "French Socialist Foreign Policy: Atlantic Relations, Defense and European Unity," in *Democratic Socialism in Europe*, ed. Bogdan Denitch (Boulder, Colo.: Westview Press, forthcoming 1979).

17. *La Nouvelle Revue Socialiste*, no. 20 (1976): 53. Also see Jacques Huntzinger, "Alliance Militaire ou alliance politique?" *Le Monde* (Paris), 2 May 1975.

18. 15 June 1976. Italics added.

19. See, e.g., Sergio Segre, "The Communist Question in Italy," *Foreign Affairs* 54, no. 4 (July 1977): 699–700.

20. Ciro Zoppo, "The Military Policies of the Italian Communist Party," *Survival* (London: International Institute for Strategic Studies, March/April 1978), p. 69.

21. George Urban, "Communism with an Italian Face? A Conversation with Lucio Lombardo Radice," *Encounter*, May 1977, p. 10.

22. Zoppo, "Military Policies," pp. 69–70, 72.

23. *Le Monde*, 16 March 1976.

24. *New York Times*, 23 May 1977.

25. Press Conference by Valerie Giscard d'Éstaing, president of the French Republic, broadcast over television, 12 April 1977. French Embassy Press and Information Division, New York (77/61).

26. *New York Times*, 19 April 1977.

27. 9 June 1977. See *Memorandum* (American Enterprise Institute, Washington, D.C.), no. 20 (Summer 1977).

28. Quoted, *New York Times*, 10 June 1977.

29. Foreign Policy Association *Outreacher*, July 1976 and June 1977.

30. Quoted in *New York Times*, 11 June 1977. Vance made this point in response to questions from Marino di Medici, Washington correspondent for the conservative Rome newspaper *Il Tempo*. Also see the transcript of his interview on ABC-TV, "Issues and Answers" (Washington, D.C.: Department of State, Bureau of Public Affairs, 19 June 1977).

31. *New York Times*, 30 October 1977. This level of stridency also characterized other analyses of the subject. See, e.g., Michael Ledeen, "The 'News' About Eurocommunism," *Commentary* 64, no. 4 (October 1977).

32. See, in reply, the letters by Stanley Hoffmann and John Low-Beer, *New York Times*, 21 February 1978.

33. The text of the statement is available in *New York Times*, 13 January 1978.

34. See, e.g., *Manchester Guardian Weekly*, 22 January 1978, as well as an editorial in the same journal on 29 January 1978. Also see Ugo La Malfa, "Communism and Democracy in Italy," *Foreign Affairs* 56, no. 3 (April 1978): 476–88.

35. *Le Monde*, 15–16 January 1978, and *Manchester Guardian Weekly*, 22 January 1978.

36. 18 January 1978. Italics added.

37. This sharp bifurcation of ideological choice tends to characterize analyses such as those in *Commentary* (cited above); Michael Ledeen's writings in the *New Republic;* Stephen Haseler's "Europe after the French Elections: A Counter-Strategy for the West," *Policy Review,* no. 4 (Spring 1978); some of the material from the American Enterprise Institute and from Georgetown University; and, in France, the approach of Jean-François Revel's *The Totalitarian Temptation.* (See, e.g., Nancy I. Lieber's review of Revel in *New International Review* I, no. 3 (Winter 1978): 9–14.

38. 18 March 1978.

39. Press conference, 2 May 1974, cited in Jacques Huntzinger, "La Politique Etrangère du Parti Socialiste," *Politique Etrangère* 2 (1975): 183.

40. *Le Monde,* 10 January 1978.

41. Pierre Hassner, "Eurocommunism and Detente," *Survival* (London: International Institute for Strategic Studies, November/December 1977), p. 254.

42. See Robert J. Lieber, "The Dilemmas of Economic Policy in Western European Democracies: Energy Problems, Foreign Policy and the West European Left" (paper presented in the Joint Country Groups Panel at the 1977 meeting of the American Political Science Association, Washington, D.C., 1–4 September 1977).

43. See Suzanne Berger, "Italy: On the Threshold or the Brink," in *Western Europe: The Trials of Partnership,* ed. David Landes (Lexington, Mass.: Heath, 1977), pp. 229–31.

44. Peter J. Katzenstein, "Domestic and International Forces and Strategies of Foreign Economic Policy," *International Organization* 31, no. 4 (Autumn 1977): 595.

45. Stanley Hoffmann, "Uneven Allies: An Overview," in Landes, *Western Europe,* p. 78.

46. Zoppo, "Military Policies," p. 66. Zoppo notes that the point had been made previously by Donald Blackner in Blackner and Annie Kriegel, *The International Role of the Communist Parties of Italy and France* (Cambridge, Mass.: Harvard Center for International Affairs, 1975), p. 30.

10

JIMMY CARTER AND LATIN AMERICA

A New Era or Small Change?

Abraham F. Lowenthal

I

Not since the days of John F. Kennedy and the Alliance for Progress has Washington lavished so much attention on Latin America as during the first eighteen months of the Carter administration. The President and Mrs. Carter, the vice-president, the secretary of state and his deputy, the secretary of the treasury, and the U.S. ambassador to the United Nations all visited the region during the administration's first year and a half, traveling to seventeen different countries. Terence Todman, President Carter's first assistant secretary of state for inter-American affairs until he became ambassador to Spain in July 1978, managed to tour all the countries of the hemisphere before moving on.

Issues to which the Carter administration has given special emphasis—nonproliferation and human rights especially—have intersected with questions of inter-American relations. Brazil, Chile, Cuba, Jamaica, Mexico, Nicaragua, Panama, and Venezuela—these and other Latin American and Caribbean countries have significantly engaged the energies of top administration officials. The Panama embroglio alone probably absorbed more of the President's time than any other single foreign policy issue during his first year and a half in office.

An earlier and somewhat briefer version of this chapter, titled "Latin America: The Not So Special Relationship," appeared in Foreign Policy, *no. 32 (September 1978).*

Will this vigorous initial concern with Latin America endure and eventually produce lasting results? Will it introduce substantial changes in hemispheric relations, even a "new era of inter-American cooperation," as President Carter has proclaimed? Or will a familiar cycle be repeated—a burst of interest in Latin America complete with visits, speeches, and the proclamation of new policies, followed by concrete decisions (or failures to decide) that weaken or even contradict the policies announced? Will basic problems go unaddressed, as they have so often in the past? Or does the Carter administration, unlike most of its predecessors, have a coherent set of concepts and approaches that will help it grapple with the underlying issues in the region? What can we learn from the Carter administration's first eighteen months in office that may help us evaluate the adequacy of its approach to inter-American policy? What does this tell us about the nature of the problems being faced in U.S.–Latin American relations?

II

It took Henry Kissinger years to discover Latin America. The Carter administration, by contrast, *began* with an expressed concern for the region, stressed often by the President. His second major foreign policy address as President was to the Organization of American States (OAS), whose headquarters in Washington he has frequently visited. After Carter took office, the first visit by a chief of state to Washington was from Mexico's president, José Lopez Portillo. Venezuela's Carlos Andrés Pérez followed soon after. In September 1977, seventeen Latin American heads of state converged on Washington to witness the signing of the Panama Canal treaties. Each visiting chief executive met with President Carter, who devoted a good part of the week to preparing for, attending to, and negotiating with his visitors. Neglect, benign or otherwise, is no longer Washington's approach to the nations of the Western Hemisphere.

Washington's stance toward Latin America and the Caribbean has changed in several important ways. First, the new administration has begun to reform the rhetoric and concepts of inter-American relations. Shopworn phrases like "Pan American community" and "special relationship" are (mostly) being abandoned, as Washington concedes that its treatment of Latin America and the Caribbean over the years often has been discriminatory and disadvantageous. The United States is not again promising preferential treatment for Latin America. Instead, this administration has focused on the growing significance of key countries in the hemisphere for dealing with a global agenda of issues equally important to North and South America.[1] The Carter administration on the whole has been treating the countries of the Western Hemisphere as they wish to be treated—as individual sovereign nations, each with interests of its own.

Second, the Carter administration mustered the courage to tackle two thorny problems from which previous administrations had shied away: Panama and Cuba. Even after Secretary Kissinger and his colleagues focused on these issues in 1974, they deliberately stopped short of measures that would have risked major domestic criticism. Candidate Jimmy Carter, too, was notably cautious on these questions during the 1976 campaign. From the outset of his term, however, Carter committed himself to revising our troubled relationship with Panama by recognizing that country's sovereignty over the Canal Zone, and to moving, on a measured and reciprocal basis, toward renewing relations with Fidel Castro's Cuba. By his first National Security Council meeting, Carter had accorded the Panama issue top billing. He rejected advice, from inside the administration and out, to leave U.S.–Cuban relations alone until the Panama problem was resolved. Instead, he began to press forward on both issues and even linked them with others, such as the recognition of Vietnam and initiatives to improve relations with Jamaica and Guyana, to demonstrate the acceptance of ideological diversity and the intent to treat all nations, regardless of their size or political bent, with mutual respect.[2]

By negotiating treaties with Panama and by successfully, if not always gracefully, pushing them through Senate ratification, President Carter concluded a necessary undertaking none of his predecessors was willing to risk. And by opening direct and public diplomatic contact with Cuba, and expressing interest in an eventual resumption of full bilateral relations with that country, the Carter administration ended an outmoded and self-defeating U.S. policy. Cuba's African involvements and the White House's somewhat irascible reactions to them have obviously complicated the eventual *rapprochement* between Washington and Havana. Whatever the course of U.S.–Cuban relations, however, the United States has improved its capacity for dealing with the challenges Cuba presents by abandoning its ossified stance of the 1960s and early '70s.

Third, the new administration has moved away from broad, undifferentiated regional policies and toward more carefully tailored bilateral and subregional approaches. This process of refining U.S. policies in the Western Hemisphere (to an extent, a return to the historical pattern disrupted by the generalities of the Alliance for Progress) made headway in previous years; the Kissinger-Silveira memorandum of 1976, for instance, set up special mechanisms for handling U.S.–Brazilian relations. The Carter administration has concentrated not only on Brazil but also on Mexico, Venezuela, and the Caribbean. Brazil and Mexico account for one fourth of all U.S. trade with less developed countries outside the Organization of Petroleum Exporting Countries (OPEC); these two countries plus Venezuela account for almost 70 percent of all U.S. trade with Latin America and well over half the U.S. investment in the hemisphere. All three countries warrant more high-level attention than they previously received, not only because of expanded U.S. investment and trade but also because of the enlarged international role these nations will play as middle-rank powers.[3]

The new administration has also recognized the potential significance for the United States of improved relations with the countries and territories of the Caribbean region, America's "third border." Spurred by the burgeoning Caribbean migration to the United States, Washington is paying attention to the region's economic problems for the first time in years. Study missions and task forces to deal with Caribbean problems have been created within the government, and a multilateral consultative group has been convened under World Bank auspices to coordinate external development assistance. Caribbean development issues are now being faced as such, rather than in the narrowly defined terms of military security that structured

U.S. perceptions of the region—between periodic U.S. Marines' landings—for generations.[4]

No Carter administration policy affecting Latin America is as dramatically new as its stand on human rights.[5] Secretary Kissinger seemed mostly indifferent, if not hostile, to this issue; the Carter administration gives it pride of place. Despite congressional instructions to the contrary, the Ford administration generally managed to support loans in international financial institutions to nations that flagrantly violated human rights; the Carter administration has already opposed more than twenty-five such loans, mostly in Latin America. The United States was previously not a party to the Inter-American Convention on Human Rights; under Carter, Washington not only signed the agreement (after years of delay) but also persuaded several other countries to do so. The United States has also spearheaded efforts to strengthen substantially the budget, staff, and authority of the Inter-American Commission on Human Rights. And the present administration has found ways— through formal and informal meetings and other expressions of interest and sympathy—to build new links with democratic opposition groups throughout South and Central America and the Caribbean.

To an impressive degree, Washington has cleansed America's sorry image of automatic identification with authoritarian regimes. Fundamental U.S. values— particularly respect for human rights and a preference for constitutional democracy—have been forcefully reasserted. The lives of hundreds of people in several countries have improved, at least in part as a result of Washington's pressures. Significant numbers of political prisoners have been released in Chile, Haiti and several other countries; and lists of political prisoners have been made available in Argentina and Chile. Commissions to investigate human rights conditions have gained entry to several countries. Reports of the use of torture have decreased. Most important, perhaps, a mood of cautious hope has begun to grow that brutal repression is no longer being legitimated. Although the Carter administration's role in precipitating the recent outbreak of elections throughout Latin America and the Caribbean should not be exaggerated, it is fair to say that the United States has been consciously and effectively reinforcing this trend, particularly in Peru and the Dominican Republic.

III

The changes cited in the previous section are commendable: paying more attention to the countries of Latin America and the Caribbean, abandoning paternalism, recognizing Latin America's potential role in helping to deal with a broad global agenda, giving priority to key bilateral relationships, and reasserting fundamental national values as a guide for policy. The new administration deserves praise, too, for resisting the recurrent strain toward intervention that has so often marked Washington's approach. Within the first two years of each of the previous four administrations, Washington had intervened in Latin America: the Guatemalan invasion of 1954, the Bay of Pigs fiasco of 1961, the Dominican intervention of 1965, and the massive efforts to "destabilize" the Allende government in Chile. It is highly unlikely that any similar adventure is being carried out or contemplated by the Carter administration.

Nevertheless, it is too soon to conclude that improvements Carter and his team have introduced in U.S.–Latin American relations will be of lasting importance. Significant questions must be raised about each of the new initiatives. Moreover, many of the toughest problems affecting the region—particularly items on the economic agenda—have yet to be faced. Whether this administration's impressive start in dealing with Latin America will ultimately amount to much depends on decisions and actions yet to be taken, as well as on trends and developments beyond any President's control.

The burst of high-level attention expended on Panama and Cuba, for example, may turn out to be insignificant or even counterproductive as a way to improve inter-American relations over the longer term. The orgy of official attention splurged on Panama, in particular, may make it much harder to get high-level attention for the economic issues at the core of contemporary inter-American relations. The administration's initiatives on Panama and Cuba were unquestionably courageous efforts to remove troublesome political problems of the past. As bridges to a "new era of inter-American cooperation," however, they seem in danger of being left hanging, precisely because the underlying economic issues in hemispheric relations remain unresolved.

Moreover, for all its talk about the individuality of the respective countries of Latin America and the Caribbean, the Carter administration's actions have been remarkably insensitive to several specific bilateral contexts. U.S.–Brazilian relations deteriorated sharply in 1977 not only as a result of objective clashes of interest (some of them long-standing) but also because of the administration's early mishandling of these relations. Particularly damaging was Vice-President Mondale's highly publicized direct approach to the Federal Republic of Germany concerning its sale of nuclear reprocessing technology to Brazil, an approach made before there was any direct U.S. discussion of the matter with the government of Brazil.[6]

After a brief honeymoon period between the incoming administrations in both countries, U.S.–Mexican relations also became strained in 1977.[7] The main reason was the Administration's somewhat peremptory proposals to deal with massive Mexican immigration. A Carter plan calling for strict measures to control the flow of "undocumented immigrants" from Mexico was sent to Congress in August 1977 with little prior consultation with Mexican authorities—or, for that matter, with Mexican-Americans in the United States. It should have been obvious that a jointly devised approach to the problem of migration would be far more likely to succeed than a unilateral one. A jointly devised approach, moreover, would have been more apt to assure Mexican cooperation on other matters of shared concern, such as guaranteeing U.S. access to Mexico's huge reserves of natural gas and its projected flow of petroleum.[8]

More generally, many individual Latin American and Caribbean countries have been hurt by specific U.S. decisions: to raise tariffs on imported sugar, to sell surplus tin from the government stockpiles in order to lower the price, to grant or deny certain airline routes, or to tighten tax regulations on business exemptions for conventions abroad. The gap between announced policies and actual decisions is nowhere more notable than in U.S.–Caribbean relations. The administration's Caribbean initiative seems to be fizzling as specific choices have to be made. State Department and AID recommendations for doubling U.S. support for Caribbean development were turned down, first by the Office of Management and Budget and then, on appeal, by the President; a much smaller increase (some 30 percent of previous aid) was approved. Caribbean development has been officially accorded high priority, but an administration that has established so many "priorities" seems unable to make such a commitment meaningful.

Washington's new stress on human rights is difficult to evaluate because it is unclear how much emphasis is being placed on the policy's several distinct, and not always compatible, objectives. The policy is supposed to win renewed domestic trust in our government and its foreign policies, regain the ideological advantage from the Communist parties of Eastern and Western Europe, provide a legitimate basis for sustained U.S. government communication with those in opposition to authoritarian governments, disassociate the United States from repressive regimes and their acts, and influence the treatment of individuals abroad. How these objectives relate to each other and which has priority in any particular instance is not so clear. Contradictory signals abound, reflecting intra- and interdepartmental disputes within the U.S. government about ends and means, as well as different evaluations of external circumstances and trends—and even conflicting criteria for evaluating them. In the relatively uncharted domain of human rights policy, broad guidelines are necessarily abstract and often unenlightening. In practice, policy is defined case by case, country by country, loan by loan, and speech by speech through an iterative process in which the personal styles and ambitions of individual participants in the policy-making process are probably more influential than any other factor.

As the human rights policy takes shape, several problems are emerging. Excessive expectations can easily be aroused, as in Nicaragua, risking eventual disillusionment. Heavy-handedness from abroad, no matter how noble the cause, can actually strengthen the domestic hold of repressive regimes, at least temporarily; this may have happened, for a time, in Chile. Policies fashioned to deal with one set of important problems—to fight inflation and stabilize economies, for instance—may contradict and even undermine efforts to promote civil and political liberties, as in Peru. Conversely, policies designed to protect individual rights may not only constrain the development of the countries denied credit by international financial institutions but may also severely damage the institutions themselves. Vigorous implementation by Washington of the human rights policy in the Western Hemisphere can conjure up ghosts of the paternalist past. Finally, the whole policy may be used perversely by a straight right-left alliance in Congress and American society as a means of avoiding the resource transfers sought by Latin American and other Third World countries. These difficulties do not argue against a major U.S. concern for human rights, nor should they obscure the considerable results the policy has accomplished. The policy's lasting impact, however, will depend to a considerable extent on how carefully this concern is calibrated. The danger is growing that exuberant and singleminded pursuit of human rights objectives may eventually produce its own backlash, turning officials away from the concern these issues should always evoke.

But economic matters, above all, present the most vexing questions about the Carter administration's policies affecting Latin America. Washington's desire to win Latin American cooperation for dealing with global problems seems tangible only with regard to the issues this country deems urgent: energy, monetary policy, and nonproliferation. The issues that most deeply concern the majority of Latin American countries—improving access for middle-income countries to the markets, capital, and technology of industrial countries; assuring more generous and more automatic concessional aid to the poorest countries; making returns from international trade in commodities more predictable and more favorable to producers; and making multinational corporations more responsive to the interests of host countries—are accorded much lower priority. Unless these and similar North-South problems are confronted, the Carter administration's embrace of the so-called global approach may turn out to be an empty shell, addressing Latin America's principal concerns less adequately than the old regional approaches.

The Carter administration's record to date on North-South issues—though admittedly restricted by recession and adverse public opinion—has been mixed at best. The administration has been struggling to resist strong protectionist pressures; at times it has succeeded. But access to markets in the United States and other industrial countries is certainly not being expanded significantly, as it must be if Latin American and other Third World aspirations are to be accommodated. To many Latin Americans, the Multilateral Trade Negotiations (MTN) under way in Geneva seem largely unresponsive to their needs; industrial countries are likely to secure greater benefits from trade liberalization than are less developed countries, at least in the short run. Even more troubling is the scheduled expiration in January 1979 of the waiver provisions of the Trade Act of 1974, which allow the secretary of the treasury to delay the application of countervailing duties to goods benefiting from favorable tax treatment in exporting countries. Unless agreement can be reached, any Latin American export to the United States currently receiving a government incentive will be subject to countervailing duties within twelve months of a U.S. manufacturer's complaint.

The news on other North-South issues is not much more encouraging. Obtaining U.S. capital is becoming more difficult, not less, for most countries of Latin America and the Caribbean. Concessional aid is relevant only for a few poor countries in the hemisphere, of course, but they are getting little help from the United States. Even if the Carter administration's request to Congress for increase in the worldwide aid authorizations were approved and funds appropriated, the increase would be small in absolute terms and would leave the United States far below the agreed UN target figure of .7 percent of a nation's gross national product. Much more credit is available to Latin American and Caribbean countries from the international financial institutions, to be sure, and this will continue to be true if the relevant congressional appropriations are approved. But the debt service paid by Western Hemisphere nations on earlier loans now consumes ninety-three cents of every dollar currently being borrowed by Western Hemisphere nations from the United States and the international lending institutions. Credit from private sources is rapidly drying up for those countries in greatest financial difficulty—Peru and Guyana, for instance. The short time-horizon of commercial banks practically assures a perverse cycle of ever deepening debt.[9]

Rhetorically, the Carter administration is considerably more receptive than its predecessors to international commodity agreements, and certainly many more U.S. officials are tied down now, either negotiating such agreements or preparing to do so, than in previous years. Concrete results are sparse, however, and likely to remain so. The International Sugar Agreement has been concluded, but Senate ratification is highly uncertain. A rubber agreement is being fashioned, but this commodity is of little interest in Latin America. Other negotiations—including those on copper—are painfully slow and unpromising.

Aside from a few scattered statements, there is scant evidence that the U.S. government will push multinational corporations (MNCs) toward greater responsiveness to the needs of developing countries. Richard N. Cooper, undersecretary of state for economic affairs, told a group of business executives the U.S. government would henceforth remain neutral in disagreements between American companies and host countries rather than automatically taking the side of U.S. corporations, but the actual behavior of U.S. embassies has not changed perceptibly.[10] Indeed, the administration has not done anything yet to repeal two pieces of legislation—the Hickenlooper Amendment first passed in 1962 and the 1972 Gonzalez Amendment—that threaten developing countries with U.S. government coercion on behalf of MNCs in cases of nationalization or expropriation.[11]

Finally, little has been done so far, despite verbal bows, to improve the terms on which technology is transferred from North to South. President Carter's proposal, announced in Caracas in 1978, to establish a "new United States foundation for technological collaboration" was notable mainly for its complete omission of any further details.

IV

The Carter administration's accomplishments in regard to Latin America, then, are at present more style than substance. Attention is being paid; still, few problems have been resolved, and several have not been tackled. The issues granted priority in Washington have been more those of the past than of the future. Rhetoric and tone have changed more than choices and actions. The setting of goals has been emphasized more than the elaboration of strategies to achieve them. The administration's major innovations have been in the most intangible arena: human rights. On matters of dollars and cents (in whatever currency), the Carter administration has so far produced only small change.

It is too early to be conclusive about what the Carter administration will signify. Initial skepticism may still be overcome as trade and tariff negotiations evolve, as specific commodity agreements are worked out, as actual investment disputes arise and are dealt with, as well-prepared projects elicit increased resource transfers for the Caribbean and elsewhere, and as the President's proposal for a technology foundation is elaborated.

It must be noted, however, that the Carter administration's first phase repeats a familiar pattern.[12] Whether calling its approach a Good Neighbor Policy, an Alliance for Progress, a Mature Partnership, or a New Dialogue—or pointedly eschewing rhetoric and labels, as Carter has done—one U.S. administration after another promises to improve U.S.–Latin American relations. Always goaded by a period of tension in hemispheric relations, successive administrations have announced reform, pledged greater attention to the needs of the area, and vowed their support (more or less flamboyantly, depending on the administration's style) for Latin America's social and economic development. In earlier days, the United States sometimes promised to help secure "democracy" in the region. "Human rights" rather than "democracy" is now the centerpiece, but the tendency is similar.

The next phase in this historic cycle has generally seen the newly expressed policy toward Latin America vitiated or even contradicted by U.S. government actions. Despite promises that they will receive enhanced consideration, Latin American interests are slighted or contravened. Despite the pretense of consultation and negotiation, Latin Americans find themselves the victims of unilateral decisions taken in Washington or New York. Whatever the official rhetoric of cooperation, Latin Americans learn that private interests in the United States can use public instruments to achieve their will. Regardless of the promises by Washington to help Latin American development, generous resource transfers untied to political concessions or special commercial privileges are infrequent. Events in 1977 and 1978—the sugar tariff increases, Washington's decision to sell surplus tin despite its adverse impact on Bolivia, the imposition (or the threat) of countervailing duties, the decision to curtail sharply the proposed Caribbean initiative, the unilateral proposals to deal with the problem of undocumented aliens—all these and more fit a classic mode.

What explains this persistent gap between a new administration's proclaimed "Latin American policy" and the pattern of decisions, actions, and omissions ultimately comprising policy? Why does the frequent resolve of new administrations to improve inter-American relations so often come to naught, or to only a bit more? What can we learn from the Carter administration's experience to date?

In focusing on Latin American policy, as administrations and their critics understandably do, we often fail to see the obvious: many U.S. decisions and actions affecting Latin America and inter-American relations are not taken for that purpose at all but are made in other policy arenas—foreign or domestic—with limited consideration of their likely impact in the hemisphere. Examples are plentiful: the sugar and tin decisions; policies regarding nuclear proliferation, arms transfers, and human rights; provisions of the tax law and its implementation; and many trade policy decisions. Such decisions often are not much influenced by regional considerations or by U.S. government personnel working on inter-American affairs. Those within the administration primarily concerned with inter-American relations may sincerely push for alternate policies. That they so often fail reflects the relative lack of priority for improving regional relations.

A second point, also often ignored, is that much of inter-American relations is shaped by a multiplicity of nongovernmental entities and processes that no administration can easily control. These entities—multinational corporations, private banks, and labor unions, for example—operate within a structure influenced by past and present U.S. decisions. Official policy can influence or constrain private actions; U.S. citizens, individual or corporate, are rarely oblivious to Washington's preference. Still, what the U.S. government decides to do in Latin America—or to refrain from doing—cannot by itself alter the main impact of the United States as a whole. In a curious sense, it is much easier for the U.S. government to manage this country's relations with Russia or China than with Chile or Peru. Latin America and the Caribbean countries are much influenced by decisions taken by Exxon, ASARCO, United Brands, Gulf & Western, Citibank, the Manufacturers Hanover Trust, or Chase Manhattan, to name just a few companies. And some of the main problems in inter-American relations—access to capital and to technology, especially—are issues on which the U.S. government has considerably less influence than nongovernmental actors.

A third reason for the contrast between announced intentions and subsequent actions has to do with the process of policy making.[13] Each new administration brings a fresh cadre of officials to Washington. They are determined to do better than their predecessors; often they bring with them concepts and policies forged in task forces and study groups. The recruits draw on this background to draft policy directives and presidential speeches, precisely the point in the policy-making process at which their influence is highest. In time, however, their influence is attenuated by the continuing pressures of special interests and sometimes by the passive resistance of the career bureaucracy.

Because private U.S. interests in any given situation can pursue their particular claims through so many differing access points in the executive branch and Congress, broad and consistent reforms of U.S. policy are hard to achieve. Any reform that penalizes some well-organized group—copper companies, sugar or citrus growers, shoe manufacturers, labor unions, church groups, or whatever—can usually be shelved or defeated by a blocking coalition assembled within the highly fragmented structure of U.S. foreign policy making. Even when the proposed reform promises to benefit substantially U.S. society as a whole, a group likely to be injured often can prevent the reform's adoption. Even when a new policy is formally adopted, an administration must ensure its full implementation at all levels of sharply divergent bureaucracies. The Treasury Department is often decisive in shaping and implementing U.S. policies on commercial and monetary matters: on export subsidies, countervailing duties, and other elements of trade policy; on the negotiation of commodity agreements and buffer stocks; on the behavior of international financial institutions—in short, on most of the substantive issues in contemporary inter-American relations. The Departments of Agriculture, Energy, Justice, and Commerce; the Export-Import Bank, the Civil Aeronautics Board—not to mention the Pentagon and the CIA—are all influential in shaping U.S. policies affecting Latin America. To be sure that all these segments of the U.S. government will cooperate effectively to pursue a new policy, an administration must be willing to give that policy significant priority. Constant monitoring, innovative coordination, and energetic follow-up are required. That kind of priority is, and must be, rare.

Another reason why new administrations find it hard to follow through on proclaimed intentions is the often underestimated and still growing role of Congress.[14] The legislative branch influences policy through general legislation (often adopted without considering its effects on the hemisphere) and by taking up particular issues in inter-American relations. Trade policy, human rights, arms transfer policy, agricultural policy, foreign aid—these and other matters important in the hemisphere are strongly influenced by Congress. Almost any new policy initiative must first run the gauntlet of congressional scrutiny, influenced by constituency pressures of all sorts, before it can be adopted. Few proposals survive this ordeal unscathed.

V

Lasting improvements in U.S.–Latin American relations are also hard to achieve for three basic reasons: the reality of declining but still remembered U.S. hegemony in the hemisphere, the emergence of sharp clashes of interest between the United States and the countries of Latin America and the Caribbean, and the absence of a coherent and accepted vision in Washington of how inter-American relations should be restructured to respond positively to these two changing facts of hemispheric life.

An overwhelming imbalance between the United States and the countries of Latin America and the Caribbean has long conditioned the realities of inter-American relations. Because the United States is so much bigger, richer, stronger, and more extensively involved around the world than any other country in the hemisphere, what is crucial for a Latin American nation may well be marginal in Washington. Because the United States is so privileged, what may appear to be mutually advantageous from Washington's perspective may seem exploitative from a Latin American standpoint. Because so many in the United States still think of Latin America as a U.S. sphere of influence, an intolerable affront to sovereignty—like the De Concini reservation to the Panama Canal treaty providing the United States with a permanent right to send its troops into Panama's territory to protect the canal—can be approved with few qualms in the United States. And because the Colossus of the North is so large, the United States casts a bulky shadow southward no matter what direction it faces. The inevitable result of this continuing disparity of all kinds of power, real and perceived, is constant tension rooted in ambitions, fears, jealousies, and resentments.

As the objective bases for America's hegemonic presumption erode, tensions in the hemisphere will probably not be relaxed but rather increased.[15] During the next few years, a new Latin American assertiveness resulting in part simply from enhanced power and also from changes in the composition of the area's leadership will exacerbate the tension. Traditional pro-American elites are being replaced all over the hemisphere by civilian and military technocrats, often of a nationalist bent. These new leaders, many of them trained in U.S. graduate schools, tend to identify their countries' interests independently of, and even through confrontation with, the United States.

Nevertheless, the likely expansion of inter-American conflict stems primarily from an objective change: the transformation of Latin American economies from inward-turned import substitution to outward-oriented export promotion. Most Latin American countries (except for the smallest) no longer care about obtaining bilateral concessional assistance from the United States. They, like other Third World countries, primarily want new international rules and practices that will improve their access to markets, capital, and technology in the industrialized world.

As Latin American and other Third World economies expand, and as their export potential and their thirst for capital and technology grow, conflicts will inevitably arise between them and the industrialized countries. The specific issues will include commodities, tariffs, countervailing duties, debt management, technology transfer, the conservation and management of resources, the terms on which capital and labor migrate, and the making and management of international regimes to govern these and other problems. As Brazil, Mexico, Venezuela, Argentina, and other Latin American countries strive to fulfill their potential, they will increasingly encounter a growing tendency of industrialized countries to defend the status quo through protectionism, the preservation of international monetary "law and order," nonproliferation policies, and the like. No matter how many trips are taken and speeches are made, therefore, a real basis for conflict between the United States and Latin America will persist.

To achieve a major and lasting improvement in its relations with Latin America, therefore, the United States would have to help establish a new international economic and political order within which the claims of Latin America and other aspiring powers are more fully accommodated.[16] A reformed international order could reconcile U.S. interests with those of Latin American and other Third World countries in ways ultimately more favorable to Third World interests than under the existing order. Substantially more of the world's manufacturing would take place in the South, for instance, and painful adjustments would have to be accepted by the North. Importantly, increased benefits from international trade in raw materials and other primary products would accrue to the less industrialized countries. The advantages derived by the rich countries from prior accumulations of capital and technology would decrease significantly. The present and prospective benefits from the world's commons—especially from the seabed and outer space—would be distributed in a much more equitable manner. The rules and regimes affecting these and other international issues would be made in forums where the interests of the countries of Latin America, among others, would be better protected. To a large extent, market forces could be used to make such a new international order work; but substantial structural change would be required to assure that markets operate effectively in a world where leverage, influence, and rewards are not so unevenly distributed.

To date, no administration in Washington has seriously attempted to change the structure of the international order from which the United States has so overwhelmingly gained. Economic concessions granted by Washington to Latin American countries (or to others) have always been provided grudgingly, in exchange for cooperation on specific political or strategic matters. Never has the United States sought to transform the nature of its relationship with the rest of the hemisphere. If Jimmy Carter were eventually to try to open a truly new era in U.S.–Latin American relations, that is the challenge his administration would have to face. Little in President Carter's first eighteen months in office—either in Latin American policy or in the other issue areas reviewed in this volume—suggests that his administration is yet ready to do so.

NOTES

1. The administration's approach resembles closely and no doubt partly derives from the reports of the Commission on United States–Latin American Relations, chaired by Ambassador Sol M. Linowitz; the "Linowitz reports" emphasized the need to deal with Latin America in a global context. See *The Americas in a Changing World: A Report of the Commission on United States–Latin American Relations* (New York, 1975) and "The United States and Latin America: Next Steps—The Second Report of the Commission on United States–Latin American Relations" (Center of Inter-American Relations, New York, 1976). I served as a special consultant to the commission.
2. On U.S. efforts under Carter to improve "badly strained relations with Jamaica," see J. Daniel O'Flaherty, "Finding Jamaica's Way," *Foreign Policy,* Summer 1978, pp. 137–58.
3. For useful recent analyses of U.S. relations with these three important countries, see Thomas Skidmore, "U.S. Policy Towards Brazil: Assumptions and Options," in *Latin America: The Search for New International Role,* ed. Ronald G. Hellmann and H. Jon Rosenbaum (New York: Wiley, 1975), pp. 191–213, on Brazil; Richard Fagen, "The Realities of U.S.–Mexican Relations," *Foreign Affairs,* July 1977, pp. 685–700, on Mexico; and Robert Bond, ed., *Contemporary Venezuela and Its Role in International Affairs* (New York: New York University Press, 1977), on Venezuela.
4. See also Abraham F. Lowenthal, "Toward a New Caribbean Policy," *SAIS Review,* Fall 1974, pp. 5–19.
5. For a general, highly critical discussion of the Carter administration's approach to human rights, see chapter 6 in this volume. A more favorable analysis, closer to my own approach, is presented by Sandra Vogelgesang in "What Price Principle?—U.S. Policy on Human Rights," *Foreign Affairs,* July 1978, pp. 819–941.
6. For a considerably exaggerated but illuminating discussion of how U.S.–Brazilian relations were mishandled, see Roger Fontaine, "The End of a Beautiful Relationship," *Foreign Policy,* no. 28 (Fall 1977): 166–74.
7. See Olga Pellicer de Brody, "La Politica De Los Estados Unidos Hacia Mexico En La Coyuntura Actual-Una Relacion Muy Especial" (colloquium working paper presented at Woodrow Wilson Center for International Scholars, 4 April 1978).
8. Richard R. Fagen and Henry R. Nau, "Mexican Gas: The Northern Connections" (prepared for a conference on the United States, the U.S. Foreign Policy and Latin American and Caribbean Regimes, 27–31 March 1978, sponsored by Joint Committee on Latin American Studies of the Social Science Research Council and American Council of Learned Societies).
9. See Albert Fishlow, "The Third World: Public Debt, Private Profit," *Foreign Policy,* Spring 1978, pp. 133–43.
10. "The Role of Investment in Expanding an Open International Economic System," address by Richard N. Cooper, Under Secretary for Economic Affairs, before the Council of the Americas, Washington, D.C., 27 June 1977. In *Department of State Bulletin* 77, no. 1987 (25 July 1977): 127–31.
11. For a convincing argument that the Hickenlooper and Gonzalez amendments should be repealed, see William D. Rogers, "Of Missionaries, Fanatics, and Lawyers: Some Thoughts on Investment Disputes in the Americas," *American Journal International Law,* January 1978, pp. 1–16.
12. Abraham F. Lowenthal and Gregory F. Treverton, "The Making of U.S. Policies Toward Latin America," *Latin American Program Working Paper* No. 5 (Washington, D.C.: Wilson Center 1978).
13. For a fuller discussion of this point, see Abraham F. Lowenthal, " 'Liberal,' 'Radical,' and 'Bureaucratic' Perspectives on U.S. Latin American Policy: The Alliance for Progress in Retrospect," in *Latin America and the United States: The Changing Political Realities,* ed. Julio Cotler and Richard R. Fagen (Stanford: Stanford University Press, 1974), pp. 212–35.
14. See Robert Pastor, "U.S. Sugar Politics and Latin America: Asymmetries in Input and Impact," in *Report of Commission on the Organization of the Government for the Conduct of Foreign Policy* 3, appendix 1 (June 1975): 221–33.

15. For a fuller development of the point, see Abraham F. Lowenthal, "The United States and Latin America: Ending the Hegemonic Presumption," *Foreign Affairs,* October 1976, pp. 199–213.

16. For a good discussion of what such a reform would mean, see Albert Fishlow's "A New International Economic Order: What Kind?" in *Rich and Poor Nations in the World Economy,* ed. Fishlow et al. (New York: McGraw-Hill, 1978), pp. 11–83.

11

U.S. POLICY STYLES IN AFRICA

From Minimal Engagement to Liberal Internationalism

Donald Rothchild

Whether moderation is politically practical or suicidal depends on the circumstances.
Arnold Wolfers, "Statesmanship and
Moral Choice," World Politics (1949)

With the advent of the Carter administration in 1977, officials and observers alike spoke optimistically of new "visions" in U.S. policy toward Africa. Indeed, the circumstances were propitious. President Carter's advocacy of human rights on a global scale and his appointment of Andrew Young as United States chief delegate to the United Nations; his call for efforts to promote racial justice in South Africa, as well as for diplomatic initiatives to end the deadlock in Rhodesia (Zimbabwe) and South-West Africa (Namibia); his determination to reintroduce sanctions against Rhodesian chrome; and his administration's promise to bring about a significant increase in economic assistance to middle Africa all seemed to augur well. An activist and affirmative concern was now to replace "a negative, reactive American policy that seeks only to oppose Soviet or Cuban involvement in Africa." [1] The United States remained as committed as ever to the maintenance of the inherited international economic system, but pursued that concern by accommodation, insofar as possible, to Third World goals and priorities.

I would like to express my appreciation to Helen Kitchen and John Marcum for thoughtful comments on the first draft of this chapter.

In adopting an accommodative approach the Carter administration was clearly attempting to exercise choice: to end the identification with white domination in southern Africa and join forces with the majority of Third World states on issues of political independence, economic growth and development, and freedom from external control. Obviously such a strategy involved contradictions of policy. Cooperation in black Africa's attack on the staunchly anticommunist governments in southern Africa seemed, on the surface at least, to conflict with global security objectives. Moreover, it was apparent that some efforts at adjusting to world demands on the southern African issue would prove to be relatively easy, but how far would a privileged country be willing to go in identifying with Third World economic interests and aspirations? It seemed apparent that unless the Carter administration could move beyond the initial steps toward accommodation and absorb the increasing costs involved in reforming the international economic system, its "liberal internationalism" would be ridiculed by the very world opinion it was designed to court.

In order to deal with these issues, it will be necessary to start by describing key contextual factors which underlie U.S. policies in Africa. It will then be possible to take note of the type of limited engagement that marked postwar administrations up to the spring of 1976. This is important to an understanding of current choices because of the continuity of alternative approaches on nonintervention and adversary action that became evident by the time of the Angolan crisis in 1975. At that point account must be taken of the initiatives begun by Secretary of State Henry Kissinger late in his term of office in negotiating a Rhodesian settlement and beginning what amounted to a general reexamination of the premises underlying American policy toward Africa. Then, following an analysis of Carter's initial "liberal internationalism" during his first ten months in office, it will be possible to outline the emerging administration debate over best possible choices in the face of competing objectives. What remains is a need to probe the feasible area for an accommodative policy style in the years ahead. If a cooperative U.S. stance toward black African aspirations is both symbolically and substantively rewarding, its noninterventionist thrust may nevertheless seem to be inadequate because of the deeply conflicting interests present in the world. Even so, the priorities statesmen set as between competing objectives are not fixed, but depend on the circumstances. The historical responsibilities and the critical nature of U.S. interests differ markedly as between diverse parts of the world. Thus, even though President Carter asserts a determination on the part of the United States to protect its interests and its friends globally, wide regional variations are apparent in applying this general formulation. Hence Africa's lack of direct threat to U.S. security interests may, in the final analysis, be the basis for its relative freedom of maneuver in a world of otherwise limited international choices.

ELEMENTS OF CONTEXT

The perceptions of interests and capabilities held by key U.S. decision makers in the formative years from 1946 to 1976 led directly to policies of minimalism and caution toward Africa. The styles of different administrations were distinctive; but their substantive involvements, with their various emphases upon stability and gradualism, entailed consistent support for the international economic system. None of this is to raise doubts about the genuineness of the backing for national self-determination and independence in the 1950s and early 1960s but only to put the values of decision makers into perspective. Once the overriding U.S. concern for the constancy and vitality of the world capitalist order is understood, the preferences of particular policy makers (e.g., on avoiding any significant disruption of Euro-African linkages or supporting moderates in Zaire, Kenya, and Zambia) become comprehensible.

The United States inclines toward a status quo outlook (i.e., in Hans Morgenthau's sense of taking the measures necessary to maintain the current distribution of power) as a consequence of its political, strategic, and material interests in Africa and of the capabilities at its disposal.[2] Its interests in Africa are real but limited: to promote values on human rights and racial justice, to secure diplomatic support at the United Nations and other multilateral bodies, to gain strategic advantage (e.g., tracking station and port facilities), to obtain raw materials and commodities, and to promote trade and investment.

The United States imports vitally needed platinum, chromium, asbestos, fluorine, antimony, and vanadium from South Africa; mica from Malagasy; cobalt from Zaire; tantalum from Nigeria and Zaire; manganese from Gabon, South Africa, and Zaire; and petroleum from Angola and Nigeria. The dependence of the U.S. economy on African raw material sources has increased noticeably in the 1970s. In particular, crude petroleum imports from all countries have risen from 29 percent in 1972 to about half of current U.S. total oil usage, and in the first six months of 1977 the Nigerian contribution of 223 million barrels (18.1 percent of crude petroleum imports) had climbed to second place after Saudi Arabia, with 261 million barrels.[3] The significance of increasing trade with, and raw materials imports from, black Africa has a noticeable impact on U.S. priorities on the southern African question. The objective of sustaining the international economy in black Africa leads policy makers to urge a tilt away from the white-dominated regimes of southern Africa on the grounds of promoting the egalitarian values of American society, as well as current perceptions of national self-interest. Yet the implementation of such a change in priorities occurs only gradually, a reflection of persisting economic, social, and cultural ties between the white communities of the West and southern Africa; middle Africa's still limited economic influence on the world system; and the continuing importance of South Africa as a mineral supplier to the world's industrialized states.[4] Given these structural constraints, the northern tier industrialized states can be expected to move cautiously toward putting effective economic sanctions into operation.

It is also becoming increasingly apparent that American capabilities are more circumscribed than once recognized, adding further impetus to a status quo orientation. Substantial imbalances in international trading accounts, the declining value of the dollar, and continuing federal budgetary deficits have all contributed to a mood of caution on external commitments. The budget deficit for fiscal year 1975 was $43,604 million, and the estimated deficits for fiscal 1976 and 1977 were $76,001 million and $42,975 million. Of total projected outlays of $325 billion in 1975, only

$5.4 billion (or 1.7 percent) was spent on foreign (military and economic) assistance in all the developing countries. And during the thirty-year period following World War II, Africa, which witnessed only one major East-West military engagement (the Congo [Zaire]), was in a poor position to compete with domestic and other foreign claimants for foreign aid funds. As a consequence, the United States ranked fourteenth among the noncommunist developed countries providing aid to all foreign lands in 1974; it allocated .23 percent of its gross national product to such purposes, considerably less than the UN target figure of .7 percent or Portugal's actual disbursements of .59 percent, France's .58, Sweden's .56, the Netherlands' .54, and so forth.[5] Declining fiscal capabilities were thus reflected in total expenditures committed abroad (although trends in aid expenditures favored Africa relative to other regions in the mid-1970s) and meant that the United States, in comparison with other powers, would become a less active agency of change than had heretofore been assumed.

These budgetary constraints on policy making were related, more or less directly, to shifting psychological and political capabilities. Thus the fact of fiscal imbalance gained political impact (and often a disproportionate one) as affected by attitudinal responses. Certainly political leaders were highly sensitive to the implications of fiscal and resource limitations. For example, Governor (later Vice-President) Nelson Rockefeller, warning in part against overspending abroad, described the United States as "close to being dangerously overcommitted." [6] The sense of strain indicated here, whether soundly based or not, reduces national determination (and capabilities), causing policy makers to shun weighty commitments and to prefer stability to revolutionary change.

MINIMAL ENGAGEMENT, 1946–76

By current Carter administration standards, all the governments in the previous thirty-year period adopted low-profile stances toward Africa. In the late 1950s, as self-government and independence seemed imminent, American spokesmen, anxious to avoid any disruption of the world economic order, encouraged African leaders to retain close ties with Europe after the transfer of power. "We support African political aspirations," a former U.S. assistant secretary of state declared in 1959, "when they are moderate, nonviolent, and constructive and take into account their obligations to and interdependence with the world community. We also support the principle of continued African ties with Western Europe." [7] If forced to choose between these objectives, a preference for international stability and orderly transition seemed apparent. In addition, the Eisenhower years were marked by a striking lack of concern for African sensitivities. Not only did the Eisenhower administration abstain at the United Nations on the vote in 1960 on the Declaration on the Granting of Independence to Colonial Countries and Peoples, but it remained largely isolated from the new African leadership, interacting as little as possible with the new African leaders at the UN or at White House receptions.[8]

As the trauma of independence came and went in the early 1960s, American policy makers began increasingly to accept the new world of African states and deal with them directly. Kennedy, bypassing European capitals as necessary, strove to build effective independent relations with nationalist leaders. "Mali and Guinea," he asserted, "show the power of nationalism to overcome an initial commitment to communism." [9] The style of politics had taken something of a turn (neutralism was no longer viewed as immoral), but the fundamental thrust (competition with Soviet expansion) remained unaltered. The United States continued to adhere to its basic objective of maintaining the Western-led international system, and its support for the UN initiative in the Congo was interpreted as a sign of the Kennedy administration's resolve in this regard. At the same time, it was determined to foster linkages based on common values rather than demand solidarity grounded on adherence to a narrow doctrinal formula of anticommunism.

If the Kennedy administration made conscious efforts to identify with African aspirations and establish personal ties with a variety of African leaders, radicals as well as moderates, the Johnson administration moved steadily toward the center, both in its policy positions and in its preference for reformist-inclined leaders, such as Mobutu Sese Seko and Jomo Kenyatta. Evidently, the Johnson administration adopted a low-profile stance on major African issues. This position might be largely explained by its preoccupation with the Vietnam conflict. With material and psychic resources heavily committed to Southeast Asia, there was little inclination to become embroiled in new regions or issues that could, it seemed, be safely left to future leaders. Hence the Johnson administration refused, on the grounds of economic viability, to be drawn into the proposed Tanzam Railway project and backed Prime Minister Harold Wilson's indecisive Rhodesian policy.

During the ensuing Nixon and Ford administrations, it is possible to distinguish two periods in African policy: Kissinger phase I, which lasted from President Nixon's inauguration in 1969 until the spring 1976 change in policy; and Kissinger phase II, which followed. As with his predecessor, Kissinger found himself taken up with the Vietnam war during much of phase I; this, plus his inclination toward "benign neglect," led him to become engaged only minimally with African issues. Nevertheless a policy tilt to the right was to become manifest. Not only did Kissinger I prefer an alignment with moderate and conservative African leaders, but he pursued policies that had the effect of identifying the United States with white racist regimes in southern Africa. In this, it would appear that Kissinger I accepted the major premise of National Security Study Memorandum 39 to the effect that "the whites [of southern Africa] are here to stay and the only way that constructive change can come about is through them." [10] Following from this premise, NSSM 39s option 2 called for a "selective relaxation of our stance toward the white regimes." The proponents of this line of argument assumed that a moderation of U.S. rhetoric and measures would encourage economic growth along with peaceful change. Although it is not clear that Kissinger embraced option 2 in its entirety, a series of actions did ensue that gave every indication of a pronounced policy tilt in this direction. Thus President Nixon failed to offer resolute leadership to Congress in opposition to the Byrd amendment, thereby acquiescing in the passage of legislation in 1971 that permitted the United States to import Rhodesian chrome and other "strategic and critical materials" in direct violation of UN sanctions. [11]

Another indication of a policy tilt was the partial relaxation of the arms embargo. The government and its Export-Import Bank allowed a variety of components, spare parts, and instruments that had military potential to be shipped to the Portuguese and South Africans. In 1971 and 1972, for example, the Nixon administration authorized the sale of two Boeing 707s and two Boeing 747s to Portugal, as well as an assortment of helicopters and other dual-purpose equipment; and in early 1974 Secretary Kissinger is said to have approved the sale of Hawk and Sea Sparrow missiles, C-130 aircraft, and small vessels to the colonial regime. Even though the United States did comply for the most part with the 1963 UN arms embargo against South Africa, it nevertheless stretched the loophole on civilian exports in such a way as to allow for the sale of such items as the Boeing 747 Jumbo jets (used effectively to ferry troops during the fighting in Angola), six L-100 transports (the civilian version of the military C-130), and an extensive military and intelligence system for ship surveillance.[12]

U.S. voting patterns in the UN further exemplified the modified Kissinger I stance on southern African questions. In the early 1970s, U.S. representatives at the UN General Assembly repeatedly voted in opposition to its allies in Africa and Western Europe on resolutions antagonistic to apartheid and colonialism. To be sure, President Nixon ritualistically denounced white racism in southern Africa in his various foreign affairs messages, but the unifying thrust of his policies made it equally apparent that orderly change was emphasized at least as strongly as the ending of apartheid. Symbolically, the United States was to cast its first veto in the Security Council in March 1970 on a resolution condemning Britain for failure to overthrow by force the illegal white-minority regime in Rhodesia. In 1972 it joined with the United Kingdom, Portugal, and South Africa to vote against a resolution (Res. 2923E) that called on all states to implement fully the UN arms embargo against South Africa, described sanctions as necessary for changing the South African situation, and stated its support for the internal opponents of the South African regime and the legitimacy of their struggle against apartheid "by all available means." The following year it joined with Portugal, South Africa, France, and the United Kingdom to oppose a resolution of the General Assembly (Res. 3163) reaffirming the legitimacy of the struggle by colonial peoples for self-determination and independence "by all the necessary means at their disposal" and called on members to provide them with moral and material assistance. Then in 1974 the United States found itself isolated and alone as it voted in the General Assembly against a much strengthened arms embargo against South Africa (Res. 3324).[13]

The Kissinger I rejection, in principle, of violent change and its insistence on bringing about reform *within* the existing structure of interstate relations represented a pronounced policy tilt in favor of the white-led regimes of southern Africa. This conclusion was not lost on South African observers, and by 1976 they had come to look to the major Western powers, and the United States in particular, for critically needed support against majoritarian pressures in the United Nations.[14] The Western tilt in the UN, then, was interpreted similarly in both white and black Africa. Its consequence was to isolate the United States and to bring it into opposition with a majority of the world's states.

FROM MINIMAL ENGAGEMENT TO CONFRONTATION

Confrontation could not, however, be contained to the United Nations, and was soon to become apparent with respect to African policy generally. In American eyes, the gravity of the conflict over Angola represented a broadened challenge to the world system they sought to uphold. As Secretary Kissinger declared: "If a continent such as Africa . . . can be made the arena for great power ambitions, if immense quantities of arms can affect far-off events, if large expeditionary forces can be transported at will to dominate virtually helpless people—then all we have hoped for in building a more stable and rational international order is in jeopardy." For Kissinger, global stability required the maintenance of some form of equilibrium between the major external actors. Hence, if the Soviet Union moved outside their immediate orbit and intervened in African affairs—sending some $200 million in military equipment, supporting teams of military technicians and advisers, and some 11,000 Cuban combat troops—it became necessary for the United States, as the leader of the noncommunist nations, to use its strength to back its allies within Angola. "While constantly seeking opportunities for conciliation," Kissinger said, "we need to demonstrate to potential adversaries that cooperation is the only rational alternative." [15] Once a military initiative of any sort was precluded by passage of the Tunney amendment in the Senate, however, U.S. diplomatic action to restore the local balance became ineffective. For the proponents of a confrontationist stance, American power had "retreated" in the face of a major African challenge. American resolve, suffering from what Rustin and Gershman portrayed as "post-Vietnam paralysis," had failed to stop what they concluded was the "expansion of totalitarianism." [16] In a repeat of the domino theory, the confrontationists contended that the implications of this action would not be lost on U.S. allies in Africa, such as Zaire and Zambia, whose reliance on the West had led to a "defeat" on the Angola issue. [17]

In resisting the argument for confrontation, why did a large segment of informed U.S. opinion remain unpersuaded on the utility of such an approach in Angola? No one seriously questioned Angola's importance as a supplier of raw materials or its strategic significance, lying alongside indispensable sea routes to Europe. How, then, explain the lethargy of opinion formers in the face of a global challenge? In the large, the paralysis-of-will argument seems less convincing than a generalized feeling, expressed in varying forms, that the limits of accommodation, with Africa *and* with the Soviet Union, had not yet been reached. One need look no farther than the (far from successful) Mayaguez incident of 1975 to find a deep reservoir of public support for an active President, at least on a short-term basis; on that occasion, approval for the way President Ford handled his job rose 11 percent nationally and 15 percent among the college-educated segment of the population. [18] Americans had not lost the will to act, but perhaps only a sense of certainty that Angola was the right involvement, at the right place, and at the right time.

An examination of the *Congressional Record* and the hearings held by the Senate

Subcommittee on African Affairs of the Committee on Foreign Relations reveals wide opposition to the official position on the necessity for preventive action. The Tunney amendment of December 19, 1975, allowed the use of funds under the defense appropriation bill to be programmed for intelligence-gathering operations in Angola but not to supply military equipment or trained personnel assistance to the hard-pressed forces of UNITA (the National Union for the Total Independence of Angola) or FNLA (the National Liberation Front of Angola). Downplaying the global dimensions of the crisis, Senator Tunney declared that it would be a disastrous policy for the United States to become engaged in military action, either directly or through proxies, in the Angola war, and Senator Kennedy drew an analogy to earlier defense appropriations for Vietnam. When put to a vote, the Tunney amendment was upheld in the Senate by a majority of 54 to 22.

A month later, the Kissinger doctrine of confrontation again received short shrift when it was discussed by the Senate Subcommittee on African Affairs. Subcommittee Chairman Dick Clark, responding generally to the secretary of state's concern over U.S. credibility as a major power should it refuse to demonstrate its resolve in Angola, remarked that "the administration's goal of achieving a military stalemate is no longer a meaningful option." He explained: "Unless the United States is prepared to send troops and advisers—and they have said they are not—or to strongly assist the South African troops to reenter Angola in large numbers—which also seems very unrealistic—it seems doubtful that achieving a stalemate is a very meaningful option." Clark warned against another option (i.e., sending further military assistance to the FNLA and UNITA) and urged instead the opening of serious discussions with the MPLA (the Popular Movement for the Liberation of Angola).[19] Thus Clark and the majority of his committee perceived American interests in terms of accommodating to the fact of MPLA power, not engaging in a costly, losing struggle against such a force, backed as it was by a global superpower. Two forms of *Realpolitik* were engaged head-on, and in this instance the confrontationalists were to fail.

KISSINGER CHANGES TACK: FROM CONFRONTATION TO ACCOMMODATION

By 1976, Kissinger became anxious over the growing costs of confrontation with its resulting isolation. In this sense, the Angola crisis had proved a watershed in U.S.–African relations. It was now evident to the secretary of state that minimal engagement with a tilt toward white Africa was increasingly counterproductive. Being the realist that he was, he altered his approach so as to adapt to the emergent forces on the continent. Thus was born phase II of Kissinger's African policy and its rationale, in North-South relations, of a movement from confrontation to cooperation. A change toward conciliation was deemed essential in order to moderate mounting Third World hostility. In Kissinger's words, "The radicalization of the Third World and its consolidation into an antagonistic bloc is neither in our political nor our economic interest. A world of hostile blocs is a world of tension and disorder." [20] Kissinger therefore sought to avoid a possibly costly collision of wills, one that might prove disruptive of the primary U.S. objective—maintaining the world economic system.

To this larger end, Kissinger redesigned U.S. policy toward southern Africa and set out in April to bring this message in person to African leaders. His aims were clear: to avoid a race war, ward off foreign intervention, promote peaceful coopera- tion among the communities in southern Africa, and prevent the radicalization of Africa. He regarded the danger as real that moderately inclined African states would be driven in a radical direction, losing confidence in Western capacity to stem the tide of possible Soviet-Cuban interventions such as that in Angola. The United States therefore sought to offer a nonviolent alternative to the festering conflict in Rhodesia (i.e., a negotiated settlement). The new African initiative was by no means an abandonment of *Realpolitik;* rather, it was conceived as a response "to a danger- ously deteriorating situation." [21]

The new Kissinger tack of 1976 had political and economic dimensions. For the secretary of state, the matter of most urgent concern to Africans was the question of Rhodesia; in Lusaka, Zambia, on April 27, he set forth a ten-point program aimed at facilitating negotiations and blocking external encroachment. Kissinger called for the establishment of majority rule prior to independence and asserted that it must be achieved within two years after negotiations had been concluded. In order to underline his commitment to this objective, he outlined the following program of action: a warning to the Smith regime that it could not expect U.S. diplomatic or material support in its conflict with the African states or liberation movements; a direct communication to the Salisbury regime stressing the urgency of a rapidly negotiated settlement; a promise to press for the repeal of the Byrd amendment; an effort to discourage American travel to and residence in Rhodesia; a declared will- ingness to provide $12.5 million to beleaguered Mozambique to assist that country to meet the costs it incurred in closing the border with Rhodesia; a willingness to help alleviate the economic hardship of other African countries neighboring Rhodesia which close their frontiers in order to enforce the sanctions program; a preparedness to consider sympathetically requests for assistance for refugees from Rhodesia; a readiness to provide support to the people of Rhodesia during the transition to majority rule; and, finally, a stated interest in furthering the peace- making process by contributing to the creation of a constitutional structure that would protect minority rights while establishing majority rule. Kissinger, recogniz- ing that the war had already started in southern Africa, was now in a position to hold out the olive branch to his critics. As he told the 31st session of the UN General Assembly: "An opportunity to pull back from the brink now exists." [22]

Kissinger also included the Namibian question in his broad reference to pulling back from the brink. Fearing that violence might escalate if the illegal South African occupation lingered on, Kissinger sought to promote movement toward a rapidly concluded settlement while an opportunity for bargaining still availed. In his Lusaka address, he described this as a propitious time for negotiations, an optimism based largely on signs from Pretoria that he interpreted as favorable for a peaceful transi- tion to Namibian independence. Consequently, convinced that a peaceful solution to the Namibian question could be worked out, Kissinger announced an American position including the following elements: a new appeal to the South African government to permit all people and groups in Namibia to express their views freely, under UN supervision, on their country's political future; a call to the South African government to announce a definite timetable for the achievement of self-determination acceptable to the world community; a statement that the United States would be prepared to work with the international community, and especially with African leaders, to determine further steps toward Namibian independence; and a declaration that the United States would ease its restrictions on trade and investment in Namibia as well as provide economic and technical assistance to Namibia once concrete movement toward self-determination was under way. The United States explicitly ruled out support for violent solutions to the Namibian dispute, but it was fully prepared to accommodate black African demands by facilitating a peaceful transition to independence in that country.

In the case of South Africa, Kissinger drew an important distinction between that country and Rhodesia and Namibia, not on the principle of majority rule but of external colonial domination. "It represents a legitimate government which carries out practices with which we disagree," he contended. Since this was viewed as a "different phenomenon" from that of Rhodesia and Namibia, it required a "different sort of influence" on the part of the United States.[23] In phase II, Kissinger explicitly disapproved of apartheid and described change as inevitable. He refused to intervene openly and strongly in the struggle against institutionalized racism in that country, however, cautiously leaving the solution of South Africa's internal affairs to domestic pressures, assisted externally by means of "quiet diplomacy." Kissinger's careful handling of South Africa involved more than a recognition of its uniqueness. It also was predicated on an immediate need to secure the cooperation of the Vorster government in smoothing the way toward majority rule in Rhodesia and Namibia. Hence goals were tempered by strategic necessity. Kissinger's pragmatism was apparent in his Lusaka address: "In the immediate future the Republic of South Africa can show its dedication to Africa—and its potential contribution to Africa— by using its influence in Salisbury to promote a rapid negotiated settlement for majority rule in Rhodesia. This, we are sure, would be viewed positively by the community of nations, as well as by the rest of Africa." [24] Thus, in something of a "tacit bargain," [25] Kissinger held out the possibility of respectability, even international legitimacy, to an apprehensive South Africa while attempting to extract critically needed support for majority rule in the peripheral areas of the southern African system. State Department officials were careful to emphasize that this appeal for South African cooperation did not involve any trades or concessions on either side.[26] Perhaps no quid pro quos were asked or offered, but a mutually advantageous exchange of interests can reasonably be read into the relationship. South Africa benefited by having its future separated from those of Rhodesia and Namibia, and the United States succeeded in securing support for systemic change in the region at minimal cost to itself. Kissinger had effectively linked South Africa to the wider strategy of accommodation; in doing so, he had redefined the southern African question, but to no one's full liking.

The response to the Lusaka initiative was mixed. To be sure, Kissinger did signal a new departure in American policy on southern Africa. Although the supportive aspects of this change were warmly appreciated by such leaders as Kenneth Kaunda, the secretary's host in Zambia, responses elsewhere were less than the "universally positive" Kissinger described to the Senate Foreign Relations Committee on May 13, 1976. Tanzania's government-owned *Daily News,* while welcoming the Lusaka initiative in cautious terms, went on to warn that war was still the only means of liberating Rhodesia. In English-speaking West Africa the response was more diffident. Nigerian authorities called off the Kissinger visit to Lagos, declaring the time to be "inconvenient" because of "other commitments of the Nigerian leaders." [27] In Ghana, where the invitation to pay a call was withdrawn on short notice, pressures exerted by the local intelligentsia and militant pan-African opinion from outside the country doubtlessly played a part in the final outcome.[28] Although Kissinger himself described the character of the American relationship with black Africa as transformed following the Lusaka initiative, it is important, in view of subsequent efforts at accommodation by the Carter administration, to note that U.S. credibility and respect were at a decidedly low ebb at this point.

The second dimension to the "agenda of cooperation" outlined by Kissinger at Lusaka dealt with Africa's economic future. Kissinger's proposals, "aimed at providing moderate African states with positive programs," [29] included the following: an "urgent" study of a new aid program for Africa; programs to deal with natural disasters and sharp swings in commodity and mineral prices (resource development, buffer stocks, and earnings stabilization); and such long-term efforts to develop the region as the training of local manpower, the transformation of rural life, the application of advanced technology, and the establishment of a modern transportation system. These measures were further elaborated in Nairobi, where Kissinger called for the establishment of an International Resources Bank with an initial capital fund of $1 billion to "help insure supplies of raw materials to sustain the expansion of the global economy and help moderate commodity price fluctuations." [30] In addition, Kissinger proposed a case-by-case effort to improve conditions of trade and investment in a variety of commodities, steps to stabilize the export earnings of developing countries, the expansion of trade in raw materials and processed goods, and a rapid and effective transfer of technology to developing countries. Clearly the United States sought in early 1976 to regain the momentum in U.S.–African relations, as well as to thwart a possible confrontation of great magnitude between North and South.

With objectives and strategy in hand, Kissinger turned to implementation. Some early indications were encouraging: Smith's willingness—even eagerness—to negotiate; [31] signs of receptiveness on the part of the African front-line state and liberation movement leaderships; Vorster's public proclamation, following his June meeting with Kissinger, of support for majority rule in Rhodesia, as well as his behind-the-scenes pressures on Smith after their September talks in Zurich; and the proposal, by the constitutional conference on Namibia, of the date of December 31, 1978, for that country's independence and majority rule. Both the U.S. State Department and African nationalist opinion criticized the Namibian proposals as not going far enough because they failed to provide for a procedure by which all "authentic" groups could participate in the deliberations.

On September 11, 1976, as Kissinger prepared to set out for Africa again, he represented himself to the press as a detached facilitator having no special position and no "American plan" in hand. Nevertheless, the series of private talks he was to hold with the "front-line" heads of state of Angola, Botswana, Mozambique, Tanzania, and Zambia, liberation movement leaders, and Prime Ministers Vorster and Smith on the Rhodesian issue revealed the existence of a framework for negotiations, if not the bare outline of a possible solution. The most critical negotiations took place in Pretoria on September 19. It was clearly a case of asymmetrical exchange. At the first meeting, held at the U.S. ambassador's residence, Kissinger, who was well briefed on the Rhodesian security situation, started by asking Smith a series of piercing questions on how he could be rescued now or in the future since he had lost the support of the United States and South Africa. Faced with three bleak intelligence reports on the matter, Smith responded by asking what Kissinger expected of him. Kissinger thereupon produced a set of proposals for majority rule and independence that purportedly had been cleared with the African front-line presidents. After an adjournment, the negotiators, joined by Vorster, reassembled at the prime minister's official residence, "Libertas," where the surrender procedure ensued. In Smith's plaintive words, "All I have to offer is my own head on a platter." [32]

From this point forward, events moved quickly toward putting the Kissinger package into effect. Smith's confidence in Kissinger's control over events was enhanced by a secret message of September 21. In it, the U.S. secretary of state suggested, rather ambiguously, that on the basis of discussions with black leaders in Lusaka and Dar es Salaam, he believed that provisions allowing for whites to retain the headship of the defense and law and order ministries could "be added" to the five-point package agreed on in Pretoria.[33] Smith thereupon carried out his part of the Pretoria agreement. In a broadcast on September 24, he noted the overwhelming pressure placed by Kissinger and Vorster on his government but nonetheless announced his "surrender terms." [34] The major points set out by Smith were the following: a commitment to majority rule within two years; a proposal to meet with African leaders immediately to organize an interim government; a statement on the Council of State's membership (half black, half white) under the interim government as well as its functions of legislation, general supervisory responsibility, and supervision of the drafting of the constitution; an outline of the Council of Ministers' composition (a majority of Africans, with the portfolios of defense and of law and order reserved for whites during the transition period), decisional process (two thirds majority), and functions (delegated legislative authority and executive responsibility); an assertion that sanctions would be lifted and all acts of warfare would cease upon the establishment of the interim government; and a declaration on the creation of an externally based trust fund to assure Rhodesians about the economic future of their country and about the effects on themselves of the changes currently taking place.

These terms represented a significant concession to Anglo–American–South African power. They did not bring an end to confrontation in the region. Ian Smith's summary of the agreement negotiated with Kissinger was immediately criticized by nationalist leaders and front-line presidents as involving serious exaggerations and misinterpretations. In particular, African leaders denied having agreed to provisions allowing the ministries of defense and law and order to remain in white hands; moreover, they described Smith's emphasis on the functions and powers assigned to the Council of State, with its heavy participation of white interests, as a "factual misconception." Certainly a comparison of the proposals given to Joshua Nkomo, president of the Zimbabwe African People's Union section of the African National Council, and the terms described by Smith substantially support the contention that Smith exaggerated the role of the Council of State when describing the Kissinger accord.[35] As a result of this dissatisfaction, the five black African presidents, meeting in Lusaka, issued a statement that ruled out an end to the struggle on the basis of the Kissinger agreement. They hailed the freedom fighters for having "forced the enemy to accept majority rule as a condition for immediate independence" and called on the British government to convene a conference outside Zimbabwe (Rhodesia) to discuss the transition to genuine independence.[36] Thus, despite Kissinger's "categorical assurance" on a lifting of sanctions and a cessation of terrorism as soon as an interim government was formed, the front-line presidents reaffirmed their commitment to further military action.

Although London authorities responded quickly and positively to the front-line president's request that the British government convene a conference outside Zimbabwe, it soon became apparent that the gulf between white and black Africa remained as wide as ever. In part, the differences that emerged at Geneva were attributable to a lack of clarity on both sides over what commitments had been made on the Kissinger package. On the one hand, black leadership, particularly the militant Patriotic Front (which combines sections of Joshua Nkomo's Zimbabwe African People's Union and Robert Mugabe's Zimbabwe African National Union), rejected the Kissinger proposals as a basis for the transition to independence. Instead the Patriotic Front demanded full powers for the liberation movement in the interim government, as well as control over the army and police. On the other hand, Ian Smith contended that the Kissinger settlement was not negotiable. "If you open the package," he argued, "then the whole package is open for negotiation." The British chairman, Ivor Richard, desperately seeking ways to facilitate an exchange among the rivaling parties, stated that Britain regarded the Kissinger proposals as "reasonable basis for discussion and negotiation," and not a package deal as such.[37] This interpretation received backing from Kissinger, who informed a television audience that the front-line presidents had accepted only the basic framework for negotiations, not the critical details of his plan.[38] The package had become unwrapped. Various alternative schemes were advanced as the deliberations ensued, but by the end of November it had become clear to all parties that this latest Anglo-American effort had not brought an end to the conflict. Kissinger's diplomatic efforts had moved the various groups toward an accepted formula of majority rule, albeit somewhat guilefully, but confrontation in southern Africa remained evident.

CARTER'S "LIBERAL INTERNATIONALISM"

The Carter administration's advent to power marked something of a shift in U.S. foreign policy style. Highly moralistic in tone and pro-black in inclination, it sought to fashion a "liberal" African approach that would shun mechanical cold-war responses to African issues and put the United States in step with black aspirations on that continent. If, in substance, there was considerable continuity with the policy outlined by Kissinger II, the "principled pragmatism" of the Carter administration meant a more concerted effort to reconcile the symbols of idealism with fundamental status quo purposes. In striving to project a positive and supportive image to black Africa, good intentions became more than moral imperatives; they were also resources that enabled a Vietnam-weary America to find renewed faith in itself and helped to restore America's liberal reputation around the globe.[39] The move to accommodation was now explicit and unmistakable.

As applied to the Third World, Carter's "liberal internationalism" brought together some of the diverse strands in the current American outlook: the desire to minimize military commitments overseas, the inclination toward loosening old alliances and establishing new relationships, the ambition to reallocate the world's wealth so as to achieve greater equality of opportunity, the demand for racial justice and human rights, and the encouragement of an open economic system the world over. By freeing Americans from what President Carter described as "that inordinate fear of Communism which once led us to embrace any dictator who joined us in our fear," the liberal internationalist was able to "rise above narrow national interests and work together to solve . . . formidable global problems." [40] Hence the liberal internationalist, who denied that liberal formulas could survive for long if limited to a prosperous, industrialized Western community of states, sought to universalize certain elements of Western political and economic experience. In very altered circumstances, a global initiative was again seen as necessary to make the world safe for democracy.

Perhaps no African initiative better illustrates the inherent globalism in the Carter approach than that toward South Africa. Whereas Kissinger had adopted a step-by-step strategy for dealing with the southern African question, separating out the issues dealing with Rhodesia, Namibia, and South Africa into distinct negotiating tracks, the Carter administration tended to apply a single regional solution to the problem of white-minority dominance. It eschewed any compromise with racism and universalized its attack on white domination in the region as a whole. The intention here was commendable and a resource in terms of fostering accommodation with black Africa; however, practical questions of strategy were soon forthcoming. For example, a London *Times* editorial described the change in foreign policy style as follows: "Before he became President, Mr. Jimmy Carter came out . . . wholeheartedly for democratic majority rule—black governments—throughout southern Africa. This means that he has nothing much to offer Mr. Vorster in exchange for sacrificing the Rhodesians—a card Dr. Kissinger kept in his hand for what it was worth. In his diplomacy the prospect that the United States would regard South Africa as 'different' in its evolution towards racial justice as distinct from Rhodesia or Namibia was preserved. Now Mr. Vorster seems to have to choose only between black rule and war with the marxists." [41] Certainly the options were wider than this would indicate. Some of the early administration rhetoric no doubt did suggest a simple, comprehensive approach, but subsequent statements and behavior have shown increasing recognition of the greater complexity of the South African problem. Even so, to the extent that Carter has denied South Africa a special place in U.S. peace-making efforts (and he seems ambiguous on this point), he has risked

foregoing the limited leverage that South Africa might bring to bear in the Rhodesian and Namibian conflicts to gain a morally consistent regional policy. It remained
to be seen whether strategy could efficiently facilitate objectives. Either Carter
could now compensate for this loss of influence by wielding a more powerful stick
against all these states simultaneously or he could suffer an embarrassing loss of face
on the continent generally.

Much of the idealism of the Carter style lay embedded in its tendency to universalize issues of political and social rights. What, then, of claims to economic equality
among countries? Here the liberal internationalist view was less aggressive in its
crusading zeal. No doubt such caution reflected the constraints imposed by the
domestic economy, mired as it was by stagflation, a decline abroad in the value of the
dollar, and budgetary deficits. Yet Africa did manage to gain a higher priority from
Carter policy makers in its aid disbursements (however, even with such increases,
U.S. assistance remained far behind a number of other countries in relation to GNP:
e.g., Sweden, France, Canada, and various Arab states). Mrs. Goler T. Butcher, the
assistant administrator of the Bureau of African Affairs for USAID, told a congressional black caucus workshop that economic assistance to Africa would amount to 9
percent of the total AID budget in 1977, more than twice the level of assistance over
the previous three years. In 1978, U.S. assistance to Africa was expected to rise to
17 percent of the total AID budget.[42] Moreover, in June 1977 the North-South
conference in Paris agreed in principle to set up a common fund for commodity
price stabilization, leaving to subsequent negotiators the task of hammering out a
final agreement on the specific purposes and objectives involved.

The Carter administration economic policy toward Africa, therefore, was more
generous in aid disbursements, more prepared to participate in cooperative efforts
aimed at leveling out fluctuations in commodity prices, and more willing to accept
diverse models of economic development. Yet at heart it remained committed to an
open international trading system—and, consequently, strongly opposed to any
preferential trading arrangements between Africa and other regions of the world
that had the effect of limiting U.S. access to markets abroad. In traditional American
terms, free trade was described by Carter policy formers as a means of promoting
the long-term development of the world's resources, providing lower prices and
greater choice for consumers, and increasing the opportunities for producers
throughout the globe. The Carter thrust would be toward pushing "vigorously" for
trade liberalizing measures in its future negotiations.[43] Freer trade would link the
United States more securely than ever to the world; and the free market system, to
the extent that it could be legitimatized in Africa, would bind these countries to the
open international economy.

In this, perhaps the foremost exponent of a free market system in the African
context was Ambassador Andrew Young. Speaking to a dinner meeting of some two
hundred South African businessmen in Johannesburg, Young spoke of the need "to
expand and improve an economic order, to draw into the system an entire population that otherwise would grow disaffected and turn to some other system." The
needs of South Africa would not be served best by radical change, but by the free
market system; this could bring about a nonviolent, productive, and humane change
"better than any other so-called revolutionary system going." In sum, stated Young,

"my argument boils down to my conviction that the free market systems can be the greatest force for constructive change now operating anywhere in the world." [44] Thus the global advocacy of human rights was joined, in a more hesitant manner, by a global advocacy of a free market system and an open international economic order.

Carter's idealism, with its pronounced tilt toward black African interests, involved a morality tempered by prudence. Recognizing that the benefits of accommodation outweighed the costs of intransigence, the Carter administration pursued the course of cooperation more zealously and more effectively than did its predecessor. Both domestic and international pressures propelled the new administration in an accommodative direction. On the domestic side, at least three groups—the professional Africanists, the black Americans, and the humanitarian, missionary-oriented middle-Americans—identify themselves strongly with liberal internationalist policies of accommodation toward black Africa. A fourth group, the apolitical businessmen, acts as a counterweight on certain selected issues (e.g., the Byrd amendment), but clearly can be influenced by a resolute government to see that its success in Africa rests with black regimes, not with white-minority rule.[45] With Carter's close electoral victory attributable in no small part to the black American constituency, this group, currently more informed and more aggressive on African questions and better led by old-line interests, as well as the congressional black caucus, than ever before, has emerged as an important element influencing the direction of policy on African-related issues. In this, the appointment of Andrew Young as ambassador to the United Nations is more than symbolic. Young's style, which may be characterized as highly accommodative to black African aspirations, has, with some notable exceptions, received considerable acceptance among professional policy makers and scholars at the UN, the National Security Council, the State Department's Africa Bureau and Policy Planning Staff, and elsewhere.[46] These organizations, deeply concerned over American association with southern African racial domination in the past, are generally determined to transform U.S. policy in an accommodative direction.

In addition to these domestic constituency pressures for an accommodative stance are changing official American perceptions of economic interest. As imports from southern Africa declined in the 1970s by comparison with black Africa (and particularly Nigeria), the high priority placed by the United States on maintaining the international economic system dictated a greater political effort to cooperate and identify with legitimate African demands. By 1975, the South African share of U.S.–African trade remained significant, but not of vital interest to U.S. policy makers. U.S. imports from South Africa during that year were $840 million, or roughly 10 percent of total imports from Africa and slightly less than 1 percent of total imports from all countries. In the same period, the United States exported some $1300 million in goods to South Africa, which was the equivalent of 30 percent of African exports and 1.4 percent of world exports.[47] Meanwhile trade relations expanded rapidly with the countries of black Africa. U.S. imports from black Africa (particularly crude petroleum from Nigeria) greatly surpassed that of South Africa, and, on the export side, the United States witnessed a swift rise in the sale of goods. Seven countries increased their imports from the United States by more than 50 percent (Nigeria, Zambia, Ivory Coast, Tanzania, Gabon, Cameroon, and Guinea) and another five showed 20–50 percent increases (Zaire, Ghana, Sudan, Liberia, and Ethiopia).[48] As William Foltz concludes regarding these changing trade patterns: *"to the degree* that foreign policy is conditioned directly by the desire to maintain good relations with countries which are strong economic partners, South African needs and desires should have some influence over United States policy, but that influence should have declined substantially during the 1970s by comparison with that of Nigeria." [49] Similarly with respect to American direct investment, the black African total ($1.8 billion in a total continental investment of $3.4 billion) was an actively expanding sector when compared with that of southern Africa.[50] The fact that much of U.S. investment in sub-Saharan Africa was directed toward the extractive sector points up the trans-African nature of U.S. strategic mineral sources. The consequences of this broad-based access to rare minerals are evident: it is essential that the United States adopt at least as sympathetic an attitude toward demands from black Africa as from white-dominated southern Africa (especially as change in the south is likely to be in the direction of majority rule). To do otherwise may be needlessly to risk future access, something which remains unlikely but not inconceivable.

Hence, emerging economic interests reinforce liberal predispositions in the United States on the southern African question, inclining Carter policy makers to identify as unequivocally as possible with black African claims. In this vein, no country has been courted in a more determined manner than Nigeria, one of the "new influentials" the Carter policy makers seek to align the United States with. Nigeria (with whom the United States did $5.7 billion in trade in 1976, or two thirds of the total with black Africa) began to reduce its past differences with the United States soon after the Carter administration came to office. For the Nigerians, "human degradation, oppressions and deprivation as rationalised and perpetuated in southern Africa by the racist regime there is a crime against which not only Africa, but also mankind as a whole must fight." [51] This, then, was a moral issue on which there could be no legitimate straddling by Western governments or corporations. To make this point definite, Nigerian officials declared that in granting new contracts they would henceforth discriminate against commercial business firms that continued to operate in Rhodesia and South Africa. The moral message was one the Carter administration could understand and sympathize with, and it responded by sending signals of support.[52] Nigeria appeared to accept Carter's sincerity on this issue, leading to an improvement in relations between the countries. For the strategy of accommodation, this restoring of a positive U.S.–Nigerian dialogue represented one of the major successes following from a reformulation of policy.

Because an accommodative policy style is particularly suitable to southern African issues, it is important to assess the Carter administration's aptitude in applying it to Rhodesia, Namibia, and South Africa. Accommodation utilized a broadly similar game plan in all three conflict situations: to come to terms, so far as possible, with moderate elements in advance of a radical takeover. What was desired was to establish regimes satisfactory to leaders in the independent African states that would be linked to the international economic order through Western capital, skills, and technology. It was in part a conscious application of the "Kenya model" to Rhodesia and Namibia in the immediate future, and, possibly in altered form, to the South African situation at a later date.

In the case of Rhodesia, a major achievement of the Carter accommodation stance came soon after taking office. The Carter administration, determined to demonstrate its unity with black African aspirations, urged Congress to move swiftly on legislation to overturn the Byrd amendment and to reimpose the ban on Rhodesian chrome imports. Strong congressional backing on this issue "would strengthen the hand of the new administration as it [tries] to reach an accommodation on the southern Africa problem in the United Nations," asserted Congressman Charles Diggs (D-Michigan).[53] Because the Carter lead on this legislation was unambiguous and effective, the Congress responded favorably; the Senate approved the measure (H.R. 1746) by a vote of 66 to 26, and the House passed the bill by a 250 to 146 vote—three days prior to Carter's March 17 address to the United Nations.

In the actual negotiations over Rhodesia's independence, however, Carter administration efforts to promote a progressive agreement lacked decisive impact. The Geneva conference, postponed on January 7, 1977, never reconvened. Instead, the various rivals pursued the negotiations on two separate tracks: the Anglo-American attempt at resolving the Rhodesian question on a basis satisfactory to all parties; and Prime Minister Smith's own venture at negotiating an internal settlement with the more moderate black leaders. The American initiative centered on the so-called Anglo-American plan laboriously hammered out by Andrew Young and David Owen, the British foreign secretary, in a series of meetings with the African front-line presidents and the contending Rhodesian parties. The plan included the surrender of power by the illegal Smith regime, a transitional administration under neutral administration, the presence of a UN force during the interim period, free and impartial elections on the basis of universal adult suffrage, a development fund to revive the economy, and an independence constitution providing for democratically elected government and the protection of individual human rights.[54]

Ian Smith and the South African leadership reacted negatively to the Anglo-American proposals. They objected to the demand that Smith resign the prime ministership to make it possible for Britain's Lord Carver to assume power as commissioner-general as well as to the provision that the future Zimbabwean army be based largely on the Patriotic Front guerrillas, with the present security forces being largely disbanded. Yet, despite this cold response, official American policy has thus far remained cautiously supportive of the Anglo-American approach. At a press conference in March 1978, President Carter reconfirmed that "the Anglo-American plan is the best basis for a permanent resolution of the Rhodesian or Zimbabwe question," and the following month, during the first state visit by an American President to any sub-Saharan African country, he told a Lagos audience that the United States would begin to explore for the earliest date when a conference of all Rhodesian factions could meet to work out an internationally acceptable formula.[55] Carter's reluctance to endorse the internal settlement, rejected widely by articulate African opinion at the UN and elsewhere, represented a concrete triumph of the Andrew Young line on accommodation. A new confrontation—including in part a defense of white interests—was anathema to liberal internationalist inclinations.

The second negotiating track, involving political exchanges within Rhodesia between Ian Smith and such moderate nationalists as the Reverend Ndabaningi Sithole, Bishop Abel Muzorewa, and Chief Jeremiah Chirau, was insulated from U.S. control. Fearful of the outcome of all-party negotiations, Smith seized the initiative and orchestrated the (partial) transfer of power. His commitment, in November 1977, to the principle of majority rule based on adult suffrage brought a positive response from moderate black leaders, who then endorsed "the desirability of retaining white confidence, and accepted Government's right to follow this course at the conference table." [56] The stage was set for meaningful negotiations leading to an "internal settlement."

After weeks of bargaining, the rivaling parties accepted terms providing for majority rule and elaborate minority safeguards. In an effort to assure white opinion, the black moderate leaders agreed to reserve 28 seats in a 100-member legislative assembly for whites, 20 of these being elected on a preferential system by whites only and the remaining 8 by a multiracial electorate following nomination by a white electoral college. This provision on reserved seats was guaranteed in the accord for a period of at least ten years or two parliaments, whichever was longer, and at the end of this time a commission would be appointed to make recommendations on further minority-group rights regarding the electoral process. Other guarantees—the independence of the judiciary; an independent public services board; freedom from interference in the public service, the police, and defense forces, and the prisons service; and guarantees on pensions and citizenship—were all to be regarded as specially entrenched provisions of the constitution. Such entrenched provisions could be amended only by a bill receiving at least seventy-eight affirmative votes, thus providing the white members with a "blocking vote" for a minimum of ten years. As Smith intended, the mutual veto was a guarantee of the status quo—if it could survive the majority's demands for transformation once the transfer of power had taken place.

The transitional government took office on March 21, 1978. Smith, chosen by lot, became the first chairman of a four-man executive council (which included Muzorewa, Chirau, and Sithole). The new regime, initially responsible for guiding Rhodesia to elections in the fall and to independence by year's end, had the difficult task of reconciling militant black nationalist opinion (the Patriotic Front) with a settlement that left white officials firmly in control of the coercive agencies of the state: the War Council, the civil service, the army, the police, and the judiciary. Thus, rather than accept the proposed general amnesty or plan to integrate into the armed forces (already four fifths black), the Patriotic Front leaders dismissed the internal accord as a fraud and called for continued armed struggle to end white rule in Rhodesia. In this, the Patriotic Front had strong international support. The internal settlement was rejected by the African front-line states and, prior to the signing of the accord, by the Organization of African Unity at its thirtieth ministerial council meeting in Tripoli. Then, in a vote of considerable symbolic importance, the Security Council approved a resolution in March declaring any Rhodesian settlement made under Smith's auspices to be "illegal and unacceptable." The depth of African feeling on the issue is evident from a speech made to the Security Council by Nigeria's Brigadier Joseph Garba, commissioner for external affairs. Describing the transitional government in Rhodesia as a " 'black-washed' racist regime," Garba stated that Africans "regarded the so-called internal settlement with utter contempt. We treated it as something contrived by the illegal racist regime with its cohorts in Pretoria in the hope of delaying its doom." [57]

The United States, which joined four other Western members in abstaining on the resolution, pulled back from the logic of accommodation. Despite the political dangers of a confrontation with black Africa (to say nothing of Andrew Young's warnings of the possibilities of a "black-on-black civil war"), some American opinion leaders (including former President Gerald Ford) nonetheless voiced support for the Salisbury accord as a legitimate effort at local self-determination. Moreover, in July 1978 the Senate voted a compromise resolution requiring the President to lift economic sanctions against Rhodesia once he determined that majority-rule elections had been held and a majority black government installed, and the Salisbury government had made a genuine effort to negotiate with the Patriotic Front. In the following month the House of Representatives went even further in endorsing the internal settlement; in a setback for U.S. efforts to encourage an all-party accord, the House members voted to lift economic sanctions against Rhodesia provided free and fair elections had been held in that country by the end of 1978. Hence, U.S. public opinion placed limits on the freedom of policy makers to exert further pressure on the various parties inside Rhodesia (African moderates and Smith) and outside (Patriotic Front, front-line presidents, and the South African government) to bring on the next stage in the negotiations. Because of right-wing demands within Rhodesia, it seemed apparent that Smith was limited in the concessions he could make prior to the constitutional referendum within the white community on the plan for majority rule. To be sure, he announced a willingness to participate in unrestricted negotiations during his controversial visit to the United States in October 1978. Prospects for an all-party conference all but disappeared immediately afterward, however, as the Rhodesian government launched a new military offensive against guerrilla camps in Zambia; not only were many lives sacrificed but also the likelihood of further Smith-Nkomo meetings. In his bitterness at the raid, Nkomo ruled out talks with Smith and participation by the Zimbabwe African People's Union in an all-party conference. Nevertheless, it does seem possible that once Muzorewa, Sithole, and Chirau are firmly ensconced in power after the April 1979 elections (made possible when 84 percent of the white Rhodesians voted in favor of the constitutional referendum in January 1979), new opportunities for formal political negotiations with Nkomo and Mugabe may become a practical course of action. In that event, the United States could remain consistent to its accommodative policy style by acting as a facilitator, helping the various parties and supporting interests promote an effective ongoing bargaining encounter.

With respect to Namibia, the United States pursued a course that roughly paralleled the course in Rhodesia. Again, a white-run administration, under severe military pressure from the South West Africa People's Organisation (SWAPO) and from African nationalist and world opinion generally, recognized the need to transfer power to a majority-backed regime by December 31, 1978. The critical question was which African group—moderate or militant nationalist—would come to power. Again, two paralleling sets of negotiations took place: "internally" between the territory's white leaders and moderate black representatives, and "internationally" between representatives for the South African government, SWAPO, and the five Western members of the UN Security Council (the United States, Britain, France, Canada, West Germany). Left to its own devices, the South African regime would clearly prefer to reach a settlement with the moderate African nationalists. As in Rhodesia, however, the United States and Britain have maintained that no settlement is likely to prove enduring that does not include full SWAPO participation in the independence government. In part at least, this Western preference for an all-party solution is based on global as well as continental considerations (e.g., the desire to close off southern Africa to possible Soviet-Cuban probes in concert with guerrilla incursions).

U.S. opposition to an internal settlement in Namibia has been unremitting. The South African-sponsored Turnhalle solution, which put forward a constitutional scheme based on ethnic representation in the National Assembly, was shelved by the South African government in June 1977. For Andrew Young, the Turnhalle approach was just another form of racism; [58] hence the plan was opposed by U.S. officials, who called instead for a negotiated agreement satisfactory to all factions.

To achieve such a comprehensive settlement, a "contact group" of five Western states began meeting intermittently as of April 1977 with South African government officials. By August, separate talks were also held with SWAPO spokesmen. Although agreement was reached on such issues as a transitional administration and elections for a constituent assembly, the two sides differed fundamentally on the number and role of South African troops remaining in the territory prior to the elections, the future of the enclave of Walvis Bay (whether to be integrated into Namibia or, in line with South African claims based on its annexation by Cape Colony in 1884, to be administered as part of Cape Province), and the release of prisoners held by SWAPO authorities.

To break the impasse, the five Western "contact" states initiated "proximity talks" aimed at facilitating indirect encounters between the main rivals. The key negotiations in this series were held in early February 1978 at the U.S. mission to the United Nations in New York. First the ambassadors and then the foreign ministers of the Western countries met separately with the South Africans (led by Foreign Minister Roelof Botha) and SWAPO (led by its president, Sam Nujoma). After initial discussion on the major outstanding points of difference, the United States presented a package proposal to the two sides that sought to find a compromise between the contending positions. The Western plan proposed to reduce the number of South African troops in the territory to approximately 1500 and confine them to two major camps prior to the elections. It also called for a cease-fire, a UN peacekeeping force somewhat larger than that allowed the South Africans, the release of political prisoners held by both parties, and UN participation in the supervision of the election and the transitional administration. The proximity talks did not succeed in bringing about an acceptable compromise, however. On February 12, Botha suddenly withdrew from the discussions, raising again the possibility that his government might opt for an internal solution. President Carter may well have had this in mind when, during his trip to Nigeria, he warned South African authorities on the necessity of a Namibian solution satisfactory to all the major contending parties. "I think if South Africa should reject a reasonable proposal and move unilaterally on Namibia," he cautioned, "it would be a serious indication of their unwillingness to comply with the legal position of the United Nations and the rest of the world. This would be one thing that can precipitate a more serious difference between us and South Africa." [59] Concern over widening the gap that existed between South Africa and the United States doubtlessly contributed to Vorster's decision to treat the Namibian question in what seemed a conciliatory manner. Thus he announced, on April 25, South Africa's acceptance of the Western proposals. Nevertheless, his agreement to the Western plan was made conditional on the assent of the various groups in the territory and, specifically, on three provisions antithetical to SWAPO's interests: a cease-fire prior to the reduction in the number of South African troops, the continued use of the South-West African police to maintain order during the transitional period, and the exclusion of the Walvis Bay issue from the independence agreement. Not surprisingly, SWAPO's leader, Sam Nujoma, held back approval and demanded tighter restrictions on South African military forces in the territory. Then, following a South African attack on a SWAPO base inside Angola, he abruptly called off scheduled negotiations with Western diplomats on the proposals.

Undismayed by this setback, the Western contact group kept up the pressure and, after months of quiet, behind-the-scenes negotiations, reached an agreement in Luanda, Angola, in July 1978 with Sam Nujoma that paved the way for a peaceful settlement of the Namibian dispute. Although the two sides remained far apart on the status of Walvis Bay, a wide measure of agreement had been secured on UN-supervised free elections, the release of political prisoners, the repeal of discriminatory laws, and the size of both South African troop levels (1500 men within twelve weeks of the cease-fire) and the United Nations peacekeeping force (5000 troops and 1000 UN civilian employees). In the words of Donald F. McHenry, the United States negotiator, the new accord was a "fragile soufflé." To underscore his point, he added: "Good food has to be consumed while hot." McHenry's intuition soon proved valid. In September, outgoing Prime Minister Vorster publicly rejected the UN's Namibia plan, an action confirmed by his successor, Pieter William Botha. Botha, who represented the most tough-minded of the potential candidates considered by a parliamentary caucus of the ruling Nationalist party, sought internal elections and a cessation of hostilities prior to a reduction of South African forces in the territory. At the outset, Botha seemed unmoved by Western appeals for compromise, and by references to possible economic sanctions. In subsequent weeks, however, signs of a partial relaxation were evident. Following a meeting in Pretoria between the foreign ministers of South Africa and the five Western states, including U.S. Secretary of State Cyrus Vance, a compromise was announced providing for dual elections in Namibia. First, a South African-sponsored election was to be held in December 1978 to select local leaders to join in the negotiations with UN officials on subsequent election procedures. Second, after the various parties had engaged in negotiations on the modalities of the voting process, a UN-approved election would take place. This agreement exposed a wide gap between Western and African positions. Although Vance described the compromise as "a step forward," the African bloc at the UN viewed it as an ill-advised concession to South African intransigeance. Nevertheless, despite strong UN opposition to the controversial internal elections, South African authorities went ahead with the December elections for a constituent assembly. The results of the voting were a foregone conclusion. With SWAPO and two other nationalist parties boycotting the exercise, the Democratic Turnhalle Alliance was able to win 41 of the 50 seats in the assembly. At this point, South African leaders decided to pull back from a head-on confrontation with the UN over Namibia's future. In late December, the South African foreign minister, Roelof Botha, informed UN Secretary-General Waldheim that his country had agreed to the UN plan on Namibia's independence. Botha invited the UN special representative, Martti Ahtisaari, to visit the territory as soon as possible to complete preparations for UN-supervised elections and to settle other outstanding issues (i.e., the size, composition, and location of the UN military force, and the South African demand that the guerrillas observe a ceasefire). Although these issues have proved difficult to resolve in the past, there is renewed hope in various quarters that an internationally acceptable arrangement can be worked out in 1979. Such an event would represent something of a success for the Carter administration's accommodative policy, as its twin objectives of conflict reduction and identification with black African aspirations would be intertwined with this outcome.

With respect to South Africa, the new accommodative approach was evident in principle but somewhat more cautiously applied in practice. Thus, administrative officers rejected any crude political tradeoffs intended to gain South African support on the Rhodesian and Namibian issues and insisted on simultaneous progress toward majority rule throughout the region. Symbolically, Vice-President Mondale asserted, following his talks with Vorster in Vienna in May 1977, that without "evident progress" toward an ending of apartheid, the United States would have to take "actions based on our policy . . . to the detriment of the constructive relations we would prefer with South Africa." In Mondale's view, "full political participation by all citizens of South Africa . . . is essential to a healthy, stable and secure South Africa." Not only did the United States oppose South African policies, but it went on to rule out any military defense of a regime based on apartheid practices. Thus the staunchly anticommunist South Africans were told that "perpetuating an unjust system is the surest incentive to increase Soviet influence and even racial war but, quite apart from that, it is unjustified on its own grounds." [60] South African whites reacted defiantly to such external pressures. Their spokesmen derided the Carter administration advocacy of "majority government on the basis of one-man, one-vote" as "nothing more than blatant interference in South Africa's internal affairs," and they asserted that such foreign pressures would prove "counterproductive." [61] Roelof "Pik" Botha claimed that a "so-called friendly country such as America" was currently a greater threat than the Soviet Union; although President Carter would not overwhelm South Africa with military force, Botha described him as attempting to do so with "finesse," slowly "smoother[ing] us to death." [62] When called to the polls to demonstrate solidarity with their leaders, the white electorate responded by giving the Vorster government the largest majority of any regime in the country's history (134 seats in the 165-seat parliament). In the face of this attack, U.S. officials, charged with prescribing a policy that amounted to "suicide" for the white minority, softened their stand on what constituted an acceptable political formula and stressed instead that they offered no blueprint and no timetable.[63] Even so, the time for straddling the racial issue had passed, in principle at least.

In practice, the United States gave substantive expression to its accommodative stance by reacting harshly to violations of civil liberties in South Africa, threatening to withhold future supplies of uranium fuel from that country unless it agreed to stricter international controls to prevent the transfer of material for an explosive device, and a positive vote at the Security Council in favor of a mandatory arms embargo on the supply of weapons and military material to that country. Although these measures were considered evidences of good intention in the Third World,[64] African leaders urged more forceful and effective action to bring about a significant change of attitude among South Africa's rulers. During Carter's visit to Nigeria, for example, General Obasanjo expressed his government's "strong disappointment" over the unwillingness of certain countries to endorse trade sanctions and the continued pursuance of "policies of outright collaboration with South Africa" in military and economic matters.[65] In fact, the U.S. arms embargo still did not eliminate all gray areas. Thus the Carter administration authorized the sale of Cessna light aircraft and Boeing 747s to South Africa and continued to extend Export-Import Bank loan guarantees to that country until October 1978 when Congress voted a prohibition of such loans in the immediate future (in the face of administration opposition). Moreover, U.S. representatives at the International Monetary Fund supported additional South African loan requests (amounting to nearly $500 million) through the first year of the Carter leadership.[66] In African eyes, then, accommodation involved something less than a total commitment to African aspirations.

Beyond tightening the administration of the arms embargo, a broad range of options are open to American policy makers for bringing pressure to bear on South Africa. The Senate Subcommittee on African Affairs, headed by Senator Dick Clark, recommended three measures to discourage U.S. foreign investment in South Africa: withdrawing facilities of the U.S. government that promote the flow of capital or credit, denying tax credits to those U.S. corporations paying taxes to the South African government that fail to act in ways consistent with American policy objectives, and withholding official endorsement of private groups that organize in defense of U.S. corporate interests in South Africa unless they support corporate guidelines and fair employment principles as laid down by U.S. governmental authorities.[67] Other measures open to the U.S. government run from diplomatic to full economic sanctions (including disinvestment, limitations on trade, a ban on nuclear cooperation, and full participation by all U.S. multinational interests in a UN embargo on petroleum products). In all this, what ought to be the central purposes in U.S. governmental concerns toward South Africa must be kept in mind: to refuse to buttress a system of institutionalized racism and help representatives of all races work out a mutually satisfactory settlement for themselves.[68] The United States is not well placed to do more than facilitate an encounter among rivaling elements, however. Lacking a monopoly of power, virtue, or wisdom, it is not in a position to impose solutions. Hence its pressures will be most usefully directed toward encouraging political exchange among those directly affected by the outcomes, while leaving the particular formulas adopted—one man, one-vote majoritarianism; proportional representation; qualified franchise; federalism; confederation; partition; and so forth—to the preferences of the South African negotiators.

THE LIMITS OF ACCOMMODATION

How far can a powerful world actor such as the United States go in accommodating to black African goals and aspirations? Given America's low involvement in black Africa's struggle for national freedom and human dignity—at least until 1976—deference now to African preferences seems to be a logical framework for current policy in that area. Thus the rejection, by Andrew Young and others, of a stance responsive to each and every Soviet-Cuban initiative on the continent, and the championing, instead, of the principle of nonintervention. To use Young's well-known formulation, the United States recognizes the need for "African solutions for African problems." In accord with such an orientation, the United States will abstain from middle African struggles, seeing in U.S. action the possibility of heightened East-West competition, as well as of aggravated tensions among rivaling African interests. As applied in 1977, such an approach was manifested in an American unwillingness to be drawn directly into a series of ventures of dubious utility: the invasion in April of Zaire's Shaba Province by some 2000 former Katanga Gendarmes ("Shaba 1"), the conflicting claims to the Western Sahara, and the Ethiopian-Somali and Ethiopian-Eritrean disputes. Should the parties to such inter-African disputes be unable to resolve their differences among themselves, the standard U.S. prescription for conflict management was Organization of African Unity mediation, not great-power interference in the struggle. Such U.S. restraint served multiple purposes. It allowed a Vietnam-weary land that lacked vital interests in the area to adopt a stance both fashionable and low-keyed, moralistic and economically prudent, domestically conciliatory and internationally circumscribed. Accommodation linked southern African engagement to middle African disengagement in a bid to find common ground between the United States and black Africa.

Nevertheless, nonintervention and linkage are distinctly different policy outcomes. Nonintervention will not necessarily further an ongoing encounter with black Africa, a low level of action hardly being aggregative in its consequences. It might indeed reduce conflict (as if conflict were automatically negative in its effects!), but whether it can go beyond this to create a sense of shared fate remains unclear at this juncture. Current signs do not indicate an expanding chain of interactions. Significantly, at the time President Carter was voicing U.S. concerns over the involvement of the Soviet Union and Cuba in Africa during his Nigerian visit, his hosts were notably indifferent toward such communist-inspired activities. As Nigeria's UN ambassador, Leslie Harriman, pointedly stated following Carter's departure: "Cubans are welcome in Africa." [69] In the broadest sense, then, accommodation may well lesson U.S.–black African tensions, but it does not automatically follow that a "cool" approach will overcome distance.

The main attack on current U.S. policy toward Africa comes from two other sources: from Africa's disadvantaged, who chafe, legitimately at times, over the pace at which global redistributions of wealth and power are taking place (on this, see chapter 4); and from conservative internationalists who question the assumption that African nationalism and established trading ties will necessarily prevail in the end over short-term Soviet-Cuban military triumphs. By November 1977, as fighting intensified on the Horn of Africa and the possibility of a major Rhodesian war loomed, the utility of an accommodative stance on issues not linked directly to institutionalized racism was called into question. Observers were quick to comment on the presence of close to 50,000 Cuban military and civilian personnel serving in 14 African countries, as well as 4000 Soviet and East European military technicians distributed throughout the continent. Moreover, it is important to note that Africa accounted for about 50 percent of Soviet arms deliveries to all Third World states by this time.[70]

For liberal internationalist strategists, active Soviet engagement in the fighting at the Horn came as a shock to their idealistic world view. That the Soviets would become involved in a massive buildup of the Somali army and establish an extensive military complex in Berbera for their own purposes was disturbing enough for those who inclined toward a benign view of Soviet intentions. Their concern deepened noticeably in early 1977, however, as the Soviets cemented close relations with the new Marxist-oriented regime in Addis and proceeded to dispatch some $1 billion in military assistance to the Mengistu government. For a time it seemed just possible that the Soviets might be able to bring about a reduction in tensions, even a federation between these two ideologically similar regimes, but Barre's determination to expand his territory so as to include all ethnic Somalis was fundamentally at cross purposes with Mengistu's insistence on holding a shaky Ethiopia together against all challenges (Somalia, Eritrea, and other nationality elements within his country). Inevitably, the Soviet straddle failed, and by October the Soviet ambassador to Ethiopia announced that his country had stopped all further arms shipments to Somalia.[71] Meanwhile, the Somalis, convinced by Iran, Saudi Arabia and, in principle at least, the United States,[72] that they would get access to Western military supplies, began a full-scale invasion of Ethiopia's Ogaden region. The outcome is well known. The Soviets provided Mengistu with all the human and material support needed for a swift military solution to the challenge in the Ogaden, thereby consolidating their alliance with Addis as well as demonstrating their capabilities and resoluteness to observers in other Third World countries.

If the Soviet Union demonstrated firmness and decisiveness—as well as ruthless opportunism—in the Somali-Ethiopian struggle, the United States, by comparison, seemed hesitant and withdrawn. The Carter administration had undertaken a review of its policy on the Horn soon after taking office; its findings, issued as Presidential Review Memorandum 21, began the phasing out of its communications station at Kagnew, as well as its long-established military aid program in Ethiopia. In Addis, the ruling Dergue acted before this policy was implemented, however, and broke military ties with the United States. It was then that American officials gave the Barre government some encouragement on arms procurement; and Barre, apparently acting on the basis of these assurances, launched his attack on Ethiopian positions in the Ogaden. To his dismay, Barre found that the Carter administration had retreated from its earlier assurances and was applying "a policy of restraint." Anthony Lake advanced three explanations for this change of position: the need for an embargo on arms sales to both sides, the urgency of giving support to peaceful diplomatic initiatives by the Africans themselves (including the OAU), and the willingness to provide economic and humanitarian assistance to the two rivals.[73] Clearly the Carter administration recoiled from checking Soviet adventurism with U.S. adventurism. Not only did it see military assistance to the Somalis as intensifying the conflict, but it recognized that such action would violate an OAU subcommission finding of August 1977 on the Somali-Ethiopian boundary dispute, which ruled against Somalia's claim to a change in the colonial frontier by forceful means. Thus the adoption of a liberal internationalist perspective ruled out an effective U.S. military response to Soviet activities in this conflict, leaving the USSR a victor by default.

Zbigniew Brzezinski, Carter's national security adviser and the most prominent official spokesman for the conservative internationalist viewpoint, has criticized Soviet-bloc involvement in Ethiopia and has warned Moscow that its activities in Africa would "inevitably complicate" the SALT negotiations. The SALT-Africa linkage was meant to signal both U.S. concern over the increasing Soviet penetration of Africa and American resolve to stabilize the continent's affairs. In Brzezinski's own words: "On the African Horn, I do view the Soviet role there seriously. I do view it in some respects as a test of détente. Does that make me a hard-liner?" [74] Brzezinski's question was apt and goes to the heart of the liberal-conservative internationalist clash. Certainly, if the East-West conflict is irrelevant in the African context, there is no need outside of humanitarian and commercial considerations for U.S. efforts at stabilizing the area. Because there are widespread fears (in both Saudi Arabia and the West) of a possible Soviet "envelopment" or "outflanking" strategy, however, globalist apprehensions seem likely to be taken seriously in the foreseeable future.

A clear indication of a renewed willingness on the part of the United States to seize the initiative in middle African confrontation situations came with the second invasion of Shaba Province in May 1978 ("Shaba 2"). Unlike the Ethiopian-Somali conflict, the invasion of Zaire by Katangan exiles from Angola (allegedly trained and equipped by Cuban forces) involved the crossing of an international frontier—a violation of the OAU's central principles on noninterference and respect for the integrity of sovereign states. The Carter administration, seeing an opportunity to dispel charges of indecisive leadership in the face of Soviet-Cuban activities in Africa, responded quickly to a request from Zaire, France, and Belgium for logistical support by dispatching eighteen U.S. Air Force C-141 transports to assist the French and Belgian military airlifts. Washington's condemnation of the invasion as a violation of Zaire's sovereignty identified the United States with black African norms and values (accommodation) while justifying a limited form of direct involvement (confrontation).

Following this initial response, Carter administration signals seemed ambiguous, wavering uncertainly between adversary action and nonintervention. Brzezinski denounced the Soviet Union for violating "the code of détente" and called for "demonstrated resolve" in the face of Soviet global competition. Carter echoed such sentiments, albeit in a more reserved manner, when he urged his NATO allies not to remain indifferent to the Soviet-Cuban challenge in Africa and allowed further U.S. logistical support for the replacement of French units with an all-African peace force composed of Moroccan and French-speaking West African troops. Nevertheless, his liberal internationalist orientation remained evident. Studiously avoiding a global confrontation, he ruled out an American military response and, in a show of support for Vance, refused publicly to link SALT with a moderated Soviet stance in Africa. At Annapolis on June 7, a "cool" Carter carefully avoided belligerency; cautiously selecting his words, he summarized U.S. policy as follows: "The Soviet Union can choose either confrontation or cooperation. The United States is adequately prepared to meet either choice." At the same time, the administration seemed to be readying for a more activist U.S. role in Africa. A presidential review memorandum, drafted by the State Department and National Security Council, reportedly called for increased economic assistance and concentration upon the peaceful resolution of African regional disputes, although some mention of providing more in the way of "defensive weapons" did appear to have been included.[75] For the time being at least, the accommodationist proponents of bringing about lasting stability through economic development still appeared to have the edge in presidential sympathies.

Obviously, as Brzezinski suggests, considerable common ground remains between the liberal and conservative internationalist positions. In the final analysis, many an American liberal internationalist would shrink from policies that fostered racial warfare, resulted in blockades of the Red Sea or Indian Ocean, or undercut the international economic system; similarly, a good number of the conservative internationalists would recognize legitimate black African sensitivities on the southern African question. As in most complicated international issues, it is not an "either-or" choice, but one essentially of emphasis. A wide area of choice exists between the polar extremes of nonintervention and adversary action. Consequently, what is justifiable cooperation in one situation is unjustifiable appeasement in another. Thus the United States can cooperate with black Africa in most matters precisely because it lacks vital interests in this area. In other contexts (for example, the Middle East) a similar posture might be highly irresponsible.

In Africa, therefore, the United States would seem to have little alternative at this time but to accept an element of uncertainty and untidiness. Old alliances and commitments are changing, and new political actors are rapidly acquiring interests. Declining U.S. power is matched by the increasing complexity of the African phenomenon. In such a situation, realism would seem to dictate a maximum effort at cooperating with black Africa—to the point, at least, that accommodative policies no longer meet the dual tests of morality and prudence.

To all appearances the optimistic, initial visions of the Carter policy makers on the possibilities of accommodation in Africa are receiving a jarring as they come up against the cold realities of domestic pressure, African and Western European alliance constraints, and global competition. Good intentions proved insufficient in the face of deeply conflicting interests in the contemporary world. Nevertheless, the enduring choices of nonintervention and adversary relations persist, requiring statesmen to choose from among competing African and global objectives. Certainly no U.S. leader can stand by while a superpower rival impinges on his country's vital interests; equally certainly, no prudent leader needlessly risks African hostility through insensitivity to continental aspirations, unwarranted interference in internal African affairs, or global rivalries on the continent over essentially peripheral issues. The points of overlap are so numerous that no present-day U.S. leader can avoid choice for long. Their statesmanship in this regard will ultimately be judged by their ability to make a correct determination of vital and nonvital interests.

NOTES

1. Cyrus Vance, "U.S. Policy Toward Africa" (speech before the annual convention of the National Association for the Advancement of Colored People, St. Louis, 1 July 1977), p. 1.
2. Hans J. Morgenthau, *Politics Among Nations* (3rd ed.; New York: Knopf, 1960), pp. 39–40. Also see Robert W. Tucker, *The Inequality of Nations* (New York: Basic Books, 1977), p. 129.
3. U.S. Department of Commerce, *U.S. General Imports, Schedule A Commodity by Country* (Washington, D.C.: Government Printing Office, 1977), pp. 2–85.
4. South Africa possesses the following holdings of total known mineral reserves: platinum, 71 percent; chrome, 63 percent; gold, 59 percent; vermiculite, 39 percent; manganese, 37 percent; uranium, 20 percent; and vanadium, 19 percent. *Wall Street Journal* (Palo Alto), 9 December 1977, p. 14.
5. *War on Hunger, A Report from the Agency for International Development* 8, no. 12 (December 1974): 12. During the mid-1970s, the United States spent some $400 million annually in sub-Saharan Africa ($250 million in direct economic aid and $150 million through UN specialized agencies).
6. *New York Times,* 30 December 1967, p. 28. Also see "Remarks by Senator Edmund S. Muskie," *Issue* 1, no. 1 (Fall 1971): 29.
7. Program of African Studies, Northwestern University, *United States Foreign Policy: Africa, a Study Prepared at the Request of the Committee on Foreign Relations, U.S. Senate, 23 October 1959* (Washington, D.C.: Government Printing Office, 1959), p. 2. Statement by J. C. Satterthwaite.
8. William Attwood, *The Reds and the Blacks* (New York: Harper & Row, 1967), p. 16.
9. Arthur M. Schlesinger, Jr., *A Thousand Days: John F. Kennedy in the White House* (Boston: Houghton Mifflin, 1965), p. 558.
10. Quoted in Mohamed A. El-Khawas and Barry Cohen, eds., *The Kissinger Study of Southern Africa* (Westport: Lawrence Hill, 1976), p. 105.
11. Anthony Lake, *The "Tar Baby" Option: American Policy Toward Southern Rhodesia* (New York: Columbia University Press, 1973), p. 214. For a participant-observer insight into these events, see Gale W. McGee, "The U.S. Congress and the Rhodesian Chrome Issue," *Issue* 2, no. 3 (Summer 1972): 6.
12. See Bruce Oudes, "The United States' Year in Africa: Postscript to the Nixon Years," in *Africa Contemporary Record 1975–76,* ed. Colin Legum (New York: Africana, 1976), p. A123; and David B. Ottaway, "South Africa Arms Embargo Too Late," *Manchester Guardian Weekly* (London) 117, no. 20 (13 November 1977): 15.
13. Statement by Elizabeth S. Landis. U.S., Congress, Senate Foreign Relations Committee, *U.S. Policy Toward Southern Africa: Hearings Before the Subcommittee on African Affairs of the Committee on Foreign Relations United States Senate,* 94th Cong., 1st sess., 24 July 1975 (Washington, D.C.: Government Printing Office, 1976), pp. 381, 387; and Tom J. Farer, "The United States and the Third World: A Basis for Accommodation," *Foreign Affairs* 54, no. 1 (October 1975): 86.
14. *Star* (Johannesburg), 9 August 1976, p. 16, and 20 October 1976, p. 1.
15. Henry Kissinger, *Implications of Angola for Future U.S. Foreign Policy, a Statement before the*

Senate Subcommittee on African Affairs of the Foreign Relations Committee, January 29, 1976. (Washington, D.C.: Department of State, Bureau of Public Affairs, 1976), PR 40, p. 2.

16. Bayard Rustin and Carl Gershman, "Africa, Soviet Imperialism, and the Retreat of American Power," Commentary 64, no. 4 (October 1977): 36, 43.

17. Colin Legum, "The Soviet Union, China, and the West in Southern Africa," Foreign Affairs 54, no. 4 (July 1976): 760–61.

18. Gallup Opinion Index, Report no. 120 (June 1975): 1–2. Also see the discussion on trends in support of the Vietnam war in Jon E. Mueller, War, Presidents, and Public Opinion (New York: Wiley, 1973), pp. 52–58.

19. U.S., Congress, Senate Foreign Relations Committee. Angola. Hearings Before the Subcommittee on African Affairs, 94th Cong., 2d sess., 6 February 1976, p. 171.

20. Henry A. Kissinger, U.S. Responsibilities in a Changing World Economy, a Statement before the Senate Committee on Finance, January 30, 1976. (Washington, D.C.: Department of State, Bureau of Public Affairs, 1976), p. 3.

21. Henry A. Kissinger, Latin America, Europe, and Africa, a Statement before the House International Relations Committee, June 17, 1976. (Washington, D.C.: Department of State, Bureau of Public Affairs, 1976), PR 306, pp. 1, 5–6.

22. Henry A. Kissinger, "Toward a New Understanding of Community," Department of State Bulletin 75, no. 1948 (25 October 1976): 500.

23. Kissinger, news conference, Philadelphia, 31 August 1976. Reported in Department of State Bulletin 75, no. 1943 (20 September 1976): 358–59.

24. Henry A. Kissinger, Southern Africa and the United States: An Agenda For Cooperation, Lusaka, April 27, 1976 (Washington, D.C.: Department of State, Bureau of Public Affairs, 1976), PR 205, p. 3.

25. See the discussion in Donald Rothchild, Racial Bargaining in Independent Kenya: A Study of Minorities and Decolonization (London: Oxford University Press, 1973), pp. 7–8. Also see the editorial in Daily Times (Lagos), 7 September 1976, p. 3.

26. William D. Rogers, The Search for Peace in Southern Africa, a Statement before the Subcommittee on African Affairs of the Senate Foreign Relations Committee, Washington D.C., 30 September 1976 (Washington, D.C.: Department of State, Bureau of Public Affairs, 1976), p. 4. For an almost identical statement by Prime Minister Vorster, see Africa Research Bulletin 13, no. 9 (15 October 1976): 4166.

27. Africa Research Bulletin 13, no. 4 (15 May 1976): 4005.

28. This conclusion is based on a series of interviews in Accra by the author at the time of the visit's cancellation. For various editorials in the local press critical of Kissinger's role in southern African affairs, see Ghanaian Times (Accra), 29 April 1976, p. 4; 11 May 1976, p. 4; 16 September 1976, p. 4. It is significant that a petition circulated at the University of Ghana, Legon, prior to the visit's cancellation characterized Kissinger as the "enemy" for his policies on the Angolan issue.

29. Kissinger, Africa, a Statement before the Senate Foreign Relations Committee, 13 May 1976 (Washington, D.C.: Department of State, Bureau of Public Affairs, 1976), PR 205, p. 5.

30. Henry A. Kissinger, UNCTAD IV: Expanding Cooperation for Global Economic Development, Nairobi, 6 May 1976 (Washington, D.C.: Department of State, Bureau of Public Affairs, 1976), PR 224, p. 5. On African resentment of U.S. refusal to back commodity agreements, see West Africa (London), 3 November 1975, p. 1294, and 16 February 1976, p. 199; and Daily Graphic (Accra), 20 September 1975, p. 2.

31. Later, Prime Minister Vorster stated that when in Zurich, he received a message from Smith wishing him "God's speed" in convincing Kissinger on the necessity of discussion with the Rhodesian government. Star, 1 November 1976, p. 19.

32. See the account in Colin Legum, "Southern Africa: The Year of the Whirlwind," in Africa Contemporary Record 1976–77, ed. C. Legum (New York: Africana, 1977), pp. A34–36.

33. Bernard Gwertzman, "How Ambiguous Kissinger Note Won Smith Backing for Plan," International Herald Tribune (Paris), 17 November 1976, p. 1.

34. Reportedly, Vorster exerted various types of pressure on Smith to get him to agree to the Kissinger plan (e.g., holding out on future Rhodesian financial commitments for military defense and closing the common border during the Kissinger visit, thereby allowing delays

to hamper the Rhodesian import and export efforts). John de St. Jorre, *A House Divided: South Africa's Uncertain Future* (New York: Carnegie Endowment for International Peace, 1977), p. 74. The full text of Smith's broadcast appears in the *Times* (London), 25 September 1976, p. 4.

35. *Times* (London), 27 September 1976, p. 7; and *Observer,* 26 September 1976, p. 1, and 3 October 1976, p. 5.

36. *Manchester Guardian Weekly* (London) 115, no. 14 (3 October 1976): 10. The front-line presidents had broad African support for this statement. See editorial, *Daily Times,* 28 September 1976, p. 3.

37. *Africa Research Bulletin* 13, no. 10 (15 November 1976): 4200–4201.

38. *International Herald Tribune,* 28 September 1976, p. 1. This led one influential weekly to conclude that "the method by which Dr. Kissinger extracted from Mr. Smith the commitment to majority rule within two years seems on present knowledge to have been not just persuasion but deceit." *Manchester Guardian Weekly* 115, no. 14 (3 October 1976), p. 1.

39. Cf. Stanley Hoffmann, "The Hell of Good Intentions," *Foreign Policy* 29 (Winter 1977–78): 3.

40. *International Herald Tribune,* 23 May 1977, p. 1.

41. *Times* (London), 25 January 1977, p. 15. On the willingness of the administration to risk losing South African support for its other southern Africa undertakings, see Bernard Gwertzman, "U.S. Recalls Envoy from South Africa for Consultations," *New York Times,* 22 October 1977, p. 8. For an explicit administration recognition of the uniqueness of the South African situation, however, see the remarks by William B. Edmondson, the deputy assistant secretary of state for African affairs, at a conference held by the School of Advanced International Studies in Washington D.C. for business executives in October 1977, p. 10. Manuscript.

42. *West Africa,* 10 October 1977, p. 2085. On the modest levels of U.S. aid programs in Africa when compared with those of Western Europe and the Middle East oil-producing states, see William I. Jones, "The Search for an Aid Policy" in *Africa: From Mystery to Maze,* ed. Helen Kitchen (Lexington: Lexington Books, 1976), p. 359.

43. See Anthony Lake, "The United States and the Third World: Economic Issues" (speech at the annual meeting of the African Studies Association and Latin American Studies Association, Houston, 5 November 1977), p. 3.

44. *Ghanaian Times,* 27 May 1977, p. 4; also see the editorial in the *Rand Daily Mail* as summarized in the *South African Digest,* 27 May 1977, p. 25. For black South African criticism of foreign private investment, and by implication Young's thesis that change can come through the marketplace, see *Southern Africa* 11, no. 3 (April 1978): 3–6.

45. See Ross K. Baker, "Toward a New Constituency for a More Active American Foreign Policy for Africa," *Issue* 3, no. 1 (Spring 1973): 12–19; Edmondson remarks, SAIS Conference, October 1977, p. 4.

46. Chester A. Crocker, "Lost in Africa," *New Republic* 178, no. 7 (18 February 1978): 16. It is important, however, not to overstate the support for Andrew Young's liberal internationalist policies. For criticism of Young's reformism by a black political scientist, see Willard R. Johnson, "Why U.S. Firms *Must* Quit South Africa," *First World,* March–April 1977, p. 11. Radical white scholars have been equally strong in their attacks on "liberal interventionism": see Immanuel Wallerstein, "Yankee, Stay Home!" *Nation* 225, no. 16 (12 November 1977): 489. Finally, NSC support of accommodation to black African aspirations is less than monolithic; on this see Elizabeth Drew, "A Reporter at Large: Brzezinski," *New Yorker* 54, no. 11 (1 May 1978): 104–5.

47. William D. Rogers, "The Search for Peace in Southern Africa," *Department of State Bulletin* 75, no. 1948 (25 October 1976): 535.

48. William E. Schaufele, Jr., "United States Economic Relations with Africa," ibid., 74, no. 1915 (8 March 1976): 295.

49. William J. Foltz, "United States Policy Toward Southern Africa: Economic and Strategic Constraints," *Political Science Quarterly* 92, no. 1 (Spring 1977): 49. Foltz also expresses considerable skepticism of the importance of South African bases for protecting the sea route to Europe. Ibid., p. 58.

50. Barry Cohen, "US–African Trade Booming," *New African Development* 11, no. 9 (September 1977): 917. Also see Donald Rothchild and Robert L. Curry, Jr., *Scarcity, Choice, and Public Policy in Middle Africa* (Berkeley: University of California Press, 1978), pp. 154–56.
51. *West Africa,* 17 October 1977, p. 2138.
52. See Andrew Young's statement at the World Conference for Action Against Apartheid, Lagos, 25 August 1977, in *Department of State Bulletin* 77, no. 1997 (3 October 1977): 446.
53. *Congressional Record* 123, no. 44 (14 March 1977): H2022.
54. *Department of State Bulletin* 77, no. 1997 (3 October 1977): 424–39.
55. *New York Times,* 10 March 1978, p. D12, and 3 April 1978, p. Al.
56. Quoted in *Africa Research Bulletin* 14, no. 11 (15 December 1977): 4641.
57. Quoted in *West Africa,* 27 March 1978, p. 589.
58. *South African Digest,* 3 June 1977, p. 22.
59. *New York Times,* 4 April 1978, p. A14. Also see his news conference in Brasilia as reported in ibid., 31 March 1978, p. A12.
60. *Africa Research Bulletin* 14, no. 5 (15 June 1977): 4445–46. Restating a similar theme during his trip to Nigeria, Carter declared that U.S. cooperation with South Africa would depend on "whether there is progress toward full political participation for all her people and an end to discrimination based on race." *New York Times,* 7 April 1978, p. A8.
61. *South African Digest,* 30 September 1977, p. 25, and 14 October 1977, p. 23.
62. *Star,* 14 October 1977, p. 5.
63. *New York Times,* 18 October 1977, p. A5; and Cyrus Vance, press conference, Washington D.C., 2 November 1977. For a questioning of the tactical wisdom of America's advocacy of majority rule in South Africa, see George W. Ball, "Asking for Trouble in South Africa," *Atlantic Monthly,* October 1977, pp. 43–51.
64. In South Africa, see Mangosuthu Gatsha Buthelezi, "Open Letter to Ambassador Andrew Young," *South African Outlook* 107, no. 1272 (May 1977): 73.
65. *New York Times,* 3 April 1978, p. Al.
66. *Sunday Tribune* (Durban), 18 September 1977, p. 3; *Manchester Guardian Weekly* 118, no. 3 (8 January 1978): 15; *New African Development,* no. 126 (February 1978): 29.
67. U.S., Congress, Senate, *Report to the Committee on Foreign Relations U.S. Senate, by Senator Dick Clark, Chairman,* 95th Cong., 2d sess. (Washington D.C.: Government Printing Office, 1978), p. 14. Also see Clyde Ferguson and William R. Cotter, "South Africa: What Is to Be Done," *Foreign Affairs* 56, no. 2 (January 1978): 269–73.
68. For a plea for interracial negotiation by an important black South African editor, see Percy Qoboza, "South Africa: A Black View," *Freedom at Issue,* no. 42 (September–October 1977): 5.
69. Quoted in *West Africa,* 10 April 1978, p. 692. On this, also note the Somali ambassador's (as well as the Ethiopian ambassador's) outrage over David Owen's speech attacking Soviet-Cuban intervention in the Horn of Africa. Ibid., 17 April 1978, p. 735.
70. *Christian Science Monitor,* 25 April 1978, p. 3; and Chester A. Crocker, "The Quest for an African Policy," *Washington Review of Strategic and International Studies* 1, no. 2 (April 1978): 72.
71. Dimitri K. Simes, "Imperial Globalism in the Making: Soviet Involvement in the Horn of Africa," *Washington Review of Strategic and International Studies,* Special Supplement, May 1978, p. 34.
72. Robert A. Manning, "Did U.S. Encourage Somalia to War?" *Manchester Guardian Weekly* 117, no. 18 (30 October 1977), p. 6; and W. Scott Thompson, "The American-African Nexus in Soviet Strategy," *Horn of Africa* 1, no. 1 (January/March 1978): 44.
73. Anthony Lake, "Africa in a Global Perspective" (lecture at Johns Hopkins University School of Advanced International Studies, Washington D.C., 17 October 1977).
74. *New York Times,* 21 March 1978, p. A16. For a blunt charge of planned Soviet-Cuban "aggression and expansion" in Africa, see *Peking Review* 21, no. 21 (26 May 1978): 18–19.
75. *Christian Science Monitor,* 8 June 1978, pp. 1, 3, and 5 June 1978, pp. 1, 3, 38.

12

THE UNITED STATES AND THE ARAB-ISRAELI DISPUTE

Steven L. Spiegel

Americans have long been fascinated—and divided—about the Middle East. "I really wish the Jews again in Judea an independent nation . . . ," wrote John Adams in 1818.[1] From the beginning of the American experiment many in the New Jerusalem looked fondly on the aspirations of those who once ruled the holiest of biblical cities. In a country founded on Old Testament-oriented Protestantism, with a frontier ideology and an optimistic sense that miracles were possible, the notion of a Jewish return to Palestine was seen by many as historically conceivable.

Nevertheless, in viewing the Holy Land there have always been two American perspectives. Zionism (both Christian and Jewish) has been balanced by a tendency composed at various times of business, missionary, and diplomatic interests that questioned a policy toward Palestine based on "sentimental" concerns and stressed the realities of international conditions and attitudes in the Arab world. In 1891 (three years before Theodor Herzl, founder of the modern Zionist movement, began his campaign to establish a national homeland for the Jews in Palestine), when William Blackstone of Chicago presented to President Benjamin Harrison and Secretary of State James Blaine a memorial signed by 413 prominent Americans containing the proposal that the Jews be restored to Palestine, the American consul in Jerusalem replied that "1. Palestine is not ready for the Jews. 2. The Jews are not ready for Palestine." [2]

Policy making toward the Middle East has been difficult for a variety of reasons.

I would like to thank several of my fellow authors, especially the editors, for their useful and insightful comments on earlier drafts of this manuscript.

First, overlapping conflicts have occurred in the region—among the Arabs, between Arabs and Jews, and between several countries on the region's periphery including Iran, Greece, Turkey, and Cyprus. The Arab world has seen many changing rivalries. In the 1960s radical Egypt was in conflict with moderate Libya; in the 1970s radical Libya was hostile toward moderate Egypt. A similar about-face has occurred between Iraq and Egypt over the past twenty years. And in the 1970s Iraq and Syria—whose regimes both originated from the Baathist party—were engaged in hostilities. Jordan and Saudi Arabia, now moderate monarchies, are ruled by the Hussein and Saudi families, which were once in fierce competition. In contradistinction to the claim of Arab unity, wars within the Arab world have taken place over the Yemen in the 1960s and Lebanon in the 1970s. Even Israel has played a part in these intra-Arab conflicts: in 1970 to aid Jordan against radical Palestinian insurgents and in the late '70s to support Christians in Lebanon.

Second, American administrations have difficulty determining policies when both sides lay claims to American support. The United States seeks friendship with both camps. Each side offers the United States its backing and specific ideological or concrete benefits. Neither side is communist. Both sides have friends and supporters (ethnic, commercial, ideological) within the United States. And to complicate matters further, Americans involved with the Middle East have varying concerns. Some care only about the regional scene—either about Israel's survival as a Jewish state or about Arab rights. Some Christian observers see in the return of the Jews to Palestine the continuation of a divine plan and side with Israel; others are concerned about missionary work in the Arab world or their theological discomfort with a Jewish state has brought them to the Arab cause. Still others view the region as a microcosm of an international morality play—they find the forces of justice and right to be on one side or the other. Some are primarily interested in Jewish refugees from Europe and the meaning of the holocaust as a reason for supporting Israel; others see the plight of the Palestinian refugees as a reason for favoring the Arabs.

The region can also be viewed in terms of global principles: as an arena for defeating international communism, or containing the Soviet Union, or maintaining democracy, or upholding international morality. These kinds of concerns have been attached at varying times to both sides. Thus, while some observers have seen the vibrancy of Israeli democracy as the best available symbol for fighting communism in the area, others have sought to thwart communism by aiding Arab moderates. The Middle East has also been seen in terms of instrumental objectives for the United States. In Israel, many have argued the need to protect the consistency and credibility of American commitments. In the Arab nations, many have pointed to concrete benefits for the United States: their oil, their strategic location at the crossroads of three continents, the potential for military bases or markets, the Suez Canal. For all these observers, the Arabs and Israelis as people have been secondary to the principles the observers cherished and sought to promote by favoring one side or the other.

BEFORE CARTER [3]

Thus, the problem successive administrations have faced in the Middle East is not only to appeal to as many competing countries in the area as possible, but also to assuage a variety of competing interests: security of Israel, oil, containment of the Soviet Union, refugees, security of the Suez Canal, and retention of business concerns. Each administration has had a particular view of how to handle the problem, even though the dilemmas have been similar. As early as the Wilson administration the problem surfaced when the British consulted the United States about the Balfour Declaration. Tactical inconsistencies that would later become traditional were evident when the United States first discouraged the British (out of a concern for Turkish sensitivities); then, a few weeks later, approved the wording of the declaration. Divisions at home were apparent in a somewhat tardy public presidential approval of British policy and in the inconsistent handling of the Palestine issue at the Versailles Conference. Later patterns could be foreseen when the President favored the Zionists, the State Department opposed them, and several Protestant missionary groups backed incipient Arab nationalism. [4]

The next American President to deal with Middle East issues prominently was Franklin D. Roosevelt, who often simultaneously made promises to both sides, leading the Jews to believe they had gained American backing for a Jewish commonwealth in Palestine and the Arabs to think they would have an effective veto power over Jewish plans for the area. Roosevelt seems to have counted heavily on the force of his own personality. During World War II he hoped to find in King Saud of Saudi Arabia a moderate, hopes that were dashed when he met with the king in 1945. The desert monarch was adamant in his opposition to Zionism. He recommended instead that Jewish refugees from Nazi persecution be given "the choicest lands and homes of the Germans who had oppressed them." [5]

Harry Truman was left with the unhappy task of attempting to reconcile competing international and domestic perspectives in the postwar world. British influence was declining; Russia was initiating a move toward influence. In Iran, Turkey, and Greece the challenge seemed clear to Truman: the Soviets must be stopped. But in Palestine the situation was more complicated. The President was caught between the blandishments of the State Department, the Pentagon, and intelligence officials on the one hand, and the Zionists and their supporters in Congress on the other. Arabists argued that the Arabs would never accept a Jewish state in their midst and that an independent Israel would be accompanied by war, an increase in Russian influence, peril to oil supplies, diminishing Western influence, and the compromise of Western bases and the Suez Canal. Zionists and their supporters argued that a liberal democracy in the heart of the Middle East could be crucial to Western interests and that a Jewish state in a portion of the territory originally declared as Palestine by the Balfour Declaration was consistent with Western, especially British, promises. They also maintained that a division of Palestine between Arabs and Jews was the only just settlement available. Horror in the West after the Nazi slaughter of six million Jews during World War II affected the debate. Many claimed that the Jews deserved a sovereign homeland, that the West had an obligation to provide a haven for the Jewish refugees from Europe.

Truman epitomized these contrasting attitudes. On the one hand, he believed that Palestine should serve as a homeland for refugee Jews; in this sense he disagreed with British policy limiting Jewish immigration into Palestine. On the other hand, he did not believe that humanitarian concerns for the refugees necessitated a Jewish state, and he sought to protect American national security interests. In this calculation Palestine seemed at best irrelevant and at worst an interference in the effort he was organizing to contain the Soviet Union.

Competing groups in the United States and contrasting approaches by the President explain the inconsistent policy toward Palestine pursued by the Truman administration. London was urged to expand immigration, which would have alienated the Arabs, but the United States was not prepared to undertake military obligations to assist its beleaguered ally in dealing with the Mandate. When the frustrated British turned the matter over to the UN General Assembly, its special committee on the problem proposed partitioning Palestine into a Jewish and Arab state. The United States supported the plan, but the State Department almost succeeded in undercutting it by proposing limiting amendments and seeking to block American lobbying in favor of the plan, which nevertheless did finally pass. Then chaos erupted in Palestine. The administration appeared to back off partition in early 1948 in favor of an interim UN trusteeship, but the United States surprised most observers by becoming the first state to recognize Israel. On the other hand, it instituted an arms embargo of the area during Israel's war of independence in 1948–49, which aided the Arabs, who had far better access to weapons supplies.

These contradictory policies often succeeded in alienating both sides. The Israelis and their supporters resented the lack of full sponsorship, and the Arabs believed (despite the original UN advocacy) that had it not been for American backing of the partition plan, Israel would not have been created. It is therefore not surprising, given the convolutions and intricacies of American policy toward Palestine, that during Truman's second term the Middle East was not a major matter of consideration. More important, the Korean war, waged during most of that period, displaced other concerns.[6]

Under President Eisenhower an effort was made to develop a "new look" in American foreign policy, and the Middle East was not unaffected. The President and Secretary of State John Foster Dulles were inclined to view the Arabs as essential to the effort to contain communism in the Middle East. Israel was seen as an impediment to a program designed to improve American relations with the Arab states. Therefore, Eisenhower and Dulles sought to promote an Arab-Israeli settlement in order to eradicate a potential interference with their projects. The effort failed. Repeated programs for initiating Arab-Israeli contacts and even cooperative endeavors were rejected, primarily by the Syrians and the Egyptians.

The administration itself was soon torn by two contrasting approaches toward organizing the Arabs to resist what was perceived as a potential communist onslaught. Led by Dulles, many sought to organize a pro-Western alliance in the area, mainly of northern states along the Russian border (e.g., Turkey, Iran, Pakistan) but also including pro-Western Arab lands that might join (particularly Iraq). This approach was the Baghdad Pact, after the alliance that eventually emerged. Other officials believed that the United States should stress relations with Egypt, the most populous and important Arab country, even at the expense of the emerging Baghdad Pact. Finally, Egypt's new leader, Gamal Abdel Nasser, rejected the alliance project, which he saw as a vehicle for the reentrance of Western imperialism. The "Egypt first" option was abrogated when Nasser, in September 1955, turned to the Russians for arms, rejecting an American weapons supply pipeline after negotiations with Washington had languished.

A new era in the Middle East began as the Russians catapulted over the line of defense erected by Dulles through the "northern tier." In an effort to salvage their policy Eisenhower and Dulles agreed to finance the Aswan Dam designed to harness the waters of the Nile. This move might yet turn Nasser back from Moscow. But the Egyptian leader again proved intractable. Dulles's eventual withdrawal of the offer in July 1956 set off a chain of events that led to the Suez crisis and altered the political map of the Middle East. With the collapse of the Aswan deal, Nasser retaliated by nationalizing the Suez Canal. The British and French then intervened to oust the Egyptian leader—to save their rights in the waterway and reassert the imperial tradition. They finally colluded with Israel, which was seeking to blunt Egypt's growing strength, its blockade of the Straits of Tiran, and fedayeen raids from the Gaza Strip. In the ensuing campaign Israel conquered the Sinai; Britain and France, pressured by Eisenhower, were unsuccessful. Israel was subsequently forced to withdraw from the Sinai by the reelected Eisenhower administration in return for American and UN guarantees and a UN Emergency Force on the Egyptian-Israeli border. With the inadvertent assistance of the United States, Nasser recovered from his military disaster and achieved an enhanced position as the acknowledged leader of the Arab world.

But American aid to Nasser did not result in improved relations with the Arab world. Despite intense opposition to what it considered unjustified intervention by the British, French, and Israelis, the administration perceived that international communism and Nasser-led Arab nationalism were in alliance. It therefore declared the Eisenhower Doctrine (which was passed as a joint resolution by both houses of Congress), by which any nation threatened with armed aggression "from any country controlled by international communism" that requested assistance from the United States would receive it if the President determined the necessity.

As Washington sought to replace the vacuum created by the political demise of the British and French in the Middle East, a variety of mini crises occurred, culminating in the overthrow of a pro-Western Iraqi government in July 1958 by what was perceived as a pro-Nasserite, pro-communist regime. Fearing that other pro-Western Arab governments would fall, the United States encouraged the British to send paratroops to King Hussein's Jordan while Washington sent forces into Lebanon to resolve a growing civil war in that country. A compromise was soon reached in Lebanon, and the area rapidly quieted. Having shown the flag, the Eisenhower administration retreated from primary concern for the Middle East, confident that it had accomplished much by confronting Nasserism directly.[7]

By the time the young and vibrant Kennedy administration came to power in early 1961 it faced an Arab-Israeli dispute that seemed to be "on ice." Nasser was suffering from a variety of political differences with the new Iraqi regime and the Soviet Union was bogged down in the temporary union between Egypt and Syria, which lasted from mid-1958 to mid-1961.

Eisenhower had stressed American relations with conservative Arabs. Kennedy moved to two factions in the American policy-making process that his predecessor had ignored by seeking to improve simultaneously American relations with the Israelis and the nationalist Arabs led by Nasser. After a lengthy study, the new President approved the first major American arms sale to Israel—Hawk missiles, regarded as a defensive weapon for use against Soviet-supplied Egyptian offensive forces. He also initiated a private correspondence with Nasser; as part of this offensive, in late 1962 he recognized the new pro-Nasser Republican government in Yemen, which had unseated the thousand-year-old imamate.

By the time of Kennedy's death his Egyptian initiative had unraveled—because of Yemen. The royalists, aided by Saudi Arabia, counterattacked and a civil war ensued. Egyptian troops intervened on the side of the Republicans, and it seemed that Nasser could threaten the Saudis militarily because Yemen borders on Saudi Arabia. When the United States could not arrange a cease-fire between the Egyptians and the Saudis and their Yemeni clients, Kennedy was pulled back toward protecting the conservative Saudi regime. Despite his preference for more progressive regimes, he felt he could not ignore Saudi Arabia's pro-American stance and American oil interests in the country. As in other areas, Kennedy's policies were becoming more similar to his predecessors than his rhetoric would have suggested. He could finesse the apparent contradictions because of the low priority that the Middle East had at the time. The area seemed quiet.[8]

Lyndon Johnson also was able to leave the Middle East on the back burner early in his administration, but he was more sentimentally attached to Israel than Kennedy had been and more inclined to favor arms sales to conservative Arabs, especially Jordan. Arms sales increased, and Johnson approved the first sale of offensive weapons (Skyhawk jet fighters) to Israel. By the May 1967 crisis that led to the Six-Day War, American relations with Egypt were near the breaking point.

When Nasser began to take steps that led to the eviction of the UN Emergency Force that had kept the peace between Egypt and Israel for ten years, the Johnson administration was preoccupied with the Vietnam war and the domestic crisis it generated. Seeking to avoid another major international crisis, it reacted in measured fashion to the growing Middle East storm clouds. American response to Nasser's blockade of the Straits of Tiran (which Jerusalem had always declared would be a *casus belli*) was largely to request Israel's delay in using the war option while the usual appeals for restraint were made to Cairo and Moscow and at the United Nations.

Israel mobilized and debated, but the Arabs united in massing troops on her borders. Washington temporized; some in the administration sought an international declaration by maritime powers affirming the rights of all nations to use the Straits of Tiran. It was hoped that this declaration would be followed by a "Red Sea regatta" composed of many nations, including Israel, that would sail through the straits affirming the international nature of the waterway. By June 5, when the Israelis attacked Egyptian forces, the international fleet had foundered on serious practical difficulties and the lack of international political support. Meanwhile, other American diplomats worked on a possible compromise with Egypt that would finesse the aggravated Egyptian-Israeli confrontation. This diplomatic initiative was proceeding during the period that Israel was encircled by Arab armies.

The Israeli government, however, feared that unless it acted, the military balance, its political position, and essential economic interests would all be adversely affected. Although the Johnson administration had discouraged an Israeli attack, it greeted the lightning Israeli victory with a mixture of relief and admiration. Now American leaders could return to the dilemmas of Vietnam without the distraction of the Middle East and without being forced to come to Israel's aid while U.S. forces were tied down in Southeast Asia. There was also general satisfaction in Washington at having successfully avoided a confrontation with the Soviet Union. The rapid Israeli victory led to respect and even an added sense that the Arabs had gotten what they had deserved. There was little inclination after the war to press the Israelis to withdraw from the territories they had captured: the Sinai desert and the Gaza Strip from Egypt, the West Bank and the eastern section of Jerusalem after Jordan had attacked on the first day of the war, the Golan Heights from Syria. Major officials in the Johnson administration did believe that Israel should eventually withdraw from the captured territories, but only in return for a viable settlement. In response to Russian and Arab efforts to gain UN backing for a formula calling on Israel to return to the 1967 frontiers, American diplomacy contributed masterfully to UN Security Council Resolution 242, passed in November 1967, which provided an agenda of problems confronting Arabs and Israelis (e.g., territorial withdrawals; navigation rights; refugees; the establishment of secure and recognized national boundaries; and the acknowledgement of, and respect for, the sovereignty, integrity, and territorial political independence of every nation in the area). Since then, Arabs and Jews have disagreed over the exact meaning of the document and the order in which agreements were to be implemented. The Arab states that accepted the resolution have favored total Israeli withdrawals from the territories captured in 1967 as an initial step to the consideration of other issues. Israel, on the other hand, has sought resolution of all outstanding issues in an interrelated package.

With the passage of Resolution 242, the focus of Middle East diplomacy shifted to the UN special representative. Gunnar Jarring, Swedish ambassador to the Soviet Union, embarked on an effort of shuttle diplomacy to attempt to bring the parties closer together on procedures and, ultimately, substance for reaching a settlement. Jarring's efforts led the Johnson administration to pursue a more passive role. Its major action on the Middle East in 1968 was to agree to sell Israel fifty Phantom jets. The United States had become the major arms supplier of the Jewish state after relations between Paris and Jerusalem deteriorated in the wake of President deGaulle's program for improving the French role in the Arab world.[9]

The Nixon administration was not satisfied with a backstage role. Instead, it alarmed the Israelis by initiating talks with the Soviet Union to determine whether or not the two superpowers could produce the framework for a possible settlement. As if to confirm the new President's analysis that the area was a "powder keg," in 1969 Nasser initiated a war of attrition along the Suez Canal, which led to constant artillery exchanges between the Israelis and Egyptians. With international terrorism increasing and Soviet-American efforts stalled, the United States released its ideas on the shape of an Egyptian-Israeli and Jordanian-Israeli settlement for the first time since the 1967 war. Announced by Secretary of State Rogers, the plan envisioned Israeli withdrawal from the vast majority of the territory captured in 1967 in return for guarantees and Arab agreements to nonbelligerency. Israel was appalled that the United States had not waited for the Arabs to enter into direct negotiations with them and viewed the Rogers plan as largely at Israel's expense. The Arabs remained suspicious.

The Israelis began deep penetration raids into Egypt in early 1970, desperately attempting to convince Nasser to resume the 1967 cease-fire. In response, the Russians dramatically increased their aid to Cairo, leading to a second Rogers initiative intended to produce a cease-fire and institute some form of American-sponsored negotiations between Egypt and Israel. After much wrangling, the war of attrition ended in early August 1970 when both Egypt and Israel agreed to the new American plan. The guns fell silent along the Suez Canal, but the Egyptians immediately violated the conditions of the cease-fire by moving sophisticated antiair-craft missiles to the banks of the canal, a feat they had not been able to accomplish while their forces suffered from Israeli bombardment. Jerusalem was left to complain loudly and bitterly at these developments and withdrew from the planned talks in protest, but Washington could do little except increase military and economic aid to Israel.

Meanwhile, the PLO had constantly been growing in strength in Jordan and seemed to threaten King Hussein's control of the country. After a spectacular series of hijackings, in which terrorists brought captured planes to an abandoned airfield in northern Jordan, the king retaliated against his Palestinian opponents. The Syrians, then closely associated with Moscow, promptly attacked Jordan on behalf of the Palestinians. President Nixon saw this intervention as a Soviet challenge and engaged in an unprecedented high level of coordination with Israel in connection with a possible Israeli invasion of Jordan. In the end, Jordanian military action, American diplomatic signals, and Israeli military maneuvering apparently combined to lead to a Syrian retreat. But the lesson for the administration (especially for the President and his national security adviser, Henry Kissinger) was that the Israelis had been important in thwarting Soviet plots in the area. The combination of Egyptian violations along the Suez Canal and Israeli cooperation with Washington over Jordan led to an enhanced Israeli position at the White House.

Simultaneously, however, the stage was set for a new situation with the death of Nasser in late September 1970 and the succession of Anwar Sadat to the Egyptian presidency. Sadat soon began to indicate some interest in a possible disengagement agreement along the Suez Canal; this led to Secretary of State Rogers' third and last diplomatic initiative, which was to occupy most of 1971. In the end neither side agreed on a partial Israeli pullback from the Suez Canal, which would have permitted a reopening of the waterway. In 1972 the administration retreated to an election-year embrace of Israel by an offer of long-term military U.S. assistance.

Sadat had plans of his own. In the summer of 1972 he shocked most observers by expelling his Russian advisers. His implicit message was an appeal to the United States to become more interested in possible association with him at the expense of Israel. Once the election and the Vietnam war had been completed by early 1973, Nixon and Kissinger began to toy with the idea of a new Middle East initiative, and quiet exploratory steps were taken. In the background a rising crescendo of public debate centered on the significance of growing Western dependence on Arab oil.

Sadat was dissatisfied with the straws in the wind and the leisurely place of American diplomacy. In October 1973, having gotten the backing of Nasser's old enemy, Saudi Arabia, and in coordination with Syria, he stunned Americans and Israelis by attacking Israel on Judaism's holiest day, Yom Kippur.

Kissinger had become secretary of state only days before and was forced to confront a major upheaval in American relations with the Middle East. During the war the political landscape in the area altered radically. The American leadership had assumed that Israel would win easily, but the early days of the war saw surprising Arab successes. Nixon and Kissinger had recently concluded agreements with the Soviet Union envisioning a mutual control of local conflicts, but the Russians openly encouraged the Arabs and initiated a major airlift to resupply their clients. Kissinger's perceptions of the Middle East and its players were shaken. His first reaction to the dawning Middle East crisis was a fear that Israel would preempt. Now a sense of concern changed to a recognition of opportunity. If a stalemate could be produced as a consequence of the war, negotiations afterward would be facilitated.

Therefore, the United States manipulated its involvement to assure that a stalemate would occur. At first, when it was believed that Israel would win easily, major arms aid to the Israelis was withheld despite past promises. After Israeli military initiatives stalled, Kissinger reversed field and approved a major military airlift to Israel worth $2.2 billion. As the war progressed, the tide of conflict reversed, especially when the Israelis took possession of an additional piece of Syrian territory (beyond what had been captured in 1967) and were closer to Damascus than ever. On the Egyptian front the Israelis had established a bridgehead on the Cairo side of the Suez Canal and were rapidly entrapping the Egyptian forces that had crossed the canal into the Sinai.

The Kremlin realized that its clients were about to suffer yet another military debacle and invited Kissinger to Moscow to discuss terms of a cease-fire. In the Russian capital the two parties rapidly agreed on a resolution that would serve as a formula for ending the war. The deal was that a cease-fire in place would occur while a proposed UN resolution would call for negotiations between the conflicting parties. The Israelis would thereby be denied a victory but there would be no insistence on an immediate withdrawal from the territories captured, which the Arabs had demanded. Jerusalem would gain a call by the two superpowers for direct negotiations "between the parties concerned," but this achievement was diluted by the stipulation that projected talks be held "under appropriate auspices." The deal quickly passed as Resolution 338 at the UN Security Council, although it did not bring an end to the war.

The Israelis soon took advantage of Egyptian cease-fire violations to complete their encirclement of the Egyptian Third Army in the Sinai. This action brought a Kremlin threat to intervene on the Egyptian side and an American nuclear alert intended to signal the Russians that the United States would not countenance Soviet intervention. Simultaneously, Kissinger agreed to a UN observer corps to oversee the cease-fire, a requirement overlooked in the original arrangement in Moscow, and began to pressure Israel to spare the Third Army.

The Arabs assumed increased importance in American eyes when Saudi Arabia cooperated in an oil embargo against the United States and The Netherlands for collaborating with Israel. Given the growing dependence of the United States on foreign oil, the embargo's effect was felt in America by long lines at gas stations and a heightened sense of an energy crisis. In addition, the Organization of Oil Producing Exporting Countries (OPEC) quadrupled oil prices over the next few months.

To Kissinger, the dangers of international instability and potential conflict with the Soviet Union were matters of even greater concern. He now set about attempting to play a major role as mediator between Israel and the Arabs in order to calm the international situation and increase American influence. In this effort he was aided immeasurably by the Saudi-Egyptian alliance and the basic decision of Anwar Sadat to move from the Russian to the American camp. American leaders had always sought a major role with Egypt, the largest and most influential Arab country. Nasser had denied this option to them; Sadat made clear to Kissinger that the opportunity was being offered. American policy makers had also long dreamed of being able to support without contradiction Saudi Arabia and Egypt. Kissinger found that possibility also within his grasp. His diplomacy over the next several months, therefore, was intended to solidify this new American diplomatic opportunity while quieting the Arab-Israeli scene. The secretary of state did not believe that this effort required the achievement of a comprehensive settlement involving the many issues and disputes between the two sides, nor did he believe that such a settlement was possible at the time. Rather, he attempted to establish a momentum that would create new diplomatic directions while the United States remained at the center of the process. Thus, he was soon traveling frequently to the area, shuttling between the major countries of the Arab-Israeli theater.

Kissinger quickly achieved an initial agreement between Egypt and Israel to return prisoners of war and facilitate the shipment of food and medical supplies to the trapped Third Army. He then set about arranging for the meeting envisoned in Resolution 338, which became known as the Geneva Conference. A session was convened in late December 1973, attended by Jordan, Israel, and Egypt, as well as by the United States and the Soviet Union. After the opening speeches it was adjourned to await the result of the Israeli elections. Five years later, the Geneva Conference had still not reconvened.

Israel and Egypt had little interest in dealing with the Soviet Union, whose presence was guaranteed at a Geneva gathering. They preferred Kissinger's shuttle diplomacy, which offered American mediation in a more controlled setting. Thus, in January 1974 the secretary of state was able to achieve an Egyptian-Israeli disengagement agreement by which the Israelis retreated to their side of the Suez Canal and conceded a small portion of the Sinai along the canal to Cairo. Egypt in turn thinned out the forces that had entered the Sinai as a result of the October war, and the two sides were separated by a UN force.

Fresh from this major diplomatic victory, Kissinger convinced the Saudis to end their oil embargo. Then, in a stunning diplomatic accomplishment, he spent thirty-three days in April and May of 1974 shuttling between the Syrians and the Israelis. In the disengagement accord he finally achieved, the Israelis gained their prisoners of war in Syria and retreated from the Syrian territory captured in the October war; they also relinquished the key town of Quneitra, the capital of the Golan, which had been captured in 1967.

Throughout this period Kissinger had been forced to deal diplomatically in an administration weakening progressively because of the Watergate scandal. Nixon now attempted to take advantage of Kissinger's achievements by traveling to the Middle East in a desperate effort to salvage his own reputation. But the visit did not have a significant effect on American relations with the Middle East, and the President returned to Washington for a rendezvous with resignation several weeks later.

Under President Ford the continuity of American diplomacy was secured by Secretary of State Kissinger's retention of his post and the strong dependence on him by the new and inexperienced Chief Executive. The first two disengagement accords had been logical outcomes of the manner in which the October war had ended. The question now was how to proceed with Middle East diplomacy. In the previous several months the Arab-Israeli dispute had gained unprecedented levels of attention from the chief foreign policy officer of the country. But over the following several months other issues dawned on the horizon: the Greek-Turkish war over Cyprus and its aftermath, the uncertain political scene in Portugal, the deteriorating situation in Indochina, the possibility of a SALT II agreement with the Soviet Union, and the emerging civil war in Angola over the selection of an independent government to replace the Portuguese. In part as a consequence, through the summer of 1974 and onward the breakdown in diplomatic momentum Kissinger had long feared began to affect the Middle East. At first Kissinger attempted to gain a disengagement accord on the Jordanian frontier that would match the agreements reached on the Syrian and Egyptian fronts with Israel. There were major differences about the scope and depth of an agreement to be arranged on the West Bank between King Hussein and the new Israeli government led by Yitzhak Rabin (who had replaced Golda Meir as prime minister in mid-1974). Before initial progress could be made toward striking a deal between Jerusalem and Amman, however, the Arab League, in an October meeting at Rabat, Morocco, declared that it regarded the Palestinian Liberation Organization as "the sole legitimate representative of the Palestinian people on any liberated Palestinian territory"—in other words, as the sole political arm that could negotiate for the West Bank and the Gaza Strip. The Arabs thereby placed the Palestinian question at the center of Middle East diplomacy and measurably increased the difficulties confronting Henry Kissinger. In many ways his diplomacy never recovered from this decision and from the effect on both sides created by Yasser Arafat's subsequent appearance before the UN General Assembly.

Attempting to collect the broken pieces of his Middle East diplomacy, Kissinger joined the Egyptians and the Israelis in discussions toward a second disengagement agreement in the Sinai. Both sides were interested, but in March 1975 the talks broke down when they could not agree on the terms and compensation for Israeli withdrawal from the key strategic Gidi and Mitla passes of the Sinai and from the Abu Rhodeis oilfields.

The breakdown created a new phase in American relations with Israel, for Kissinger clearly blamed it on the Israelis. President Ford declared a reassessment of American policy in the area. During the reassessment the United States did not initiate new arms deals with Israel and clogged the military supply pipelines. Meanwhile, a variety of future diplomatic options were discussed, including a return to the Geneva Conference setting. In the end, however, the obvious interest in returning to the talks on the part of both Sadat and Rabin (as indicated by Egypt's reopening of the Suez Canal and an Israeli unilateral military pullback in the Sinai) contributed to an altered atmosphere. By the end of the summer a deal was complete. The new factor that made agreement possible was the inclusion of an American civilian observation team with sophisticated equipment in the strategic passes to assure compliance on both sides. The accord, signed in September 1975, included several memoranda of agreements between Israel and the United States under which the United States undertook to compensate Israel economically for the loss of the oilfields, which had provided 50 percent of her energy needs. The United States also promised economic aid on a long-term basis and the continuation and increase of military assistance; Washington committed itself to cooperating diplomatically with Israel in preparation for a Geneva Conference and promised not to deal with the PLO until that organization accepted Security Council Resolutions 242 and 338 and recognized Israel's right to exist.

On the face of it, these promises represented a major intensification of the "special relationship" between the United States and Israel. Certainly many in Israel, as well as American pro-Arab observers, believed that the agreements amounted to an intensified courtship between the two countries. As subsequent events were to demonstrate, however, verbal commitments could be redefined and even ignored as American personnel and predispositions altered.

The American-Israeli relationship was changing as the effects of the October 1973 war began to be felt. Not only was oil wealth increasing the attention paid to the Arab states and the Arab cause but Kissinger could not resist the opportunity to nudge the Russians out of the Middle East in favor of an expanded American influence, which meant closer relations with several oil-producing nations. Thus, American arms sales to Iran and the conservative Arab states increased dramatically during the Ford era, while American businessmen hastened to take advantage of the growing wealth of Arab oil producers to compete for contracts and sales.

While the infrastructure of a new relationship between the United States and the moderate Arabs was being constructed, the diplomatic momentum stalled completely. Syria angrily accused Sadat of betraying the Arab cause by reaching a second disengagement accord with Israel; President Assad thereby rejected the option of a second Syrian-Israeli disengagement agreement. Meanwhile, internal confrontation in Lebanon between Palestinians and leftist Moslems on the one hand and Christians and right-wing factions on the other erupted into a full-scale civil war that occupied the Arab world through the remainder of President Ford's term in office.[10] The same difficulties in American relations with the area remained: (1) the issue of growing Arab petro-power, (2) the dilemma of reaching an Arab-Israeli settlement, (3) the determination to contain the Soviet Union, and (4) assorted issues related to the energy crisis. It fell to a new team, led by Jimmy Carter, to handle these problems.

THE CARTER BACKGROUND

The Carter administration entered office confronted in the Middle East with a continuing Arab-Israeli dispute, a temporary cease-fire in the Lebanese civil war, the growing international significance of Arab oil producers, and diplomatic differences with the Soviet Union over an approach to the resolution of outstanding Middle East issues. Unlike Ford and Kissinger, the administration sought new initiatives in approaching these problems through a comprehensive scheme that attempted to deal with each major party in contention and each major issue. In the early months of the administration Secretary of State Cyrus Vance traveled to the Middle East and Carter met with Arab and Israeli leaders. In a series of statements at news conferences and town meetings, the President also identified the key items in dispute and hinted at possible solutions.

First, he dealt with the necessity for Israeli territorial withdrawals; in the tradition of previous administrations, but more clearly, he stressed only "minor adjustments to the pre-1967 borders." Second, Carter became thè first American President to indicate that the United States favored complete Arab-Israeli normalization as a viable objective. He suggested that Israel's borders with each of her four neighbors "must be opened up to travel, to tourism, to cultural exchange, to trade, so that no matter who the leaders might be in those countries, the people themselves will have formed a mutual understanding and comprehension and a sense of a common purpose to avoid the repetitious wars and deaths that have afflicted that region so long." Third, Carter also became the first American President to endorse the idea of a Palestinian homeland.[11]

In an effort to bring the parties together to achieve an Arab-Israeli settlement, the administration at first sought to reconvene a Geneva Conference attended by every key regional party and co-chaired by the United States and the Soviet Union. As part of this enterprise, Washington and Moscow agreed to a joint communiqué, released on October 1, 1977, in which the United States for the first time accepted the phrase "legitimate rights of the Palestinians," which until then was viewed as code in Arab diplomatic parlance for displacing Israel with a Palestinian state. The administration of course took a more restrained definition of the wording. The communiqué also indicated that representatives of the "Palestinian people" should participate in a Geneva Conference; it advocated "normal peaceful relations on the basis of mutual recognition of the principles of sovereignty, territorial integrity, and political independence"; it also suggested a role for Soviet and American guarantees as part of any settlement.

The controversial idea of involving the Russians in the peace process was much criticized in Congress and the press. Though it officially remained administration policy, it was displaced in public discussion by President Anwar Sadat's astonishing visit to Jerusalem in November 1977 and the diplomatic efforts that revolved around Egyptian-Israeli contacts. Once negotiations between Cairo and Jerusalem foundered, administration efforts were devoted to resurrecting the talks. The major issues in dispute included a formula for handling the future of the West Bank and the Gaza Strip and a declaration of principles broadly covering all Arab-Israeli issues. These agreements could be followed by negotiations leading to a final

Egyptian-Israeli settlement and the entry of Jordan into discussions about the West Bank.

By midsummer 1978 the Sadat peace initiative had ground to a halt. Sadat refused to conduct future talks with the Israelis and called on the United States to become a "full partner" in Mideast diplomacy. The Carter administration feared the worst—a total breakdown of the peace initiative followed by a war followed by an oil embargo and the end of its close relations with Saudi Arabia. In this light the desperate gamble of Camp David was conceived involving Presidents Carter and Sadat and Prime Minister Begin personally.

Few observers anticipated major gains from the Camp David meetings; indeed, on the eve of the September 1978 summit, prospects seemed bleak. Nevertheless, in terms of personal and national interests each side had much to gain from an agreement. Carter feared war in the Middle East if failure resulted and believed his low standing in the public opinion polls would be improved by a summit success. Begin, more popular at home than Carter, had long favored a strategy of making peace with Egypt as a means of lessening his country's crushing defense burden and reducing the likelihood of another major war with the Arabs. A success would also enhance the political image of his Likud coalition, which had gained power in 1977 (after twenty-nine years of Labor party rule in Israel). Sadat had risked his political career, his reputation, and even his life to travel to Jerusalem in November 1977; he seemed loath to admit error and return to the Arab fold and confrontation with Israel, a course of action being urged on him by many Arab states. Egypt's armed forces were ill-prepared for war; the majority of the populace was clearly tired of the conflict with Israel and resentful over the wealth of the oil-rich Arab states compared with the poverty of their own country. Sadat was anxious to resurrect his country's shattered economy and infrastructure, while the average Egyptian had high hopes of the practical benefits peace would bring.

Despite this calculus of benefits to each of the three parties from a summit success, the problems at hand and a distrust generated by thirty years of conflict led to several near-breakdowns during the talks. Through most of the discussions Carter and his aides shuttled between the two antagonists raising potential compromises and conveying suggestions from one side to the other. In the end two documents were agreed on and signed at a dramatic White House ceremony. The first consisted of a framework for the conclusion of a peace treaty between Egypt and Israel; the two countries agreed to seek completion of the detailed negotiations necessary before a treaty could be signed within three months. The basic compromise was shortly approved by the Israeli Knesset after a grueling seventeen-hour debate. It included a phased Israeli withdrawal from all parts of the Sinai (including Israeli settlements and airbases) to be completed within three years of the conclusion of the treaty in return for diplomatic and commercial normalization of relations between Jerusalem and Cairo. In addition, UN forces and limited-force zones would separate the armies of the two states.

The second agreement was more complex and bound to cause controversy. It dealt primarily with the rubric for settling the West Bank/Gaza issue. Under the terms of the agreement, a five-year transition administration would be established by a committee consisting of Egypt, Jordan, and Israel; West Bank and Gaza Palestinians might participate on the Egyptian and Jordanian delegations. This committee would arrange for full autonomy in these two territories by an administrative council to be "freely elected by the inhabitants of these areas to replace the existing [Israeli] military government." Under the accords, security during the transition period would be provided in three ways: (1) the Israeli armed forces in the West Bank and Gaza would withdraw to "specified security locations"; (2) "a strong local police force" would be established, which might include Jordanians; and (3) the borders would be patroled by joint Israeli and Jordanian units.

By the third year of the five-year transition period, negotiations would begin among the four parties (i.e., Israelis, Egyptians, Jordanians, and representatives of the West Bank/Gaza administrative council) to determine the final disposition of the West Bank and Gaza. Meanwhile, Israelis, Jordanians, and administrative council representatives would conduct negotiations on a final Jordanian-Israeli peace treaty. At the end of the process, arrangements for the West Bank and Gaza would be submitted for approval to a vote by the inhabitants of the two areas' elected representatives.

These arrangements present substantial compromises by both sides. Israel had already offered the Palestinians autonomy under the "Begin plan" presented months earlier to President Sadat, but the Camp David agreement was more specific concerning Israeli commitments and the exercise of future Arab authority and did not provide Israel with as many safeguards in implementing the plan. Moreover, Israel now accepted the goals of resolving "the Palestinian problem in all its aspects" and of providing "full" autonomy to residents of the West Bank and Gaza Strip; the Jerusalem government also recognized the "legitimate rights of the Palestinian people and their just requirements." These phrases could be used against Israel in future negotiations. Indeed, many Israeli critics of the plan argued that Begin had authorized a process bound to end in the establishment of an independent Palestinian state on the West Bank and Gaza Strip, which could, in their view, threaten Israeli security. The Israelis retained the right to maintain military forces in both areas and did not necessarily agree that either the forces or Jewish settlements would be withdrawn from the territories after the five-year transition. They did not commit themselves to complete withdrawals at that time, and the delicate Jerusalem question was sidestepped when letters were later exchanged indicating the differing positions of each of the three governments that participated at Camp David. Of particular importance, the five-year transition was not slated to begin until the administrative council was established and inaugurated. If serious delays were to occur in arranging for elections, the portion of the accords applying to the Gaza Strip and the West Bank might become academic.

President Sadat agreed to a document in which the PLO was not even mentioned by name and in which the Israelis did not commit themselves as a precondition to accept basic Arab demands. Nevertheless, he could reasonably argue that the second document provided a framework that, if accepted, offered opportunities for the satisfaction of Arab objectives he himself had achieved in the context of his dealings with Israel.

The risks of Camp David were thus asymmetrical. For Israel, the agreements involved potentially severe security and economic problems in the long term by relinquishing the considerable military advantage of holding the Sinai; by giving up promising oilfields; by enduring the painful economic dislocations involved in moving people, equipment, and materiel back to pre-1967 Israel (estimated to cost several billion dollars); and by possibly destabilizing the West Bank and Gaza Strip. For Egypt, the political and economic risks of isolation in the Arab world were critical immediately. This danger came to fruition when the involved Arab moderates—Jordan, the West Bankers, and Saudi Arabia—joined the radicals in rejecting the Camp David accords.

These Arab conservatives, especially the Saudis, feared that acquiescence in the Camp David accords might increase their vulnerability to radical assaults. King Hussein feared for his throne; many West Bank leaders feared PLO assassination attempts. For the Saudis, the growing turmoil in Iran in the fall of 1978 led them to question the efficacy of American protection, precipitating a greater tendency than usual to acquiesce in radical initiatives.

When the "Washington talks" at Blair House convened to negotiate the precise details and wording of an Egyptian-Israeli peace treaty, the hostile attitude of many key Arab states and the growing isolation of Sadat delayed the successful completion of the negotiations.

The Egyptians sought to link the peace treaty to progress on establishing an autonomous entity in the West Bank and Gaza in the belief that it would more adequately test Israeli intentions, and more important, would cover their Arab flank. On the other hand, the Israelis sought as weak a connection as possible, out of fear that if they committed themselves to a timetable for completing the arrangements for autonomy, West Bank Arabs would be granted veto power over the Egyptian-Israeli peace process. In other words, if autonomy could not be instituted on schedule, the Egyptians might delay or even terminate normalization with Israel. To the Israelis, dividing issues into manageable proportions could facilitate a durable settlement and simultaneously test Egyptian intentions.

THE CARTER POLICY RATIONALE

In this debate the Carter administration tended to agree with the Egyptian perspective because of U.S. intention to maintain close relations with as many Arab states as possible and deal with as much of the Arab-Israeli problem as might prove feasible. The key motivations of American officials can be found in concern over the possibility of the Arab-Israeli conflict's creating instability or anti-American attitudes within Arab oil-producing nations. The basis for understanding the administration's approach lies in its fundamental premises. From the outset there were basic tactical differences with Henry Kissinger's policies, but the conclusions of the Carter administration were not different from those of the former secretary of state. Affected by the shocks of Vietnam and the Yom Kippur war, Kissinger and his Democratic critics who rose to high office shared a pessimistic belief in the limitation of American power and in the country's need to adjust to the new forces developing in world politics. Kissinger, by comparison with his successors, concentrated on the Russians more and on Third World forces less, but all shared a deep-seated fear of another oil embargo, a fascination with the increase in Saudi power, and the opinion that the future in the Middle East lies with the Arabs.

To Kissinger, the key state in the Middle East was Egypt, and the central problem facing American policy in the area was to block the Russians from a major role. To Brzezinski and his comrades, the key state in the area is Saudi Arabia and the central problem, energy. Israel had a role to play in Kissinger's approach, but is of little value to the United States in Brzezinski's.

Prominent Democratic foreign policy advisers have written a great deal about the Arab-Israeli dispute and how to solve it; thus their views are hardly secret. The result is a doctrine that, in its broad outlines, has become the intellectual basis of the current American approach. Labeled by former Undersecretary of State George Ball "How to Save Israel in Spite of Herself," the adherents of the doctrine propose that because they are friendly toward Israel, they understand better than the Israelis (and their supporters) what is best for the Jewish state.[12] In one form or another these analysts argue that it is right for Israel to return to the 1967 borders because (1) the Arab confrontation states are ready for peace, (2) the Palestinians deserve a home-land, and (3) a smaller Israel ensures Middle East stability. Basic to their approach is the conviction that Israel cannot have both territory and peace. Many argue that Israel must be pressured to return to the 1967 boundaries because without a settle-ment the Arab moderates will lose control, thereby diminishing American influence or opening the door to Russian reemergence; the Arabs will start another war or there will be another oil embargo. Those who maintain these views argue, paradoxi-cally, that Israel's interests (and, conveniently, America's as well) can be simultane-ously secured by taking actions the Arabs favor.

The centerpiece of the approach is linkage of the Arab-Israeli and energy ques-tions. As Brzezinski himself once wrote,

> *It is impossible to seek a resolution to the energy problem without tackling head-on—and doing so in an urgent fashion—the Arab-Israeli conflict. Without a settlement of that issue in the near future, any stable arrangement in the energy area is simply not possible.*[13]

This linkage of the Arab-Israeli and energy questions means that Saudi Arabia must be central to any analysis of the administration's approach to the area. Were the Saudi kingdom to fall to a Qaddafi, the economic future of the West would be severely jeopardized. But if the current Saudi leaders were to turn against the United States by dramatically raising oil prices or lowering oil production in the years ahead, the consequences would also be lethal for the West. Therefore, America must not act in a manner that will lead the Saudis and their allies to question their trust in the United States or lead other Arabs to question Saudi policies.

A number of corollaries result. The United States can no longer afford to ignore the radical Arabs because it must be assumed that they possess the power to ruin the structure of American economic and political power in the Middle East. A further corollary is an inter-Arab domino theory: any accretion of radical power is a poten-tial threat to the conservatives (i.e., the Saudis). Moreover, the economic and political damage caused by OPEC—and its most central power, Saudi Arabia—must be tolerated and the United States must adjust to the "interdependence" the new conditions have created.

The result is an intriguing combination of passivism on the Middle East energy issue mixed with activism on the Arab-Israeli question. The Carter administration believes that OPEC cannot be broken. When combined with its definition of the need to solve the energy question and the linkage of that problem to the Arab-Israeli dispute, the policy results in attempts to solve the conflict immediately. Conveniently, an Arab-Israeli settlement is seen as possible because of the perceived moderation by all the confrontation states and Israel. Even Syrian President Assad was at first labeled by Carter a "strong supporter in the search for peace." This belief that the Arabs would be prepared to accept a normalization of relations as part of any settlement explains why Carter became the first President to endorse the Israeli claim to a genuine peace rather than a mere arrangement of nonbelligerency. The administration believes, however, that Israel can earn normalization only by major concessions.

The sense of urgency demanded more than confidence in Arab moderation and explains Secretary of State Vance's four visits to the area in the first year of the administration, early and frequent summits with Arab and Israeli leaders in Washington, repeated presidential statements about territories and Palestinians as well as normalization, the preoccupation in the fall of 1977 with reconvening the Geneva Conference by the end of the year, the constant fear that Sadat might soon withdraw his peace initiative, and the convening of the Camp David summit and the concern over the linkage issue in its aftermath.

An Arab-Israeli settlement "in all its parts" was stressed in order to gain the confidence of the Saudis in American leadership and to maintain, by extension, Arab confidence in what Washington perceived as a growing primary Saudi role in the Arab world. The lesson drawn from the Lebanese civil war was not the lesson assumed by many of Israel's supporters: that the PLO was on the wane. Rather, the administration concluded that Saudi Arabia was capable of exercising leadership and providing a stabilizing influence. Key U.S. officials determined that the Saudis had taken the steps necessary to bring the war to a close after Syrian intervention. The Saudi role in moving Somalia away from the Russians reinforced this stabilizing image. But the crucial significance of this most conservative of Arab monarchies was increased manifold by its perceived function as international banker, oil price regulator, and the world's most critical oil producer.

Instances of the special U.S.–Saudi relationship in the Carter era can be recounted easily: (1) On his visit in May 1977, Prince Fahd was given a royal welcome. Carter commented that "so far as I know, between ourselves and Saudi Arabia, there are no disturbing differences at all." (2) The private Saudi claim that they sought a Palestinian state on the West Bank and Gaza Strip was followed up seriously, and a flirtation with the PLO undertaken. (3) Saudi Arabia was the only Arab state included on Carter's original itinerary to the Middle East at the outset of 1978; no pretense was made of the need to balance the visit with stopovers in other Arab states or Israel. In the administration's perspective, the trip was not part of Arab-Israeli diplomacy but of the "new influentials" policy, though to the local parties themselves, political symbolism was present nonetheless. (4) Sadat's visit to Jerusalem was at first received cautiously in Washington, until the Saudi reaction could be ascertained. At the same time the administration refused to insist on a public Saudi statement of support for Sadat's initiatives. Instead the Saudis were promised by the President that they would receive F-15 jets, and the announcement of the sale was made at a delicate point of Egyptian-Israeli negotiations and despite widespread controversy because the Saudis claimed they would judge American willingness to sell the planes as a litmus test of their "special relationship" with Washington. (5) The President was prepared to confront Israel's supporters on Capitol Hill in mid-1978 in fighting fiercely and successfully for the acceptance of his Middle East arms package to Saudi Arabia, Egypt, and Israel. (6) The administration responded cautiously and mildly when Saudi Arabia sought in the interests of Arab unity to wean Sadat away from his peace initiative in the summer of 1978, and when the Saudis reacted negatively to Camp David and joined the Arab radicals at an anti-Sadat, anti-Camp David summit in Baghdad in early November 1978.

The administration stressed Geneva, comprehensiveness, Arab unity, the Palestinians, and even a Russian role in the peace process because it sought an Arab world organized under Saudi leadership as a means of assuring the stability of inter-Arab politics and oil and monetary flows. This objective meant that a peace settlement would have to be as comprehensive as possible so that no party involved in the area would have an incentive to undermine it. Comprehensiveness at first meant a "Syrianized" American policy, for Assad was the key Arab leader with ties to both moderate and radical camps. This objective also demanded the involvement of the PLO at a peace conference in order to assure that the organization would not torpedo an accord. It also demanded that the Kremlin, as co-chairman of Geneva and as Washington's competitor, be neutralized through involvement. The administration optimistically assumed that if both the PLO and the Russians were involved in the process of reaching a settlement, an agreement could be obtained and all would accept it and abide by its terms. These calculations explain the Soviet-American communiqué of October 1977, the administration's flirtation with the PLO in 1977, its emphasis on a Palestinian homeland, and its endorsement of the then controversial phrase, "the legitimate rights of the Palestinians."

The Carter administration's preoccupation with comprehensiveness also helps explain its initial hesitancy over the Sadat visit, its lack of enthusiasm for Sadat's early idea of a Cairo Conference in December 1977, and its early overtures to Assad to join the new peace process. At first the Sadat visit raised the specter of several developments that had been feared in Washington: a moderate-radical split in the Arab world, with a major threat against the conservatives from the radical forces; a Soviet-American split, with an accompanying Kremlin effort to ruin a comprehensive peace; a separate peace between Israel and Egypt, which would strengthen Israel but might jeopardize the conservatives led by Saudi Arabia and might lead to a permanent state of conflict and radicalization in the Arab world. It is not surprising that American doubts about Sadat lessened as it became clear he would not accept a separate peace and would insist on a declaration covering Palestinian rights in specific form.

With Sadat's position clarified by early 1978, it was possible for Washington to conceive reinvolving not only the Jordanians but also gaining future Syrian and Russian participation.[14] As for the PLO, American discouragement with Arafat was clear; the administration now favored neutralizing the organization through Palestinian self-determination on the West Bank and Gaza after a five-year transition period. At Camp David the basis for fulfilling this modified policy was established.

But how was American influence to be exercised? In any situation there is a subtle distinction in the imposition of leverage: economic, political, or military pressure designed to force compliance can be juxtaposed against confidence-building measures intended to induce cooperation with one's objectives.

The Carter administration's definition of the energy crisis and the Arab-Israeli problem predisposed the balance between pressure and confidence-building measures. Since Saudi importance had been stressed in early analyses, inducements such as increased arms sales were likely. On the Israeli side, pressure was more probable because Israeli concessions were seen as necessary to produce a rapid settlement.

Seen in this light, American-Israeli disputes over settlements in occupied territories, over the definition of Resolution 242, and over the future of the West Bank were consistent with preconceptions built into the structure of the administration's policy. For the first time, an incoming administration rejected its predecessor's deal with Israel when the sale of concussion bombs was canceled; in addition, the sale of the latest FLIR night-vision equipment was delayed; despite oral promises by Kissinger, the sale of Israeli-built Kfir jets to Ecuador was vetoed. Meanwhile, several co-production agreements with Israel were not approved: for example, an Israeli request on F-16 co-production and the co-production of a sophisticated military communication network between American and Israeli firms. On the other hand, the sale of Hawk and Maverick missiles to Saudi Arabia, which the President had criticized during the campaign, was allowed to go forward, and American participation in the rebuilding of Egyptian Mig-21 jet engines and airframes was approved.

The most-debated aspect of administration aid policy in its first eighteen months was the package sale in 1978 of 15 F-15 and 75 F-16 fighter aircraft to Israel, 60 F-15 jets to Saudi Arabia, and 50 F-5E jets to Egypt (the first offensive weapon offered Cairo since 1955). After a bitter fight, the administration succeeded in preventing a congressional veto of the sales. Israel's supporters claimed that the offers to Israel had been unnecessarily cut below Jerusalem's requests and that the sales to Egypt and Saudi Arabia would jeopardize the peace process and the Middle East military balance. They also claimed that the package concept was an abrogation of the September 1975 accords because Israel had been promised the jet fighters irrespective of sales to Arab states. The administration claimed the sales were in the interest of the United States by rewarding President Sadat for his peace initiatives and by maintaining the trust of oil-powerful Saudi Arabia. It denied that the sales would tilt the military balance against Israel and was confident that the fighter aircraft sold to Egypt and Saudi Arabia would not be used against the Jewish state. The administration further maintained that if the United States did not sell advanced aircraft to Saudi Arabia, other states, especially France, would do so and in larger numbers and with fewer safeguards and conditions. Some opponents of the package claimed that the equivalent French jets were not as sophisticated or as effective as their American counterparts. Others argued that the possibility could not be excluded that Saudi Arabia would purchase comparable jets no matter what the United States did.

The arms package was reflective of the pattern of influence the administration had assumed. The number of fighter planes to Israel was cut, and the sales were tied to arms for the Arabs. The opposite approach was employed with Saudi Arabia and Egypt; they received arms as an incentive to resist raising oil prices and to continue the peace process.

A similar pattern was expressed after Camp David when the administration was reluctant to support Israeli claims for large increases in assistance to finance the moving of sophisticated equipment and material from the Sinai to the Negev. Meanwhile, the White House pressured a reluctant Congress to approve economic aid for Syria despite President Assad's opposition to the Camp David accords and continuing clashes in Lebanon between Syrian peacekeeping forces and Christian militiamen. The pattern was in turn reinforced by the anti-inflation program at home, which led high-level officials to hesitate about such major new foreign aid efforts as Israel was requesting on the grounds that the United States simply could not afford them.

THE CARTER POLICY AND RATIONALE: A CRITIQUE

Confronted with a desire to conduct amicable relations with states that were hostile to each other, successive American governments have developed a delicate balancing act over the years, rooted in an understanding of conflicting American interests.

By the time the Carter administration assumed power, the balance might be described in the following terms. The Middle East lies astride three continents (Europe, Africa, and Asia) and thus is in a critical location affected by, and in turn influencing, politics and policies in many countries. Several states in the area possess vast petroleum supplies, which are constantly becoming more crucial to the conduct of international politics as the possibility of future energy shortages increases. As oil prices have skyrocketed, states like Saudi Arabia and Iran have become important as potential markets for goods and services, for the international influence their petrobillions allow them, for their role in international finance, and for their ability in cooperation with other OPEC countries to regulate the flow and price of oil.

Given this growing importance of many countries in the area, and their proximity to the Soviet Union, the Middle East has continued to be a locus of potential superpower confrontation and a potential source of Russian aggrandizement that could severely threaten American economic and strategic interests.

The Middle East is also the location of one of the world's few remaining liberal democracies, Israel. This country is closely tied to the United States by common heritage, shared values, and moral commitment. Effective protection of the security of Israel is a sign of American trustworthiness abroad and bolsters the American reputation for credibility. Many participants on the American political scene who are concerned over continuing turmoil within and between countries in the area argue that Israel is also a source of regional stability in that she represents a stable and strong pro-American presence in an area of political instability and huge gaps between oil-rich states and poverty-stricken states. They see the Israelis in the region as a factor encouraging pro-American political forces through their military power, their active intelligence services, and their very presence. In this view, backing of this self-reliant and pro-American land is potentially the safest means of thwarting Soviet aims in the region because (1) it has been the most forthright and consistent opponent of Kremlin designs and pro-Moscow regimes; (2) in the Israeli-American special relationship Israel stands as a model for other regimes in the area, demonstrating the attractiveness of the Washington connection; and (3) the Russians know there is one country they cannot control in the region, i.e., Israel's existence prevents a Russian hegemony. Skeptics of these arguments claim that the existence of Israel has offered the Soviets opportunities to penetrate the Arab world because the Arabs continue to need arms against Jerusalem. The usual response to this position is that if Israel had not come into existence, the United States and the Soviet Union would have been involved in the area on competing sides within the Arab world and, given patterns in other regions, the United States would likely have aligned itself with the weaker Arab competitors.

Those who stress the utility of Israel point out that in some prominent cases Jerusalem has influenced the outcome of internal Arab conflicts. They cite as examples Israel's role of support for King Hussein in the September 1970 challenge to his monarchy by the PLO and Syria; Israeli assistance to Christians in the Lebanese civil war; Israeli warnings to Sadat in the summer of 1977 about impending Libyan-sponsored coup attempts against the Egyptian and Saudi regimes. They also mention the once solid and quiet cooperation between Iran and Israel as an example of the role Jerusalem could play if given greater prominence in American security calculations. Some of Israel's supporters do not carry the argument that far and prefer to rest their case on fundamental American commitments to democratic societies. All observers agree, however, that every President since Truman has reaffirmed the commitment to a democratic Jewish state in the Middle East, creating in and of itself a substantial interest in terms of historical policy continuity and a bedrock of domestic support that no administration can easily ignore.

The Carter administration has differed from its predecessors in the greater stress it has placed on the energy issue by comparison with the Soviet problem and, tactically, it has been more prepared to consider comprehensive rather than step-by-step solutions. Those who seek to judge the administration must weigh the adequacy of its response to the Middle East dilemmas raised during its tenure and the ability of the administration to juggle accurately the delicate balance of interests affecting American policy toward the Arab-Israeli dispute.

There is something of a tradition in American foreign policy of linking the Arab-Israeli dispute to whatever is perceived to be the major global issue. Thus, Eisenhower and Dulles thought they could resolve the problem of organizing the Arabs against communism by solving the dispute; Nixon and Kissinger assumed that settling the Arab-Israeli dispute would check Russian advances in the area. The linkage of the Arab-Israeli conflict to other questions has always been much debated. For example, it is unlikely that Nasser would have accepted the Baghdad Pact even if Israel had never existed because of his reluctance to become involved with any vestige of Western imperialism. Similarly, a Kremlin decline developed in the area when significant Arab states (e.g., Egypt, Sudan) became disillusioned with the Russians even while Israel occupied most of the territory captured in 1967.

The main conceptual problem the Carter administration faces in linking the Arab-Israeli dispute and the energy crisis is that the connection may not be as clear as many observers and government officials believe. As Elie Kedourie argues, "it is unsafe to link the two issues in a manner such as to lead to a belief that the supply of oil can be made secure by a settlement of the Arab-Israeli conflict." [15] Many ignore the nature of the distinction between the two problems. If the energy crisis were resolved, the Arab-Israeli issue would still exist. Similarly, if the Arab-Israeli dispute were settled, the energy crisis would continue.

> *It by no means follows that a settlement—even a pro-Arab settlement—of the Arab-Israeli conflict will necessarily safeguard American interests in Saudi Arabia. Such a settlement will not do away with radicalism and instability in the Arab world, and will thus by no means lessen the threat to the present Saudi regime. It may even, conceivably, increase it. . . . The Saudi regime needs the friendship and protection of the USA just as much as, or perhaps more than, the USA needs Saudi friendship and good will.* [16]

The two problems interact on one major axis: in the case of an Arab-Israeli war, oil supplies could be disrupted. This contingency could arise either by retaliatory acts by frustrated Arab oil producers (e.g., embargoes or price hikes) or by an Israeli raid on Saudi oilfields—especially if Saudi Arabia were to become involved in a military confrontation with Israel.

Because a war once caused supply disruptions, the result is a tendency to seek a settlement as an end in itself, for economic reasons, without sufficient regard to the traditional caveat that poor arrangements may actually create security deficiencies and increase the likelihood of war. This approach creates the crisis-management diplomacy distinctive of American Middle East policy since 1973.

There are inherent risks in so strong a preoccupation with a settlement; the intimate involvement of the United States in Arab-Israeli diplomacy with energy questions as a background may raise Arab expectations and Israeli fears to such an extent that the chances of diplomatic failure are actually increased. The Nixon, Ford, and (especially) Carter administrations have been willing to confront the dangers of activism on the ground that the alternatives were more stark. American leaders, unaccustomed to dependence on foreign sources for required natural resources, have been impressed by the figures of rising oil imports and Arab oil revenues, with the added leverage they give Arab producers in international financial markets.

Many fear that Arab oil producers might choose to punish the West if they become displeased with the progress of Arab-Israeli diplomacy. But the Arab producers have essential limitations on them—encouraged by their military and political dependence on Western powers, their economic interests, their inherent caution, and practical difficulties. Under conditions of surplus, the costs of playing politics with oil are likely to be considerable, whereas under conditions of scarcity, the costs to the Arabs would be diminished. Whether conditions of plenty or scarcity prevail in international markets is likely to be determined by rates of economic growth in the advanced industrial societies, new oil discoveries, effectiveness of conservation efforts, the rate at which new discoveries can be brought on line, and internal political conditions in oil-producing states (e.g., the disruptions caused by situations similar to the crisis in Iran). A host of factors is likely to affect pricing and production decisions, of which the Arab-Israeli conflict is only one. Similarly, despite the petrodollar surplus of such countries as Saudi Arabia and the resulting preeminence in international finance it gives them, they cannot easily transfer their funds to another currency base than the dollar because the most obvious alternatives (West Germany, Switzerland, and Japan) are not seeking petrodollars, and these currencies cannot provide sufficient liquidity. The viability of the dollar in international exchanges cannot be as easily undermined under current conditions as many may believe.[17]

Despite past performance and the logic of national interest, Saudi Arabia in particular could choose to take precipitous steps that might hurt the West. A prudent American policy must take every conceivable contingency into account, but a prudent policy must also not help to precipitate the worst of all conditions. The Carter Presidency has at times come dangerously close to the latter situation. By taking Saudi threats seriously and advertising their efficacy (as in the publicly presented rationale for selling Riyadh F-15s in 1978), the United States could actually force the Saudis to raise the stakes in order to maintain credibility with radical Arab critics. The Saudis fear that Arab disunity could increase pressures on them from a variety of quarters; if they are a part of the Arab consensus—even radical—they believe they protect themselves from attacks on the regime. Thus, only weeks after the administration justified its sale of sophisticated jets to the Saudis, in part on the basis of the efficacy of the harm Riyadh could cause the West and in part on Saudi moderation, the Saudis were actively organizing opposition in the Arab world to Anwar Sadat's peace initiative. Later they were unwilling to back the Camp David accords and organize support for them in the Arab world. In this sense Carter policy may well be on the road to creating a self-fulfilling prophecy out of the Israel-oil connection.

Unquestionably the United States needs a good relationship with Saudi Arabia to facilitate the flow of international oil and the health of international finance. But Saudi Arabia is also a militarily and politically weak country whose ruling family is sorely dependent upon the United States for protection and support. The relationship is therefore reciprocal; to act as if it is unilateral, as the Carter administration in effect has done, is to create discontinuities in the political balance between the two states and potentially to create the very dangers the administration seeks to prevent.

Some observers argue that American pressure could result in political instability in Saudi Arabia and elsewhere in the Persian Gulf. Caveats like this one contribute to American reticence toward Saudi Arabia. Yet political instability within oil-producing nations is more likely to result from indigenous movements and activities, as well as from American inability to take protective actions on behalf of these countries, than from U.S. pressure.

Many observers have wondered whether the administration has not overemphasized the Palestinian-Saudi energy connection at the expense of fundamental geopolitical concerns. Even if the West Bank entity envisioned in the Camp David accords were to come to fruition, the problems of Iran, the future of the Persian Gulf, a growing Soviet presence among countries peripheral to the area, and the fragility of oil-rich pro-American regimes would remain. These analysts have questioned whether American policy makers have become so fascinated with the new role of petrodollars that they have failed to measure power adequately.

In the perspective of analysts with these concerns, perhaps American officials have spent insufficient time and taken inadequate account of the real dangers posed to American interests by the growth of Russian strength on the periphery of the area because of their ideological preoccupation with economics and the Palestinian question. These analysts stress that moves toward the Soviet Union in Ethiopia, Afghanistan, and South Yemen plus the turmoil in Iran have cast a shadow over the politics of the Persian Gulf. They worry that political instability and radicalism may rise in the gulf as a result of forces only marginally related to the Palestinian and Arab-Israeli questions. In that case pressures on the Saudis would increase, as would the possibilities of oil supply disruptions. Administration spokesmen respond to such criticisms with the arguments that the United States has no choice but to adjust to altering world conditions, that a different strategy would not have been more effective in thwarting political crises in such countries as Afghanistan and Iran, and that the Palestinian issue was the most obvious source of political instability in the area—especially affecting the key oil producer, Saudi Arabia.

The tactics the Carter administration has used in relation to Middle East diplomacy flow from its premises and the sense of urgency encouraged by the energy crisis. The basic tactical problems with the administration's approach refer to its tendency toward comprehensive solutions and its specific handling of both the Arabs and Israelis.

The administration has consistently insisted on the most comprehensive version of any diplomatic process available. Before Sadat visited Jerusalem, it flirted with the PLO and gave Syria—the most radical of the Arab states on Israel's borders—a virtual veto over preparations for Geneva. In involving the Russians in the peace process it similarly strengthened the hand of the radicals in the Arab world at the expense of the moderates. These efforts were never likely to succeed because they forced the Arabs to unite around the least conciliatory consensus available.

The administration was saved from this approach by the Sadat initiative, but it immediately retreated to its previous concerns for comprehensiveness. The Carter camp emphasized the importance of linking a separate Egyptian-Israeli deal with an overall peace settlement, especially with a declaration of principles covering the Palestinian question. This route inevitably led to tensions between Washington and Jerusalem, for it involved concessions by Israel before the talks had actually begun. The administration feared that without such a declaration, Jordan would never enter the talks and Sadat could not proceed to make a bilateral deal with Israel on the Sinai. But the approach had inevitable corollaries. By insisting on a comprehensive formula, the administration made it more difficult for Sadat to pursue a separate approach or accept major compromises. Why should he amend his position when Carter was still pressing Israel? How could he appear less protective of Egyptian and Arab interests than was the President of the United States?

At Camp David the administration gained another reprieve from its self-imposed commitment to comprehensiveness, a reprieve it again refused to accept. On the surface the Egyptian-Israeli agreements did provide a separate peace with an appropriate cover for Sadat's Arab flank, but the administration chose to view the Camp David accords as a package and to stress their comprehensiveness. When the Jordanians, Saudis, and West Bank residents refused to accept the accords in the period after Camp David, the United States might have signaled that it was prepared to sponsor even a separate peace if no reasonable alternative existed and until the moderate Arabs altered their positions. Instead, Sadat was again forced to adjust to signals emerging from Washington that the United States did indeed regard a linkage between the two documents as essential and that a comprehensive approach to the Arab-Israeli problem was mandatory.

In its handling of the Arabs the administration has shown a constant tendency to back Saudi preferences. Since the Saudis were interested in Arab unity as a means of protecting themselves from the radicals, American designs inevitably worked to undermine any effort to achieve an independent Egyptian-Israeli connection. Jerusalem's diplomacy was aimed at achieving just such a conclusion. Therefore, there were bound to be fundamental differences between Jerusalem and Washington, which in turn encouraged the Arabs to resist compromise on the assumption that Israel would be pressured by the United States, which obviously disapproved of the diplomatic stances Jerusalem had taken.

As usual, the American-Israeli connection was a central factor in Middle East diplomacy. Here the Carter administration confronted a major paradox. As key patron of Israel, Washington was an appealing ally for the Arabs because they assumed she could press concessions from Jerusalem. On the other hand, because of American domestic politics and Israel's internal unity, American leverage was not as great as it appeared. The trump card that America had long offered to induce Israeli concessions was American guarantees and largesse. This balance had worked famously in the September 1975 accords that concluded the second Egyptian-Israeli disengagement agreements. The problem with Carter policy was its tendency to lean so hard on the Israelis that their incentive for concessions and their trust in the United States were seriously diminished.

An example of this process occurred shortly after Camp David. In his skepticism King Hussein submitted questions to the administration concerning the accords. Assistant Secretary of State for Near East and South Asian Affairs Harold Saunders was soon sent to Amman with replies to the king's questions. The answers he brought with him were rumored to contain assurances that Israeli settlements on the West Bank would be withdrawn as part of any future peace agreement—a report that gained substance when Saunders met with Arab notables in Jerusalem and commented that the United States regarded the eastern sector of the city as "occupied territory." The Israeli government felt that it had to respond to this challenge, both because of the internal pressures the Saunders statement generated and a fear that no answer would hinder its negotiating stance. Therefore, it shortly announced an expansion of existing Jewish settlement facilities on the West Bank, which led the Egyptians to harden their position on the issue of linkage in their negotiations with Israel.

The administration's enthusiasm for comprehensiveness has itself led to the expending of precious political capital that undermined the Jerusalem-Washington relationship and was also hurting the Jerusalem-Cairo connection. Curiously, from the time it arrived in Washington, the Carter entourage seemed to welcome a confrontation with Israel, presumably on the assumption that this would aid its relationship with Saudi Arabia. Even before Prime Minister Begin was elected, the administration was engaged in a range of disputes with the Rabin government over such issues as the Palestinian question and the extent of Israeli territorial withdrawals in case of a settlement. Carter had reversed the letter or spirit of several Ford-Kissinger decisions on direct and indirect aid to Israel, and it was an open secret in Washington that the President was displeased with Prime Minister Rabin's perceived rigidity. In this sense the administration's later difficulties with the Likud government were an extension of its initial assumptions—before Begin came to office and before Sadat visited Jerusalem—that the road to a peace settlement must be paved with Israeli concessions.

By the time crucial Egyptian-Israeli negotiations began, administration stands were already looked on with suspicion by the Israelis and their American supporters. As a consequence of such actions as the Soviet-American communiqué and the Middle East arms package, much goodwill had been squandered by the administration, and its effectiveness as a mediator was undermined. The impressive Carter performance at Camp David was nonetheless achieved, but the administration shortly returned to disputes with Israel over the future of Jerusalem, the extent of aid for Israeli transfer of equipment and material to the Negev, and the length of time the expansion of Israeli settlements on the West Bank would be suspended after Camp David.

Despite Camp David, there are limits to the concessions Israel will make without the confidence of a close relationship with Washington—a confidence the Carter policy has consistently eroded. Therefore, the administration's continuous conflict with Israel has actually lessened the prospects for successful future negotiations, especially over the West Bank. Camp David was possible because of a confluence of interests and a parallel willingness to make concessions that occurred between Egypt and Israel. The United States facilitated negotiations at Camp David, but it did so through the technique of personal interaction and the innovation of an informal atmosphere—not by affecting the preexisting calculation of interests by Sadat and Begin. By taking stands threatening to Israel and lacking a balance of parallel concerns generated by the parties themselves, the Carter administration could jeopardize the possibility of future agreements.

Since the United States can help the Arabs to regain other parts of their territory only by a close relationship with Jerusalem, the undermining of that connection actually risks the continuation of American credibility with the Arabs. In the long run, if the United States does not fulfill Arab hopes and proves incapable of exacting concessions from the Israelis, it runs the risk of Arab disillusionment with Washington and diminishing cooperation in the economic areas that primarily concern the Carter administration. Ironically, the absence of confidence-building measures vis-à-vis Israel may well mean ultimately a loss of American influence in the Arab world.

Arab unhappiness with the results of Camp David and a tendency to blame the United States suggest the perils of mediation. These could be exacerbated measurably if future negotiations proceed poorly; and the more delicate issues become, the more essential Israeli-American coordination will be. The surprising and disappointing fallacy in the Carter administration's approach to the Middle East has been its seeming assumption that American-Israeli dissonance would not undermine American objectives vis-à-vis the Arabs. While this disagreement can and did lead to temporary Arab satisfaction, by impeding the American ability to achieve agreements the Arabs favored, the long-run implications were for a weakened American role in the area. Failure to understand the importance of retaining Israeli confidence as a means of achieving American objectives has been the Achilles heel of the Carter policy from the outset.

CONCLUSION

The Carter administration has been typical of its predecessors in its concern for the Arab role in the Middle East, in its determination to uphold Israel's security, and in its willingness to work for an Arab-Israeli settlement. But an unprecedented sense of urgency has keynoted Carter's approach. Like Eisenhower, but unlike most recent American Presidents, Carter has been prepared to confront Israel and her supporters. He has gone further than his predecessors in publicly etching out the contours of a possible peace settlement. While he has placed less stress on the communism question in the Middle East than any President since Roosevelt, he has stressed the energy issue in his conception of the American role in the area more prominently than any Oval Office occupant.

Perhaps President Carter has differed most distinctly in his willingness and determination to pursue a comprehensive Arab-Israeli peace as a central goal of his administration. This objective is a crucial but perilous endeavor that could meet with failure on a variety of fronts at home and abroad. The future of the Middle East, of the Arab-Israeli dispute, and perhaps of the Carter Presidency will be determined by the skill and talent the administration brings to bear on the subject and by the degree of success it ultimately achieves. Though the early record of the administration was not always encouraging, observers could only hope that administration aims would in the end be accomplished.

NOTES

1. Reuben Fink, *America and Palestine* (New York: American Zionist Emergency Council, 1944), p. 20 The citation refers to a letter written by the former President to Major Mordechai Manuel Noah.
2. Quoted in Frank E. Manuel, *The Realities of American-Palestine Relations* (Washington, D.C.: Public Affairs Press, 1949), p. 72. On the Blackstone Memorial, see Fink, *America and Palestine*, pp. 20–22.
3. The material covered in this section will be explored in greater detail in my forthcoming volume, *The War for Washington: The Other Arab-Israeli Conflict*.
4. Richard Ned Lebow, "Woodrow Wilson and the Balfour Declaration," *Journal of Modern History* 40 (December 1968): 501–23; and Manuel, *Realities*, chap. 5, 6.
5. William A. Eddy, *FDR Meets Ibn Saud* (New York: American Friends of the Middle East, 1954), p. 34.
6. Truman's Palestine policy is discussed in Robert J. Donovan, *Conflict and Crisis: The Presidency of Harry S. Truman, 1945–1948* (New York: Norton, 1977); Dean Acheson, *Present at the Creation* (New York: Norton, 1969); John Snetsinger, *Truman, the Jewish Vote and the Creation of Israel* (Stanford, Calif.: Hoover Institute Press, 1974); and Harry S. Truman, *Memoirs: Years of Trial and Hope*, vol. 2 (Garden City, N.Y.: Doubleday, 1956).
7. Eisenhower's Middle East policy is discussed in Peter Lyon, *Eisenhower: Portrait of the Hero* (Boston: Little, Brown, 1974); Townsend Hoopes, *The Devil and John Foster Dulles* (Boston: Little, Brown, 1973); Kennett Love, *Suez: The Twice-Fought War* (New York: McGraw-Hill, 1960); Dwight D. Eisenhower, *Mandate for Change: 1953–1956* (Garden City, N.Y.: Doubleday, 1963); idem, *Waging Peace: 1956–1961* (Garden City, N.Y.: Doubleday, 1965); Herman Finer, *Dulles Over Suez* (Chicago: Quadrangle, 1964); Robert Murphy, *Diplomat Among Warriors* (Garden City, N.Y.: Doubleday, 1964); and Sherman Adams, *First Hand Report* (New York: Harper & Row, 1961).
8. Kennedy's approach to the Middle East is discussed in John Badeau, *The American Approach to the Arab World* (New York: Harper & Row, 1968).
9. The Johnson Middle East experience is discussed in Lyndon Johnson, *Vantage Point* (New York: Holt, Reinhart and Winston, 1971); Theodore Draper, *Israel and World Politics* (New York: Viking, 1968); William B. Quandt, *Decade of Decisions* (Berkeley, University of California Press, 1977), chap. 2; Walter Laqueur, *The Road to Jerusalem* (New York: Macmillan, 1968); Bernard Reich, *The Quest for Peace* (New York: Transaction, 1977), pp. 41–99; Nadav Safran, *Israel: Embattled Ally* (Cambridge, Mass.: Harvard University Press, 1977), pp. 381–431; and Jonathan Trumbull Howe, *Multicrises* (Cambridge, Mass.: MIT Press, 1971).
10. A great deal has been written on the Nixon and Ford foreign policy and the place of the Middle East in its framework. The interested reader may wish to consult Richard Nixon, *RN: The Memoirs of Richard Nixon* (New York: Grosset and Dunlap, 1978); Tad Szulc, *The Illusion of Peace* (New York: Viking, 1978); Matti Golan, *The Secret Conversations of Henry Kissinger* (New York: Quadrangle, 1976); Insight Team (London Sunday *Times*), *The Yom Kippur War* (Garden City, N.Y.: Doubleday, 1974); Quandt, *Decade of Decision*, chaps. 3–9; Marvin Kalb and Bernard Kalb, *Kissinger* (Boston: Little, Brown, 1974); Reich, *Quest for Peace*, pp. 99–455; Edward R. F. Sheehan, *The Arab, Israelis, and Kissinger: A Secret History of American Diplomacy in the Middle East* (New York: Reader's Digest Press, 1976); John G. Stoessinger, *Henry Kissinger, The Anguish of Power* (New York: Norton, 1976); and Safran, *Israel*, pp. 431–594.
11. The Carter statement is printed in *Presidential Documents*, vol. 13, no. 13 (Washington, D.C.: Government Printing Office, 16 March 1977), p. 361. See also *New York Times*, 11 March 1977.
12. For a sampling of the discussion in American journals at the time, see Zbigniew Brzezinski, Francois Duchene, Kiichi Saeki, "Peace in an International Framework," *Foreign Policy*, Summer 1975; George W. Ball, "How to Save Israel In Spite of Herself," *Foreign Affairs*, April 1977; Stanley Hoffmann, "A New Policy for Israel," *Foreign Affairs*,

April 1975; and Richard H. Ullman, "After Rabat: Middle East Risks and American Roles," *Foreign Affairs,* January 1975.

13. Zbigniew Brzezinski, "Recognizing the Crisis," *Foreign Policy,* Winter 1974–75, p. 67.

14. See, for example, the interview with Zbigniew Brzezinski, "Issues and Answers," American Broadcasting Company, 10 December 1977.

15. Elie Kedourie, "How to (and How Not to) Seek Peace in the Middle East," *Encounter* 50, no. 5 (May 1978): 47.

16. Ibid., p. 48.

17. I have consulted with Dr. Arnold E. Safer, Vice President–Economics, Irving Trust Company, New York, on these economic calculations. Although the conclusions are my responsibility, his assistance is greatly appreciated.